Mike Martin

Siân Phillips

Public Places

SIÂN PHILLIPS is an acclaimed theater, film and television actress. Her stage work has ranged from roles in classics such as *Hedda Gabler* and *The Three Sisters* to musicals such as *A Little Night Music* and *Pal Joey*. Most recently, she starred on Broadway in Israel Horowitz's *My Old Lady*, but she is best remembered for her role as Livia in *I, Claudius*. She lives in London.

Public Places

My Life in the Theater, with Peter O'Toole and Beyond

Siân Phillips

Faber and Faber, Inc.
An affiliate of Farrar, Straus and Giroux
New York

Faber and Faber, Inc.
An affiliate of Farrar, Straus and Giroux
19 Union Square West, New York 10003

The Library of Congress has cataloged the hardcover edition as follows:
Phillips, Siân, 1934–
    Public places : my life in the theater, with Peter O'Toole and beyond /
Siân Phillips.—1st American ed.
        p. cm.
    Published in 2001 by Hodder and Stoughton, Great Britian
    Includes index.
    ISBN 0-571-21128-3 (alk. paper)
        1. Phillips, Siân, 1934–   2. O'Toole, Peter 1932–   3. Actors—Great
Britian—Biography.   4. Actors—Wales—Biography.   I. Title.
PN2598.P418 A3 2003
792'.028'092—dc21   2002042602
[B]

Paperback ISBN 0-571-21119-4

www.fsgbooks.com

10   9   8   7   6   5   4   3   2   1

To my daughters, Kate and Pat, who have helped me, and to
those who helped all of us, the people who
'lived faithfully a hidden life'.

Private faces in public places
are wiser and nicer
than public faces in private places

     Orators by W. H. AUDEN

They change their climate, not their lives, who rush
across the sea

                              Horace

Acknowledgments

My sincere thanks to my editor at Hodder, Rowena Webb, and to my agent, Mark Lucas, for their good advice and support throughout. I would like to thank Peta Nightingale at LAW for the invaluable editorial suggestions and Stephanie Darnill, my copyeditor, who gave so generously of her time. Without Nina Humm, who not only can read my writing but has a firmer grasp of the chronology of my life than I, the book would not have come to completion. I owe her more than I can say.

William Corlett has been unstinting in his help and encouragement during a year in which he and Bryn Ellis have smoothed my path. In many ways I owe a huge debt to Thierry Harcourt for reading the book as it progressed and for being so candid in his opinions, as was Sarah Randall who may know more about some aspects of my life than I do.

Bob Willoughby has been more than generous in allowing me to choose from his magnificent collection of photography taken in South America. I am grateful to my theatrical agent, Lindy King, for her forbearance when I was obliged to steal time from acting in order to write. Above all, I thank the friends who have stood by me during the past year – in particular Fabi Waisbort, the best sort of friend with whom to travel a difficult road.

Public Places

Chapter One

March 1975

Naples Airport and I'm frightened. Coming after the black winter months in London and the weeks of filming on the icy Suffolk coast, the March light of Italy is blinding me. And the noise is confusing me. London and its airport must have been busy but I feel that we have emerged from near silence into this aggressive, lighthearted tumult. Years of disciplined dieting have left me stick-thin and as I shuffle the travel papers and passports and begin to worry about the baggage, I am aware that there's nothing much in the way of protection between my frame and the demands that are being made on it by this expedition. No ordinary journey for me or for the tall figure standing a little to the side, detached, aloof and rather grand but in fact carefully positioned so as not to be conspicuous and finding the place of maximum safety in this press of people. If I'm scared, he must be terrified. Not that he's showing it. Only a slight over-stillness and a too-studied air of relaxation betray him.

He is not supposed to walk more than a few steps, forbidden to lift anything heavier than a teacup. There is no certainty that he won't suddenly need the resources of a well-equipped hospital. I have on me the number of a helicopter ambulance service and the address of an approved hospital. His medical records are in my suitcase along with a letter from our doctor, Gerry Slattery. Don't leave London, they all said, the doctors who have become familiar to me these last months. And here we are in Naples Airport on our way to the San Pietro Hotel outside Positano. More importantly, we're on our way to Sr Carlo Cinque, the

I

builder, architect and proprietor. We are the hotel guests from hell.

Left to me, we would still be safe in Guyon House, on Heath Street in Hampstead, just up the road from Dr. Gerry Slattery and the Royal Free Hospital (the umbilical cord attaching me to Men's Surgical has yet to be cut). As usual, confronted with the prospect of O'Toole standing alone against expert opinion and common sense and people who know what's best for him, I crossed the line and stood with him against Them. 'He's not an alcoholic,' they told me. 'He just drinks a lot.' When he became aggressive they always made themselves scarce, I couldn't help but notice. 'See you tomorrow,' they'd cry, trooping out into Heath Street as the first glass shattered. They have been very present at the hospital, looking grave and concerned.

The sense of the folly of this adventure and awareness of the responsibility I've taken on myself have kept me awake for a week past. And this comes at the end of the worst time in my life; standing vigil while he hovered between life and death, returning to an empty house only to change clothes and deal with the journalists anxious to verify the show-business facts of a life that they believed to be coming to an early end. They didn't try to hide what they thought and offered sympathy. Only Jules and Joyce Buck, our partners in Keep Films – our 'family' – knew what was really going on. We spoke briefly at night. They knew too much, feared too much, to be interested in chatting or speculating. Night after night I sat, alone, on our bed in the big, gleaming house. Manolita, much, much more than the 'daily' and one of the few people to know anything of our private life, had been there all day, cleaning as though she were banishing fiends, conquering illness with antique wax. She brought from her house little plates of food and left them in the fridge and these small kindnesses were enough to tip me over into short, violent bursts of weeping, never a long, healing, outpouring of grief. There were too many moments every day when I had to assume a bright face; even the children and my mother, away in Ireland, and his parents, in a flat off Haverstock Hill, are not to be told how bad things are until the last moment – should the last moment come.

For a while I even fooled myself. 'All this is to be expected, I suppose,' I said to Sister in a sensible tone after a particularly bad night. 'It will get better, won't it?' Her eyes filled with tears and she looked away before leaving the room without speaking. Then I knew we were in more trouble than I had realised. 'Be prepared for the worst,' I was then advised and during the next few weeks I forced myself, alone at home, to come to terms with the fact that the person dearest in the world to me was possibly never going to return to himself but would slide from this comatose state into his death and I would never speak to him again.

I had never before felt such grief. When the worst thing in the world happens it seems incredible that one should be able to get up and bathe, get made up, phone for taxis, wish people good day and lie. Lie all the time. 'Oh, you're giving yourself a bad time,' said my closest friend, Ricci Burns, when we met in the street. 'Stop making a drama. He's going to be fine.' Oh Rick, if you only knew what it was like in that side ward.

Against all the odds one day, many weeks later, he opened his eyes in that side ward, ripped out his tubes and irritably demanded sustenance. The tubes were replaced and it was explained to him that he'd been 'really quite ill'. He didn't seem interested and quickly graduated to what we called 'flat' food – little pools of pureed who-knows-what. The family returned to London, the house grew light again, and not quite as gleamingly perfect. And he came home. 'I *told* you it was nothing too awful,' I said to everyone. Dr. Slattery and the surgeons and Manolita and I looked at each other in mute fellow feeling. All our lies were coming true, but the shadow of death had come very close.

The question of drink was not broached. Gerry Slattery must

have explained the score to him. Large quantities of vitamins and packets of something new and helpful called Valium were deposited in the house. O'Toole insisted that the bar – just opposite his large leather chair – was fully stocked and the wine cellar kept full. He just didn't drink. No discussion, no help required. It was an extraordinary turn of events. He'd always been bookish and an easy, fluent writer. Now he became a slow, painstaking writer of sonnets. I could not even imagine what went on in his head as he embarked for the first time since his mid-teens on a life of sobriety. My admiration for him increased even as I found it difficult to keep up with his frantic intellectual curiosity; everything was considered and questioned down to the most trivial newspaper stories. It was exhausting. Admiration and respect struggled with resentment. In the past I and the girls, Kate and Pat, could have done with a sober, present husband and father but nothing that I could have said or done would have stopped him drinking. He stopped now to save his life – which is reasonable enough and thank God he has but – but, I wish he could have stopped for our sake.

My mother, who had come to live with us in London after my father's death in Wales in 1962, flung herself into the role of matron; cauldrons of beef broth were prepared in the kitchen and she mastered the art of flat food. The children, aged twelve and fifteen years, learned not to lean on his stomach but otherwise enjoyed having a father captive in bed instead of one that dashed in and out of the house, worked behind closed doors, surrounding himself with people. I never talked to him of the time in hospital but he must have thought I looked the worse for wear and after a few weeks he urged me to accept a job that I had thought I couldn't possibly take. Each night, scared, I called him from Suffolk and he, tucked up in bed which he referred to as his 'teapot', assured me that he was enjoying his life as a dormouse. Dressed as Mayflower pilgrims in a film made for American TV, we froze all day on the desolate beach and I returned to long, dreamless sleeps in the hotel. I discovered a tiny brewery that made exquisite beer. That and the fresh air began to repair me. I went home to my beloved dormouse.

'I need to go somewhere nice to recuperate. Not too much sun. Quiet. Nice.'

'Go? Where? You're not even supposed to be *up*. Not for ages.'

'I'll *get* up.'

'Categorically, NO. We stay in London.'

'Oh. Hello. My name is Siân O'Toole. I'd like to make a reservation. Is your hotel suitable for a semi-invalid?'

'Is there total privacy in your hotel?'

'How far is it from your hotel to the nearest hospital?'

'What do you mean, you're not even open yet?'

'I see, sorry to have troubled you.'

O'Toole's partner, Jules Buck, and I looked at each other in despair. We'd been on the phone for hours. North Africa, France, Italy, Austria. Nothing.

Then suddenly, 'Oh, we have *total* privacy – a suite hanging over the Tyrrhenian Sea. No, we are not open but we will open for you and look after you like family. We will respect the ill-health and never make anything of it.'

Oh blessed, blessed Carlo Cinque. Just let us get to you quickly now. We are an odd little procession. I've got a porter and the bags are piled high on a cart and he wants it to be the fastest cart in Naples Airport. I want to slow him down so that the third figure bringing up the rear can seem to saunter as though his mind were on other things. Each step is painful, I know. Tapping the porter on the shoulder, I shake my head and apologetically pat my chest. I don't have the Italian to say, 'Feel a bit woozy'. But, hands raised in comprehension, he nods sympathetically and we proceed at a regal pace and he keeps a brotherly eye on me until we reach the waiting car.

Good as he is at 'disappearing' in a crowd, people are beginning to recognize O'Toole and as I'm carefully eased into the back seat I try not to look at him on the other side of the car, nonchalantly negotiating himself into the seat beside me. I can tell it's a miracle of small, self-controlled, slow movements. The half-smile disappears once he's seated and we're pulling away from the curious crowd. I'm so relieved I could weep. As for him, I think that in the last forty minutes he's done enough acting to last the year and now we're silent and grateful that the pressure is off. Well, I am. Who knows the state of mind of someone who has been in what doctors call 'unacceptable' pain ('torture', I'd call it) and who is now, after a close brush with death, biting all the hands that have helped and fed him because he *must* try to return to what *he* thinks of as normal living. O'Toole on the ropes is beyond sensible help. Only crazy people can lend him a hand. No, not that. He needs crazy people who are also rational. Madness has to walk hand-in-hand with common sense to be any use to him. And that's my talent. It would be nice to say only great love can help in these extremes but I don't think that's it. Fear and anxiety and grief have left me empty of soft emotion but I can't see this person without seeing my shadow behind him. And I don't feel I exist without his presence, informing my voice, my behaviour, even when he's there only as an irritating grain in my shell and I'm forming layers of disagreement along with the shiny, graceful insights I get from observing him at what I think of as his best. Even after all these years I'm not sure that I don't make up this state of mutual dependence, the 'oneness', this very special state that is never discussed. Maybe it only exists in my head and that has worried me in the past; now it doesn't matter. We're on yet another crazy, possibly doomed journey.

There's a tiny chapel – hardly that, maybe a shrine – on the roadside. In a less anxious state the twists and turns of the Italian Riviera road would have left me a wreck but today

I'm not worried about my skin. Steps! Damn! Lots of steps! No one said anything about steps. The hotel is out of sight below us. How far below? Very slowly we begin the descent. If there are hundreds of these steps we're not going to make it and this place will be impossible for us to stay in. So what do we do? There's a turn in the staircase and a lift door appears in the rock. We step inside and descend, emerging into a lovely room – a huge foyer looking out at the ocean. There seem to be seven people to help us to our set of rooms and the terrace, already flaming with bougainvillaea, does truly hang over the Tyrrhenian Sea (is this the 'wine-red' sea? It's lovely but about as wine-red as ink).

This feels like home. Are the Italians alone in their talent for purveying luxury in a way that has one reaching for words like 'simple', 'homely', 'unassuming'? Since 1970 I've spent almost five years building a house in Ireland and immediately I feel here much as I feel on the West Coast in Connemara. Even the ground under our feet is familiar; solid rock everywhere around, above and below. Who or what guided us to this place? I'm overwhelmed with a sense of good fortune. Maybe our luck has turned. Luck is important. O'Toole is lucky. Leaving him to potter around the rooms, I set about fine-tuning our life here. Breakfast quite early, big jugs of fresh juice mid-morning. No alcohol. The simplest of small lunches. More fresh fruit juice at the cocktail hour. Dinner as much like lunch as possible. The minimum of attention. Telephone calls only from my mother or Jules (and they won't ring unless there's an emergency). I unpack and within hours his books and papers (O'Toole never attempted to master the art of travelling light when in 'civilized' surroundings) cover the tables in the enormous sitting room. My books are piled high in the bedroom. Carlo has raised the drawbridge for us and we are alone.

I've stayed in some of the loveliest hotels in the world but never in one that met all the urgent needs and desires of the moment as did the San Pietro. As the weeks went by we began to tackle the corridors and the steps to the foyer and the dining room. At first we were the only guests and it *was* like being in the West of Ireland. Service was impeccable but running through everything was a streak of idiosyncratic joie-de-vivre that was peculiar to Carlo. There was a St Bernard (suffering in the warmth of Southern Italy) who came and yearned mournfully at the food on the table. Outside there were grumpy penguins living in and around the pool. The parrot in the dining room shrieked obscenities learned from the village builders. The builders . . . When we learned the story of the making of the hotel I knew that we were right to feel at home. In the West of Ireland, before you build anything, you buy gelignite and you blast yourself a flat space on the granite. The boys cycle out to you with a bit of 'jelly' in the basket and, cigarette in hand, survey the impossible terrain, then they lay their charges and murmur, 'Better get back there now, missus', before the ground explodes. 'Would ya like a little bit of that over there blown off?' 'Mmm, I think a terrace looking out at the—' 'Sure thing. Better move back a bit.' Pow! And there's your terrace – just where you wanted it.

Carlo Cinque, who ran a successful hotel in Positano, thought he'd like a quiet place just for himself and, having bought the San Pietro chapel, perched on the edge of a cliff outside the town, he and a few of the village boys 'jellied' a bit of a ledge and, having cut some steps down to it, he built himself a few rooms and a kitchen. His friends kept borrowing them so he blasted away another ledge and built a few more rooms and on it went. Most wonderful of all (and if he was proud to tell this tale he never found a more admiring audience) when he decided that this was now a proper hotel and maybe should include access to the beach, he decided to make an elevator through the cliff to the sea shore hundreds of feet below. A couple of village boys came and surveyed the problem and quickly said they were ready to start. Carlo gave them the go-ahead and provided the explosives. (A less confident man might have feared for his hotel.) Off they went. One boy descended through the rock from the hotel ledge and the other ascended from sea level. They blasted away and one day they met – smack on target in the middle – and there was the elevator shaft. It's sad that this is an extraordinary story. People, understandably people in remote neighborhoods, have talents and skills and don't question them. Closer to urban communities they lose their confidence and learn to bow to 'experts in the field', experts on building, parenting, meteorology, elevator construction. Well, I hope nobody wages a guerrilla war in Southern Italy. Those men are invincible, natural engineers.

We were told that we were too early, alas, for the annual, month-long visit of the famous Welsh actor Hugh Griffith and his wife, Gwnda (one specially designated member of staff would tactfully head him off as he made for the edge of a cliff late at night, glass in hand), but a few guests appeared in the dining room as time went by – charming, quiet Americans mostly. Carlo and they and O'Toole and myself began to meet for 'drinks' before dinner. Innocently, they would urge us to have a glass with them. Carlo never betrayed his anxiety at these moments. Nor did I. O'Toole was a model of tact and sweetness, saying he'd 'not been very well' and would have a fruit juice. They, worlds away from the hells we'd inhabited, said, 'Well, when we get home, there'll be no more wine, Fanta only, so we're going to have a glass *every night*.' Oh God, they were so nice and I loved the glimpse into their nice, safe lives. 'Why *not*?' we chorused, raising our glasses of fruit juice and Carlo nodded, beaming.

Normally a sound sleeper, even in the most desperate of circumstances, I lie awake in this Eden. James Herriott's books are making me laugh in the wind-down part of the day. Siegfried seems to be such an O'Toole character; I read aloud to him and he recognizes his own maddening habits and it makes him laugh also, before he falls asleep. After that, with the lights out, in the profound silence I lie awake, listening. When I was a little girl I would creep across the landing to see if my parents were still breathing but that was out of fear that I would be left alone in the world. This is different. I feel that if I don't stand vigil he might stop breathing after all. I fall asleep at dawn. Only the dark hours are dangerous. Exhausted, I fall asleep again after lunch. I think that my fears are concealed but one day we decide to take the famous elevator to the deserted beach. Entering the cave below we look around, admiring the arrangements, the bar that would operate in season. We stand there looking out at the sea, which looks different at close quarters, more real, less like a set. Above us rises the press of hundreds of feet of rock. My feeling of dread is profound and when O'Toole says, 'Well, I think we've seen enough of this', I gratefully get into the elevator and return to the familiar warm, sunny lounge high above the painted sea. In our suite I climb on to the beautiful ornate day-bed in a corner of the sitting room – and sleep, and sleep. When I wake, O'Toole is sitting there looking at me. 'You were afraid, weren't you?' I nod, eyes full of unshed tears. 'Don't fret,' he says, stroking my head. Does he mean that there's nothing more to worry about? Does he mean I'm allowed to feel nervous about rocks? Does he mean he's going to be all right? I nod and resolve to try not to fret.

We now have a lovely pattern to our lives. We've so rarely had patterns. Rising, we have breakfast in the sitting room. (Who brings breakfast? I see no one.) Then we prepare for The Walk. It becomes a little longer each day. The hotel car follows us and at first we're lifted the last kilometer into the town. There we buy the New York *Herald Tribune* and sit outside drinking coffee and doing crosswords or playing word games. There are few people about. Then the car takes us back to the hotel and we lunch in the dining room. Now that visitors are beginning to arrive the foul-mouthed parrot has been banished. Also the St Bernard (we know that he stands in the kitchen, drooling over the preparing of lunch). The penguins also have had to go. The hotel still doesn't look quite 'there' in brochure terms. It's the gardens, of course. Carlo and I go to Naples and buy hundreds of plants. (This time the road *does* scare me half to death.) Over the next week I spend a few hours a day digging and fertilizing and planting and *voilà*! There we are. Every suite has a beautiful, planted, fed and watered garden. By now, I almost feel I'm on the staff and I'm happier than I have been for a long, long time. One day O'Toole and I walk *all* the way into Positano. Triumph! We peer at Zeffirelli's villa down on the beach and hear stories of the goings-on down there. Nureyev hurling heavy objects down from road level is one I particularly like to contemplate. Having been around during the time of Rudi's worst excesses it doesn't surprise me in the least that he should have been thrown out of the villa. Though frankly, by O'Toole standards he's not so bad and I, for one, would never have kicked him out.

Life is calm, a bit like our early days in Connemara when we first acquired a small cottage and a little land. It's not so much having a time to think and reflect, rather it's inhabiting a space in which not to think at all. There was a time in 1960 in the desert when I felt like this. Nothing happened. Living closed down to existing, getting through the day, like a tree. Or a cabbage. Maybe there's something wrong with me. I love life at its lowest level. One thing is clear: I have never felt such love for O'Toole as I feel now. I was all loved out, slumped like a boxer, beaten in my corner. I thought I knew all the turns in this maze he and I inhabited and there was nothing that could dismay or surprise or delight me. Wrong. Where did it come from, this huge, even surge of love? Not from pity. I could never feel pity for such a dangerous, disruptive human being. Sympathy? No. I've never almost died so I don't know what that feels like. Well, this is the place we've arrived at after so many exhausting twists and turns and stops and starts and ups and downs and false endings and I've learned one thing: to accept what comes my way. I'm not going to try to work it out, the reason for this intensely happy time.

Chapter Two

Nineteen fifty-seven, when we first met, seems a whole lifetime away . . .

'Marry Siân and become a famous couple in the theater.' Emlyn Williams talking over the supper table, Micheál MacLiammóir nodding enthusiastically. The two matchmakers smiled on us. We were in our early twenties and it was only a matter of weeks since, after a long estrangement following our first play together, John Hall's *The Holiday*, he'd appeared in the early hours of the morning at my window in Ladbroke Square and swung himself back into my heart and my life. No, he'd never left my heart.

Now, we were sitting in a dark night club arrangement that Clement Freud used to run high up under the roof of the Royal Court Theater in Sloane Square. We raised our glasses though the subject of marriage had never been mooted before and I don't think either of us was keen on the idea, and I was still married to Don, from whom I'd run off to come to London and RADA. For now, it was more than enough to be together. I was dazzled by him (and I could tell that he was fascinated by me). We knew from our time together on tour that we got on very well. We were good company for each other and had no trouble adjusting our living habits to suit each other. I'd never stayed up late but I got to love it. He began to enjoy seeing the world in daylight hours – streets and parks as well as the dark interiors of bars. We shared erratic eating patterns, a love of music, singing, guitar playing, people watching. Our likes and dislikes chimed. The only slight difficulty was drink. Before I met O'Toole I had never even tasted beer or whisky.

On tour he had introduced me to Highland malt – single and blended – and I had liked small quantities of both. Beer and Guinness were utterly beyond my comprehension but I realized that an appreciation of draft Guinness was pretty essential in my new life and I persevered, sipping the hated drink slowly during evenings when O'Toole drank his own age in the stuff. Everyone we knew drank so much; incredible quantities of alcohol were lowered on every conceivable social occasion. I was cautiously intrigued.

Drink apart, it was easy living together and with wonderful sex thrown into the mix it was ecstatic. He was still in Willis Hall's *The Long and the Short and the Tall*, his first big London success, while I played lead after lead in live television plays, also successful and making a great deal of money. We would meet in his dressing room after my rehearsal ended, before his performance began, and eat high tea together; the same meal every day. Huge plates of anemic scrambled eggs on white bread toast and mugs of tea, sent in from the workmen's café round the corner. While he did the show I would spend the evening watching bits of the play or looking after the new friends we were making, the people who flock to a new success. They were, on the whole, truly nice people, some of whom became part of our lives – people like Dr. Slattery and his wife, Johnny, and R. D. Smith, the radio producer, and his wife, Olivia Manning, the novelist; but already I could distinguish between them and the people who came to devour, whose eyes lit up if he said something outrageous and unsayable, who became excited when he crossed the line between high spirits and being hopelessly 'jarred', as the Irish put it. I was made uneasy by them.

I became used to working really hard all day (fortunately I never had to sit down to memorize anything, lines sank in after a few readings) so that I was able to join O'Toole after the show, ready for whatever the evening had to offer. After the play the company would move back next door to the bar where a few hours previously they had been enjoying themselves as the 'five' was rung. Bowing to the inevitable, the theater had rigged a line relaying the calls through to the pub – there wasn't much hope that the hard core of the company, Ronnie Fraser, Bob Shaw, Bryan Pringle, O'Toole, was going to leave the 'craic' and get into the theater at the 'half' hour call which is given thirty-five minutes before the play is due to begin. The 'five' sounds ten minutes before curtain up and at that point they would straighten up and stampede for the theater, pausing only to wipe their fingers under the hot-water pipes and rub the dirt on to their faces. It took them a matter of seconds to discard their clothes and pull on their 'distressed' army uniforms. A dab of Vaseline rubbed into the dirt and they were on stage, looking as though they'd spent a long time in make-up to achieve that diseased, desperate, jungle-damp look which the play demanded. They drove Lindsay Anderson, the director, mad. The expert on army behavior brought in to make them look like soldiers had a nervous collapse and left. I don't suppose any of them behaved as badly ever again but they and the author, Willis Hall, were unstoppable. Had they not been a triumph they would never have worked again. As it was – who argues with success?

A member of the company who did not racket around London was Peter's understudy, who was called Michael Caine. When O'Toole hurt his knee badly and was told he'd have to go 'off' for surgery, he refused flatly. 'What – and let Mick on stage?' he said. 'No chance, thank you very much.' It was a compliment from one good actor to another. Who knew what Michael got up to? He was focused, quiet and circumspect.

Observing the boys, I realized that in fact they'd all done a huge amount of work and that they were desperate to conceal the fact. I heard the story of the 'foreigner' in Dublin who suddenly realized to his nervous amazement that the men standing next to him at the bar were members of the inter-national rugby team he was about to watch playing England. 'And they played a *blinder*. *And* they *won*.' Playing a 'blinder' was crucial. So was winning. The company's behavior was a pose, and none of them believed you could just stroll on stage without preparation and be wonderful, but that was the impression they liked to give – no one more than O'Toole.

There was something else to it as well. I think there was a revulsion against the 'actorish' English actor who went home after a quiet day of organized rehearsal, had a small sherry and settled down to a few hours of 'study' after dinner; the sort of actor who appeared in well-made plays and led a middle-class life, as respectable as a banker, who, after the show, tied a silk cravat around his neck to protect his white shirt against the remnants of Leichner make-up, numbers nine and five. Plays were altering and the lads were going to show that they were the new breed of actor, born for the occasion; unconventional, bohemian, with no pretensions to belonging to the polite society of 'civilians'. No use expecting polite speech and middle-class behavior from this lot. The Lord Chamberlain was being challenged to allow unheard of words on the stage and they were the guys to whom such speech came naturally. Stage make-up was considered 'poncy'. It was all very understandable and rather attractive. Exciting, certainly. It was over simple and no actor who cared about theater would have maintained a prejudice against the great writers and actors of the Thirties and Forties, but for a while in the late Fifties it was no bad thing to seem to be rebelling against everything that had gone before.

It was a mercy that we were all so young and in possession of endless energy. When the pub shut there would be a muttered conference and then a large part of the crowd would drift into taxis and cars and find themselves in basement flats in Paddington and Bayswater. How did anyone know where the parties were happening? It was all a mystery to me.

These gatherings weren't recognizable parties either. 'It's just a piss-up,' explained O'Toole. I don't ever recall going further north than WC2. Hampstead was reserved for exquisite Sunday lunch around Johnny Slattery's kitchen table. She would feed at least six actors as well as her own family and it was often the only 'proper' meal that we found time to sit down to eat all week.

More or less the same fifty people found themselves together late at night several times a week; actors from the London shows. All the new Australian actors in town were there, arriving bearing crates of Fosters lager (Ken Warren from *Summer of the Seventeenth Doll* was a host several times a week). The actors were mostly young, those unencumbered by domestic life, and guilty young actors who *did* have families and went home at dawn to ruffle the sheets and take the children to school. There was always a sprinkling of actors from an older generation who were curious to see what was going on. Willis Hall was an enchanting leader of the pack. Describing a more sedate version of an actors' party he said, 'Oh awful. You know – white wine in cups and young girls being sick.' There were very few rehearsal rooms and companies moved from church hall to church hall – St Thomas, St Luke, St John. One day Willis, checking his diary for the next rehearsal, shook his head and said without looking up, 'If I get knocked over they'll think I'm the fuckin' Pope.'

Robert Bolt was another nightly companion. He used to like to visit the theater where his first West End play, *The Flowering Cherry*, was playing. Anxiously eavesdropping, he usually heard good, enjoyable things about himself. Not always. (One of his favorite remarks was a grumpy, 'It's all right, I suppose – if you like a great play'.) I listened to his worries and didn't talk about mine, but I remember a night after I'd been to a party at the German Embassy (I did so many translations of German classics on television that I was on their guest list for years) and Robert and I were slumped,

I in full evening dress. Conveniently forgetting that, acting on advice, I'd turned down three film contracts in order to become what people in those days called a 'real' – a theater – actress, I moped a bit and shed a maudlin tear and said, 'I was sent for by Mr Vidor for a big movie and he's just DIED!' Robert, who'd been going on about the problems of being a writer, wrenched his attention on to my life for a moment and tried to console me. 'Oh my poor girl. Sudden death *does* seem a bit hard. But cheer up.' We both started to laugh at ourselves at the same moment and reached for another Fosters.

There were after hours clubs. Jerry's, which I knew when Sean Lynch ran it (he later married the formidable and talented Annie Ross and they opened Annie's). There was the Kismet run by Raj and his father, just off St Martin's Lane. Jack's near Orange Street was approached through an unmarked door alongside a plain black window. This seemed to be harder to join than the Garrick; only death left a membership place open. Joan Littlewood of Statford East held court there and as far as I could make out they served only steak and baked potatoes. The Buxton was the jolliest place, situated in a quiet street behind the Haymarket across from the stage door of the Haymarket Theater. I liked it because it was the only place where I ever got to eat anything (a lunchtime sausage and a scrambled egg high tea left me ravenous by midnight. Tough, over-cooked steak and frozen peas were the staple diet and so good.) The Buxton was a bit more like an actors' restaurant of today, but there were no customers outside the profession and it had an illicit air about it. One memorable night in 1953, John Gielgud, newly knighted, and newly convicted of soliciting, squeezed his way through the crowded club. John was loved and revered in the profession but few knew how best to deal with what must be an embarrassing time for the great actor. Stumbling, he put a hand on Emlyn Williams's waist to steady himself. Without looking round, Emlyn in ringing tones cried, 'Four months!' When the laughter subsided, relief and comradeship pervaded the room. Some time afterwards, looking up from his mail, O'Toole said, 'This is ridiculous. I've been thrown out of the Buxton for bad behavior and someone wants to put me up for the Garrick – oh, sod them all.' And he trashed both letters.

The tail end of the night was my favorite part. Often still hungry, the two of us would walk down to the all-night tea and sandwich stand in Covent Garden and order huge white china mugs of tea and hot sausage sandwiches which we ate sitting opposite Lloyds Bank, alongside Boulestin's great restaurant. Fortified, O'Toole would say, 'Okay. Now for a little climb', and he would scale the wall of Lloyds. The first time he did this I was terrified and tried to dissuade him. I was upset by what seemed to be mad, dangerous behavior. In a remarkably short space of time I came to accept the behavior as fairly unremarkable – what did that say about the state of my mind? – and I sat nursing my tea, sitting on the low wall with the tramps who liked to hang around near the cheerfully lit stand, watching him as he negotiated the familiar footholds. He was sure-footed. And lucky. The regulars at the stall knew him as 'Pete' and gave him a little cheer as he finished the descent.

When it was time to go home, we would retire to our tiny room in Ken Griffith's flat in Belgravia, facing the side of the National Coal Board building. Ken Griffith and Doriah Noar were like guardian angels to us and we lived for next to nothing in SW1. If Doriah caught us standing still for ten minutes she fed us nourishing meals. We slept in a double bed which rested on about £75,000 worth of stamps ('Covers', as I learned to call them); part of Kenneth's passion for the Boer War. He adored and admired O'Toole and the feeling was mutual. He made me welcome, partly because I was a fellow countrywoman, but he had grave doubts about the union. When we were filming in Cardiff, he walked me round the Temple of Peace saying, 'You cannot marry this wonderful man. Understand, he is a genius but he is not normal.' I replied, 'He is the most normal man I've ever met.'

I meant it but what did I know about him, this super-normal man? Something and nothing, and everything. He was Irish and he came from Leeds, from the same neighborhood as Keith Waterhouse and Willis Hall and Albert Finney. His father was an off-course bookmaker – feckless, a drunk and occasionally violent. His mother struggled to keep the family afloat. A Scots Presbyterian, she loved the Catholic Church, its kindly priests and candles. Beautiful, with a low husky voice, she was given to quoting Robbie Burns and loved to stay up drinking tea – or preferably whisky – and exchanging stories with her children, O'Toole and his sister, Patricia. I could tell that both children were bright and I was baffled by parents that wouldn't have fought to keep their children at school. O'Toole's sister had made an early exit from the bosom of the family and set about making up for their lack of education by joining the Wrens. Later, having achieved a coveted job as an air-hostess, she had just made a brilliant marriage, and here was O'Toole, one of the brightest young stars on the London stage, via National Service in the Navy and two years' training at RADA. I had never been to the north of England, except on tour, and couldn't quite make out what his upbringing had been like. His father had come to visit when we were on tour, playing *The Holiday*. He'd arrived, looking dapper in a good suit and a sharp felt hat, no overcoat against the cold, long Irish face like a fiddle, a lop-sided half smile and a permanently raised right eyebrow.

'Where are you staying?'

'I don't know – I don't know.'

'Any luggage?'

'No. Stop fussing. Don't spoil everything with *details*.'

He sat in the front row of the stalls and when O'Toole entered he raised his hand in salute. Outside the theater as we made off for a drink after the show, he didn't refer to the performance but he pointed to the front of the theater, at O'Toole's name featured prominently. 'Look at that,' he said. ' "O" as big as a cartwheel.' He wasn't much of a theatergoer.

I don't know what he thought of me. O'Toole's friends saw their free spirit being sucked into a conventional relationship and, with no special ill-will towards me, they tried to put a stop to it. I didn't mind. They weren't to know that we had a *new* kind of equal partnership and that the last thing I had in mind was domesticity – as alien to me as it was to him.

My friends, advisors, employers were equally appalled and bluntly said that he would destroy my career, that I needed taking care of and bringing on and that O'Toole would trample all over me. They must be mad, I thought. We both love the theater above everything. What can go wrong? For the first time in my life I am living with someone who respects me as an equal and he *will* look after me. Gradually, I lost my support system – the older actors and the directors and producers who were good to me dropped away. But work was still plentiful.

When I left RADA, MCA was the agency I went to, but, with their approval, I had signed an exclusive contract with Douglas Uren, a businessman who was interested in the theater and chose to make an investment in me. He guaranteed me an income whether I worked or not. But I liked working – all the time. I realized that my private life would have to alter now and I was willing to adapt – sometimes in unexpected ways.

O'Toole looked at my wardrobe of good clothes and said, 'You look as though you're in mourning for your sex life – all this black and violet. Give it here.' It was late at night and it was raining as he gathered up armfuls of organza and wool, bags, shoes, gloves, frocks, hats, suits and, opening the window, flung thousands of pounds worth of clothes on to the wet cobbles below. I had a momentary pang of regret but spoke only to say, 'But what will I wear?' '*My* clothes,' he said grandly, gathering me into his arms. I would have liked to retrieve my things but the new woman in me thought, 'Maybe he's right. That's an old-fashioned way of dressing.' So we became the only couple in town who shared a wardrobe. Winter and summer we wore colored cotton trousers and canvas shoes and lumberjack shirts and big, thick, knitted fisherman sweaters. I had to roll his trousers up, of course, which made me look like a waif (he looked like a handsome pirate). My next TV role was that of a sexy publican's wife who was no better than she should be and after the show they gave me the skin-tight frocks and six-inch heels. So for months I veered between looking like a tart with a heart and the shrimp boy. I was so deliriously in love I couldn't understand why everyone around me was worried. 'You are going to ruin your career' was the constant warning. Indeed, it was as though he wanted to eradicate my life before I met him, but I was a willing accomplice.

The Long and the Short and the Tall ended, not having transferred well to the New (now the Albery) Theater in St Martin's Lane and while O'Toole began to figure out his next move I went on from TV play to TV play. It was the time of the single play when the writer was still king, so working in television was not unlike working in the theater. Many of the plays were written specially for TV, otherwise we did stage plays barely adapted for the screen; three acts with thirty seconds in between to change clothes and re-dress the set. Everything that went out on the screen was live. It was pandemonium in the studio. If anyone got injured they were dragged out of the way. During a flu epidemic I watched a sound engineer faint and fall off his seat high above the studio floor and since I was carrying around a bucket into which to throw up, I didn't have much sympathy to spare. In one play at this time an actor died on a set of a mine shaft and the rest of the company had to crawl over him, sharing his lines among them, until someone managed to extract his body. There were no rules to speak of. It was like travelling without a map.

We would rehearse for four weeks and after three weeks we'd get into costume and pop into a small studio, pose for stills and play the 'trailer' – live. Then we'd do the show and, having done it once, we'd have a few days off and then we'd go back into the studio and play the 'repeat' – live again. Prompting was out of the question. There was very little anyone could do to help. Being on screen alone when an actor was 'off' was a nightmare and we became used to ad-libbing – not very well in my case. I doubt if the watching audience was fooled as I sat there one night saying, 'Well, I thought that *GEORGE* would be here now. *GEORGE!* Is that you I hear on the path? Well, my goodness, there's no one there. I could have sworn that was *GEORGE's step*. Oh, *GEORGE* there you are – darling, you seem out of breath.' (You bastard.)

Only people who never lived through these experiences talk of the 'wonder' and 'immediacy' of live TV. Immediate coronary, more like. But it was all we were used to and very early on I began to see that television was going to be the most powerful and influential arm of show business. Many actors were snooty about it for a long time. Some of the directors had moved over from radio or the theater and were pretty pedestrian, but there were also wonderful directors who were devoted to the new medium. When Sidney Newman joined the BBC he galvanized everyone and kept agitating for more boldness, more close ups; he didn't want to see any more 'photographed plays'. 'Get *in* there,' he yelled at cameramen. 'This has to be a close-up.' When you think about it, it stands to reason that close-ups come in ones or twos. At that time I was doing a rather 'sensitive' play for a sensitive director who was petrified when Mr Newman came in to watch our final rehearsals. He looked at the five actors in the scene and, feeling he should be moving in, he whispered desperately to the camera crew, 'Come on boys, in you go. Make this shot – a *close five*'. The fallout was awful.

O'Toole was offered three short films made for television. *End of a Good Man*, *Once a Horse Player* and a little airplane drama with Patricia Neal who had quit Hollywood and stardom for life as Roald Dahl's wife in Great Missenden. (I'm not sure that he explained to her where Great Missenden was. She was a little non-plussed and, unbelievably, she was finding it hard to find work and quite glad of this tiny film.) When we went to stay at her house we had to pretend to be married or her housekeeper would have resigned on the spot. Oh, the Fifties.

One of these short films was chiefly remarkable for introducing into our lives a woman who helped provide the glue of our relationship, the Abbey actress, Marie Kean, who was moonlighting in London for her chum, director Charles Friend. Immensely struck by O'Toole, it seems she'd tactfully nudged him so that his acting might be rather more than less visible to the camera whose existence he didn't appear to notice much. He in turn was hugely impressed by her. He knew all about her work and the Abbey Theater, Dublin, was of course almost a holy place to any theater-lover, let alone an expatriate Irish actor.

He introduced me to her at dusk near Victoria Station and before the evening was over we were a family. Older than we were, she was like a big sister, a big sister who didn't pull rank. A voracious reader, she had a prodigious memory for books and for people and a humorous outlook on the world that was to make my life possible and was at the same time the undoing of me. I learned from her not to take personally the abuse uttered in drink. 'Sure he was drunk at the time' was supposed to wipe out all hurt. Men, I learned, were given to excess and behaved like children 'when they had drink taken'. In *vino* was never in *veritas*. Drunken talk made no sense. Had no relevance. Women shrugged tolerantly and loftily in the face of masculine stupidity. Clever women never nagged. Clever women dodged the flying crockery and went away where they could get some peaceful sleep and never in the morning referred to the excesses of the night before. Clever women never made men feel guilty. I tried to learn these lessons. Up to a point they made my life tolerable. In the long run? I don't think the deception could be sustained.

A wonderful actress, Marie had a great love of food and drink and good company; something of a fine disregard for clothes and interior decoration (the minutiae of housekeeping passed her by completely). Shrewd brown eyes missed nothing and the lips could assume a threatening curl. I realized at once that we had come by our best friend. Somehow, then and ever after, she managed to love us both.

Chapter Three

Each Sunday for three years, I would take a train or fly to Wales from wherever I was acting in the theater or rehearsing a TV play and present *Land of Song*, a program of light music with links which I wrote and delivered in Welsh and English. English was not allowed in the charter for TV Wales and the West but my bits of inserted English meant that we were taken up by the network and I spoke fast, hoping no one would notice which language I was speaking. The ratings were high and I was extremely well paid. That sort of job brought in a great deal more than I could earn playing a star part at Stratford, for example.

One Sunday O'Toole decided to come to Wales with me. As usual the journey became complicated. I think we went by way of Bristol – never a good idea if one wanted to arrive anywhere on time. I managed to mislay my presenter's dress and did the show, after racing against time to write it, in my trench coat, hoping it looked more Left Bank French than desperate. O'Toole mingled with the extras for fun and everyone was charmed, at which point he said, 'Let's go to Dublin', and we adjourned to the small, almost deserted airfield that was Rhoose Airport until we found a plane that would go to Ireland. We were due to go West, the mythical West I'd been hearing about since I met O'Toole.

In Ireland we hired a car and set off – O'Toole confident, although he didn't have a driving license and had learned to drive on holiday in the Swiss Alps. (Kenneth Griffith to O'Toole on a vertiginous road, 'I say, old son, you're doing very well but should you be trying to change gear with the hand brake?') First we called in to see Johnny Slattery's brother, Dick Wilkinson, and his wife, Bridget, in their farm, Balcorris House at Santry. A day and night later we were still there. It was my first experience of Irish country house life and it was like being in a Chekhov play: the beautiful house in some disarray, a house full of drifting people (some never identified), rain, large meals with no discernible beginning or end, sad old dogs, cheerful old people, melancholy conversations and bursts of wild hilarity. Drink.

It was O'Toole who decided that we should move on. Too late to go West. (This was to become the first of many abortive attempts to go West.) What about going to Marie Kean's flat in Dublin? It was spring and the fields outside the farmhouse were yellow with thousands of daffodils. (Very un-Welsh that sort of farm crop. Could it be an Irish custom to farm daffodils among the cows?) We were given a carload of daffodils to take to the city. Arriving at Marie's, we hauled the flowers up five flights of Georgian stairs in the house in Lower Baggot Street. Marie had the ham and cabbage almost ready. She went back to the kitchen and, surrounded by daffodils, O'Toole clutched me and said 'Have my children'. Without pausing for breath I said, 'Yes'.

Thank God for contraception, or I could have become one of those women with nineteen children clutching at their skirts. Our first child was no sooner suggested than conceived. Marie, the witch, claimed to know this the following day. Never having given obstetrics so much as a passing thought (I'd never held a baby or particularly wished to) I forgot about the consequences of the long, joyous spring night – illuminated, it seemed to me, by the shine of scores of daffodils, pungent with the smell of bitter vegetation, remembering only that I'd – well, what had I done? Plighted my troth were words that seemed to fit the bill. Thrown my bonnet over the windmill. Cast my lot with. Now, had he said 'Marry me' I would have shuffled a bit and said, 'Oh I don't think you really mean that' and 'I don't really know about that' and we would have moved on to bacon and cabbage and Guinness and conversation and a simple, lovely night like any other, but the unwanted proposal didn't come. Not then. Not ever. And I began the one great journey that underpinned all the hilarious, foolish, reckless journeys that characterized our life together.

Five weeks later it dawned on me that I must be pregnant. I didn't tell anyone, especially not my agent at MCA, who grew restive as I turned down a long-term project. To do her credit, she was very satisfied with my contract with Douglas Uren which freed me from the necessity of taking job after job but I felt guilty now and booked myself up with a great deal of highly paid TV work and, as a nod towards what I should have been doing – theater – I agreed to do a play for the reopening of the Hampstead Theater Club with a translation of *Siwan* by Saunders Lewis, the great Welsh writer who had written for me and befriended me and helped to change my life by leaving Wales for London and RADA. James Roose-Evans was to direct this limited run and I figured the thirteenth century costume would conceal my interesting condition. Someone would have to be told. 'Someone – sometime, please – soon,' nagged Marie. Yes, but not yet. O'Toole and I were both pleased but I could tell that no allowances were to be made for this happy event. Life went on exactly as before and I was lucky that so far I wasn't visited by any of the inconveniences of pregnancy. Rude good health persisted, unmarked by fancies, moods and morning sickness or, should I say, rather there were no symptoms which I was able to identify, but what power was it that made me so blessedly, stupidly unworried about tomorow if not some kind of hormonal change? Any fool except me could see that it wasn't going to be possible to continue my present way of life; getting up early, working all day, staying up late, sleeping too little, eating when and if the opportunity arose. I didn't have to worry about smoking because no one suggested that it might be better to cut down, let alone give up. 'Relax, have a cigarette!' we all cried to each other; 'Have a drink!' And where were we to live? *How* were we to live? Would O'Toole help me with the baby? (That didn't seem likely but one never knew.) When would I have to give up work? (Last minute, I thought.) When could I resume work? (As soon as possible.) What did having a baby cost? Did we make enough money? The months went by and few of these questions were formulated, let alone addressed, except for one. O'Toole took a short lease on a fourth-floor flat in Bryanston Street.

Before we moved something happened that was to alter us both completely. 'People don't alter,' said O'Toole, 'they adapt. Or die.' Maybe. But make a huge, major adaptation and you end up pretty altered. Or so it seems. And if you *seem* altered then you *are* altered.

O'Toole's agent asked him to go and see a film producer called Jules Buck. I knew who he was because my agent had asked me to come and meet him at the MCA office near Hyde Park Corner. I couldn't confess that I was going to be too out of shape to be in the film so I went along half-heartedly, wearing a really boring 'good' dress that I'd just been given after playing a middle-class character in *The Tortoise and the Hare*. (Already it didn't fit properly around the waist.) Mr Buck, very American, smoking a big cigar, wasn't mightily impressed, I could tell and my agent was willing me to snap out of my lethargy and sparkle a bit. For the first and only time in my life I was asked to 'turn around'. I couldn't believe my ears. I turned on my sensible shoes, and felt the first spark of interest and amusement which lasted for the short remainder of the meeting. (It was a dull part anyway but I knew I'd never have to worry about how to play it. The part went to a sensible English Rose with a small, unpregnant waist.)

And now O'Toole was going to be seen for the same film, *The Day They Robbed the Bank of England*. Would he have to do a twirl as well? Or was it just girls? When he'd been gone for about an hour – just round the corner to Groom Place – the phone rang and Jules asked me to pop round as well. Jules and his wife, Joyce, were enchanting. I was ashamed that I had written him off in MCA as a crass American mogul. He was very funny and very Jewish. Joyce was the most beautiful and elegant woman I'd ever seen; sophisticated, witty and with such stories! Everything was going swimmingly, I could tell, and I was sure that O'Toole would be offered the quite nice part of the Irish 'boyo'. They were talking about Hollywood, telling hilarious tales about people who didn't seemed quite real to me, Olivia (de Havilland), John and Walter (Huston), Sam (Spiegel), Marilyn (Monroe), Dmitri (Tiomkin), George (Axelrod), Joan and Eric (Ambler), it went on and on.

Jules was part of the exodus from Hollywood to Europe as the studio system broke down. He and Joyce had just moved to London from Paris where they'd been working and sharing a life with Jacques Tati and his wife. This was almost too much to take in at one sitting. Hours went by. Joyce, ever the good hostess, provided a picnic dinner. Drinks came in huge, beautiful tumblers. The drawing room was the most lovely domestic drawing room I'd ever been in; clean and fragrant, dark walls, gleaming walnut and mahogany furniture, blissfully comfortable chairs, softly gilded picture frames and drawer handles and bits of ormolu glowing here and there in pools of light. Joyce noticed my look. 'Twenty-seven sources of light,' she said. (It was the first of many lessons I was to learn from her.) I marvelled and settled down for more delicious small eats and stories.

It seemed a shame to come back to the present and O'Toole's part in the film. And it seemed a *real* shame when O'Toole, who didn't have any other decent options, grandly said that he didn't want to play the part under any circumstances. Horrors. Dismay. He would, however, consider the part of the upper-class English officer. Jules, who was very taken with the Irish Irishman who reminded him of a former business partner, John Huston, was severely jolted. I nodded off but at five o'clock in the morning I was nudged out of my chair and joined the other three in a toast to a new company, Keep Films – directors Jules, Joyce, Siân and Peter – and we toasted O'Toole's coming appearance as an English officer in Jules's movie.

Chapter Four

I settled into the flat O'Toole had found – a fourth-floor eyrie in Bryanston Street. Doriah helped me move. Before he began Jules's film, O'Toole had a good part in another film, *The Top of the World*, which was to be directed by Nicholas Ray. We expected a great deal as we went to meet him; he'd been married to Gloria Grahame and he'd directed *Rebel Without a Cause*. Like all visiting Americans, he was installed in a sumptuous flat in SW1 (they didn't seem to consider living anywhere other than Mayfair or Belgravia). He was oddly disappointing; distracted and unfocused. But he wasn't drunk – maybe he was ill? O'Toole met his director at the tail end of an interesting career.

What had seemed a wonderful opportunity, playing opposite Anthony Quinn, quickly turned into a farce and O'Toole's mood blackened. Anthony Quinn was very honest with him. When O'Toole pointed out that his balaclava came down to his eyes and the frozen dirt covered the little bit of face visible between the cap and his beard, Quinn said, 'Listen kid, it's taken me twenty years to get to be first over the title. If you think I'm letting you loose on the screen with me think again.'

It was a disaster of a job. O'Toole turned to Jules to get his name off. More and more we were turning to Jules. He was beginning to regulate our lives. For instance, income tax was something O'Toole intended to think about some other time. While we were living with Ken and Doriah in Dorset Mews Douglas Uren and the accountants at my agents, MCA, saw to it that *my* affairs were in order and I was half horrified and half impressed by O'Toole's cavalier attitude towards law-abiding existence. His attitude towards most of the practicalities of life was nonchalant, to say the least, and Jules had a great deal to contend with. He urged O'Toole to acquire a driving licence for his car and on a wet morning in 1959 the newly hired instructor drew into the Mews and off they went, O'Toole a little hung-over but in great high spirits, brimming with confidence. He had, after all, driven in France and Switzerland, and London traffic held no terrors for him. Ken Griffith was apprehensive, and he was justified; in the few minutes it took to do a three-point turn and head out of the Mews into Wilton Street, connecting with one of the pillars on the way, an executive decision was taken inside the car and the BSM official requested that he be brought back to the mews. O'Toole obliged and as he got out of the car the shaken instructor wished him a firm 'Goodbye', adding mysteriously, 'a wink is as good as a nod to a blind horse, sir'. O'Toole seemed surprised by the man's attitude and promptly forgot all about taking lessons. Instead he bought an Irish driving licence for thirty shillings. Decorated with harps and shamrocks it was, surprisingly, valid in the UK. Then he made plans to buy a sports car he rather fancied. Jules was not happy but for the present he turned a blind eye to motoring and set about dealing with the Inland Revenue and its neglected place in O'Toole's life and he also turned his attention to the matter of my divorce.

In 1959 it was not possible to live in sin, as we were doing, and conduct a reasonable public life. Having a child out of wedlock, which we were about to do, was asking for trouble. Urgency was therefore in the air; but divorce was no easy matter. Three years of separation had to elapse before we could apply for a divorce. Before that, there had to be proof of infidelity or unreasonable behavior. Private detectives did a roaring trade; men and women were made to sit in bed with each other while a prearranged photographer burst in upon the bedroom scene, after which they accepted the check, donned their clothes and left, breakfast uneaten. My husband wouldn't (why should he?) give me grounds for divorce, nor would he prosecute me, so I was stuck with another year to go. A year too much, Jules decided, assuming, correctly as it turned out, that we would shortly be the subject of public curiosity and scrutiny. Having something to hide would make life impossibly difficult. I maintained a kind of lunatic calm and didn't worry about the arrangements. Jules's (now 'our') lawyers got me divorced by proxy in Mexico. The papers were signed and O'Toole and I were free to marry – in secret, of course – and we chose to be married in the only registry office in Dublin.

As usual there were cliff-hanger moments on either side of the ceremony. Fog at the airport and over St George's Channel meant that we only just made it to the registry office. One of the requirements made at the office was that we should have been, for some weeks, resident in Dublin – O'Toole at the Wilkinsons' house in Santry and I, care of Marie Kean in Lower Baggot Street; (Marie was our best man and Joyce gave me away) so when I launched into a breathless apology and, finger pointing heavenwards and circling, began, 'I'm so sorry – there was terrible fog –' O'Toole grabbed my raised hand, turned my index finger down and, rotating it, finished the sentence '– around St Stephen's Green'. He had the nerve to wink at the registrar. Too late I remembered the Irish method: be seen to observe the proprieties and do what you damn well please.

I had never enjoyed a wedding; this one didn't seem any better than most but it was, at least, full of incident and quite wonderful in the early stages of the day. As far as I was concerned, O'Toole and I were indivisible. There was nothing I wouldn't do for him and he said as much for me. But a wedding? It seemed irrelevant and brought out the worst in both of us.

* * *

Three o'clock in the morning in a Dublin shebeen. O'Toole, great, diminutive actor Harry Brogan, Marie Kean, Joyce Buck and myself and the host sit around a scrubbed wooden table in a first floor back. A child in his pajamas sits half asleep in an armchair next to the fire. The linoleum is worn but was once patterned to look like Axminster carpet. No two walls are papered alike and any one of the patterns could easily be said to dominate anything near it. The ceiling of the beautifully proportioned Georgian room is papered blue, studded with gold stars. A sheet hangs on one window and a flimsy curtain gathered on a wire covers the other. The table has disappeared under Guinness bottles and there's a bottle of Jamesons whisky as a nod towards Joyce Buck's superior status as an American. Harry Brogan loves Joyce Buck. I may be the bride but the early morning wedding is already forgotten and the star of the shebeen is Joyce.

We've just seen Harry on the stage of the Abbey. The moment we sat in the Circle we all fell asleep; the four of us waking in terror in that awful silence when there's a 'dry' on stage. Once they were back on track we all fell asleep again. (What would you do on your wedding night but catch the show at the Abbey? It seemed reasonable to me at the time.) The party had been moving around the city since curtain down. There had been Breakfast at the Dolphin where the Irish gourmets were said to order 'Four tomato soups, four mixed grills, four large Irish and hurry up with the Irish'. God, I was hungry and glad to be in the Dolphin. From pub to pub we crossed and criss-crossed the city, gathering well-wishers, famous or just entertaining. Liam O'Flaherty recited a poem for me. For me? Not at all. This wedding ceremony didn't signify. It was just an excuse for a all-nighter, but I didn't feel done out of anything in the way of ceremony.

Now there are just the five of us left standing – or rather, sitting around the table. O'Toole and I have to be back in

London in the morning and it's decided that we really should go to bed. Harry, looking older with each glass of stout and not wanting to be parted from Joyce, says, 'Would ya like to go to the Ladies now? I'll take ya. My old mother told me how to look after a lady.' 'I'm just fine,' she says firmly (what a test for a Jewish Princess and how brilliantly she's doing). Attempting a different tack, he says, 'Have ya ever read *Ulysses* by James Joyce?' 'No,' she says faintly, 'but I think I'm in it.'

We acquire two taxis. Marie and Joyce sweep into the night and we set off to deliver Harry Brogan home. We aren't to know that, great actor that he is and fully deserving to be the center of our attention on our wedding day, his party piece is to refuse to say where he lives. We drive around for what seems like hours and he grows more and more skittish and it becomes harder and harder to maintain the respect due to great actors, '*even when they're drunk, Siân*'. Finally, I think we may have tipped him out and returned to Lower Baggot Street. None of us can be called sober but I develop a disdain for the tone of the evening and adopt a dignified *froideur* towards my bridegroom. Marie opens the door and I sweep in without a word. O'Toole follows, laughing sheepishly. 'I think she's a bit cross with me.' The phone rings.

Joyce: 'Siân, please, dear – come over to the Shelbourne and get some *sleep*.'

'No, I'm fine – really. Thanks. Good night.'

Putting the phone down, I turn into the bedroom saying (according to Marie), 'I might as well go on the way I'm going to start.'

Where is Jules? Back in London planning deals. Wise in the ways of our business, I doubt that he thought it worthwhile interrupting business to attend a wedding that, to outside eyes, seemed unlikely to last. Volatile young actor takes up with young actress. Same actor becomes an international movie star and *stays married* to the same young actress? Hardly.

*   *   *

Back in London, a married woman. Oh, this is good. Proxy divorces made in Mexico are not recognized by English law. I don't want to be finicky but it seems to me that I may be bigamously married and there are those who have been known to take a dim view of bigamy. I don't like to complain; it seems mean-spirited after all the trouble people have taken over the arrangements. All the same, the sooner I'm properly divorced, the better. Getting divorced after the marriage ceremony could arouse comment, so how on earth are we going to manage that without attracting publicity? We manage it! I dress in a voluminous raincoat of O'Toole's and my mother's riding hat and use a Christian name, long abandoned but legal. We drive at dawn through the fog from London to Shrewsbury, missing death by inches as a four-ton truck screams to a halt in front of our wrongly overtaking bumper. It's so early and so foggy and so horrible that there's nothing to do but look each other in the eye and thank God that we're all alive. In court, the judge implies that Don is well out of this irregular situation and he's right. We drive away and I am now legally an O'Toole person. It feels astounding and enlarging. O'Toole – '"O" as big as a cartwheel', as his father had said.

If you put your mind to it, the press is easy to evade. Every so often we fail. When I was being made a Druid of the Gorsedd of Bards we had to take a taxi from the National Eisteddfod in North Wales all the way to London, I didn't mind the aggravation so much as the expense. I'm no longer sure how well-off we are. Media attention is pushing us into living like film stars – a taxi from North Wales, I ask you!

Finally I've given in and bought two maternity outfits. One dress – mailbox red. One red and black suit and a present from O'Toole, a silk shirt covered in a design of playing cards. Nothing more eye-catching could have been devised. And I'm trying to lie low.

The fourth floor of Bryanston Street is lonely; horribly lonely. And the decor is pure Peter Jones – nicely painted or reproduction furniture, well-made shiny curtains. Blameless. Dull. If I hadn't observed Joyce's living arrangements I might have rather liked it. Now it's lowering my spirits. O'Toole goes off early for a gloomy day of filming in his balaclava with his back to the camera. He says he's learned from Quinn – they quite like each other – how to upstage on a film set. (Quinn is upstaging *him* of course at this point, but who knows when that little skill might come in handy.) There are polar bears who are dangerous and can't act and a Japanese actress who can't talk – or act. At night he comes grumpily home and sometimes he goes straight out again. Some nights he doesn't come home at all after work. I know what he's doing. He's leading the life we used to lead together but now I'm the wife and not really eligible. Anyhow I can no longer stand about in bars; it would look irresponsible and inappropriate. I acknowledge that I never much liked pubs and clubs anyway. I've given them a try and now I shan't bother with that life anymore. But I don't mind O'Toole living it because it's what he's used to and he *does* love it. Occasionally after work, I call him a taxi to go to the Salisbury. Discomfited he says, 'I can't have you getting me a *cab* to go on a bender.' Well, I can and I don't know why he should find that so hard to understand.

The Top of the World was to be followed by *The Day They Robbed the Bank of England.*

The question of his nose came up, and was dealt with very casually. Little did we guess the furor that would follow. The nose was kicked in while he was in the Navy playing rugby against the Swedish police team and every cameraman who had to photograph him had complained of the time involved in shooting around the bent gristle, lighting it out. So much easier to push it back and straighten it to where it was before. It didn't take a minute to do. The media outcry was incredible. I was disbelieving when I read that his 'character' had disappeared. His nose was now 'retroussé'. He had 'sold out'. His so-called 'friends' said it was symptomatic of his changing life. I was so sorry for him. I think he found it very hard to recover from this ill-considered cruel stupidity. What, I thought angrily, had two-tenths of an inch of gristle to do with talent? Other actors might have insulated themselves by moving into the company of equals only; O'Toole obstinately refused to do that. His obstinacy was ill rewarded. I felt nothing but contempt for those smart-asses who saw psychic value in a rugby-bent nose.

Left alone in the flat I have time to take stock. I can't see the way forward at all. My agent isn't speaking to me, she's so fed up. There are jobs I want and I can't accept them. There are jobs I need and I can't go after them. Jules talks of a future framed around O'Toole's career, whatever that might turn out to be. It isn't acknowledged anymore that I am an actress. I'm depressed and completely cut off from everyone I've ever known in my working life. I'd thought I'd show them how well this was going to work. Now, I have my doubts. But I don't want blame or sympathy.

When I see the stills of O'Toole in *The Day They Robbed the Bank of England* looking every inch an upper-class officer, I know he's made the right choice of role. It's not going to be a great film but he's obviously going to be very good in it, and the film won't be bad either. I'm ignobly happy to note in the rushes that the girl's part is hopeless. O'Toole is behaving himself. His new partner is pleased. So am I.

I may be worried and confused and depressed but I do love this man, that's the only thing I'm sure of. He comes home one day with a lovely red MG motor car, bought with his film money. 'Get your passport,' he says. 'We're off.' He's going to show me his favorite city in the world – Venice. We leave at once. The problems are left behind in Marble Arch in W1.

Chapter Five

Two weeks of refuge from London. The November weather was foul but neither O'Toole nor myself much minded the cold and the wet. We arrived in Mestre, outside Venice, and it was hideous. 'Just you wait,' said O'Toole gleefully 'you won't believe what you see.' Then, more purposefully, 'Wait here.'

'Why?'

'Just wait here.'

There was a limit to the amount of money that could be moved from country to country but there was some kind of illegal scheme – something to do with petrol coupons – that enabled one to augment one's foreign currency and O'Toole had been told about it and was about to give it a try (I suppose). One of the things I most liked about O'Toole was that a great deal of the time I didn't know what he was up to. He didn't expect help either – just non-interference. I read my book while he trawled the bus station.

After a few hours he was back looking jubilant and I assumed we were in funds as we set off down the Grand Canal. Yes, it *was* all the things I'd been told and all the things I'd read but O'Toole loved it so much and expected me to share his feeling that I soon became tired of enthusing and was hungry and cold, I began to feel a bit unwell and not a little grumpy. Naturally, we didn't have hotel reservations. 'Wait here with the luggage.' He was soon back having found us a lovely room in the Gabrielli Sandworth on the Riva degli Schiavoni. It was dark and wet but I realised that the window had the loveliest view I've ever seen, across the water to the campanile and cupolas of Santa Maria della Salute.

This should have been such a lovely night and it wasn't. I was six months pregnant. My body was letting me down somewhat in that I suddenly felt I'd like to go to bed but O'Toole was so anxious that I should see and love everything that we walked and walked and walked in the rain before subsiding into a restaurant where the warmth and the food and the wine finished me off and I fainted away. I could hardly believe that we were scurrying 'home' through the rain, up and down slippery steps and I was actually crying with irritation and we were having a row about Hy Hazell's *legs*! Best he'd ever seen. How could he be so brutal as to prefer Hy Hazell's legs to mine? Grabbing a pillow and an eiderdown I flounced out to spend the night in the bath, where I slept like a lamb and woke feeling loving and happy and when I looked out of the window my spontaneous reaction of wonder and admiration would have satisfied the most demanding lover of the *serenissima*. We didn't refer to Hy Hazell or her wretched legs.

My great, abiding love for Venice didn't catch fire for years but from that first visit I was over-awed and over-impressed and wanted more, much more. I was glad to have a respite from my problems. O'Toole was also escaping problems. After the huge impact of *The Long and the Short and the Tall*, and the film work that followed, he was restless. Now, after a few days in Venice he said 'Let's see if it's warmer down South,' and handing me the map said, 'Let's go to Rome.' I'd never been asked to map-read before. 'Turn right, here,' I said and by late afternoon we were heading towards Yugoslavia. (I think Rome was a left turn.) Soon it was dark and we were high in the mountains on a horrible road and when we came to a checkpoint where soldiers with serious-looking guns wanted visas (visas? What were they?) O'Toole reversed hurriedly and thought for a moment. I knew what he was going to say. Extracting a bottle of emergency brandy from the back of the car, he said, 'Wait here. It'll be all right,' and disappeared into the darkness.

When he came back he had a sheaf of papers and he was smiling. 'Off we go,' he said, accelerating alarmingly, and we shot past the waving, smiling soldiers.

'What did you do?' I asked.

'Just trust your uncle,' he said, smiling wolfishly.

What could he have been doing? Yes, I'd trust him to get us out of any mess, I thought, but the journey over the mountains was unremittingly awful. Although I was ready to trust him with my life in a crisis, I couldn't fail to notice that he was a terrible motorist. In the total darkness I could sense that we were perilously close to the edge of the road and that the darkness beyond the road was that different darkness of nothing but space. It stood to reason (I thought) that as we climbed, the drop on our right became greater. Every muscle tensed, I sat bunched up, stifling the squeals and whimpers that threatened to surface as we swung around the hairpin bends on that terrifying road. I longed for the drive to be over. Even more, I longed for it to stop for a bit.

My prayers were answered and O'Toole braked suddenly as, into the middle of the road, ran the first person we'd seen for hours. She was old and draped in black shawls which rose and fell like wings as she waved her arms up and down. Satisfied that she had our attention, she darted to my side of the car and launched into an urgent torrent of what I supposed to be Yugoslav – or Serb – or Croat. Apologetically, I shook my head and she immediately switched to a violent mime, holding her head and rocking from side to side and moaning horribly. 'Oh my God, help me get her into the back,' said O'Toole, catching the urgency of the moment. It took us a few minutes to realize that we were failing to get her into the car, not because she was infirm and hampered by layers of clothing, but because she was putting up a spirited resistance. Discomfited, we stopped being good Samaritans and stood back from the lively little bundle of shawls, still wailing, but now wailing with a note of irritation. There was something we weren't comprehending and she was losing patience with us. Clutching her head with one hand, she pointed into the darkness with the other and took a few steps, gesturing to us to follow her. I realized that any fears I entertained that we might be about to be set upon and robbed was an utterly inappropriate emotion at this point in a promising and developing adventure. I was learning to strangle at birth these petty feelings of caution and prudence. It also occurred to me that while I was exhausting myself during the white-knuckle ride O'Toole might very well have become *bored* as he flung the car around the turns in the road and to him this could well be an agreeable diversion. Briskly I brought up the rear of the little procession as it disappeared on to a rough path. Very soon we came upon another little group (more moaning) and I realized that the old lady wanted to load a child on to us. Obligingly, stumbling back to the car, we heaved the boy into the back seat and he was followed by a couple of men who got into the car, nodding approval and pointing at the road ahead. They wanted us to get a move on. O'Toole performed a racing start and we roared off, leaving the old lady in the darkness.

I couldn't make out if the boy had terrible toothache or acute stomach-ache. O'Toole concentrated on driving like a man possessed (I cannot begin to describe how much worse the driving became) and I kept an anxious eye on the passengers and they in turn kept nodding approvingly at me. We were doing the right thing. Whether more was required than making speed in the dark we had no way of knowing. As we approached a town the two young men leaned towards the front of the car, one head each side of O'Toole, and began to give directions, speaking very loudly and slowly in Yugoslav and making simple, clear gestures. The car was filled with a new smell – sweet and faintly rotten at the same time. What was it? We drew up at what turned out to be a very dimly lit, bare hospital and out hopped the men, half carrying, half dragging the boy. As they ran for the door they made expressions of gratitude, more simple mime and much pointing vaguely in the direction of the heart. 'It was nothing,' we mimed back, shaking our heads from side to side, 'glad to be of use' and we pointed at *our* hearts. We felt a bit flat now that we weren't an ambulance anymore and when a couple of men in coveralls carrying bags of tools (plumbing tools, I thought) indicated that they wouldn't mind a lift, we leapt on them as the most welcome of passengers and off we tore through the sparsely lit streets. I realized that we hadn't seen another car since we'd crossed the border. We were a novelty in our bright red MG.

The town center of Zagreb was bleak; nothing much happening it seemed, not many people about, the few shops with lighted windows were uninviting (the window-dresser's art hadn't penetrated Yugoslavia). One of O'Toole's talents lies in his nose. Standing in a strange town he turns his head this way and that, picking up little smells and sounds, like an animal, then he sets off, making unerringly for the best place to eat and drink or the only place still open after hours. Zagreb, however, had him nonplussed for a moment. Beaming, our plumbers directed us to what looked like a grand town hall. Entering from the gloom and cold outside was like entering paradise. There was no food in evidence but I felt there must be some, somewhere. Not having eaten since breakfast, I was ravenously hungry, but I forgot my empty stomach as I took in the extraordinary scene.

We were in what had once been the ballroom of a grand baroque hotel which the People had taken over with a vengeance. Figures still in drab working clothes filled the huge, brilliantly lit room, drinking, dancing to fiddle music, having what could best be described as a party. The story of our adventure as an ambulance and taxi service was told at once and we were immediately the center of a large, noisy, extravagantly friendly crowd of workmen. An old lady in long skirts appeared and, clucking at my interesting condition, took me off for a much-needed toilette, shrieking with mirth as she showed me how to negotiate the hole-in-the-ground toilet. It seemed rude to ask her to wait outside so I peed as best I could to her accompaniment of more gales of laughter. 'Please, I have to be alone. I'm an only child. Intimacy doesn't come easily to me.' No. Instead I nodded at her toothless smiling face and, having washed my face and hands, launched into more 'How can I thank you?' behavior. Bereft of a single word of Yugoslav, I developed a kind of Japanese mime; a little bow from the waist while indicating my heart. Rock-hard sausage appeared just for me. Delicious. I identified the sweetly corrupted smell which hung in the air everywhere as the smell of ingested slivovitz, divine corrupted apples.

A few hours later, excusing myself on the grounds of my advanced pregnancy – this time my bow was accompanied by a triple hand gesture; tummy to heart to tummy – I went to bed. O'Toole stayed behind to explore the true nature of slivovitz and to do a bit more taxiing while I was shown to a room high above the celebrations which looked as though they might well continue 'til morning.

Lying flat – *not* hurtling through the night, *not* expecting every moment to be my last – was negative pleasure enough but it was augmented by the sign above the table, 'Your commands by telephone will be obeyed instantly'. I didn't want anything but I picked up the Bakelite receiver. Dead. I went to sleep smiling. This wasn't Rome, where we'd meant to go, but I felt very lucky to be here alive, lying flat in Yugoslavia.

Walking around town in the morning we saw that the theater was as grand as the hotel. 'Better go and make ourselves known, then. They may give us "comps" for the show.' (Like all tourists we were short of money, in spite of the petrol coupon scam.) All we said at the theater was that we, like them, were actors. There was someone who spoke a little English and he believed us and may even have thought that we were important actors (it could have been the effect of the car, which was still attracting a good deal of friendly envy) and with much hand-shaking (and bowing from me) we were told to present ourselves at the theater and we would be 'passed' in to see the play that evening.

We felt under-dressed when we were shown into a prominent box at stage level, but it was clear that no one was dressed to suit the splendor of the theater and we settled down to enjoy the performance. Four and a half hours later we were still there, hanging on to the arms of our chairs, glassy eyed, stupefied with boredom. The play wasn't even in Yugoslav, it was in an obscure Serbo-Croat dialect. It looked faintly fifteenth century. There were lots of children in the audience and they also looked a bit glum but I could tell that the play was meant to be a comedy. 'I know what this is,' hissed O'Toole viciously. 'You know that one performance of some ancient bit of culture you have to give every year to justify the Arts Council grant? Well, this is *it*. The Serb equivalent of *Gamma Gurton's Fuckin' NEEDLE!*'

During the ensuing week, hurtling from country to country, we saw four plays. Three times the offering was *Boeing Boeing*, the most popular play in Europe that year. Probably the most popular play in the world. We didn't see any German theater because O'Toole suddenly took against the thought of being in that country and we drove across it without stopping. Never in my life have I been so glad to see a veal escalope as I was when we got to Linz in Austria late at night. (Hunger was one of the leitmotifs of this breathless trip.) In Switzerland I developed violent toothache and O'Toole decided that the best dentists in the world were to be found in Italy and only the best would do for me. (I fancy he was thinking of barbers' poles and a long operatic tradition.) Useless to say that any old dentist would do, so after an evening of *Boeing Boeing* in Schweizerdeutsche, off we set for Milan. I held brandy in my mouth for hours until it grew hot and O'Toole drove and drove like a demon along these frightening straight Autobahns. (He had never before encountered big, straight roads.) He got me to Milan in record-breaking time, slightly drunk, the pain all but banished by fear. After a lot of *'porco misere!'* and *'Bruto!'* and no anaesthetic because I was pregnant, the Professor of Dentistry put his knee on to the arm of my chair and pulled and pulled, encouraged by shrill cries from two admiring young assistant dentists. Finally, he reeled backwards across the room triumphantly, holding aloft a large back tooth.

O'Toole finished off the brandy – well, it had been a gruesome experience – and we turned the car towards Holland where Hélène (Van Moeurs, my old friend from RADA) lived and where she was playing Molière at a theater in The Hague. Apart from the terror I experienced all day in the car I was loving the trip. O'Toole was loving the trip. He was the perfect travelling companion; each day was a challenge and a hilarious adventure. He was like a Pied Piper, collecting people wherever we went. No one knew who he was but everyone wanted to spend time with him and I was content to look on, but I was beginning to weary. The pace was gruelling and I wasn't making concessions to my pregnancy. I had never had many close women friends and now I thought that it was a good moment to have Hélène look over my new life, my new state.

The theater at The Hague is so beautiful – like a meringue. It was, I was told proudly, 'the Stradivarius of Europe'. I was glad that we weren't seeing *Boeing Boeing* yet again but even Hélène had to admit that Dutch is not the ideal language for Molière. The play sank heavily like unleavened dough and lay expiring on the beautiful stage.

We got into the car and (a by now exhausted) O'Toole drove from The Hague to Hélène's home in Amsterdam. Hélène – sturdy, strong, fearless and practical – silently climbed the stairs to her flat. 'Does he always drive like that?' she asked as I joined her in the kitchen. 'Ye - es,' I replied guardedly.

'He should never drive *anything*', she said. 'He's *lovely* but
I thought we were going to die on that journey.' In a way I
was relieved that she felt as I did; I had begun to think that I
was being feeble minded and wimpish out there, on the road.
On the other hand, her reaction told me that I had a genuine
problem on my hands. I didn't drive and I was terrified of cars
and now was at the mercy of a terrible driver. 'You put a stop
to all this,' she said briskly, chopping vegetables. I looked at
her – so reasonable – and thought I couldn't begin to explain
that it was completely outside my remit in the relationship to
'put a stop' to anything. 'And another thing,' she said. 'You
should be resting and eating properly.' 'Oh it's okay. I do
normally,' I lied.

After supper I went to bed, uneasy. Our life together would
be lived very much at O'Toole's pace. I had played fast
and loose with so many men that it was a huge relief –
and a lifting of responsibility – to be involved with a man
whom I could not hoodwink. There is something so attractive
about being wholly known with all one's faults and vices
and now it was a huge relief to be seen through. I couldn't
at the time see how childish and truly irresponsible I was
being. The idea of female service and support to men had
been taught only too well in Wales and the childish part
of me felt this to be right and proper. The Ireland I was
beginning to know was male dominated as well. The idea
of a wife with a career, demanding rights, was laughable in
the Fifties.

I lay there in Amsterdam and saw that if things went awry
over the birth of the baby and my ensuing life, then the
problems would be largely of my own making. Hélène made
a supper dish which I have never forgotten. Here's how she
prepared it. Chop and cook every root vegetable you can lay
your hands on (making sure you have carrots and rutabegas to
make the final mixture pink). Vigorously mash the whole thing
and pile it high in a large shallow dish. Make an indentation

at the top of the pyramid and into it place half a pound of butter . . . eat.

Then go to bed and try to worry about your life and career. Sleep will soon take over.

Chapter Six

S afe in London again. A mere two weeks have elapsed. So much has happened but the wonderful journey has done nothing to solve our problems. There's a Welsh poem that ends '*A groeso fôr, Ni newid onid air.*' ('Crossing an ocean only gives you a change of air.')

I sense O'Toole is profoundly dissatisfied with almost everything that has happened since Willis's play. The movies he's made have proved mildly interesting, profitable in a moderate way but they were not what he wanted. The ones he did want have not come his way. There isn't a good play on the horizon. We have a rare council of war and decide that the best thing would be to go back to the beginning and restart in the theater. Almost at the same moment there's an offer from Stratford for him to play Shylock and Petruchio and Thersites in Peter Hall's new company. It's so obviously the right thing to do that I can hardly believe our luck. I don't know what Jules thought of his partner's decision to disappear to Warwickshire for six or seven months but he's extremely graceful when we all meet for dinner. About a week after the offer is accepted I do a very delayed double-take and think, 'But how will *I* manage in Stratford?' The baby will be born at the end of February before the opening of *The Merchant of Venice*. I would hope to go back to work in the spring but Stratford? Notoriously difficult to live in, I'm told. How will I manage? And O'Toole's salary will be low – but then I have an income and a reasonable bank balance. But is having a baby within the terms of my contract with Douglas Uren? My agent is already cool towards me and I no longer have a single friend or advisor to turn to. And where will we live? Pregnancy is making me feel completely powerless. My body, which has never let me down, seems to belong to someone else. And I'm lonely. I'm not accustomed to being isolated from people but my life with O'Toole is absorbing all my energy and excludes everyone I've ever known. There is no question in my mind that my loyalty should lie with him but it does seem hard to have to cut my ties with everyone else. I see no one. I begin to draw close to Jules and Joyce Buck. They are my new family. Denise Sée, the company lawyer, becomes a valued advisor – but she's not principally *my* advisor. Nyman Libson is to be our accountant. He and his wife and family, Sue and John, are to me the impossible-to-attain perfect family. Again, they are to be O'Toole's advisors, not mine, but I like them all, on sight. When I'm with them I admire them so much that I lose all confidence in *my* family life. Brutally, I don't have a family life. It's fashionable in our circle to despise uxoriousness, domesticity, bonds, ties, fetters. We're standing in some kind of no-man's-land, me and my unborn baby, because motherhood is suspect as a shackle on the masculine genius/worker/provider. Cyril Connolly's 'somber enemy of good art – the pram in the hall' is familiar to all of us.

Before Stratford I do Saunder Lewis's play in Hampstead. It's well received but in translation it just doesn't work as it does in Welsh. 'Lovely Siân recalls the days of Mrs Pat,' says one big headline but I know that Mrs Patrick Campbell played Hedda at the Hampstead Theater when she was fat and truly past being convincing! (Still, no one seemed to notice I was pregnant.)

One television play and then we're off again! Where? O'Toole wants us out of the flat in two hours. It's late. Why? Never mind. It's an adventure. I never really liked this flat. But where to go? My mother's brother, Davy, newly widowed, has a house near my old family home, Tŷ mawr farm. We can go there. I call him and he seems glad of the prospect of our company. Another journey through the night, this time from London to West Wales. No Autobahns, thank God. As we climb in the dark towards the Black Mountains, I roll down the window and take deep breaths of the air which is different from any other.

Gwaun-Cae-Gurwen.

This is going to work out very well. O'Toole in preparation for *The Merchant of Venice*, is reading the whole of the Old Testament – two fields away from Tŷ mawr farm, where I was born, where my grandmother, Mrs Thomas, Tŷ mawr, read the Good Book every day and was said to be able to write out the whole of it from memory. I'm not a good cook but neither Davy nor O'Toole are gourmets so I make very ordinary meals and sit reading at the table in the house on the Betws Mountain and watch Davy dealing with school and local government work and O'Toole in the other armchair, burying himself in the family Bible. Our evenings are long and silent and agreeable.

The best bits of our life together, like these months in the country, could not be imagined and would not be credited by people who see us out and about in London. O'Toole's friends wouldn't believe the sort of life we lead when we're alone. We keep it to ourselves, like life in a Persian garden – secret and unseen.

My tutor from university days, Moelwyn Merchant, is free to discuss *The Merchant* with O'Toole. We visit him near Caerleon and the men talk Shakespeare line by line and we women talk obstetrics. Is it being pregnant that excludes me from everything interesting? I hate Women's Talk. I'm sure that having a baby will be a breeze and there's nothing to talk about. I want to talk about Shakespeare. I feel mutinous.

And yet I have more fun with this Irishman than I've ever had in my life. One night he decides to cook dinner – he's never been known to cook anything. 'Oh yes. I can make French toast. The best French toast. Just leave me to it.' As the stove explodes into flames and we wrestle it, covered in blankets, out of the house on to the mountainside and the entire kitchen needs repainting and we have no supper, the three of us stand in the flame-lit cold garden and rock with laughter. It's been sad in this house since my Aunt Maya died. It took this conflagration to restore life and ordinary happiness and it took O'Toole to light the fire. He has an invincible drive towards joy and life.

My uncle has to go to Westminster on Council of Wales business and we volunteer to drive him to the station in Neath and pick him up a few days later. We set out after dark to collect him and on the hill to Rhyd-y-Fro the car goes out of control on black ice. This is it. We're in an uncontrollable spin. I remember from my school days that there's a big drop on the right. For what seems like miles we career from right to left and I pray that we shan't meet another car. Finally, we crash into a bank and come to a halt. When we pull out we have a young sapling embedded in the back door of the car. 'Whew! That was close,' says O'Toole, cheerily, 'but if we get a move on we'll still be on time.'

Through the moments of danger O'Toole said, 'Put your feet on the dashboard. Keep calm.' And I said, 'Don't worry about me, I'm all right. I'm prepared.' And I *was* prepared and I was not frightened. And he *did* get us out of trouble and we *were* in time for the train.

Davy, when he get into the car along with the young tree, splutters, 'What—?' 'Oh, just a little tap,' says O'Toole and Davy beams, reassured, as he leans away from the buckled door. How does O'Toole do it? Davy would have wanted an explanation from anyone else. He also is under the spell. It's no wonder that my family feels about O'Toole much as I do. Who wouldn't? He says the awful, confronts the impossible and shrugs it off as though it were nothing. He doesn't *care* that his car is ruined and that he can't buy a new one. His priorities that night of Davy's return were to avoid getting us killed and then to meet the train on time. Both were accomplished and he was contented. And so were we.

The family has moved away from Tŷ mawr on the Betws Mountain to the richer lowlands further west. My parents now live in East Glamorgan at Dyffryn House. It seems odd to look up the Betws across the meadows at the farm where I, my mother and my grandmother were born and to think it belongs to someone else. I don't mind that. It never was technically *mine*, but it is mine no less now than when I inhabited it. Property is a mystery. There are things I own that don't feel mine at all but some things are mine forever.

The new farm is in Whitland. When the proposal to move was put to my grandmother, John and Meriel, my uncle and aunt, expected it to be the beginning of a long period of persuasion, emotional and painful. Elizabeth – Mamgu, my grandmother – sat in the house that her grandmother had built and looked at the business proposal and having thought for a bit said, 'So, when do we move?' When she drove away, almost ninety years of age, she looked straight ahead.

O'Toole is taken down to Whitland. The farm is set in beautiful countryside, gentler, easier, more profitable than the slopes of the Betws above Gwaun-Cae-Gurwen. The house is a traditional long house, at one end is a room with a deep and high inglenook and that is where my grandmother sits. O'Toole and Uncle John and some of the boys sit up late in the 'top room', drinking whisky. John and the boys are up and about early, back at work. So is my grandmother whose life is geared to six o'clock milking by hand (days long gone). When O'Toole descends at ten o'clock she greets him in that intimidating way, each English word weighed and considered, 'Good day to you'. She's slightly wrong-footed by her lack of English which is lucky for him, and never having encountered suede, she has spent quite a while trying to get a shine on his desert boots. Almost blind, there is very little she can do that is useful but she has to do something – something now reduced to washing up and cleaning the seventeen muddy pairs of boots and shoes in the kitchen corridor every morning. While O'Toole sits at the table I quickly cook us a Welsh breakfast and put both plates on a corner of the big table. I'm about to sit when her voice emerges from the semi-dark of the inglenook. 'Siân! *Tend* to Peter.' I realize that she expects me to serve O'Toole – pour tea, cut bread and wait on him before I give myself breakfast.

His eyes light up with amusement. It is inconceivable that I should disobey her, nor would I wish to challenge that touching certainty in her voice. She knows how things should be done. But this is a woman who ran a farm while her husband gossiped, and whose mother knocked her drunken husband down the stairs to his death. They are fearless and frightening these women but part of their strategy seems to be that lip service should be paid to the god-like quality of Man. As I stand between Mamgu and the table, I can see the funny side of this breakfast ceremony but I don't want to carry her teaching into my life and times, not even as a joke. I don't want to bend the knee – but then, I can't run a farm either. I feel lost between two worlds.

Chapter Seven

January 1960 and I was almost at the end of my pregnancy. O'Toole and I finished taping the Saunders Lewis play, *Siwan*, this time for TV in Wales, and then we moved to Stratford-on-Avon. Dr. Slattery had referred me to a doctor in the town. I made myself known to him and I liked him. He was reserved and quiet. I had been booked into a cottage hospital. We were to live in 'Mount Pleasant' (promptly re-christened 'Mount Unpleasant' by O'Toole). It was the house occupied during the 1958 season by John Osborne and Mary Ure (and a right nasty time *they* had there, I was told). We hoped we would have better luck with it.

It looked all right; a big double-fronted Edwardian house, two stories high with a grand porch, almost a porte cochère. There was a lawn at the front and a rough private lane that led down through the fields to the road into Stratford. At the side, the drawing room side, there was a huge dilapidated conservatory. I loved the drawing room – big, with huge, comfortable neutral colored sofas and armchairs and a large stone fireplace. There was a big dining room (the table seated about twenty people), a somewhat gloomy morning room furnished with reproduction oak furniture and at the back a big 1950s kitchen. The master bedroom and its bathroom were lovely – windows south and west like the drawing room below. There was another bathroom and two bedrooms and out at the back there was a stable wing which would be taken by someone else in the company. I wondered nervously who my close neighbor would be. I didn't notice the door at the back of the big front hall. Fool that I was, this was the door leading to the most important object in my life for the next six months. The door led to the cellar, and the cellar contained the Boiler, the monster which had to be fed with coke before we had heat or hot water in the rooms above.

We didn't have much in the way of possessions so I called a taxi and went into town to buy extra china, linen and cutlery. Meriel, my mother's sister, had sent me lovely bed linen and my mother sent me a superb Welsh throw. I looked at the immersion heater in the bathroom and wondered how to live economically in what was a very big house. What did it cost to run a house? Damn it, why didn't I know these rudimentary things? I was heavy now – and resenting it – but, finding the cellar, I started shoveling coke. O'Toole was going to start rehearsing at any moment. He had discovered that there were two or three more possible Shylocks standing by in the wings in case the wild Irish boy didn't come up to scratch. Could this be true? If so, the pressure on him was awful and I decided he didn't need to know about the coke boiler. (But *was* it true?) Now I was alone most of the time. The boiler was a monster and all my worries about the impending birth and my inability to run a house were centered on the problem of getting the elderly central heating system to work properly. I didn't know anyone here in Warwickshire – and there were no neighbors. My family was a long way off and anyway, I wanted to be able to stand on my own feet. There was no one to help with the cleaning. With the confidence of the healthy and ignorant I was not in the least worried about giving birth but I was terrified that I would not be able to run our lives once the baby was born. Would I get the food right? How did you tell the difference between a cry of hunger, a cry of pain or a shriek of bad temper? I was painfully aware that I had never spent *five minutes* in the presence of a baby. Would I be able to keep the heat and water going? Would everything come naturally?

Feverishly I read my Dr. Spock over and over again. We

didn't have any prospect of help with the house or the baby and I tried to give myself a crash-course in housekeeping. Marie Kean in Ireland sent me a large hard-backed manual on domestic science and it quickly became dog-eared and dirty with furniture polish, detergent, cooking fat and blood. My hands were covered in small cuts. Apprehensive and clumsy, every time I began a simple task I cut myself – on sardine tins, chopping knives, the shovel in the cellar, blades of grass.

Alcohol had always been a major factor in our life together and, coming from a non-conformist, teetotal Welsh background I had been charmed by the guilt-free, amusing nature of drinking-to-excess as practiced by the Irish. There was something so wonderfully un-English, un-Welsh and un-Scots about Dublin society where if you needed to see your MP you called round to his favorite bar, after hours, where he was busy getting very drunk. Everything functioned but there was a refreshing absence of bureaucracy and a totally un-British attitude towards life. And how merrily I laughed when I learned that the process of casting a play in Ireland began with the question 'Is he all right', 'all right' meaning back in circulation after a spell in hospital, drying out. The funny stories about drink were legion and no one enjoyed them more than I.

From being only a part of life, enjoyed in an endless festive atmosphere, drink became a dominant factor in my daily life. And I was alone now, no partying friends making jokes, and suddenly I was vulnerable and afraid. I was surprised but not shocked to find that my free spirit, my equal partner, expected me to take care of myself, clean the house, wash and iron and provide meals and be on parade when needed. This was the standard male expectation at that time. And I was faintly ashamed that I was so ill equipped for the job. I *was* taken aback however when I was told that the baby, when it arrived, was not to interfere with my husband's work. That *wasn't* what I'd expected at all; I think I'd rather hoped that I and my baby would be the center of admiring attention (it's possible that a cradle with muslin drapes featured in this fantasy). Now our roles in life were made separate and strictly defined and I mentally revised the scenario of my life within wedlock. I couldn't begin to think where *my work* fitted into this and there were no discussions on that subject. I made meals at night and threw them away uneaten before I went alone to bed. Sometimes there'd be a dawn demand for something to eat; more often I would wake to find O'Toole asleep in an armchair, an overturned glass beside him. I looked out to see if the car was all right and wished I could take an axe to it. His driving when drunk had become my chief worry and source of fear. I tried not to think of the journey from Stratford to Mount Unpleasant. Every night I tried and every night I failed.

Stratford, the marshy graveyard of showbiz relationships. On Monday mornings the platform at Leamington Spa was damp with the tears of furious actors' wives, returning to London tight-lipped and red-eyed after a ghastly weekend. I couldn't leave. And I didn't want to. I was damned if I was going to join the list of Stratford casualties. Stubbornly, I resolved to find a way of living through what was shaping up as a testing time.

What happened next would have defeated me utterly had I not been so near to the birth of the baby and had I not thought – rightly or wrongly – that O'Toole was beside himself with nerves and worry. I was aware that his professional future depended on this performance as Shylock. There had been a few setbacks and missed opportunities and his drinking habits had led to a few hilarious and possibly damaging episodes. The bottle of whisky that fell out of his overcoat pocket as he sat down to talk to a producer, Cubby Broccoli, who wanted to see if he might replace someone with a 'drink problem' (at that time only Americans talked of drink as a 'problem') had added to a burgeoning legend. Now, he needed this job and needed to do it well. He was prepared, maybe over prepared, but he was still unconvinced that he had the confidence of the management. His moods became darker and his drinking became more dangerous. Every morning he pulled himself together. Doubtless the knowledge that he believed he was being watched made matters worse. I was completely on his side even as he tried to push me away. My admiration for him as an actor was enough to withstand the anxieties and miseries of this life of insecurity.

When drunk he was savagely critical of me and my ego was taking a severe beating. When he imitated me, I could see there was some truth in his cruelty but I recalled Hélène Van Moeurs at RADA, out of patience with the psycho-babble of the day saying, 'Ego? Little ego? To hell with ego! If my ego is so little and so feeble, it can go and take a running jump. I'll do *without* my ego.' I resolved to banish *my* ego, batten down the hatches and sit out the storm. Is it possible that you perversely push away your support just to test how sound it is? I felt he was doing that to me, trying me to the limit. That was the only interpretation of events which made sense to me but this may have been my way of justifying my acceptance of a situation in which I was learning not to answer back, not to argue, not to defend myself. Sobriety brought wonderful interludes of repentance and irresistible charm, when I believed myself supremely loved and needed, but when I was made to feel like a useless encumbrance I believed that just as fervently. I was living with the good cop and the bad cop in one person.

Meanwhile O'Toole justified his erratic behavior towards me in the most unexpected way imaginable. He was the last person I would have expected to take the high moral ground over anyone's behavior, let alone mine. Now he did just that. I had never made a secret of my past or made anything much of it either, never having had to live among people who subscribed to the Fifties double standard for men and women. The thinking of the time was that nice girls 'didn't'. Girls didn't really enjoy sex. Casual sex was fine for men but out of the question for women. Women were, by nature, monogamous and men were naturally promiscuous. Lest all this should seem to be something left over from Victorian times, biological arguments were produced to show that women were chaste in order not to become accidentally pregnant and men were promiscuous in order to ensure the continuation of their genes. Women were either Madonnas or Whores of Babylon. The idea that girls might have sex because they liked it, or for affection, or for fun, or for company, or out of boredom or loneliness was not entertained. If they did it they were Bad. I had lived a life of carnal pleasure outside wedlock, completely guilt-free. Now, as the weeks went by I came to accept the fact that my position was fairly untenable – in fact I had no position at all. In between whiles there were passionate reconciliations but I lost my spirit and doubted that I would get over this. I was disenfranchised and very little trouble to live with. A quiet girl.

This is how I saw things in early 1960, but I was pregnant and I was living – trying to live – a new, different life and perhaps my view was distorted. Even then I could see that my wish to keep up appearances *was* ludicrous and O'Toole was right to despise my petit-bourgeois desire to keep our problems secret. When he was drunk he publicly exposed his view of my character and at that time I couldn't endure the humiliation. The best I could do was to remain impassive but it was a very long time before I learned not to care what people thought. At that time I cared desperately – I wanted a private life, lived privately.

February was the longest month that year. I saw no one, spoke to few. My parents occasionally telephoned and we talked about immersion heaters and heat conservation and the boiler. O'Toole's big sister, Pat, who lived in a rich suburb of Birmingham, called and offered to help. She had married well and was living the most comfortable and orderly of bourgeois lives; a life I wouldn't have admired or wanted until now when, insecure and adrift from the certainties of my life, I envied her the calm, the certainty, the regular meals, the rock garden, the rose beds, the expensive reproduction furniture, the dogs, the housekeeper, the attentive husband who left the house and returned at the same time each day. I didn't want her or anyone else to visit me and see or hear what my life was like. It hadn't taken long for my Celtic guilt and pessimism to rise to the surface and I now felt that I was to blame for everything that was happening to us. All the attitudes I had despised as hypocritical or retrogressive reared up to mock me. I had been wrong all along about everything – especially my instincts. Seeing that I was low in spirit, Pat took matters into her own hands and in a rather feudal manner drove her housekeeper over to Stratford and left her with me for a few days.

Austrian Gertrude quickly took charge and for a while all was quiet and the smells of comforting middle-England meals soothed me more than any kind words could have done. I watched her moving around the big house, taming it, and felt admiring and inadequate. After she left, I found myself alone again but now the house was orderly and well stocked with food and cleaning material.

Before I had time to become anxious again – the baby was due in a week's time – I fell ill with influenza. I didn't know where O'Toole might be and I could no longer climb the stairs to bed or descend to the boiler so I made a bed on the couch in the drawing room and lit a fire. I don't know how long I lay there, alternately shivering and perspiring, but one night after dark fell I awoke to find my doctor in the room re-kindling the fire. He'd become worried because I hadn't kept an appointment and, failing to reach me on the phone, he had driven up to the house and when no one answered the door he'd peered through the drawing room window and, seeing me lying on the couch, had broken into the house through the crumbling conservatory. I was too ill to eat and he left me with plenty of water and a roaring fire and went away, saying that he would be back in the morning. In the morning, miraculously the flu had gone away as abruptly as it had arrived and slowly I got up, bathed, washed my hair and began to tidy the makeshift encampment in the drawing room.

Unexpectedly, O'Toole appeared after work and was sweet and solicitous and made me sit down while he cooked supper. I was astonished by his re-appearance and sat there meek and vacant in the morning room; a room I would not normally sit in, it was so dimly depressing. I was given an enormous over-cooked plate of fried food and it was one of the best meals I've ever eaten. Some things do come naturally to one and suddenly I knew that I felt different. O'Toole's timing had not deserted him. He'd come home just in time to drive me to the hospital to have our baby.

Chapter Eight

I've always felt apologetic towards my daughter Kate, not least because her birth was one of the most humbling and in a way annoying experiences of my life. It was unlike anything I could have imagined and it *hurt* and my physical well-being, my athletic body, was useless to me. I simply couldn't get the hang of what was going on. Whatever it was, it was out of my control and I didn't like it. Lying alone, cold and fractious on a gurney in a hallway, I grizzled quietly to myself, a passing nurse flicked my shoulder with the back of her hand and said sharply, 'Come on, come on. Pull yourself together.' She gave me the mouth-piece of a gas and air machine and left me to 'pull myself together'. And I would have done had I been able. Rubber nozzle over my nose and mouth, I breathed deeply again and again before I realized that there was nothing but stale air in the machine and that the situation was getting nastier very fast. I didn't really want to see Miss Brace-Yourself of 1960 again but she reappeared with a colleague and they wheeled me out of the sad, dark corridor into a warm room with a very bright light overhead. I lost track of time. The pain worsened, the light grew brighter, brighter and then became completely white until the room was all brilliance and the light made a loud buzzing noise in my ears and I fell into blackness.

Waking up in bed in a ward, I thought I must have had a baby and I waited for someone to bring me a cup of tea. 'The best cup of tea you'll ever have in your life,' I'd been told. Ordinarily I didn't like tea but I really wanted this cup of reward-for-having-a-baby tea. When it didn't come I thought,

'Well, that's just about typical of this whole experience.' As soon as I was able to sit up and look about someone came and I was told that there was nothing to worry about but there was some complication about the baby's blood, which had to be changed. It seemed as though that was a lot to worry about and I lay there miserably. There was no way of demanding information. Demanding anything was out of the question in a 1960 hospital, but one had no reason to fear that best efforts were not being made on one's behalf. After what seemed an age, they brought me my baby. I looked at her, completely separate, already getting on with her life, and I wished I could feel that I'd *done* something. I wished I hadn't fainted before she was born. I felt as inadequate as I'd feared I would. I didn't know how to feel or what to do next. I held her and she seemed pretty solid. Whatever happens, I thought, I'm going to rear you properly. I didn't feel emotional. Just very, very determined.

There was a gypsy girl in the ward (a gypsy with no husband; how low can you get?). She and I were the only ones with no regular visitors at visiting time. (Visiting times were strictly ordained and maintained.) I tried to sink down below the sheets and pretend to be asleep lest anyone should come over and be sympathetic. Roy Dotrice's wife was right opposite and I didn't even want Roy's pity at that time. Just once O'Toole came in at the right time bearing a white television set! Televisions were still out of the ordinary and we couldn't watch this one – there was no aerial – it sat in a corner, silent and glamorous. One night, when all the lights were out, I awakened to hear the sounds of drunken revelry from the grounds outside – O'Toole and a car full of actors had left the pub or the party to come and serenade his daughter. Hoping no one would wake up and complain, I lay silently in the dark, looking at the ceiling until they went away.

I didn't feel very well. Sister said I was to feed Kate, as we decided to call her, in a small side room where I could be alone.

Sitting there one afternoon, I overheard my doctor talking to the Sister. Referring to the gypsy girl and me, he said, 'Keep both of them in. Neither has a suitable home environment.' I'd read that tension was bad for breast-feeding so I tried not to tighten my grip on Kate as she lay there. I couldn't look at her for shame. I had no suitable home for her to live in.

A few days later in the ward, we were both in better shape. The breast-feeding – so important to get right – was on track at last and I felt notably less of a failure. Kate looked quite wonderfully normal and even amusing. '*Kätchen lumpen*', I called her to myself, little lump of a Kate. Child of Stratford, she's called Kate, not Katherine, for Shakespeare's Shrew, she is 'Kate, sweet Kate, the prettiest Kate in Christendom'. O'Toole was due to play Petruchio after *The Merchant* opened and Peggy Ashcroft would play the Shrew. Before that, in a month's time, I was going to play Kate in another *Shrew* at Oxford. Many of O'Toole's friends became fathers round about this time and the preferred names were Kate and Emma. As I looked at my Kate a ladybug flew through the open window and came to rest on her shawl. I love ladybugs and in my shaky state I took it to be an omen – she was going to be all right. I hardly liked to think 'What about *me*?' No matter where I turned, this was not a 'me' time. But it was my deep-submerged question.

My experience during our winter weeks in Stratford had been so unnerving that I was anxious to resume what was to me the security of working life. I was able to do television plays until four weeks before Kate was born and then, four weeks after her birth, I would go back to the theater. I would start rehearsing *The Taming of the Shrew* in London. Kate would come with me. I didn't know how to organize this but Ken and Doriah were letting me stay with them during the week and I would return to Stratford at weekends until I was ready to open at Oxford, when I could commute by taxi each day. If anyone thought this was a mad plan, not a word was said. It was up to me to pull myself together again and I was silently determined to try.

The cry of all new mothers – 'What did I *do* with all the time at my disposal before I had a baby?' Mount Unpleasant has become a school where the sole subject is Reality. Indulgence is a thing of the past. Every moment is taken up with learning how to take care of another life and the demands change every week. Armed with Dr. Spock's book, I am efficient and determined to prove I am when the nurse comes visiting. I pass the test; the breasts are working like clockwork, Kate is functioning smoothly like a little engine but there is something wrong here. I am so anxious to get everything right that there is little room for spontaneity. Housekeeping is still a monstrous, alien task. Now there are visitors to see to as well and even if they only want cups of tea, rushing between the sink and sitting room, cutting bread and making sandwiches, keeping my eye on the clock for Kate's next meal, exhausts me. Washing up, cleaning, tidying the sitting room against the next wave of guests, running down to the cellar to feed the boiler, hand-washing clothes (no washing machine), ironing (what is the secret of the knack of ironing? If I do it the *Good Housekeeping* way I shall have time for nothing else). All this is unwelcome activity and, try as I may, I don't like it. I don't like it because I'm not good at it and practice isn't making me better. I love Dr. Spock because he makes me feel successful. I hate *Good Housekeeping* because it makes me feel a failure.

Meanwhile the tension heightens. Only a few weeks to go to the opening night of *The Merchant*. Occasionally, some of the actors roll in, ostensibly to see Kate, actually to settle down, drink and gossip or worry aloud about their jobs. One night I go up to her and someone has dropped hot ash on her foot and I'm so full of bile I find it very hard to be civil to these genial fellows. They seem to inhabit another world; carefree, joky. I'm jealous, of course. This was *my* world. Well, now it isn't. Maybe it won't ever be mine again. Soon I'll go away but I don't want to leave O'Toole alone here; it isn't much of a home but in my absence it could disintegrate completely.

My mother-in-law comes for a brief visit. We haven't met since I visited Leeds as the Girlfriend. I'm struck again by her good looks and her beautiful, whisky-soaked, 'Tallulah' voice. Desperately trying to be the good daughter-in-law, I go along with everything she suggests. It's really difficult not to react when she urges drink on her son. I can't understand why she doesn't know that 'Just one more small one, son' can be the beginning of the end of an evening. When it comes to breast-feeding time she sits in on what has hitherto been a private occasion. 'I worked in a hospital you know.' Beside myself with misery, I grit my teeth and submit as she seizes my breast and rearranges it. O'Toole, reentering the drawing room at that moment, sees this piece of intimacy and roars his revulsion. Doors slam and the car is heard roaring off. He won't be seen again for some time, certainly not until tomorrow. His mother shakes her head, disappointed to be left with me and an empty whisky bottle. Too late, she shrugs and backs off. Thank God for the beautiful white television set. We watch everything, including the 'Interludes', periods when a potter's wheel slowly revolves to the accompaniment of gentle music.

After a few days she leaves and O'Toole returns and we are reconciled happily. His mother thinks he doesn't care for me. He doesn't when she's around. When later, his father arrives we have an easier time but Patrick Joseph is not my cup of tea. We go on what is for me a mind-numbingly boring visit to Warwick races and I win money and he winks and says, 'Another sucker born.' (I don't think so, sir.) When I look at him I see the man O'Toole has told me about. The father sitting the little boy on the mantelpiece. Arms outstretched, he says, 'Jump, boy. I'll catch you. Trust me.' When the child jumps, the father withdraws his arms and as the child falls to the floor he says, 'Never trust any bastard.' O'Toole thinks this is an admirable story. I find it despicable, so I can't warm to the man. He *is* charming, in a way, but I would hate to be his wife or child.

Producing a baby has done nothing to improve my status at home. I don't know why I had been so sentimental as to think it would. Most people become embarrassed when my public trials begin, late at night. I'm not sure they believe what O'Toole says about me. Much as they like and admire him they think he has a 'bad' side, a side that creates chaos and confusion and madness and I, as the closest person to him, come in for the bad as well as the good. Only he and I know exactly what the dialogue is about and we do not fully understand the struggle between us. Those who don't like me rejoice. A childhood friend of his comes to visit and is hateful. Even at our worst O'Toole and I are close, and the friend feels I've usurped a special place to which I have no right. One night, when O'Toole has finished abusing me and collapses into a deep sleep, his friend looks at me across the drawing room and, picking up from the coffee table the big salad bowl full of uneaten, dressed salad, smiles as he slowly empties the oily contents on to the pale green carpet. I can't defend myself. I can't complain to O'Toole because I know he wouldn't dare to take my part against this free spirit – the 'poor' artist, from his past life – the person who belongs to a world that he may be about to leave for success and fame and money. The friend picks up the half-empty bottle of scotch and, still smirking, saunters to his bed in the guest room. I want to garrotte him. I am left to pick up the lettuce leaves and wash the carpet and fetch a rug to cover O'Toole, asleep in an armchair. I am not sad but full of loathing, loathing for O'Toole's servility towards his friend and for my own inability to jerk the situation into normality and reason.

Chapter Nine

Kate was four weeks old and I was rehearsing the *Shrew* in London but was home in Stratford for the opening of *The Merchant of Venice*. The season had already opened with *The Two Gentlemen of Verona* which was not bad but no great success either, so a great deal depended on this second play of the first Peter Hall season. And suddenly the wild Irish boy lived up to the worst expectations and disappeared into the Warwickshire air. Where was he? It was very simple, though shamingly no one at the theater thought to ring me at home in Mount Unpleasant. He did what few people would have expected, he went to bed. Knowing how tough he was under his somewhat ramshackle, airy-fairy manner, I didn't fear the worst. He'll play, I thought. Occasionally, he took a cup of tea, mostly he wanted to be left alone.

When the theater did begin to ring the house he refused to take the calls. 'He's not feeling very well,' I said, unconvincingly. Undeniably, he was under stress – and he *was* only twenty-seven – but in the back of my mind I wondered whether or not this behavior wasn't due to what he saw as a lack of support and confidence from the management. I had a faint suspicion that he might be thinking along the lines of 'You want to field someone else? *Four* someone elses? Go ahead. Do it.' The house was quiet. Kate, whom I was beginning to think of as a true theater child, was amenably good-tempered in her cradle at the far end of the drawing room.

Opening day tomorrow. I have to arrange some kind of party here at the house. Jules and Joyce will come before the show and Mrs O'Toole will be at the performance. I'm working on the assumption that he *will* play and I wash my hair and look out an old pre-Kate frock and ask the Shepherds at the local pub, The Dirty Duck, ('The White Swan' to the Brewery) if they will look after Kate during the performance.

The day of opening night and by now the calls from the theater are coming here thick and fast. O'Toole is still in bed, not speaking. I wish I knew what he was up to. I clean the house and see to Kate. No food is required in the bedroom. There are moments when I could take a club to him but the minute anyone complains about him I become his chief defender. Jules and Joyce arrive. It's teatime and the situation is becoming critical, to say the least. Now, thank God, Jules will take all the phone calls and we will take turns to visit the bedroom. On one of my visits O'Toole extends a hand and says softly, 'Come to bed, girl.' I do and we are reunited after the long arid weeks since Kate was born. I dress and go downstairs. Jules goes up and I hear him saying, 'Listen, kid, if you're not going down there *I'm* going to play Shylock and God knows, all I've got is the nose for it.' Suddenly, all is laughter and bustle and excitement and 'Where are my clean clothes?' 'How about a cup of tea?' 'Where's the car?' 'What's the time?' 'For God's sake everyone, get a *move* on.' And he's gone. It's almost time for the performance. We look at each other, Jules and Joyce and I. It's their first O'Toole experience. We're perched on a cliff edge, danger passed, giddy with relief. But what comes now? 'Let's go to the theater,' says Joyce.

Theater at its best, that April night, 'One of the great nights in the theater' they called it. Those of us who were there in Stratford looked at each other, smiling, knowing that this was a night to cherish for a lifetime. At the wild curtain calls I sat in my unbecoming dress, tears rolling down my face. Whatever it cost, and now I had no illusions as to the price of life with O'Toole, I was going to do everything I could to help cherish this talent. Joyce nudged me. She was in full, beautiful, glamorous, first-night mode. 'We have to go back. He'll be *mobbed*.' Child of Hollywood, she was used to high excitement, not realizing that by English standards this night was an extraordinarily heightened occasion. Backstage I had a brief moment with him alone. He was laughing. Clutching me with make-up encrusted hands he whispered in my ear, 'You're not going to believe this. Peter Hall was the first in here and he said, "We're going to be the youngest knights in the history of the theater." Is he completely mad?' I went to pick up Kate from the Shepherds, got a taxi back to the house and settled her for the night before greeting the guests at the party I'd hastily organized.

I tried to put a brave face on it as they asked, 'When will Peter be here?' I didn't think he would be home for some time. This was going to be Hamlet without the Prince. His mother was inclined to make a drama out of his absence and I spent some time reassuring her, telling her lies she didn't believe and she didn't help me by pretending to believe. I was nonplussed and caught off-guard, had no answer when a guest, non-theatrical and a stranger to me, inquired, 'Aren't you jealous? He could be anywhere, with *anyone*.' It didn't seem to be the moment to unravel my feelings, not even in the cause of polite hospitality. I filled her glass and moved on, smiling. She was insensitive but I had to accept that she voiced a question that must have been present and unspoken by many of our acquaintances.

I would have been astounded to have seen him on this of all nights, handing round the canapés on his own Axminster, surrounded by admiring, well dressed guests. At the same time, I would have liked him to have wished to share the moment with me in some way but it was his moment with no obligation to share it. I knew him well enough to know that he had a need as keen as a need for food and drink to be abroad, alone, obliterating the tensions of the weeks of anxiety as he had geared up to prove himself in this great part and earn his place in the front line of actors. For all his bravado, the understandable doubts and misgivings of those around him had kept him on the rack. Knowing nothing of science, I imagined that his system must be poisoned and curdled with left-over adrenaline churning around him with nowhere to go. Eventually, he would reach the point of oblivion and collapse somewhere. That worried me only in so far as I was concerned for his physical well-being. I wasn't jealous. Unless I had made a massive misjudgment, there was nothing furtive or squalid in his character and however outrageous his behavior he retained a certain style.

Standing in our drawing room with the party subsiding gently around me, Kate safely in her crib upstairs, I dealt with the smallnesses of opening night, passing food around, pouring drinks, promising to pass on congratulations, laying aside the presents and cards and when everyone was gone and the big house was quiet, I cleared up and washed up; tired, cross at being left alone at home, proud of his great achievement, glad to have got through the day and resentful to be the prey of so many conflicting feelings. '*Tout savoir est tout pardonner.*' Too much *savoir* puts one at a terrible disadvantage. It might be healthier to be able to look at things solely from one's own point of view. I put myself to bed and listened to Kate making small animal noises as she slept. I could hear her father's great voice in my head.

At this time O'Toole composed a song and would sing it, smiling. 'A sweet crime I sing you, a sweet, sweet crime. There's a dainty way to rape and a sweet way to kill but I know something still.' Love and destruction walked hand in hand that spring.

Chapter Ten

For me it was wonderful to be at work again. I was lucky in Frank Hauser, my director, and even more so in my leading man, Brewster Mason. Large, good-humored and self-assured, he had what was in those days an original approach to the relationship between the Shrew and Petruchio. Eschewing the paraphernalia of the war between them – the whips, the threatened violence which had characterized the famous 'wooing scene' – he said to me, 'Just establish yourself as a shrew – for whatever reason you choose – but when you come on for our first meeting, fall in love at first sight and I'll do the same and we'll see how we go.' I inquired nervously about the laughs, the funny 'business', and he shook his head and said, 'Trust me. No business. Let the play do the work. It *will* be funny.' Even Frank wasn't sure about this and I was only three-quarters convinced and very nervous. Only Brewster maintained his god-like calm, making time to put me in his car and run me home at lunchtime to breast-feed Kate in Doriah's flat in Belgravia.

My part was very active and after four weeks of vigorous rehearsals my milk dried up. Dr. Slattery had wanted me to breast-feed for four weeks and now I'd done eight so I thankfully moved Kate on to formula feeding and life became a great deal easier when I returned to Stratford and prepared to open the play – which worked like a dream! As the wooing scene approached I suffered a moment of terror; no props, no business, nothing but the words and a rather bare stage. Almost immediately I heard the first big laugh – another line and a huge laugh – a riposte and a roar of delight from the audience. The play really does work on this 'straight' level. Who'd have thought it? Not I. Thank you, Brewster.

We came in for a good deal of admiring attention from the academics in Oxford and from the press as well. Full houses always. Bianca was the gorgeous Samantha Eggar who had the most exotic beaux imaginable (Graham Greene seemed to be one of them or am I dreaming this?). She wore tattered jeans and cowboy boots and her boyfriend (Dandy Kim, renowned in the gossip columns – or am I dreaming this too?) picked her up in a jeep. What chic! No one else drove a jeep rather than a racy car. We shared a dressing room and she was forbearing about my taste for vinegar and chips. O'Toole was wonderfully admiring, especially lovely to Brewster and asked if he could 'nick a few readings'. Brewster, charmingly flattered, said, 'But of *course*.'

It was great to be back on stage in a wonderful part. Ted Hardwicke, O'Toole's close friend from Bristol, was in the company. Sometimes he drove me back to Stratford in his Morgan, and even *I* could tell that this was a special car and that he was a wonderful driver. He was also a lovely man, discreet and tactful. Son of Sir Cedric Hardwicke, an international movie star, he must have been accustomed to the very grand side of show business but maintained an impeccable, unassuming charm. I would say that he was more talented than his famous father, but I don't think he'd be glad to hear that. He told me stories about his time at Bristol with O'Toole when they used to entertain the talented young cub reporter Tom Stoppard (not so long ago Tom Straussler) in their humble dressing room. They played the smallest parts in their first year and invented fantasies about their unimportant characters. The road sweepers or footmen or ostlers which they played were actually the true leading parts in the plays in which they appeared, they only *seemed* to be unimportant. Occasionally the fantasies threatened the balance of the play and they were threatened with suspension if the 'complex business' they invented for door opening or floor sweeping or coat hanging wasn't cut out – *at once*. They'd spent an enviable three years acting together in the same company.

The atmosphere at home had become difficult as we approached our opening of the *Shrew*. I think O'Toole got scared for me, maybe he feared I was not as good as he would have wished me to be. I turned up for rehearsal one day wearing dark glasses to hide my eyes, red from a night of wakefulness and weeping. Frank was cross and shouted, 'For God's sake, take off the glasses!' As I did, the company grew silent and looked away, embarrassed. Nothing was said.

During the run I experienced a disturbing and revealing incident. The night had been endless with accusations and inquisitions. When had these interrogations begun? Long after we'd first met, after our long months of exploratory conversations where we had told each other everything we could think of about ourselves! I'd never talked so much in my entire life and I'd never been as open and honest with anyone. Discovery, marriage, houses, cars, a baby; it was as though it had been too wonderful, too exciting, too fast, too easy. Within a couple of months of Kate's birth when we moved to Stratford, everything began to come apart. What price now my belief that I was right to throw in my lot with O'Toole? What price my self-confidence in my own way of running my life? What about my rejection of the narrow morality of my non-conformist upbringing and my self-belief as I did what I pleased on equal terms with men? Hadn't I been proved right as my behavior led to this wonderful union with the unconventional, totally lovable man? It was as though one day my husband made a huge, delayed double-take and found my past behavior no longer just appalling but utterly unacceptable. Gradually, I came to see myself in the same, poor light. I was completely alone in that house, in that town and ashamed and frightened and only occasionally moved to answer back or to apply reason to the situation. Part of me didn't believe in his change of heart but part of me was heartbroken to be the cause of such blackness in O'Toole and such unhappiness in both of us and also, after Kate was born, to be responsible for bringing her into such an agonized home.

On this particular morning in early May, when usually O'Toole would have been expected to fall asleep, the row continued until it was time for me to leave for the Oxford theater to play a matinée. There was silence – maybe he had gone to sleep somewhere. Mindlessly, I set about packing Kate's luggage for the day. The taxi arrived and I began to load the trunk when I saw the driver's eyes lift and his expression changed. Looking over my shoulder, I saw O'Toole on the leads of the roof. There was silence all around. I couldn't read his expression but he looked – well – spectacular and impressive. He swayed precariously. I was aghast but it didn't occur to me to stay. I *had* to leave within minutes or run the risk of missing the matinée. Running into the house I called the only person I could turn to, my doctor. He promised to come over immediately. I got into the back of the taxi with Kate and said, 'Drive off, please.' Sitting there, looking straight ahead, I began to close my mind to the happenings of the night and the nightmarish scene I had just left. I was conscious of my lack of a 'normal' response; it was as though the effort of living with extreme behavior was numbing my reaction. I thought ahead to the theater and the prospect of doing two shows. Kate would stay with me in the dressing room, as usual, until I would hand her over to the wardrobe mistress as I went on stage. I felt a flicker of anger against O'Toole. It just wasn't *fair*. Living from day to day was proving exhausting and almost impossibly difficult *and* I had a job to do. I needed help and felt sabotaged at every turn. I couldn't sustain my anger. 'It's your fault,' whispered a voice in my head and how could I ignore the fact that O'Toole himself was in torment. 'Life isn't fair' was one of his often repeated remarks and I was slowly learning the truth of it. But clear in my mind was the conviction that I had to do my job meticulously with no concessions to my hopeless state.

We gave two good performances and, briefly, unbelievably to an outsider, I was very happy. On my return home I found the house in darkness. I hadn't been to bed for two days and once I'd settled Kate for the night I fell into a long sleep. When I awoke, O'Toole was home. We didn't speak of what had occurred.

Kate was now approaching five months old. I was still nervous of child-rearing, had worn out one copy of Dr. Spock and was into my second, but my life was transformed by the advent of Lonnie Trimble.

Our house in Stratford had become a kind of ramshackle hotel for people who wanted to see the plays and stay over. Working closely with the tourist industry, British Railway timetables made it impossible for people to see a play at Stratford and get back to London again on the same day, so our spare beds and couches were constantly occupied and once, in fine weather, there were makeshift beds on the lawns, as well. O'Toole was lavish in his offers of hospitality. More often than not he wasn't there to attend to his guests and very often I had no idea who they were and hadn't been warned to expect them. I muddled through the day from one nightmare meal to the next. His salary of £45 a week was going nowhere towards covering the cost of this generosity. The laundry alone was a major problem and I learned how to remake beds with roughly dried sheets, plugging the iron in at the bedside and ironing only the top of the sheet where it turned over. Fortunately I had my weekly income from my contract with Douglas Uren and had money left over from my pre-marriage days with which to help subsidize our life. Even so, it was a bit worrying.

Kenneth Griffith, most blessed of guests, arrived and solved some of my problems. He had made the acquaintance – I never discovered how – of a young, black, ex-marine from Atlanta, Georgia, one Lonnie Trimble who, having tasted life in the Navy, found it impossible to resume segregated life in the South. He was in England with no job, no work permit and needing some kind of humble employment for three years so he could become a legal resident and fulfill his ambition of becoming a chef.

Me: 'Well, Kenny, thank you very much, but I sort of thought that I needed a *nanny* right now.'

Ken: 'Yes! And *he's* your *man*!'

Well, why not? He could read Dr. Spock as well as I and he could cook a great deal better than I could, so it had to be a good move. It worked well in another, more subtle, way. I suspected that O'Toole was feeling half-guilty about the changes in his life; acquiring a wife and child was bad enough, renting a big house was a bit worse, employing a *servant* was beyond the pale. Which is why Lonnie was perfect; he was no man's servant. In his head he was already the boss of a catering firm. He wasn't an early bird either and I took him a cup of tea to awaken him in the morning. Oh, but he was fearless in the kitchen; an unexpected twenty people to supper brought a happy smile to his face. Faced with the usual request for a 'cup of tea and something on toast' from O'Toole, he sulked. Possessed of endless patience, he played with Kate; she emptied a box of matches and he picked them up. She emptied, he picked up. She was in heaven. We did the marketing together (it had never occurred to me before that you *planned* your meals and bought everything in one fell, weekly swoop). He was six feet four and jet black and beautiful. In the crook of his arm he held Kate in her beautiful white shawl which Sidney Poitier had unexpectedly sent me after we'd met at dinner one night in the White Elephant in London. 'All very well,' sniffed a Stratford housewife in an audible whisper in the greengrocers.

'It's the *children* that suffer.' Lonnie loved the sun and spent hours lying in it on the lawn. 'What are you doing,' yelled O'Toole as he drove off to the theater, 'trying to get a tan?' and sometimes, 'Get out the Leichner Five and Nine, I've got some really racist people coming for supper.' Lonnie looked at him from under half-closed eyes and shook his head with good-humored disdain.

Under his easy, masterful control the house assumed a semblance of normality. Now at least there were two of us ranged against the chaos. When times were bad between O'Toole and myself, he became an invisible presence in the house; to all intents seeing nothing, hearing nothing. It must have been an outlandish solution to his immigration problem. I could only hope that it suited him as well as it suited me. We didn't discuss it. He arrived in time to prevent a total collapse on my part. The scenes and inquisitions that had murdered the weeks before Kate was born resumed after her birth and I sank deeper into despair. I had never heard of post-natal depression, my books hadn't mentioned it. Babies, as far as I knew, arrived bringing good cheer and happiness unconfined, but I was getting more and more unhappy.

One night after hours of more close, drunken questioning about my past – and yes he was now right to doubt my veracity, I was lying with a will about everything. My instinct to tell him the truth had brought me nothing but trouble, and pins under my nails would not drag more confessions from me. The table overturned, doors slammed and the car raced erratically down the long drive. I walked out of the house reeking with fear and suspicion and noise, lay in the wet, long grass on the untended lawn in my nightgown, unable to stay inside. It was almost dawn but I didn't feel the cold. My wish was to get ill and die. 'Let me just *leave*,' I wished. Even as I made the wish I was shocked by my cowardice. Incapable of killing myself, what did I want to happen? That the harmless damp should carry me off while I wasn't looking? Desperate as I was, I couldn't bear to be so feeble. I sat up. It was quiet; in the distance the lights on the road led to Stratford, the theater, actors, my past life, the only life I knew how to live. As dawn broke I heard the country noises around me and I returned to my senses. I looked at the house, the scene of more misery than I could have imagined possible. Kate was inside, sleeping in her basket. What was I thinking of? So long as she was there, I would have to be there. Getting up, I returned to the house and sat on the floor, leaning against the wall, waiting until she woke. I might have forfeited my right to what I had imagined was my due as a wife and mother – protection, tenderness – but all her rights as a daughter shall remain intact, I swore to myself.

I don't recall O'Toole hurting anyone when drunk. He broke things and made a great deal of noise. I didn't fear for myself but the noise and the destruction terrified me. I hadn't quite acquired the knack of never answering back and sometimes unable to resist speaking up for myself I would add fuel to the flames. When he erupted out of the house, running in bare feet into the dark across the Warwickshire fields out of sight, beyond the lights of the house, I stood alone crying tears of rage and helplessness.

My nerve was gone; a raised voice, a loud noise – nothing much in themselves – these were enough to frighten me. Sitting alone, trying to find a solution to my helter-skelter home life I did the stupidest thing imaginable; for the first and only time in my life I called my parents in Wales and asked for help. My father had retired from the police force and he and my mother were running a further education house in the country outside Cardiff and enjoying the work and their pets and hobbies and generally living a more comfortable life than they'd ever had before. I had not lived with them since moving on to University but I visited as often as possible and they were completely charmed by O'Toole and impressed by his talent. Of course, they were ecstatic at the arrival of a granddaughter. The consequences of my phone call were appalling. My father, realizing I must be desperate, believed me to be seriously at risk and, hundreds of miles away and powerless, he collapsed. It was left to my mother to find a friend, Joyce (director Herbert Davies's wife), to accompany them on the long car journey from Wales to Stratford. When O'Toole, sobered, learned what I had done he was angry and appalled; it was the first time that an outsider had been allowed into our private torment. There was nothing to do but wait for them to arrive and for once he said little. He seemed contemptuous that I'd felt the need to lean on someone else. I didn't know what to think. I had lost all sense of self, all sense of pride in myself. I doubted my motives, my abilities. And yet, I was sure of my duty as a mother. And there were moments when I thought I couldn't be as bad as I had come to believe. Was *everyone* out there, in the world beyond the lawn and the field to the road, virtuous and good? I thought with envy of the Company in the town, going to work, going to the pub, having fun, misbehaving – and all in some way acceptable to O'Toole where I was not.

My parents and Joyce Davies arrived and there was a good deal of shuffling of feet and tea making. My father looked awful. I felt guilty all over again. For the first and only time there was a proper 'family' talk and I didn't much like it. I had to confess all over again bits of my past in order to explain why O'Toole was so angry with me. I remembered my friend's sister being expelled from Chapel for sexual irregularity and felt much as she must have felt. People went away in pairs, regrouped and whispered. I just sat there in a pool of shame. Finally all five of us sat together and the consensus of opinion seemed to be that 'We all make mistakes' – we now had to 'Go forward'. I wasn't too sure whose mistakes we were talking about but I felt it was better not to inquire. We seemed to have arrived at a measure of calm. O'Toole had some time off from work and he announced that my parents were going to take Kate to Wales for a week and he and I were going, at last, to the West of Ireland. This was the most unexpected outcome. O'Toole charmed them all over again. I would never be able to forget the events of the last few days. I didn't expect anything good to happen again but everyone was now smiling and making sandwiches and everything was behind us, it seemed. I was unbelieving but I was relieved to be out of trouble, even if just for the moment. O'Toole was adorable to me, as only he could be, and he was taking me to the West – the precious, mythical West he'd talked about so much, the home of the troublesome O'Toole clan, I was told, after they'd been banished by Cromwell from the eastern side of Eire. I was back in favor. I was forgiven. Why? For how long?

Jules's film, *The Day They Robbed the Bank of England*, was due to open in London in a few days and we were to go to that after our visit to Ireland and before I returned to Wales to pick up Kate and resume life in Stratford. I couldn't quite believe what was happening. Had I done the right thing after all by calling in my parents? My father's face was bitterly changed. I didn't know what he'd said to O'Toole but it was evident that the episode had cost him dear. His worst fears for me had almost come true. His expression haunted me. Even as he smiled and joked and said how pleased he was to be taking Kate to Wales and was glad to assist, I could see fear and defeat in his eyes. I recognized his look because I now had been taught fear and defeat. I was an unworthy wife, an uncertain mother and a troublesome daughter. My theatrical vows were neglected and broken. He never lost the look he wore that day and that was my gift to him, the man who would never harm me.

My mother, harder, more realistic, didn't address the problem, the discussion or the resolution. She took me aside, looked at me and said in Welsh, 'Understand, if you want this to work – and for Kate's sake you must make it work – from now on you're going to have to stand in a very small space.' The unspoken question, 'What are you going to do?' hung in the air. I knew she was right. I had seconds in which to think as bags were packed, the fridge was emptied, doors were locked, cars were loaded. I didn't look at my mother or answer her. O'Toole was looking at me, smiling. He held out his hand and I could no more resist him than stop breathing. I waved goodbye and with a lightness of heart that comes from doing the inevitable, if doomed, I took my husband's hand.

Chapter Eleven

After all that O'Toole had told me about the Eire beyond Dublin I was nervous when we arrived. What if he'd exaggerated? What if I couldn't enthuse? But, like Venice, everything was just as it had been described and at the same time better. The weather alone was wonderful to me and assuaged a homesickness I never dared acknowledge. It was weather Celts are used to and love; damp, unpredictable, changeable, unreliable, enlightening. Jack Yeats, the painter, talking of the problem of painting in the West said, 'The light has legs,' and everything does change even as you look at it. In the West, the countryside is a mixture of the lush – the Gulf Stream nudges past the coastline, cabbage palms intrude exotically, fuchsia hedges riot around the brutally barren little fields – smaller than one could imagine – bounded by lumps of granite. Cromwell, consigning the native Irish to the West, sent them 'to Hell or Connaught'. Coming from farming stock I was appalled by the agony of farming this landscape which looked at times like the far side of the moon. And the people – this was a foreign land and it was home to me. As a Celt, I was used to listening to stories, hearing people sing for enjoyment, wasting time talking, but these people were something extra, something from a past I'd only been told about. The gift of story telling, now barely a memory in close-to-England Wales, flourished here from acknowledged spielers to your neighborhood grocer or the bus driver. Language was supreme. I remember that in London O'Toole and I were one night trying to find the Stratford East Theater. Hopelessly lost, we stopped a local East Ender who turned out to be an Irishman.

He directed us, 'You go down that road until you come to nothin' at all and you turn left.' Thanks for nothing. Going 'down that road' we came to a bomb site which *was* 'nothin' at all' when you think about it. So we 'turned left' and there was the theater. At the time I thought that man was a poet. Now going West, I realized that he was just an Irishman.

Coming to a crossroads we saw two men, *not* hitching a lift – nothing so vulgar – they were looking expectantly in the direction in which they wished to go. We stopped and they got in, my first Irish countrymen: the tall, serious, thin one in the front with O'Toole and I hopped into the back with the small, cheery, fat one. (How did I know to give up my place to the natural leader?) We drove in silence for a while and O'Toole asked his passenger if he'd ever been in England. 'Yes,' was the taciturn reply. My small, fat friend dug me in the ribs. 'He was in Dartmoor and Pentonville.' Oh, gosh. 'Yes, he was trying to shoot policemen and needless to say, he missed.' We both heaved with merriment in the back. The tall, thin, would-be murderer asks, ruminatively, 'Have you ever been to Brighton? When I left Pentonville I went there. Beautiful. England is beautiful.' I didn't really know what to say to that. They got out, thanking us in a sprightly, somewhat Japanese way that I remembered from Yugoslavia – a touch to the heart, the head, and then open the palms and bow from the waist.

In the Great Western Hotel in Kerry, as we sat in the garden the bartender approached us unsteadily, tray tilting perilously away, he treading the lawn carefully as though he was negotiating very long grass. 'Bin and Binjer Jeer?' he intoned sonorously as we clutched at our falling glasses of gin and ginger beer.

I love, I love, I love this place. I want to live here. I think this is what Catholic Wales was like before Non-Conformism laid its hand on it. That's unfair. Non-Conformism has done so much to save us as a nation, made us remember we are different from a nation that has a ruler wedded to the Church of England, it's sent us underground, which produces another kind of strength and energy. But the joy of this place, the lack of shame, is overpoweringly attractive. It is with difficulty that I embrace my husband at times, but I unreservedly adore his country, the things that made him. He may not have been born here but he is a boy from Connaught.

Another time, we sit in Frank Kelly's pub, Kings, on the square in Clifden (the centerpiece of the square is a half submerged concrete public lavatory). As we drink our Guinness – 'Takes forever to draw, half a minute to drink' – a long faced man asks, 'Are you here for the funeral?' 'No,' I say. 'What funeral?' 'Peter O'Toole's daughter.' 'Oh, my God.' 'No, Peter O'Toole. Peter's daughter.' 'Sorry?' 'Peter O'Toole. Peter's daughter's funeral.' 'Oh, I see. Yes.' Looking around I see that I am surrounded by men who look exactly like Peter O'Toole, long faced, blue eyed, thin, almost skeletal, tall, beautiful in a Sam Beckett sort of way. This is O'Toole country. I want to live in it.

How could I have imagined a mere two days ago in Warwickshire that I would be sitting here in Ireland totally happy with my decision to stay married. I didn't just marry O'Toole, I married a country and I am ecstatically happy with my decision. This country is part of my child's inheritance, she is half Welsh and half Irish. I'm proud to have made her this.

And looking at these poor little abandoned farms – hearing stories of people's grandmothers found dead, lips stained green from eating grass – I dimly understand something akin to the Welsh experience, the fear of something beyond poverty, the total annihilation of one's right as a human being. Is the dread bred into his bones as it is into mine? If so, we have a difficult time ahead. How can the blind lead the blind? In a relationship, opposites are better. When he says, 'I'm done for', I think, 'Yes, of course you are'. What use is that? I think I see his truth and he knows more of my truth than anyone. We are completely 'suited', and we have such a chance of riches. He buys me a red-dyed bawneen jacket. If only we could stay in Ireland. This is the land of lost content for me, which is absurd because I encountered it only yesterday.

We lingered too long and now we had a wild race against time to get to London in time to change at Dorset Mews and get to the opening of *The Day They Robbed the Bank of England*. My hair was a windswept disaster and I didn't have time to get made up and I vowed I wouldn't again be such a good sport. I looked awful.

The film was very well received and O'Toole was first rate as the English officer. It wasn't a great part but playing it was a good move, I thought.

It was a better move than I could have imagined.

Back to Stratford. The trip to Ireland and the opening of the film have had a miraculous effect on our home life. We're happy. The days get longer, the elms and laurels round the house stop dripping, everything lightens. Lonnie cuts the lawns. Max Adrian has now taken the stable block and the moment I meet him I recognize a lifelong friend. He becomes Kate's baby-sitter or rather she shares his bed when he's resting. With Lonnie on board, I no longer dread the guests and the rickety domestic arrangements seem bohemian and amusing rather than desperate and slovenly. And what guests! Celebrities come and go. Sometimes Lonnie is the only person to see them. Anthony Quinn arrives for the weekend from America, the current girlfriend in tow. He beds down in Mount Unpleasant very gracefully and more or less ignores his gorgeous companion who sits in the drawing room and sobs for the entire weekend. Tactfully we also ignore her, walking round her armchair and leaving cups of tea within reach along with fresh boxes of Kleenex. He decides to take us to dinner and as I call the only decent restaurant he hisses, 'Book it in my name.' I call this restaurant at least once a week but I oblige him. 'Who?' says the Warwickshire lad on the phone. 'Anthony Quinn.' 'Anthony what? Can you spell that.' 'Q-U-I-N-N.' 'Is that Siân?' 'Yes.' 'Well, why didn't you say so, girl.' I replace the receiver and he smiles across the room. 'Got a good table, huh? Always pays to *use* the name.'

Elizabeth Taylor wants O'Toole to be in a rather dubious version of *Anna Karenina*. We've read it and it's horrible and O'Toole has turned it down but now Eddie Fisher is dispatched to Stratford to woo him afresh. Just for the fun of it, O'Toole nips up to the Dorchester for talks, wins £100 from them at poker and buys a new set of clothes, and having thrown his old ones away comes home looking gorgeous like a peacock. No *Anna Karenina* of course. Everything is fun. He's inundated with illustrious visitors but the only solid job offer on the table after his colossal success in *The Merchant of Venice* is a schools' broadcast for the BBC. We both vow that we'll try to remember this. Huge successes are more often than not followed by absolutely nothing.

I am approached to be in a play with Gladys Cooper and that is hugely tempting but just for the moment I feel I have a chance to mend my life with Kate and O'Toole and I decline. O'Neill's play *A Moon for the Misbegotten* at the Arts is more seductive still but now we are getting along so much better I will stick out what remains of the season in Stratford and fill in with radio and television. Now, unaccountably, life is good; I'm a good Irish wife; Marie is here; I feel useful in Mount Unpleasant. I'm living again with the man I married and he is the only person I can imagine living with.

Now most nights Kate and I are invited to supper after the show in one of the two restaurants in the town. She is an amazing child and sleeps in her basket under the dining table. (In the theater at Oxford she slept in a skip in the Wardrobe.) I don't think she ever utters a sound when she's out for the night. We don't go to the parties, of course, but at least I hear about them now and I feel a little as though I'm part of the season.

Patrick Wymark comes calling and when he gets drunk he puts classical music on the record player and conducts an imaginary orchestra for hours on end. He reassures O'Toole, who at twenty-seven is playing Petruchio to Peggy Ashcroft's fifty-two-year-old Kate, that she will *give* him more than any other actress alive. She has a reputation for being predatory towards her leading man and I can't help but feel nervous that she will be *too* generous with her attentions. But I remind myself that, at fifty-two, she's ancient and past such follies. She invites us to tea at the lovely house she's rented outside Stratford – strawberries and cream on the lawn. Hanging in the hall is her Vita Sackville-West type hat and rain coat. 'I walk to work,' she declares briskly. I'm afraid she *does* look struck by O'Toole but I don't think it's anything for me to worry about.

Sam Wanamaker and his wife invite us to tea as well (I hate tea but I like these invitations – they're a Stratford institution). They have a wonderful half-timbered house and beautiful garden. There are young girls – daughters? – in the kitchen but they don't join us. Kate's Moses basket is placed on the lawn and when I turn to see if she's all right I see her covered in blossom from the tree above. Her arms are raised and she's smiling in the soft pink shower. No one remarks on the sight but we all smile and the picture is engraved in my mind as *the* picture of my daughter as a baby in Warwickshire.

These were the more sedate aspects of our intense social life. The parties I didn't go to sounded a lot of fun. Jackie McGowran was in the *Shrew* company. He was one of the most famous Irish actors working in England at that time and 1960 was the height of his excess, the watershed of his drinking life. (At the end of the season he checked into a drying-out clinic under our former flat in Bryanston Street.) In his apartment in Stratford there were two goldfish called King Lear and Cordelia. During a party, in the early hours of the morning, Jackie slipped out of the sitting room and got busy with the frying pan. He re-emerged, ashen, saying, 'Jayses – I feel like a fuckin' cannibal. I've just eaten King Lear and Cordelia.' He'd had them on toast.

Dinsdale Landen and his beautiful wife, Jenny, woke one morning (at her insistence, 'There's someone in the room, Din.' 'Oh, don't be silly, darling') to find a damaged car, *in* their very damaged bay window. There was an explanation for this but at the time it escaped a hung-over Dinsdale. There was so much bad behavior during this season that people flocked to the town to see what this outrageous bunch of actors were getting up to. Mercifully, on stage, they were wonderful but it was touch and go at times. The Shepherds who ran the Dirty Duck were invaluable allies in times of crisis. One day Jackie McGowran before a matinée, blind drunk since the night before, said in the Duck, 'I can't go into the theater in this state – I'm a disgrace to my profession.' He was on a warning so it was imperative that he should play the matinée. 'Look, Jackie,' said Dinsdale, 'put your clothes on back to front and they'll think at the stage door that you're coming *out*, not going *in*.' 'Right, aould son,' said Jackie, beginning to take his clothes off. O'Toole mixed him a 'cocktail' of beer, mustard and tobacco from cigarette ends, guaranteed to make anyone throw up. Jackie drank it down, shook his head and said 'Great, aould son, great!' and proceeded to put his clothes on back to front. He played the matinée and never threw up.

The Stratford *Shrew* was a joyous production (Peggy carried Kate on at one matinée) and with other actors it went on to enchant London audiences, but it had had a difficult birth. John Barton's production was set in a winter-gripped Italy. The company was clad in furs and wools (a bit at odds with the text). There were endless scene changes and the difficult part of Biondello was played by a child. Peggy had decided to play Kate as a stroppy, angry, militant suffragette (shades of the CND demonstrations of the time). Came a night when Peggy shut herself in the dressing room in tears of despair and refused to come out. Rehearsals were abandoned. The following day, the furs and wool were jettisoned and the wardrobe department raided for sunny Italian clothes, the scene changes were halved, Dinsdale replaced the child and O'Toole persuaded Peggy to stop being Major Barbara and just come on and fall in love with him. She did and she was sensational. It was odd, seeing her do the 'gags' that Brewster had worked out for me but she did them so wonderfully that I was forcibly reminded that, in acting, it doesn't matter who *gets* the idea, it's how well you *execute* it that matters. She was heavenly and seemed younger than her Petruchio, who was more than young enough to be her son. The opening night performance was a great occasion but I didn't organize a party. The tense opening of *The Merchant* – the party without O'Toole – meant I never again expected an opening night, mine or anyone else's, to be pleasurable, or fun. But I was happy he'd 'done the double', as his bookmaker father would have said.

Chapter Twelve

O rdinarily I would have been disappointed that the proposed foreign tour of the Oxford *Shrew* was cancelled but, given the volatile state of my domestic life, I recognized it as a piece of good fortune. I was far from giving up my efforts to redeem myself in O'Toole's eyes but part of me just wished for a miracle; a change of heart on his part. The likelihood that he would turn round and agree that he was over-reacting to my 'past' – which was no worse than that of most of the actresses he admired and respected and which had never been concealed from him – receded as the weeks went by. Every so often our bubble of normality was punctured by scenes of appalling verbal abuse and these were to continue at unexpected moments. I realized with regret that in his eyes I was not a woman deserving of respect. There wasn't a stage play on offer that would not keep me away from Stratford for unacceptable periods, so I began to consider television plays again.

Wilfrid Lawson was one of the greatest and most revered actors of the first half of the twentieth century. A driving accident in Hollywood had left him with a legacy of ill-health and he continued throughout his life to be a spectacularly heavy drinker. He was a great actor and it wasn't his fault that subsequent generations strove to emulate his drinking exploits and his outrageous behavior as well as his talent. When I was considering a play by Kenneth Jupp, *Strangers in the Room*, O'Toole happened on the proposed cast list and said, 'You *have* to do this play. It's the chance of a lifetime to act with Wilfrid Lawson!' Richard Pasco, Donald

Houston and I were the leading players. Mary Ellis was going to appear and Wilfrid was to play the relatively small part of my grandfather. It was a good play but I went into it as a designated handmaiden to the great Wilfrid. 'Look after him,' said O'Toole sternly. 'Whatever it takes, DO it.'

I did. Wilfrid, playing a part that absorbed less than 10 percent of his ability, reined in his astounding talent and behaved meekly during rehearsal. The producers were on the alert for the smallest backsliding into drunkenness. Mary Ellis loathed him and his reputation, and *still* he was adorable. Remote and unfathomable – but adorable.

During rehearsals I had an urgent dental appointment and Wilfrid offered to look after Kate! (As usual I had her with me in her basket in London.) I couldn't believe this – I was so in awe of him and he was completely undomesticated. 'Where will you be?' I asked. 'At the Kismet,' he replied. The Kismet – the afternoon drinking place in Cranbourne Street, peopled by drunks in between licensing hours in the pubs, where the owner, dear Raj's father, cooked delicious but dubious curries in the rudimentary kitchen over a blackened stove. Never had a baby graced these premises. And a baby in the charge of Wilfrid Lawson? No. Yes. Why not?

I went to the dentist and rushed back to the Kismet and . . . Wilfrid and Raj's father had looked after her beautifully, so we stayed on for more convivial hours but even O'Toole was taken aback when I told him where Kate and I had spent the afternoon.

After that I was Wilfrid's willing slave and when we went to Manchester (without Kate) for the broadcast I was the first person dressed, packed and in the foyer of our hotel when Wilfrid was evicted for roaming the corridors in the night shouting for 'Aggie'. I knew that 'Aggie' meant something to Wilfrid. She meant nothing to anyone else. There was a story of him going to Germany to do a television show. In his scene he had to say, 'Kneel, serf,' and then proceed with some faintly ridiculous speech. The lines escaped him. 'Kneel, serf,' he intoned then, searching around for a suitable continuation, he went on, 'I have fought with Aggie' – long pause – 'the one-eyed Dane' – pause – 'several times' – pause – 'recently.' 'Cut!' said the horrified director in hushed tones. Wilfrid turned to his equally shocked fellow actor and murmured, 'That was a close shave,' pleased to have got away with something. He wasn't aware of being dismissed from the show and sent home to England. Who was 'Aggie'? Now she was here in a Manchester boarding house. I wouldn't have dreamt of abandoning Wilfrid and we taxied around until we found an Aggie-proof boarding house. The landlady liked him on sight. He kissed her hand and we were given lovely rooms and special breakfasts.

He repaid me by trying to give me a few acting notes. One of them: 'That big scene – don't play it like Lady Macbeth, it won't stand it. Never impose more weight than a scene will take. That's showing off. Never show off.' When we came to broadcast day for ABC television (the Aereated Bread Company, Wilfrid called it) he fell off the wagon. Chlöe Gibson, the director, was incensed. Mary Ellis was beside herself and Wilfrid stole every scene he was in; drunk but great. I sat on the arm of his chair (he was my grandfather) and acted away, laying down yards of text while he made holes in his biscuit with a pencil he happened to have handy. Even I was fascinated by this bit of business and I realized that my fascination with 'characters' and my slavish admiration for good actors was not going to be a help in my career. He was drunk as a skunk and all I wanted was for him to get through the show. As though he needed my help.

I was asked to join the Royal Shakespeare Company for its move to London and the first Aldwych season. I hadn't been on stage for a couple of months since *The Shrew* just after Kate was born and this seemed to be a gentle return. They were the dullest parts I'd ever been asked to play but I so wanted to be in the company. Events at home overshadowed this small decision. David Lean had seen *The Day They Robbed the Bank of England* and decided on the spot that he wanted O'Toole to play Lawrence of Arabia. Sam Spiegel – no admirer of O'Toole's – offered it to many other people including O'Toole's friend Albert Finney who, it seems, turned it down because he didn't want film stardom at that moment and Marlon Brando who turned it down goodness knows why. David's choice was always O'Toole. Sam desperately went on suggesting other actors, *any* actors. O'Toole went to London to do a test, the same test that Albert had done. His partner, Jules, an old adversary of Sam's, insisted that he test in uniform as well as robes. He looked great in both. David's instinct was confirmed and even Sam had to capitulate. O'Toole was undeniably Lawrence.

'It'll be a six-month shoot,' said Sam. Jules warned that movies on this scale took twice as long as scheduled. Sam insisted that it was a six-month job. O'Toole's contract with Stratford ended with the 1960 season, in the autumn with *Troilus and Cressida*, but he had expressed a wish to play *Becket* by Anouilh in London the following spring. He and Peter Hall went to the States to see Anthony Quinn in the play on Broadway. It was O'Toole's first visit to America and he fell in love with New York. For a city boy it was *the* city above all cities and it became his favorite playground. As a country girl, I wasn't sorry that he liked to visit it alone.

He was morally committed to *Becket*, five or six months away. Also on offer was the biggest film opportunity of the decade which should end in five or six months. When Sam Spiegel reluctantly gave in to David Lean's insistence and announced the casting of O'Toole as Lawrence, there was consternation at the theater. O'Toole was characterized as a traitor to his profession. Life at home descended again into chaos. The brief interlude of shared days and meals eaten together was over. I lost my precarious happiness. Sadness, which I didn't think to characterize as depression, crept closer and colored the days and nights gray.

I could still take my pick of the best television on offer but my confidence was at rock bottom. O'Toole despised radio and television, media in which I'd grown up. Welsh-speaking theater was, to him, not theater at all. The Welsh were completely outside the mainstream of 'real' life and art. I took him to meet Saunders Lewis in Cardiff. During lunch at the Park Hotel, he told Saunders this; Saunders took it badly and rushed out of the hotel to disappear from my life for five years. I thought that if he dared to treat our greatest Welshman in this way, there was nothing he wouldn't dare to do to me. At the nadir of my life at this time, the BBC came to Stratford to film a day in the life of one of the 'bright young hopes of the British Theater'. My agent said I *had* to do it. I slunk out of the house and spent the day walking around Stratford being interviewed in scenic spots, smiling, looking confident, talking about my 'exciting life' and my 'glittering future' and wishing I were dead.

Peggy Ashcroft summoned me to tea and lectured me on O'Toole's folly in 'selling out'. Surely, she said, I could use my influence to make him see sense and play Becket for the RSC rather than Lawrence in the movie. Much as I admired her I felt unfairly invaded. She was so enviably in the right, and at the same time so comfortable, so successful, so middle class, so English. I wondered whether she had ever been asked to refuse the chance to become an international movie star, in a great part, written by a wonderful writer, directed by one of the best living directors. Given my training and inclinations, I agreed with her and, asked to choose, I would have accepted a play rather than a film. But the world had changed and was changing very fast and in my heart of hearts I feared that my recent choices and the one Peggy was advancing were mistaken. And I wondered if she had any idea how little influence I wielded. Aloud I said that I felt it would be wrong for me to try to influence events. We parted frostily. I didn't want to alienate the great woman but even at a time of resentment and fury with him, my loyalty to O'Toole was absolute. I couldn't discuss him. Not even with her.

Our life spiralled further out of control as his professional problems grew more oppressive. He was being made to feel guilty and unworthy by day and at night he had the responsibility of two major parts and was on the receiving end of a huge amount of adulation. I felt that I and Kate and the house were just too much for him to deal with at this time. Had there been no love, no need on his part, it would have been easy to turn aside and wait for his life to return to something approaching normality. As it was, there were times when he clutched at me as though his life depended on me. And there were times when he couldn't bear to look at me and I had neither the years nor the sense to know how to find a balance. All too often now I found myself accepting his view that my behavior before I met him was something for which I had to atone. Marie Kean was the only person who was allowed to witness the worst of these scenes. On a brief visit she tried to make light of things for my sake. 'Look now. He can't have expected you to live like a NUN until you met him.' 'But he *does*!' 'Not at all. He's just having a bit of a bad time and it's up to you to put up with these Moments of Truth and it will all blow over.'

The Moments of Truth, as I learned to think of the hours when my character and morals were scrutinized and found wanting, grew more frequent and one night, more intense, more anguished than ever before, I decided that I could no longer continue to live in this fashion. As the car hurtled down the lane, I looked about me and vowed that I would never again spend the dark hours in this house which had become so hateful to me. I assembled Kate's things and packed a suitcase for myself. For the remainder of the night I restored the house to perfect order, working mindlessly until the sun was high in the sky. I bathed and called a taxi.

It was a couple of days since I'd slept but I wasn't tired. I fed Kate and took Lonnie a cup of tea. On a deep level and beyond expression, I was angry. I couldn't work out the consequences but I knew I had to leave Stratford, taking Kate with me.

It was a beautiful morning. I sat on the front step and thought I must be slightly deranged to be so happily affected by a perfect English summer morning, looking at a view Shakespeare might have seen. There had never been a moment in my life where my concern with my own affairs couldn't be entirely diverted into pleasure in my surroundings. That *must* be a kind of madness, I thought, not for the first time.

Barely more than a year since I defied everyone as they predicted that I was embarking on a course that would ruin my life and my career and if I'd laid about with an axe I couldn't have made a better job of fulfilling their prophecies. The stupidest thing I'd done was to allow Keep Films, at O'Toole's urging, to buy me out of my highly unusual and good contract with Douglas Uren. I had hoped that ending the contract would help our situation but all I'd achieved was to place myself in a very vulnerable position. I had to take a job as soon as possible. I was short of money.

The taxi was late but the best imaginable house guest appeared. Gary Raymond, slightly taken aback to be given a pram containing Kate and asked to wheel her around the lawn for a while, obligingly fell in with the unusual social arrangements. He'd been at RADA with O'Toole and had made a name in movies almost immediately (he'd just appeared in *Suddenly Last Summer*). Much too gentlemanly to ask questions, he helped us into the taxi when it arrived and I left him in Lonnie's care to enjoy the delights of Stratford, a place I devoutly wished never to see again. I reminded myself that I shouldn't make too operatic an exit since I would have to return to rehearse *Malfi* and *Ondine*, the plays which would open the RSC season at the Aldwych in December. How

I would organize that was impossible to imagine. For the moment I should content myself with the mundane business of finding shelter and quiet and getting some sleep.

Ken and Doriah's mews in London provided all that. I saw no one except Jules and Joyce briefly. I had cut myself off from everyone I had ever known and now I was much too proud to look them up, admitting I'd made a terrible mistake. Jules and Joyce were sympathetic but I reminded myself that they were in business with O'Toole; the three of them were about to take off on the exotic journey that is the beginning of a great career. I would probably have no part in this; already I felt part of the past. I don't know how people like Ken and Doriah preserve their integrity – discreet and unintrusive, they found it possible to shelter me and Kate without for a moment taking sides or even wanting to know what passed between me and O'Toole in Stratford.

And what *had* passed? Nothing that made any sense. O'Toole found it intolerable that he was not the first man in my life and he found my past beyond pardon. I found it intolerable that I should be blamed for having a previous life and then I came to blame myself for it as well. Was that really what made our lives so dangerous and hideous? Looking back, the only reality was that we were hurting each other beyond reason.

Chapter Thirteen

I spent a few weeks hibernating in London. Returning to Stratford to rehearse the new season was difficult. I found lodgings in a quiet back street and my landlady took care of Kate while I was at work. I ran home at lunchtime to feed her and returned home as soon as rehearsals were over, taking care that I was not followed. For two weeks I remained hidden. At night I sat in our room, reading, but inevitably in the end I was followed and found and O'Toole insisted that I be moved to his sister's house outside Birmingham. From there, I could commute to work every day and his sister's housekeeper would look after Kate. I felt like a Victorian serving maid who'd got into trouble and whose life was being organized by the Young Master. Had I had only myself to think about I wouldn't have agreed to any of this but I was now a mother and, good as my landlady was, my digs weren't ideal for Kate. I sat on my single bed and looked at her in her basket. What right did I have to subject her to this improvised existence which was the best I could muster? I had to admit that O'Toole's arrangement was better for her. I'd spent all my savings on that profligate season at Stratford and, my contract terminated, I now had no private income, only what I earned each week.

My brother-in-law, Derek Coombs, and his wife, Pat, were generous and tolerant. Their house and its comfort and security had an alarming effect on me. Arriving, I sat at the end of one of a pair of seven-foot couches and burst into tears. For two days I sat there and wept, rising only to see to Kate. I couldn't stop crying. The warmth and the comfort debilitated me completely. Derek and Pat looked in from time to time and just let me get on with it – whatever *it* was. Later, Pat said she thought I would never stop. She drove me to the train each day and picked me up at night and I marvelled at her kindness (I still do). She must have had better things to do with her time. I thought that my world had come to an end, but Derek and Pat didn't seem to understand this. I thought that if these good people understood how 'bad' I was and how my badness had led to the destruction of my life, they wouldn't want me under their roof. Sitting on the train to Stratford I wondered how on earth I had come through life before O'Toole with no carnal guilt. Now, I felt guilty about everything I'd ever done or felt.

Not only guilty but scared. Scared because not only was I heartbroken and sad, I was incompetent. All my life, through bad and good, I had been able to perform. Now, suddenly, at the beginning of this engagement with the RSC, I couldn't act. The prospect of walking on to the rehearsal set was terrifying. The prospect of 'doing it' in front of an audience was so terrifying that I couldn't entertain it. Was this the thing I'd only read about – stage fright – or was it life fright? To whom could I turn? There was no one except O'Toole and he was the prime 'fixer' and solver of acting problems. When he called me to see how Kate and I were doing, I slipped in an acting question. He responded immediately and effectively. Sensing I was in trouble, he told me to call him with a progress report. From that time on we talked acting every day. My tormentor had become my savior. Wouldn't it be nice, I thought, if we could solve acting problems all the time? We seemed so hopelessly bad at everything else.

We didn't meet. I was informed by Jules that O'Toole had rented a mews house into which I and Kate were to move when the company moved to London. What did this mean? Did it mean that we would resume life with O'Toole? I couldn't ask.

One November morning weeks later we *did* meet. He met

my train from Birmingham and drove me to the theater where
I was rehearsing. Parking the car, he said. 'Bit of a problem.
I'm to be taken to court because Anouilh is allowing *Becket*
to be performed only on condition that I play Henry.' It was
odd to be sitting so close to him. Reluctantly I acknowledged
to myself, looking at his left shoe and his hand resting on his
knee, that I loved him as passionately as ever. Focusing on his
problem, I said, 'I very much doubt, saving your presence, that
Anouilh has ever heard of you.' He looked at me for the first
time, my conspirator, and an evil Irish smile suffused his face.
'Hmm,' he said. 'Maybe I'll just nip over to Paris.'

In Paris, it seems that John Huston's mistress at that time,
the wonderful actress Suzanne Flon, also a friend of Jules and
Joyce, took him to see Anouilh who said, 'I am enchanted to
meet you but who are you?' Anouilh wrote a letter saying he
did not care who played the part and by November 10 O'Toole
was free to play Lawrence of Arabia.

We opened *The Duchess of Malfi* at Stratford while I was still
living in Birmingham. Max Adrian, with whom I played my
erotic scene, making love on a tombstone – he in Cardinal's
robes – was a tower of strength. Stephanie Bidmead got me
through the worst of my stage fright. O'Toole was wonderfully
supportive on the phone (the house in Stratford had been given
up and he was in London). I don't think I was very good but
my sights were so lowered that I was grateful to be 'on stage',
picking up my cues, making sense. It was the lowest point in
my professional life but at least I was practicing my profession
– and that was something.

Why was I so passive about my living arrangements? The
stuffing had been knocked out of me but I couldn't understand
how I'd been brought so low, so fast. There must have been
something in me – some infection at the core – that lay there
waiting to be exposed, biding its time to spread through my
system. O'Toole was the only person close enough to me

to probe that core and his terrors happened to chime with my failings. We clung to each other like drowning people, incapable of helping one another, unwilling to let go. We both had an instinct towards health and we kicked away from each other, only to return for another possibly fatal embrace. But health lay in being together as well. Parting for good was inconceivable. It wasn't an option for me nor, it appeared, was it for him. I don't think I hoped for happiness but I couldn't stop trying for resolution. Ken Griffith's words came back to me: 'Do you really think you can sustain being Mrs Edmund Kean?' I loathed the romanticism, rejected the exaggeration of the notion of the wild, doomed genius. But, all the same, I *was* hitched to an acting genius, according to some and I *was* attempting the impossible.

When *Malfi* opened, the rollercoaster life at Mount Unpleasant had taken its toll and I was very far from being the healthy, optimistic, confident young woman who had arrived in Stratford at the beginning of 1960. I was doggedly following Helen's dictum, and managing without my 'wretched little ego' but it was hard to get through the days. I had no idea what life held in store for me. Was I to live in our London mews house alone? Sometime soon O'Toole was to go to Arabia to acclimatize; learn to ride a horse, a camel, stay with the Bedouin who were going to make a major contribution to the making of the film, learn some Arabic, get fit.

I was astonished to read in the newspaper that his contract stipulated that each month I, his 'cherished' wife, should be provided with an airline ticket to visit him in Jordan or wherever he might be filming during the making of the film. What did that signify?

We moved to the Aldwych Theater and after *Malfi*, the company opened *Ondine*. Peter Hall's wife, Leslie Caron, was the water nymph and was ravishing but the play, like most of the French plays I was ever in, didn't travel well.

What a company it was, though. Peter Jeffrey, Ian Holm, Gwen Ffrangcon-Davies, Eric Porter.

So I returned to London to a little mews house in Hyde Park Gardens, a house rented for a year by our Company, Keep Films. O'Toole was in residence and charmingly anxious that I should approve the arrangements. Bemused, I settled in. It was as though the previous eleven months had not occurred. I was wary and faintly disbelieving as he took me out and we posed for magazine and newspaper features. My new helper – Swedish Marianne – was installed, Kate was promoted to a bigger cot and it seemed insane to embark on questions and recriminations. I wondered if I would ever lose the mistrust that had lodged in my system. I ignored it and faced forward, undeniably happy again.

Lonnie had moved on to a job cooking for the American boss of Pan Books just around the corner. It was a hectic job; he was all the help there was. He wore three uniforms in rapid succession each day. One for cooking, one for cleaning and one for serving drinks. On the evening of a dinner party, when the front door bell rang, he ran to answer it, tearing off his white cooking jacket and replacing it with a dark one as he majestically opened the door and took the coats. He served drinks wearing white gloves and from time to time hurtled back to the basement kitchen to keep dinner on track, tearing off his upstairs jacket as he ran. White gloves were replaced for serving at the table. Occasionally, English food flummoxed him. One night the telephone rang at 7:00 p.m. and an anguished voice said, 'Siân! Siân! Hurry! Hurry! Tell me, what is this mint sauce they're talking about for the lamb. Is it meant to be hot or cold?'

Domestic life was sweet and calm. Even when Marianne dropped all O'Toole's precious 78 rpm jazz recordings and couldn't look up she was so horrified by what she'd done, O'Toole shook his head tolerantly and said, 'Accidents.' His behavior was unnervingly benign. Then, a few days before

Christmas he went missing. I was upset but not as worried as I would have been a few months earlier. All our cars had been wrecked or abandoned and he was no longer driving so I had no fears for his safety. It was dismal preparing for a Christmas that might or might not happen. I trundled up the Edgware Road in the winter dark with Kate in her pram, assembling a small tree and colored lights and presents and food. On Christmas Eve I said goodbye to everyone at the theater and returned apprehensively to an empty house. Marianne left and Kate and I were alone. Obviously he wasn't coming home. Was it worth preparing a Christmas lunch – the first I'd attempted? Before I went to bed the front doorbell began ringing insistently. There was a great deal of noise in the mews and O'Toole was at the door, laden with presents for Kate, beaming with pleasure, so pleased with himself and pleased to be home that I didn't have the heart to spoil everything by pointing out that he'd been gone for days. After a bit he said, 'Have you looked out of the window?' 'No.' 'Why don't you?' There, sitting perkily outside the house was a powder blue Morris Minor car with a huge ribbon around its middle and a massive bow on top with a banner reading: 'Happy Christmas Siân, with all my love, your Peter'.

I struggled with a confusion of emotions; guilt for having thought that he wouldn't be home for Christmas, pleasure at being given such a magnificent present and fury at being given a present which he must surely know I wouldn't use. When I was at RADA I had been involved in a traumatic accident which had led to a spell of reconstructive surgery. My terror-soaked experiences in O'Toole's cars when he drove when drinking in Stratford had left me with an abiding fear and hatred of the combustion engine. But it did look lovely, sitting out there, motionless. The atmosphere in the room became positively Dickensian as we hugged our good fortune to ourselves. The fire glowed, Kate beamed, my recipe book was open at the page reading 'How To Cope With Christmas'.

The days that followed were happy until O'Toole, deciding that he would like to bid farewell to Bristol before leaving for Arabia, borrowed my car and, while I went back to the Aldwych, drove west on his sentimental journey. In bed after the performance I was awakened by the phone. 'Is that Siân?' 'Yes.' 'Ah, well' – West Country voice – 'now I'm very sorry about this but I'm afraid we've had to lock Pete in the cells. We thought you ought to know.' 'We' was the constabulary. Jules, awakened in turn, promised me that he'd take care of things. He rang me back to say that O'Toole, much the worse for wear, had absently driven 'my' car, full of actors, into the back of a police car which in turn was full of dozing policemen, who weren't best pleased. He was processed through the court with the minimum of fuss and the maximum of dispatch and packed off home by train. I never saw the car again and I was pleased about that. On this occasion it truly was the thought that mattered.

Chapter Fourteen

There was excitement in the small house as O'Toole prepared to leave England in the early part of 1961. The film company had set up an office in Amman in Jordan and another, the home office, in Mayfair in London and mail was sent to and fro in the company bag. Filming was not due to begin until May but the preparations were well under way. The King was firmly on board as an ally and had placed the army and his own Bedouin desert patrol at the service of Horizon Pictures. I was told that O'Toole would be sent into the desert and would be completely out of reach of the phone or letters for long periods. We had been enjoying a wonderful time and I didn't like the thought of being separated for so long but in a way it was fortunate that we had endured that time of misery at Stratford. Being apart was not going to be much fun but it wasn't as bad as parting unhappily or even living together unhappily. The alcohol consumption had already been reduced drastically; in Arabia drink would have to be banned completely except for the odd infrequent break in Beirut, the nearest fleshpot. The heat at times would be over 120 degrees and we learned that it is impossible to live and work in that heat encumbered by a hangover.

This piece of information was part of a comprehensive briefing that took in manners and morals as well as food, drink and hygiene. O'Toole was reading everything that had been assembled for him; Lawrence, his campaigns, the geography of Jordan, religion, the background history of the 'fertile crescent', and we were meeting people who were involved with Lawrence himself. Anthony Nutting had been appointed advisor; an expert on Middle East affairs, he was a wonderful source of information and good gossip. Lunch with Captain Basil Liddell Hart at his house in Medmenham brought home to me the scale and nature of this job. Even to me it no longer felt like a job; this was the biggest adventure of a lifetime. Making a movie on this scale was a bit like mounting a military operation. I was aware that, David Lean apart (his confidence in O'Toole was absolute), there were doubts again about the maverick Irishman. Would he be able to submit to the unrelenting discipline, the physical hardships that awaited him? Did he have the strength of character? How would he manage, hundreds of kilometers from the nearest water let alone a welcoming bar? Did he have the 'right stuff' in him? The whispers were incessant. It was Stratford all over again. I had no doubts at all. I knew how hard he drove himself when he was working. I also knew that he wanted this film and all that it would bring. Jules, knowing as neither of us could that O'Toole's life was about to change completely, asked O'Toole suddenly one night, 'Do you *want* this? *Really* want it?' There was no need to answer yes as their eyes met. In his words, he wanted it so much he could taste it.

I buried any nervousness I may have felt about our future and joined in the excitement. I was ashamed to admit even to myself that the future frightened me. I was not at all sure that *I* wanted all this. I was not even sure that I would have a part in it. I was not sure that I liked the film world. I didn't voice any of these doubts and braced myself against the trial of the coming months which Kate and I would spend alone. 'Months?' said someone. This picture is going to take over a year and then some. My heart sank. Smart restaurants, interviews, photo sessions, eight shows a week at the Aldwych for me, and too many people packing into our small mews house, an endlessly ringing telephone, happy noise – and then silence. He was gone. It was as though he'd taken all the color and light with him. For a week I mourned and moped and grieved then

I began to look about and realized how very fortunate I was in my job, in London, in Hyde Park across the road, in the shops of Connaught Street, in my lovely bedroom in the front with Marianne and Kate tucked in at the back but I couldn't even imagine what the desert was like. What his new life was like.

Naturally, during the bad times at Stratford my eczema, which I had suffered since childhood, had raged out of control and I'd developed abscesses inside my ears. At the theater this was a problem. I was getting over my bout of stage fright but many nights at the Aldwych I couldn't hear anything much; it was like acting in a thick fog. My friend in the company, Stephanie – Steve – Bidmead who, having had health problems of her own and overcome them, recognized a fellow casualty and took me under her wing. She made coping with the deafness into a game. On stage or watching me from the wings, she would raise an index finger a mere centimeter and that meant 'speak up' and lower it fractionally to mean 'stop shouting'. Once I had arrived at the correct pitch she'd give me a big wink and get on with her own performance. Gradually, I learned to tell if I was too loud or too soft by the feeling in the resonators in my face but without Steve I don't know how I would have survived the early months of 1961.

The first wonderful letters had begun to arrive from Jordan. I read them over and over again, sometimes I read them aloud to Kate who looked benign and indifferent. I pinned a photograph of her father near her playpen. This was foolish, I know, but I was not quite sure how to behave and I was also sure that Dr. Spock didn't tell me everything about babies in general and Kate in particular. I sang her the song that O'Toole composed for her and used to play to her on his guitar (the only thing which had survived Stratford unbroken and which had now been packed and sent to Jordan).

Why do I laugh? Why do I sing?
Why is there music? Birds on the wing?

Kate is charming
Kate is charming

Who knows? Maybe she recognizes it, maybe not. I'm not sure of anything. Looking back at my younger self a mere year ago I cannot believe that I was ever so confident, so sure of myself. Now I'm uncertain of everything and, in particular, unsure of my own ability. It seems that once one's confidence is destroyed, nervousness seeps into every area of existence. I look at Kate and she looks back at me and I wonder am I doing right by her? We're a bit like a couple of comfortably installed hostages. I've learned to organize and manage and we share an orderly life but a life lacking in spontaneity. There is nothing to indicate when my period of atonement for my past might end – maybe never. I have overcome the pointless fits of frustration at not being able to do anything to put matters right. My childhood dream of having done something so bad that it is unpardonable and unforgivable has come true and all I can do is to ensure that I lead a life which is, and is seen to be, beyond reproach. My old, pre-O'Toole life is as though it never was.

I have a few new, permitted friends and acquaintances; Jules and Joyce keep an eye on me, Derek Bowman, a journalist on the old *News Chronicle*, comes round and patiently picks the bits of ham out of the omelettes I absent-mindedly make for him. Tom Stoppard, an old friend of O'Toole's from Bristol, temporarily fills the space I like to reserve in my life for the person-a-million-times-cleverer-than-I and brings me out-of-print books. He's going to be a full-time writer. John Libson, our accountant's son, soon to be an accountant himself, rescues me from the ladies' seminary I've created for myself and takes me for spins and Chinese meals. He, also, is a lot cleverer than I am and solves domestic problems as well as fiscal ones. Stephanie Bidmead stays over sometimes and we talk about everything except my private life. I don't think that she knows O'Toole at all. If she does, she never mentions him. Then – heaven sent – Marie Kean arrives from Dublin to do some filming in London. Now we're four girls in this little house. Marie and I step out after the show at night and within days she raises my spirits. I doubt that I'll ever again be as high-spirited as I once was but this will do to be going on with and I thank God for Marie, the funniest woman I know.

As the season draws to a close, O'Toole begins agitating for me to end the engagement. Understandably, since the Royal Shakespeare Company took him to court over *Becket*, he's taken against Stratford in a big way. This is a shame and inconvenient for me. My natural 'home' is obviously in the theater and my natural place in the theater is obviously within a permanent company. It is equally obvious that to make my life in the Stratford company would be regarded by O'Toole as totally disloyal, almost grounds for divorce. I don't know how I'm going to proceed but I do know that I have to finish at the Royal Shakespeare, go to Jordan (which I want to do) and only then come back and worry about my future. The values of the Forties and Fifties still prevailed in the Sixties and it would have been unacceptably disloyal of me to have defied my husband and thrown in my lot with people whom he regarded as enemies at that time. My mother had told me that I would have to stand in a very small place to make this marriage work and I was prepared to do that but I was quite unprepared to give up my work. I would try to have it all.

I have changed agents and am now represented by John Redway & Associates but I am being held to my contract with MCA and am paying two lots of 10 percent on every job. O'Toole is going to be paid £13,500 for making *Lawrence*. The other actors will make a great deal more but Jules says this is all fine and all is going according to plan – whatever that is. He doesn't say. My RSC salary is completely swallowed up by the cost of employing Marianne, the nanny, and the cleaner who comes with the house. During the day I'm able to do radio work and I make commercial recordings of plays as well so I get by but I do have to keep working.

Alarmingly, people assume that I don't need to work now that I'm a 'film star's wife'. They also assume I might not *want* to work and that if I do, I'll want to do only very smart work. These are problems which I had not anticipated. Even more worrying is the attitude I detect in my own camp. Keep Films, our company, is establishing itself; accountants, book keepers, lawyers, secretaries are being assembled. Naturally, everything exists because of O'Toole and everyone's effort is directed towards his work and well-being. I am very much a willing part of this team and I can see that my co-operation is essential to the enterprise but I am mortified to realize that my work hardly figures. It's as though my life before Stratford is completely wiped out. I'm known as a wife on a difficult assignment, a mother and – oh yes – an actress. Sort of. (Nice for me to have something to do in my spare time now that O'Toole's away.) Jules, who is genuinely fond of me and whom I like hugely and depend upon hugely, is heard to say, 'It's all right for her to work so long as it doesn't get in Pete's way and so long as he isn't embarrassed by her.' This is crushing but this is my life now and somehow I shall have to find a way of surviving as an actress. To protest and to demand a toe-hold of my own would be perceived as grotesque and graceless. This is 1960 and women – wives – are meant to be helpmates not strident nuisances. And this *is* a great, important and testing time for O'Toole and I *do* want to help. In the back of my mind I harbor the hope that, when he is able, and if ever he is able to accept the fact that I was not a virgin bride, O'Toole will be my ally and help me out of this difficult situation. He may disapprove of my past but he does also love me, and to others – never to me – he is extravagant in his praise of me. Michael Langham says that when he was thinking of mounting a production of *Cyrano*, O'Toole, approving my casting as Roxanne, wrote: 'Her voice is a great bell that rings in my heart.' To Marie he said, 'I'm marrying the best young actress in the country.' This astonishes me. I feel like a goose girl with bare feet over whom O'Toole has thrown a beautiful cloak that hides the rags underneath. I may have to buy my own shoes.

Ondine at the Aldwych comes to an end. The parts I've played have not suited me much – or rather, I don't feel that I've been able to do anything with them. For many reasons the season has been an uphill climb all the way. I'm not sorry to come to the end of it but I am desperately sorry to leave the company. Two recent memories of the play; exquisitely beautiful Leslie Caron in the title part, and the night when, processing as part of the Court up from the orchestra pit, on stage right and moving diagonally up stage and off, stage left, I felt my fourteen-foot train (suede, trimmed with fur, designed to look like velvet – don't ask) to be more than usually difficult to negotiate. Looking back I saw my Mother, the Queen, in the person of Gwen Ffrangcon-Davies on her hands and knees on my train, myopically peering at it in a puzzled way and presumably wondering why the stage cloth was moving. I dragged her about thirty feet but she seemed none the worse for wear when she was helped up in the wings. (Not a titter from the respectful audience.)

Kate has been taken to Wales to stay with my parents who are delighted to have her all to themselves. With a few pairs of trousers and a lady-like divided skirt and a sun dress for private wear and a few pairs of long-sleeved garments so as not to offend anyone on the street, I'm heading for the Middle East. I've been reading all O'Toole's research books but I don't really know what to expect.

Travelling in a nice new American tweed suit, I walked into a wall of heat in Amman Airport. Exhausted and overpowered by the heat, I immediately fell under the spell of Jordan. The

With Brewster Mason in *The Taming of the Shrew* at Oxford Playhouse in 1960 (*Studio Edmark*)

At 'Mount Unpleasant', with Jackie McGowran and Jill Bennett

With Joyce Buck and Kate in a pub at Stratford

In *The Duchess of Malfi* with Max Adrian and Pat Wymark at The Royal Shakespeare in Stratford, in 1960 (*Angus McBean © The Harvard Theatre Collection*)

My first camel ride in Aqaba

Watching the filming of
Lawrence of Arabia in
Jordan

(*below*) At a mansaf in
the desert with O'Toole

In Beirut during a break from filming

In Seville with O'Toole during the last stages of *Lawrence of Arabia*

On tour with Kate during *Lizard on the Rock* in 1962

With Michael Bryant and John Phillips in *Gentle Jack* at the Queen's Theatre in 1963 (*Angus McBean © The Harvard Theatre Collection*)

With Wilfrid Lawson in *Strangers in the Room* – a play by Kenneth Jupp – in 1960

With O'Toole in his dressing
room on the opening night of
Hamlet at the National Theatre,
Old Vic (*Jack Nisberg*)

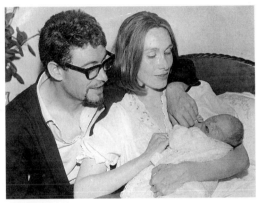

(*right*) The arrival of Pat in 1963
(*Independent Newspapers*)

In the film of *Becket* in 1963

With the family
at Guyon House
(*Jerry Bauer*)

Marie Kean

(*above*) My father in 1961

(*left*) Debbie Condon and Kenneth Jupp

(*below*) Christmas in Venice: (*from left to right*) Joyce Buck, my mother, Elizabeth de la Cour Bogue, Harry Craig, Joan-Juliet Buck, Pat, Kate, myself and Shana Alexander

With Sam Beckett working on *Eh, Joe*
(*Michael Peto*)

(*right*) With Mark Eden in
The Night of the Iguana at the
Savoy Theatre (*Lewis Morley*)

(*left*) Vivienne's portrait for her
exhibition during *The Night of the
Iguana* (*Vivienne, London*)

flight had been endless. Hungry, I looked longingly at a street
vendor's tray of pungent food. 'Uh-huh,' said the Columbia
official as he followed my glance, 'never. Not ever. Asking
for trouble.' The car bumped along what was little better
than a dirt road and we drove to the best hotel in Amman,
the Philadelphia, a ramshackle affair with flimsy doors and
furniture – but still those wonderful spicy smells everywhere.
And the sounds! Chaos in the street below and on the radio,
music that seemed to go on and on and on without a break.
'Ghastly din you can't get away from,' said my American
escort. I looked at him in his beautiful jacket and slacks
and polo-necked cotton shirt, shiny shoes, manicured hands
and thought he must be having an awful time since he didn't
seem to like anything about the country. I couldn't wait for
him to leave. Before he abandoned me for the night – in the
morning I was to be taken south to Aqaba where O'Toole
was based – he pointed out the Royal Palace on the dusty
hill, one of the 'jebels' I'd been reading about. It was an
undistinguished, squat, sandstone house and on another hill
there was a biscuit-colored piece of suburbia where Columbia
Pictures had made its home.

Left to myself, I leaned out of the window (arms covered
in case anyone looked up) and marvelled at the scene below.
There didn't seem to be a rule of the road, or if there was no
one observed it. The men in their robes looked exactly like
the men in every drawing I'd ever seen in childhood Bible
classes. I'd never been in a place where everything matched
up to my mental picture of it, but I couldn't have known what
the sound would be like, or the smell. I don't know how long
I hung out of my window before the muezzin began to chant
and the wonder was complete.

Reluctantly, I withdrew into the spacious, ugly room and
began the long struggle to summon room-service and, having
eventually raised someone, to order some food – *any* food
– and then to get it delivered. When eventually it came it

was nothing like the delicious concoctions sold on the street. This being the best hotel, the food was a muddled attempt at European hotel food, but nothing could lower my spirits and I ate the grey meat and watery boiled vegetables, then bathed in tepid water and, lying on top of my artificial silk bedspread, fell into a deep, contented sleep.

In the morning I woke early, dressed and hung out of the window until the company car arrived to take me to Aqaba. Breakfast was a bit of bread left over from dinner. I couldn't face another struggle with room service. It became hotter and hotter as we descended to the southern coast. The heat in the car was almost unbearable. The heat outside was just as bad. We passed no other traffic, occasionally I saw a little cluster of small dried mud-colored houses that looked as though they'd been assembled from a child's outsized building kit. When I saw a few Bedouin on their camels I swallowed hard and pointed. The driver nodded, bored. I almost burst into tears; I had never, ever seen anything that looked so totally *foreign*. Everything, every single thing that was happening was intoxicatingly new and unknown – maybe unknowable. By the time we drew into the tiny settlement that was Aqaba and bumped along the track to the Columbia Pictures encampment on the shore of the Red Sea, I already felt in some way altered just by being in this place. I wasn't concentrating on myself and certainly wasn't ready for what greeted me.

Chapter Fifteen

Aqaba – a dirt track through a sketchy village then, slightly apart, a military-style compound; a dining mess, a few hastily thrown up rooms around a cement yard on a beach bordering the Red Sea, rudimentary lavatories, showers and a few un-smart trailers. The film was in pre-production, O'Toole was one of the very few actors present and he'd been installed in a trailer. There was very little room. The walls were completely covered with sheets of paper on which he'd hand-written useful Arabic phrases and a daily addition of ten words to a growing vocabulary. One end of the trailer was filled by the over-sized bed. There were no home comforts but there was Arabic, Arabic everywhere, then books, papers, and a little ledge holding soap, towels, toothpaste and brush and bottles of Ambre Solaire. I had very little luggage and I found a small cupboard where I could stow my things. O'Toole was wearing long boots, trousers, cotton shirt and a belted cotton robe, his camel-riding gear. We were both shy and tentative as we greeted each other. He looked extraordinary, a thousand times fitter and healthier than he'd ever looked, his eyes were clear and for the first time in his life he was tanned, his curly black hair had been straightened and bleached. He looked – I couldn't quite think what he looked like. Then it came to me. He looked like a movie star.

Someone brought us tea. The heat was stifling. He began to pass on to me the lessons he'd learned about how to live here and in the desert where he would take me soon. He'd been living with the Bedouin camel-patrol as they travelled around the desert and clearly he'd formed a great attachment to them and their way of life. It sounded wonderful to me. He described the nights sitting outside the black tents, grateful for the cooler air after the horrendous heat of the day. They would sit, leaning on their saddles, still holding the sticks they held in their right hands while riding. Total silence, except for the occasional noise made by a sleeping camel and no conversation, unless someone had something useful or amusing to say. I couldn't quite imagine the absence of small-talk. Silence in society makes me feel uneasy. They would draw meaningless patterns in the sand with their sticks and the patterns looked like exquisite Arab calligraphy.

Enthralled, I forgot the heat and my inappropriate clothes. When could *I* go to see The Boys, as he called them? The atmosphere changed at once. 'Maybe not at all' was the reply. It was a totally male society. Women were never seen. I began to wonder where I would fit, even temporarily, in to this new life O'Toole was experiencing. He continued to talk about these wonderful people, their skills, their hospitality, their code of honor and I realized with dismay that we were moving into the familiar territory of my *lack* of 'honor'. It wasn't possible, was it, that we were reprising the awful, circular debates of our wretched months at Stratford, debates that I had assumed to be behind us for ever. Exhausted and incredulous, I couldn't think of anything to say except 'Well, shall I go home then?' I sounded cheap and chipper. 'Maybe that would be best,' was the reply and O'Toole slammed out.

I sat there in the little oven of a trailer. I had loved the journey, I loved what I'd seen of the country, I longed to go into the desert, I longed to be reunited with O'Toole. A part of me had now become so accustomed to failed expectations, to finding that nothing turned out the way I expected it should do that I didn't waste time crying. I began to puzzle out whom I should talk to in order to get a car back up the length of the country north to Amman. The door opened, O'Toole entered and swiftly, without speaking, we fell into each other's arms and laughing and crying we started all over again. It was the beginning of one of the best times of my life.

I'd thought I was a brisk creature of damp and cold, changing skies, winds and mountains and now I'm gladly ravished by the baking, dry, unbearable heat, the cloudless skies, the slow pace one has to learn in order to survive the long day between dawn and sunset. O'Toole gets us both up at five in the morning and we drink sweet tea with mint and shower and dress and tidy our tiny living space before the heat begins. We lie in the sun for ten minutes only; the rest of the time we stay covered up like the Arabs. Nevertheless, very quickly, I become brown and my hair bleaches itself. I've never looked like this before.

Gradually I meet the huge unit. Phil Hobbs, the location manager, has built a large village here, some of the men already dislike the climate and the lack of comfort (with much more hardship to come when filming starts) and they begin to ask to be sent home. The airlines are doing a brisk trade. It seems to be the luck of the draw; hating this place or loving it. There are very few women here. Barbara is the continuity girl and she's already up to her eyes in work. The most colorful members of the unit, the property master and his brother, Eddie Fowley and Dave, live slightly apart from everyone else and Eddie has his wife, Doris, with him but she is never seen except at night when Eddie returns from the day's 'recce'. Leila Lean, David's Indian wife, is installed in one of the concrete bunkers, windows shaded against the light. She's brought over a hundred saris with her and a huge, stringed instrument irreverently referred to as the 'joke banjo'. She doesn't emerge during the day. David has already gone into the desert and doesn't return to base.

Eddie Fowley is an amazing man. Blackened by the sun, stripped to the waist, he's ready for anything. I'm told that he's the man who built *and blew up* the bridge on the River Kwai. He has a large truck and no matter what outlandish request is made to him, he lifts his head belligerently and bites out a command, 'DAVE! In the *TRUCK*!' He speaks in capital letters and he's never been known to be found wanting. David Lean rightly treasures him.

People in these early stages are still trying to shake down into some bearable kind of life together, getting ready for the long, hard haul. I've never been on a location like this (I don't suppose there *are* many movies planned on this scale). The problems are mind boggling; I listen in the mess as they begin to discuss the question of trucking water, daily, hundreds of kilometers into the desert, some of it unchartered. How much water is needed by each person daily? Canvas villages will have to be erected, latrines dug, field kitchens built at speed. Huge quantities of salt tablets are flown in and every table has a huge jar of them along with the HP and ketchup. If you forget to take regular handfuls, with no warning at all you gently keel over as you stroll along. Sweat dries even as it's produced and sometimes one is so dehydrated that three tablespoons of salt in a glass of water have no taste at all. Occasionally we walk into the village proper. There's nothing much there but there is a lean-to café and we begin to eat forbidden local food – it's delicious – much nicer than our British-style canteen food. Leila Lean accompanies us and is grateful for the change of diet. We suffer no ill effects. The unit doctor shakes his head reprovingly. There is a Mayor of Aqaba and he sits outside his run-down house looking across the bay at the Jewish settlement, another small village, Eilat, which seems to be full of builders and – especially – electricians. It changes daily and one can just make out that they're building and installing lighted signs. It's odd to be sitting on this side of the bay, one mile and three or four hundred yards away from the Jewish side. Barbed wire divides the two places, the divide is mined, I'm told, and the stretch of no man's land is patrolled by soldiers in long frocks and bandoliers. What is the Mayor thinking as he sits hour after hour playing with his beads and glowering moodily across the bay? He's a bit jealous, I'd say.

Sam Spiegel, the producer of the film, is, of course, Jewish and his yacht is moored in the bay. He daren't come ashore, which pleases David Lean no end (no interference). There's trouble when the rumor is put about that this is a Jewish film with a Jewish unit. King Hussein comes to the rescue and drives into the desert to address the army and especially the camel patrol – his special 'boys' – and says he is entrusting the safety of the enterprise to them. They adore him – this is like watching Henry V on the eve of Agincourt – they'll do whatever he asks them to do and it's pretty plain that he loves them, as well. It's very unlike home.

The King is sophisticated. Sam tries to be smart. When the concept of Ramadan is explained to him he nods sagely and says, 'Ah yes. Just like our Lent.' The King is kind enough to pretend he didn't hear.

O'Toole and I on a rare visit to Amman are invited to the Basman Palace. It's very, very modest. Not pretty. We sit in large British-style, uncut moquette armchairs and are mightily impressed by the King, who is small with a bass voice and a wonderfully handsome head. I reflect that he's lucky to be a king not an actor; it would be such bad luck to be so handsome and so much smaller than the most petite of actresses. People – not just the Bedouin – love him. Over and over I'm told how brave he is; recently he had his appendix out without anesthetic and walked out of the operating room. I'm suitably impressed.

Not long into Operation Lawrence, the King takes a fancy to the chief telephone operator at the production office. John Sullivan, the charming, good looking head of stunts and O'Toole's stand-in and companion, steps out of the romantic frame and, within the year, Miss Gardiner becomes Queen of Jordan and the phones never really work properly again. It's a bit like Alice in Wonderland here. Anything can happen.

Finally, I'm to meet the Bedouin – not in the desert – on a piece of scrub behind the little town. O'Toole and about six Bedu are practicing with their camels. Racing camels are called *thalools*. They go from zero to thirty miles an hour in under a minute. The motion, I'm told, is almost impossible to understand and being a horse rider doesn't help because the camel rocks forward and back and up and down and you don't know what to do for the best. We do a lot of greeting and bowing. I'm decently covered and wear a divided skirt and desert bootees and socks. They seem very jolly – full of jokes – and contrive to look blood-thirsty as well, hung about with guns and bullets. I understand as they gesture towards me and one of the camels that I'm being asked if I'd like to try riding. Shooting a glance at O'Toole, who is good humoredly non-committal, I say, 'Why not? Well, of *course* I want to try.' It seems polite. They show me how to lock my legs around the pommel, hand me a whip and up rises the camel.

Well, this isn't too bad. It's rather lovely, being so high up, trying to get the hang of the motion as the beast begins to walk on. I look at them for approval; they nod. We're all in a good mood. Stepping forward, the man who seems to be the leader lifts his whip and, smiling broadly, gives my camel a brisk crack along the backside. I can only just hear the beginning of merry laughter behind me. I'm rocking at speed forward and back, hitting the big wooden 'nails' of a pommel front and back with each horrible movement. Lurching up and down and sideways I land just to the left of the saddle, then to the right. This seems to go on forever before I fall off. Well, no, I *don't* fall off, I hang upside down, my legs and feet are locked and I know that so long as they stay locked I can't *possibly* fall off and no power on earth is going to unlock my legs. I thank God quickly for all those years of training at gymnastics. I may be hanging upside down but I'm staying calm. But where are we going? I lift my head slightly and see that we're heading in the direction of a lot of barbed wire. Land mines? No man's land? This is not good. I'm thinking what to do when I sense another camel tearing along and overtaking me. The rider begins to beat my camel about the nose and she begins to turn in a circle and turning, decelerates, eventually slowing down to walk. I'm able to hoist myself back up into the saddle. The rest of the company has caught up with us. They're still laughing! I nod and smile and roll my eyes to heaven. I can see that this is one of the funniest things they've experienced in days. Too late, I remember – they love practical jokes. Down goes the camel and off I get, very shaky in the legs. 'After all that would you like to go back to the trailer?' asks O'Toole solicitously.

'Mmm – maybe.'

'You all right?'

'FINE.'

'Okay, then.'

A small jeep is summoned and I bump back into camp. Blood is now seeping through my shirt front and back and I stand in the shower to peel it off. Half a bottle of Dettol and a tin of lint and plasters later I'm as good as new. And when after lunch O'Toole sees my torn midriff and back I'm able – truly – to say that I'm just fine. Actually I'm more than fine. I feel I've passed some kind of test. I'm having the time of my life.

Thanks to The Boys, O'Toole is now a really good camel rider. I'm overcome with admiration. No one prepared him for all this at RADA. He's learning to keep his eyes open in the blinding light of the sun. They're pale blue and sensitive to light and all he wants to do is scrunch up his face and close his eyes but that isn't going to do. I can see why he's so fit – this is like being in the army except the hours are longer and he'll have to wear a bit of make-up. The day arrives when I'm to be taken into the desert to the black tents. We pile into a jeep with enough cigarettes for us both, a shovel for going to the loo and a straw mat for digging out when we get stuck, a compass and off we head into the desert.

Hours go by. He's becoming used to this terrain; we're miles away from Aqaba and I don't see how he knows where to go, there isn't a road. Occasionally we get bogged down and have to lay down the mats in order to get started again. It's incredibly *clean* here. When we stop the silence is profound – no birds, no insects, hardly a breeze today.

Suddenly O'Toole nudges me in the ribs. There, ahead in the distance, is the most romantic scene imaginable: in the middle of nothing, the long, low, worm-like shapes of the black tents – woven wool with rugs hanging from the 'roofs'. Camels are lying alongside and they *do* look like moored boats, necks raised like elegant prows. As we approach Getaifan Abu Tai (the grandson of the great Auda, played by Tony Quinn) emerges, dropping the door flap behind him. The women are inside the harem and we won't see them. We're invited to sit, and leaning against the large camel saddles on the ground I fondle a pommel, exploring the large, flat head of the nail-like shape, which crashed into me not so long ago. Greetings are elaborate and take a while. Then small cups of tea are prepared, sweet, sweet tea with mint, '*shai ma nana*'. I've learned the basics, '*hamdilla*', '*shwkran*' and '*afwan*', and nothing else. We sit under a black awning, shaded from the sun and are joined by three or four men, all in full fighting rig.

The men have become fascinated by some of the paraphernalia of film-making. Mascara has become a favorite toy, little mirrors also. Laying down their rifles, they peer at their eye make-up admiringly and laugh with pleasure. Occasionally you see these fierce-looking soldiers stroll hand in hand past the tents where the wives and children remain out of sight until the strangers are gone. It looks unselfconscious and totally charming. And here's the famous social silence I've been hearing about. We smile at each other – the formalities have been observed and we lapse into quiet. They draw patterns in the sand with their canes. I find I'm doing the same with my index finger. At first I have a real compulsion to fill in the pauses but once the pause is beyond help there's scarcely any point. Occasionally, catching someone's eye, I exchange a smile. Intermittently, someone does say something – there isn't necessarily a reply and the silence continues. Once I've become accustomed to this I find a wonderful state, a state of wakeful relaxation. Nothing need happen, nothing needs to be said. Hours go by and we finally take our leave, return to the jeep and make for the long drive back to camp. I realize that now *we* are hardly talking to each other either.

Night falls and the sky above and all around seems to dip below the line of the earth. I've never been so aware of the night sky and the stars and I wonder if I might be able to stay overnight out in the desert sometime. We have supper and I go to bed. O'Toole works on his vocabulary while I try to assimilate the experiences of the day. One thing I realize now is that the desert Arabs are a good deal more sophisticated and tolerant than their small-town brothers. In the heat I took off my jacket revealing a very short sleeved bodice. No one batted an eyelid.

This was the first of many visits to the black tents. Much later that year we sat for hours with Getaifan and his friends and after we'd made the long trip back to base camp by Jeep there was a flurry of activity and shouts in Arabic. Looking out, we saw Getaifan, who'd galloped after us on his camel. While we'd sat there with him, his wife, inside the tent, had silently given birth to a baby – a girl. He wanted to know if he could name her after me. Later, on a rare break, O'Toole and I made for Beirut and in the gold market we bought Siân Abu Tai, Auda's great granddaughter, a gold chain and we hung a ruby on it. On our return we gave the chain to Getaifan to give to his wife and when we next visited him he beckoned to me to come inside the back tent. It was an honor to be allowed into the women's quarters; dark and cool and hung with bright carpets and shawls, Siân was produced and unwrapped from yards and yards of swaddling clothes and there was her necklace, fastened round her belly with the ruby nestling in her navel.

That was the only time I was allowed inside the black tent. I was however invited to a Mansaf. O'Toole, who was acquiring Lawrence-like status in the desert, was asked to settle a blood feud between two families. We sat for hours in the shadow of the ruin of a Crusader castle while our interpreter did his best to guide us through the byzantine complexities of this ancient family row and when everything was settled to everyone's satisfaction, as darkness fell, a huge fire was lit and a sheep was killed and cooked and we ate it – *all* of it. I was ravenous and it was delicious – *all* of it. Meat was a rarity and we felt very privileged to be allowed to share what was truly a feast.

The first day of shooting arrived. The long preparation came to an end around the time of my birthday in mid May. I accompanied O'Toole and the unit into the farthest reaches of Jebel Tubeiq. Here and there are faint traces of eighth-century settlements. It is vast; one of the most inhospitable, awe-inspiring places on earth and, on the face of it, a mad place in which to try to shoot a movie. We received a message to join Eddie Fowley, with rough directions as to where we'd find him. After a long bumpy drive we came upon the truck in the huge empty landscape. Eddie had produced a roll of plastic 'grass', a table and striped umbrella, yellow paper daffodils – the Welsh emblem – and he served us 'cocktails' of fruit juice in glasses with little parasols and glacé cherries, all produced from the famous truck. I had been there for a month and now, when filming started, I went home, riding with one of the unit members on an errand to Amman. We got lost, we got stuck again and again and eventually reached the road that ran north-south through the country. Amman seemed incredibly noisy. I spent the night there and when I started a rare headache, prompted by misery at having to leave, someone sent out for some pills. When I got home to London Jules called me and said he'd just got a bill from the production office: 'Mrs O'Toole – one packet Aspirin'. We paid up.

Chapter Sixteen

B ack in London I missed O'Toole terribly. Picking Kate up from my parents' place in Wales, where they'd all had a wonderful time, I brought her back to Hyde Park Gardens.

Jules had decided that we could now afford to buy a permanent home in London; our situation had stabilized to the point where we both wanted to put down family roots. Lying on my couch suffering from flu, towards the end of the Aldwych season, I'd received a visit from Henry Woolf, a friend of O'Toole's from Bristol. He had presented what must have been the first performance of any Pinter play at Bristol University so I credited him with impeccable taste. I couldn't stir myself to go house-hunting and play in the theater at night and I asked Henry if he would mind taking the house agents' lists and begin looking for a suitable house. After a few days he came back saying, 'Now, I know your top price is £8,000' (that was the price of a house in, say, Little Venice) '– but I've found a house which is £14,000 and needs *everything* doing to it and you *have* to buy it.' I went to see it. It was inconvenient, big, needed years of 'improvements' taken out, but it was beautiful and Henry was right, we *had* to have it. It dated from 1740 and was built on five floors, all listing slightly to starboard. There were big cellars that ran under Heath Street and it had been one of the group of five Hampstead houses where felons could be 'secured' overnight, before police stations were established. Ownership would give us grazing rights on the Heath. The top floor was level with the top of St Paul's Cathedral and there was an uninterrupted view, almost unchanged since the eighteenth century, down past gardens and small suburbs to the City. The view decided me. Promising Henry that should he ever need it one of the bedrooms was his, I put in a bid for £13,500 which we didn't have and dumped the problem of paying for it in Jules's lap.

O'Toole wrote wonderful letters from the desert – I wished I were there (maybe I would never return, I thought). I had left the RSC, as requested, and got myself a West End play produced by Peter Bridge. It was called *Lizard on the Rock*, written by John Hall, and was due to open in the West End in seven weeks' time and who knew when it would end? It didn't occur to me to take time off. Harry Andrews and Anthony Oliver were my leading men and it was a lovely company throughout that pitched in to help me when we went on the road and Kate – eighteen months old and now walking – came along as well, as did Marianne.

Kate had a badly 'wandering' eye so she wore patches and thick pebble glasses and had to endure her daily eye exercises. All the actors were careful with their language when she was around, solemn and adorable-looking with her owl-eyes. However, on our last week on tour we walked into our bedroom and the first thing she did was to go over to the bed and test it for the quality of its mattress. 'Good,' she approved and then, dropping her little toy satchel, said cheerily, 'Oh fuck,' as she picked it up. Not a very good start, I thought. I looked at her, busying herself with settling into the room, and thought regretfully that maybe we should abandon the 'born-in-a-trunk' existence and establish a more conventional life and vocabulary for her.

The house is bought! I don't even *ask* Jules how he managed it. Joyce will help me 'do' it while I'm in the play. O'Toole will come home for a break in September and I'd like at least a part of it to be ready for him. Meanwhile our lease is up at the Mews and Marie Kean, who is working in London, Marianne, Kate and myself move temporarily to an apartment in a large building on the Edgware Road. It's hot and the noise with the window open is deafening. We keep it shut and swelter. I tread a path between the Phoenix Theater, Heath Street in Hampstead and this very strange building on the Edgware Road. It *looks* quite grand but there's something odd about it. The corridors are spacious, the elevator doors elaborately decorated, but one morning the whole of the front large elevator has been removed and is lying across the corridor. There *was* a bump in the night, but now there's no one about. It's a bit like being on a sinister movie set.

The play has not, alas, been well received. It's the tail end of a verse-revival that began with Christopher Fry and continued with T. S. Eliot. The action takes place in Australia and as usual I have to toil away extra hard to achieve a tolerably presentable accent. Australians who see the play say, '*You* are what we sound like! People always exaggerate the sound of Australians.' My friends with good accents seethe.

As Heath Street was built and lived in for a long time by a family called de Guyon I re-name it 'Guyon House'. The last owner was the writer E. Arnot Robertson, whose best-known book was *Ordinary Families*. Happily married to her sailing husband for the whole of her adult life, when he died, it's said she lost her will to live and her death was unhappy. The price of the house reflected this sad event. The dining room and the master bedroom are lovely, the stairwell is beautiful, but every other room (and there are lots of them) is a studio with a hot plate and a sink. I keep meeting actors who've lived in the house. It's a piece of old Hampstead and in a way I'm rather reluctant to start dismantling and clearing it out, restoring the fireplaces and making up-to-date bathrooms.

The kitchen which lets on to the garden has the same beautiful bowed wall that rises almost to the top of the house and every deep window ledge, three to each floor, is piled high with bundles of letters and I long to start reading them but don't. One day when I go up to measure something or other, Mrs Robertson's son is building a bonfire in the garden – a bonfire of letters. Now I wish I'd stolen just one bundle.

Restoring the house is going to be a massive job – expensive as well. I wonder how long it's going to take me. 'Six months?' I inquire. Joyce Buck, who is going to help me, looks at me pityingly. 'It takes about five years to do a house like this properly.' Five years? 1965 before I'm through? I can't believe it. I questioned my other mentor in matters of building and decorating, Ricky, John Huston's wife who has just spent an age 'doing' St Clerans near Galway, one of the most beautiful houses in Europe, where I holidayed before Kate was born. She looked at No 98 and said, 'You should be through in five years.'

As usual, I hadn't thought through the practicalities of what I was up to. Now I began to learn about plumbing – *American* plumbing, plumbing that *worked* – wiring, lighting, how to recognize a good bit of furniture at the bottom of a pile of rubbish, learning what needed to be fixed, who could do the fixing, who was best at making lined, interlined, weighted curtains, where to find the best lamp makers, lamp*shade* makers. There was a never-ending list of things to be learned. And if something wasn't right, whereas my inclination would be to say wearily, 'Oh, I'll put a plant in front of it; it won't show,' Joyce made me take it back and have it re-done. Ricky Huston even criticized the look of the forty door hinges I'd bought and I had to take them all back and start another search for the perfect hinge. I was grateful for all the help and all the lessons but I was completely exhausted all the time because I was acting, as well.

Marie, Kate, Marianne and I moved into the house in despair that it would ever get finished. There wasn't a window that closed or a door that locked but none of us felt nervous; NW3 was a civilized, safe place. The nursery was finished – a beautiful Vie Bohème apartment at the top of the house, furnished, carpeted and curtained with a new bathroom and kitchen and sitting room and balcony and the view to St Paul's. Kate and her nanny, Marianne, were installed in style while Marie and I put our beds in adjacent rooms on the floor below and camped out. The play was over but I was still busy, now doing television. One morning – having done a gruelling, taped performance of a Shaw play with Cyril Cusack and Alan Badel at Granada the night before (it cost a fortune to stop the tape so you had to try to keep going) – I was awakened in my empty room in Hampstead by Joyce saying, 'Come on, come on! We're supposed to be in the Fulham Road looking at dressers in forty minutes.' I moved in a daze from antique shops to little basements full of promising treasures to rehearsal rooms, to studios.

My best moments that summer were spent at the BBC in Portland Place. Martin Esslin was presenting modern European plays and I was in quite a few of them and made my first acquaintance with Genet and Ionesco and Marguerite Duras. I couldn't believe my luck when I read that I was to play *The Afternoon of M. Andesmas* with Ernest Milton. We had a wonderful time together and I couldn't get over that amazing voice which I'd heard imitated by so many actors. *There* it was in the flesh and I was talking to it! He'd taught O'Toole at RADA, where he was adored by all the rebellious, young actors. He was a wonderful actor himself and had been an exquisite young man but, old now, he was undeniably, incredibly 'mannered'. O'Toole had seen him outside RADA in Gower Street chasing after a bus, crying, 'Staap! S t a a p! You're killing a genius!' I was very nervous around him at first but in no time at all we were sharing Chinese meals – still a bit of a novelty for me – in a restaurant on the first floor of a building above Boots in Piccadilly Circus. I'd always been fond of the company of elderly gentlemen and he came high on my list of Fascinating Old Men.

Life was good in Guyon House. The fine weather meant it didn't matter that the whole place was in uproar. Kate had her lovely flat and the rest of the house was an adventure playground for her – the garden was a wilderness and we began to explore the little streets behind the house. I bought a little boat for us to sail on Whetstone Pond. There was work to do at every turn but there was also calm, and Jules and Joyce saw to it that Marie and I saw a bit of high life as well. We were taken to the new White Elephant restaurant in Curzon Street – opened, so it was said, so a few prominent actors, Albert Finney among them, could dine in style *without wearing ties* (extraordinary in 1961). Life was changing; there was a wave of Italian restaurants. The owners and maître d's became as famous as pop stars, Leslie Linder at The Elephant, Mario and Franco in Soho and later all over the West End, were the top of the heap.

I was changing a little as well. I realized that my clothes weren't good enough for my social life. Marie laughed sardonically when she recalled how in the early days of our relationship with Jules and Joyce, I got 'decked out' as, she called it, in my only 'good' dress, a white shirtwaister from Jane & Jane with ropes of beads from a department store and high heeled gold shoes from Pinet. Arriving at the Bucks' front door, Jules greeted me warmly and innocently called up the stairs, 'Joyce, don't *dress*, honey.' I felt I'd better do something about my appearance but it wasn't easy. My head was faultless; my producer, Peter Bridge sent me to a new salon in Bond Street, owned by Vidal Sassoon, for a hair cut and color job for *The Lizard on the Rock*. Vidal chopped off my perm and I emerged with dark red hair. (The author had specified smoky and I couldn't quite work out the connection but Vidal Sassoon was extremely confident and no one dared to argue with him.) I now had straight hair. Oddly enough, it looked just like that of my first form mistress, Miss Inkin, the person I'd most wanted to resemble when I was a little girl. (She *had* been ahead of her time in those days of upswept rolls and permanents.) Joyce Buck took me to a tailor who made me some plain dresses and jackets. I bought *plain* black and brown court shoes from Pinet. A *plain* black bag from Hermès, *plain* gloves from Harrods. Then, I discovered, at Liberty, clothes that I really liked; American clothes by a designer called Bonnie Cashin, wonderful, soft, unlined tweed, piped in colored suede; canvas sports clothes, piped or edged in leather; swingy leather coats; cashmere sweaters with hoods; bean-bag caps in wonderful colors. I wasn't dressed '*up*' but I was *well* dressed in a way I liked. Evening clothes would just have to wait until I had more time and more money. Money was a bit of a problem. Every cent I earned was going into running the small household of women and dressing myself and taking taxis, a vice I wasn't to cure for many years to come.

One morning, as I was nervously setting out to make a recording of *Measure for Measure* with Eric Portman, I opened the morning post to realize that I just couldn't pay all the household bills that month. I stood at the top of the big house and was suddenly appalled by its size, and by the number of workmen scrambling around in it. Kate and Marianne sat at the breakfast table. How had I imagined all this was going to be maintained? I called Jules and, to my astonishment, he was completely unfazed and mightily reassuring and he said, 'And, of course, you should have an allowance.' Well! He – or rather, our office – would take care of the major building and decorating expenses and I would receive £60 a week with which to run our lives. I was completely enchanted and never thought to change that magic sum of unearned money which came my way henceforward. For the next twenty years I spent £40 on the house and each week I kept £20 of it for myself and thought myself very fortunate.

At work that week I was rather depressed. Eric Portman gave me his terrible cold. I *had* to show up but he didn't always show up and I lay under a grand piano nursing my temperature. Fortunately I'd played Isabella at RADA so I knew it quite well. When he did come to work he gave the impression of being overwhelmingly sad and I was glad when the job was over. Not for the first time I reflected that doing a part more than once was really difficult. If one had been – or thought one had been – good the first time round, one was very loath to alter the 'good' bits to suit a new production. If one hadn't been good in the part there was a feeling of desperation in the effort to get it right the second time around.

Months had gone by since I'd left Arabia. O'Toole and I had kept up an intense correspondence but we longed to see each other and he arranged my return. I took Kate down to my parents in Wales and left London as soon as I could. I was to fly out with Anthony Nutting and go straight to the canvas village in El Jaffre. El Jaffre, the huge, mercilessly hot plain, which made Tubeiq seem almost hospitable by comparison. My parents were overjoyed to be getting Kate again, the building works were coming along nicely and Joyce was spending a large part of every week in Hampstead overseeing the Irish team of builders. She never bought a spoon or a cushion or a table without taking me to see twenty spoons, cushions and tables and making me choose. I don't know where she found the patience. Slowly, I learned from her and soon my choices earned an approving nod from her. I was a good pupil but she was a wonderful teacher.

This time round the Middle East was even more enthralling than I'd remembered it to be. Many members of the unit had disappeared but the stalwarts were very much in evidence, thinner, more weatherbeaten and more determined than ever to see this film through to the end. O'Toole was more assured and he looked magnificent. He'd been having daily master classes in film-making from David Lean. (This job must be the equivalent of twenty ordinary ones.) Still there was A. G. Scott, (Scottie the Hair) successfully translated from Mayfair and in charge of the bleaching and straightening, still dapper and well-dressed; Charlie Parker, head of make-up, still cussing and feuding, being brilliant and impossible at the same time;

Eddie and Dave Fowley, indomitable, calm as though they were making a film on the back lot at Shepperton. Leila Lean was banished alas – her concrete bunker, never visited by David, was now occupied by an actor. We also were installed in a bunker at base and O'Toole had acquired a kind of 'body servant' Shwfti (what was his real name?). He would say, craftily, 'Shufti – *Mufti-Klefti*' (I see – I steal). It was hard to make life comfortable, even in a small way, and Shwfti would 'see and steal' little things to make our life cozier. He was a handsome boy, adept at killing vermin and keeping his eyes and ears open. Little happened in the camp that wasn't reported to O'Toole by Shwfti. He didn't travel into the desert and then I was glad of a reprieve from his constant twenty-four-hours-a-day presence, serving us, spoiling us, organizing us, guarding our door day and night. O'Toole didn't seem to notice him but I was always aware of those inquisitive little brown eyes intent on interpreting our smallest change of expression. There were times when I couldn't accompany O'Toole to work and then to get away from Shwfti I would sit on the deserted beach reading or playing the guitar. If I was very still I would quickly become surrounded by hundreds of tiny sand-crabs. A deep sigh on my part was enough to make them disappear in two seconds. Eilat, across the bay, was pushing upwards; each night one could see more neon signs than before. The climate here on the Red Sea made life difficult so they must be spending a fortune on air-conditioning, unknown on this the Arab side of the barbed wire.

One day as I watched the filming, we were all crouched under umbrellas or in the shade of trucks while O'Toole, dressed in heavy khaki, sat mounted all day in the intolerable heat doing the same scene alone, time after time after time. No one knew *why* it was being retaken. No one could ask. The director was always God. I've heard that, great though David was, he liked to enhance his power by breaking down his leading actors, and when they were broken, build them up again so they became grateful or dependent. No one moved in this vast, silent landscape but I saw a few of the old hands exchange knowing glances. It did begin to look as though this was O'Toole's day for being broken down. I sat there under a truck knowing that O'Toole was *never* going to be broken down in this way. Calm and contained, he turned his animal and walked back along the camera track and waited patiently for the word 'Action'. Each take was faultless. Scotty looked pained. Even Charlie was subdued as he checked the make-up and walked slowly back to the unit, so far away from that solitary figure sitting alone in the hateful sun. Some eight hours later there was a simple word, 'Wrap'. It was the end of the day's work. O'Toole slid down from his horse and walked stiffly towards his jeep, parked in the distance. Everyone looked depressed. It had been a murderous day of unspoken conflict. Suddenly, I was compelled to run after David walking back to his vehicle. I didn't know him – I had hardly ever spoken to him. 'What in the name of God was all that about?' I demanded. His handsome face contorted as he replied, 'Actors! Actors! They have the easiest job going. Who gets here first in the morning? The technicians! And who gets the glory? *Actors!*' There was nothing to say to that and anyway I was now appalled by my cheek in ticking off a genius. We walked away from each other and I joined O'Toole in his jeep. He didn't ask what had occurred between me and David and I didn't tell him. I put my arm around his shoulders. Two things were clear to me suddenly. I couldn't bear to see him being badly treated, especially not at work where he was entirely correct in his behavior and second, he had put me through so much that I had no fear of anyone. I had heard him say, 'I've been worked over by experts', well, so had I now. No one would ever be able to try me as he, the expert, had done. But now it was just a matter of getting through the evening quietly before he had to resume the fight tomorrow.

On the morrow, there was no fight. Work flowed enjoyably. David and O'Toole were sunny and the unit blossomed. Show business . . . When I was last here I was asked to help Maurice Ronet (the French actor who was to play Ali) with his English. David wanted him to play a scene on camera with Omar Sharif – newly arrived from Egypt. What no one knew was that Omar was to be looked at for the part Maurice had been engaged to play. David loved Omar and Maurice was dismissed (with $30,000, I was told. Seemed like a *lot* of money to me). O'Toole christened Omar 'Cairo Fred' and they were by now firm friends. They were the constant elements in the picture but all the big stars arrived to play supporting parts and O'Toole said he felt like a boxer waiting in the ring for the new heavyweight champ to show up. Anthony Quinn arrived and borrowed my eyelash curlers. He was on the run from a buxom blonde who pursued him all the way to Aqaba, God knows how she managed it. (I'm not sure that she didn't eventually succeed in getting him to the altar.) Things were altering at base. It was becoming clear in the film world that something extraordinary was going on and visitors began to arrive, never staying for more than a few days, with the notable exception of George Plimpton, who actually tried riding a camel.

Out in the desert everything remained inviolate – David saw to that. He and Barbara, the continuity, were, by now, living together. He and Barbara and Freddie Young, the brilliant lighting cameraman, formed part of a private nucleus in the huge unit. John Box, the designer, was another member of the closed circle. Every time I was around John I would pick up the crumpled drawings he discarded and threw away – wonderful drawings and watercolors which I straightened and ironed and packed away for framing at home.

There were wonders every day which I could hardly believe. In El Jaffre, the route to work was signposted by mirages, which never changed from day to day. The jeep travelled mile after mile over the chalk-white ground 'crazed' from the dry heat and when one saw 'Westminster Abbey' up ahead, one bore east until one came to 'The Lake' and turned north past 'Dickins & Jones' until one saw the real trucks and the real location. The landmarks remained constant, more real than reality. The silence of the movie set was always alarmingly wonderful. Everyone strained not to allow any of the detritus of our living arrangements to escape. A single paper cup rolling away across a virgin distant sand dune to be retrieved on foot was enough to stop work for hours. David and Freddie squinted at the sky and waited and waited for everything to be perfect while Sam Spiegel became mad with fury at the measured pace of filming. And, of course, he couldn't come into Arabia to see what was going on. David smiled evilly and sat in his chair happily waiting, waiting.

We took a short break in Beirut. The morning after we arrived in that most glamorous of cities, I leaned out of my hotel window and in the street below two men from the surrounding hills shot a young girl, a family member who'd brought disgrace on them by descending to a life of sin in the big city. 'What'll happen to them?' 'Nothing, it's their right.'

The Middle Eastern correspondent of the *Daily Mail* was someone O'Toole had known on *The Yorkshire Post* and we were invited to a drinks party in his flat. We passed a very pleasant hour or so and only afterwards did I have reason to remember a quiet chap we'd been introduced to that night – Kim Philby. It was unsettling, being in a city and I was glad to return to the desert. When I left Jordan this time I knew that I was unlikely to return. I realized that I'd rarely been happier, anywhere.

The month in the Middle East had gone by very quickly and I missed O'Toole but equally I missed the smells and tastes of the Middle East, and I missed the never-ending music incomprehensibly going on and on – and on. I didn't need reminding that if I weren't married to O'Toole and if he didn't wish to have me with him, I would never have experienced this adventure. I did however have an unexpected legacy from Arabia when I was suddenly presented with the ultimate in what I called Petruchio's servants, people who were undoubtedly good at something, but absolutely useless at what they had been engaged to do. When O'Toole finished in the desert, he determined to *do* something for Shwfti and contrived to send him to live with me and Kate and Marianne. To what end I had no idea. The house didn't suit him, our meals didn't suit him; he slept in Kate's small bedroom with a scimitar under his pillow. After the show I would return to find the small sitting room out of bounds to me as he lay, unsmiling, smoking on the hearth rug. His cigarettes smelled strange. One day, before a matinée when I'd cooked and cleared away lunch, I said, 'Shwfti, during the afternoon could you please wash the dishes for me?' He looked up from his favorite spot on the hearth rug and made no response. Holding the look between us, he slowly closed his hand on the wine glass he was holding and red wine and blood trickled down his wrist. There wasn't time to stop and discuss this new development in our relationship so I left for the theater without another word. After that, mindful that to him I was a mere woman, I was tentative in my dealings with him. He began to explore London. I had no idea what he got up to but was relieved when a few weeks later he was picked up in Soho, arrested for drug dealing and deported. He was never mentioned again, the scimitar was tidied away and we repossessed the sitting room which smelled once again of Virginia tobacco.

The Hampstead house is progressing. Life is changing rapidly. People are taking an excessive interest in us as a family. One day I walk into an empty second floor room in Guyon House and find a journalist and a photographer poking about in a cupboard. The phone rings all the time with requests for photo sessions and interviews. The house, we are agreed, is not to become the subject of magazine layouts. For one thing,

O'Toole has begun to acquire art and the last thing we want to do is advertise to burglars that this might be a likely place into which to break and enter. Also, we want Kate to have a private life untroubled by publicity. Columbia Pictures' publicists are jumping up and down with irritation. I now have enough of the house done for O'Toole on his return to have a room in which to talk to people, a room with a bed where we can sleep, a front door that locks and for meals we'll just have to use the nursery kitchen or have picnics. Mercifully, food does not loom large on his domestic horizon.

On September 28 Sam shut down the production of *Lawrence* in Jordan. David was dismayed; there were many wonderful locations, Petra included, that would never now be used. And the charge at Aqaba would be the charge at – well, somewhere in Spain. The suspension of business was all to do with money and – contrary to popular belief – had nothing to do with screenwriter Robert Bolt's imprisonment; he was jailed in September 1961 after a CND demonstration in Trafalgar Square. It wasn't a horrible experience being jailed as he was in an open prison but they wouldn't let him write so it wasn't very convenient and, besides, Sam wanted Bob at his beck and call. He tried to persuade Jo Bolt, Robert's first wife, to cajole Bob out of jail. Little did he know that Jo had conceived a rich and abiding hatred of him and his way of life, and what it might do to their life (hers and Bob's). Finally, Sam convinced Bob that the entire unit would be thrown out of work if he didn't allow himself to be sprung. Shoulder to shoulder with the workers, Robert allowed Sam to secure his release and I don't think he ever got over the mortification of realizing that he'd been 'Spiegalized'. His release was convenient for Sam and that was all. It earned him Jo's contempt and made him feel thoroughly guilty. Meanwhile the picture closed down in Jordan simply because Sam wanted it moved.

Activity at the house accelerates as O'Toole is expected home for a break. Everyone is feeling the strain. I desperately want him to be pleased with what I've done. This is our first real home and after a bad start our life together has moved, imperceptibly but surely into calmer waters. And I've made a friend. (Marie doesn't count. She is more like family.) During the run of *The Lizard on the Rock* throughout my visits to Vidal Sassoon I'm looked after by a young man; years my junior, still in his teens, but almost from our first meeting I sense that Ricci Burns is a friend – a potential friend anyhow. The changeable circumstances of my life make me slow to admit anyone beyond a certain point but I suppose only children always have their antennae out for potential brothers and sisters. Ricky feels like a potential brother. He seems to read my mind. He makes me laugh. He's smart where I'm naïve. He has a terrific sense of style. He's brutally honest with me but he's on my side. I'm immensely cheered to see him always. I think I'll keep him to myself for a while.

The homecoming is a stupendous success. The bags are laden with robes and coffee pots in three sizes and brass pestles and mortars for crushing cardamom seeds for future Arabic coffee (never made). There's beautiful, bad quality glass that breaks almost at once. O'Toole is bigger and handsomer than ever – he looks absurdly fit and if Kate doesn't really know who this is, like the rest of us she's fascinated and excited. We all want to touch him. The builders have stayed behind and share a glass of champagne with us as everything is inspected and admired. I have a feeling O'Toole at this moment is taking in little if any of the detail of plans for the rest of the house but we're all pleased and happy. What must it be like for him to be back in England after all these months and still only half way through this huge job. There's a break of at least four weeks and he'll have to keep everything bubbling in his mind in spite of the long pause and the inevitable distractions of London life.

After a few days' rest he begins to examine the house more closely and he falls in love with it; I can tell. Because of the complications of re-plumbing the old house, we've had to push

many of the central heating pipes that festooned the dining
room ceiling up into the room above and Joyce has had the
notion of building a platform over them. This becomes the
'stage' and the room becomes the actors' Green Room. It's
also known as the Marcus Luccicos room and there is a plaque
on the door commemorating the character in *Othello* who is
mentioned once, never appears and has no lines. Already it's
the most used room in the house.

With one or two hiccups, he and I have been getting on better
than I could have imagined during our Warwickshire life. I had
not dared to hope that we could be as happy as this and the
house seems to set the seal on this exciting, light-hearted phase
in our life together. He runs up the ninety-seven stairs several
times a day, revelling in the beautiful eighteenth-century stairwell. We have an uncomplicated month together, the three
of us, and then it's time for him to leave again. I tell myself
that this is no more difficult than the life of hundreds of
servicemen's wives. If I want to work and let Kate have a
settled life then I have to learn to deal with separations.

When he resumed it is in Spain and as soon as I am
able I visit him in Seville. My mother takes care of Kate
again. Now he's surrounded by actors – Claude Rains, Jack
Hawkins, Alec Guinness. There are infantile, highly enjoyable
unit jokes based on the 'th' sound in the Castilian dialect.
They stay at the Alfontho Trethi and Alec Guinness, encountered in the street on Sunday morning and on being asked
where he's been so early, replies sonorously, 'Confethione'.
They're all happy to be acting in the interior scenes. The
unit, after the rigors of Arabia, is ecstatic to be what they
call 'ashore'. Sherry is a penny halfpenny a glass. For ten
shillings (fifty pence) you can eat as many prawns as you
are able and finish the evening blind drunk as well. There
are a few catastrophes at work; men in the grip of ferocious hangovers fall off ladders and are sent home. Only
the wild men on the unit regret the hardship and the beauty

they've left behind in Arabia. I feel that David Lean is one of them.

O'Toole can see now that the film is going to absorb two years of his life. This is an unusually long time and the strain on him and indirectly on me is considerable. He is having to maintain concentration and immaculately good behavior while coming to terms with the fact that his status is altering by the month and that the rewards – or recriminations – lying in wait are, in the world of entertainment, huge. I have a foot in two camps and make a quick adjustment to a way of life that will persist; one that combines the extremely ordinary business of shopping and cleaning and stripping and mending furniture and spending my hours in very unglamorous theaters and TV rehearsal rooms with occasional well-dressed, chauffeur-driven forays into a much grander sphere. Mrs O'Toole is treated very differently from Miss Phillips. I learn to take it as it comes. Ever a realist, I am not bothered either when people jostle me out of the way in their need to get near the rising star. I did object when little Gina Lollobrigida actually put her stiletto heel through the arch of my foot in her hurtling frenzy. Unrecognized and unacknowledged, some moments later in O'Toole's dressing room I handed her a quadruple single malt whisky and watched happily as, gulping unthinkingly, her eyes began to roll, and I took a malicious delight in reading that she'd been unable to turn up for work the following day because of a 'virus'. Ordinarily, I was all sweetness and understanding but she managed to get on my nerves.

I can hardly believe that, in spite of the unusual circumstances (or maybe because of them) our life has become so harmonious. Our times together are both hilarious and tranquil – not for a year had there been a mention of my Past. Did that mean it was forgotten for good? I didn't dare to relax my guard completely but nor did I allow the small fear to spoil the present. There is no one else I would prefer to be with. We talk and talk and talk again as we used to.

That was what I missed most during our estrangement, the uninterrupted conversation. Of course, now from time to time our conversations have to continue on paper and he writes such wonderful letters that I am almost reconciled to the separations. Some of the letters are written in pencil and the writing grows faint with re-reading.

No Christmas leave for the *Lawrence* unit. I have work to do and I take Kate to Wales and try to be cheerful for her sake. We do eye exercises daily but the eyes are not improving. It hasn't been nearly as much fun, working on the house in the cold and dark of winter. Marianne has left for home and I embark on a series of mostly awful nannies. Now that we're becoming famous, some girls come for the interview just to have a look at the house; one stays overnight and is gone when we wake in the morning. Because of the lack of good help leaving home is becoming a problem and much of my TV work is at Granada Manchester which has the most adventurous TV drama department in the country. I worry all the time and hurry home the minute work is over. All the young mothers I meet tell me horror stories about unreliable nannies. I don't really know how long I can go on like this and I think I am going to have to work only in and around London. Before that I solve the problem temporarily by asking my parents to take Kate to Spain to visit her father. They can all holiday and I can go on working without having to worry about child-minding. When they go south to Marbella my father, handsome still, has a lovely time at a bullfight with glamorous April Ashley, now Lady Rowallan. O'Toole didn't spoil everything at that moment by telling him – as April herself would have done, given time – that she had begun life as seaman George Jameson. April – a really good sort – was adorable and put herself out to entertain my unworldly father.

Later in the year I spent a few weeks in Almeria, where Columbia filmed the charge at Aqaba. O'Toole and Omar had rented a frightful house full of hideous religious objects;

there were figures of saints with seeping, lit-up bloody wounds, a sacred heart that pulsated. Every classical statue in the house had its sex organs removed. Living there was unnerving. Robert Bolt was the brightest presence. In spite of the rigors of working for Sam – and he did hate being 'Spiegelized' – he maintained his good manners and his good sense. His marriage was in difficulties, however, as was Omar's, whose sister had come to join us in Nightmare Towers. There was a strange mother and daughter duo there as well, the sort of people who trail around in the wake of film crews and one is never quite sure how they pitched up or why. The Twist had begun to sweep the world and everyone in the house practiced it day and night. The noise was deafening and that and the lack of privacy made me long for escape, which we did briefly to a charming little place called Torremolinos. Sitting in a restaurant on a cliff we saw a British ship sail in. Taxiing down to the coast, we waved and waved until someone sent a boat for us and we had a lovely afternoon and evening in the bosom of the Navy. What is it about sailors that makes them the best of all hosts?

I didn't want to leave O'Toole but I was glad to leave the overcrowded house in Almeria. With the exception of the trip to Torremolinos and meeting April and catching up with the Navy, it hadn't been a successful visit. O'Toole had been distracted, or tired or worried or bored, who could tell? Any of these would have been understandable but I had not yet learned to stand apart emotionally and I was hopelessly affected by his moods. Now that we had become so close again I could not bear the occasions when we were not of one mind and heart. He was as bad as I was; absurdly possessive and jealous of my attention. My unthinking, polite response to another man, no matter how unprepossessing, caused him distress so I learned to tailor my behavior to the occasion. It wasn't difficult.

I'm told that Columbia Films is spending millions of dollars on O'Toole's publicity. Can this be true? It seems an incredible amount of money. Jules is convulsed with mirth when we discuss this. 'What's so funny?' 'Never mind, kid.' I *do* mind. It's lonely once Kate has gone to bed. Marie has gone back to work in Dublin. Almost all the Irish actors I know have a cut-off point beyond which they do not care to stay in England and three months is the most that Marie seems able to endure. Alone in the building site at No. 98 I keep busy, acting in television. There isn't a commercial play I like and the Royal Shakespeare Company is now out of my reach. People say, 'You're always busy. You're so lucky.' No, I'm not. There is a world of difference between being courted, chased after, getting first bite of the cherry and keeping busy, mopping up the crumbs that fall from the big table. I think – no, I know that during the last year or two I've missed some big chances and have missed them because of my character, or a lack of it. Will I get another chance? I doubt it. Life isn't that sweet. The best I can do now is to persist somehow. Nothing will make me give up that first childhood resolve to be an actress, but I'm going to have to be a quiet sort of actress. It may be that I shan't succeed in being any sort of actress at all, but I'm going to try. I see clearly that all the career mistakes I have made I would probably make again, so I have to accept that my life is going to be problematical and the problems are of my own making. This doesn't make me feel better.

Chapter Seventeen

Because of work and my need to be at home with Kate, I didn't visit O'Toole when the unit moved for a brief time to Morocco. I wasn't to see him again until he returned to England – we were reunited in the early autumn of 1962. The foreign locations are over at last. The remainder of the film will be shot in England. There's been a stupendous homecoming – the hall looks like a souk, he's been shopping in Morocco. There are piled up carpets everywhere, one of them so big it will only fit into the big, empty first-floor drawing room; there are robes from Ouarzazate, and Kate and I sit there covered in luxury, speechless. 'God has come home.' It is heavenly.

Joyce and I have made a ravishingly beautiful bedroom on the first floor back; walls upholstered in rough grey and off-white silk fabric, dim gilded lights, dull, gold curtained windows, a beautiful Louis XIV desk in the Georgian bay – she's made me walk all over London for six months before settling on this one. I've found there is a 'fair' price for a good piece of furniture. There's no such thing as a bargain but some pieces are marginally nicer than others, marginally cheaper too. I've looked at scores of desks including the supreme examples at the Wallace Collection and this is the best one going at £400 and I'm so keen on it I pay for it out of my most recent fee. It's almost an object of devotion for me; dark red wood inlaid with dull metal strips, the top pulling out to seven feet wide. I lie in bed and look at it and wonder at it, so plain and so beautiful. In a junk shop just off Gower Street I acquire a Louis XV chaise-longue in bad shape and have it done up and with a couple of plain English eighteenth-century night tables at the bedside and plain lamps and a huge, spectacular bedhead made out of a semi-circular picture frame picked up on a pavement in the Kings Road for £40, mended and upholstered with a pad covered with the wall fabric. I'm in the perfect bedroom business all right. Once inside that door there is total tranquillity. He's *got* to love it. He does.

Our bedroom sits behind the first floor drawing room which is a big empty shell. There's no money left to do anything to it at present. I can't mess about with the structure of this pretty house to produce an en-suite bathroom (so desirable these days), as it would destroy the proportion of the first floor, so our bathroom is on the second floor and it's quite beautiful – but it does involve a run up the stairs. O'Toole decides that he'd prefer his own bathroom which means running *down* the stairs to the newly made ground floor shower room. We've shared so little domestic life together and I realize that he doesn't see me getting made up and I don't see him shaving and this seems just fine to me. In many ways we're too close for comfort and this bit of apartness is welcome. The happiness of our time together in Jordan, in the Lebanon and in Spain was no illusion. In grey, damp Hampstead I can tell that we have turned a corner and we are truly happy.

Elated by our good fortune, we decide to have another child and I become pregnant at once. (Thank God for contraception, I breathe, yet again.) I am still unsure what the future holds. The film is not finished and already our life has changed utterly. We're invited everywhere but we don't go anywhere much. Every day there are requests for interviews, photographs; hardly any are granted. We lead a quiet life with very occasional forays into society. People come to us.

It was at home in Hampstead that I first met Rudolf Nureyev. He was presented to us by the writer Eric Braun as a brilliant, homeless waif. 'Not quite,' I thought as the slight figure pursed his lips dramatically and raised his hand to his heart and *retreated* a few steps, instead of advancing to take my hand, outstretched in greeting. He struck a pose, standing in the Green Room with his back to the window overlooking New End Hospital's Men's Surgical. 'The kind of woman who gets me into trouble,' he said to the interpreter, throwing his head back and watching my reaction, which was to smile, shifting my feet awkwardly. I wasn't embarrassed for me. I was embarrassed for *him*; he was too theatrical by half. Nureyev swooped forward and kissed my hand and, at that moment, the door opened and O'Toole entered. Rudi dropped my hand like a used hankie and it was *his* turn to smile and shuffle and come over girlish as he fell under the scrutiny of a pair of eyes every bit as potent and confident as his own. We knew next to nothing of the ballet and meeting Nureyev was like encountering an exotic, amusing animal – a bit of a show off.

Nothing could have prepared us for our next meeting after he had rapidly become the huge star and partner of Margot Fonteyn. One didn't need to know anything about the ballet to realize that he was phenomenal. One didn't need to like ballet to love watching him, much as one could be enthralled by watching Cassius Clay in the ring while knowing nothing and caring less about boxing. Rudi conquered society as well as the theater and the way in which he exerted his social power was a measure of a rapidly changing social structure. Young turks could get away with anything in the Sixties.

At a dinner given in Belgravia there was considerable excitement among the ladies because Nureyev was due to come on after a performance. It was a cold night of frost and snow. He arrived when we were still at the table, he swathed in woollen scarves and sweaters and carrying a duffel bag full of dirty practice clothes which he dropped in the dining room, making for the drinks tray and picking up a smallish bottle of plum brandy which he lifted to his lips. The large throat opened and relaxed like a singer's and he drained the bottle in what seemed like seconds while we all watched in silence. The room was, not exactly frozen – everyone was too delighted – but it was halted, wrong-footed; there were glad cries of welcome, some only half-uttered, people had begun to rise but didn't know if they should continue. Rudi's next move completed the confusion. He seemed to levitate on to the table and, slightly smiling, he danced down its length, sure-footed and dignified, extending his arms and deftly but forcefully lifting off a postiche here, a top knot of ringlets there. The cries of alarm and anguish were overlaid with uncertain laughter. The ladies were going to love and appreciate him no matter what he did to them. I wondered what O'Toole – no stranger to the outrageous – was making of this new Rudi. Margot had also arrived, perfectly groomed, smiling and imperturbable as though Rudi's behavior was the most natural thing in the world. I was pregnant and wearing a heavy, green Dior velvet dress and jacket, trimmed at collar and cuffs with heavy jet beads. The heat and the excitement proved too much and as I stood chatting to Margot I knew I was going to faint, faint right on to her, squashing her flat. As I began to fall I felt someone catch me and when I regained consciousness I was floating in a stairwell and I realized after a moment that Rudi was carrying me above his head. He was drunk and I weighed a ton, what with the unborn Pat and yards and yards of expensive Christian Dior, lined, inter-lined and beaded. There seemed to be a little procession. O'Toole and Margot followed us and they in turn were followed by a few ladies who, slightly unnerved, decided to leave us in a very pretty nursery, upholstered and curtained in pale, grey toile de jouy. I recovered and we chatted for a while until Rudi began to throw up violently. I don't think he missed a wall, a chair or a piece of carpet. Margot and I looked on while O'Toole came into his own. The great dancer was as drunk as a skunk and needed to be packed off home. Rudi wanted to curl up and sleep. 'Come on, mush,' barked O'Toole, 'you can't sleep on the town hall steps. Here we go,' and seizing him by the legs he began to bump him down the thickly carpeted stairs. Rudi seemed perfectly happy with this method of descent but in the hall below there were anguished cries of 'Be *careful* with him', 'Take care of his *feet*'. 'To hell with his fucking feet,' muttered O'Toole as Rudi giggled to himself, and louder, 'Just get us a cab.' As we negotiated the icy pavement, the assembled diners called out with more pleas for caution with the precious feet. Margot and I tiptoed behind the ungainly, slipping, lurching couple ahead. Rudi was angelic in the cab; smiling, well content with his evening, delighted to be looked after so glamorously, wanting to kiss us all.

O'Toole and he went out on the town alone sometime later when the Twist was still at the height of its popularity. In Al Burnett's club they were dancing with a couple of hostesses and O'Toole heard the rather bored girl, gracelessly twisting near Rudi say, 'Are ya Polish?' 'No!' growled Rudi, concentrating on a very muscular bit of twisting. 'I am *Tarrtarr*.'

Sam had ordained that the film be ready for public viewing by December! David was inclined to argue that this was completely impossible but Sam had craftily secured a Royal Première and since the Queen would attend, it had to be ready. A royal opening was important for the success of any movie. David was once a brilliant editor and he *had* a brilliant editor, Ann Coates, working with him now, but a large amount of the editing had already been done as he shot the film. He would, for example, cut in the camera to make it impossible for anyone to alter his concept. One day he asked O'Toole to casually move the cigarette to the 'wrong' hand during a scene which had been requested but which he didn't want used – the continuity was broken and the scene became useless. Even so, it was a mad rush and he moved a truckle bed into the cutting room and stayed there day and night.

I went to work on a modest TV film at Elstree, *This is not King's Cross*; Michael Craig was one of my leading men. He drove a Jaguar and, sensing I was under some pressure, he kindly named himself 'Radio Jags' and became my personal cab company, picking me up in the morning and returning me to Hampstead every night. O'Toole was now fully occupied doing press and publicity. Jules still seemed to be nursing some private joke as he organized O'Toole's busy days. I joined Jules and Joyce and their daughter, Joan-Juliet, and Peter at night after my rehearsals. I went home to bed alone. I wasn't really a part of the circus. Not yet.

December 1962 and the only London pea-souper I remember. There must have been others but I didn't notice them. When we worked in North London, I rose early and walked from Heath Street to rehearsals at Swiss Cottage, clutching at the walls, unable to see my hand in front of my face. Sound was so muffled that one collided with people before becoming aware of another presence. Cars veered dangerously and silently on to the pavement. It was frightening but everyone was imbued with the spirit of the Blitz. Mich Craig slowly, slowly drove me home at night. I had a beautiful brown woollen robe that O'Toole had brought me from Arabia and one night I went upstairs when it became obvious that he wasn't going to be coming home for dinner and lay on the bed reading until it was time to take off the big robe and go to sleep. No O'Toole. I was only a couple of months pregnant but I was thankful for quiet times. (A non-appearance at dinner and no phone call didn't rate highly as a bad time). I fell asleep and at five o'clock in the morning I was awakened by the telephone, always on my side of the bed. I looked around. Still no O'Toole. Picking up the phone I heard Uncle Davy's voice. In Welsh he said how sad he was to tell me that my father had just died in a hospital outside Cardiff. To my shame and surprise I realized that I was feeling a flood of relief, before it was followed immediately by acute grief. I put the phone down and sat on the side of the huge bed looking at the wall. Cold, I pulled on my heavy robe. As I sat there I realized that I had spent my life worrying about my father. He had probably done the same for me. Neither of us had been able to do much for the other. He may have heaved a sigh of relief when I married O'Toole and became his responsibility (as men of that generation would think) and now for a second I had breathed relief and release. I felt bad but I could understand why that feeling had come for a moment.

What to do now? I didn't know where O'Toole was and it was a measure of my acceptance of his need for freedom that I had no idea how I might reach him. He didn't carry identification, or keys and hated to be contactable. I wasn't sure if this was a pose or a genuine wish to maintain a measure of liberation in a life that was becoming more and more constrained by approaching fame. Whatever the reason, this behavior was part of the rules of the house and I didn't have too much trouble incorporating it into my life, though I did have mixed feelings when roused to respond to his insistent ringing on the door bell in the early hours. But even then I thought there was something rather touching about his being so sure of his welcome. And I *did* always feel welcoming.

Now, calling Michael Craig, I left it to him to inform the company that I wouldn't be at rehearsals for a day or two and he volunteered to drive to Hampstead and get me through the fog to Paddington. I packed, went to the nursery to talk to the Nanny and make sure that she could cope for a while; played with Kate – she had been adored by her grandfather – and I felt sad for her, unknowing that she'd lost a great, tall, handsome supporter from her little corner in life.

Mich Craig picked me up. I wrote a note to O'Toole and left for Paddington, Michael driving through the white wall of fog, to begin the long train journey to Wales. Oh those train journeys packed into claustrophobic compartments; no buffet, very little heat, no privacy. My father's death was such a shock I couldn't truly confront it. He'd been unwell and I'd brought him to London where Gerry Slattery had arranged a meeting with the Queen's heart specialist, a Welshman. 'Don't worry,' he'd said. 'Live normally, eat and drink whatever you'd like. Don't fuss.' 'There you go,' I'd added, briskly, willing him to be well and strong and willing him not to be ill, willing him not to die. 'Don't *fuss.*'

Lawrence of Arabia was due to open in a few days. Would I be there? O'Toole had bought me a dress in New York and amazingly it fitted; Joyce Buck had organized a coat to go over it. Ricky Huston had loaned me a reliquary to wear as jewelry and Ricci from Sassoon would do my hair. How? Where? I didn't care.

My mother was in black, observing the formalities, sitting alone while people came to pay their respects and talk of my father. I'd never seen the Welsh ceremony before and I was faintly and irrationally irritated by the formal demonstrations of grief. My mother *had* to look sad all day. There must have been moments when she would have liked to smile – but no – all was unrelieved gloom. Davy, her brother, was there, making arrangements and suddenly, out of nowhere, there was O'Toole. I was overwhelmed with relief. I adored him in the role of rescuing cavalry.

He'd found my note and, abandoning Columbia Pictures and the publicity machine, had hurtled down to Wales by taxi. His arrival changed everything and everyone for the better. My mother cheered up and resumed a little light cooking. Davy and O'Toole went to the pub and Davy looked uncharacteristically cheerful when he returned. Funeral arrangements speeded along, interspersed with little drinks (normally, unheard of) and then he was gone again to London. Before leaving he told my mother and Davy that I was pregnant and that also helped to alter the atmosphere for the better. I arranged with my mother that as soon as she felt able, she should come and live with us in London. I didn't doubt that O'Toole would be generous hearted enough not to question this decision and I was right to take his generosity for granted. He could be awful but he wasn't mean and at moments of crisis he displayed a shining grace that lightened all around him.

December 9 was the day of the funeral and I was overcome with grief afterwards. Icy cold, I went to the railway station in Cardiff and sat bolt upright during the three-hour journey to London and the première of *Lawrence of Arabia*. Jules had told me to go to Claridges and there I found him and Joyce and Joan-Juliet and O'Toole and his sister and Derek, her husband. My clothes were there in the suite and so, blessedly, was Ricci, who washed and fixed my hair, tweaked my dress and chivvied me into presentability. We went to the movies and in my sad state I didn't see an inch of the film. The Queen was there but as a wife I wasn't needed in the line-up so I was able to slump a little. Afterwards, it seems there was a party for about five hundred people. I don't remember it at all. But I do remember going to Tony Nutting's lovely house in Chelsea and sitting there until dawn when, leaving the group, I walked alone into the street and got a cab home. The fog was over. I bathed and changed my clothes at home and was picked up by Mich to go to Elstree to start filming.

I didn't see O'Toole for days; I was putting in long hours at the studio and he became the hottest young property on two continents. I knew that life had changed yet again but everything was happening at two removes from me – and anyway, there was a show to do.

Chapter Eighteen

Guyon House is reorganized to accommodate my mother. She will have the second floor front as a bed-sitting room and her bathroom is almost en-suite. (This house is always going to be slightly cockeyed.) Kate is delighted she'll be one staircase away from her Mamgu (specially dear mother – the Welsh for grandmother) and I am delighted because now I'm going to be able to leave home and go to work without fear. (Since Marianne's departure to Sweden I've been glued to NW3.) On the other hand . . . I bid a mental goodbye to the kitchen, my mother will want to take over. But on the other hand, I can't cook well and don't much like it so why *not* hand over? On the other hand, am I going to enjoy resuming life under my mother's thumb? But we haven't lived together since I was sixteen – I'm grown up now and this is a big house, there's room for us all. On the other hand, she's never witnessed anything like O'Toole's drunken rages (no less alarming for being less frequent) but I don't intend that she shall, neither she nor Kate. (I add green baize-lined double doors to the list of work for the builders.)

Christmas is approaching, our first Christmas in Guyon House. My mother arrives. She's sold her furniture and almost all her possessions. 'Good!' I nod breezily and set about settling her in. She adapts to London life without missing a beat. Lying awake at night, thinking of her on the floor above – also lying awake? I wonder have I done something wonderful for her? Or have I asked her to do something incredibly difficult? I'm three months' pregnant and selfish and I don't dwell on the problem. There are no cozy chats. Not that we ever had any. The

Christmas holiday is here and we have immaculate Christmas and Boxing Day dinners and lunches – organized by Mamgu of course. The kitchen holds inexhaustible reserves for all who are invited or who drop in or pass by. The turkey is perfect, the puddings are my mother's vintage puddings made last year. O'Toole is not given to family occasions but even he goes along with this perfect festive regime. Kate bangs her turkey bone on her plate at the huge dining table. There's a massive fire in the newly uncovered eighteenth-century fireplace. The big tree shines in the hall. But I don't allow mourning. I miss my father so much and don't know how to express it so I don't allow *any* expressions of grief. I cannot bear to talk of him. My mother, still dressed in black, smiles and cooks and greets strangers and becomes 'Mamgu' to everyone. We don't speak of my father. And I know I'm failing her.

My pregnancy is beginning to show so I find a clever dress and do a television play with young Robin Phillips, feeling a bit too old to be his lover. It's the first time I've ever felt like that. Time is knocking on. I'm almost thirty and that seems so old. Robin wasn't very happy and it didn't surprise me to learn that he became a director shortly afterwards and directed Maggie Smith's glittering seasons in Canada. Just at the moment Maggie is involved with O'Toole and Marie Kean in London, preparing a reading of Sean O'Casey's *Pictures in the Hallway* (this is O'Toole's response to International Super Stardom). Arriving to rehearse at ten o'clock and finding the door open, Maggie drifts in past a builder or two and finds herself in Marie Kean's bedroom where the great Irishwoman is discovered fast asleep in a gold lamé evening gown. Maggie's day is made, I think. She's wreathed in smiles and Maggie, wreathed, spreads the smile over a half-mile radius.

When I am too heavily pregnant to work, O'Toole decides to do a play in the West End. *Baal* by Bertolt Brecht, his first appearance in London since the ill-fated *Oh Mein Papa* and

The Long and the Short and the Tall in the Fifties. And
O'Toole is not going to take a fee. 'How good,' they say. I
wonder about that. I feel that such a magnificent gesture really
undermines people who have to make a living in the West End.
After registering my protest and seeing it ignored, I shut up, but
I'm disturbed. I suspect that O'Toole's altruism is tinged with
guilt. Being a movie star is perceived in this country to be in
some way a disgrace. Albert Finney turned down Sam's offer
to play Lawrence because he didn't want to become a movie
star. (He went on to make movies for Woodfall productions,
nevertheless.) There's something about success that is regarded
with suspicion and the received wisdom is that movies are not
for 'real' actors. But I can see that our world is changing – it
has changed. (And do these self-appointed critics have any idea
how *difficult* it is to become a movie star?) I'm worried that
Jules is being too accommodating when every fiber of his being
must be screaming, 'No *Baal*! No dirty leading man in filthy
rags singing dodgy songs in a not-too successful Brecht play.'
Instead (and probably wisely) he says, 'Sure, play it until the
next movie. Sure, do it for nothing.'

The next film? Finally, I see why Jules had been chuckling
to himself at any mention of O'Toole's future. Wise, from
their years at Fox, to Sam and his wiles, Jules has somehow
slipped past Sam and Columbia an agreement for O'Toole's
services that does not extend beyond *Lawrence of Arabia*.
On the day when Sam tells O'Toole that his next four films
will be X Y Z and A, Jules says, 'I don't think so.' Sam
explains that over the next seven years O'Toole, like Omar,
will play whatever he decides he should. 'I don't think so,'
repeats Jules, softly. Lawyers and vice-presidents open files
and scrutinize O'Toole's contract with Columbia Pictures
beyond 1962. 'Hell let loose' is a mild way of describing what
happened next. People were fired. People hastily resigned.
Well into their million dollar campaign, they realized that
they were promoting an actor they didn't 'own' and, what

was worse, they had to go *on* promoting him for the good of the movie.

Jules and Sam were old hands at the game of dog-eat-dog but Jules had scored the revenge of a lifetime. Knowing the background, I couldn't do anything but salute Jules. I had never doubted his business sense but I was bowled over by his capacity to wait for his cooled revenge.

Jules and Sam had been partners in Horizon Pictures, which had produced *Treasure of the Sierra Madre*. As young things they had seen their furniture dumped on the pavement for non-payment of rent. John Huston (the third partner) had gone out hustling for production money. Joyce Buck's father had sent a check to ensure that Kate Hepburn continued on into the jungle for the shooting of *The African Queen*. Their association had been long and eventful. All the same, I was slightly worried that Jules – like all of us involved in the family firm – was over-charmed by O'Toole. Much as I adored him as a man and revered him as an actor, I was well aware that O'Toole could be horribly wrong about many things. It wasn't easy being the one person who would risk telling unpalatable truths and I had a feeling that no one would ever compete with me for that job.

Baal – well, worth doing, I suppose. I wasn't sure. It was, like all O'Toole's projects, fraught with dramatic incident. His dresser, on the night of the dress rehearsal, screamed, 'This show is cursed', flung the clothes on to the floor and fled into Charing Cross Road, never to return. The beautiful Jocelyn Herbert sets were changed by a gauze 'wipe' that traversed right to left and left to right and took for ever to move so the play lasted almost five hours. In the middle of it all O'Toole summoned George Devine to come and 'fix' it, ignoring the director's feelings. What a time they had! George Devine (who ran the Royal Court) and Jocelyn Herbert were lovers, the director had to be shunted sideways – it was exhausting just listening to the backstage drama. They opened and everyone fairly hated the play. A large portion of the audience slammed out each night crying, 'Disgusting'. But – was it all worth it? O'Toole looked awful on stage, which he wanted to be as a change from the beauty of Lawrence, but why, I wondered? The public isn't in the least bit interested or impressed by versatility. Marie and I went to the opening and nodded our approval of best efforts, but we both wondered, why bother? The play opened on February 7 and had to close at the end of April to accommodate the beginning of O'Toole's first picture as a co-production between Keep Films and a big outside company. The chosen film was *Becket*, based on the Anouilh play he had not done for the RSC.

May. *Becket* begins with Richard Burton. I haven't seen him or worked with him since I first took up with O'Toole after I left RADA. He's now involved with Elizabeth Taylor and against everyone's guess and wish has left his wife, Sybil. Of course, Elizabeth represents the great uncharted sea of superstardom and Richard has always wanted to be a superstar – a *wealthy* superstar. There's a story of him – a favorite of Daphne Rye, the H. M. Tennent Ltd casting director – at an all night party, sitting in a circle of young things who were asked to declare their ambitions. 'I want to be the greatest Juliet since Ellen Terry.' 'I want to play Hamlet as it has never been played.' 'How about you, Richard? What do you want to be?' The reply was simple. 'Rich.'

Thanks to Elizabeth, he is now going to *be* rich. Very rich. They both come down to the pub near Shepperton Studio and eat more food than normal people can imagine putting away. I'm a healthy eater (to say the least) but Elizabeth Taylor's food consumption leaves me standing . . . 'Those fat pigs,' snarls Kate Hepburn in disdain at such indulgence. I don't know. A part of me admires that kind of robustness. Another part sides with Miss Hepburn; such unbelievable self-indulgence *can't* be right – or can it?

Richard seems sheepish but rather pleased with himself, I

think. Not sure where he stands with us in his new role. Nor am I. As his wife Sybil's husband, he would have fitted perfectly into our life, but now? O'Toole senses that I am holding back rather and doesn't push to accept many invitations to the Dorchester or anywhere else.

Elizabeth and Richard are at the height of what is called the 'Scandale'. They seem to love the notoriety and the publicity. One night, Elizabeth wants to go to a theater in St Martin's Lane. We arrange seats. Elizabeth is very small. She wears a huge, turquoise turban. Word spreads (how, I wonder?) that the Seductress is at the theater. In the interval we arrange drinks to be served in the manager's office, front of house. 'No,' she cries to our horror, 'we're next door to the Salisbury. Let's go to the pub now!' St Martin's Lane is fairly heaving. Someone clears a path. All they can see is a turquoise hat. 'Oh,' cries a woman, 'the bitch! I'm so close, I could spit on her.' Unaccountably, Elizabeth finds this charming. She beams. 'It is so awful,' she says winsomely to O'Toole, 'not being able to go anywhere in peace.' 'It might help a bit,' O'Toole replies tartly, 'if you took off that fuckin' turquoise busby.'

There is something wonderful about her appetite for being noticed. Richard? No, I don't think so. He looks faintly embarrassed. But it's so obvious that he's willing to pay the price of fame. O'Toole may be disconcerted to be confronted by Stardom in its complete, unacceptable – but true form. He can have this, if he wants.

In 1967, very generously, they offered to take the children to stay on their yacht *Kalizma*. Over my dead body, I thought; it's hard enough trying to bring them up sane in NW3, never mind on a luxury yacht.

The same year, quite by chance, we flew to a film festival together, a beautiful festival in Taormina in Sicily where the Italian Oscars are given out. There was a confusion over tickets and Elizabeth snapped her fingers and got some boxes produced out of nowhere and the four of us cluttered up the front of the first-class compartment. We drank champagne all the way to Italy (I was right to avoid them, it was impossible not to behave excessively in their company). Elizabeth was very good natured. Richard was – Richard, and I remembered that even *reasonable* behavior on the part of royalty or celebrities is translated into *wonderful* behavior; the expectation is so much less, I suppose. When we got off, Rich and O'Toole and I looked dishevelled and blowsy. Elizabeth, who was royally drunk, looked stone cold sober and the photographs reflected this. 'Camera cleans her up,' said Richard philosophically.

At Taormina all the film stars were mobbed by screaming crowds. We stayed in a pretty and very uncomfortable hotel. Staying in the rooms (formerly monks' cells) was out of the question and in order to do some sightseeing and visit restaurants, we braved the boisterous fans who never left the front courtyard. After a day or two they grew bored with the stars and life was very pleasant for everyone. Richard and Elizabeth, on the other hand, remained closeted in two tiny rooms where they sat squashed in with their hairdressers and assistants. 'We're not going out till The Night,' said Richard. 'By then, they'll be MAD to see Elizabeth – it'll be a riot.' He was deadly serious, I realized dismally. He was right, of course; Elizabeth, the only star who hadn't been seen, was nearly killed by the pent-up enthusiasm as she left the hotel. On The Night, Richard said, 'Watch this, it'll be a sensation. The light will go on *there* but *she* will come in *here*.' We were in a Roman amphitheater – rubble everywhere 'backstage' – the auditorium, beautifully lit by candles issued to the audience as they arrived and then sat with their backs to the ocean. O'Toole was suitably, sincerely grateful in bad Italian. My friend, Silvana Mangano, brought a loving house of fellow countrymen to their feet, striding on casually and exiting smartly, then Elizabeth was introduced and didn't appear – didn't appear – didn't appear – and finally she was picked up in a light in the wrong place, picking her way through the uncleared rubble to the podium. It seemed a lot of trouble for very little return.

Much later, Richard and I sang some Welsh songs. A minor princess who seemed to be setting her cap at him was not best pleased. Elizabeth suddenly summoned him and we exchanged a wry smile. 'Mabel calls,' he said. One thing I remember about Elizabeth was that she had a terrific voice, clear and incisive, always interesting, no affectation. Richard and I had other, sadder, meetings as he lost his robust constitution and the years of excess took their toll. But he got what he wanted: 'Take what you want and pay for it.' Didn't he just!

Kate is three and already, as my mother says, she is a 'bit of a character'. She wears her round, metal-framed glasses with a forbidding air, peering suspiciously at the world, pinning my mother to her chair with demands to be read to. We're heartily sick of *Ant and Bee* and *Janet and John* and I begin to read her poems and stories that I find entertaining. She tolerates almost everything – even the fourth leader of *The Times* – but remains loyal to *Ant and Bee* in particular. Between us, my mother and I run the house. Manolita, the daily help, comes every day and cleans and mends and helps organize our lives.

Becket is a long movie and is being shot at Shepperton. Peter Glenville, who has a sound theatrical pedigree, is having no trouble at all with his stars, O'Toole and Burton. The press tries to create stories of tension and potential mayhem but even they have to give up in the end. The journey from NW3 to Shepperton is long, so the weekdays are calm; O'Toole leaves in the early hours of the morning and returns late with barely time to greet everyone and have dinner with me in the Green Room before going to bed early. Saturday is a bit of a lost day when he sleeps and sleeps, but Sundays are enchanting and we all lunch in the dining room before O'Toole and I take a walk around Hampstead and then sit and read until it's time to prepare for another hard week. Quiet, dull and totally happy, those months.

However happy I am, I feel I cannot forget the circumstances surrounding Kate's birth and I make up my mind that I am going to protect myself and the next baby from the remotest chance of drama and over-excitement. How to contrive this? Marie suggests that I come to Dublin for the birth and everything falls into place. Having a child on Irish soil will compliment O'Toole and put me beyond his reach at the same time. It works! Everyone – except my mother – is happy. It's seen as a charming gesture, but it's actually self-preservation on my part. So, three weeks before Pat is due to be born in June, I fly to Ireland and move into a back bedroom in Marie's flat at Lower Baggot Street. She's booked me into the Stella Maris Nursing Home (staffed by nuns) and Declan Meagher, a friend of Dr. Slattery's, will be in charge. I'm told to prepare a bag and the list includes a bottle of chloroform and a large pad of cotton wool; I find myself packing for myself a pair of white silk pajamas of O'Toole's. I may be wanting to do this my way but I also need to feel close to him and wearing his clothes will help me, I know.

The June days are perfect and long. Marie cooks wonderful meals (the Irish potatoes in June are heavenly). I lie on my bed high above the Dublin rooftops and I think I may never have such a relaxed time again. Marie is at work at the theater but her flat is lined with books so I read and read and read and look west out of the window. Joan Huet, a friend and stage manager, and Marie and a couple of the boys from the company decide that maybe we should speed things up a bit (I might sit there, reading and dreaming forever). 'Into the car,' they cry. 'Off to the Wicklow Mountains.' Joan brings her stage manager's stopwatch. In the mountains we stop here and there. 'Small gin for the lady,' say the boys. I scarcely drink but gin and orange doesn't taste like alcohol at all. After a few hours of bumping around the country roads, I feel a twinge.

'Oh Jasus – great,' they cry, relieved, and we speed back to town, Joan recording twinges on her stopwatch. When we reach the Stella Maris, she confers with the nuns while Marie and the boys bring my little bag up to my very nice room – two beds (bathroom en-suite). 'Ouch,' I exclaim at the next small twinge. 'All right. Everyone away now,' says an adorable nun. 'Did you feel a little pain? Aren't you the good girl? Here!' And drenching a pad of cotton wool with chloroform, she plants it on my face.

I'm told later that Declan shot across Dublin for the birth and, as an ex-Irish Rugby International player, was non-plussed to hear the unofficial Welsh Rugby anthem issuing from the prone, unconscious body beneath him. '*Sospan Fach, yn berwi ar y tân, sospan Fawr, yn berwi ar y llawr.*' 'I didn't know,' he said, 'whether to pass the baby or score a try.' All unknowing, I woke up in O'Toole's silk pajama top. 'You've got a beautiful baby girl,' said the saintly (I'd elevated her) nun. 'Oh, thank you. How nice,' I replied and looked at the perfect, pink happy bundle. Could anything be more perfect than this? This is the way to have a baby, I thought, as I drifted off to sleep again.

I woke up to find great excitement going on. O'Toole from England had ordered champagne and Guinness – enough Black Velvet for the city, it seemed, and the city was turning up. The bath was out of commission because it was full of ice and champagne. The room was full of Irish actors. I regarded the assembly calmly. I've done this my way. My baby was calm and untroubled and I was calm and untroubled.

So, Kate was born in Shakespeare's country but Pat has been born on Irish soil and I feel I've managed things very well. Jim Fitzgerald, a lively young director, drops in for a drink. Pat sleeps resolutely through the incredible din. Jim feels a little tired and says, 'D'ya mind?' as he rolls into the other bed in the room. He's still there twenty-four hours later. 'Ah, the craythur,' snaps Marie, irritably. 'Who cares?' I say. The nuns just smile.

O'Toole arrives. Jules and Joyce, also Peter Finch; various nobs. I'm concentrating on Pat. She is a miracle baby. I wonder if her manner reflects the way she was born, women only, no problems at all. She's easy. I'm easy. O'Toole leaves and returns to *Becket*. On my bed is the script of the movie. They need an actress who can speak old Welsh, find appropriate music, sing it and play the gittern at the same time. What kind of competition did I have to beat off to get *this* job? Yes. I'll do Gwendoline when I get home. But it's not a great part.

Robert Bolt sends me the script of his new play *Gentle Jack*. Again, it's not a great part but Edith Evans will be in the play. I have adored her for so long and nothing would give me greater pleasure than to sweep the stage so I could watch her – so, Yes! Of course I'll do it. Dame Edith . . . Can she be as wonderful as I think she is?

I feed Pat who is completely content and untroubled. Jim Fitzgerald wakes and says, 'Oh Jasus, where am I? I'm late for rehearsal.' He's a day late.

Marie makes me get up and get out to Bewleys for a coffee. I don't feel so good. Give it another day, she says, and then she puts us on a plane to England, where there's a *proper* Nanny. The first ever for me. Elizabeth de la Cour Bogue has arrived via Jack and Doreen Hawkins, almost snaffled by David Niven and then Lauren Bacall on the way, but she's *OURS!* Young, smart, upper-crust, great with horses as well as children. What have I done to deserve this? Doreen Hawkins, I bless you for ever. And Mamgu is in residence. And there's a crib swathed in pink. And there's a grim, cross-eyed, three-year-old sister. When she's seen holding a pillow over the baby's face with a pair of scissors in her hand, I think The Baby (even I can see 'The Baby' is a term of opprobrium) should be moved three floors down out of Kate's reach. Poor Kate, who had such a horrible birth and who has gone through so much already – has she any vague notion how she's been seized and rescued and re-seized and moved from pillar to post? And now here's this blissful creature who has never known a moment's trouble.

When Kate was born she was one of many children born to Royal Shakespeare Company members that year – all girls. Someone asked if my husband minded not having a son. I – so completely sure of my welcomed and treasured existence in my parents' lives – was amazed at such a question but, when I remembered it, much later, I put it to O'Toole. As I expected, he was as amazed as I and said that a houseful of women would suit him very well. When Pat was born, again I heard a sympathetic 'still no boy'. O'Toole and I looked at each other in mute amusement. What is this obsession with boys? Our friend Robert Shaw longed for a son and went on producing child after child until he succeeded in getting a boy. Such persistence was a source of wonder and amusement to O'Toole and we decided that two children was enough and so the houseful of women was established. When Pat was brought home from Dublin, Guyon House was up and running and it was much, much easier to ensure that O'Toole was not aware of the noise and tumult that a baby trails in its wake.

An infrequent visitor to the nursery on the fifth floor, he came up with me one night very late to see Pat in bed when she hadn't been too well. He was charming and she was charmed. Days later she asked me, 'You know that man – not the one with the beard, the other one who came to see me – who *is* he?' It had never occurred to us that his infrequent presence in London, coupled with the constant changes in appearance, could be so totally confusing to her. After that I made sure that I scattered around stills of their father in whatever new persona he had adopted for the current movie or play. These misunderstandings evaporated as the girls grew older but even so, Pat didn't exactly distinguish herself at her primary school by claiming that she knew the Bible *very* well and that it was a movie, starring her father.

Chapter Nineteen

*B*ecket continues without incident. O'Toole and Burton have both vowed to stay on the wagon. There's been no trouble and then one night they both fall off the wagon at the same time and meet up in some horrible dive (there are few pretty dives in 1963) and, partly appalled and penitent, go home for an hour or so and turn up on time for the first scene of the day, still drunk and hanging on to each other. They do a good day's work but the lapse has been noted.

I turn up to do my scene – quite complicated with all the music – but it goes smoothly and quickly. They incorporate my music into the theme of the movie. I go home to the girls.

Pat O'Toole continues to be the dream baby. Blonde, serene, she lies outside in the garden at Number 98. I, my mother and Liz, the daily, dote on her from a distance. She makes no demands. She smiles, the sun shines. Life is deceptively easy during the summer months. She's called Pat because I'd got it into my head that she was going to be a boy called Patrick and when they asked me her name in the nursing home, I couldn't think of anything different.

Soon it's time to start work again. *Gentle Jack* will now include Kenneth Williams, who is a great friend of Robert Bolt, and Michael Bryant, one of the best actors in England. It's a very classy show. Robert comes to stay with us while we rehearse. On the first day we're required to wear hats and skirts and gloves. Trousers are allowed on day two, thank God. Robert is conceiving a real dislike of the Dame. It's true that she hasn't read the play. It's true that she's demanding that Hardy Amies should design her a ball gown in stiff taffeta for all her daytime scenes in the City office. No one dares question her about this. They all moan in private. She sees that there will be rostra, six to nine inches high, here and there. 'I can't possibly act on those,' she cries. 'I'll have to wear slippers.' Carpet slippers and Hardy Amies frocks. No one dares comment. 'You seem very relaxed,' she accuses me in a cross voice. I'm petrified and I'm trying to *act* a relaxed, upper-class girl. I shake my head. She glowers. Gretchen Franklin learns that I'd like to improve my tap dancing. 'I'll teach you,' she offers. And does, until the Dame tracks down the source of the noise. No more tap. I have a passion for oranges. She hates oranges. No more oranges in the theater.

But the Actress is everything I'd thought she might be. All day at rehearsal and every night during the run I stand and watch her and I can't see what she's doing. She gets laughs and I can't see how – there doesn't seem to be any preparation – no special light, no good place, no clean 'feed'. She just gets a laugh if *she* thinks it's a funny line. If she doesn't understand something she says it with no expression at all. She never 'helps' the dramatist, never papers over a crack in the script. Faced with a bit of bad writing she suspends her acting until the moment is over and then carries on. The behavior is aristocratic.

Producer Binkie Beaumont is brutal to her when the play does badly on the road. In the broad alleyway to the stage door he barks, 'Come on, come on,' after a performance in Brighton. 'Do your magic! Pull the play together.' What a hope! He should know her better than that.

We play Brighton for a month. She and Kenneth Williams stay at the Royal Crescent, traditionally the stars' hotel. I stay in a suite at the Albion and have the girls there with me a great deal of the time. When Dame E. and Kenneth go home they share a miserable wilted salad and as they go up in the lift the friendly night porter nudges the Dame in the ribs and says, 'Enjoy your grub?' According to Ken, not once does she acknowledge his presence.

In the wings, at night, she stands, smoothing down her taffeta dress, making a horrible crackling noise and muttering to herself. She fairly *hates* this play. They told her she was playing a modern-day Elizabeth the First. Well, of course, her part is nothing like that at all and she hasn't read the other bits of the play. 'Remember *Nina*,' she says to no one in particular (*Nina*, a play few of us had seen, was a great failure and she left it on a stretcher), rustle, crack, rustle. Norah, in the prompt corner, hisses fearlessly, 'Please, SHUT UP, Dame Edith!' She smoulders a little and then resumes the crackle, rustle, crackle, mumble, mumble, until she has to enter in her carpet slippers and grand frock. I'm more enslaved by her than I could have thought possible. Robert cares for her even less than before. When she died, he happened to be staying with us and I said, 'Look who died!' Eulogies were pouring in. Robert looked at the tributes in *The Times* and delivered his own, terse, obituary: 'Well, she was no use to me.'

In Brighton – it being almost the Christmas season – there's a misconception that *Gentle Jack* is a children's show about Jack and the Beanstalk (grand managements like H. M. Tennent Ltd. don't think that they need to advertise or let the public know what to expect). When a dog is disemboweled quite early in the play the hatred wafting across the footlights is palpable. Occasionally people tut-tut at us in the street. This doesn't augur well for London.

While I was rehearsing *Gentle Jack*, O'Toole accepted an engagement in London which he'd be able to fit in before going off to shoot *Lord Jim* in Cambodia. It was to play Hamlet in the Laurence Olivier production of the play which was to open the National Theater (housed at the Old Vic). Before we opened on tour in Brighton, I attended the first night. It was a huge occasion, a landmark in the British theater. As I took my seat in the stalls I felt all the symptoms of acute stage fright. Bob Bolt took my hand and gave it a shake but I couldn't respond, my tongue had stuck to the roof of my mouth and I could only nod in answer to his encouraging 'Come on, girl, it's only a play.' It *wasn't* only a play (and he didn't believe it either). It could have been worse, I reflected. A few months previously Larry had asked me if I would like to play Ophelia. I was speechless and O'Toole had spoken for me, saying that they ought to cast someone really young (I was thirty at the time – no juvenile). For a moment, just a moment, I had felt dashed (and Larry looked quizzical) but within minutes I thought that I had probably been saved from myself. I was *not* a juvenile but would I ever have turned down such an opportunity? Now I sent up a prayer of gratitude that I was not backstage, coping with my own terrors and worrying about O'Toole as well. Even so, sitting out front was a nightmare; the play and the building were bedevilled. Buses thundered past the side of the unfinished building swathed in tarpaulin and this *Hamlet* was a pale shadow of the performance O'Toole had given at the Bristol Old Vic in the mid-Fifties. Sean Kenny had made a lovely set that rarely worked. Only too often the company climbed down from the lofty bridge that hadn't met in the middle and continued the performance on the flat apron in front of the safety curtain. Since they were giving these performances uncut (nine hours on matinée days), some of the evening performances interrupted by technical glitches were interminable. The public didn't care. They flocked.

Larry seemed intent on making O'Toole look like a clean, well-dressed, young master. O'Toole went along with everything – pudding basin hair-cut, Lord Fauntleroy collar. Larry wrote him God-like notes and letters. 'My son, in whom I have such pride . . .' Some temporary cleaner swept these into the bin and I got the blame. I thought O'Toole was badly served by Larry and for once he was too obedient by half. But it's very hard *not* to be subservient around one's idol.

When we arrived in London the critics savaged *Gentle Jack* and Robert was terribly upset. He'd thought it was his best play. We played on while *Hamlet* closed and O'Toole prepared to play the lead in the film of Conrad's *Lord Jim*. Jean Simmons and her husband, director Richard Brooks, and their children had come to lunch at Guyon House to talk about the project before leaving England. 'No script to be seen until we've started shooting,' said Richard Brooks. The Conrad novel was a wonderful subject but I couldn't quite believe that O'Toole was breaking his cardinal rule: no script, no deal. Jean Simmons looked as harassed by domesticity as I. Our children got wet and dirty in the garden. My mother beamed at the Jean Simmons she saw in her mind's eye, not the tired mother scraping mud off small Wellington boots.

It was time for O'Toole to leave (for 'the high China seas' I read in my atlas) and I would be able to join him there as soon as I was free. Pat was thriving, Kate was at kindergarten (and already her life was an endless round of parties). I'd grown to enjoy the long period of home life, only rarely threatened by alcohol owing to the daily pressure of work, and I didn't want it interrupted, but this was a pointless regret and I didn't even voice it. It was easier to deal with these separations if we didn't have farewell scenes.

While I was playing *Gentle Jack* I accepted, as a day job, my first 'real' movie, *Espionage*, albeit made for TV, and the first made for TV in the director's long and fascinating career. 'Oh, you'll have an *awful* time,' said his contemporaries. On the contrary, Michael Powell and I found ourselves working together extremely happily. The great Powell and Pressburger days were behind him but films like *The Red Shoes* and *Peeping Tom* were fresh in people's minds. He and Anthony Quayle, my leading man, between them gave me a month's seminar on movie acting and it was the first really interesting job I'd had in about two years. There was an actor in the movie whom I found dazzling. Marie knew and admired him also and we used to inveigle John Wood round to Heath Street for sketchy suppers, lots of drinks and tons of adulation which just slipped off his back unnoticed.

Michael Powell took me under his wing and began to make plans for a movie future for me. But he'd fallen on hard times himself and none of his projects for me came to fruition. I sensed that he was whistling in the dark, but I felt very privileged to get to know him and his wife and talk, talk, talk about films in his flat in Melbury Road.

Dame Edith, who wasn't good at names, usually addressed me as 'Mother-of-two'. I feel like a 'mother-of-ten' and I'm a full-time daughter again but finally I've had to learn how to run a house properly – even I can tell however that I'm very tense and over-anxious. There are lists everywhere; menus for the children, menus for us, notes to the daily, memos to myself and just about anyone I see who passes me on the stairs. And I feel I would like to be four wives – four separate wives: one, sleeves rolled up, seeing to the nuts and bolts of daily life, doing the odd bit of carpentry and furniture removal; one for dealing with the delicate, personal secretarial work that can't be handed on to an office; one for fun and one for going to the hairdresser, the dressmaker, the chiropodist, the manicurist and looking smart, and entertaining like a lady of leisure. Then, there's Miss Phillips, the Equity member, to accommodate somehow. I'm keeping a tight grip on things but every second of every day has to be accounted for and I'm losing even more weight and on my way to becoming 'thrillingly thin' as my friend Debbie Condon describes the emaciated, model-size figure I had never thought to possess. Deb is a beautiful American supermodel, married to our friend, playwright Kenneth Jupp and we spend what little time off we have with our friends and business partners, the Bucks – including daughter, Joan-Juliet – and Ken and Deb Jupp. I keep two diaries, one big desk diary and a

small Hermès agenda which I carry around. Ah, Hermès . . .
Yes, life is becoming very 'Gucci, Pucci, Cucci' as I heard a
disgruntled husband mutter while he trailed up Bond Street
behind his busily shopping wife. The diaries intimidate me
at the beginning of every week. Kate's eyes require constant
attention, the patches have to be moved regularly from eye to
eye, so every page bears a note saying 'Left', 'Right', 'Both for
a bit', 'Check-up, Mr Wybar' (Mr Wybar, the saintly oculist
of Wimpole Street, is the man who features most regularly
in my diary, accompanied by Mr Cuthbertson, the equally
venerated dentist). The travelling is tiring even to read about.
The lists read like incomprehensible gibberish within weeks of
being written.

1964: Feb. Close play. Girls on holiday with my mother.
Fly to Cambodia 26th. *Lord Jim*. Move to Hong Kong 28th.
Depart to Japan by March 3rd, Kyoto on 5th. 11th opening
of *Becket* in New York – organize hair and dress. Party P.
Glenville. March 13th leave for London. Children. Kate to Mr
Wybar. Work on drawing room. Learn lines. Be in Manchester
March 17th. Film in Southport. Sleeper to London arrives 5:30
a.m. Dinner Ken and Deb. April 3rd *Tom Jones*. April 10th
Bermans and Wig Creations. Costume pick-up. Ireland. Soup
Bowl Restaurant, Molesworth Street today. Girls to Marie
Kean – and so on and on unremittingly.

The circus moved on when O'Toole went away on location
and life at the Ladies' Seminary settled into a quieter rhythm.
There were seven of us, sometimes eight: my mother, Elizabeth
the Nanny, Manolita, the treasured daily housekeeper, Pilar,
the au-pair, Marie Kean, Kate and Pat and me. During the
year I did more television and began another play for the
West End. Out of the blue I was asked to do a play, *Hogan's
Goat*, on Broadway and declined at once. I could see that
there were several ways of organizing family life, given our
circumstances. More and more movies were being made on
location and more Americans seemed to be based in Paris and

Rome, so the chances were that O'Toole would work away from home in Europe. Many actors liked to travel their 'homes' – wife, children, nanny, secretary, friends – with them. O'Toole firmly rejected this. Some mothers, when they travelled, took the children with them, travelling a tutor if necessary. My mother and I between us decided that the girls' life should retain in its own routine, regardless of our activities. I would try to work around their lives. They were not to go away to school and that way O'Toole would be able to see them whenever he was at home whether it was term or holiday time. My going to New York while O'Toole was in Europe was out of the question. The New York producers and my agent were put out by my continuing resistance. Finally they wrote testily, 'You know there is an actress in America who is *longing* to play this part.' 'Well, I'm afraid you'd better give it to her then.' So, Miss Faye Dunaway got her first Broadway break and very good she was, too, I was told.

Instead, I did a French play with my friend Max Adrian. It was a fantastical work by Marçel Aymé, translated by Kitty Black, and it was the first of many French plays I was to perpetrate over the years – all flops – but I liked them and *Maxibules* was one of the most spectacular failures. No amount of work in rehearsal and on the road could make it acceptable to the English audience. After a faintly improper (for 1963) scene I had to say 'I'm disgusted'. 'So are we,' came a cry from the upper circle. 'And I'm going home,' I continued. 'So are we!' replied our self-appointed critic.

As the curtain fell on opening night someone hissed, 'Don't take the rag up again, for God's sake!' 'Nonsense!' barked Max – heart of a lion – 'Take it up!' He held my hand tight as we got the bird; my first experience of being booed and hissed. They threw money at the stage. Four days later we were off, but I'd had a lovely time working with Max and I *still* liked the play.

The television play was more successful. It was a very

interesting piece of work, *The Other Man*, by Giles Cooper.
I played opposite a reserved, young John Thaw and Michael
Caine and Granada generously allowed us seven weeks in
which to rehearse and film the play. On the long railway
journey to Manchester, Michael – also quiet and rather self-
contained – outlined his strategy for the next stage of his
career, at the end of which he said, 'Within a year, I'll
be in movies in a big way.' I nodded, doubtfully. I didn't
question his ability but I didn't see how he could be so
sure of a thing like that. Just over a year later I noted
that he'd been absolutely correct in his strategy and in his
prediction.

One night while I was doing a stage play on tour in
Guildford, the well-known agent Harvey Orkin took the
train to see the show and travelled back with me in our car.
Before I dropped him off in the Fulham Road, he handed me a
script and said, 'Read this, I think you'll find it funny and you'd
be very good in it.' It was days before I got around to reading
the screenplay and when I did I found it brilliantly funny. I'd
never heard of the author. The part Harvey wanted me to look
at was fine but the men's parts were wonderful. Harvey wasn't
my agent and I didn't know him very well and I wasn't sure
what he thought I could do with the script. When I showed
it to O'Toole his eyes lit up. I was so pleased he agreed with
me – it *was* brilliant. When he took it off to our office, which
Jules had set up in Belgravia, I hoped that he would like it
as well. O'Toole would be wonderful in the leading part
and I wanted to be in such an original movie. The author
was invited to London and I was intrigued and enchanted
to open the door to a small, droll, shy character who settled
cautiously into a corner of the big couch in the Green Room
and was sufficiently moved to pull himself together to pay me
a compliment on my dress as I brought him tea. Good. He liked
me, and he warmed to me even more when I complimented him
on *What's New Pussycat?* which is what he'd called the script.

O'Toole entered the room and the coziness was at an end. 'All right – thanks,' O'Toole smiled and nodded affably but firmly at the door. Evidently I was dismissed. I said goodbye, hoping I looked as though I had lots of other interesting things to do and went up to the nursery. I was a bit put out but even more I was bemused. For someone to be flown across the Atlantic for a chat was wonderful and extraordinary. Less wonderfully, I never saw Woody Allen (for he was the short, shy American) or the script again and was never told what had been discussed over tea.

As the weeks went by I realized that our company, Keep Films, was actually going to co-produce *Pussycat*. During a meeting one day I gathered that 'my' part was going to be offered to someone called Capucine. I was mortified at first but I did appreciate that O'Toole loathed nepotism and it was a measure of his slightly cockeyed respect for me that he strenuously avoided doing me any professional favors. (I saw a photograph of Capucine; she was *incredibly* elegant!) We never discussed this development of casting and I confined my interest in the movie to events in the production office – drama enough.

Because of the attention of the paparazzi, and an attendant court case, O'Toole insisted that the movie he was shooting in Rome be moved to France and so began several years of filming in Paris. All the movies were co-productions with our company, Keep Films, so we kept an apartment at the George V and Jules and Joyce and I flew to and fro as though we were bussing to Putney. O'Toole built up his art collection and I bought my clothes from the big houses and there was much pleasure in our life but it seemed to me that my hold on my place in our life was so precarious that, like a mole in the night, unacknowledged even to myself, I began to build a little power. Rather pathetically, it took the form of making sure that I myself remained extremely thin; ultra-fashionably thin. Anorexia or bulimia was totally alien to my healthily greedy appetite but discipline was second nature to me and I now put myself on the strictest of strict diets. Eating only in the best restaurants in the world, I read the menu, looked at the elaborate food and ate a lamb chop or a piece of fish and a grapefruit every day for lunch and dinner. Sometimes I drank wine, mostly I drank water and I was so thin that I was much in demand by designers to model their clothes. I was flattered to be asked and, more to the point, bought my grand clothes cheaply at Dior because I was exactly the same size as their German house model, Christine, and at the end of the season I could buy the clothes she'd been wearing during the shows. I don't think O'Toole even noticed my strange eating habits or my clothes; if he did, he never remarked on them, but being thin – never giving way to temptation – made me feel stronger and more in control than I actually was.

Of course, I was addressing the wrong problem in the wrong way, controlling the wrong thing.

Chapter Twenty

During this period O'Toole found a way of 'remembering' my birthdays, our anniversaries and Christmas presents. 'Let me off the whole thing,' he said. 'I'll give you things to cover all occasions.' And he did. He'd begun to collect Etruscan jewelry – wonderful, intricate objects, unbelievably crafted before magnification. Most were things to look and wonder at but some were wearable – just. The gold was unalloyed so a chance bump in the night could seriously damage one's favorite bangle. I was happy with this arrangement; there was no suspense about one's birthday being forgotten, no marking of the anniversary to worry about – and Christmas? Well, one less thing to worry about at that time of year could only be to the good.

On Joyce's advice I took my Etruscan collection to Mme Claude de Muzak on the Left Bank in Paris who made beautiful, gunmetal-bound vitrines. I took a few of the more robust looking pieces to Boucheron to be fixed for wearing. The workroom there refused to touch them because they were afraid of destroying them. The man I talked to there asked me if I minded that he'd shown the collection to someone at the Louvre. 'Well, heavens, no, why would I?' I asked. 'No, you don't understand. This is something that should *be* at the Louvre.' 'Oh dear. Yes, I see.'

'O'Toole, do you want this to go to the Louvre – I don't mind, really?'

'Do I fuck? It's *yours*. Take it home.'

And there it sat in the drawing room for years and as the years went by there were more and more vitrines. They were so beautiful and they were *mine*. I couldn't quite believe my good fortune.

But those years in Paris were such a time of unbelievable beauty; beautiful things, beautiful places and acquisitions. The paintings were lovely: a quiet Bonnard for the wall opposite our bed, gorgeous vivid Brós for the entrance hall, a Braque for the drawing room. The drawing room at home was ravishing. Most of our Jack Yeats's paintings were hung there and we had seven big oils; the weakest of all (according to our friend, art dealer Leslie Waddington) was the one I liked best, *False Morning Promise*, a clown on a raft sailing into heaven knows what sort of day. Milton Avery, the American, was the painter I best liked to live with. O'Toole bought a few, lone seagulls on a grey American coast. Jules and Joyce gave us a lovely grey bird against a blue sky as an anniversary present. I looked at it in the front study every day and loved it more and more. My only outright possession and my favorite painting was one that O'Toole gave me one Christmas when he had missed six planes from Orly to London (in all fairness the distance from the bar to the gates was, in those days, enormous). Lionel, the chauffeur, and I went to the airport at lunchtime and waited in vain – came home; went out again, came home – and so it went on all day and finally the children went to bed and so did my mother and dinner was thrown out and Lionel went alone to the airport. Late at night a very vague O'Toole was delivered to the front door, apologetic and not very well but clutching a smallish parcel which was my Christmas present. When I saw it all was forgiven. It was a painting by Paul Klee. Called *Little Hope*, it was a small, sad face painted on burlap in 1939. I couldn't believe that I could own anything so extraordinary. Every day after that I unlocked the drawing room door and snatched a look before locking up and going about my day.

Joyce Buck was a wonderful companion in Paris. She and Jules and her daughter, Joan-Juliet, had lived there for years – part of the time as neighbors of their colleague, Jacques

Tati, when Jules was producing *Mon Oncle*. (He introduced Jacques Tati to America.) Jules hadn't even got to the point of pronouncing 'Peugeot' properly, but Joyce had taken the whole thing very seriously and had learned French, and young Joan-Juliet to all intents and purposes *was* French. When we came to Paris at weekends Joyce took me around art galleries and antique shops and framers, restorers, carpetmakers – I saw aspects of Paris I would never otherwise have seen. At night we went to the smartest restaurants – lamb chops and grapefruit for me – the newest nightclubs (hell on wheels) and one night, I cannot imagine why, Joyce and I – so correct, so controlled, so proper, so not wanting to get our hair messed up – went madly out of control, got drunk in a Russian restaurant, danced all night like dervishes, while our bemused husbands sat, mournfully patient at the bar, looking on. One of my (four) hair pieces fell off. I kicked it into touch without missing a step and cried, 'Leave it! The waiter will get it.' 'Is she often like this?' asked a tired out and sympathetic Regine, queen of the night-club scene. 'No,' said O'Toole, puzzled and truthful. John Shepbridge, the producer, danced with Joyce – watched by an unbelieving Jules. 'Oh John,' she said the following day, 'was I dreadful?' 'My dear,' said John, 'I don't remember a thing.' Joyce, who did remember dancing lewdly, said to me, 'There *are* good guys. They're the ones that say they don't remember a thing.'

During the late Sixties especially, O'Toole spent a great deal of time filming in Paris but my attention was mainly on life at home with the girls and my work in London. I do remember learning that my hero, Hugh Griffith, had been fired off *How to Steal a Million Dollars*, one of the films we co-produced during this period, after persistent bad behavior, culminating in a naked stroll down the corridors of the George V with 'Don't' struck out and 'Do' substituted before 'disturb' on the card he held in his hand. What is the matter with these film people? They themselves are *so* badly behaved, so cynical, so seriously amoral. An inebriated, naked stroll down a corridor doesn't seem to me to warrant dismissal. In one of the movies, beset with problems, almost the least of the problems took the form of a leading actress who, having completely flipped her lid, was discovered up a gantry with slit wrists dripping blood on the upturned faces below. Deprived of alcohol, she'd been drinking eau de toilette and had to be coaxed down and packed off to the hospital. The more I saw of the movie world, the more astonished I was at the nonsense people got away with.

Audrey Hepburn (in *How to Steal a Million Dollars*) was so lovely. She was surprisingly tall and when we were introduced I was shocked to feel her tiny, fleshless hand – like holding a bird's claw or a small cat's paw. She lived a life of iron discipline that made me feel self-indulgent, watching the rushes twice; once alone and once with her make-up man, making notes; filming from noon till 7 or 8 p.m., eating only a little dry salad then going through every still photograph taken during the day (hundreds), rejecting all that weren't flattering, then home to the hotel, alone, for a little more dry salad and back to the studio in the morning for more rushes, more consultations and two hours in make-up before the day's work began. I realized that she was a woman playing a much younger girl and that the work behind this successful deception was enormous and gracefully embraced. It wasn't vanity on her part, it was attention to business. I didn't much like her husband at the time, Mel Ferrer. He installed her in Paris, sent her out to work and decamped, all over Europe having, as far as I could see, a fine old time.

When *What's New Pussycat?* was being shot, I spent my time at the George V and went sightseeing each day rather than go to the studio too often. Romy Schneider was a pillar of professional good sense, but I couldn't warm to Capucine who was playing 'my' part, though she was perfectly amiable. I thought she was a little dull. It was difficult to see how the director, Clive Donner, managed to keep the whole thing chugging along on schedule. The stories we heard told in the office back in London were alarming and Peter Sellers, whom I revered as an actor, went down rather in my estimation. Since his heart attack he was uninsurable and after the financial disaster of *Cleopatra* caused by Elizabeth Taylor's near fatal illness when she was shooting in England, film companies were very aware of the dangers of employing actors who were not in good condition. O'Toole, also a huge admirer and sympathetic to his plight, had pushed and pushed for engaging Sellers and finally the company had agreed to take the risk. At this point Peter Sellers, 'agreeing' to do the film which he desperately needed and wasn't wanted for, said he would only do the movie if he was given first billing over O'Toole. Executives reeled back, laughing feebly at this piece of madness and were totally nonplussed when O'Toole calmly told them that he didn't give a damn and Sellers was to be given anything he asked for. Jules was fit to be tied and even I thought it was a bit over-casual, but O'Toole refused to discuss the matter. So P. Sellers was given everything he demanded and he got top billing. Then when they started shooting he took against Woody, throwing out huge chunks of script and wiring music-hall entertainers in England for gags which were then inserted into his scenes. I was disappointed to see that O'Toole condoned this behavior. They refused to rehearse with Woody Allen and I don't think Peter Sellers ever realized that he was dealing with a comic talent every bit as great as and even more complex than his own. Clive juggled the personalities and managed to run a very efficient, hard-working unit and produced a funny film.

Sellers came into my life some years later when O'Toole was filming *Man of La Mancha*. He pitched up in O'Toole's suite of rooms at the Excelsior Hotel in Rome and installed himself on the sitting room couch. He was having personal problems so he was depressed and couldn't return home to England because of taxation problems. Tiring of his guest, O'Toole urged him to go and stay with me in Hampstead, where he could be hidden from the Inland Revenue and would find the study day-bed much more comfortable than the Excelsior couch.

Our house, when O'Toole was away, centred around the activities of the girls; their diary was crammed with dancing classes, parties, visits to the dentist and oculist, homework, tests, sports and holidays. (I was amazed that they could fit so much into each day.) Now, we were told to expect the movie star and his chauffeur. I myself was also busy, so my mother made a wonderful Boeuf Bourguignon which would only improve as the hours went by and we awaited the arrival – time unspecified – of the Sellers team. When the doorbell rang I rushed for the door and saw more Louis Vuitton luggage than I had ever seen outside an antique shop (at that time there was no Louis Vuitton shop in England and it wasn't widely familiar). This was not luggage for a short stay I thought, with a sinking heart as I yielded up my study and day-bed. When '*Boeuf*' was mentioned, the two men started back, 'Didn't Petey *say* I was a vegetarian?' said Peter. 'No dear Petey didn't,' I said grimly. 'Well, he may have done,' soothed Mamgu. 'It's not a problem.' As we tore down to the basement kitchen she wailed in Welsh, 'What do vegetarians eat?' 'Vegetables,' I snapped. Liz the Nanny and I plundered our big cellars under Heath Street, returning with mountains of carrots and cabbages and potatoes and onions. 'Okay Siân, you upstairs to give them drinks and keep them distracted,' ordered my mother, back in charge. 'Liz, start peeling and fetch someone to help you.'

Within an hour Peter Sellers was exclaiming over the best home-made soup he'd ever tasted. 'Can I have this every day?' 'Of *course*,' said my mother, sweetly. Downstairs Liz and the au-pair and I cleared away mountains of peelings and began assembling the next day's pyramids of vegetables. When my mother came down, beaming, I held up a large cauldron and pointed at the dregs. 'What's that?' (In Welsh) 'Bones.'

'Vegetarians don't eat *bones*.' 'You can't make soup without bones.' I gave up the unequal struggle and for a month Peter Sellers thrived on what he thought was vegetable soup and glumly picking my way round the L-V trunks, unable to use my phone or get at my books, I thought, 'Oh, what the hell, it won't harm him.' Like many great comics, Peter was not much fun at home. He was depressed. At night, I would let myself in and try to tiptoe past the study and fly up the stairs unnoticed. On the nights when I was waylaid we would sit in the Green Room next door and Peter would talk of himself, explaining to me how impossible his life was and how sad. He had made a film with Sophia Loren and conceived an unrequited passion for her. Listening to him I couldn't believe that anyone so smart in his own field could be so stupid as to misunderstand the situation so utterly. How could he imagine that a practical, ambitious woman from a poor background – protected by Carlo Ponti, her powerful, film-producer husband who devoted his life to promoting her career – would, for a moment, consider endangering her position for a romance with a mere actor. I wasn't much use to him and I didn't become a close friend. As soon as I could I left the house and joined O'Toole at the Excelsior in Rome. The girls came to Rome as well and O'Toole laughed evilly when I arrived, worn out by my house guest and his self preoccupation. 'How *could* you?' 'Ah, get off. Don't make a fuss. There's no harm in him.'

Naturally, Mamgu became a confidante of Sellers and got to like Bert, the chauffeur. Peter had embraced an Eastern religion, we supposed, and she didn't much like the Eastern scrolls hanging over the bookshelves or the chanting which filled the ground floor from time to time but she liked looking after him. I stayed away till he was gone.

I'd been bumping up against famous people since I was a girl so it wasn't exactly difficult having to live with celebrities and I knew enough not to expect them to be fascinating when they were off duty, but alas, many huge stars were really heavy going. There is a kind of self-absorption that infects their behavior and makes them less interesting than they might otherwise be. I'd been raised to have respect but not to be 'a respecter of persons' and I couldn't shake that off. There were glorious exceptions. I loved my time with Wilfrid Lawson, I would have given anything to know Ralph Richardson better, the time I spent with John Steinbeck and his wife, Elaine, is indelibly etched in my memory, as were the few evenings I spent with Jacques Tati and his wife. Laurens van der Post was even better than I could have imagined from reading his books and I was perfectly happy to be a kind of third hand-maiden on the left for Edith Evans because I admired her so much.

Kate Hepburn, whom I first met when she was filming *Lion in Winter*, was interesting and in many ways admirable, but I couldn't help feeling envious of the way in which she seemed to have her life organized so as to have things all her own way. Her seemingly simple life was in fact kept oiled and running by retainers of long standing. Her companion ('Phy-lisss!' would go the shout whenever she wanted anything) travelled with her and organized her living arrangements. She wore gorgeous, glamorous clothes all her life until, cleverly, realizing that, no longer youthful, she couldn't compete with young actresses, she devised a marvellous uniform; colors of beige and red, black or white; slacks and smart gifted or purloined men's sweaters or jackets. Her years with Spencer Tracy suited her very well – a wife with none of the wife's boring jobs – and she admitted as much to me. When O'Toole, who was very smitten by her glamorous, unusual presence, was moved to say, 'My God – if I was thirty years younger I'd have given Spencer Tracy a run for his money', we looked at each other, slightly cross-eyed, wondering which of us had been more insulted; Kate for being considered too old to be desirable or me, who, all things being equal, would have been discarded in favor of a young Kate. It wasn't something to be thought about too closely, so we both smiled sweetly. When, in 1970,

Kate was playing in *Coco*, the musical, in New York, O'Toole and I dined at her house before leaving for South America. As we left, she grabbed me by the arm and hissed, 'You let him push you around – stop it. I'm spoiled. *Get spoiled!*' I nodded, smiling, and thought I'd like to see her try getting her own way with O'Toole, were she thirty years younger. Not a chance. I remember her as spoiled and selfish indeed but what wonderful common sense she had. And she took what she wanted and paid for it, and, I would hazard, has rarely had occasion to regret her choices.

On the whole, O'Toole kept me out of his professional life. Very few people were invited to Guyon House. We gave at the most two large parties and one tiny Christmas morning cocktail party, distinguished only by a very woozy Robert Stephens falling right through a rather nice chair. He was living with my friend, the remarkable and beautiful Pat Quinn (whose mother I played in *Shoulder to Shoulder*, the TV series about the suffragette movement). They married subsequently and were perfect for each other. An Irish friend of mine went to them for lunch one day and round about teatime Pat – not quite herself – served some meat, then a little hors d'oeuvre, then a pudding, then said, 'Oh God, I forgot the veg,' and left the room never to return. 'Please excuse Patricia,' murmured Robert. 'She's frightfully unhappy today.'

It was so mightily encouraging when Robert made a return (almost from the dead) to play Falstaff and get knighted. The most extraordinary things happen in our profession. I'm sure Anthony Hopkins would agree that he was, in 1978, the least likely candidate for international super stardom and respectable knighthood. Then he went to America, made some awful movies, temporarily renounced the theater, nearly killed himself in a car, joined AA, and became one of our senior, respectable ennobled actors. Hepburn was one of Tony's first mentors in the movies. O'Toole, against the wishes of the American producers and the casting director, had insisted on engaging him for *Lion in Winter*. (John Castle was another of his 'finds' and Nigel Terry also – a remarkable, very Cornish actor.) When Tony played his first scene with Kate she took him by the shoulders and turned him away from her. 'There's the camera – over there. It needs to see you.'

Most of the actors I knew and liked were people I'd worked with but one actor, very close to O'Toole, became someone I treasured although we never worked together. Donal McCann was hugely talented. The son of a sometime Lord Mayor of Dublin, he'd been raised in the Big House and during his childhood had suffered an enormous tragedy. Entrusted with his younger brother's safety on the way to school, he'd looked away for a moment and his little brother had darted into the road and was run over. Donal never recovered, never escaped the demons that pursued him after this and he drank to excess for much of his adult life. He and O'Toole played *Godot* together many times, learning it holed up in the Shelbourne, sleeping in twin beds and working every moment that they weren't sleeping. They were wonderful together in the play, with Niall Toibin playing Pozzo. One day Donal came to visit O'Toole in Guyon House. His chum was spending the day in bed and not even for Donal could he be disturbed. We sat together till lunch time and Donal refused to come to the dining room to eat. I returned to the Green Room after lunch with the girls and we sat there as darkness fell. By this time Donal was into his second bottle of vodka and I, sipping cold tea, was getting sleepy. Nodding off, I jerked awake to dimly make out something odd about Donal's silhouette as he sat on the Green Room 'stage' with his back to Men's Surgical beyond the garden. He was on fire, having dropped his cigarette into his curly black hair which he was in the habit of teasing with his right hand as he talked. I crossed to the drinks tray and, picking up a soda siphon, turned it on to Donal and put out the fire on his head. He blinked a bit and held out his glass for a refill. Years later, when I was on location in Dublin a slim athletic figure darted across the road and embraced me. I could hardly recognize the teetotal Donal. His work, which had always been good, became even more wonderful. *The Steward of Christendom* at the Royal Court, not many years before his untimely death, was a never-to-be-forgotten piece of acting.

Godot is one of my favorite plays and McCann and O'Toole surely approached the intention of the author. The author . . . Sam Beckett. So beautiful, so vain. Blind as a bat and didn't wear glasses. Exquisitely dressed in cashmere polonecks and soft tweeds. A cross-Channel swimmer. And an opinionated bigot in some ways, I thought. I sat in a flat in Manchester Square and listened to Beckett and O'Toole, fascinating and good-looking, as they became drunker and drunker and through a haze of tiredness and boredom I heard Mr Beckett say, *Godot* can never be filmed. No film with dialogue has *ever* succeeded. Buster Keaton is the only film actor worth considering.' Sitting there, slightly outside the adoring throng at the great man's feet, I thought, 'Oh puhleez. Give me a break' and, aloud and unheard, said 'Excuse me,' and left. Standing in a fog-bound Manchester Square I began to laugh as I searched for a cab. Here I was wandering around W1 on my own because I was bored to death by a great playwright who I thought was talking rubbish about the movies.

In 1966 I worked for Sam, and it was an extraordinary experience. Jackie McGowran came to my dressing room at the Vaudeville Theater where I was halfway through a long run of *Man and Superman* with Alan Badel. He was carrying a copy of *Eh, Joe*. We'll do it at the BBC,' he said. 'You will speak the "play" – a monologue lasting twenty minutes. You won't be seen and the camera will remain on me throughout.' What a lovely, easy job, I thought as I agreed to go the following Sunday to a flat on Haverstock Hill and work with Mr Beckett himself. There were very few preliminaries and I began to read for him. It wasn't an *easy* read but I thought I was doing quite well until, after about ten minutes, I caught sight of Sam's face contorted with what looked like pain. I plowed on and when I'd finished there was a long silence. Then 'I don't know where to start,' said Sam, faintly. I was too sorry for him to be upset on my own behalf and I urged him to be as brutally frank as he wished and please to believe that if he *told* me what he wanted I *would* be able to deliver it to him. I don't think he believed me. It took two weeks of grinding work to get the twenty minutes anywhere near what Sam wanted. He banged his hand on the table like a metronome; three beats for a full stop, two for a colon, half for a comma. Three speak, speak, speak. Half speak speak. Two speak stop. I gave up trying to interpret the monologue and learned it like a piece of music, hanging on to that text like a stubborn dog with a bone. Finally came the moment when Sam nodded from the control cubicle. Michael Bakewell who was producing and Jackie who was hanging about looking anxious, both looked relieved. I had a bit of time to spare before going to the theater and I asked Sam if I could try another take; one for me. He shrugged but maybe he thought I'd earned a small favor after all we'd been through, so off I went, hoping that enough of Sam's rhythms had become second nature to me because I wasn't thinking about them on this take. When I'd finished Sam said, '*That's* what I meant all along' and I could have hugged him except I didn't dare. I could quite see why whole companies had gone on strike during rehearsals of his plays and refused to work if his time-beating hand wasn't removed. But I was glad I'd hung on; it had been quite an experience to remember. Patrick Magee and Jackie McGowran and Billie Whitelaw were Beckett 'naturals', the rest of us had to work quite a bit harder. And there's nothing quite as wonderful as having the author around. What would it be like to be able to pop up to Admin to ask Shakespeare what exactly did he mean on page thirty-two?

A pattern of sorts emerged. O'Toole's work took precedence

over everything. His large office in Belgravia presided over by Jules was organized so as to keep him busy as much of the time as possible. Jules, who had spent his earlier life with some of the major players in the movie business, had a theory that work was the only thing that kept some of the more 'highly colored characters' sane. And much as I would have liked to have been able to have more of O'Toole for myself and the family (maybe even to take a holiday), I had to admit that Jules might be right. While he was preparing for a big movie, O'Toole was an angel; hard working, moderate and a benevolent presence in the house. When he was actually filming he was quiet, self-disciplined, a little 'absent' even when at home. Once work was completed, very often after a six-month work period, he became a different person, erratic and unpredictable, turning night into day. Then he would sleep and sleep and wake penitent and chastened and spend days being attentive and charming – overwhelmingly charming. I never saw anyone fail to forgive him completely, no matter how badly they'd been hurt and I was as susceptible as any of them. This roller-coaster life would continue only until his attention was engaged by a new job and then quiet times would be resumed. It was my good fortune to love and be loved by this extraordinary man and it was my deep misfortune to be as incapable as the next person of expressing my anger at his unfair, unjust behavior. No one else in my private or working life had ever been able to treat me as he did. I was part of a huge conspiracy directed towards protecting O'Toole from the painful consequences of his behavior. It didn't make me feel better that bigger, stronger, cleverer people than I shared the urge to protect him.

Walking out on him was not an option. Unbelievable as it may seem, life in Guyon House was happy; it was a big house and the children, my mother and Liz led busy, enjoyable lives in very comfortable, beautiful surroundings. They took holidays in Ireland in a cottage we had acquired in the Sixties, and we began to plan an Irish home, on the large piece of land O'Toole had acquired. Taking a meat-cleaver to all this seemed pretty selfish. And there was so much of our life that I loved. Trying to figure out how to proceed, I decided that the only truly awful thing that could happen to me would be for me to become sour and resentful. I had *truly* to get over my feelings of hurt pride. I also had to stop identifying with O'Toole, feeling embarrassed or guilty when he behaved badly in public, and above all I had to learn not to accept as truth his icy criticism of me as – when drunk – he ordered me out of the car or restaurant or our house. 'Who owns this house?' was the frequent Dr. Jekyll challenge. I never liked to point out that we owned it jointly. On the whole – with a few mutinous lapses – I managed to embrace survival strategy and in the process I became harder and rougher around the edges but it made the bad times bearable. Someone asked me, 'How do you manage to combine your busy private life with your career?' O'Toole answered for me, 'She doesn't have a career. She has jobs.' No, I thought, but let the moment pass without comment.

I didn't show my hurt over my summary rejection from *What's New Pussycat?* and I got my reward almost at once. A few years previously I'd been asked to be in *The Night of the Iguana* by Tennessee Williams. Vanessa Redgrave, who'd made a *very* good start to her career and had great support from her husband, Tony Richardson, was to play Hannah Jelkes and I was asked to play a part I was totally unsuited for – Maxine – the character that Bette Davis had played when Margaret Leighton had done the play in America. I fell completely in love with the role of Hannah and felt bitterly frustrated not to be asked to play her. I was so right for the part. So was Vanessa, of course, but that wasn't my concern at that moment. I'd turned down the offer and in the event the production didn't take place. Now the play came to me again; Richard Shulman and Philip Wiseman had acquired the rights and were going to mount it in Croydon. Croydon . . . the

Ashcroft Theater in the Fairfield Halls complex wasn't exactly the most appealing of theaters. I said 'Yes', of course. I just wanted to play Hannah Jelkes but it was a damned shame that it was going to take place for such a short run in one venue.

I'd seen the movie of *The Night of the Iguana* with Richard Burton, Deborah Kerr and Ava Gardner and hadn't thought much of it. It was given wisdom that once a play had been filmed it could not be mounted as a West End production, so I was lucky to get Croydon. And I would be able to commute.

As I read the script I realized with dismay that it wasn't the same script I'd read when Woodfall Productions held the rights, before the film was made. The cuts really bothered me and I began to ask if I could reinstate bits of the play that for no reason I could see had vanished. I became a terrible nuisance, bargaining for a line here, a speech there. Philip and Richard were patient but firm – we *had* to perform the new version. Gradually I discovered that some of the cuts had been made at the insistence of Bette Davis who hadn't been too happy with the way her part was received as they began touring (Maxine just isn't as good a part as Hannah). Tennessee, I was told, was obliging beyond belief, chopping away at his play with a will. I was astonished; the playwrights I'd met were touchy about altering commas, let alone brilliant chunks of text. Temporarily deflated (I'd seen myself as the author's champion), I began rehearsing the new version but as the weeks went by I began to slip back the bits I couldn't bear to be without and Philip turned a blind eye.

This was the best part I'd been given for years and I became over-enthusiastic and probably tiresomely obsessed by the play. Philip Wiseman, a quiet, bookish American in English tweeds, was a marvel of discretion. Somehow he reined me in – he admitted afterwards that directing me was a bit like handling a jumpy, highly strung race horse – and we arrived safe and secure at our opening night. I fell in love with the Ashcroft auditorium. Philip had 'placed' the production so well in it that it felt wonderfully comfortable. I enjoyed going to the stage in a lift that also carried boxers or wrestlers (half-dressed muscular men, raring to hit something) on their way to the sports arena. It was very relaxing to be in a dressing room that totally defied one to pretty it up. There were half-pint glasses of half drunk beer on the dressing table with its layer of dust and grease. I didn't even bother to make a 'place' for myself. I don't know if anyone sent flowers; they certainly didn't make it to the dressing room. Mark Eden was the Reverend Shannon and I was lucky again that he also possessed the temperament of a gentleman. As I nagged and altered things and rehearsed and re-rehearsed and over-rehearsed, he got on with his own work and helped me where he could and resisted what must have been a justifiable temptation to take me by the shoulders and shake me until I quietened down. I think I was as much of a nuisance as is possible to be within the walls of a theater.

On opening night the play went wonderfully well. The following day I got up early and went off to model some clothes for an Irish designer. I was in the middle of a long photographic session when Philip tracked me down and asked me if I'd seen the papers. No, I hadn't (I hadn't thought the national press would come to Croydon). 'Well,' he went on, suppressing what even on the phone I could tell was huge excitement, 'we have rave notices across the board and our pick of five London theaters into which to transfer. Be at the theater early and we'll talk.' I went back to my photo session more thoughtful than excited. Already I was worrying about the transfer; would our show work as well outside the confines of what had become to me the 'dear Fairfield Hall'? The phone went again. Audrey Wood, Tennessee's agent, sent a message of congratulations and said that 'Tom' (Tom? I didn't know that Tennessee wasn't called Tennessee) would be coming to London for the West End opening. Back to the clothes and the posing. 'Chin down, eyes up, button the jacket.'

Eventually I'm through and dash home to see the girls and then take the train to Croydon. The journey gives me time to think. My mother says the phone has been ringing all day with requests for interviews and photographs, the house is full of bouquets; she's quietly pleased. I feel odd. It's four years since I was the subject of this kind of attention and something has happened to steal the joy from the moment. I feel – what? Apprehensive. A bit of me seems to have broken and I don't have the confidence to enjoy all this fuss. It's as though I'll wake up to find that a mistake has been made. 'Not you! Whatever made you think we meant you?' And what if it *was* a kind of mistake last night at the theater? What if I can't do it again? Keeping these fears hidden I put on a brave, bright face and join the high-spirited gathering at the theater. It is wonderful for Richard Shulman and Philip and I'm genuinely happy for them. We'll choose a theater tomorrow. What larks! I'm glad to get to my dingy dressing room and put on my dingy clothes. The only way I can maintain my equilibrium is to think about nothing but the play from now on. Let the rest wash over me. See to the children. Attend to the play. This unexpected turn of events has thrown into sharp relief how badly I've reacted to the events of the last few years and how low I've been brought. For whatever reason I've arrived at a state of mind where I cannot feel that anything I do is of any consequence whatever and I'm worried how this success might affect my relationship with O'Toole. Might this change? If it doesn't, is it something I might be able to turn to my advantage? Or will it always apply a little brake to my efforts?

Chapter Twenty-one

Playing eight times a week really suits me. Many of my friends hate it and they hate being in a run. Not I. To me there is no greater pleasure than steering a good production of a good play through the different circumstances that occur each night. Each night is different and not different. Flops are another matter. I've had more than my share and can get fed up with a bad play in a week, but even then, there's a kind of perverse satisfaction in getting a bad job done well. I've been stage-struck since I was six, and sat in Swansea Empire watching a pantomime. Will I go on feeling like this forever, I wonder.

At the moment I'm as happy as can be, ensconced in the Savoy Theater. Tennessee – Tom – did arrive and stood on his seat in the front row and over-did his enthusiasm. Richard Condon (the novelist and Debbie Jupp's father) rushed a massive basket of flowers down the aisle and had a noisy row with an usherette who wouldn't let him hand it up to the stage (for fear it contained explosives?). There were flowers everywhere and I remembered that on my last opening in London, just a few months ago, someone had thrown copper coins on to the stage and there had been the noise of booing and hissing, rather than cheers.

Nothing had happened to alter my reservations about opening nights. I'd worn a nasty, mustard-colored old frock to work so that I wouldn't be tempted to go out to celebrate afterwards; straight home as usual, a relatively early night and up early with Kate. Later, when the play settled down, I began going out to parties with my new best friend Tom but I think I was a bit of a disappointment to him as a date. My neuroses were far too well submerged and I could have only a flimsy grip on his attention. As we entered a room I would watch him as he prowled around for a while before homing in on someone who, a surprising number of times, would turn out to be in the throes of a breakdown, or recovering from a failed suicide attempt or about to do something disastrous. Nose to nose, they would chat for hours.

On other levels, we got on very well and corresponded from time to time after he returned to America. He sent me a poem he wrote for me. I got to know Audrey Wood, his agent, as well and they sent me all his new material for many years to come. I admired him above all the authors I knew so I suppose that pre-disposed him to like me too.

Soon after we opened, O'Toole returned from France where he was filming and when he came to see the play he was generous about my performance. To Ken Jupp he said facetiously, 'Blimey, they'll be calling me Mr Phillips in a minute. I'm off!' and hopped back to Paris. When the film finished he went into rehearsal for a new play by David Mercer, *Ride a Cock Horse*. It was long, very long, and had a difficult shape. In two parts, it consisted of six duologues between the hero and his wife, his girlfriend and his older mistress. It was a marathon part for an actor. It was also, I was given to understand, a '*pièce à clef*' about well-known contemporary writers. It was so well written and so depressing. (My life, in comparison, seemed peachy, I thought gratefully.) The ladies of the company were Wendy Craig as the girlfriend, Barbara Jefford as the wife and Yvonne Mitchell as the unhappy mistress. Rather them than me, I thought as I made my way to the Savoy.

David Mercer began to visit the house to work with O'Toole. A great deal of alcohol was consumed. Then, when O'Toole began rehearsing and cut out the drink, David would arrive and drink alone and finally O'Toole would retreat to the bedroom to work, leaving my mother to cope with the brilliant but very touchy playwright. I, thank God, was out of reach at the theater. My mother spent hours listening to David talk about his parents so one night when he arrived dressed in a railwayman's overalls, mourning the death of his railwayman father, my mother ministered to him and finally he spent the night on the Green Room couch. When it was revealed later to her that his father was in fact alive and well, my mother – endlessly patient – was *almost* annoyed with him.

Between shows at the Savoy on matinée day. A knock and then the door opens before I can say 'Come in' – O'Toole, followed by Michael Codron the producer. Drama. At rehearsal, they've lost (or shed) Yvonne Mitchell. Can I open in Nottingham next Tuesday? I open my mouth to say 'But what about my play?' and they say they'll buy me out of the last two weeks of the run (Bernie Delfont, a friend, is one of the producers). I don't want to miss two weeks of *Iguana* but it doesn't occur to me to deny O'Toole. Also, it's a challenge. I don't like the David Mercer play and I don't think that, at my age, I'm very well suited to a part based on Penelope Mortimer in a bit of a decline. All the more reason to try, I think perversely.

So I'll travel to Nottingham the day after I close Tom's play on Saturday and open on Tuesday. 'When will I rehearse?' O'Toole considers. 'Well, now, let's see. Learn it and go over the moves with the stage manager and we'll rehearse you *after* we open. We have four weeks on the road.' Heavens – this *is* a challenge. I've never opened a play without rehearsing it. It's an endless part; two duologues of over half an hour. If I pull it off, O'Toole will be so grateful. And I'll be doing him a favor. Michael Codron is strangely silent. I wonder if this is O'Toole's harebrained idea and he doesn't like to object. We're all going along with the idea. Gordon Flemyng, who had made such a good job of directing the TV play *The Other Man*, which I did with Michael Caine and whom I introduced to O'Toole, is directing the Mercer play. I didn't know he worked in the theater at all.

Nottingham is a nightmare. O'Toole has decided that we will only play the biggest of theaters and, confident of doing good business, he will clear all production costs before we come into town. There are banners reading 'O'Toole' all over the streets and the run is completely sold out before we begin. I've never seen anything quite like this and I've played with some of our biggest theater stars. I learn my lines and write down my moves from the prompt copy. I share a suite with O'Toole but hardly see him. He's deeply involved with David Mercer who is drinking heavily. Every night we have dinner with him and Gordon in a private dining room in the hotel. I still haven't rehearsed. I haven't dried on stage and I haven't stood in the wrong place but I haven't the faintest idea what I'm doing. It's utterly horrible. The little bit of confidence that grew during the months of success at the Savoy drains away now in the first week of playing *Ride a Cock Horse*.

They cut chunks of the play. Every night the stage manager comes round at the half and says things like, 'Take out pages twenty-four and twenty-five, the top of forty-five, two lines at the bottom of fifty, this section on fifty-one.' I barely know the original text, learning cuts every day as well is torture. The play is down to about four hours long. Now O'Toole declares, 'Go faster. Top all the laughs and let's see if we can't cut fifteen minutes by playing faster.' 'Topping' laughs means coming in at the crest of the laugh and moving on smartly; it's a struggle, in a huge theater, to be audible without shouting when you're speaking over a huge laugh. We all manage. Floundering about a bit, I catch O'Toole on stage looking at me quizzically. 'Are you going to *do* it like this?' he mutters sardonically in the middle of the scene. I'm fashionably flat-chested. Message from the management: 'Get her some falsies.' This is hell.

'When do I rehearse?'

'Tomorrow.'

'Oh, thank God.'

At seven o'clock I wake, alone, in the suite. At 9:30 a.m., walking through the foyer to go and rehearse with O'Toole, I meet him and Gordon Flemying coming *in* after a night on the town.

'Hello, darling, where are you off to?'

'To rehearse with you.'

'Ah, sorry about that, darling. Bye. See you for a spot of late lunch?'

Each day I go to the theater and go through my lines but I'm no nearer playing this part properly. I hate this play now. I hate the dinners at which D. Mercer gets drunk then gets on the hotel phone and recites soliloquies from it to someone who must be driven mad. It's all so depressing. But the money is flooding into the box office. Who is in charge? 'I'm going to complain to the Management,' I think and then, remembering that this is a co-production with Keep Films, I realize I *am* the Management.

The torment continued. Being confused, nightly, in front of thousands of people may not rank high in torment on a global scale but it *is* major nastiness on a personal scale. Gordon, the director, managed to avoid me, Barbara and Wendy had their own problems and O'Toole never did rehearse with me. We opened to a sold-out, limited run in London. The big Piccadilly Theater seemed quite cozy after our huge touring theaters. Production costs had been paid off. I supposed that, as usual, O'Toole was not taking a salary. I don't know how the play was received by the critics (I'd recently stopped reading reviews), but it was a huge commercial success. People – Kenneth Tynan notable among them – came again and again. I hated every minute of it. O'Toole and I had completely different timetables. I would rise early, see the girls, see to the house while he slept. Seething with resentment, part of me longed to have a huge row with him. Who else, I wondered, would treat me with such colossal disrespect? No one I could think of. But he was marvellous in the play and he loved it and he had a huge job to do each night: how could I have a row with him? And if I did, how would he torture me on stage? I didn't delude myself that I was smart enough to cope with an angry O'Toole, certainly not in front of a packed house. Each day at five o'clock I would eat a plate of scrambled eggs, go to the West End, walk about a bit, go into the theater and go up to my dressing room, call home unnecessarily to check everything was still all right, throw up, get made up, do the show, afterwards descend to dressing room Number One if we had mutual friends in to see the show, occasionally I would go to dinner (always if the Bucks or the Jupps were around). The rest of the time I went home alone. It was odd. And faintly embarrassing.

And yet O'Toole gave me one of the best opening night presents I ever received. He remembered that, many years ago, fleeing from a failed relationship, I'd had to leave behind my mother's complete set of Charles Dickens which I'd been reading since I was a little girl. He bought me a lovely edition of the complete works. The boxes were delivered to my room just as I was throwing up and hating him and I was overcome with gratitude and love and misery all at once. Fancy his remembering something that had happened so long ago. Fancy his knowing how much I missed those books. He always knew things about me that no one would guess at.

It felt as though the whole town flocked to Dressing Room One. One regular visitor – and he didn't even watch the show – was Robin Douglas-Home. He irritated me hugely and was for ever insisting that we should go with him to a gaming club in Mayfair. O'Toole, son of an unsuccessful gambling bookmaker, liked gambling but had successfully disciplined himself not to indulge. Week after week, day after day, Robin Douglas-Home haunted the theater and, finally, we went with him. I watched, impassive, while O'Toole lost almost £10,000 in half an hour. We smiled and accepted a glass of champagne and drifted into the night, still smiling, but I couldn't speak for fury.

The play and O'Toole's pace of life are taking their toll. He begins to bleed from the nose on stage. Night after night there's blood everywhere but the audience doesn't seem to notice. I never cease to be amazed at what the audience simply doesn't see. No one can understand why he's losing blood every night but Gerry Slattery says it's time to stop. The play, which is only slated for a limited run, could actually run forever but everyone has been paid and a profit has been made so it's decided to close the show two weeks early. There is a God, I think. I'm just about as low in spirits as it is possible to be. One of my teachers from RADA and a friend of O'Toole's as well sees that I'm in a bad way despite the bright smile after the show. The following day he sends me one of my unread notices for *The Night of the Iguana*; only months ago W. A. Darlington the senior critic of the *Daily Telegraph*, it seems, had written, 'If she never acts again she has proved she is a great actress.' I look at it in stupefaction. I feel that I've now spent months acting badly and doubt that I was *ever* any good. The review gives me no consolation. Going about my daily business; dealing with the domestic details of our life, occupying myself with the children, listening to my mother and my treasured daily help, Manolita, writing letters for O'Toole, I am well aware that the way I do my job doesn't matter to anyone except me. But it does matter terribly to me whether I act well or badly.

We never worked happily together, sadly for me. *Ride a Cock Horse* was a push-push experience – all bad but usually there were good aspects as well as painful ones. *Goodbye Mr Chips* was an example of a pull-push engagement. I was cast in a roundabout way and felt that O'Toole was not pleased that I'd been given the part of Ursula Mossbank (which Terence Rattigan based on Tallulah Bankhead). I spent some time during the student riots of 1968 in Paris, marooned in the

George V with Herb Ross who was to direct the film and Nora Kaye, formerly a prima ballerina and now Herb's wife and collaborator. We got along famously and Herb asked me if I'd like to be considered for the part of the actress – along with half a dozen of my contemporaries. When we were able to return to London I duly presented myself at the studio and read for Herb, who had never seen me act. He gave me the part and, to our dismay, when we came to film the party sequences O'Toole declined to rehearse with me, leaving me to walk the set with Herb and with Ossie Morris, the lighting camera man.

I retired to my dressing-room and stayed there alone, going over the scenes until I knew them backwards, sideways and upside down. I was terrified of the ordeal ahead but determined not to be found wanting. Called to the set, I sat on my own, waiting. O'Toole sat alone, some distance away. Afterwards, Herb said it was like sending into space astronauts who didn't know each other. He was nonplussed and I didn't know either why O'Toole behaved as he did. I guessed that maybe he was overwhelmingly concerned that I might not be any good and simply couldn't deal with his nerves. But that was my guess. In the event the scenes worked like clockwork without the usual preparation and despite the complex set we 'got' the scenes in one take. No mention was ever made afterwards of the tensions of the day. 'What was that about?' asked Herb. I shook my head, as mystified as he was. O'Toole was affability itself when he returned home. I loved watching him work on that film and thought that he gave a great performance in a so-so movie. When he was made up as old Mr Chips I looked for him in the canteen and, not recognizing him, walked past him. He made a lovely old man. We rented a house in Cerne Abbas in Dorset where the bulk of the film was shot and the girls and I spent wonderfully happy weeks there.

Trials, like the hateful first day of filming, served me well in the long run. There was very little I couldn't handle and very few actors who scared me, however 'difficult' their behavior. Surviving O'Toole in a bad mood made me very self-reliant. When in 1970 I came to work with Rex Harrison on *Platonov* I was aware that he had a fiendish reputation for being ungenerous, to say the least. His behavior didn't alarm me at all. Interestingly, in Wilfrid Lawson's opinion he had the edge on his contemporaries: Sir Laurence and Sir John and even Sir Ralph. 'Took the wrong turning,' Wilfrid said sadly. Rex's rages were apocalyptic and strong men paled as he tore a phone from the wall one day and threw all the furniture off a set he didn't particularly like. Watching him, I could imagine what a great Lear he would have made. Knowing him to be ruthless in appropriating whole scenes for himself, I was determined not to be eclipsed and once he saw that I had more than done my homework and that I wasn't frightened of him, he let me 'in' and although it was always as dangerous as acting on sheet ice, acting with him became truly thrilling and rewarding. I admired him almost more than anyone I had ever worked with.

Chapter Twenty-two

Meanwhile, our domestic life was going through one of the welcome, quiet periods. O'Toole and I were working hard and my mother became the point of refuge for neglected guests. O'Toole was lavish in his offers of hospitality and equally protective of his working time (easily bored, as well). People would arrive and find themselves adrift and alone in the Green Room. A great deal of the time I didn't know who was in the house and if I returned late from the theater to find a party in full swing I shot through the hall and up the stairs to the bedroom before my presence was registered. I really liked getting up early and seeing the children in the morning.

My mother actually enjoyed staying up and talking, especially to the writers. For instance, she was the one who scooped up and took down to the big kitchen a figure that I'd stepped over in some exasperation as I left with Kate early one morning. He'd obviously been asleep on the hall floor for hours. I called her later to find out who the derelict drunk was. 'Oh a lovely boy,' she replied. 'Yes, but who?' 'Wait a minute now, James – James *Baldwin*, that's it. I've just ordered his books from the High Hill Bookshop. He's had a wash and eaten a good breakfast. *Brilliant* man.' She guarded O'Toole's privacy ferociously and was known as 'The Dragon' by some of our more frivolous friends ('They've got nothing but time to waste, that lot,' she sniffed). I felt a little faint one day when I heard her on the phone saying, 'No Sir Laurence, I'm afraid it is *impossible* for me to disturb Peter. He is *working*.' 'No' (more emphatically), 'it is *impossible*.' 'Mummy, are you sure about that?' She turned, wide-eyed and shocked. 'He's *working*.' She worshipped him and the two of them would sit up late into the night playing Scrabble and talking, talking. She got rid of our cook and catered for his every whim – surprise lunch for eight, midnight snack for him, endless pots of tea at all hours, breakfast for people who hadn't been to bed.

It was a big house and because of the increasingly valuable art collection, it couldn't be left empty. Even so, with constant vigilance, dozens of internal locks, alarms and bars, we were still burgled twice; once very audaciously through the bars at the front of the house, well lit by a lamp post in Heath Street. It was a rather Hampstead-type break-in: the (very slim) burglar left with a valuable painting cut out of its frame, leaving behind a comb and a bloodstained copy of that week's *New Statesman*.

Good daily help was crucial but finding it wasn't my great talent, especially as I tended to muddle up the people I'd interviewed. I must have been more dozy than usual the day I engaged Miss Statema; Dutch, almost six feet tall, stately in somber clothes. 'What d'you think, Mummy?' Mamgu, who would have been the one to perceive the softer side of Genghis Khan, enthused, 'Wonderful choice. Immaculate.' When Miss Statema became ill, almost at once, my mother tore down the hill to her basement room, bearing flasks of hot soup and home-made bread, and Miss S. was back at work in no time, but looking subtly different. It was the clothes! No longer somber; many shades of pink and the apron had been discarded. She looked almost modish. The following week she appeared in a dated but very dressy light wool 'afternoon frock' and the following week I was halted in my tracks in the front hall as she sashayed by in a lilac taffeta dress with a sweetheart neck and puffed sleeves, ballerina-length skirt, the ensemble finished off with elbow-length lace mittens and silver, open-toed dancing slippers.

She had a bad habit of throwing away a Hoover bag every week and I'd narrowed my good housekeeping down to the task of curing her of this wastefulness. Now, not quite daring to remark on her sartorial tribute to Christian Dior circa 1947, I overtook her, stood barring her way at the top of the stairs to the basement and began, 'Em – Miss Statema, once again I must *insist* that you reuse the Hoover bags.' Towering above me malevolently, she stretched her right arm out behind her and, swinging it round, whacked me accurately across the face. As I reeled sideways into the (mercifully) closed door, she drew back and waited, strangely serene, as I gathered myself sufficiently to say, rather feebly, 'Em – I rather think you're going to have to – er – leave.' She nodded graciously and swept out saying, 'Send on my National Insurance Stamps.'

Determined not to share the house with any more sinister people, my very next choice was a small, round and cheerful, apple-cheeked woman who looked down to earth and healthy, as though she worked out of doors.

O'Toole was reading in the ground floor study so I asked her to work very quietly as she moved around the hall and Green Room. She nodded cheerfully. Descending from the nursery that afternoon I heard the lusty strains of music from below. 'Come and join us! Come and join us!' she sang and as I peered down the stairwell I could see her, duster in one hand, bucket in the other, not doing much in the way of work, *marching* up and down outside the study as she sang. Running down the stairs, I hissed, 'Hush! Hush!'

'Oops,' she beamed and disappeared down to the basement. I knocked on the study door and went in to apologize. O'Toole was sitting in his wing chair and looked amused. I joined him and while we chatted our new daily left by the front door and as we glanced out of the window we saw her put down four bulging plastic bags and open up the doors to the big dustbin enclosure. She began riffling through the bins, singing to herself. I opened the door. 'Where exactly did you say you lived?' 'Oh, here and there,' she said breezily. I realized I'd employed a lady tramp who'd fancied a day or two indoors.

Mostly I left the interviewing to my mother and it was she who found Manolita, one of the nicest women I'd ever met. We became close; she did her job perfectly and a lot more besides, and I became godmother to one of her children. We never discussed anything personal or intimate but she knew more about my life than anyone else in the house. Her discretion was absolute and I was grateful for her.

I used to tease O'Toole for acquiring what I called 'Petruchio's servants', charming, feckless people, hopeless in any job. Now, *he* got lucky as well and in fact the whole family benefited when Lionel Bryant was appointed as O'Toole's chauffeur.

One of his previous jobs had involved driving Montgomery Clift while he was filming *Suddenly Last Summer* and rendering everyone mad with confusion and exhaustion (and a young O'Toole was interviewed with a view to replacing him, should he fall apart completely). His drivers came and left on a regular basis. He never went to bed. He never told them where he was going – or why – or where he might be going next. They hung about all night and sometimes all day and, overcome with fatigue and deafened by wifely complaints, they resigned. Young Lionel Bryant heard the horror stories at the prestigious car hire firm where he worked and became intrigued by the challenge. He liked Monty Clift's acting so why not have a go, he thought, and volunteered his services.

Warning his wife, Margaret, not to expect him home much, he told her, 'I'm going to drive Monty Clift and I'm not quitting.' And he didn't. Monty, with a drink or two taken, liked to travel lying on the floor of the limo with his feet out of the window. This raised eyebrows as they pulled up at smart restaurants, so Lionel always shot round to open the door, addressing him as 'Sir', daring the doorman to be disrespectful. He liked to tease at five o'clock in the morning, going round and round in the revolving door of the Dorchester. No one could use the door, he was impossible to catch. The staff liked him and were tolerant. Lionel found him to be as

congenial as his acting was wonderful and, enduring nights in
the countryside tramping through fields, looking for 'cows to
stroke', he stayed with Monty and grew to like him more and
more. He didn't quit, but Margaret Bryant was rather pleased
when the movie finished and Monty went home to America.
Driving Judy Garland, he felt sorry for what he saw as her
under-privileged children and gladly spent days playing with
them in Battersea Park. 'But you know, the little girl – she
never talked. Just sat in the back of the car, singing, singing
all the time. Drove me mad, all that singing.'

Now some benevolent act of fate directed him to us. It
was Jules who engaged him and it was the most perfect
piece of casting he ever accomplished. He was part of our
family for thirteen years. He was O'Toole's driver but when
O'Toole was away he drove me or Mamgu or the girls (Liz,
the Nanny, had her own car). A Leo, he was an organizer
and a bit of a bully, in a quiet way. No use getting into his
car and saying 'Shepperton'. He really needed to know why
Shepperton? Was it a nice visit, or an ordeal? Did we need to
be dead on time or keep them waiting a minute or two? And
how was I feeling? I learned to tell him what the day held;
how easy or difficult it was going to be and then he would
work it all out and it would always be to perfection. I was
surrounded by Leos: Jules, O'Toole, Lionel, Derek Coombs
(O'Toole's brother-in-law), and they all had to be top dog.

Lionel wore Rolls-Royce livery at times but he knew I was
unimpressed and cared nothing for cars. I overheard him
outside my dressing room at Pinewood, standing next to
our brand new Rolls. 'So what's the Boss's wife think of
it?' asked his friend. 'Her? All she wants to know about a
car is "Where's the ashtray?".' He was like a brother to me
and loyal to O'Toole and fond of my mother and protective
of the children. Sometimes, when O'Toole was hard on me,
these feelings were in conflict with each other and reconciling
them put years on his life – literally, sapping his strength. While

he remained at his post, I remained at mine. Does this seem absurd to outsiders? I suspect that only Lionel and I would fully understand the situation.

My mother, Manolita, Liz and Lionel formed a protective shield around me. I might have had difficulties at work but I had more security at home than I had ever before experienced and I had no fears for the girls. Even so, I never forgot the need for caution and I took nothing for granted. The balance achieved was delicate and I prayed we could all maintain it.

Chapter Twenty-three

At last, the closing night of *Ride a Cock Horse*. I've been writing lists for a week at home and I've packed the bags and they're ready at the theater. During the last show I clear out the dressing rooms. Lionel drives O'Toole and me to Heathrow and we catch a plane to Venice – just the two of us for two weeks. All the ugliness of the preceding months drops away and we move on to a level of total harmony, total happiness. His nose stops bleeding. I stop throwing up. We beam at each other, hold hands. This is what our doctor, Gerry Slattery, calls 'Time out of life'. But surely this is the problem. 'Out of life', above the humdrum, on journeys, in crisis, in danger even, we are in perfect accord, and happy, ecstatically happy a good deal of the time. Faced with ordinary life, surrounded by people and obligations, we become stiff, disjointed, dysfunctional, resentful. Nervously I put in a bid – can we try to make work a *part* of ordinary life, not something divorced from everyday life? He looks at me with those old eyes and nods as though he knows what I mean but that's as far as it goes. He knows how hurt I am, how much I've hated him over the last months and effortlessly he makes it all better. I don't understand his magic. So how am I ever going to make sense of my life? I don't think anyone could ever know me the way he does and I do have this urge to be wholly known. So does he. We know things about each other that we never articulate or share with anyone.

Cold, misty Venice. Unpoetically I think of it as the great poultice; the badness is drawn out of both of us, everything is healed. I grow smooth and soft and stop protecting myself.

Familiarity with Venice has bred more and more love for the city. We have been coming here every year since we met. This time we've brought James Morris's book on Venice. We walk all day carrying his book and find Othello's tomb, with strawberries carved on it and as we approach the district called the ghetto (I think the word *getto* means metal works), we hear the clink, clink of hammer on metal. One morning we meet a lovely American (there are very few visitors in this weather) and he says would we like to explore the lagoon with him? Of course we would, and we set off in a small boat to look for the island where the dug-up bones are put when the city graveyard is full up. 'It doesn't exist,' we've been told. Following a slim Edwardian guidebook, we cross and criss-cross the lagoon, finally bumping up through the mist into a bank of reeds. Pushing in, we reach solid ground and in the silence, hear the rustling of tall dry reeds stuck here and there with bones. It is an island of dry bones pierced by grasses. Sam Beckett talks of a 'bone orchard' and here it is. We don't want to walk on the bones so we push off again into the mist, cold and silent and glad when we get 'home' to the bar of the Danieli where we're staying and the company of Gastone de Cal, the head barman, who has now become a friend.

We're building a little family in Venice. Gastone began it all and introduced us to the four-star gondolier of Venice, Gino Macropodio. He's doubly endeared to me because he has a wonderful tenor voice; Welsh tenors sound like Italian tenors and Gino makes me feel at home. We sing duets. Then we meet Gastone and Gino's friend, Buzz Bruning Jr, who is American but has become a Venetian resident, owning a house next to the Frari. He is writing a cook book with his friend, the Cavalieri, who is a great gourmet and a war hero. We all dine out with the Cavalieri's sister, Maria, who is in her late seventies and is hugely admired by all the young men for her sprightly gait and terrific appetite. 'Look at her eating,' says

Gino to the young waiter. The gaze in fond admiration as tiny Signora Maria tucks into a dinner that would satisfy a bricklayer. Sometimes Norma, Gastone's wife, brings their little children along for dinner as well. Each night we are three or four generations at one table, all having a good time, enjoying each other. A generation gap is maybe the first sign of a sick society.

Gastone, Buzz and Gino finally introduce us to their friend, the Great Toio, 'Toio Piazetta' as he's known. He has a restaurant on Giudecca – a restaurant? It's a room with one table and the people at that table eat whatever it is that Toio's wife and mother-in-law are cooking for the family in the room beyond. Toio feels that he was meant for greater things and at night he escapes from the bedroom window and makes for the piazzetta next to St Mark's Square and there he spends his time hanging out with his friends, moving slowly from bar to bar. He doesn't speak Italian, only Venetian, and even Gastone and Gino have trouble understanding him. I spend entire evenings sitting next to him, desperately trying to get the drift of the stories he tells – he never stops talking. Many of the stories are to do with the war and bunkers. The minute we hear 'bunkers', pronounced 'Boonkerrs', we know we're listening to a joke and in time the word is enough to start us laughing – which inspires Toio to tell *more* funny war stories. Never in my life have I spent so many hours genuinely laughing at stories I don't understand at all. Dear, exasperating, rotund, bellicose Toio.

For years, as I got to know the city, I felt more and more that there was a deep reserve within the Venetians and even O'Toole, usually adept at nosing out secret places, admitted that there was something he could not penetrate. It was as though, overrun by and living off tourists, the city with its great past resolutely kept something of itself to itself as at the same time it entertained, cosseted, cheated, spoiled and took advantage of the hordes that invaded it except in the depths of

winter; hordes without whom it could not live. In a city where
the inhabitants live with an awareness of the past ('So we all
clubbed together and built this.' 'When was that?' '1732.'),
tourism must be a bit of a come-down. Our feeling of being
politely excluded lasted until our visit following the close of
Ride a Cock Horse. It was winter. We flew to Venice but in fact
we were diverted to Milan, landing in torrential rain. There, we
were put on a bus to Venice and when we arrived – it was still
pouring with rain – the driver said, 'Okay, everyone back to
Milan. You cannot go into Venice.' O'Toole looks at me and
jerks his head towards the exit. Without hesitation I make for
the door. 'No, you cannot disembark. There is nowhere to go.'
'Thank you. All the same—' pushing forward. 'No, madam. I
must insist.' 'Keep going' (O'Toole from behind). 'Frightfully
sorry, I have to get off. Thank you, goodbye. Just need the
bags.' O'Toole, following, stuffs a bundle of notes into the
driver's hand and he releases the bags from the hold.

Well, here we are. It's so quiet, unusually quiet, in Mestre.
There's a lamp outside a deserted building and underneath it
we pile up the bags and I sit on them. O'Toole gives me a
book and says, 'Look after the bags and have a read. I'll be
back. Just wait.' I read. It's still raining. When he returns –
there is still no one about – he says, 'Okay, I think we're on,'
and we manhandle the luggage to a jetty which is in pitch
darkness. The bags are loaded into a little motor boat. We
speak in whispers. Why? Off we go. Why does the trip seem
so strange? Well, for one thing it's dark – totally dark. It is
the middle of the night but there are no lights at all. We go
down a deserted Grand Canal and encounter no other traffic.
Here and there windows are lit by candlelight. This is a view of
Venice no one has seen since the nineteenth century; Venice lit
by candles alone. We turn off the Grand Canal and see a bridge
ahead. The driver turns round and motions to us to lie down.
Obediently, we lie down on the floor. So does the boatman.
He cuts the motor and as we approach the bridge which seems

dangerously near to our heads, he lifts his legs and begins to 'walk' slowly along the underside of the bridge. He gestures to us behind and we follow suit, pushing the boat down in the water. We have to 'walk' with bended knees and, emerging the other side, we straighten up and look at each other. The boatman raises a thumb. We nod. What on earth is going on? We're in a dark, empty stretch of water and there are *things* bumping into us. What are they? As we approach the Danieli Hotel I realize that we are working our way through broken masonry, bits of timber, and drawing close to an unfamiliar looking jetty. It's the top of a balustrade and there, back-lit by a huge, flickering candelabra, is the massive bulk of Bruno, the doorman. He looks amazed and, arriving at the boat, lifts me over his head and, reaching the top of the mahogany reception desk, he sets me down on it and returns for O'Toole and the baggage.

The Danieli is under water. I walk along the top of the desk and begin to hop and skip through the flooded foyer on stepping places made of pieces of furniture. Gastone de Cal, the head barman, hasn't gone off duty and is standing on a little island of tables, looking amazed and overjoyed. No one has managed to get into Venice for twenty-four hours. Traffic is not allowed on the Grand Canal after dark. There are no guests in the hotel, they've all left. What do we do now? 'Have a drink!' Normally, O'Toole would be only too glad to sit down and celebrate our feat in getting into the forbidden city. Tonight – this morning – he can see that things are bad; the staff are trying to save the ground-floor furniture. 'Come on, Siân,' he says. 'Get some wellies. Let's get to work.' They find waders for us and we spend the next few hours carrying chairs and tables up the main staircase, rolling up the staircarpet and hoisting everything that can be moved up to the first floor. I never had such a good time at the Danieli as I did that night. Finally, at dawn, we take our pick of the empty rooms. Gastone explains that we'll have to move from bathroom to bathroom as there's no plumbing and there's no electricity and are we *sure* we want to stay. Are we sure? What could be more fun than to camp out in this beloved, familiar, romantic hotel.

We've been coming to Venice for years unremarked among the glitterati of the world, avoiding high society and any occasion remotely smart. Now, we are famous in the nicest way. Wet and shabby in our waders, we seem to be the only guests in the city. As the water subsides we have our own brooms and we help sweep out the filth from Florians and the little shops around St Mark's Square and, finally, after years of being visitors we discover real, hidden, secret Venice. It's a rich reward for a bit of discomfort and no running water. The Venetians let us in and we spend weeks of pure pleasure, getting wet and dirty and sitting in people's back parlors and being entertained in their favorite wine shops, far off the tourist track. All our new friends are 'experts' on their city and we're dragged to and fro, sightseeing all day long from the eye-opener of grappa first thing in the morning to the nightcaps at the Danieli.

A member of the hotel staff who has become a companion and guide in his off-duty hours shows us paintings, dirty and unlit, in small churches where he produces a torch so we can stand and admire silently with him. He's as proud as though he were the painter. We go into little bars serving food, which we have passed by dozens of times on earlier visits. 'No tourist has ever walked in here. Good wine – *our* vineyard.' The wine is alarmingly robust but very welcome in the cold morning air. It's also purple and stains our tongues and lips an ineradicable, lurid but rather fashionable Mary Quant color (it looks better on me than on O'Toole who looks as though he's in some louche Carnival scene). Our friend's father is a painter – a very special painter. Sworn to secrecy, we visit his studio in an unremarkable apartment in an unfashionable street. The sprightly, elderly Venetian is busy grinding his 'colors'. All around are astounding eighteenth-century paintings. After a few hours of sitting around and admiring and drinking tiny beakers of wine ('I know the vineyard – very good', I read in our good guidebook that the Venetians don't drink; I'll be lucky to get home with half a liver intact), and after a spot of lunch – blissful home-made pasta with tiny, almost transparent, brownish shrimps (I also read that Venetian food isn't up to much!) Sr X confides that his business is forgery.

This doesn't pose an artistic problem for him as it does for many forgers who feel their 'own' art, just as skilled, is unappreciated. He lives for paintings, loves Guardi, in whom he specializes. 'It's only embarrassing,' he says, 'when I have to go to authenticate something for a museum, sometimes in America. I see it is mine and I hate to disappoint them. I have some Guardis in most of the big museums. Not too many.' He has been busy during the last few days. The high tide has 'liberated' eighteenth-century paper from a basement around the corner and his flat is festooned with washing lines of drying paper. 'So good to have the real thing.' He prepares his paints exactly as Guardi and Canaletto did, but the paper and canvas is always a problem and now the flood has brought him a rich windfall. As we leave, he presses a small canvas into my hand and gives me his cousin's address. When I go there he is busy making eighteenth-century furniture. His family has, for countless generations, been making furniture in the same manner. He gives me an eighteenth-century picture frame. He's so *proud* and so he should be; this isn't reproduction, this is top of the mark deception. Our time here is becoming more and more splendidly unreal.

At night we have to wait in an improvised bar until the night staff come on because the night electrician at the Danieli is the best tenor. We learn Venetian songs and I improvise an alto line. We sing until dawn. High tide is a horrible thing but the Venetians are behaving like blitzed Londoners and we have the time of our lives.

I think we love travelling because it stops us from thinking about ourselves. Ourselves – oh, so difficult. Armed insurrections, hunger, thirst, danger – oh, so easy. To move ahead. To move. Interesting. Binding. We never failed to have a good time while engaged on the many journeys we made together. Neither of us was a passive tourist and life, while we moved about together, was arduous and exhausting and exhilarating. Some of our journeys, marooned in provincial railway stations or stranded in unpromising, unpicturesque spots would have bored and frustrated many but we always found something interesting to keep ourselves amused. Most of our journeys were, however, more exotic; some were dangerous. Tedious, uncomfortable, glamorous, perilous; it didn't really matter what the conditions were, I think we both travelled for the sake of travelling and consequently we travelled well – almost always.

My trip to Cambodia in 1963 was unexpectedy brief. I arrived in a daring skirt made by a new designer called Mary Quant. It was demurely box-pleated but it rested an inch and a half above my knee (a bit like my school uniform, which I detested). I had square-toed, stubby-heeled shoes and a modishly straight hair cut. O'Toole was appalled. We had a vehement, all the more intense for being whispered, exchange when he suggested I went home on the next flight. 'What have you come as?' he asked in horror. Fortunately I was able to reassure him that my luggage contained below-the-knee skirts and ordinary shoes and on the spot I was able to shake my hair into a less fashionable shape. I hated him for greeting me in such a way but understood by now the tensions of reunions and – I hated to admit it – he was quite right about the clothes. Skirts were getting shorter and shorter; the one I wore to Cambodia was a restrained version of the London fashion. I had to agree with him when he asked rhetorically, 'What is a tall, thirty-year-old, mother-of-two doing dressed in clothes that would look well on a twelve-year-old?'

We may have been good at travelling but we were bad at reunions and, rather embarrassed by our own behavior, we made for the hotel and a soothing bath. A spider, larger than any I had ever seen, fell out of the beautifully folded towel. 'They wear hob-nailed boots here,' said O'Toole, glumly. 'Clump, clump, all over the place.' At the night shoot the film lights sizzled with large, dead, fried night bugs. This place was all snakes and bugs. The loo was a wicker contraption on stilts. the prop-man – prop-men are always my favorite people on a film set – said, delicately, 'Siân – now, not to worry, but we had a really nasty snake in the ladies' tonight and they always go in pairs, so be really careful when you – you know.' There was a snake called the Two-Step. You got bitten and then two steps later you fell down dead. O'Toole sent me on a trip round Angkor Wat. 'Wear boots because of the snakes.' I set off into this amazing place and spent the day there. There were soldiers hiding in the bushes, guarding the bits of art that might get chopped off and taken home. Good for them. I wondered if O'Toole had been thinking of 'liberating' a little art.

That same week, news came that the political situation was rapidly worsening and American and British nationals were advised to leave at once. The film unit was disbanded and dispersed quite fast. O'Toole ignored the official evacuation and preferred to trust to his own wits and I had no doubt my best bet was to follow him. 'Let's go to the airport,' he said. There were no planes. I was installed in the ladies' lavatory. No luggage (the contentious skirt was now in the possession of the attacking army). How do I know what I'm going to hear next? 'Here, read this and *wait here*, darling.' I had a guidebook to Angkor Wat and nothing else except my passport which seemed strangely useless in what appeared to be an armed insurrection. I sat on the floor in a cubicle in the ladies' lavatory and read about what I'd seen during the day. It kept me busy for over an hour until a familiar hand appeared under the door. I touched it. 'Open up,' breathed a voice and I opened the door and O'Toole crept in. 'We've got a plane.' (There were few left in the airport.)

'Oh, good.'

'But not for five hours.'

'Oh hell.'

We sat on the floor of that horrible lavatory, alternately whispering and reading and actually having quite a nice time (I learned a lot about Angkor), until the appointed hour when we straightened up and cautiously moved out and on to the runway. O'Toole thought he recognized our small plane. 'Okay, run!' he whispered and we belted out across the airfield and up the staircase. It was the right plane. Money changed hands and we were off. Where to? 'Don't ask.' We landed in Hong Kong where O'Toole had been filming before arriving in Cambodia. O'Toole hadn't trusted the film company to get us out of a war zone but once in Hong Kong he summoned the might of the company to get us an hotel. They may not know about politics but film companies sure know hotels. We were directed to the newly built Mandarin and rolled up – dirty and hungry, no baggage – to inaugurate the Presidential Suite. There was a lot to play with; lying on the vast bed I opened curtains, raised televisions, altered the temperature – I'm not sure I didn't run a bath while lying down. O'Toole proved surprisingly adept at acquiring toothbrushes and paste and combs and shampoo and also summoned tailors to the room to measure us for clothes. I ordered a modest frock (skirt on the knee) and a jacket and coat and O'Toole ordered a few pairs of slacks and shirts and a jacket or two.

He showed me around the Hong Kong he had become familiar with and into the bar frequented by 'Hot Pants Molly Malone' (a bit of a disappointment), whose card he'd retained. Who wouldn't? Then he ventured into more interesting territory. 'There's this square mile owned by a feudal war lord.' 'Ah yes.' 'But no one goes there. The police don't dare. Let's go and have a look.' 'Sure.' I was in my new Chinese 'Chanel' coat and dress, still clutching the Hermès handbag (the only thing I'd brought out from Cambodia). Our taxi driver said, 'No! No! Please!' as he set us down. 'Just wait here,' said O'Toole sweetly. 'No, sir! You cannot go there. Not the lady.'

'Be all right, old son,' murmured O'Toole as we ducked into a dark alleyway, the entrance to the forbidden city. So this was the place where criminals went, knowing the law could not pursue them. 'Now, are you sure . . . ?' 'Come *on!*' After a few twists and turns I felt horribly conspicuous. There wasn't a lot to look at, either. My Hermès bag seemed to be sending out signals. 'O'Toole—' 'Yes?' 'This is very interesting but do you notice how the women are taking the children indoors?' 'Yes.' 'D'you think this is a bad sign?' No reply. The dark, narrow, fetid alleyway ahead was now deserted, save for a few moody-looking young men.

'Mmm, don't look frightened. Just turn around casually, make a left and *stroll* back – no, *STROLL* dammit.' As we turned around we saw that the street behind us had emptied as well. Was this prior to some act of violence? Or did they think *we* were dangerous? We strolled, God, how hard we strolled. I have no sense of direction and couldn't think how to get back to law-abiding, everyday Hong Kong. O'Toole sauntered confidently, his casual amble at odds with the vice-like grip in which he held my hand. Light ahead. Daylight. Not quickening our step, we made for what turned out to be a version of Oxford Street, and our taxi – thank God O'Toole had a great sense of direction. The driver practically wept when he saw us. I suppose it would have been very awkward for him if he'd reported back to Columbia Pictures without its star.

'Yeah, well – you can't think about all that,' said O'Toole, recovering his high spirits as we made for the Mandarin. 'You go back to the hotel. I've got a chance to buy a little bit of Korean something or other. Bit dodgy. Tell you what – have a read and just *wait for me.*'

I waited for a long time in that huge suite before he returned with a lovely bulky piece of bas-relief – horsemen rushing into battle.

'Excuse me, but I'm awfully itchy.'

'Well, so am I.'

'How strange.'

Strange indeed that the first guests in the Presidential Suite should be lousy from their spell in the public lavatory at Phnom Penh Airport. They fumigated the rooms – and us – and O'Toole said, 'Let's go to Japan.'

Chapter Twenty-four

As we walk down a Tokyo street, nasty as the Edgware Road and twice as noisy, I glance into a small sandwich bar and see an empty piece of Formica countertop and on it, in a jar, a single branch of flowering cherry. Behind the deep-fryer is an open door leading to a postage-stamp of garden – cool and quiet. It's a tiny, powerful piece of calm and beauty holding its own against the tumult. Pressing forward into the unbearable over-congestion of the street, I feel excitedly that once again I am in a truly foreign place – already I've encountered ten things I do not comprehend. I decide not to try to understand anything and begin to review the contradictions of the day. Mrs Kawakita is our contact as head of Toho Films. She is tiny, dressed in traditional costume, perpetually smiling and polite. I'm told that grown men have been known to cry after bruising business encounters with her. When things get really tough voices remain low, but terrified underlings in the outer office fancy they see Western blood seeping under the door before Mrs Kawakita emerges, head nodding, smiling and eyes lowered, a favorable contract completed.

I tower over her in my Hong Kong pretend-Chanel and feel, as I try to gauge my bows to correspond with and not exceed hers – otherwise we'll be here all day – that she looks quaint and a bit odd in that get-up. It takes only a week for me to begin to marvel at the beauty of her hair and make-up, the complexity of her dress, the delicacy of her movements and the subtlety of her expression, while feeling more and more like a clod-hopping land-girl; too big, too loud, too vulgar of face. Even my perfume – that year Mitsouko by

Guerlain – seems too obvious by half. I feel *ugly*, is the short word.

We have elected to stay in a Japanese hotel. Walking up the white-lined corridor to the suite, we notice tears here and there in the paper walls. 'Looks as though someone bad with props, like Johnny G, has been here,' remarks O'Toole. He is great with props. I am not, as I demonstrate within minutes of entering the huge, empty, beautiful set of rooms. Exploring what might be a bedroom, I withdraw the wooden bolt in the wall in order to open a window and find that I have the entire wall in my hands and am precariously balanced, leaning outwards over a lovely moss garden one floor below. I dare not move. I breathe, 'Pete – Pete! Help! Help!' It seems an age before O'Toole, thinking he hears something, drifts into the room and, anchoring me around the waist with one arm, takes possession of the wall with the other and, shaking his head resignedly, much as he does when I mess up a bit of business on stage, replaces the wall and leaves me to unpack while he goes in search of a bar.

I tiptoe around the dividing screens. So much in the rooms is so light and breakable but at the same time the deep, narrow bath, the bedroll which is laid out at night only, the headrest, the dark wooden floor, are so confidently heavy and in their correct, immovable place that I am constantly wrong-footed as I move around, at one moment behaving rather patronizingly like a grown-up in a doll's house and the next submitting to an alien but mightily convincing arrangement of objects.

O'Toole returns, having discovered not only a bar (the Japanese are crazy about whisky, it seems) but a massage parlor below where a little lady *walked* up his spine. I settle for a shampoo and set but even so my little lady shampooer does something unprecedented to my skull. We're two Brobdingnagians in paradise. 'I'll bet they laugh at us,' says O'Toole. 'Apparently we smell awful and they call us "the Big

Noses".' He's probably right. My nose – rather unremarkable I always thought – seems to be growing.

Sleep. Such sleep. My first night on a Japanese bed-on-the-floor. No book, no radio, no television, big darkness, the polished floor near my right hand and sleep that I can almost taste.

In the morning, film representatives come to call. They're discouraging about the possibility of buying art. 'You'd swear they don't *want* to sell anything,' says one. 'I've been rooting around for ten years – nothing.' O'Toole nods gravely and we promise to ring the office if we need anything in the way of restaurant reservations, cars and so on. This must be a horrible job, looking after movie stars and their whims. We have a couple of numbers we've found for ourselves. Eureka! Kurosawa rings back; he's filming *The Red Doctor* and we're invited to watch him. Our cups run over completely when the most famous of all Japanese actors, Toshiro Mifune, calls. It's going to be very hard to behave like rational beings around these two men. They're like mythical beasts to me. I owe my knowledge of them to O'Toole and am overwhelmed now by the magnitude of my debt to him. I don't actually want to meet these men at all. But I do want to *watch* them; however, meeting is a part of all that.

The set of *The Red Doctor* is wonderful. If this were movie making then I would want to do little else but make Kurosawa movies. He is a master, Kurosawa – and he's tall! He's a good-looking cowboy of a Japanese. His mother is tiny and she cooks and runs the kitchen on the film set. It's like filming in his parlor, except one is aware that he is one of the most illustrious directors in the world, but oh, the difference from anything I've seen . . . He doesn't act great. His mother doesn't treat him as great. The unit mills about like family retainers, the actors behave with modest dignity; no one is treated exceptionally well. But there it is – hanging over the ramshackle location – the impact of great quality. Watching movies being made is low on the list of spectator sports but I could have sat on my orange box for months – and I didn't understand a word of text. It seems the financiers are exasperated by the length of the shoot; Kurosawa is being hounded and harried. His great talent and reputation don't save him from being treated badly. I make a mental note once again *never* to feel bad when I'm badly treated. Much better talents than mine are treated shamefully by people who are actually only trying to hang on to their jobs, trying to save a bit of money.

Toshiro Mifune appears! This is a star! He, also, is tall, another Japanese cowboy and when he walks he displaces a lot of air . . . It's a pleasure to see him and he and O'Toole fall on each other. O'Toole has adored 'Tosher' since he was a boy in Leeds; it must be wonderful to stand on Japanese soil and embrace one of the best Japanese actors, and to find that they like each other on sight! I hang back slightly and watch the meeting. They arrange to see each other later.

Where do we meet? I'm getting used to the unexpected and don't blink when we enter a huge, ghastly, dark, pleasure-drome where they serve – of course – many kinds of whisky. Toshiro loves whisky. O'Toole loves whisky only too much and becomes a mad person when he drinks it, so he's forsworn it and I'm impressed when he refuses one now. Whisky is a big treat. Toshiro is buying. O'Toole is choosing – who knows what? – it's not whisky and I'm silently overcome with admiration. He wants to make a good impression on Mifune but not at the expense of turning into a mad person. They talk through an interpreter and I sit, enjoying this meeting, hating the venue and only vaguely understanding what is being discussed. The noise is *tremendous*! This is worse than Annabel's.

We now have a longer list of phone numbers. I'm getting to understand that in this country, without a personal rec-ommendation, it is very difficult to reach anyone significant.

Kurosawa and Mifune between them pass us on to the best kimono maker in the country, the best antique dealer and the best lacquer man and we make calls and wait. Then we embark on a series of visits that feel a bit like auditions.

And in the interim the film company arranges visits to the theater. They are touchingly eager to please a big Star and I think that they must be keenly grateful for an easy few weeks now that the Star has the Wife in tow. Nothing is required except visits to special monuments and trips to the theater and they must wonder what we do with our time. 'This play goes on all day, you don't have to stay,' we're told as we go backstage at the theater. Backstage is huge. Actors sit in front of cheval mirrors, hands on knees, legs apart. Silently they look at themselves as they are transformed into the character they will inhabit for the rest of the day. Old men become young girls. Young men become elderly. I believe it all. Here, in the ordinary light of day, the atmosphere is church-like. Out front, I settle into an uncomfortable seat next to an old lady who is sitting on her feet. On the floor in front of her is a primus stove and food and tea. The play opens with the most compelling entrance I've ever seen an actor make: slow, slow, lateral walk to the acting area but the acting, the diction are at first grotesque and after a mere ten minutes, totally believable and natural. The audience gasps and cries as one; red ribbons are as real as the blood in a Peckinpah movie, blue cloth is a believable, impassable river. The movie representative appears in the aisle to 'rescue' us. No way am I leaving. My old lady busies herself with a bit of cooking and I wish she'd offer me a bite, as we settle down for another couple of hours of drama. Eventually, shaken and exhausted and exhilarated, I emerge into the Tokyo afternoon. We have an evening appointment, otherwise I *could* have stayed there all day. Why? I find it quite difficult to sit through a long play in London. I've read about people sitting through a day of theater in Ancient Greece and wondered how they could do that. Maybe there has to be this degree of mutually accepted tradition and commitment before the experience becomes possible. Come to think of it, I'm rarely convinced – this carried away – in a theater at home. Back in my empty Japanese room I sit and wonder at the day.

Our phone calls lead us to people who are distinguished artists and not about to start making a sale to just anyone; not even at the say-so of their important and successful friends. Sometimes it's O'Toole's reputation and charisma that gets us by but sometimes it's my patience and sincere admiration that wins the day. We sit day after day in what looks like a council flat in North London (except our feet are dangling over a fire-pit under the dining table) and gradually the Lacquer Man brings out small objects for our consideration. Kurosawa has explained to me that this man marks a tree he will use in ten years' time and he waits and waits for it to mature and his output is wonderful and prized but tiny and he will never be rich but he is the greatest lacquer artist in Japan and, sitting in his dowdy living room and knowing nothing, even I can tell that he is great. My ideas are getting such a shake-up. Actually, I'm learning to forget what I've been absorbing over the last ten years. What was that? Style, I suppose. I'm unprepared for the person who lives in an unappealing house like this, wears undistinguished clothes like this, eats dull food such as this, but thinking back, I recall that Johns the Postman in Cwmllynfell, in my home in Wales, drank too much, looked like a cleaned up tramp, lived in a little house with a Mabel Lucy Attwell calendar on the wall and antimacassars on the uncut moquette chairs and wrote Welsh poetry, the complexity of which would bear comparison with the best Greek poetry. And now, I'm sitting in a little living room with nasty wallpaper and awful little ornaments and the man of the house is showing us great art, wrapped up in tea towels. O'Toole can see that I'm making an impression and he leaves the negotiating to me. Well – I don't talk about *money* – I ask about being *allowed* to *acquire*.

Eventually, we leave with eight superb bowls. I've had such an intense few nights with this man but I don't say, 'We'll be in touch'. What would be the point? He hasn't any idea of who we are but we have connected quite strongly. Maybe he can see that I will remember these few days forever. I hope he can. I will.

The Kimono Man is a bit more of a showbiz character, more accustomed to visiting stars. We order kimonos that bear no relation to the ordinary kimonos sold in the shops here or in England. (When they wore out I tried to have them copied and no one could master the intricacy of their making.)

Art is so much more difficult to find. The film people – Westerners who live in Tokyo – are almost right when they say that the barrier between 'us and them' is as good as impenetrable. We sit, night after night, drinking tea in suburban houses. Occasionally, our host says 'Let's go and visit X' and off we trundle to another little sitting room and drink more tea. Still no art appears. A week goes by before a bundle is produced and, unwrapped, proves to be an actor's mask from the eighteenth century – holly wood, painted for the Old Man's character. The owner gestures to me to put it on and I do and I am very moved by the gesture and, taking it off, I sniff a bit, and pass it to O'Toole. He puts it on and the company roars with laughter to see the beautiful star face transformed to decrepit old age. He lays it reverently back on its cloth and we drink tea for hours. As we leave, the mask is bundled up and pressed into O'Toole's hands. Our interpreter must have agreed to pay; these negotiations are always rather lordly.

The Mask Man hands us on to another dealer and after many nights in back rooms we buy almost my favorite object of all, a terracotta head, so simple it is scarcely formed at all.

When I say 'we', that is of course completely misleading. O'Toole chose to spend a major part of his earnings on art and I was an enthusiastic helper but he was spending *his* money, not mine. I spent a large portion of *my* earnings on antique furniture but I never felt a great sense of ownership except in a few, emotional, instances. I rarely bought art. Here, in Japan, I'm becoming acquisitive. I buy an eighteenth century scroll – I want to live in a low, Japanese house. I want a garden of mosses. I'd like to be smaller, quieter, less scrutable.

Chapter Twenty-five

B ack in Heath Street in Hampstead, fitting our acquisitions into this lovely fortress of a house and our life in it continues to be workable, as well as intermittently ecstatic or unbelievably dreadful. We've acquired a family of cats who live downstairs and a bulldog called Scobie who lives in the basement and in the Green Room and who absorbs a great deal of household energy. O'Toole bought him as a protector for the houseful of girls he has to leave behind when he goes filming. Fierce to look at, Scobie became a well-known feature of street-life in Hampstead, plodding out twice daily on what looked like a glum walk, occasionally slipping his lead on the Heath and once, during such a moment of freedom when the fair was paying its Easter visit to Hampstead, charging up the steps of a fairground trailer – he wasn't named after a jockey for nothing – and, unable to stop, smashing his way into a china cabinet. 'Very good china,' said the vengeful and formidable old fairground woman when she visited us and her eyes alighted on O'Toole's name here and there in the Green Room, and then, taking in a poster on the wall, 'Royal Doulton mostly – and some *Limoges* as well, and then there's the *crystal*!' 'Yes, yes,' I said soothingly as I pressed bundles of notes into her hand.

Scobie had already been in a spot of bother with the law and I didn't feel he was well placed to survive more trouble. Although every time one of the many burglar alarms in the house went off at night, he greeted the police, tail wagging, dribbling affectionately on their trousers, he'd taken against being loaded into a Black Maria when he, along with his young walkers, had been arrested on an apple pillaging expedition and hauled off to Rosslyn Hill police station. The schoolboys obediently trooped into the sinister van but Scobie exerted all of his not inconsiderable strength, summoned up the indomitable spirit of his breed, and would not budge; policemen overbalanced and sat down suddenly on the pavement, helmets rolled down the road and as passersby clutched each other, crying with laughter, Scobie glowered at everyone and phone calls were made to the house to 'Get this damned ferocious beast out of here. NOW!' It was my mother who hurried down the hill and murmured reproachfully, 'Oh, Scobie!' and he trotted over and sat at her heels. She apologized to the recovering officers, glared at the boys cowering in the van, and in the voice that could still make me jump with fright said, 'And as for you. Just you wait . . .'

At home, when he inadvertently knocked someone to the ground, he stood there mournfully, breathing hard, bestowing the odd wet lick on the prone figure until, to his evident relief, it righted itself. He arrived 'toilet-trained' but he'd got the message wrong and would stand for hours on the Heath, longing to pee, legs crossed, practically hopping with anxiety. Then, once back in the house, he would lean against the closed door in the hall in a 'Thank God' position and the floodgates would open. He had to be sent back to school to re-learn the lesson but he was never entirely sure that he'd got it right. Nor had he when he appeared in the film *Great Catherine* as the dog belonging to the British Ambassador, played by Jack Hawkins. He rode to Shepperton in the Rolls, sitting motionless up front and dribbling steadily on the upholstery to Lionel's frustrated fury. 'I'd like to *murder* him,' he muttered. He lived for thirteen years and was the longest lasting of O'Toole's Petruchio's servants – adorable and totally useless in the job for which he'd been engaged.

Scobie personified our home life – sweet and slightly cockeyed.

In spite of my earnest efforts, there were times when I found it almost impossible to contain my frustration over work. Time and again I failed to embrace my hero Sydney Smith's dictum, '. . . If my lot be to crawl, I will crawl contentedly; if to fly, I will fly with alacrity; but, as long as I can possibly avoid it, I will never be unhappy.'

Desperate to be 'flying', in a place where it counted in those days (and London seemed to be the only place that really signified), I jumped at the chance to play Cleopatra at the Vic. O'Toole wanted to know all the details of the production (none of which I knew), saying that a 'true professional' would not embark on such a job without making sure that all the conditions were perfect, down to the smallest piece of casting and costume. (He added that the play rarely worked.) Very differently situated from him, I was not in a position to make demands and exhaustive inquiries. Nor was I convinced that a guarantee of perfection was any guarantee of a successful outcome but as the arguments raged at home and they became more concerned with my character and less about the job, I withdrew from it and domestic harmony was instantly restored, but I was sick at heart as I resumed a modest crawl.

I lost *The Cherry Orchard* in much the same way. When I began to quiz my old friend, director Frank Hauser, about the casting he was outraged that I should be interfering in his production plans. That was the reaction I expected and I wasn't surprised when he withdrew his offer and didn't work with me again for a good ten years. I was disheartened to see how little courage and confidence I was able to muster at home. Defiance was out of the question.

Almost at once, in 1966, I came near to losing *Man and Superman* as well. This time, the order from O'Toole was not to play it without acquiring a major star for Jack Tanner (a role that O'Toole had played brilliantly at the Bristol Old Vic). Philip Wiseman, the director, and Richard Shulman, the producer, were bemused but obligingly, as requested, offered the part to a few movie stars who they knew were never going to accept the job (and who took months before they bothered to reply). Finally, reality overtook everyone and a list was compiled of major theater actors who might reasonably want the huge part as well as being able to perform it. As we looked down the impressive list the crumpled, exhausted production team, *longing* to get on with the job, paused at one name and we read no further. Everyone wanted one of the most exciting actors in the country, only too infrequently seen in the great parts he was born to play. It was just as well that Philip and Richard and I were equally enthusiastic because it became clear that Alan Badel was as reluctant as any Hollywood tyro to respond to letters or to return phone calls. Weeks and months went by and in despair I called Alan's wife, Vonnie. (Their house was more of a fortress than ours.) Vonnie lifted the phone and there was a very guarded, 'Yes?'. 'Vonnie, it's Siân and I'm desperate. Do you think Alan will do the play?' 'Well, I think he should.' 'But *will* he?' 'Leave it with me.' I did and within days we had a message of acceptance. O'Toole approved. Well, how could he not?

When Alan turned up to read the play with a good but hastily assembled cast, Philip and I were only slightly put out when we slowly realized, chatting with Alan over coffee, that he had turned up to rehearse *Arms and the Man*. A copy of *Man and Superman* was hastily but casually slipped on to the table where Alan would sit. I watched him touch it, his face revealing nothing, as he made a mental readjustment and prepared to sightread Tanner. It was the beginning of a long, incident-packed journey which culminated in one of the longest commercial runs of any Shaw play. The highs were glorious and the lows difficult to look back on without shuddering.

The opening night at the Arts was, on the whole, a low. Alan, busily teasing Philip because he belonged to that hated breed –

directors – neglected to thoroughly learn his part. Philip was exhausted from directing the play while keeping out of Alan's sightlines. I was dazed with fatigue from keeping the peace between the two of them and was far from having figured out how to play Anne. Also, I couldn't help noticing that Alan – my friend – having summoned up all his formidable resources in order to get through the long opening duologue with me was playing it brilliantly but also was playing it pressed up against the backdrop while I (his friend and protector against the wrath of the management) sat, pinned in my chair, down stage. To the uninitiated this is called 'upstaging' someone. I loved acting with him and forgave him completely. O'Toole, in England for a while before leaving for Warsaw to film *Night of the Generals*, arrived at the theater in a state of mixed emotions and passed out drunk in the corridor backstage, so we made our entrances stepping over his curled-up figure in the corridor. What little stock of embarrassment that remained to me evaporated forever that night. Alan went on a few weeks later to be superb and although the long run threw up its share of weekly crises, it was for me one of the most exciting, if erratic, of jobs. During the year Alan and I worked on *Antony and Cleopatra* in our spare time and hoped to mount a production of the play and when that collapsed I thought I really wasn't *meant* to play the part, except in my head.

My mother in the play was played by Marie Löhr who, despite the disparity in our ages, became one of my closest friends. Marie, well into her seventies when I met her, was stately, on the stout side, and beautifully dressed in the grand clothes of an earlier time. In spite of a streak of sheer naughtiness which she retained from a youth studded with some startling romances and adventures, she had the air of a grande dame and it wasn't difficult to see her as the actor-manager she had been in her heyday. Living alone now in a small flat, she had developed a few idiosyncratic habits but her awareness of the absurdity of a great deal of daily life – her own included – quite exempted her from being perceived as eccentric. Lest she should miss something interesting, she kept both radio and television running softly as she dealt with her correspondence and, in order to keep her beloved canary near her when she released him from his cage, she sprinkled bird-seed on to the crown of her head so he was never away for long, returning to peck away among her shiny, white curls. This seemed very sensible to me and I would forget about the seeds and it was Marie who would lift her hand halfway to her head, as we sat down in a restaurant, raise an index finger, mouth pursed in comic disapproval, and sail majestically into the Ladies to remove her hat and shake out of her hair the forgotten remnants of Joey's breakfast, before returning to further enslave an adoring bunch of waiters who would never have seen her act, but who knew she was Somebody, all right. Her exquisite manners were camp in a ladylike way and fragments of advice she passed on to me were all too few and so lightly produced as to be in danger of passing unnoticed. She never talked about herself or of the past except when, knowing her better and better, I would press her to look back.

There were great gaps in the story always, but I pieced together enough to make me wish that she'd kept a journal. She'd been an actress since she was sixteen or seventeen and described the scene up and down Shaftesbury Avenue or the Charing Cross Road as dozens of young actresses ran from theater to theater to be seen or to audition for jobs. There is a wide walkway along the side of the Garrick Theater where we were playing at the time and she remembered it being full of girls – young ladies – all in hats and gloves and carrying little bags with their spirit heaters and curling tongs for smartening up the hair before they went on stage. She became Sir Herbert Beerbohm Tree's leading lady in *Faust* when she was eighteen. He was an actor-manager who was a law unto himself and when Marie lost her voice he suspended rehearsals and sent her and her mother to Brighton for a week with his own recipe for throat medicine and instructions that she was not to speak until she returned to London. She did as she was told and the play opened triumphantly when he felt that it and she were good and ready.

Marie's mother (I never heard her speak of a father) was an actress called Kate Bishop and Marie was utterly devoted to her. They were living together when Miss Bishop died and when Marie described her last illness her jauntiness deserted her and the sense of loss was fresh in her voice. Her mother loved and had a way with birds and as she lay dying, small song birds sat on the headboard and on the piled-up pillows and even on her hand where it rested on the coverlet. 'She smiled and smiled at the end,' said Marie.

She herself made a glittering career, becoming an actor-manager and ran a fine house, somewhere on the river. When she took one of her own productions from her theater in Shaftesbury Avenue to New York, she re-cast the play and an actress called Margaret Bannerman was given her star part. The play did not do well in America and she was obliged to come home, where she found that her husband had taken up with her replacement. She lost everything – jewels, furs, grand house – and even saw Miss Bannerman wearing her jewelry. An excruciatingly painful divorce followed and in court the judge – an admirer of Marie's – asked plaintively, 'Who *is* Margaret Bannerman?' 'I could have kissed him,' said Marie, her eyes glistening with malice.

When she toured she – an expert player – travelled with her own custom-made, collapsible billiard cues, along with a great deal of luggage. She loved the company of men and she acted with most of the matinée idols of her day; occasionally when certain very renowned names came up she would look a little absent and the conversation would halt and I guessed at a *tendresse*, to say the least, but knew better than to ask her to reveal more than she had already volunteered. She was a lady.

Her beloved mother had been a contemporary and a col-league of Ellen Terry and as small children, Kate Bishop and Ellen Terry had both been engaged as fairies at Bristol, where Mrs Kendal (Madge Robertson) was actor-manager of a stock company. It was awesome to me to realize that some of the voice exercises passed on to me by Marie had been taught to her mother in the middle of the nineteenth century.

After playing my mother for about nine months in *Man and Superman*, things went well for a while; she played in a film and on television with O'Toole and was made much of by visiting Americans who were inclined to whisk her off to the Connaught which she loved. Then she had a few falls at home and decided that it was dangerous for her to live alone. Lacking family to live with, a good friend, with the very best intentions, moved her from London to a nursing home in a quiet, prosperous part of Brighton. Lionel moved her in our Rolls and the trip was, he said, hilarious. She was completely disorganized and he did most of the packing before they set off, hours late. They had lunch on the way and he installed her in her nice room in the large, soundless house. Then, I think, the laughter ended for Marie. She sat in her room, with some of her own good furniture around and whispered, 'I don't see anyone here. They're all *old*, I think.' She became slim again, and then thin and all her lovely clothes had to be given away. She went on dwindling and very soon she was gone, and I miss her still.

Philip, Richard and I worked together for a third time. We missed acquiring the rights to *A Streetcar Named Desire* by a matter of hours only, but Tennessee sent us a re-written version of *Summer and Smoke*. He called it *The Eccentricities of a Nightingale* and we tried it out at the Yvonne Arnaud Theater in Guildford. Our doubts about the reaction of the stockbroker belt to Tennessee were dispelled in the first few days. Our reception and favorable press led us to believe that we would have no problem in finding a home in the West

End after one month in Surrey. London was however packed with plays and we grew anxious as the days went by and every play in town seemed set to run and run forever. Then, like a miracle, we were offered one of my favorite theaters, the Vaudeville. It was a rush job; closing in Guildford on Saturday, we had to open in the Strand on Tuesday. The revolve at Guildford on and around which Nicholas Giorgiardis had devised a beautiful, elaborate set, was as wide, if not wider, than the proscenium arch at the Vaudeville. Catastrophe. We needed to borrow £5,000 in order to move the set and re-jig it to fit the new theater. I turned to our company – Keep Films – and, to my surprise, I was told that 'they' ('they' included me, surely?) needed to inspect the management's fiscal health and to 'think' about the transaction. Clement Scott-Gilbert and Richard Shulman, the producers, went to the office armed with their bank statements and balance sheets, confident that all would be well. The following day we were all mortified to be told that in Jules's opinion, Tennessee Williams was too 'chancy' a playwright to merit such a loan. To general stupefaction, we closed the play and sent the set to be broken up. Of all the blows Keep Films dealt me over the years, that one was the most difficult to overcome.

During this time I made infrequent forays into the London that was called the 'Swinging' London of the Sixties. From time to time I read with bewilderment that we were part of the set that embodied it. Nothing could have been less plausible. When I wasn't working I was usually at home with the children and O'Toole was far too busy working or doing the crossword to meet most of the film stars who came to London and called on Keep Films. As a director of Keep Films, I was occasionally deputed to pick them up from the Dorchester or the Grosvenor House and get them in to Tramps or Annabel's, the first places they wanted to visit. I would have done one, sometimes two, shows before I picked them up. Once installed inside, we would make conversation for a moment or two. 'And what do *you* do?' 'Oh, I work in the theater here in London but I have small children – do you mind if I leave you now?' For me to spend an evening in Annabel's was torture; the ceiling was too low, the music too loud. Twice I went there with Jules and Joyce, sat on the banquette, ordered a drink and fainted clean away.

One night after the show, my dresser gave me a message to go to Tiberio – a lovely restaurant off Curzon Street – where the acoustics were so bizarre that from certain tables you could hear every word spoken at some of the other tables (since deals were made at each table at lunchtime it really paid to know exactly which were the vulnerable spots). I couldn't get a taxi from the Garrick Theater and sprinted over to Mayfair, where I joined a large table nearing the end of dinner. They were all beautifully dressed in the fashion of the day: soft silk shirts for the men, stiff, beaded frocks for the women, hairpieces, false eyelashes, false nails. I sat down recognizing all the famous people – nods and kisses. Peter Sellers! How nice – yes; hello, yes – all round the table. There was one little woman I didn't know – not an actress – speak to her later. Later was a bit too late. The one person I failed to recognize was Princess Margaret. It was only when she switched suddenly into HRH mode and tremors ran around the gathering that I realized my mistake. I rather admired her in her wrath. Lord knows what had inspired it on that night.

Chapter Twenty-six

London – the end of the decade. Another film offer, to be directed by Peter Yates who had recently made *Bullitt*. I was to play a doctor, working opposite Warren Beatty. 'I absolutely can't. So sorry. But thanks.'

At home, O'Toole said, 'Are you *sure* you don't want to do this film?'

'Oh, absolutely. South America! With the girls coming up to their entrance exams. Not a chance.'

'But South America,' he kept on insisting, 'a wonderful place. Oh, you should go. The girls could visit after their exams.'

Eventually I said, 'Well, maybe. And Warren Beatty is a nice man, they say. And South America does have wonderful vegetation . . . oh well, all right. *Murphy's War* it is.'

After I accepted, O'Toole stopped talking about the film. I went off to the medical center and was jabbed in dozens of places. I went off to the Quaker Centre in the Euston Road to learn about their attitude to foreign ministries (I was to play a Quaker). I concentrated on life at home, especially on Kate's entrance exam to a school I had chosen above all others – the North London Collegiate. Visiting, I had embarrassingly dropped a little curtsey to the Headmistress, Madeleine McLauchlin. My mother was also besotted by the school. We *had* to get both girls in, somehow. (We entered them for Camden and Francis Holland as well, just in case.) My mother was appalled by the results of the new methods of teaching: classroom walls being torn down; grammar despised; mathematical tables not to be learned, nor poetry memorized;

the children measuring the walls of their classroom and shaking
powder from cocoa tin to cocoa tin and doing unbelievable
things with empty egg boxes. Not only had Harold Lever advised
Harold Wilson to close down every legal tax avoidance scheme
so that high earners like O'Toole now paid nineteen shillings and
sixpence in the pound in income tax ('Go abroad at once and stay
there,' was the advice. O'Toole refused and elected to stay), but
the Labour Government that we fought for was now – it seemed
to me – also destroying the education system to which I owed
my present life. The National Health Service was still intact. But
for how long? At the moment it was the education system that
worried my mother and me. She went to a few PTA meetings
and I watched in awe as she rose to speak against the new system.
The hostility and derision were palpable. After one meeting, a
man sought us out; ignoring the headmistress, he talked to my
mother. 'I just want to thank you – I didn't have the nerve to get
up but thank you – I'm a Maths lecturer at London University
and I'm appalled at the ignorance of incoming students and the
rot begins right here at primary level.'

'I *know* that,' said my mother, grimly. Unsmiling, they
looked at each other and parted, too upset to say goodbye.

'I'm taking them out,' said my mother. 'How d'you mean?'
'They have to know how to read and write and add up and sub-
tract and multiply and divide or they'll never get into a decent
school.' I envisaged scandal and endless newspaper attention.
'Just say they're not well. Get a note from Gerry. I'll teach them
at home.' 'For how long?' 'Give me four months.' Feebly, I
begged sick notes from Gerry and wrote letters describing
fictitious family dramas. My mother held classes in the dining
room and I took grammar and literature in the Green Room
then, feeling like a deserter, I left for South America and my
mother was left with the task of getting the two little girls into
a *decent* school – the sort of school that, thanks to Rab Butler
(a Tory), had been mine by right. The world turns.

*   *   *

'So I'm going to do this job?' (To John Miller, my agent.)

'Yes, dear. Oh, by the way, Warren Beatty isn't doing it.'

'Really?'

'No, he wanted too much money. The producers are being a bit careful; even your part now incorporates three others – a man and two women.'

'I see.'

This is a week before I leave for South America and I say, 'So who *will* be playing Murphy?'

John looks amazed and embarrassed. 'Oh, don't you know? Er – well – O'Toole is the star of the picture. It seems he's mad about South America.'

I return to Hampstead, hatchet faced. *Ride a Cock Horse* had been a never-to-be-forgotten, horrible experience. How would we get through a four-month movie together?

'Aw, come on – it'll be *great*,' he smiles. The study desk is piled high with books about Simón Bolívar, Eldorado, Pre-Columbian art, Spanish primers, dictionaries. I look at him, quivering with excitement, all his attention directed at the desk.

My mother appears, beaming. She's been won over. So much to *learn*, how lovely.

'Don't worry about anything. Sort everything out when we get there. This is going to be a *great adventure* – just you wait.'

Caracas, Venezuela. The Caracas Hilton, isolated in what is a large, hot version of the new Spaghetti Junction in Birmingham and no possibility of going out for a walk. There's a grand welcoming party to wish the film well. The big garish reception room is full of the most beautiful women I've ever seen congregated in one place; their skins range from black to brown to café-au-lait to olive and the effect is devastating. I remember that Miss Venezuela is usually a starry presence in the Miss World line-up and am astonished to realize that the dazzling good looks that are so extraordinary in London are the norm here in this part of South America. And there's something else, as well, the rich pungent smell of expensive perfume and leather and cigars adding up to – what? Later, unwrapping the beautiful piece of jewelry nestling in my bouquet, the gift of a stranger (no address, thank goodness, or I'd have to return it), I realize that the smell is the smell of extreme wealth. Caracas may have been beautiful once. No longer. The slums, a huge shanty town a stone's throw from our smart hotel, are large and appalling. I'm glad to get away to start filming. Our base will be Puerto Ordaz and we're to live on a Greek boat and travel by Hovercraft to our locations in the huge delta of the Orinoco. 'No!' shriek our new acquaintances. '*Nobody* goes to the Green Hell.' I've brought all the wrong clothes, as usual, and leave almost everything in Caracas. The delta will be sulphurously, stiflingly hot.

It was. We tried to settle in on board the rather run-down Greek cruise ship. It wasn't a success. The cabins were cramped and, making a stab at running a happy ship, a nameless person put out cheery messages over the ship's loudspeaker. There was a lot of 'Wakey, Wakey! Savoy Grill now open' at breakfast time. Within a week we were all desperately trying to get away from each other – and there was no means of escape. I tried to learn some Amerindian, laboriously compiling a phonetic dictionary of useful phrases I might use in the film in my role as doctor. We got on with wardrobe fittings and make-up tests and grew more and more restless – no filming in sight. On our first outing in the huge Hovercraft we encountered very rough water (no one had realized that the Pacific meets the Caribbean hereabouts and the waters are always rough). All the windows smashed in and we took on a great deal of water. My hairdresser, who was calm about most things, shrieked that this was *it*. No more Hovercraft! There was rumbled, sea-sick assent from the unit and we limped home to

the accompaniment of audible prayers. So, no way of getting
to work and, on board ship, a mutiny. We were taken off and
housed in the Rasil Hotel in Puerto Ordaz and helicopters and
trucks were ordered to get us into the rain forest and deeper
into the delta. All this was desperate for the company and
for Peter Yates, the director, who couldn't begin filming. It
was decided that it was by now cheaper to continue than
to abandon the film. Not having any responsibility beyond
knowing my lines and staying upright in the killing climate,
I was loving the beginning of the adventure. O'Toole was still
up to his eyes in books about Simón Bolívar, the liberator
of Venezuela and the difficulties – the near impossibilities –
brought out the best in him. Our companion was Philippe
Noiret who, until fairly recently, had been a senior member
of the Théâtre Nationale Populaire, the TNP, in France. We
ordered ourselves brightly colored cotton pajamas and bought
identical straw hats and called ourselves the Theater Nationale
Orinoco, the TNO – The tay en oh. We divided our leisure time
between the only two restaurants and our sitting room where
Philippe unveiled his cache of champagne and I contributed a
large Cheddar cheese and Branston pickle, sent from Jermyn
Street by Joyce. Philippe had packed *A la recherche du temps
perdu* in French and we looked at each other in amazement
as I opened my trunk and revealed my complete Proust – in
English. Working conditions were appalling but we had a
high old time. Peter Yates was kindness and forbearance itself
and somehow, slowly and painstakingly, the film got made. It
wasn't a 'smart' film but it was a really good adventure story
and how else could we ever have lived in such an outlandish
place, for so long?

On my last day I'd been filming alone, and was one of only
a few people waiting to be lifted off by helicopter. The chief of
police, an unpleasant man who'd been a heavy presence during
the last few weeks, treating the movie as a holiday, was fooling
around in one of our dug-out canoes on the Orinoco. A few

of his men stood on the bank and as we waited there, barely paying attention, tired after a long day, one of the policemen on the bank took out his gun and shot his disliked superior. As my mouth opened, the unit member standing alongside me clamped his hand on my arm and hissed, 'Shut up. Turn your back and look inland.' I obeyed and we stood there for what seemed a very long time, ignoring the cries (of joy? protest? who could tell?) behind us. The helicopter approached, my friend pushed me into it and we lifted off from the delta for the last time. The scene below was quite calm. I'd learned a great deal in four months and knew enough not to talk about what we'd witnessed. I didn't discuss it with anyone when I returned to the hotel. I was scared and fascinated in equal measure by the absence of anything resembling law and order as I'd been raised to perceive it. It was a lesson we'd had to learn quickly: that the so-called absolutes, the codes of behavior we'd learned to live by, meant nothing here in the remote corners of this continent.

Chapter Twenty-seven

'Everything that can go wrong, will go wrong and at the worst possible time.' So says Murphy's Law and the months of filming on the Orinoco convinced everyone that the Law contained an incontrovertible truth. Even after we moved to the comparative comfort of the Puerto Ordaz hotel, the Rasil, the company still faced the problem of transporting the large unit to work each day. Tracks were cut through the rainforest, tracks which within a week would become impassable under the rampantly returning vegetation. We were soon made to understand why 'nobody goes to the Green Hell'; almost invisible, clouds of small insects bit or stung every scrap of exposed flesh and the steady drip, drip, of sweat drove the sound operator mad. One night the river rose fifteen feet and our set disappeared and once, at three in the morning, I was awakened by an Irish crew member who'd been sent to fetch the all-important barge which figured hugely in the film (as Philippe Noiret's home and O'Toole's torpedo carrier) in order to sail it to a new location. Maybe no one else answered the phone or maybe he was too nervous to confide in anyone more important. 'Siân?' he whispered urgently. 'Siân – THE BARGE IS SUNK.' He'd encountered treacherous waters in the sea to the east of the delta and, alive and not too shaken, was making his long way back to base in the casual manner peculiar to those men who like working in inhospitable places. It was left to me to pass on the dreadful message which galvanized the set department into heroic, round-the-clock work as they reproduced the eccentric vessel. I worked alone for a week with 'my' Indians who played my patients in the film, all of us running for our lives day after day, while enemy planes bombed us and shot at us and the village burned all around. I returned to base thinking that the climate was beginning to get me down and that, moreover, I'd pulled a muscle in my upper back and was having trouble breathing and maybe I should let the doctor have a look at it. 'Got a few days off?' he inquired. I nodded. 'Good,' he said. 'Stay in bed. You're just recovering from pleurisy.' He understood completely that the symptoms of pleurisy could seem like part of the rather poorly feeling that afflicted us all as we struggled to get through the day. Life on the ground was difficult but the movie was largely about aeronautics and the Frank Tallman team of American aviators had been engaged to do all the Second World War stunts. They purveyed the glamour of danger and they were such stars! Their wives – blonde and glamorous – were never seen, except at night, dining with their dashing husbands. Of course, not everyone realized that Gilbert Chomat, with the camera strapped to his helicopter, had to do everything the Tallman team did. We became fast friends with Gilbert (he *wasn't* starry) and the three of us made trips over the rainforest every weekend. One day he told me, 'You know, this job is too dangerous for a family man – all my helicopter pilot friends are dead. I have four small boys and a beautiful wife in Brittany. I will do only one more movie after this – *The Blue Max* in Ireland.'

Gradually, it occurred to me that O'Toole had a purpose behind all the flying around over the massive delta of the Orinoco. We had been collecting Pre-Columbian art for some time and had been assured by a Venezuelan government official in London that there was none to be found in Venezuela. This seemed improbable, if not impossible, so he began to scout about for likely settlement areas. Sheltered spots on rivers seemed favorable and indeed when we were able to touch down and walk to the waterside, we occasionally saw signs of past occupation. One day we arrived at an unusually pleasant curve in a river tributary. We stood there breathing in the calm of the place, when O'Toole whooped – a ghastly Irish sound – and darted to the mud bank. He extracted a beautiful parrot-head handle which must, once, have been attached to a big bowl. The Pre-Columbian art was surrendering to us, falling out of the soft earth. Gilbert and I tentatively joined in the 'dig' and loaded the helicopter with twenty-five beautiful 'bits'.

After that we made frequent weekend forays, not always fruitful, but I can't remember spending more pleasurable times. We found a great many objects – almost two hundred in all, including one entire pot, very precious. I thought that the existence of art was denied through ignorance but our visit to Angel Falls opened my eyes to a darker purpose and frightened me.

O'Toole: 'Angel Falls! We've got to go there.'

'It's hopeless. They're invisible most of the time.'

'We've got to *try*, though.'

Gilbert said, '*I'd* like to try.'

Bob Willoughby added, '*I'm* in!'

Bob Willoughby, the famous prize-winning photographer, had worked on foreign locations with O'Toole before. He contributed to all the major picture magazines and now, frustrated by the physical difficulty of travelling to our locations, he made it his mission to get us to Angel Falls and then to attempt to travel to the remote reaches of the Orinoco, where it flows through the Amazonas territory, not far from the border of Venezuela and Brazil. He was preparing a book of portraits of women and was desperate to photograph the Waika tribe. He went to work to obtain permission from the government for an expedition.

'But *when*? *How*?' I asked, disbelievingly.

'Oh, later,' said O'Toole, cagily. 'Maybe not at all. Forget it.'

I knew better than to try to question him further so I *did* forget all about these wild plans until, with a free weekend ahead, I was told to pack a few toothbrushes and a change of underpants and socks and be ready to leave the Rasil Hotel at dawn. I knew we were going to try to land on top of Angel Falls. I also knew that the film company would knock us out and lock us up rather than let the four of us do anything so foolhardy. I spent a sleepless night, guilty and pleasurably excited in equal measure. We were on the little airstrip at daybreak and found Gilbert waiting at his helicopter. He explained to me that we didn't have enough fuel for such a long trip but that I wasn't to worry because O'Toole and Bob had learned from someone called 'Jungle Rudi' that there was aviation fuel stored nearby his place in Guiana. It had been there for years and the metal drums were all rusted but *no doubt* it would get us to Angel Falls and then home again. No doubt. Oh, yes. But this was no time for doubts. We were off.

The Guiana Highlands lie in a corner of Eastern Venezuela, Bolívar State. This is El Dorado, the Terra Incognita between the Orinoco and the Amazon. Sir Walter Raleigh was here; one hundred men and five rowing boats and no luck at the end of the journey. Of course, there *has* been gold here. Until the discovery of the Rand goldfields of 1886, Venezuela was the largest gold producing country in the world. We're after water not gold. Angel Falls, named after the great aviator, Jimmy Angel, whose plane got stuck on the summit.

'Going down,' shouts Gilbert over the noise of the helicopter and we land in a landscape unlike anything I've ever seen. The river and the trees where we stand are dwarfed by the *tepuis* all around; massive, squat, sheer-sided, table-top mountains that seem to belong in a work of fantastic fiction. An unkempt figure appears. Somehow, Gilbert, after flying for hours with no sign of human being, has located Jungle Rudi, who greets us. They confer and Gilbert says we'll be back later.

'Now hold this.' I'm given a small piece of helicopter and see that Gilbert seems to be taking his machine apart and the men are neatly piling up everything that can be safely detached and soon there's nothing left but the frame and the seats – no doors, no sides, nothing to hang on to except the frame of the seat in front. 'Okay,' he says cheerily. 'Let's go.' He and O'Toole are in great high spirits. The summit of Angel Falls is more often than not out of sight, blanketed in thick cloud, so it had been far from sure that we would be able to land there but now, it seems, Gilbert thinks we have a good chance. Bob and I scramble into the back seats and hang on as we whoosh up and away and the ground, only too visible beneath our dangling feet, recedes and at the same moment the rain begins. We're drenched in minutes and that, coupled with the unaccustomed, terrifying feeling of naked vulnerability in a foreign element so disorients me that it is moments before I realize that the shrieking noise I can hear is coming from me. We fly into cloud and that is calming but as we emerge from it I realize that we're going to put down on a piece of flat ground that to my fevered, disturbed senses doesn't seem to be much bigger than a grand piano. I clutch Bob's arm and scream, 'I can't look! I can't look!' 'Nor can I,' he shouts, 'and I'm taking the pictures!' As we make a perfect landing I open my eyes. 'Get out carefully on the *left side only*,' says Gilbert. 'We have no more than five minutes, then we must lift off before the cloud descends again.'

The summit of the *tepui* is spongy (no wonder Jimmy Angel's plane got stuck there) and it's covered in mosses and ferns which, so I've read, grow nowhere else. I've got gloves and pruning scissors and plastic bags in my pocket and I begin collecting. I believe Gilbert when he says that there's nothing but emptiness on the right-hand side of the helicopter and I stay on the left as I'm told, too frightened to look anywhere except at what lies directly under my feet so, standing where No Foot Has Trod is somewhat wasted on me; I'm seeing very little. The sound of water is deafening but I can hear O'Toole laughing at my RHS gloves, or my cowardice, or both.

'That's it,' calls Gilbert. 'We have to go.' We obediently

jump in and rise sideways and then, dropping slightly and moving in close to the side of the *tepui*, we come face to face with the falls as they emerge from rock and I realize that Gilbert is going to descend *with* the sheet of water thundering down the side of the mountain. I've heard of downdrafts (or is it updrafts?) and the dangers of what we are doing, but after the trials of the morning I have no fear left and I am able to admire both the beauty of the sight before me and Gilbert's skill as we gently drop 3,212 feet to the ground below. Purged and quiet, we disembark weak at the knees, floppy like rabbits and smile our gratitude at Gilbert who is looking very pleased, as well he might. We return to the fuel dump and re-fuel, Bob filtering the precious stuff through a nylon stocking while Gilbert spoons it off.

The adventures were not over and the day ended on a somber note. After reassembling the helicopter, we flew a short distance, O'Toole and Gilbert conferring and searching around – for what? Suddenly they spotted a lone figure standing on a piece of level scrub near a small shack. It was Jungle Rudi's home. We put down, switched off the engine, and I followed the group making for the little house where we sat drinking brandy and Jungle Rudi told us a fantastic tale of plots, of genocide, of danger. As he talked on and on, directing his attention to O'Toole only, speaking in an urgent, low monotone, I tried to separate the real, the probable, the believable from the improbably fantastic. I was tired and the brandy, taken on an empty stomach, was distorting my reason while at the same time in a way enhancing my acceptance of this strange scene. Rudi, his shotgun close to his right hand, talked of the destruction of huge tracts of land, flooded in the service of hydro-electric power. 'You think it is physically possible that they have warned Indian tribes impossible to locate even by expert anthropologists?' he asked rhetorically. I remembered that the student revolt I'd seen begin in the capital when we first arrived had been quelled in record time and when I'd asked how it had been stopped our Caracas friend, Mr Perez-Canto, had airily replied, 'Oh well, they shot quite a few.' I looked down at my precious bag of plants on the ground between my feet. This was a terrifying, beautiful, unruly place. I tried to rearrange my ideas of fair play and justice and my notion of the way things should be done. The intolerable was only too possible. But why was he telling this to O'Toole? 'They'll get me soon,' he said. 'They'. I began to withdraw. He could be just a lonely man, deranged by isolation. 'If you have art made by these so-called inartistic, ignorant, valueless people be very, very careful.' We had been digging and collecting for months, and yes, everyone *had* said that the Venezuelan Indians produced no art worth speaking of. That was the official line. I began to feel depressed, too tired and too inadequate to evaluate what was going on. Rudi and O'Toole walked together as we returned to the helicopter. I looked with relief at Gilbert's healthy Breton face and Bob's slightly skeptical, confident American sideways glance.

We were too tired to shout above the noise of the helicopter and sat silently as we flew over the seemingly endless rain-forest. The last quarter of an hour of the journey found us sitting up, very alert and tight-lipped, while the red light on the chopper's panel glowed red for empty as we headed for the makeshift airfield. O'Toole kissed the ground when we landed safely and we headed off to the café to toast Gilbert and his dazzling skill. Back at the hotel, we sauntered through the coffee shop as though we'd been on a short taxi ride. I felt shaky but I swung my plastic bags of plants as though they contained a little shopping. O'Toole sat down and ordered a coffee. No one was to know what we'd been up to but Bob couldn't suppress his elation as he took off at speed to develop his pictures in his makeshift dark room. 'Nice day off?' asked someone. My eyes felt as big as saucers and I was sure I didn't look normal after the wonders of the day, all too much too absorb and digest, and I could do no more than nod and smile as I headed to bed and oblivion.

The Spanish Conquistadors had left behind forts which, unlike any subsequent buildings, caught the breeze and made the days bearable. The hospital scenes in the movie took place in such a building and while we were shooting these sequences the girls and my mother came to join us in Puerto Ordaz and made the long journey through the rain forest to watch the filming in the fort. Watching people filming is not a spectator sport and they were relieved to be let off to explore the pleasures of the American oil company compound which had, glory of glories, a swimming pool and a Coca-Cola machine. Even the Caracas Hilton was more fun for the ten and seven year old girls. So good to see the three of them; my mother had done a terrific job in my absence and under her coaching Kate had passed the entrance examination to three good schools and was all set to go to our first choice: the North London Collegiate School for Girls. My mother had a determined gleam in her eye as she talked about Pat's future. Pat, blonde, immaculate – a stranger to bad hair days – shrugged and smiled non-committally. My mother permitted herself a half-smile and I could see that Pat had a date with my mother's classroom-for-one in the big kitchen in Guyon House.

When they left, we embarked on the last phase of the movie. Fate was kind to our director, Peter Yates, who had struggled so hard against awful odds and filming was almost uneventful. When it was over, there was a concerted, mad rush for the exit. Our cases remained unpacked, however, and I assumed that we were to make a leisurely departure, returning via Caracas, the capital, where we had friends to visit. The telegram from our lawyer, Denise Sée, puzzled me. 'Poor Kate and Pat,' it read, 'to think of them as orphans . . .' Orphans? 'What does she mean?' I asked O'Toole. He looked at the telegram and tossed it into the wastepaper basket with a laugh. 'Good old Denise.

Nice try,' he said. 'Try? What?' I persisted. 'Oh, everyone is behaving hysterically,' he said, soothingly. 'Pay no attention. We're going to make that little trip I was talking about and Dr. Inga Goetz is coming down from Caracas to help us on our way.' Dr. Goetz was an anthropologist and I'd read her book about the Yanomama Indians. I'd also read about the difficulty of reaching the head waters of the Orinoco and I'd thrilled to the accounts of head-hunters and abandoned missions and missing travellers. It had made exciting reading, all right, and I was rather inclined to leave it at that, but already Bob was organizing water purifying tablets and was all set for the trip. O'Toole's contribution to the packing was a couple of bottles of brandy and a few gifts of tin kettles and machetes and sheets of Yanomama words he'd been given by Dr. Goetz. 'You could learn these,' he said encouragingly. I didn't waste time arguing. It was very clear that O'Toole was going up the Orinoco and if he was going then I was going. I visited the only store in town, and found three plastic ponchos, folded small. I couldn't find anything else to buy. And it was difficult deciding what to wear, so far from the Army & Navy Stores or Tropicadilly in London. In the end I wore a cotton Yves St Laurent safari jacket and a Herbert Johnson cotton bush hat (they qualified as suitable because of the words 'safari' and 'bush'). My trousers were stuffed into a pair of Charles Jourdan 'riding' boots. I remembered buying an anti-bug burning device from Harrods. It lay unopened in my trunk along with the complete set of *A la recherche du temps perdu* which I'd intended to read and hadn't. I slipped it into my little rucksack along with the brandy and a toothbrush. It didn't seem enough somehow, so I added some chocolate bars.

Even so, we seemed to be woefully unprepared but I could see O'Toole's reasoning. We only had two or three weeks at our disposal. If we loitered, trying to make adequate preparations, we simply wouldn't make the trip at all. 'Remember,' he said, 'Englishmen once went up Everest in tennis shoes with a packet of sandwiches.' I supposed he was exaggerating but I rather agreed with the notion that anything was possible until it turned out to be impossible. 'Okay,' I said and bought more chocolate.

Dr. Goetz arrived; German, tall, middle-aged and very sprightly. We were in business. The four of us flew in an alarmingly small plane to the small settlement called Ayacucho (I could have done without being told that this meant 'corner of death'). There, she helped us find a suitable small boat (the soapdish, O'Toole christened it) and a pair of guides. They were incredibly uncharming and shook their heads gloomily whenever Dr. Goetz addressed them. We only had room for one man but they were adamant that they wouldn't accompany us alone and conveyed to Dr. Goetz that they would only go 'so far'. It seemed that most of the missions along the river had been abandoned and only two remained. Dr. Goetz would accompany us to the first one and persuade them to let us stay overnight. As we began our journey the following morning, sun shone and the river was alarmingly wide, as it had been where we'd been filming hundreds of miles to the east. The noise of the outboard was deafening and we were silent as we stared at the 'green wall' which was the vast rain forest on both sides. At least the river had a shine on its mud-colored surface. O'Toole had decided that he wouldn't bother with water purifiers so we were to start drinking river water as soon as possible 'to get our systems going'. Bob looked incredulous. He was weighed down with the latest thing in camera equipment and water purifiers.

It took us a day to reach the mission; a day spent looking at not very much. It seems absurd but remote jungles and rain forests viewed from the river do present dull, almost blank, high 'walls' of green. I began the journey sitting up straight on the bit of bench that was to be mine during the entire journey, eagerly looking about. After about four hours I sat slumped, wishing I could at least identify the trees which made up 'the wall'. It looked impenetrable and I wondered uneasily how we'd manage when we pulled in.

The landing place looked very small when it appeared, protruding into the immense river. We tied up and Dr. Goetz, who was familiar with the place, led us through the trees on to a serviceable pathway which led in turn to the clearing and the somewhat ramshackle mission building. The nuns were welcoming and indicated that they would be very happy for us to eat with them and to stay overnight. We were ravenous and fell on the food which was laid on a trestle table in a dilapidated room, bare of furniture save for a few benches. The meat was wild pig and was delicious. We were shown to small cells containing narrow wooden-framed beds with straw mattresses. I scarcely remembered undressing and the sun was high in the sky when I woke and scrambled to get ready to leave. Dr. Goetz sat with us and gave us a last briefing before she returned to Ayacucho and then to Caracas. The bad news was that one of our guides refused to come any further. It seems he was now voluble with horror stories of the dangers ahead but I couldn't understand a word he said. Dr. Goetz said that we should of course be careful but that in all probability we wouldn't find any native Indians. She had made thirteen properly organized expeditions and not all of them had been successful in this regard. She wished us luck and reminded us to use our Yanomama words, especially *Shori noji* (good friends) and to be as cheerful and as amusing as possible, should we be fortunate enough to find ourselves surrounded by the Yanomama.

Rested and fed, we were in high good spirits as we set off on our own and the rain began to fall. It didn't just fall, it leapt on us and jumped up and down. I fished out the plastic ponchos and we each retreated into a little brightly colored tent. We were wet by the time we arranged them over our little places (Bob draped his over his cameras) and then the rain penetrated the neck fastening and ran up our arms as we tried to smoke. We couldn't even look up, the rain was blinding and the noise was deafening as it landed on the metal soapdish and bounced off our ponchos. There was now a wall of rain between us and the wall of the jungle. There was nothing to do except stare silently at the floor and occasionally glance sideways. The remaining guide was malevolently fed up, as well he might be. I'd given him my chocolate bar, which he accepted with palpable disdain. I wished I could speak to him; we might have enjoyed a bit of a moan together. We seemed to have been travelling for a week already and I thought I sensed him wondering where we would sleep and would there be anything to eat except chocolate. Bob and O'Toole were full of high resolve and in no mood to be bothered with trivial details.

Out of the corner of my left eye I see something – the first *different* something I've seen all day. On a smooth outcrop of rock shining in the rain, backed by the dark green jungle wall, stands a person – a small, stocky figure, legs braced, arms raised, holding a huge bow, taller than himself, the arrow poised for flight. Snuggled under my pixie hood I figure the bow is six feet high, so the man is only four feet something. The arrow is trained on the soapdish. I nudge O'Toole with my foot. He's sitting opposite me, staring at the ground. He looks at me through the rain. As subtly as I know how, I indicate the bank to my left. He looks and sees the naked figure. As he stiffens, Willoughby, behind me, follows his gaze and automatically his hands tighten on his camera. 'No,' breathes O'Toole. 'Leave it.' Our guide is oblivious, thank God, and we pass up river – oh, so slowly – and the arrow slowly swings around to follow us until we pass out of sight into the rain-soaked dusk. We can't discuss what happened, conversation is impossible, and we plow on. In a way, that little incident has made me less afraid. We've gone over Niagara in a barrel and there's no going back and that makes everything simpler. I no longer have any hope of knowing what time of day it is, or indeed what day it is, but suddenly the rain stops and we see a lawn – I swear – a lawn. It's like a vision, too Pre-Raphaelite bright to be real, and there, standing on the edge of the lawn is a figure in black robes with a huge white Old Testament mane of hair and long, spade beard. It says something for my state of mind and the amount of brandy I'd ingested that I have no recollection in what language we communicated with this priest. But we dined with him in a ramshackle shed and he showed us his work. He was making a dictionary. Yanomama to – what? I'd never make a decent explorer. I don't remember. I fancy it was Armenian. He looked Greek. There was no one left in his mission. And there were no missions left up river. He told us there had been trouble with the Yanomama – there was danger and we should turn back, now.

We ate bits of meat picked from small rib cages (what *were* we eating, I wondered). Now that we were at rest and the rain had stopped, we could hear noises again: birds shrieked and later frogs croaked and crickets filled the air with their sound. We slept in hammocks. I wasn't worried about what lay in store. Only later did I realize that I was living entirely in the present.

Onward up river. Against advice, we are not carrying guns (just as well, I think – my aim is probably as bad as my sense of direction). The rain is intermittent now and the boys have thrown away their red cloaks. Mine is stuffed under my seat, just in case. It's so incredibly boring, this trip up the exotic river. I'm now thinking of the jungle wall as green concrete. Where are we? How far have we come? What will the source of the river – miles away – look like, if we get there? Is it worth it? Plod on. Drink brandy and river water. Smile at guide a lot. He doesn't smile back once. I'm half asleep most of the time. There's a hallucinatory quality about my waking moments.

A small girl appears in a tiny clearing in the forest wall. O'Toole shouts at the guide to pull into the bank. The water is high but he manages to moor near a small spit of land and we disembark. Reality intrudes as the small child grabs O'Toole's hand and begins pulling him into the forest. Bob and I fluster out of the boat and set off at a run after them. The guide doesn't budge. Waist-high branches and creepers slash across our bodies as we try to keep up with the pair ahead. The little girl is so small that she can run under the impediments. How is O'Toole coping? We're slowing down to a trot and, breathless and scratched, we reach a clearing. Ahead is what looks like a huge, blond ski-slope and I realize it's a massive thatched roof made of palm leaves yellowed with age – it must reach from forty feet down to a little wall-opening just four feet high. The small girl drags O'Toole through the opening. Keen not to be left behind, we half crawl, half stumble after them. We are in a big *shabono*. I've never seen one from the air but I'm told that from above they look like doughnuts. From ground level they are much more elegant, the roof rising to an open circle, and below as many as forty families occupy a segment each of the circle; hammocks swing in two or three layers over fires which can be reached by hand from the lowest hammock. Behind the hammocks against the wall are makeshift shelves, holding little more than baskets, it seems, and on ground level, pet birds and parrots play. Babies are at all times attached to their mothers. Dusk is falling, it's raining again. The noise of the rain on leaves mingles with the shrill noise of female voices. *That's* what's so odd. There are no men here. And Willoughby and O'Toole have disappeared. I remember what Dr. Goetz had told me, 'Say "*Shori noji*" – often! Smile! Lift your eyebrows as often as possible. And allow them to explore your body. They need to know what you are.'

There must be fifty small, small women pressing around me, not one reaching my diaphragm. Tiny hands pull at my St Laurent shirt. The buttons give (well done, back at the workroom). My black silk trousers give way at the waist and rip down the length of the zipper. My hat is torn off and my hair detached from its rubber band. They scream with laughter – these small, big-breasted women – I'm revealed as an androgynous, flat chested, wide shouldered, slim hipped, flat stomached – what? So much exercise, so much disciplined dieting to a perfect catwalk size eight to ten has resulted in hilarious entertainment for the ladies of the upper reaches of the Orinoco. I tie my clothes back on – I'm not enjoying this much but am trying to keep smiling – and hope that my genuine goodwill is going to get me through the ensuing night. O'Toole and Willoughby appear from the side of the *shabono*. It seems that most of the men are away on a hunt. I'm so dazed I don't ask how they *know* this. 'This is quite lucky for us.'

'We're to be taken to sleep now.'

A little group of women walk us back into the forest until we come to another clearing and there we see a group of nuns. Now, I do feel I'm hallucinating. I'd read that some of the Yanomama, while not accepting Christianity, quite like to live near a mission in order to trade goods. This must be the second of the last remaining missions. These sweet-faced women lead us to a trestle table and yet again we eat unidentifiable bits of meat attached to small ribcages. After much nodding and miming of gratitude we retreat to snug hammocks under a broken-down barn roof. I remember my Harrods anti-bug coils. I light the coils and place them under our hammocks and I lie there listening to the forest noises, looking up at the broken roof, wishing I hadn't read so much about vampire bats.

All night the air was filled with music. The women, alone in the *shabono*, ululated and sang for the success of the hunt. I made that up. They sang all night but I don't know what they were singing about. The men were away hunting. They may have been wishing them success or just enjoying a hen night.

In the morning we thank the nuns and make our way back to the *shabono*. The women are having a kind of lie-in after the musical efforts of the previous night or maybe this is how they spend their days. They lie in their hammocks playing with their babies, decorating them with paint and feathers. The older children play on the floor with the family pets. One woman is working; she is weaving a basket, lying down in her hammock, using her two hands and one foot. The vine is held away from her by her huge big toe. I notice that they all have large big toes that stand away from the other toes. A few men appear and try to engage O'Toole and Bob in some kind of game. We can't work out what they want but we do a lot of eyebrow work and smile obligingly. The women roll out of their hammocks and we follow them as they all trot a little way away from the *shabono* (they never seem to move at walking pace; everything is done at a run). Ah – it's to be a contest of strength. They're producing the huge bows and arrows we saw the young man holding on the river bank. O'Toole is almost twice as tall as these men, the contest seems unfair. Everyone is in huge good humor. Some of the men are laughing so much they can barely stay standing. They're calling O'Toole something and I write it down so that Dr. Goetz can translate it later. The men give O'Toole a bow and arrow and stand alongside him. He's not a bad archer and now he good humoredly prepares to shoot with them. Their arrows fly into the air and O'Toole is left struggling. He cannot release the arrow no matter how he tries. They now lie on the floor, they're laughing so much. These tiny men have shoulders and arms like heavyweight boxers at the peak of fitness. We are now *loved*. O'Toole is patted on his bottom and is obviously being told what a great fellow he is. We trot out our bits of Yanomama and throw in lots of '*Shori noji*'s; greater harmony could not be imagined. The women have got used to me and stroke my clothes and my flat chest, fondly amused this morning. We can't stay, fearful that they might feel they have to feed us – and they don't seem to have anything in the way of food. Almost all of them accompany us (at a run) through the rainforest and down to our boat. The 'guide' and boatman looks appalled and stands apart, hatchet-faced, as we indulge in a prolonged leave-taking and O'Toole produces gifts from our little store of machetes and beads and tin cans. I've never had such a social success anywhere.

As soon as we set off up river it begins to rain again. I can tell that the river is very high. Today, we're seeing things. They were there before so have we only now learned to notice them? I can't believe that but we are now seeing birds as they sweep across the water: macaws, I recognize; dark green kingfishers also – although they don't look much like the kingfishers of Carmarthenshire. As I look at the jungle wall, I see an ibis, high up, miss its footing and fall gracelessly down four or five 'floors' of tree. It finds a landing place and, effortlessly elegant again, sits there, pretending nothing embarrassing happened. I catch O'Toole's eye and see that he has been observing the same comical scene.

The rain stops and we are able to look around again. I don't know what time it is – my watch became waterlogged days ago – and it is very hard to be sure how many days we have been travelling. There is a smooth rock and a piece of beaten earth alongside it that could be a landing place. We are very tired and very hungry and quite disoriented (probably a bit drunk as well). Pulling in, we set off into the rainforest. There *is* a path of sorts. The vines and branches lash cruelly across our waists and chests. We're too tall for this vegetation. On we go, each sunk in our thoughts, and suddenly there is another *shabono* but the drama is *outside* this time – we gradually realize we have walked straight into a hallucinogenic ceremony. There are no women in sight. The men are naked, save for the belt which holds the foreskin tucked up in its correct 'public' place. We freeze on the spot and no one acknowledges our presence. Squatting down, one man, clad only in a loincloth, is about to blow the hallucinogenic dust into the nostrils of another man. I've read about this often so I know what to expect but nothing prepares one for the explosion of mucus; the eyes, the nose, the mouth – everything runs violently. As I'd read, this pain seems to go on for half an hour; then, for the next half hour, the shaman (the wise man) receives auditory instructions and advice for the tribe, then he goes to the river and washes and takes another half hour to recover. So we watch the full one and a half hour experience.

Instinctively, we felt that we shouldn't linger in this place. There was none of the friendly curiosity we had experienced earlier. We laid our gifts on the floor, machetes and tin kettles, and while they were unsmilingly picked up and examined we nodded and smiled, said, '*Shori noji!*' and tried to melt into the forest, backing away as casually as we were able. I had found the ceremony alarming. Bob, of course, had snatched some photographs and O'Toole, who prided himself – with reason – on his nose for trouble, murmured, 'Don't hang about, my dears. Back to the soapdish.' Once we were out of sight of the *shabono* we turned and ran back to the river and continued towards the source. We didn't make it but we stopped after travelling a very respectable distance. The BBC was in Venezuela making a documentary that year. They were making a proper expedition in a Hovercraft with guards carrying submachine guns and it seems that we managed to get four hundred miles further up river than they did. And this gave us a good deal of childish satisfaction at the time.

The return to Ayacucho dragged. We had none of the excitement of the beginning of the adventure and time was running out and we ought to be thinking of returning to England where, in a few weeks, filming would be resumed in the studio. O'Toole was in a 'Let's push on' mood and we took only brief rests on the long journey. The guide was handsomely rewarded for his pains. For an unguarded moment he looked surprised as he swiftly counted the notes O'Toole thrust at him. He hadn't realized that he'd been working for one of the great over-payers of the Western world. We hired a Cessna in Ayacucho and flew to Caracas. Coffee and beds and baths and a spot of scrambled egg were just beginning to feature in my thoughts when we flew into a violent storm. I was too tired to be frightened and looked at the men in disbelief as the little plane was thrown about and the pilot began to shout incoherent bits of advice to us over his shoulder. It was obvious that we had to escape from the storm so down we went – all the way down, in fact. The pilot managed to land and we stood in the middle of nowhere with our bits of luggage – mainly Bob's equipment – until the pilot succeeded in raising a local taxi who was startled but game when we asked him to drive to Caracas, five or six hours away. Bob and O'Toole pressed a great deal of money into the pilot's hand and off we lurched – it was a *very* old car; all of it rattled but we slept like infants and it got us to the Hilton, pulling up with a noisy flourish alongside the Bentleys and the Rolls-Royces.

Bob's wife, Dorothy, was waiting for him. 'We're going to Machu Picchu,' they said. 'Not without us,' said O'Toole and I went upstairs to pack and change the air tickets and telegraph London to say that we were safe and *almost* on the way home. I called Dr. Goetz before we left Venezuela. She told us that the name O'Toole had been given was 'High Mountain'.

We rendezvoused with the Willoughbys in Cuzco and obediently followed all the rules for acclimatizing to this altitude; no alcohol and a four-hour sleep, then very slow movement for a while. In the 'best' hotel our sheets were grubby and I took them off and we fell asleep under the rough blankets. (Why should we assume that the blankets were cleaner than the sheets, I thought lazily, and at the same moment thought, 'What does it matter?')

Awakening, we strolled – slowly – around Cuzco, marvelling along with all the other visitors at the wonderful stonework. O'Toole and I have a special interest in stone. Connemara in Ireland is a land of granite, the drystone walls of Ireland are beautiful and varied. Looking at the massive drystone walls of Cuzco, we decided that we would try to build a drystone house in Connemara. Like all the visitors, we wanted to go to Machu

Picchu. In 1970 it was still an uncomfortable trip and along with a cartload of other tourists we felt slightly adventurous. There was no place to stay, it was a bit like going to Petra ten years previously, and we were well able to rest curled up under a rock. Nothing can prepare one for Machu Picchu and nothing one can say can add to the descriptions or convey the wonder of it.

We moved on to Lima where O'Toole had a contact in the art world. Bob and his wife left us after the one conventional meal we were to enjoy and they also gave us money; we had run out but there was something called a credit card and it gave you money, no matter where you were. O'Toole and I were mystified and impressed and grateful. Lima was the noisiest city I had ever been in – or was I now unused to urban din? O'Toole went off to 'meet a man – don't ask' and I 'Wait here'. To pass the time, I pressed my dried plants (my mother would be fascinated to see them) and repacked our luggage and sat looking at the dark street. This city scared me somewhat, though I didn't know why. At four in the morning O'Toole returned, exhausted, bearing a few plastic shopping bags. 'Pack these – don't look. God, I'm tired.' Fully clothed, he stretched out on the bed and slept. This man slept better and longer than anyone I knew. Dutifully, I didn't 'look' and I packed the objects in the luggage. When O'Toole woke, we left for the airport and home. In Bogotá we landed unexpectedly and the plane was kept on the ground for hours. 'Sorry, love,' he said. 'I think the game's up. Don't forget you really *don't* know what's in those bags.' I tried to read and not contemplate the punishment for the unlawful liberating of works of art. Suddenly we were off! I couldn't look at him. It was the luck of the Irish, dammit. I felt sick.

In the Green Room of Guyon House, my mother and Kate and Pat and Liz and Manolita unpack and drink tea. 'Oh, thank God for a decent cup of tea,' groans the Irishman. 'Where's the jewelry?' 'What jewelry?' 'You *know* – the

jewelry from Lima.' 'Was there any? You said not to look.'
'Oh Jaysus – I'm surrounded by eejits.' 'Wait, wait,' soothes
my mother and goes to search through the rubbish. 'Is this
what you were looking for?' she says, holding up a ratty plastic
shopping bag. 'Could be,' and he drops the most beautiful old
necklaces over my head. The Pre-Columbian masks are put
aside to be sent to our British Museum friend who will 'blow'
the flattened gold back into shape and then they will be sent
to Claude de Muzak in Paris to be mounted. We all look at
the beautiful, battered, soft gold faces. The girls stroke them
and I can't feel too guilty about any of this.

We leave for Ireland almost at once. Arriving at the cottage
in Connemara, I unpack my plants from Angel Falls and see
the *Irish Times* on the table. 'Air Tragedy', I read and before
I pick up the paper I know it will tell me of Gilbert's death
on *The Blue Max*. A small piece of something or other fell
from above and cut Gilbert's rotor blade. It only takes a little
something to destroy a helicopter and in this case five lives
in Brittany. We look out over the fuchsia hedges, down to
the Atlantic; the never far-away melancholy of this piece of
Ireland rises up to chime with the desolation we're feeling.

Chapter Twenty-eight

Since my schooldays I had never had anything much to do with people of my sex and age. I spent the most interesting times working with adults where I was 'the girl'. Then as I grew up and played leading parts, I worked largely with men. The other women I worked with were usually considerably older than I was. In private life I was a wife – a wife obliged to keep her private life very private and defined to a large extent by the identity of a husband. As a young mother I felt redefined by my children. Was it my imagination, or were young women years ago constantly in some kind of competition with each other? Certainly there were, as always, too few jobs for too many of us actresses so that competition was understandable. Those women whose ambition was to marry well seemed also to pursue a solitary path to their goal. As the wife of a rich, talented, glamorous man I was from time to time painfully aware of the unabashed, predatory behavior of the women we met. From time to time I was astonished to observe that even women whom I regarded as friends were not above making a barely veiled attempt at seducing my husband.

Safe within my small circle of women whom I liked and admired, women whom it was not possible to define especially by their gender – well behaved, hard working, amusing, clever, good looking – I looked out somewhat nervously at the liberated woman of the late Sixties and early Seventies.

So when I was asked to play Mrs Pankhurst, the leader of the Suffragettes, in *Shoulder to Shoulder*, a six-part series that Ken Taylor had written about the movement and the women involved in it, even as I unhesitatingly accepted the producer

Verity Lambert's offer, at the same moment I thought, 'Oh, this is going to be hell on wheels – six months, virtually living with fifty women.' Half the plays were to be directed by Moira Armstrong, the other three by Waris Hussein – how would he cope with us all? – and even one of the camera operators was female. I could imagine the rows, the tears, the gossiping, the cliques, the jealousies that lay ahead.

The range and diversity of the personalities cooped up together in close quarters for long hours each day as we worked six, sometimes seven, days a week gave rise to amusement and absorbing interest rather than irritation. I realized that I'd turned some kind of corner when I found myself polishing Patricia Quinn's skin-tight leather dress – which she was wearing at the time. It had been bought in a shop in the King's Road in which I wouldn't have been seen dead but I could appreciate that it looked terrific on Pat. I played Mrs Pankhurst, the leader of the Suffragette Movement, Patricia was my daughter, Christabel, and Angela Down played Sylvia. Angela was as reserved as Pat was extrovert, I hovered somewhere in between and we became the little family which was the nucleus of the drama. Georgia Brown developed the idea for the series along with Midge McKenzie and Georgia played a leading part as well. Ken Taylor was the writer and as we all became experts on the politics of the turn of the century he grew to dread our pleas for extra scenes – especially 'good' bits of the story that we didn't want left out. If he'd listened to us the series would have been fifty hours long. Verity Lambert, the producer, presided effortlessly over the huge undertaking, helped by the best of buccaneering company managers (shortly to become a producer himself) Graham Benson who, on our first early morning filming call in the damp, grey countryside outside Halifax (which was playing Manchester, 1890), appeared in the makeshift make-up room bearing trays of champagne and orange juice 'to cheer things up a bit'.

We stayed cheered up for the next seven months, all of us running more or less complicated private lives, and no one pleaded tiredness or illness or heartbreak or buckled under the worries of organizing homes and husbands and parents and children by remote control. There wasn't one woman who gave less than her best and I was buoyed up like a cork on the ocean. The men in our lives were a trifle bemused, as well they might be. Many of them found themselves at home while we worked late. This was a different kind of life we were leading and it made us all a little different. Waris Hussein, who shared the directing with Moira Armstrong, accompanied us when we let off steam occasionally and went out on the town, dancing for hours, and Graham Benson made sure we were all packed off home in good order. This was all quite unlike working in a more usual mixed-sex show where the men went out on the spree and the women rushed home to catch up with the housekeeping. I'd never had such a good time and my confidence began to grow. Observing how other women struggled to reconcile the many demands made on them with varying degrees of success and often with utter failure, I began to realize that it was impossible to do everything properly; that feeling slightly inadequate and very guilty all the time was a state common to us all. The current wisdom was that it was easy to Have it All, to Do it All. I had been photographed many times in my 'perfect' room in my 'fashionable' clothes with my clean, 'adorable' looking children, 'successfully combining my busy working life with my beautiful domestic existence', as the caption would read. What a lie! I thought, with relief. I knew now that I wasn't alone in finding the effort of running three or four lives almost impossibly difficult. It was comforting to feel part of a huge, struggling, largely silent sisterhood. Men weren't expected to help at all; if women wanted to work they had, somehow, to manage everything so as to inconvenience no one and many of us learned for the first time to admit failure and to ask for and give help.

More than a few of us had health worries as well. 'Pains peculiar to ladies', as I'd seen them quaintly described, were ignored, as were minor illnesses and even major illnesses were overcome with a minimum of drama. Both Verity and I were hospitalized with suspected breast cancer. When we went to visit our producer after her exploratory operation, she was holding an IV fluid bottle in one hand, a telephone in the other and gesturing at the champagne with her foot.

The moment that there was an indication that I might have breast cancer, Gerry Slattery whisked me back from Bristol where I was spending the weekend with O'Toole, who was doing a season of plays at the Old Vic. I was booked into the London Clinic at once, pausing only to tell Verity that I'd be back at work as soon as possible. She was reassuringly matter-of-fact; with fifty women on board for six months, these crises were depressingly frequent. The watchword was 'Don't get excited; just deal with the situation minute by minute.' O'Toole was more fearful than I was but he went on rehearsing.

It was winter and before I drove down to Harley Street for surgery, I went to one of my favorite Hampstead places, the High Hill bookshop, to order the Christmas books for the girls and for my friend Ricci Burns and his mother, Lilian. Standing there, suddenly I wasn't able to maintain my chirpy attitude and I wondered morbidly if I would *be* there in Guyon House at Christmas time. I trailed back up the hill, feeling sorry for myself. There was no one at home in whom to confide. My mother most certainly wasn't to know; not many years past she'd survived a double mastectomy and I didn't want her to have to confront another, frightening cancer episode. It would be silly to worry the girls and I had waved them off to school as casually as I was able. As usual, my only confidant was Ricci Burns. I called him and he didn't let me down. 'Oh, my God, I can see it all! You're sitting in that house and you've convinced yourself you're going to die! Stop it! Don't be a drama queen!' I took his advice and stopped organizing my funeral service.

O'Toole came to London from Bristol to receive an award and called in to the hospital on the eve of my operation. I think that hospitals and illness distress him beyond measure and am glad when he hurries off. As I'm on the brink of feeling alone and sorry for myself, the nurse comes in bearing a massive, magnificent bunch of red roses; it looks incongruous in this expensive but spartan room. When I look at the note I rejoin the land of 'normal', functioning people. It reads, 'Wear these in your hair tonight, love Ricci'. Ricci – thank God for him. I feel like Frida Kahlo in a Buñuel film as I snuggle down to sleep, broadly smiling, surrounded by red blossoms.

After the operation the next day when I came round, they give me my 'Permission to perform a mastectomy' form to tear up because the papilloma which had bled so alarmingly had proved to be benign. My first thought is to call the BBC to say I'll be back at work the following day. I call home. Lionel isn't available to bring me home; he's picking up actors and bringing them to Guyon House before they all set off for another week's rehearsal at Bristol. A little groggy, I thank my nurse and go out into Harley Street to look for a taxi. I feel lucky, standing there, listing slightly to starboard, under the weight of my roses. At home, the Green Room is alight with laughter and story-telling – there are some expert raconteurs in there, sitting and then jumping up to take advantage of the small stage. It's lovely but it's not for me today. O'Toole and I have a short, relieved moment together but I can tell that I'm expected to have moved on. That moment when I was at the center of the domestic stage is over. Downstairs, Lionel looks mightily relieved when I flash him a grin. (He would have wanted to pick me up and bring me home, I know.) My mother, knowing nothing, looks a bit disgruntled that I've been away for a night for no good reason. Climbing the stairs from the basement kitchen I meet the troupe setting off for Bristol. I have another brief moment with O'Toole, then they're gone.

As the big Georgian door closes a profound silence descends on the house. Thanks to Manolita, everything looks beautiful. The big hall with its black and white tiled floor glows with the dull brass of the Persian chest, opened to reveal a tumult of oriental silks. The Bró paintings with their violent, vivid mop-headed trees are startling against the grey walls. The stairwell is hung with a large stone bas relief from China and rubbings from Angkor and deceptively quiet Picasso etchings. Turning into the bedroom with its big bow window shuttered against the winter light and, beyond the garden, the men's surgical ward of New End Hospital, I know that three floors below me, Scobie, the bulldog, is plodding to and fro under the fig tree, mute and mutinous; willing someone to let him in. Not I. Not today. My mother and Manolita will be clearing away the cups and glasses and ashtrays in the Green Room. Liz is in the nursery, the children are at school and the bedroom is extra silent. I drop my bag and sit on the bed facing my treasured Louis XIV bureau plat. The walls of cupboards are shut and behind them, I know, there is perfect order; hanging cupboards filled with clean, pressed clothes, blouses filed in order of color, trousers, all black and white. Shoes, polished and lined up on brass rods – all fitted with their shoe-trees – everything rising unseen to the high ceiling. Gloves are neatly arranged – leather, cotton, suede, string. There are monogrammed handkerchiefs and underwear in scented bags. I know exactly what lies, invisible, behind the blank walls, the multitude of potentially chaotic garments which could fill the calm room, unfurling themselves, filling it with color and confusion. Manolita's devotion and my anxiety keeps everything at bay, subdued and in its place. There is nothing in this beautiful room to indicate that I live here. Turning back the dark tapestry spread on the bed I switch on my bedside lamp. Lying down, I think gratefully that when I am alone, there are no surprises in this room, Manolita has seen

With Alan Badel in *Man and Superman* in 1966 (*London Life*)

(*above*) With O'Toole before curtain up in *Man and Superman*

Marie Löhr, my friend and my mother in *Man and Superman* (*Vivienne, London*)

With Rex Harrison in *Platonov*
in 1971 (© *BBC*)

As Ursula Mossbank in
Goodbye Mr Chips

(*above*) With Patrick Barr in
Tennessee Williams' play *The
Eccentricities of a Nightingale*
(*Surrey Advertiser*)

Fashion shot with my best
friend, Ricci Burns

The edge of Angel Falls with O'Toole
(*Bob Willoughby*)

Being explored by the
Yanomama (*Bob
Willoughby*)

Enjoying the moment as Peter fails to pull the
bow any further (*Bob Willoughby*)

Making friends (*Bob Willoughby*)

The house at Connemara on the
Sky Road

Kate and Pat laying the
foundation stone

As Mrs Pankhurst in *Shoulder to
Shoulder* (© BBC)

As Hesione in the BBC production of
Heartbreak House in 1977, with
(*from left to right*) Sir John Gielgud,
Lesley-Anne Down and David Waller
(© *BBC*)

The BBC Television production
of *How Green Was My Valley*
in 1975 (© *BBC*)

(*right*) With Brian
Blessed in *I,
Claudius* in 1976
(© *BBC*)

(*below*) With Dan
Massey in *The Gay
Lord Quex* at the
Albery Theatre in
1975 (*Zoë Dominic*)

'The last of the summer wine' – *Daily Express*

With O'Toole and the girls during the filming of *Caligula* in 1976 (*Jerry Bauer*)

As *Boudicca* in the Thames Television production (© *Thames Television*)

With Robin, just after our wedding, in 1979

In my first musical, *Pal Joey,* performed at the Half-Moon and at the Albery Theatre in 1980

With director David Lynch in *Dune* in 1983

With Keith Baxter in *The Inconstant Couple* at Chichester
(*Sophie Baker*)

As Mrs Patrick Campbell in *Dear Liar* – this is the John Bates costume which got its own round of applause
(© *Catherine Ashmore*)

After delivering the Royal Television Society
lecture, support from the inner circle of friends:
(*from left to right*) William Corlett, Kevin Moore,
Bryn Ellis, Pat O'Toole and Edward Duke

In the sunshine with June Havoc in Connecticut
in 1992

to that, and I am comforted by our unspoken stand against the misrule and chaos that threaten to engulf me and this house. Yea, though I walk through the valley of the shadow of death, my folded clothes, my shiny shoes, my gloves and my clean handkerchiefs shall comfort me.

Lying there, I know no one will disturb me until the girls get back from school. Few people know this ex ex-directory line and anyway, who would call me in this fortress? I realize that I *had* said goodbye to all this, thinking of my own mortality in a way I had not done since I was a little girl, much preoccupied with death.

The next day I was back at work, feeling terrific.

I was on the whole blessed with rude good health but illness dogged much of our lives together. When I first met O'Toole he was living with Ken and Doriah Griffith in Belgravia and Doriah confided in me, half-admiring, half-scandalized, 'He sits there drinking alternate gulps of white ulcer medicine and Scotch. *And* he's smoking Gauloises!' During the Stratford season his ulcers got worse and he was urged to go into hospital. More or less organizing his own treatment, O'Toole ordered gallons of white 'stomach medicine' and the kitchen was piled high with Complan. Naturally, he continued to stay up late and drink and smoke prodigiously. When he returned to London after the season, he was completely well again. His extraordinary restorative power, aided by a huge capacity for sleep and a healthy appetite, continued to stand him in good stead. My mother and I worried quietly and were mightily relieved when he underwent a cure before each job. And of course he emerged at the end of a job tired but healthy, after a prolonged bout of discipline. It was the in-between times that were difficult.

Chapter Twenty-nine

In the early Seventies, inexplicable episodes of bad health began to occur. A few years earlier we had acquired the small cottage with a piece of land in 'O'Toole country' on the West Coast of Ireland. Our plan was to acquire yet more of the adjoining land and to build ourselves a family home. As we planned the new house we all squashed into the one-storey croft with two bedrooms and a living room, lean-to bathroom and kitchen, an attic bedroom for the girls under the roof, one turf fire for heat and a Calor gas cooker. Even when I was working and couldn't accompany them, the girls and Liz and my mother spent all the school holidays in Connemara. The girls were given a life that almost duplicated my childhood, disappearing after breakfast and returning at night to a house where there was no television or radio; just talk and books by night and freedom and security by day for girls who had at one time been on the receiving end of kidnap threats in London. In her seventies, my mother was returned to her youth. Her country skills were recollected and became useful again. Isolated and a bit out of our depth, we were dependent on her store of knowledge and that, I suppose, is what ought to happen in a family, but modern life is rarely conducive to this happy state.

The cottage boasted a garden which had been neglected for years. Brambles and sycamore seedlings, twenty-foot-high thickets of old hydrangea bushes, flowering green-white in the shade, stands of bamboo thickening over the kitchen garden. The soil was superb; friable and dark, chocolate brown (obviously this garden had once been beautifully looked after) and everywhere in the small front garden and in the copse at the side of the house, fresh, green-leaved plants in among the montbretia, all increasing healthily inside the overgrown boundary hedges of fuchsia. I admired the plants and looked them up in my gardening dictionary. My mother and I looked at each other in dismay; 'Bishop's Gout-Weed, Devil's gut,' we read, 'otherwise known as *ground elder* – the most virulent of weeds. Almost impossible to eradicate.' What to do? It was everywhere. We couldn't poison the whole garden – we wanted to start replanting.

Depressed, my mother flew back to London with the children and O'Toole and I, with some time off, stayed behind, for a few days as we thought, and I fretted over the monstrous weeds – the smallest piece of root left in the earth would grow into another plant and it would even go on growing out of earth thrown on the rubbish tip. It was like something from another planet and I began to regard it as a personal enemy and was sitting on the doorstep, wondering moodily what to do about it, when I realized that O'Toole, sitting behind me in the house, was distinctly unwell. Unwell enough to go to bed without argument. Unwell enough not to object when, the following day, frightened, I called the local doctor. He was also worried. O'Toole had dreadful stomach pain and there didn't appear to be an explanation for it. He was too ill to be moved and so began a month of misery. Our patient seemed barely conscious at times and lay there – just enduring pain. The local doctor came and stood, worried, at the foot of the bed. He spoke to Gerry Slattery in London. There was nothing to do but try to keep him as comfortable as possible. Eventually the pain diminished somewhat, and, exhausted, he lay there, drifting in and out of sleep, too weak to move. Twice a day I hand-washed sheets wet with perspiration and laid them out on the brambles to dry. I left the bedroom window open and a few feet away from the bed inside, and sick at heart with worry, I began to work on the ground elder, gently uprooting it by hand. All my misery and fear went into that weeding. Every few minutes I glanced at the bed through the window and for three weeks I worked my way slowly through those innocent-looking, monstrous plants.

When O'Toole was able to stand and walk, I felt that, together, we'd conquered something mysterious and dangerous. The garden also had been tamed, the ground elder banished, the beautiful soil sieved and checked over again and again for a fragment of evil, white, fleshy root. Powerlessness in the sick room had given me the tenacity of an animal, working out there on my hands and knees by day, while at night I listened for his breathing until I fell asleep, exhausted.

Back in London, we were none the wiser. What had it been, pondered Gerry and a few of his friends from the Royal Free Hospital. Well, no sign of anything now. O'Toole went back to work on *Rosebud*, a movie that would take him to seven or eight countries. 'All over for good, let's hope,' said Gerry. But it wasn't over. In Paris, O'Toole became very ill indeed and his make-up man, Bill Lodge, called a halt to the unequal struggle to go to work every day. Otto Preminger, the director, stopped the film without a murmur, got O'Toole into the American Hospital and sent for me. I did little except loiter, worried, in the hospital and spent the rest of the summer days of 1974 alone in the hotel, never straying far from the phone.

There is always a professional need, shared by all actors high and low, to keep illnesses a secret from the press and the public. In my case, this created an additional divide between me and the girls and the outside world as well. O'Toole's parents and his sister were not to be told anything but good news – Jules and Joyce and my mother (up to a point) and I were isolated in our falsehoods. The girls were asked not to talk about their father. And I wasn't told what was wrong.

Otto Preminger was capable of being a difficult director, but he was what Joyce Buck called a 'six o'clock pussy cat', turning into the nicest person imaginable once the day's work was done and certainly, to us during our troubled month, he was kind and considerate over and above the call of duty. I did see the other side of him once during the filming of *Rosebud* as for no good reason he demanded take after take from Richard Attenborough. There were actors of every nationality in the movie and I was very proud to be, if only by similar training, on Richard Attenborough's 'team'. Throughout the trying day he remained polite and calm and solid as a rock, never allowing Otto to affect his work adversely.

Script writer Roy Clarke had been co-opted and flown to Paris to improve O'Toole's dialogue (in a script written by someone else). I met him at the hospital and he gave me the few bright moments I enjoyed during that sad, worrying summer. We shared a coffee after one of our visits to the American Hospital and were sitting silently outside the Café de la Paix, watching the crowds go by. It was July 14. Roy, in his North Country voice, broke the silence. 'D'you know what day it is today?' 'No.' 'Ah, well, at home tonight they'll all be asking "What did *you* do for Bastille Day then?"'

When O'Toole recovered from his mystery illness and we'd spent some time quietly in the hotel suite while he convalesced, he packed me off home. I was loath to leave him; he looked frail to me, but as usual he hated to be seen to be looked after and I knew Bill Lodge, his make-up man, would watch over him. Before I left I visited the set as they shot a street scene. The only actor I met that day was Peter Lawford, who looked appallingly ravaged. We sat together in a café and I had to make my excuses and leave; there was something unbearably distressing and depressing in his manner and conversation.

I flew home, low in spirits, and the film dragged on in an undistinguished fashion all over Europe. I had finished work on *Shoulder to Shoulder* and then played Mrs Patrick Campbell for the first time in a TV series about Jenny Churchill. Richard Shulman and Philip Wiseman and I tried to reunite to do Tennessee Williams's *Camino Real* but our plans failed.

Sara Randall, the most creative of agents, had commissioned a treatment of the story of Frieda, D. H. Lawrence's wife, and was beginning to negotiate with the BBC who were interested in producing six hour-long plays, each dealing with Frieda's relationship with a significant man in her life, beginning with her brother, Baron von Richthofen, the First World War flying ace. I began to read all the material available and my enthusiasm grew in spite of an encounter with Sir John Gielgud in Sloane Street. We were on opposite sides of the road, both dressed identically (except he was in brown and I in black) in long, Yves St Laurent trench coats with Herbert Johnson fedoras. John, who seemed to know *everything*, even in the planning stage, called across to the underground side of the road, 'Shawn, Shawn' (he never mastered 'Siân'), 'why d'you want to play that boring German cow?' Taking all my books and Tennessee Williams's new short plays, which his agent, Audrey Wood, had sent me, I left for Connemara and some serious gardening and building. The children were at school and my mother and Liz were left in charge.

Moving swiftly through customs, I located the driver and began the long journey up the West Coast into Connemara. I had a house to build!

'You throw your hat into the air and where it lands, there you build your house.' Leo Mansfield, the architect, told us this and we had stood solemnly on a hill above the vanished village of Eyerphort, which was where we'd bought the land and the small cottage we'd been staying in, and up went O'Toole's hat and we scrambled to the spot where it landed before it disappeared, borne away on the wind over the Atlantic. 'Is it always as – er – as – breezy as this up here?' I inquired. 'Pretty much,' was the reply. All the other houses in Eyerphort, past and present, were built down below in the southern shelter of the hill. Even the Castle near Clifden was sheltered (but nevertheless, all its trees had been destroyed in a famous, vicious storm). The cottage nestled down below the inhospitable spot where we were – barely – standing. But what a place on which to perch! We seemed suspended in air; Atlantic to the south and west, an estuary to the north and to the east Clifden, out of sight, and the Twelve Bens beyond. It was a difficult site from every point of view. It was high and obvious above the coastline and I racked my brain to think of a way of building an unobtrusive house. It was not going to be easy to get planning permission. I asked Leo to draw an elevation of the house. Soon discarded were all my ideas of a long Japanese house ('Yes,' said Leo, 'those low, over hanging Japanese roofs are very nice-looking. First bit of a storm and your house would be up in the air on its way to New York'), or a Roman house built around an atrium ('Have you ever looked inward week after week at an atrium under driving rain?').

Leo was an expert on the Irish vernacular and he persuaded us to build a low house of stone that snaked down the hillside, like a Welsh long-house, its stone walls merging into the granite boulders everywhere. Granite. Ever present in the west. Not far away to the south in the Gaeltacht there were fields as small as dining tables surrounded by lumps of stone taller than a man and beautiful drystone walls; works of art everywhere. The first thing to be done was to level a piece of ground and that meant calling into town for a few experts in the art of handling gelignite. The explosions were dramatic and swift and accurate. In the grey, bitterly cold, wet afternoon, I looked at the flattened site – looking much the same as it had a few hours earlier but without the big outcrops of living rock. There was no water, no electricity, no refuge from the violent wind. Would we ever be allowed to build where the hat had landed?

Winning permission took a long time and I became versed in the arts of patience and very un-English diplomacy. In Wales, I remembered, petitioners came to Uncle Davy's door at all hours but there was a faint effort to abide by a set of rules formulated in Westminster. Here in Ireland, I couldn't make out what the rules were that I was trying to bend. I wrote letters, submitted plans, tried to convey my good intentions, went to meetings, submitted to interviews and waited and waited and waited. And then, one day over a year later, it was over. Permission was granted to begin work on 'The O'Toole House'. Aware of the great favor extended to enable us to build this high above the spectacular coast, I redoubled my efforts to make a tactful house. Leo Mansfield was the perfect architect for this project and he not only designed the house but he taught me about stone and weather; the effect they had on the life of the inhabitants of the west and how they determined the style of the houses. I came to see that there was nothing random about the little crofts; every feature was there for a purpose and it became an absorbing game to build a house with six bedrooms, almost as many bathrooms, central heating and plumbing, while incorporating as many aspects as possible of the traditional Irish house. There was the huge hearth in the main 'room' where the turf fire was never allowed to go out and over which hung an iron pot where we could cook all our meals, should the need arise. Near the fire was a recess and a day-bed where the oldest (or sickest) person could sleep near the fire, the floors were made of slabs of stone cut from the cliffs of Moher, each one bearing the imprints of fossil remains of worms. Indoors we used them convex side up and outside, on the wide walkway surrounding the house, we turned them and showed the concave side. The roof was made of the Bangor blue slates of my childhood home, shipped over from North Wales. The doors and stairs and roofs were of pine, the door furniture was a cheat – I bought all the 'traditional' black iron from Beardmore's in London – but the outer walls were the real thing and gave me a thrill of pleasure every time I looked at them. It wasn't easy, finding someone who could drystone an entire house, but I had seen writer Richard Murphy's barn in Cleggan which he'd had built by John Cosgrove, a local mason who spent a large part of the year odd-jobbing for the Council.

The Harbour Bar at Cleggan had become a center of my activities as I searched for local craftsmen to work in the house. Eileen O'Malley was my ally in this. She had inherited the bar from her father, Matcher O'Malley, whom I had met on my first visit to the West as a girl when O'Toole and I had spent the entire day sheltering from the driving rain and mist, huddled next to the turf fire in the empty bar while Matcher leaned on the half-door looking out. Two cars passed through the village that day. When night fell and we decided we had to make a move, a lone customer, soaked to the skin, joined us in the bar and uttered a greeting. 'Ah,' said Matcher. 'A wet day and nothin' but cars goin' wesht wesht wesht all day.'

In this same bar I sat and tried to beguile the local building talent (O'Toole called me the Mata Hari of Galway County). Their expertise was hidden under a veneer of jovial insouciance and the menial work they did for the local Council mending roads, flinging up cinder-block bus shelters. Eileen O'Malley arranged a meeting for me with John Cosgrove. It was inconclusive and another was arranged. After a day's gardening I would clean up, shake out my black St Laurent skirt and sweater and set off for Cleggan, praying that this time I could persuade Mr Cosgrove to build me a house. 'No. No. No,' he demurred again and again after we'd skirted around the subject for an hour or so. 'I've only ever made barns – a few auld walls.' 'But a house is a few old walls,' I pleaded. After weeks of to-ing and fro-ing to Cleggan, he agreed to 'have a go' and began to order stone from a quarry nearby. He brought his son of nineteen with him and I spent hours watching as he selected the granite blocks he needed for each course and asked his son to fetch them and make more 'shtwff' with which to bind the narrow gaps (shtwff – stuff, was a mixture of straw and mud). Miraculously the walls rose.

To ease John's mind, I'd promised that the builders would

build a cavity wall inside the stone wall so that, as winter approached, we would have an independent shell to the house but, as it turned out, John and his son ascended at the same speed as the builders with their cinder-blocks. It was beautiful. I remembered the morning in Cuzco when we had looked at the dramatic pre-Columbian drystone courses at the base of the Spanish buildings and determined to try to make a smaller, Celtic version of this Inca marvel. After the house was completed, someone complimented John and said he must be very proud to see his work. 'Ah, Jaysus no,' he said. 'Every time I pass by I'm afraid to look at the yoke in case it's fallen down.' Nothing could ever overcome the modesty of this man whose skill was of such a high order.

Our first, small cottage, which we now called Mamgu's cottage, drew water from an old, small well on a nearby meadow. It was known as a well that had never been known to go dry, not even in the worst droughts. Now, we needed a much bigger well, high up on the hill. Matter of factly, Leo said that he'd order along a dowser. This was a magical development in the building process and on the appointed day, O'Toole and myself, Mamgu, Liz and the girls were out on the meadow waiting – for what, we weren't sure. The ordinary looking man in flannels and a sports jacket and a raincoat walked about with his home-made dowsing rod and we watched, entranced, as it occasionally kicked upwards between his hands. 'Just about *here*,' he said finally, as the hazel twig almost flew out of his hands. 'Have a go,' he offered. 'Have a go?' We looked at each other, wide-eyed. The man had just made our house possible (a house without water is no house at all). On his say-so, we were about to spend a great deal of time and money. Were we, also, capable of this extraordinary feat? Well, I wasn't, nor was Mamgu, nor Pat. Liz said she thought she felt something but O'Toole and Kate walked about, their hazel twigs twirling like things possessed. It was still a mystery but it was all systems go for building.

The artesian well was sunk and quite soon we accessed a huge supply of water – we drank it in wine glasses standing in the rain. Halfway through the building the well ran dry after a quarry across the estuary indulged in some over-enthusiastic blasting; we suffered panic-stricken days until the dowser returned and found us another source. Searchlights were put up in the meadow overlooking the estuary and I stood alone in the shell of the house, watching the men drill day and night in the driving rain. The meadow looked like a Texas oilfield. 'If they strike oil I'll commit suicide,' I muttered to Mamgu as I crept off to bed in her cottage. Down and down they drilled into the rock and 176 feet below ground they found water again. I've never been so relieved in my life.

I travelled between the building centers in London and Dublin and Connemara. I bought the *Readers' Digest* do-it-yourself-building book and learned as I went along about plumbing and damp courses and electrics and generators and septic tanks. Working towards moving the family in was like working towards a big opening night. The children, my mother and Liz had been living it up in an hotel in Clifden as we hiccupped our way towards completion. At last, we were ready. Everything worked. The family arrived. 'Fill every bath,' I cried. 'We have limitless water.' The men waved goodbye and drove their trucks and cars across the lower meadow to the road and off they went for good. 'How's the water?' 'It's grand but it doesn't go away.' The men had laid the pipes too near the surface and had flattened the whole system as they drove away. We now had a houseful of water and no means of getting rid of it. There was nothing in Liz, the Nanny's past to prepare her for this (her name was not Elizabeth de la Court Bogue for nothing – she was rather grand), but sending for more joints and bits of pipe, with the *Readers' Digest* book open at our side, we, together, re-built the drainage system and went to bed in a house with perfect plumbing. They say that building a house makes you a philosopher. I don't know about that, but it teaches you many things. The chief of which, in my case, was patience.

There was a time for the girls when, I suspected, they would have preferred to spend their holidays pounding the pavements of the King's Road rather than clambering up and down the West Coast. Temporarily, they had an uneasy time of it but I was sure it would soon pass. O'Toole and I went to Connemara, together or separately, whenever we were free of work and between 1970 and 1974 I spent every moment I could there, working on the new house, and often this entailed making the long journey for one afternoon on the site. I was as happy as a clam; rising at daybreak and spending the whole day out of doors, a piece of cheese in my pocket and the kettle and coffee situated nearby in an open window so that, filthy and often wet, I need not enter the house until it was time to come in and scrub myself clean and begin preparing dinner. Pat rode a bit and went visiting. Kate, on strike from country pursuits, read indoors whatever the weather. Occasionally I bribed them to help me carry water or push wheelbarrows of weeds to the bonfire, but this was not really how they wished to be spending their vacation. They were pathetically pleased when we drove into the town and were able to watch a bit of television before dinner.

Guiltily, I occasionally gave up a day's gardening and organized an outing. My excursions were cursed with bad luck (or bad judgment) and inevitably we found ourselves hopelessly lost, miles from anywhere, or trying to cross a huge bog in the pouring rain, or arriving at our destination to find that the castle was shut or the people we were visiting had gone away. The girls were remarkably patient and there was nothing in the way of outright rebellion but I did discover from Liz that they raised their eyes to heaven, shaking their heads gloomily when they knew that one of what they bitterly called 'Mummy's little expeditions' was being planned.

Our neighbors, Ann and Eddie Pryce, who farmed on adjoining land, called round regularly and we all sat drinking tea and chatting – 'wasting' time. Old Mr Feste Pryce, Eddie's father, lived with them and my mother always brought him a gift of black-brown, solidly compacted 'plug' tobacco, wrapped in silver foil. The gift was received with a gracious nod and a smile and little else. In fact, I never heard Feste speak until one day, as Liz was driving me back from a shopping expedition to Clifden, we saw Feste and his friend Tommy, not doing anything as obvious as thumbing a lift but definitely looking hopefully in the direction of home some fifteen miles away. We stopped and they nodded and climbed into the back seat. As we drove along the coastal Sky road, high above the Atlantic sparkling in the spring sunshine and studded with the tiny islands of the West Coast, I heard Feste say to Tommy, 'You know, one life is too short to enjoy all this beauty.' He had lived in the same house, looking at this same view, for over seventy years.

The road that ran past our land, and in some places through our land, simply circled the peninsula and returned to Clifden, so visitors were few and far between. When the big house was completed, high on its hill, we could see cars approaching from a great distance and one night as my mother and I prepared dinner and O'Toole read near the big fire, the girls, who had been hanging out of the gable window, watched a car approach and then they saw it stop at our gate and, wonder of wonders, the occupants began the steep, stony ascent to the house. Callers! 'Mummy! Mummy!' they cried as they hurtled down stairs. 'There's an old tinker woman coming up the drive!' When I answered the knock at the kitchen door and peered into the dusk it took me a moment or two to make out behind the shawl wrapped around the raincoat and the scarf tied over the hat, the wonderful features of Kate Hepburn and behind her, looking considerably more respectable, her companion, Miss Phyllis, and film director

Tony Harvey (who had directed *Lion in Winter*). Abashed to have made such a huge mistake, the girls remained mute for the rest of the evening, sitting at a respectful distance, gawping at the most unusual film star they had ever met. I felt a bit like Moley showing off his house in *The Wind in the Willows*, as I recounted the story of the building of the house and Kate was every bit as obligingly admiring as Ratty as she inspected and approved the arrangements. I think she really did like the plain, solid rooms. She had been to visit Brian Friel to talk about a script and she now wanted to talk to O'Toole, but first she concentrated on my problems with the drains and the septic tank – still so fresh in mind. 'D'you know,' she said, 'if I had a daughter, d'you know what I'd have her train to be?' We leaned forward. 'A *plumber*!' she pronounced forcefully. The girls, pop-eyed, looked nervous.

Not everyone liked my efforts. Robert Shaw, with whom I had a mildly competitive friendship, began building his family home at much the same time as I did. Robert had spent years being dissatisfied with his progress as an actor. Too long a period carrying spears and playing small parts had left him feeling disgruntled and unappreciated, and the on-off success led to his losing patience with the profession and he determined to be a writer instead. His first novel, *The Sun Doctor*, was a success and he was well reviewed. As is the way of things, he immediately became a star actor, the most notable of his movies being *The Sting* with Robert Redford and Paul Newman and *Jaws*. Rich and successful, he was rebuilding and converting a bishop's country residence in a much gentler part of Western Ireland. He bounded up the half-finished steps into the living room. I waited proudly for him to comment on the enormous flags I'd had cut for the floor and the great wooden 'upturned boat' ceiling and the walls, four feet thick against the constant winds. There was a long pause and he said, 'What are you *doing*? Where are the *carpets*? Where is the *comfort*? You can't live like *this*, from *choice*. You're *mad*.' We agreed to differ and turned our attention to the safer topic of gardening. He quite admired my plans and said, 'I'll bet I get mine up and running before you do.' I was delighted by the challenge and fancied my chances for once. I was desolate when, soon after, Robert died suddenly, and I always paused on the spot where we had stood outside the house, and thought of him looking down towards the sea and seeing a garden which had not begun to exist.

My life in Connemara was becoming dangerous. It was by far the best part of my existence and I became more and more obsessed with the huge garden I had in my mind. There was a massive amount to learn; for one thing it was difficult for me to learn to think Big. O'Toole generously called me Capability Phillips as I wrestled with walkways and woodlands and planned vistas and hired backhoes. One day, I thought to myself, I might just stay here when it is time to return to London. Then what would happen? Would I be able to change my life completely? Could I really live there in isolation except for the family visits? These faint, uneasy thoughts remained in the back of my mind but they were sad days when I was driven away to Clifden and then to Shannon Airport. Not since I was a small child in Wales had I felt such an attachment to a place. I looked out of the back window of the car, printing the scene on my mind, as though I might never see it again.

Chapter Thirty

The four years spent building the house in Connemara had demanded such an investment of time and emotion and hard work that now, on its completion in 1974, I felt it to be the center of my life. There wasn't a scrap of it from the damp course and the insulation to the material of the blinds and the drawer holding the teaspoons that I hadn't scrutinized. O'Toole had let me have my head and when he'd been in the country he had taken a keen interest, not in the furniture and door handles, but very much in the structure of the house; the thick walls, the roof and, above all, the huge fireplace and main chimney. We shared the intense excitement as the walls rose and we walked around the shoreline, learning to identify the spots where one could first glimpse the house. We stood, leaning on the west wall where our bedroom would be, and looked at the sunsets. I don't recall that we ever exchanged a cross word while we were in Ireland. But we didn't spend all our time in Ireland and life in London was very different.

It's hard to describe how fragmented life became when O'Toole was not working. Although he was protected by Jules and the staff at the offices of Keep Films, he was nevertheless besieged on all sides by people who wanted his help, his advice, his money, his company. The hordes of journalists who wanted to talk to him were often fascinating people in their own right and they had the time of their lives with O'Toole, who was a newspaper junkie. Once they'd penetrated the defenses, O'Toole found it impossible not to throw himself wholeheartedly into whatever project they had in mind. When he was drinking, sober-sided writers would be whisked off on a pub crawl they were not to forget in a hurry or, stone cold sober, he would spend hours a day with foreign newspapermen, pouring his enthusiasm and energy into giving them a guided tour of Hampstead or Soho. It seemed mean to begrudge the fine time they were having but I *was* mean and resentful when O'Toole returned home too exhausted to do anything but rest. It didn't help that I was able to see that my problems were largely of my own making. O'Toole was what he was and avowedly had never intended to make any changes in his behavior. 'If you don't like me, leave me alone,' he would say, wearily, taxed for the umpteenth time in his life with not behaving like a 'normal' husband or father.

More threatening and only half in jest was the question 'Who owns this house?' It went without saying that the owner of the house made the rules. He and I had both grown up at a time when male-dominated households were normal, so part of me enthusiastically embraced the task of being a 'good' wife; supportive, undemanding, avoiding censure, basking in approval (also, alas, atoning for my past). Few men would willingly give up such a delightfully agreeable domestic arrangement where clothes could be dropped on the floor and reappear washed and pressed, rooms tidied by unseen hands, children raised and fed. Men in those days were not ashamed to say they had 'better' things to think about, the implication being that women did *not* have anything better to think about. Astonishingly, this attitude held even when women were occupied in the same profession as their husbands. Some brave spirits protested against all this and altered the structure of their lives. They were regarded as strident, tiresome, unattractive. I was not a brave spirit. Had I been partnered with any of the other men I'd ever associated with I wouldn't have thought twice about moving with the times and staking my claim for equality. Indeed outside the house I found it only too easy to assert myself, had no qualms about appearing strident, tiresome, unattractive, but

I was linked with the most powerful man I'd ever met, whose chauvinism was equalled only by his attractiveness. 'If you don't like me, leave me alone', indeed. He patronized me; called me 'a silly girl' and there were times when I didn't like him at all. Did I want to leave him alone? No, I did not.

But I wasn't a masochist. I *was* loved – hugely. How did I know? Simple; if you *feel* loved, you *are* loved. There were times when I was thanked for my help. There were times when he asked for my forgiveness and pleaded for my forbearance. There were times when we just had fun. And we were bound by shared prejudices and shared likes in books (a shared fondness for P. G. Wodehouse, which we would read aloud to each other, is not a bad reason for staying with someone).

When, as a girl, I first left Wales and home and safety, Saunders Lewis wrote to me saying, 'You must learn to live your life on the knife-edge of insecurity.' I had learned to do just that, for a time, but now I was unable. I was standing in the 'small place' my mother had predicted for me all those years ago in Stratford-on-Avon and not only was it small, it occasionally shook beneath my feet. The measure of balance we had achieved was flawed; it was too dependent on my conduct. Were I to be 'difficult' or argumentative, the whole structure of our life would collapse. Then what, for example, would happen to my mother who had come to live with us? She ran the house, made up the accounts, painted the odd ceiling, did all the washing, but if I were dismissed there would be no house for her to take care of. And the children? I would think twice before depriving them of the kind of life they enjoyed in Guyon House. All the money I made was spent on the house, on clothes for the girls and my mother and myself. I saved nothing. Keep Films took care of our medical insurance and Jules said there were now trust funds set up for the girls in Ireland and that they would be entitled to a cottage each on our land. But all that would be in the future – they were eleven and fourteen years of age in 1974. Could I start from scratch and provide for them in the manner to which they were accustomed? I didn't have any idea – I doubted it. On the surface all was well and everyone in the house took the future for granted and, much as I tried to stifle it, my resentment grew. 'She is my rock,' I would read in the newspaper, or 'She is his still center.' 'Without her to lean on . . .' What sort of woman was this solid, immovable object? She earned her keep but what kept woman didn't?

Unable to bear the pain when love and approval were withheld, I began gradually to reduce my dependence, to loosen the ties that bound us so tightly, so lethally. Less ecstasy, less despair would make my life more bearable and I couldn't think beyond this.

In early 1975 it was as if all the small and inexplicable episodes of illness that O'Toole had suffered over the previous five years gathered themselves into one life-threatening attack, so large and frightening that it obliterated all other considerations for many months.

Coming home from a prolonged reunion with his friend, the writer H.A.L. Craig who had just returned to London after a long absence, O'Toole couldn't conceal the fact that he was once again in dreadful pain. Harry looked sheepish and left and I put O'Toole to bed. As usual, he didn't want to see a doctor but I was so worried by his state that I went against his wishes and called Gerry Slattery (also a friend of Harry Craig). As we had done so many times in the past, Gerry and I sat, one on each side of the big bed in the dimly-lit bedroom, and Gerry chatted calmly, trying to piece together the events of the last twenty-four hours. It was pitiful to see O'Toole attempt to talk, even to joke as he answered Gerry's questions. Almost apologetically, Gerry said suddenly that he thought O'Toole should go to the hospital. Normally, this would have produced voluble objections ending in stubborn refusal. I was alarmed when O'Toole now remained silent, overcome with pain which was evidently greater than any he had endured and denied. Gerry indicated that I should follow him as he made his way down to the study. Always in the past we had stood in his room while he reassured me that there was nothing to worry about. Even after wild drunken episodes ending in collapse he had told me that all would be well in the morning.

Now, almost apologetically, he said that O'Toole should immediately be hospitalized. Within minutes, it seemed, O'Toole was taken out into the gathering dusk and I was left to collect together a few things he might need, then follow them by taxi. What was I thinking of? I packed the *Times* crossword, the book on the night table, a toothbrush and an extra night shirt. I couldn't get a taxi so I ran to the Royal Free in Pond Street. There was nothing for me to do at the hospital. Everyone – Gerry included – had disappeared into the business end of the place, where no 'civilian' may follow. I walked down Pond Street towards South End Green and the Heath and sat on a bench but I couldn't sit still and I walked back up the hill, past the hospital to the taxi stand on the main road, standing there where there were strangers for company. Eventually, I returned and sat alone in the hospital.

Finally, Gerry appeared, looking drawn and grey. I could tell that he was miserably unhappy not to be the bringer of good news and I asked him what I should do. He told me to go home and go to sleep. 'But I want to *be* here when he comes round.' 'Siân, it's not quite like that. It'll be some time before he can see you.' I didn't know much but I could see that things were as bad as they could be short of – no, that was unthinkable. I asked the Sister if she would telephone me if there was any change and climbed the hill to Guyon House, standing dark and empty. The girls and my mother and Liz were all in Ireland for the holidays. Manolita would come in at nine in the morning but no one else would come. The phones were silent. Only Scobie, the bulldog, rumbled and snorted, grumbling to himself in the garden. I went down and unlocked the garden door and he shot into the house and up the stairs to the ground floor, pounding into the Green Room where he liked to spend his evenings. I put the lights on for him and went to sit alone in the study. I couldn't go to our bed upstairs and it was dawn when I went up and, entering, saw the bed and the sheets thrown back where he'd been lifted out, and I sat in the chair near the door and wept. If he was allowed to get better, never, I swore, would I ever entertain a disloyal thought, never would I feel resentment, never would I complain. I would do *anything,* so long as he didn't die. Dammit, I thought, I shall *will* him not to die.

I don't know how long I sat there before I stopped crying, got up and made the bed. Going downstairs I fed Scobie and went up to my bathroom and took a bath and put on more make-up than usual. Then I called Jules who I knew would be awake in order to make his calls to California and told him what had happened. Jules, the fixer, the do-er was frustrated when he realized that there was nothing he or I could usefully do, but he had to do something so he drove from Belgravia to Hampstead to see me. When I opened the door he was surprised to see me dressed and painted and assuring him that O'Toole *would* be all right. He nodded obligingly but not very convincingly and said that he'd been talking to Gerry and wanted to go to the hospital to see for himself how things were. I wondered what Gerry had told him.

At the hospital we were allowed to enter the room where O'Toole lay motionless and connected to a battery of instruments. Nothing happened and we were ushered out again. Jules went to the office; he had somehow to withdraw O'Toole from public view without actually admitting that he was seriously ill. There are people in every court room, theater and hospital who ring the papers with 'stories' (and are rewarded very poorly for their pains) and indeed by the time

I was home, the phones were ringing. 'Was it true that Peter was at the Royal Free? Was it true that he was terminally ill? Did he have alcoholic poisoning?' . . . and so on, endlessly. I explained to Manolita what had happened and left the house to walk around Hampstead until it was time to go to the hospital again.

At first, I found the papers relatively easy to deal with; I had had long practice in being evasive without being too infuriating but as the days became weeks and my will to stay optimistic crumbled, it became harder and harder to put on a brave face – or in this case, a brave voice. One night after I'd been sitting in O'Toole's room for most of the day, I went home and sat despondently on my side of the bed. Picking up the phone, I heard the voice of a journalist I knew quite well. 'Look, Siân, it's Peter here. I know it's late but you're a sensible girl, you know what I'm up against and I want to do a good job – could you give me a hand updating the obit?' I couldn't think of anything to say to him but 'No' as I put the phone down before bursting into tears.

As time passed in that side ward I learned to operate the system of tubes and gradually lost my terror of the paraphernalia which had so intimidated me at first. Sister was unhappy and Gerry was so worried that he could scarcely bear to speak to me, unable as he was to give me reassurance and hope.

And then one day it was like sailing into a calm dawn at sea after a stormy night. O'Toole opened his eyes and they were *his* eyes. He couldn't lift his head but he gave me a lopsided grin and my heart filled with relief and love. We held hands and didn't say a word. One by one the nursing staff popped their heads round the door and smiled and nodded. There was very little talking. 'Very good. Very good,' said Gerry, nodding vigorously, his eyes almost shut, his head tilted back. 'He'll outlive us all, kid,' said Jules brusquely and shook his head as if to wipe out the horror that was past. I felt like a different person. O'Toole was different. We went home thankfully and quietly, so quietly. He went to bed to convalesce. My mother and the girls returned. We had him to ourselves! We had him. I had him. His girls revelled in him. When I looked at him I saw many people, people he did not know who were him, the people who, high up in the Royal Free Hospital, had hated me, reviled me, pleaded with me, adored me, all while he slept. And now he was back. Let us rest.

'I need to go somewhere nice to recuperate. Not too much sun. Quiet. Nice.'

Oh, no.

I had been so reluctant to take him abroad but the month in Positano had been transforming. He'd been right again. Now we came home and began to consider the next step in our new life – a life that seemed like a gift.

Chapter Thirty-one

'*Please* let me come with you.'

For the first time, I was pleading to be allowed to accompany O'Toole on location. The response was a firm, dismissive 'No'. He looked surprised that I should even raise the possibility of such a change in our routine and saw no reason that he should break the habit of a lifetime. I understood that it was important to him to be alone and independent while he worked but I was far too worried about his health not to try to persuade him that he needed to be looked after. He had escaped death by such a narrow margin. Did he fully appreciate this? Or was he deliberately erasing it from his mind? Whatever the reason he refused any discussion. I couldn't bear to see him, frail but straight-backed, determined to be as he was before, rejecting sympathy and help. In a way, I thought his behavior brave and admirable but of course I didn't want him to reject *my* sympathy, *my* help. My part in the grim struggle we had endured had made me feel that I was indispensable to him, that our partnership had advanced to another level and it was a crushing blow to discover that I also was expected to dismiss from my mind the terrors, the pain, the discovery of a new well-spring of love, the perfect happiness that had followed the despair. I tried to show how profound was my disappointment but the habit of not being a nuisance was too strong and I gave way to his decision with reasonably good grace. I couldn't conceal my sadness but it went unnoticed amid the usual flurry of preparation for departure. Someone asked me what was the name of the film that he was going to shoot and who was the director and I realized that for the first time in our life together I had no idea and didn't really care.

How to explain my feelings to myself? I could hardly believe the alienation that had occurred. Never, not at the lowest point of our relationship, had I thought of leaving O'Toole; I had hated him, resented him, wanted to smite him and never entertained the possibility that I wouldn't spend the whole of my life with him. And now for the first time since we met I felt totally separate from him. It was almost as though my O'Toole *had* died at the Royal Free down the road. How *could* he behave now as though nothing had happened? Near-death had happened, a new beginning had dawned and now another sort of death was happening.

I made plans to return to work myself. I had foolishly assumed that I would be away in Mexico – New Mexico? I wasn't sure which. Now Sara advised me to do a play in the West End, partly because it would be rehearsed in London and would preview there as well so, at least, I could be at home while I worked. The play, which was one of the scripts I'd read without great enthusiasm in Positano was *The Gay Lord Quex* by Pinero. John Gielgud was almost alone in loving the play but he *did* admire it enormously and had now persuaded Eddie Kulukundis to produce it. The Edwardian settings and costumes were hugely expensive and it was to be a lavish production. For the most part my scenes would be with Dan Massey (who played the eponymous hero) and Judi Dench, whom I'd never before worked with but admired enormously and wanted to act with, not least because I was told it was the greatest fun imaginable. I could do with a bit of fun, I thought.

O'Toole was to be gone shooting *Foxtrot* in New Mexico for three months at least. His movies often took a good deal longer than this and Jules was vague even now about the actual date of ending. It was strange to be leading a normal everyday life while grappling with such inner turmoil. And no one noticed;

life went on as usual for the girls and my mother and Liz. The house ran on oiled wheels, Manolita and I scarcely needed to consult each other as we began to pack the big trunk and the suitcases; assembling everything that might conceivably be needed during O'Toole's time away, pasting the list of contents inside each lid. And as the hours and days went by I felt my presence becoming more and more indistinct. It wouldn't have surprised me if one of the family were to have walked right through me where I stood in the hall, an invisible person, as doors opened and shut, telephones were answered, children ran up the stairs, everyone absorbed and full of purpose. Everyone except me. I knew with certainty that I couldn't return to the old life with its long separations and lack of shared experience. When the day came to say goodbye to O'Toole, I felt I was saying goodbye to him forever. I had been incapable of making him understand what I felt, how urgently I needed to be with him now. He had a hard task ahead of him and I could read the determination in his face and in the set of his shoulders. He would not yield to weakness. He would survive whatever the cost. I admired him for that but I was admiring him as I would a stranger and that left me desolate.

It was May – a wet May. I went to work as he went to the airport. What did he feel? I had no idea. It was hard to be bright and cheerful as I met the *Quex* company for the first time. Dan Massey was an old friend and he made me laugh as we were photographed in the rain in the churchyard outside our rehearsal room in Piccadilly. 'Great start,' he said, looking at my wet, ruined hair-do. That night I sat alone in the study. Were it not for the presence of the girls, the house would have seemed very gloomy. As it was, when they climbed the stairs to their apartment all the rooms on the ground and first floors were very quiet indeed and save for my desk lamp in the study, unaccustomedly dark. I went over the events of the morning and our farewells to each other. O'Toole had no idea how I felt, I was sure of that now. His farewells had been as they would usually be before a long absence and he would expect everything to be as usual when he returned in late summer. And of course I would be here – why would I not be? The future had yet to be resolved and I had no idea what it would hold. How quietly it had come about, this revolution in my life.

When I had asked O'Toole if I should come to visit him should the play not enjoy a long run he'd responded, 'No, no, you'd hate it. Cabo San Lucas is the arse-hole of the world.' Now I rose and took down the atlas and looked it up. Baja California didn't seemed to be horrible at all. I had always visited him however awful the locations and I was puzzled by his determination to keep Cabo San Lucas out of bounds to me. What did I know of O'Toole's life in Mexico?

Before he became ill, he returned from filming *Man Friday* in Mexico and dumped the usual pile of unanswered mail on my desk, and there was one letter written in a neat, childish hand that especially caught my eye and for some reason I put it aside instead of throwing it away with all the other mail, much of it too fatuous to need answering. A girl called Anna wrote sadly that she had obviously misunderstood all that had passed and – God, save her – I thought, apologized for her presumption. There was a greeting-card type of poem as well, a pathetic little adieu. I remembered that a Mexican girl called Anna had been given a job on a co-production of a film we had made without O'Toole. Was it the same girl, I wondered, but only for a moment.

It had not occurred to me that he might have another reason for wishing to be alone when away on location. I had always been too occupied trying to burnish my tarnished reputation in his eyes, trying (in vain, I sometimes thought,) to convince him that I was trustworthy, faithful beyond reproach. He was quick to criticize looseness in other women also and loud in his condemnation of what he called 'fouling your own doorstep' and I had assumed that he applied the same stringent standards to his own behavior as he did to mine and certainly, with the small exception of the sad note from Anna, I had never been confronted with a whisper of infidelity on his part. Nor had I ever read anything of the sort in the mass of newspaper articles about him. Nor had I ever felt that his affections might be engaged elsewhere. When he first became famous, O'Toole had been as taken aback as I by the deluge of attention from women and I was left to deal with the intemperate behavior and the surprising outpourings of respectable young women who ought to have known better. He was pursued by every manner of woman and I was astonished that he was able to deal with the avalanche of flattery with such grace and restraint. His close friend, Kenneth Griffith, said to me, barely controlling his laughter, 'D'you know – he looked me straight in the eye and said, "I have never been unfaithful to her".' I wasn't sure how he expected me to react and he, sensing my confusion, changed the subject. Now, as I thought of it, I wasn't at all sure that I regarded it as any of my business what O'Toole got up to during those long absences, provided it did not affect our life together. It wasn't anything we'd ever talked about and now it didn't matter in the least. All the same, I was mildly curious about Mexican Anna – if she still existed in his life or whether she had ever signified in it.

During the remaining weeks of May I spent my evenings at home and went to work by day, scarcely registering the considerable storms brewing in the rehearsal room. Like most sad times, this was laced through with comedy, verging on farce. Dan Massey, the same dear Dan – who wrote such elegant, witty letters, who was such a tower of strength when I put my back out while we were rehearsing *Alpha Beta* together in 1972, who made a game out of our violent fist fight in Act One and laughed me out of my terrors that I was disabled for life, that same Dan was now despondent, black, bowed, scarcely speaking to anyone. He and John Gielgud did not get on. Worse, they scarcely spoke the same language. Dan, who had just played an acclaimed Lytton Strachey, his first 'character' part, wanted to apply the same principles of research and heavy appearance-changing make-up to Lord Quex. Unfortunately, *The Gay Lord Quex* was a jolly, young man-about-town, handsome as all get out and a devil with the ladies. Nothing much else to think about.

There was a huge cast, four sets, four changes of costumes – and at the end of it all not a great deal in the way of a story. Judi Dench was playing the little manicurist and John admired her as much as he disliked Dan. When I laid aside my personal unhappiness and began to look around I became fascinated by John who came to work each day with a completely new set of ideas. He and the designer devised sets, each of which had a round object in the middle (make-up display counter, table, fountain) and occasionally he would cry, in pain, 'Oh for God's sake stop going *round* and *round and round*! You look as tho' you're dancing round a maypole.' We were – there was nowhere else to go. Occasionally, he would get up and demonstrate how an Edwardian lady would enter, speak and sit and that was magic. Descended from the great Terry family, he'd kept his eyes open around all those Terry aunties when he was a youth and it was a privilege to be given a glimpse into the manners of another age. But the rest of the time we limped from bad to worse. 'No. No. No! Why are you doing that?' 'Because you told me to.' 'When?' 'Yesterday.' 'But that was another *life*.' He and Dan stopped talking to each other completely. John could not understand why Dan couldn't just bounce on and be a charming roué. Dan retreated further and further behind elaborate make-up drawings.

Judi Dench was the cleverest actress I'd ever watched working. While she wasn't 'getting' the part, she remained calm and cheerful and good humored and then, after about three weeks, she came in and declared that *finally*, after puzzling and puzzling, she'd got hold of the end of a string and, with any luck, if she pulled on it – that would be the solution. And it was! More than anyone I'd known she had a formidable, a huge, actor's intelligence and the solid good sense to get her through the vicissitudes of production week. When she came on at the dress parade in her specially designed dressing gown, Gielgud shrieked, 'Oh God, you look like Richard III.' Many leading ladies would have been put out (Peggy Ashcroft would certainly have locked herself in the dressing room, weeping), Judi – secure in her performance – probably consoled the unfortunate designer who had to make another costume in a hurry.

Almost four weeks into rehearsal, Judi and I decided that maybe we'd better work out our own moves on our own (John's were getting more and more wild). It seemed almost sacrilegious to doubt him but we *did* have to open and soon. That night we went to see John in his play, *No Man's Land* by Harold Pinter, which he was playing with Ralph Richardson. He was so sublime that, of course, we decided we *were* being sacrilegiously insubordinate and henceforth we would slavishly obey his every whim. 'Did you really like it?' he smiled when we went round afterwards. 'D'you think it's a good play?' (So patrician.) 'I'm frightfully lucky to be playing it, you know.' (Lucky? He?) 'It's only because poor Larry's dead – dying – I mean so much better, thank God.' He beamed at his own success in avoiding a faux pas. An awed hush settled over the dressing room. It isn't often you see a legend strut his stuff.

John thought I looked like Mrs Patrick Campbell and he taught me some lovely bits of what he called 'plastique', but when I came on in my ballgown – plumes in my hair – he wailed, 'Sit down, *Shawn*.' 'But John . . .' (common sense overcoming my reverence) 'I've only got to say five lines and get off. It'll take hours if I sit center stage.' 'I know, but I want you to *sit* in the middle.' 'John, it doesn't make *sense*. I'll be trailing this costume around for minutes with nothing happening.' 'I know, I know, but you must *sit down*. You look so *tall* when you're standing up.' I think this gave Dan the only smile in a dire dress rehearsal.

John was so sweetly apologetic when we opened badly. He gave Judi and myself the most beautiful presents. Neither Judi nor Dan could face doing the obligatory radio interviews. We had all said from time to time – John – 'Wonderful, sublime actor but cannot direct *traffic*'. My old friends at the BBC said *someone* had to do this interview, so I went to Broadcasting House and was vague about the virtues of the play and confined myself to remarks where I could be truthfully praising of John. He sent me flowers and then a card, thanking me for being 'more generous' than he deserved. I turned it over and the picture was of a policeman directing traffic. My blood ran cold. It was a privilege to be in a flop directed by this complex, brilliant man.

The weeks went by. No word from Mexico. I didn't have a number where I could reach O'Toole and anyhow, he didn't like the telephone. And in a way, he had a point; the wires don't support emotion or need over great distances.

During rehearsals I had seen Judi – so much more observant and more caring then I – restrain one of the young men in the play when he made as if to strike John after a particularly tactless piece of direction. I hadn't been paying any attention at all but I felt sorry for the pretty youth who sat, mutinously pouting, Judi's restraining hand on his arm. At the same time I thought how callow to react to John in such a way. It was another few weeks before I could take the time to look around at other people and their problems. The young man should have been all right in his part of a glamorous officer but John had completely incapacitated him. 'Come on and *take the stage*!' he would cry. After four weeks of John's direction he could scarcely walk straight, let alone dominate a scene.

Not my problem, I had no scenes with him. Didn't even know his name.

Weeks went by and predictably the 'notice' to end was put up. Only a fortnight more to play. I had been to the BBC to talk to producer Martin Lisemore about playing Beth Morgan in *How Green Was My Valley*. Still faintly tanned from Positano I wore a beautiful pale, pastel Missoni dress. When I went to talk to him, Ronnie Wilson, the director, joined us and said, 'This is the part of a *mother*, you know.' 'Yes,' I said, thinking maybe my new Maud Frizon shoes were a mistake. 'Look,' I said. 'I am Welsh and I *am* working class. I may be thin but I *am* a mother. Thin, tall mothers do exist, you know.' They smiled and dismissed me. I've never 'gone for' jobs and now I think maybe one should *dress* for them? No. If they can't see I can act this part a change of frock isn't going to help. Ah well. The play was ending and I didn't think I'd got the television part, so what to do with myself? I would go to Connemara and garden and perhaps as I wrestled with that inhospitable, rocky terrain I would begin to see what I should do next.

Chapter Thirty-two

The girls and my mother and Liz were already on holiday as usual in Connemara. July 1975 was the hottest in years. The theater was as hot as Hades and I was grateful to get out of my sodden costume and hurry into the alley alongside the Albery Theater. I stood there, looking for Lionel and wondering where he'd put the car.

'Would you like to go for a drink? I've got a friend in and we're both going for a jar.'

It's the young man who was at odds with John. I'm *so* flattered. No one asks Mrs O'Toole out. Not ever. 'Well, there's the chauffeur . . . and I have an appointment early in the morning. I don't think so.' 'Only a drink.' 'Well, all right. We could pop over to Macready's' (a really depressing actors' club in Covent Garden. Damp.). I was a member so that left me more or less in control of the evening. Lionel drove the three of us to Macready's and it was shut. I was at a loss. Whenever O'Toole was away I never went out unless escorted by Jules and Joyce and I only knew really expensive places. 'Look – both of you come back to Hampstead.' We piled, rather uneasily, into the Daimler and, arranging to meet him early in the morning, I said good night to Lionel, and took the young men into the house, to the ground floor Green Room, unlocking the door to the basement floor and the wine cellars reaching under Heath Street.

The drinks tray held only spirits so we all went down to the cellars for wine. The night was still unbearably hot and I opened up the door to the garden, as well. It was so strange to be alone and using the house in this way. It made me feel rather grand and powerful to be entertaining alone in it. It was *partly* mine, after all, this place I lived in. Drinks. Music. (I *never* played records at night.) We sat and chatted until I thought it was time to end the evening. One young man (what *was* his name?) left and the other helped me lock up the cellars and garden and before we'd made for the front door his hand was on mine and the key was thrown aside. I couldn't believe what was happening. I had felt myself to be in an aunt-like position to these men and had no wish to complicate my life. I was well aware that the solution to my problems did not lie in displacement activity and, hopeless with names, I didn't even know who this person was. Knew nothing about him. And I welcomed this happening. Even as I thought to myself that I was making a dreadful mistake, I could feel a smile forming on my face. A smile of approval to some submerged self. Accustomed all my life to untroubled, wonderful sex, the worries and heartbreak of the last six months made this coupling something more extraordinary than usual. I was asleep when he left in the morning. Descending to start the day I looked at my handbag, where I'd left it in the study the night before. My wallet had disappeared. 'Serves you right, you fool,' I thought without rancor. 'He callously turned you over and you deserved it – and it was, in a way, worth it.' I laughed and was abashed later when I saw my wallet, intact, on the Green Room table. I knew so little of this man that I thought he might be a thief.

I went through the motions of running my house, distracted by my extraordinary behavior of the night before and surprised by my lack of guilt. I felt – almost exhilarated. No, maybe not quite that, but certainly elevated above the rut in which I'd been living. Going to work at the theater was another matter. I was deeply embarrassed when I made my first entrance that night, feeling as though the audience was pointing at me and whispering, 'Well, there's a fast woman.' I didn't see Robin – I'd checked his name in the program and discovered that he was the son of one of my favorite British film actresses, Eleanor Summerfield. His father was also famous but I didn't know him, Leonard Sachs, best known as the chairman of *The Good Old Days*, the City Varieties Music Hall. I also figured out that Robin must be sixteen years my junior. Well! That was something new. But the play would end soon and that would be the end of the matter. Just a few weeks of awkwardness to get through. The fact that it *wasn't* the end of the matter was every bit as much my fault as Robin's and I felt that 'fault' *did* enter into it, even as I took pleasure in the fault.

Robin and I spent a weekend together in the empty house, camping out in the nursery, and it was domestic in a way that was quite new to me. Robin could cook rather better than I could. He prepared meals and we cleaned up together and it was highly unusual – wrong, but intriguing. He was a bit forward, I thought. Cheeky, in fact, and disrespectful in a cautious sort of way. No one had ever been bold with me. Monstrous, maybe, diabolical even, but cheeky? No. I rather liked it. My pedestal was niftily kicked into touch and I assumed my place as a grubby, voracious creature, sweating in the August sunshine and praised, and flattered – I had never been so eloquently, endlessly flattered – just for being myself. Or rather, less than myself. When the play ended, we parted, he to Greece with his brother and I to wind up business in London before joining the girls and Liz and my mother in Ireland.

The unbearable heat of 1975 turned my head and before leaving for Ireland I spent a wonderful week with an actor whom I had known and admired for the last twenty years. I knew he liked me but we had both behaved so well until now when we didn't. What was happening to me? I felt that I'd burned my bridges as far as O'Toole was concerned. There was no way in which I could pretend to be the person he'd left in May. I didn't even want to be. Behaving badly was making me happy. Of course, Robin would have been outraged by my behavior after his departure and I didn't give a damn about that either (though I didn't tell him so). As I boarded the plane for Ireland, I felt terrific.

My brief time with Robin had stopped me shrouding my body in Celtic decency or shame and I gardened in my bikini, covering up only if I saw someone approach – I was a guest in holy, Catholic Ireland and had no wish to give offense.

Martin Lisemore actually managed to get through to Mamgu's cottage telephone, assisted by Miss Heffernan at the Post Office. Yes, they'd like me to star in *How Green Was My Valley* with Stanley Baker and could I get back to London quite soon for pre-production. I told my mother the news. She lifted her gaze from our gardening notes only to say, 'Well, let's hope it's better than that last try.' She was referring to the Hollywood movie based on the novel in which the parts were all played by American based Irish actors because the Welsh cast was unable to cross the Atlantic in wartime. We continued planning the next stage of the garden. Did she notice I was different, I wondered? *Was* I different?

Back to London, alone. Robin was back from Greece and it was entirely due to me that we met again. Well, maybe he would have braved the castle keep, but I rang him and arranged a meeting in Kensington Gardens. I still felt that there was something odd about us but there was also a growing sweetness. He was so incredibly encouraging. No man in my emotional life had ever been encouraging or helpful or paid one so much attention. I could tell Robin all my fears and difficulties and he didn't sneer at me or belittle my feelings. I was warily impressed. Part of me now identified with the previously traditional male figures in my life and I sometimes thought, 'This man must be mad. He's so nice, there must be something wrong with him.' Then, 'No, wait a minute, this is really agreeable, this care and attention.' Occasionally, I worried about his attitude to work. During September as I prepared for six months at the BBC he was recalled and recalled for an important series. He didn't get the part and said, sincerely, 'The man who's got it is *wonderful* – and I'm happy I've got *you*.' Well, such generosity of spirit was alien to me and what did he mean he 'had' me? This was proceeding too fast and yet – he was getting something very right and maybe I *was* his already.

Something strange had happened in August. I received the only letter O'Toole wrote to me from Baja California. On what was the night I had first slept with Robin, O'Toole had had a strange experience. I had 'appeared' to him. In the letter he pledged his troth to me anew, implying that he regretted what had drawn him to Mexico but he did not elaborate on that. He wrote things I would have been so happy to read even four months previously. I couldn't respond. But my silence seemed to go unremarked.

In late August O'Toole returned and quickly settled down to London life. He resolved to take more of an interest in the running of Keep Films, so every day he would leave with Lionel and spend most of the day in Belgravia. His energy was prodigious because he was no longer drinking. The doctors had been uncompromising on this – he must never drink again. Another bout of illness could be fatal. Gone were the days of sleeping until lunchtime, of feeling slightly under par until the drinking began again. I could scarcely imagine how he managed this revolution in his life. As he interfered in everyone's business, read, made notes, wrote poetry, looked at his mail for the first time, tried to understand balance sheets and filled every moment of the day with activity, a friend said, 'Only Peter would try turning not drinking into an art form.' As for us, his assumption seemed to be that everything had settled down as he wished it to. We chatted a great deal less though and he seemed as unaware as before that there was a change in me. I was in pre-production for *How Green Was My Valley*, seeing Robin occasionally for a brief walk, usually in

Kensington Gardens. I was astonished that no one ever asked me where I was or what I did. It was amazingly easy to be deceitful.

I left for location in Wales and O'Toole came down with me and dressed as a collier and for a lark appeared as an extra. Stanley Baker played my husband. I'd been wary of him, a tough guy among tough guys. He turned out to be professional in the extreme, courteous, well-prepared, so tactful when, drawing on a wealth of experience, he suggested an alternative, maybe a better way of shooting a scene. He held the cast and unit together in the most unobtrusive way imaginable. When he got to know and like me, he would share his lunch with me on production weekends. 'There you go,' proudly handing me a perfectly nice but unremarkable cheese sandwich. 'Ellen made these.' Ellen, his wife, was perfect in his eyes. We worked well together and people would suggest that maybe we'd become very close. 'You know that look, in that scene – come on. Tell.' Nothing could have been more absurd to either of us. My admiration for him grew and grew.

For six months we lived in each other's pockets, Ronnie Wilson directing this bunch of volatile Welshmen, Martin Lisemore, the producer, keeping a close eye on us all. I travelled from Hampstead to the BBC rehearsal rooms in Acton each day, ran the house, spent a good deal of spare time at the North London Collegiate School, saw the children at night and also Marie Kean, who was staying with us, and went through the motions of being Mrs O'Toole, a role which no longer had any credibility for me. Once Marie said suspiciously, 'What are you up to? Why are you more cheerful than usual?' But no one else noticed my altered state. Very occasionally Robin and I would manage an early dinner together and I discovered a whole raft of cheap restaurants that no one I knew would ever dream of visiting. My liking for being adored was gaining ground. I'd never in my life met a man who was so unafraid to show his feelings, who didn't seem to want to protect himself or take control of the situation.

How Green Was My Valley drew to an end. My actor friends from Wales, who'd been commuting to London for six months, declared that they now had to get jobs to pay for this job, during which they'd spent their salaries in the bar of the Paddington to Cardiff train. There had been a great deal of drinking. On the day of the arrival of Beaujolais Nouveau, Stanley had arrived with the first shipment in his car and the entire company, floating on a sea of red wine, had been sent home early with a severe reprimand.

We held the 'wrap' party in the basement flat of one of the designers. I took part in the cabaret playing Stanley, dressed in his flannel shirt, corduroys and boots. The room was lit by candles placed against the walls. I'd treated myself to a new St Laurent suit in shiny black ciré fabric and as I perched on a side table, talking to Mike Gwilym, who had played one of my sons, he said, 'Siân, don't move,' as he placed his arms around me and hugged me tight. My jacket, too close to a candle, was on fire and melting horribly. The room was packed and mercifully no one saw him put the fire out. Later, as we were searching for my new black raincoat and realized someone had taken it by mistake, Mike, thinking back to the cabaret, said, 'Oh, poor Siân, what a night you've had; you've lost your raincoat, burned your new suit *and* you made a fool of yourself.'

Before I went to the party, when I was still in my dressing room wearing my worn Beth Morgan dress and cracked boots and white wig, Martin Lisemore came in bearing a large pile of scripts. 'Here, have a look at these and tell me if you want to play the part I've marked.'

As I took off my aging wig and make-up for the last time, I flicked through one of the scripts – 'nearly bald, ancient, she looks up at Caligula' – oh no, not *another* geriatric part. Turning back, I read a scene which made me laugh. Flicking forward, I realized that this was a very camp script, very well written by Jack Pullman. I got Martin on the extension. 'That was quick.' 'Yes, well, I'm obviously doomed to play old bags forever and this does make me laugh – and we've had a *nice* time over the last six months – haven't we?' 'Is that a "yes", then?' 'Why not.' By the time I left the building I'd agreed to play Livia in *I, Claudius*.

The incessant activity meant that I had very little time in which to review my private life which was, frankly, absurd. It was also becoming nicer and nicer and that was absurd *and* bad. I had a husband with whom I was living what a cynic would call a 'normal' married life – not much in the way of communication and totally satisfactory sex. My lover would have been horrified, I realized, had he been aware of this. Young and romantic, he took it for granted that I would have broken off 'relations' with my husband. I didn't care to disabuse him.

For the first time in my life I had a life of my own which was nothing to do with either of these men and I had no intention of sharing it with either of them. I took good care of all our properties (we had now acquired a flat in the West End as well), went on working on the Irish garden, maintained the Irish house and two other Irish cottages and the house in Hampstead ('maintenance' was a major part of my life). And, my main, big jobs aside, I made broadcasts, wrote book reviews, appeared on television shows, went regularly to the girls' school, organized their weekends, went to the cinema with them and supervised lives which, more and more, ran like clockwork. Everyone was having a perfectly fine, busy time. Although I was a part of many people's lives, it seemed to me that I was still shadowy and superfluous. Except to Robin. To him I was becoming more real – more a possible, valid part of his life. To me, this seemed still ridiculous. There was no way in which our relationship could become 'real', it seemed to me that it could exist only in its present clandestine form. And what would be the outcome? I supposed that it would simply fizzle out. Then what would I do? I would be sad, I was sure of that. O'Toole, leading a completely sober life, was understandably preoccupied with his own problems. The drinks table across the room from his favorite chair was laden, as usual, with bottles. Drink was *pressed* on all our guests. Dr. Slattery prescribed large quantities of vitamins and they were conscientiously taken, also Valium, something new, beneficial and harmless, it was said.

Pat became more and more locked into her life at school and with Mamgu and Liz, and Kate began to rebel fairly seriously and demanded to be allowed to leave school after taking her O–Levels, going instead to an A–Level tutorial college in town. She also demanded to be allowed to go on holiday with a mixed sex group. All this was tricky but pretty standard, I thought. Kate had always been somewhat beyond my control. I admired her independence of spirit and was amused by her escapades and there was very little I could do to alter whatever course she'd decided upon. Until I realized this, we'd lived at loggerheads. Now, I told her what I thought and left her to make her own decisions. O'Toole said he would have a talk with her but that she should be allowed her freedom. I didn't really feel I was in any position to *tell* her how to behave. I'd done everything my parents wished of me: stayed at school, gone to university, married – well, maybe I'd gone slightly wrong at that point – but eventually I'd settled down in a spectacular way. And where had all that got me, I wondered? My life was unravelling and I was endlessly postponing the day of resolution.

But at Christmas I decided that I had to end the affair with Robin. He was devastated and the scenes were prolonged and painful; I also was distraught and very unnerved to realize how attached I had become to him. However my problems were twofold and separate and it was impossible to deal with the difficulties of the marriage while conducting an affair. The parting lasted all of three weeks. We were reunited, feeling relieved but more confused and muddled than ever. We saw each other little, we walked in the park in the cold. We were happy and not happy.

In 1976 O'Toole went to Rome to film *Caligula* with John Gielgud, Malcolm McDowell and Helen Mirren. He rented a house on the Appian Way and began to study Spanish; Mexico still held a potent attraction for him and he determined to learn the language properly. I discovered, by chance, that he had acquired land there and was thinking of building a house. '*Another* house!' I thought indignantly – as though I didn't have enough to look after. Then, realizing that I wasn't meant to know about it, I also realized with some relief that I wasn't going to have to look after it, either. So, what did this signify? The language lessons, the Mexican real estate? I remembered Anna and his strange letter describing my appearance in his dream, almost hallucinatory in character. Was it possible that he, also, was looking for a way to terminate or alter this seemingly unbreakable relationship? That would be too easy by half, I thought ruefully. There was a horrendous time ahead and no way of avoiding it.

Cowardly, I put it out of my mind and concentrated on *I, Claudius*. Robin was a constant on the periphery but I was beginning to realise that to my sorrow, the affair was going to have to end again. I was simply too busy and too involved in other business to move it 'center stage' and it was scarcely fair to Robin to keep him on the sidelines. I postponed the moment. There is something so strange in living a life which is totally chaotic in one aspect and so completely happy and coherent in the other. *I, Claudius* was, after a bumpy start, one of the most pleasurable, carefree jobs I'd ever had.

I'd worked with Herbie Wise, the director, before at Granada when he was part of just about the best drama department in television. He and Jack Pullman and Martin Lisemore and the designer Tim Harvey, and head of costume, Barbara Kroenig, and head of the BBC's superb make-up department, Pam Meagher had been working on the series for a very long time before that first read-though at Acton. I'd worked with or known many of the actors involved: George Baker (not for the first time I was playing the mother of someone who was my senior), Brian Blessed, John Hurt (an old friend), Pat Quinn (my daughter in the Suffragette series), John Castle (whom O'Toole had 'discovered' for *Lion in Winter*), Patsy Byrne (whom I'd been with at Stratford). Herbie laid down the ground rules early on. I had all sorts of ideas about the subtlety of my character, Livia. Derek Jacobi, in one of his first big television parts, was still doubtful about how he was going to play Claudius; we all had our little private problems. After the readthrough – pretty dull – Herbie said, 'Okay, let's get up and try a bit.' We played a few scenes. He looked appalled. 'Look,' he said (in effect), 'we don't have much time and we are certainly not playing some kind of English costume drama. *This* is how we're going to do this show – BIG, up-front, poster paint. It's *my* decision. No negotiation.' Consternation and tears (men, as well). Reluctant performances at rehearsals, wails (very British) of 'But this is so *obvious*.' Remorseless, he whipped us on towards the first episode. It was a nightmare. One of my big scenes came right at the end of the last twelve-hour day. 'Sorry, Siân. We have ten minutes to get this. Get a move on.' Somehow, we got it done – on the run. And it was over. Episode One was finished and we were committed to this somewhat un-English style of acting. Would it be good or awful, we wondered? Herbie was confident. Martin was thinking hard.

Chapter Thirty-three

During the rehearsals for Episode Two we all calmed down. Derek was still saying that he might give up the part, Brian was a bit mutinous, but then Brian always is gloriously mutinous. I sat there, rehearsing a scene with George and Brian on the main set (what we called 'the family parlor'). It was a family squabble scene and I noticed, at the end, that Jack and Herbie were smiling, pleased. 'Tell me,' I said. 'Is this a Jewish comedy?' There was a pause before they beamed and said that they hadn't wanted to say anything so crass but, yes, that was more or less what it was. After that I did as little 'acting' as possible. And the less I did the more approving Herbie was. After the first few weeks everything became terribly easy and hugely enjoyable.

Even so, we had no idea that we were making a classic. As new cast members joined the show, they were sent to a viewing room to see what we'd shot so far. Time after time they came back to the rehearsal room looking doubtful. Close friends said, 'Oh dear, this looks really *strange* – I don't think it's going to do well.' It was so lovely to be in that we stopped caring about the outcome, successful or otherwise. In the summer my character, Livia, 'died'. Martin and Herbie took me to lunch and said we might be on to something. Already, I had begun to worry about my 'life' again and didn't pay much attention. The girls flew back from Ireland and together we went on to Rome to visit their father.

The villa on the Appian Way – pretty enough – had become a 'Petruchio' house, staffed by typical O'Toole Petruchio servants. There was a pool, but it needed cleaning; the sitting room was festooned with wires and recording equipment (Spanish lessons were in full swing). Meals were provided by a small Italian who was prone to fits of hysteria and who was running a busy sideline in stolen jewelry. Where did O'Toole *find* these people? What did the gardener do? Why did the cook confine himself to frying aubergines?

Our visits to the set were even more bizarre. John Gielgud stood there looking grand and pretending not to notice that the girls flanking him were bare breasted and carrying dildos. In the trailer, Helen Mirren and Malcolm McDowell were beyond caring and very funny about their experiences. O'Toole was playing Tiberius and as I watched, he nearly drowned, swimming in a huge red robe, surrounded by up-to-no-good under-age boys (Tiberius's 'minnows'). It was so strange to leave the set of *I, Claudius* (which can't have cost much), which had been researched, old BBC-style, for a year before shooting began and to walk on to this huge set with all that *Penthouse* money behind it and where the actors were paid vastly more than any of us at home and to see it all going horribly wrong. The costumes and make-up and sets were a mess and as for the script . . . I said nothing.

Kate's boyfriend from Ireland pitched up and came to stay. Michael from Clifden was one of the nicest young men I'd ever met and I was sorry that they were meeting at sixteen, when neither of them had spread their wings. They seemed so perfectly suited (certainly *I* was perfectly poised to be *his* perfect mother-in-law), but they were very young. When they disappeared to her room I felt that maybe we should exert some kind of control over them and asked O'Toole to sort out their living and sleeping arrangements. Telling me that I was a little out of touch, he promised to deal with the situation and I was glad to leave it to him. As for us, we had very little to say to each other; my head was still full of *Claudius* (which I had to return to for a 'ghost' scene) and my infidelity; he, for his part, was preoccupied with his Spanish and only in bed did we come together easily, mindlessly, pleasurably.

Jerry Bauer, a photographer who always took our family pictures and who now lived in Rome, came out to take photographs and he released a strange, sad picture of us to the press. It was captioned 'The Last of the Summer Wine'. It looked just that – the end of something.

The girls and I returned to London, leaving O'Toole in Rome, and I began rehearsing a play about Janet Achurch, the actress who created Candida for Bernard Shaw and who ended her days, a great nuisance to him, in a fog of drugs and drink. It was a BBC/TV production, written and directed by Don Taylor. *Frieda*, Sara said, was progressing well. Although she had set up the series through Keep Films, James Cellan Jones, the head of drama at the BBC, would ultimately be in charge. I admired him enormously and knew I'd be in safe hands. It was a very big project, six hours of television, and I looked forward to working on it for the whole of the following year, with any luck. O'Toole returned and began to film for the BBC as well. Jack Gold, an old friend, directed him in an adaptation of a book by Geoffrey Household, *Rogue Male*.

It was I suppose a measure of the gulf that had opened between us that my duplicity, my unhappiness, my withdrawal of myself seemed to go unremarked for so long. Not having any clear idea what I wanted to do I did nothing and dreaded the storm which would surely break over my head one day. In the back of my mind I calculated that when everything was known, I wouldn't have to make the decision which seemed so beyond me, I would merely have to react to events – whatever they might be. That was more or less how things happened, but they seemed to happen in slow motion and time spread and lengthened as it does in dreams. Finally, when O'Toole noticed that something was seriously amiss – and why did he, I wonder? – he sprang into attack mode and began interrogating me, something to which I was only too accustomed and I reacted like a frightened rabbit, much as I had all those years ago when we were first married. I couldn't tell him about Robin at first, not wishing to unleash the eloquent and derisive reaction which I could hear before it was spoken.

Secondary to this selfish desire was a wish to protect Robin; the contest between him and O'Toole seemed painfully unequal. Even worse, the passion I had felt for Robin was diminishing; his violent reactions to our partings had made me realize that he in his youth couldn't fully deal with the situation we had created. My recurring concern was the effect of all this on the girls' lives. Robin couldn't be expected to understand this. He wasn't a parent and had never met my children. All he wanted was me. And I worried about my mother who was oblivious, it seemed, to all that was going on around her. Closed doors and raised voices were things to be complicitly ignored in a house in which alcohol figures so largely. The habit of not acknowledging unpleasantness continued now that sobriety reigned in Guyon House. I went as far as to make it clear that I was unhappy and that I would like us to part and eventually I confessed Robin's name. Useless to say that he was a symptom not a cause, useless to say that all I *really* wanted to do was to live apart, on my own.

Somehow, for months we managed to work, plan future work, live our lives without confiding our problems to anyone. We slept little, argued a great deal, advanced not at all. O'Toole still spent a great deal of time as a more active partner of Keep Films, putting in hours in the office when he wasn't working. He and Jules worked on *Frieda*, among other things, and one day as I sat waiting for a taxi in the parking lot at TV Centre, Jim Cellan Jones called out to me and told me that after all the work the BBC was abandoning *Frieda*. The BBC felt that the demands made by Keep Films were simply too expensive and our company wanted to retain too much control. 'The next time you want to do something,' said Jim, 'do your own negotiating.' It was the end of two years' work. Sara was aghast. I was disbelieving; no one at Keep Films called me to explain what had happened. O'Toole said nothing.

Janet Achurch's photographs featured heavily in Shaw's letters and the BBC went to a great deal of trouble to produce a good photograph of me as her. The play had turned out very well and the photograph was so good that it was decided to make it the cover of the *Radio Times*. Then *Rogue Male* entered the lists and they called me from the BBC to say I'd lost out to my husband. I wasn't surprised, or annoyed. By now I was old in the faith and nothing if not a realist.

Events accelerated. Robin turned up one day to meet me for a snatched coffee and said he'd told his parents about us. I wasn't pleased but said nothing. In the same week, O'Toole summoned Robin to meet him in his palatial office in Belgravia. Robin had called him and asked for an interview. He was glad to have things come to a head but I felt sorry for him and I feared for him. He seemed strangely unafraid and unaffected and as far as I could make out, he more or less asked for my hand. I don't know how O'Toole responded. The situation was careering out of control. I wanted my hand to myself. O'Toole told me to end the affair once and for all and I felt that ending the affair *was* inevitably the right thing to do but not so I could stay within the marriage. The cheap jokes and the scorn strengthened my wish to leave. To leave and live alone.

But once again I ended the affair and again I was surprised to be overcome with sadness, more affected than I had anticipated I would be. I gave Robin my most treasured small possession and said goodbye and went home to bed where I stayed, crying into my pillow like a foolish girl – as I never *had* done as a foolish girl. I couldn't believe that I was behaving in this way. No one seemed to notice that I wasn't up and about. Life at home became a torment. Autumn dragged into winter and I began to see Robin again. There didn't seem to be any reason not to and I did miss him frightfully. I missed having someone to put me first. It was as potent as any drug.

By Christmas of 1976, which was spent in London, O'Toole and I had both reached exhaustion point. Sidney Gottlieb, O'Toole's friend and a hypnotherapist, came to visit and said that something had to be done; we were living a life of unbearable tension. O'Toole refused to discuss a plan, wouldn't release me in a coherent way and I couldn't just jump ship. But, feeling desperate, I did once again terminate my affair with Robin – this time for good, I thought.

I'd become immensely fond of the ugly BBC Television rehearsal rooms in North Acton where I spent so much of my time. There were sometimes thirteen shows in rehearsal so the crowded canteen at the top of the building was like an actors' club. I began to rehearse *Heartbreak House*. Sir John – by far the most illustrious member of our profession in the building – seemed unaware of his status. He adored gossip and scandal and each day he began pointedly looking at his watch a good five or ten minutes before the lunch break began. Once in the canteen he would stand there holding his tray, transfixed by the 'famous' faces all around. 'Look, look!' he hissed one day and I followed his gaze to a table at which sat a very young actress/model/singer/dancer, mainly famous for going to other people's opening nights. 'So?' I said, 'what's so special about her?' 'Oh, *always* photographed going through airports,' breathed John, admiringly. So different from Rex Harrison. When we were embarking on a long rehearsal period for his first ever television play (*Platonov* by Chekhov), he entered the canteen on the first day, a glamorous vision in oatmeal tweed with a cream silk shirt. Startled, he joined the queue as indicated, helped himself to a little food, then looked disbelievingly at his tray and at the plain, noisy room and, setting down the tray, turned and walked swiftly out of the building in search of his chauffeur and the Bentley and disappeared to fetch a little light lunch from his house in Belgravia. He could be seen each day after that, moodily picking at a little cold salmon in the back seat of the car.

When I finished *Heartbreak House*, the bitch – reality – began to nip at my heels again. Life at home was grim for me, living as I was in a kind of limbo; not allowed to leave, obliged to stay – for how long? I didn't know. I felt like a fly in a web, only half alive, wrapped in barely discernible threads. I was lonely. It was unthinkable that I should confide in anyone and I missed Robin's company. Everything around us was beginning to disintegrate; Lionel left to take up another job. For me, this was like losing a brother; although we never ever discussed family problems, in his privileged position he saw and heard everything and was the only person who knew exactly how I was placed. Much as he might wish to, he never ventured to defend me but he was, I knew, deeply upset when I was treated badly. I knew that I could not see him again until I regulated my life. A regulated life seemed beyond our grasp. At one stage it was suggested that we might separate, divorce, and continue to live in the same house – we were thrashing around like animals in a net. O'Toole began to fall out with Jules – Jules, who had run our lives, arranged our finances, organized O'Toole's life in the movies, dealt with every manner of trouble imaginable. In my view, for me to confide in Jules would have been disloyal to O'Toole and worrying and embarrassing for Jules, so I kept my distance and, deprived of the company of Jules and Joyce – my 'family' for as long as I'd been married – I was completely isolated.

O'Toole announced that he was going to Mexico alone to recuperate from his illness. It says a great deal about my half-paralyzed state that it never entered my head to quiz him about his life in that country or his possible attachment to someone there. I asked O'Toole if I might go and spend some time alone in Connemara. He pointed out that the Irish house was not mine and that my presence there was unacceptable. I realized that I had indeed seen the Sky road and the house on the hill for the last time. Ordinarily, I would have been heartbroken, but now it just seemed to be one more blow, much like any other.

The weeks of February dragged. Looking at my diary I see that I went to school to talk about Kate's future. I went to listen to a recording I had made of *Antony and Cleopatra* with Robert Stephens and Ronald Pickup, under the direction of Martin Jenkins at the BBC. I tidied my papers, filed everything to within an inch of its life, rearranged books, answered O'Toole's mail, avoided our friends. Why didn't I take some action of my own? My mind darted from one problem to the next. What would happen to the family if I left? Where would I live? I had never saved money – all my earnings went into the houses, furniture and furnishings, and my clothes. What would I live on? O'Toole warned me that the scandal, when made known, might mean I would find work difficult to come by. And what would happen to my mother? Would I be able to take care of her? There were too many questions to which I had no answer. I was immobilized with no one to talk to in my secret life. And worst of all, I didn't feel I had the *right* to do anything. My capacity for altering my life seemed spent and I waited to hear what O'Toole thought I should do.

He was away in Mexico for six weeks and I kicked my heels in Hampstead. We were not in touch. When he returned it was only for a day or two before he left on private business in Bristol. He had arrived at a solution during his stay in Mexico – it was just as well that one of us had done so. It was clear to him that I should leave Guyon House. I had no reason to disagree with this decision but I didn't know where to go and when he returned from Bristol a few days later I had made no plans at all. It was February 21 and I agreed with him it was right that I should leave home the following day at four o'clock. Still I did nothing, made no provision. I couldn't argue with his disdain at my paralysis; I rather agreed with him that such feebleness was despicable. Had he not helped devise a means of departure, I might have continued for months to sit, half dead, in that lovely house.

On February 22 he assembled the household; my mother, Kate, Pat and Liz, meeting in the Green Room; the girls and Liz sitting on the big couch, my mother in an armchair and O'Toole in the high Prides leather wing chair I had bought him when he had hurt his back. I sat in the most disadvantageous chair in the room, a Charles Eames chair I had given O'Toole after a particularly well-paid TV job. It was low and luxurious and in its embrace I appeared indolent and relaxed. Unbelievably, I lounged there and told the people to whom I was closest that I was 'exhausted' and needed to leave home for a 'rest'. The family looked at me, silent and uncomprehending. I'd finished what O'Toole called my 'Father Xmas version' of the events of the last two years. No one spoke. Finally O'Toole rose and said, 'Well, that's that then.' He was brisk and benevolent as he moved to the study. It was clear that I was dismissed.

I went to the bedroom, while the family dispersed over the other four floors of the house. I felt numb beyond tiredness as I began to pack, barely acknowledging to myself that the scene I had rehearsed and played had been deeply humiliating. I knew that I would never see O'Toole again; he prided himself on his resolutely unforgiving nature and I had no wish to expose myself ever again to being patronized in this lordly way.

Swiftly, I reviewed the situation. My mother would stay and run Guyon House – she did not know and was not to be told that I would not return. The girls' lives would continue uninterrupted. They went to school at Edgware, so it was important that they remained where they were. Liz was, by now, part of the family and I knew they would be looked after properly and enjoy all the benefits to which they were accustomed. On that day in February I had nothing to offer them. It would not have occurred to me or to anyone in our circle to question O'Toole's decisions. I had sometimes observed people formulate an unspoken question in response to some draconian pronouncement on O'Toole's part, but I never saw anyone defy him or question him. Not once.

I began to fill two suitcases – black things only, something to wear to BAFTA which was coming up, one pair of black shoes, one black bag, a few toilet things. Where could I go? O'Toole had told me that I wasn't to tell anyone that we were parting. He said there would be unwelcome publicity if anyone found out that I wasn't living at home. I accepted this and it worried me but in a way, in spite of my efforts to free myself, I was still identifying with him, even against myself. I was looking at the situation from his point of view, not mine; I realized that I wasn't going to be able to handle this change in my life on my own but I couldn't ask any of 'our' people for help – it would place them in an intolerable position. Everyone was nervous of 'The Guvnor'. The only person I could think of who would not be made nervous by helping me was Ricci – Ricci Burns. I called him at his hairdressing salon in George Street. 'I'm leaving home and I have to be out of here in forty-five minutes.' He asked no questions. 'Take a cab and go straight to my flat in Portman Towers. Leave the bags there and then come back here to the salon to see me.' I called a taxi on the bedroom phone and looked around for what I knew would be the last time ever. The room had altered a little and was not quite as perfect as it had been when Joyce and I first designed it. The bed now had its back to the bow window since the night O'Toole had set fire to it when it was placed against the wall, but the room was still beautiful; my 'things' lay behind closed drawers and cupboards.

The months of turmoil were over.

I lifted both bags and walked downstairs and out into

the street to wait for the taxi. I met no one on the way out; the house was sweetly scented, shining and quiet and, like water, the air closed behind me as though I had never been there.

Chapter Thirty-four

Ricci was wonderfully, reassuringly flippant and dispelled the effect of the endless gloomy drama that had prevailed for so long at home. 'Silly cow, get over this nonsense. Say you're sorry and *go home*, for God's sake.' Lilian, his mother, said, 'Have my room. I'll go away for a week – but *listen* to Ricci, please.' She was fond of O'Toole and he of her and we had spent many happy hours together, the four of us but, like many people, she liked the *idea* of us, the O'Tooles, and knew little of our private life. 'So,' said Ricci when he came home from work, 'you *look* all right. Who have you left him for?' When I told him that there *had* been someone and that it was all over and I was planning to live on my own, he simply didn't believe me. 'I love you but you're lying. I know you.' Ricci and I were so different and so close. He understood me very well and his advice on most matters, even complicated professional matters to which he responded in a purely instinctive manner, was always good and I listened to him even before Sara with her experience, or O'Toole with his huge knowledge of the Business. Now, he was wrong and we bickered and argued as we cooked supper and we went on arguing for weeks to come.

He found me a small service flat in Curzon Street and I moved in and began to heal physically. I couldn't remember when I had last slept so well. I was still smoking as heavily as ever but I didn't drink at all and I lived a hidden life in the flat, seeing no one except Ricci and Lilian and my mother, Liz and Pat. In the evenings, I hung out of my window, watching people entering the Mirabelle restaurant below. My life had changed utterly overnight. (The Mirabelle was probably a thing of the past, I thought.) Our joint bank account was closed and naturally my small allowance ceased; my medical insurance was cancelled; however I was strangely untroubled as I felt myself becoming rested, stronger and more contented. I had enough money in my own account to live on for the present and I went on working.

I hadn't seen Robin since before I left Guyon House and thought never to see him again. The madness that had possessed me was over. Now living at home with his parents, he found out where I was and asked if he could come to see me. I realized that it no longer mattered to me whether I saw him or not. When he arrived I explained that I had to go out and left him in the flat to wait – or not – till I returned. He was still there at midnight and we spent the night together and it was hugely agreeable but I told him that I didn't even wish us to meet again. He accepted this, remarking that it seemed such a shame that someone who liked sex so much should consign herself to a celibate life. For a moment, I couldn't follow his thinking. Then I remembered that he had no way of knowing that I had maintained a sexual relationship with my husband. Feeling only momentarily guilty, I assured him that celibacy was probably going to be just fine and we parted. Forever. I realized that I was mightily relieved to have simplified my life.

A few people had to be told where I was. They were sworn to secrecy. Sara (to whom I'd been introduced by Ricci), was wonderful to me. I'd stuck by her early on in our relationship when she'd been hospitalized with a mystery ailment – and now she repaid the debt of loyalty with interest. As a sideline she read scripts for Keep Films and developed projects for O'Toole. Now he told her to choose between Keep and me. Unhesitatingly she chose me. Not only that but she called me every morning to check that I was all right before she opened the office. My accountant, John Libson, the son of the Keep

Films accountant, the great Nyman Libson, also showed that he was not going to abandon me and between us all we tried to find a financial path forward. It was realized that since I didn't know what O'Toole might suddenly do with regard to my mother or the girls, I had better try to buy a house that would shelter all of them – a four-bedroom house, in fact. How to do this? Out of the blue I received two large checks – rerun fees for lengthy serials – and John reminded me that, on his advice some years previously, I'd left some film money outside the UK and now it could be retrieved, legally and tax free. I could buy a house! I could hardly believe it. Ricci and I found a house for me in an early Victorian part of Islington.

Miraculously, we kept the story of my separation from O'Toole out of the papers but I now told my mother the truth. She knew better than to suggest we might patch things up. Marie, who was staying at Guyon House while filming, spent her evenings with me and she also knew better than to suggest that the rift between O'Toole and myself could ever be healed.

Islington in 1977 had not become fashionable; the Georgian bits were fairly desirable but the Victorian section I was to buy into – built on a square mile of old market garden – boasted not too expensive, solid, well-built, airy houses with decent gardens. I found the house through Peter Brooke in the King's Road, a firm I remembered from my undergraduate days and renowned for its blunt descriptions ('Horrible flat in a bad neighborhood, in need of repair, looks for a loving, mad buyer', etc). John D. Wood and Chestertons were snooty and depressingly pessimistic. It was raining. At Peter Brooke they took me in, gave me some tea, told me to sit down and get dry and reassured me that I'd have no trouble buying a house with the money at my disposal. And I didn't. Sara knew that I now needed to make regular money and between us we saw to it that I didn't spend an idle day. Ricci found me a larger flat in Chelsea and it was easy to move my few belongings to this new, secret address. Only Sara, Marie, my mother, Ricci and John Libson had the phone number.

I was preparing to play Boadicea for a Thames Television series called *Boudicca* and was spending a large part of every week in Kingston-on-Thames in an indoor riding school, learning to ride bareback on the nastiest horse I'd ever met – Jasper, who knew that I was vulnerable and took advantage. At weekends, bleeding and barely able to walk, I saw Pat and my mother and Kate, who, I fancied, was rather glad to have got rid of the Wicked Witch of the West and, looking at it from her standpoint, I didn't entirely blame her. She was at a rebellious age and, no doubt, behaved better when I wasn't there. My mother didn't think much of my flat, after the splendors of 'home'. The girls rather enjoyed puttering around it – it was smaller than their nursery apartment. It seemed that they had deduced correctly that the marriage was over and no one reacted with regret or sorrow or surprise. Pat said consolingly that she only had one friend with two parents living together. There was no possibility that they could move from Hampstead while they were at school, even had they wished to but I assured them that very soon I would have a house large enough for all of us, should the need arise.

Organizing the house purchase was eventful to say the least. *Boudicca* was shot on location all over southern England. I would repair, painted white – or blue – as the script demanded, to the nearest telephone kiosk to plead with my charming young lawyer at Harbottle & Lewis to speed things up. 'How can I *force* her to complete?' 'Oh, it's very easy.' 'Really?' 'Yes, you take hostages and every day when she doesn't do it, you shoot one.' I stopped nagging him. My life was complicated by the fact that, following O'Toole's instructions, I was pretending to everyone (except those in my small, close circle) that I lived in Hampstead in the family home. In order to be picked up at 5:30 a.m. by the Thames TV car, I had to rise at 3:30 a.m. in my Chelsea flat and then get myself up to Heath Street and wait in the street until the car arrived to pick me up and at night, after I was dropped off in NW3, I had to make my own way back down to Chelsea again. Tired and furtive, I felt like a member of MI5 on a dangerous mission.

Towards the end of March I went to the British Academy dinner and award ceremony. The organizers wanted to arrange a suitable escort for me when they learned I wouldn't be attending with my husband. I resisted this vigorously; I was really enjoying life on my own and didn't feel the need for an escort. (I had a small dalliance with a really charming writer but decided I couldn't cope with a relationship and firmly told him so with a new-found honesty that I, at least, found refreshing!) I had been nominated as Best Actress for *Livia* and *Beth Morgan* but hadn't really had time to think about the possibility of winning. Ricci pulled me together and organized my appearance – my dress and my hair – and off I went alone in a taxi. I sat halfway up the auditorium next to a well-known comedian who told me that my position in the auditorium meant that I was *not* going to be a winner. I rather agreed with him and we were both surprised when my name was called.

After the ceremony I found a taxi and went straight home to Chelsea, preoccupied as usual with the problems of the morning pick-up in Hampstead. As I paid off the cab and fished out my front door key, a figure appeared from the shadows. It was Robin. He'd watched the ceremony on television and had come round to congratulate me. How was it that he always managed to find out where I was and be there to do something really nice for me? I had not been planning to mark the occasion at all, but now we sat up and had a celebratory drink together. He still lived at home with his parents in their house in Bayswater. 'Mind if I stay over?' he asked, trying to sound casual. He *was* forward. And sweet. I would have preferred him to go home but it seemed a bit mean, considering the fact that he was the only person who'd bothered to say 'well done'. 'Okay, but just for tonight,' I replied. He agreed and went home the following day and I got on with my life.

The post arrived bringing a typed confession for me to sign. I called Sara, asleep in bed, to ask what I should do. 'Sign nothing,' she cried and gave me the name of a lawyer to consult. Now, I was not only trying to buy a house by remote control, I also had a divorce lawyer to see every week. Trevor Williams – the most gentlemanly of lawyers – became a fixture in my life and I met him regularly for the next three years. Having completed *Boudicca*, I was on my way to try on crinolines at Bermans for a BBC serial called *Off to Philadelphia in the Morning*, when O'Toole demanded a meeting where I was to hand over the signed 'confession'. We met on the pavement and I told him that my lawyer would not countenance my signing such a thing. When he learned I had engaged a lawyer he was enraged. Engaging a lawyer, it seemed, was as bad a deed as having an affair had been in the first place. 'Goodbye,' he snapped, turning towards his chauffeur waiting at the curb. 'Goodbye,' I replied faintly but resolutely and turned into the costumer's fitting room. It was still only 10 a.m. and I *shook*. They laced me into my Victorian corset and slipped on my opera singer's dress – pale blue taffeta – I heard a buzzing in my ears and the faces around me approached and receded and the voices grew loud and then indistinct and I felt myself beginning to fall and mercifully for a while I was released from the dreadful day.

I came to, laid out on an elegant couch in the big fitting room, worried, sympathetic figures hovering around me. I wondered how on earth I was going to survive this battle with O'Toole. Obviously the first step was to get on with the fitting so I could do the next job. I apologized and began to get up. My dress felt strange and oh, *merde*! I couldn't believe it – as though things weren't bad enough, for the first time in my life I had wet myself (and ruined yards and yards of expensive silk). 'Oh Lord,' I began, confused and embarrassed, 'I don't know how to apologize.' 'Hah!' barked an elegant young man and deftly tore the soiled length of silk from its moorings at my waist and consigned it to oblivion. 'Think nothing of it,' he said firmly, and calling out 'More silk!' went on with the fitting, and on I went, one step at a time, with very little idea where I was heading or what I would do when I got there.

After about a month Robin telephoned me – we hadn't been in touch at all since the British Academy Award night – and asked if he might come round to visit at the weekend. I was still in hiding and welcomed the company. He stayed the night. The same thing happened the following weekend and a few weeks later he left some of his things in the flat and before long he began spending the greater part of every week there. I was out at work during the day so it made sense that we should stay indoors in the evening. But weekends were difficult. I was nervous of being seen in the street near the flat and it wasn't easy being cooped up indoors, especially when the weather began to improve. On the whole we got on reasonably well but already I could see that there were difficulties ahead. At weekends I cleaned and laundered and shopped and cooked. Robin loved sunbathing above everything and while the sun shone he lay beneath it, methodically 'working' on his tan. As I hoovered and struggled to come to grips with domestic arts I'd never before had to try to master except briefly at Stratford – which was a long while ago – I looked malevolently at the oiled, brown body on the balcony. O'Toole's words to me after he'd met Robin crossed my mind. 'Watch out for those small, brown eyes,' he'd said, 'and remember, you can't afford him.'

As I worried about the girls and my mother, saving as much money as I could and working all the hours I could, I thought to myself, 'This is very pleasant in many ways but it is going to have to stop,' and finally I plucked up courage to say to

Robin that he could not possibly move with me to my house in Islington, when my life would cease to be a clandestine, hole-in-the-corner affair and become 'real' again. 'I cannot see you in the road with my Pickford's removal van,' I told him, trying to make light of it. 'Oh I don't see why not,' he replied breezily. 'I can take care of the whole thing for you.' And he more or less did. When the mood took him he could get a lot done. I was fully occupied with work and my visits to the lawyers' office; mountains of paperwork arrived regularly from O'Toole's lawyers and I had to sit for hours every week, answering all the points and trying to distance myself emotionally, but I came away from each meeting distressed and shaken. It was comforting to have someone take care of me. Robin organized deliveries, took messages and actually moved into the house while I was away at work and saw to it that we had a table at which to eat, somewhere to sit, somewhere to sleep, a stove and fridge. With a sudden rush of energy he even built me a broom cupboard, bought groceries, prepared meals and was charm itself to the girls and my mother, who was impressed by the broom cupboard. I had now accompanied Kate on her first day to Davies College where she would do her A–Levels and my mother was still at Guyon House to see Pat through her O–Levels (Liz would be in Hampstead as well). Pat couldn't possibly travel from my house in Islington to school in Edgware each day. It wasn't perfect but it was workable and now I *did* have a house in place, in case of emergencies.

This house was the first I'd ever lived in where I took care of everything myself. I cleaned it, did the laundry, struggled with the ironing and, book in hand, I began cooking in earnest. Meals for ten or twelve people became the norm. Robin's family and our friends and the girls sat around the big dining table and, ironing excepted, I began to enjoy the intense domesticity. There were still moments when I wanted to murder Robin as, if the mood took him, he rested while

I wrestled with a new job *and* put in long hours in the kitchen, but on the whole it had a great deal of charm, this new life. Robin acted very little but this didn't seem to bother him. (For how long? I wondered.) My mother gave us a small, cheap car and for my part I began to familiarize myself with public transport. My life could not have changed more completely and although my vision of myself had been of someone living alone, unencumbered by the demands and irritations of a permanent relationship, there was something rather wonderfully absorbing about living with someone with whom I got on very well indeed, although we had little in common. It was shaking me up in an interesting way and I did, for a while, adopt alternative ways of looking at people and events. And it was exhilarating to feel that I was in charge of our lives. I said what I pleased, did what I pleased, within reason, and nothing in my life made me nervous or afraid. If anything annoyed me I could walk away from it. A horrible thought gave me pause; I was behaving rather as middle-aged men behave when they abandon their wives and take up with a younger, good-looking bimbo with whom they appear to have nothing in common. If that was the case it didn't reflect well on me or on Robin – and there *was* genuine affection between us. Nevertheless, I read something which gave me food for thought. It seems there are two periods in a woman's life when she throws her bonnet over the windmill; one is when she is about twenty-four and the other when she is about forty. At more or less those ages I'd first flown against all advice and married O'Toole and, much later, taken a young lover. It was humbling to feel like a textbook case. But, best of all, I wasn't living in, and being reminded that I was living in, a house that belonged to someone else. The house was constantly filled with people, and I could invite whoever I pleased.

Gradually, the house which had begun as a pretty but empty shell took shape. Each time I completed a job I 'did' another room or carpeted the stairs or bought curtains or china. Like many only children, I had been over attached to my 'things'; pencils, pens, books. I liked to arrange my room exactly as I wished, not really wanting to share my time or my possessions, and very often preferring to be an observer rather than a participator. I had carried much of this behavior into adulthood but now I changed my ways. I had lost this attachment to my possessions. I would never again see 'my' garden in Ireland and if ownership is 'that with which man has mingled his labour' then it surely *was* mine. The Irish house and all my books and notes and furniture were gone, but I realized now that it was the work of building that I most enjoyed, not sitting around luxuriating in the result of that work. As for the beauty of the place, it didn't belong to anyone and it was imprinted on my retina. Every so often I would wish to be standing there. I would feel blowing into my heart 'the air that kills', see in my mind's eye 'the land of lost content'. But those moments were few and I grew to love my bright, cheerful house in the busy, dusty streets of N1, off the unlovely Essex Road.

Robin began taking an interest in horticulture and together we improved the garden at the back of the house – he, learning to lay York stone and build steps. He had no way of knowing that nothing a man could do would impress me more. Everything that we had, we shared with friends and he helped me turn my private life outwards for the first time.

Chapter Thirty-five

Denise Sée was our Keep Films company lawyer – poached by us from United Artists – small, like a pouter pigeon in a grey barathea business suit and shiny black shoes and briefcase, iron-grey hair cut short, in private life a cordon bleu cook, devoted to her husband and her dachshunds. She was content to let her appearance lull her opponents into underestimating her formidable mind and killer instincts, and she took me in hand when I was a young wife under considerable pressure from the paparazzi. 'Whatever the provocation, don't answer back. Never complain. Never explain and above all do not engage in litigation.' I thought of her words each week as I climbed the stairs to Trevor Williams's office in Holborn. It seemed now I couldn't avoid litigation. O'Toole had teams of expensive divorce lawyers who flew wherever he was filming and lengthy affidavits would then come winging to me in London and there was nothing for it but to continue to sit with Trevor and slowly refute them, point by point. O'Toole still had the power to make me laugh and Trevor was occasionally scandalized by my inappropriate reaction to a particularly ridiculous statement. At one stage, O'Toole's lawyers were changed for reasons I could only guess at, and we all went back to square one. There seemed no reason why this divorce business should ever come to an end.

Denise pointed out that she had years ago secured half ownership for me of one of our properties, the house in London. That was all I could legally claim from the marriage, but I requested the rest of my clothes, my grandmother's furniture, my mother's silver and a guarantee that the girls would be assured money for their higher education. O'Toole quite rightly supposed that nothing would induce me to embarrass the children by opposing him in open court publicly raking over my difficulties within the marriage. Also, I didn't feel like presenting such a simple and consequently incomplete picture to the world. In many, so many, regards our life together had been thrilling and happy and exactly what I wanted. And my high regard for O'Toole's many virtues remained intact. Of course, as Trevor pointed out, this would be construed by the opposing side as weakness; and it soon became clear that his lawyers *did* think that I was stupid, which I wasn't, and my lawyer incompetent, which he was not. Trevor suited me because he was not a thug and not combative but even he said that he was bound to point out that it was absurd that I should walk away with so little after twenty years. He added that he understood my reasons for leaving quietly and even sympathized with my stance. There was a moment when it seemed as though I would have to fight to keep the house I had just bought with my own money but the claim was abandoned. Even so, it took almost two years to reach an agreement by which I willingly gave up everything I might reasonably have laid claim to. It was a sad and sorry affair and I was to see all my jewelry – the accumulated birthday, Christmas and anniversary gifts – for sale at Sotheby's. I tried never to think about the divorce the moment I closed the door to Trevor's office and he found the case so depressing that he said he was disinclined to accept another divorce suit. By the time I was divorced, Keep Films had ceased to involve Jules. Naturally, Joyce and I resigned as directors and the Bucks began to think of returning to America.

Trevor took me for a farewell lunch near Chancery Lane. 'There you are,' he said. 'Free – free to make the same mistakes all over again.' I laughed uneasily. It was the winter of 1979 and I'd been working flat out since I'd left Hampstead in 1977. I was driven by the need to achieve some financial security but, or maybe because of that, the work had been variable in quality. The West End play I did, called *Spine Chiller*, was so bad that it acquired a cult following. Friends crept in to see it week after week – to laugh. In January 1978 we received a notice that pronounced confidently, 'This is the worst play of 1978.' It is difficult, going 'on' night after night in a terrible flop. My friend Fenella Fielding called and asked me to get her tickets for the mid-week matinée. I pleaded with her not to come, but she insisted. When the day came I forgot that she was out front and trudged back to the dressing room after the matinée to put my feet up before the next performance. There was a knock on the door and I heard the unmistakable Fielding tones. Opening the door, I moaned, 'Oh God, Fen, I'd forgotten you were in. Please don't say anything. I *know* what it's like.' 'No, no,' she reproved, 'persevering out there in a turkey like this is useful. It *builds muscle.*' And it does, but one wouldn't want to do it too often. My dear friends Edward Hibbert and Edward Duke – both unknown to me at the time – sneaked in regularly for the curtain to the last act where, dressed in Balenciaga, I sank down, center stage, cradling the dying, very black murderer in my arms and he looked up and whispered 'Mother' as the curtain slowly fell on my astonished face. Not as astonished as the audience, believe me. George Baxt, the author, a witty, clever novelist, became a firm friend and ever after we wondered how we had sleepwalked our way into such a disaster.

On top of everything I went down with violent food poisoning the night before we opened that play on the road and I saw the truly sweet side of Robin's nature. He was keeping me company on tour (and that also was a first for me and very agreeable) and now he sat up all night, holding my head, wringing out towels, cleaning me up. I'd never been taken care of in this way – not by anyone – and of course I liked it. But not enough to entertain the prospect of marriage and that was being proposed more insistently and with greater frequency.

The mere thought filled me with fright. And there was the question of the age difference. Once again, I brought up all the arguments against such a lopsided union. What about children? It seemed unfair that he should be denied a family and while it was physically *possible* for me to have children, I didn't want a second family and couldn't see how I could fit a child into my already overcrowded life. He assured me that he had no interest in being a father and that he had thought through all the problems. All he wanted was that we should be married and he wasn't going to rest until we were. I persisted in saying that – like him and me in the street with the Pickford's van – I couldn't *see* it. He pointed out that we were having a perfectly nice time, living together, so why *not* get married? The argument went on and on. Well, it wasn't exactly an argument; he remained good tempered and rational – and adamant, and I shook my head and feebly waved my hands about. Of course, it was *hugely* flattering as well as worrying – and wrong.

The day my divorce became final he came home with a special licence. I was aghast. He'd arranged a party after the wedding ceremony and we'd tell our friends then. We would get married first thing in the morning on Christmas Eve to avoid the press. 'For the last time,' he said, 'give me one reason why *not*.' It seems feeble to say that I'd been ground down, but I'd run out of arguments and yes, we *did* get on better and better. Something was working, that much was obvious.

There wasn't time to do much in the way of preparation for the wedding. I prepared a buffet supper for about fifty people. My main preoccupation was to avoid publicity but I bought a new grey skirt from Browns and fished a nice old St Laurent coat from the back of the wardrobe. Robin's family attended.

The girls were on holiday and my mother didn't choose to attend. I wasn't surprised or upset. Ricci and Sara came to the Rosebery Avenue registry office, neither of them approving or hopeful of a happy outcome. At the party at home as the news slowly circulated, not a few people asked, '*What* do you think you're doing?' I said, 'Look, I'm not doing. It's done. Don't ask.'

I entered the Eighties, nervous, dreading the newspaper attention, but determined to keep a straight back and maybe Robin had been right – life at home was now more relaxed than ever. Ricci determined to try to be pleased for me. Sara said, 'Keep your own bank account.' Almost everyone was unexpectedly kind and understanding. Inevitably, in time the press became involved and the papers made a huge business of the age difference. I tried to keep my comments on marriage to a minimum, pointing out that it was people who'd been married only once who were in a position to be knowledgeable and wise about the institution. What did I know?

Reading the tabloids one day I noticed with amusement that O'Toole had moved a Mexican girl called Anna into the house. (He renamed her Malinche after Simón Bolívar's mistress but she could have been the Anna of the sad note and poem.) So I had after all been right to feel curious, had I? How did he manage never to relinquish the high moral ground, I wondered, unable to keep from smiling at his nerve. My mother completely astonished me. She was still running the Hampstead house and over Sunday lunch at my house she said, 'You know that Malinche has moved in. She had a *beautiful* pair of expensive, new boots yesterday. I said to Peter last week, "I will look after Malinche as though she were my own daughter".' Well! I was lost for words. I was glad that she was taking what could have been an awkward situation in her stride but did she have to be *quite* so enthusiastically generous towards my successor?

Robin and I were apart a good deal now. He went off on a provincial tour and I got ready to go away to film a TV series about Sean O'Casey in Ireland. Before I left I tried to find a new stage play. After the débâcle of George's *Spine Chiller* I redeemed myself slightly with *You Never Can Tell* at the Lyric

Hammersmith, the play that opened the new theater there. Our first week was gruelling as the construction workers moved out and earnest efforts were made to clear away the drunks from their usual pitch outside the stage door before we embarked on four days of openings – for dignitaries, the press, fund raisers and, finally, Her Majesty the Queen (the drunks were back for that, I noticed). Smoke alarms went off, the sprinkler system was activated and there were police dogs everywhere sniffing at one's make-up. I love Shaw but Mrs Clandon is one of those heavy-duty parts that are all hard work and no jam. Paul Rogers was superb as the Waiter and it was a uniformly good cast, but even so, I wasn't sorry when we closed. The plays sitting on my desk weren't spectacular. The best script by far was not a play, it was a musical. But I'd never done a musical. I could read music after a fashion but I'd never sung alone in public, so I laid it aside and went on reading the plays. But I kept coming back to the musical. No harm in talking to the director, Robert Walker (what on earth made him think that I could do this show, I wondered). He was breezy and confident on the phone. I explained why casting me was a terrible idea. 'Nah, nah,' he responded. 'Give it a go. It'll be great.' I was beginning to think he was deranged. 'What's he like?' I asked around. The answers were uniformly favorable: 'talented, bit of a maverick, deeply attractive, law unto himself'. Mmm. I knew the score of the show because I'd been playing the LP at home for at least ten years. 'I'd better come and meet the musical director,' I suggested. If he says 'no' I shan't do it. 'Yeah, okay,' Robert agreed equably and so I found myself in a house in Islington nervously (and presumably very badly) singing through Vera's numbers from *Pal Joey*.

'Yah, great,' said Robert casually. He didn't seem to be paying a great deal of attention. 'What d'you think?' I asked John Fiske, sitting at the piano. 'You'll be all right,' he said, 'if you start taking singing lessons right away and keep at it. Call Ian Adam, he'll get you on.' I walked home through Canonbury hardly believing that I had just agreed to star in an American musical. Of course, it was only for a run of six weeks and the theater was in the Mile End Road. No one I knew would be there to see me fall on my face. I bought a tuning fork and hoped that Robert Walker knew what he was doing.

Before I had time to begin getting nervous about my new job, I read a TV script that made me laugh so much I almost fell out of bed. It was one episode of a very long and successful Tyne Tees serial called *Barriers*. Unbelievably (in view of the nature of my role) it was targeted at older children. Over-riding the dampening comments in the production office ('She'll *never* do it.' 'It's only *one* episode.' 'It goes out late *afternoons*/early evening.') Malcolm Drury, the casting director, said, 'Nothing ventured . . .' and mailed me a script. Even as I finished it, I reached for the phone and accepted the job. I was to play a slightly dazed, glamorous middle-European, retired opera singer, a widow who'd been married to a very small, rich man called Mr Dalgleish who left her lots of money, a castle in Scotland and two Rolls-Royces and she employed two chauffeurs – very young and beautiful, in pasted-on trousers – 'Two – in case one gets tired, you know'. As it turned out, my contribution apart, the series was very moving. Who had dreamt up this extraordinary character? I turned back the pages and read 'William Corlett'. I looked him up. Former actor, theater playwright, award-winning novelist, TV writer – award-winning TV writer – for some reason I had never come across him. Paul Rogers was the star of the series and Benedict Taylor was the juvenile lead. It would be lovely to work again with Paul, one of the best actors in the country, and I could just fit this in before *Pal Joey* and *Sean O'Casey*. What could William C. be like? Would I get to meet him?

I called Robin to let him know that I was off, picked up

a dress from St Laurent, negotiated the hire of a sable coat for myself and, with no time to fit a wig, packed a Graham Smith turban. I did *love* dashing around as and when I chose, answerable to no one. It occurred to me that maybe I was enjoying my freedom too much. Undeniably there was an element in it not only of making up for lost time, but of getting my own back on everyone who'd ever cramped my style. Robin might have more trouble to deal with than he could have anticipated.

In Newcastle, Maggie Bottomley, the producer, gave a lavish dinner for Paul, Patti Lawrence (who was playing his secretary), William Corlett and myself. It was a riotous evening and we ate and drank too much and I was in no mood to stop but Paul coughed gently and indicated the lift and bed. I couldn't wait for morning when we would drive to Bamborough Castle and begin shooting. Mr Corlett – Bill already – had made me laugh more than anyone I'd met for a very, very long time. We had a wonderful time, freezing all over Northumbria (thank God for the sables). Maggie provided real champagne for the picnic scenes and every night Bill and I thawed out, listening to *Pal Joey* and then, already replete with location catering food and sips of champagne, laid into huge dinners. By the time we took the train back to London we were fast friends and planning to do more work together. We were also a good deal fatter. I felt I'd acquired a brother and I blessed casting director, Malcolm Drury for sending me the script and Sara for encouraging him to do so.

It was March and *Pal Joey* was not due to start rehearsing until June. I knew all the lyrics and I took the tapes with me to Dublin where I would stay in Baggot Street with Marie Kean while I played Countess Markievicz in the Sean O'Casey series. Because there was a TV strike on I had a great deal of time off and Marie and I spent far too much time going to restaurants and staying up late at the Arts Club where she was a member. This was another aspect of my new life in which I was revelling – and far too enthusiastically; for the first time drink was a huge pleasure, with no worries attached. I could drink as and when I pleased because there was no fear that I would be setting a bad example or laying the ground for trouble ahead. If anyone became drunk and objectionable, I could walk away if I pleased. I no longer had to be the good caretaker and it was terrific – for a while.

Waking one morning with a terrible hangover, I looked at Marie and said, 'This, alas, has got to stop.' On the spot I renounced my brief career as a bar fly and began to *run* to Marie's masseur's clinic every morning for a treatment before running on to work at the TV studio in Donnybrook. Life in Dublin was just as much fun on tea and orange juice as it had been on wine and I began to get fit. I might not be any *good* in *Pal Joey* but I was determined to be 'able' for it. I loved working at RTE, and especially enjoyed working with the wonderful Irish actor, John Lynch, who played Sean O'Casey, and only disliked having to learn to handle a rifle. I don't think I managed to make it look more menacing than a handbag.

When I finished in Ireland I joined Robin on tour in Scotland and we spent a lovely week in Edinburgh before returning to London together. He was a skillful driver and I always felt safe with him. Driving down what Ralph Richardson used to call 'the backbone of England' was an unexpected pleasure. I was astonished to see that so much of this small island was still green, unpopulated and unspoiled.

London. *Pal Joey*. My life closed down to contain nothing but the show. I met my vocal coach for the first time and from now on I would see Ian Adam four times a week and every day I would practice his exercises at home. Without Robin I could never have done *Pal Joey*. Well, I *would* have done it, but with great difficulty. Ian, my music teacher, lived in Knightsbridge, I lived in Islington, *Pal Joey* rehearsals took place in the East End and there were wig fittings with Brian Peters in W1 and costume fittings in Soho. Without Robin's willingness to drive me all over London every day, to wait for me, to pick me up, to deliver me back to work and to have something prepared for dinner at night, I don't see how I would have managed. I was being paid £60 a week with no prospect of earning more. It would have been ruinous for me to take taxis all over London and public transport would never have got me to my appointments on time.

I was on a strict diet again (I'd given up dieting when I met Robin). The script demanded that the clothes for Vera in *Pal Joey* had to be simply wonderful. The Half-Moon Theater budget was £200 for six outfits. Impossible. Among my new circle of friends were two of the top British designers, John Bates and Bill Gibb. Lunching at John's apartment one Sunday, I tentatively asked if he might consider designing me just one outfit in which I could sing 'Bewitched, Bothered and Bewildered'. 'I'll do the lot,' he said, casually. 'If I don't have time, Billy there will do them,' indicating Bill Gibb. I was speechless. 'Mind you,' said John, 'no bra – no underpinning and you need to be *thin*.' 'Thinner?' I asked, standing up straight and breathing in. ''Fraid so, dear.' John set about making a breathtaking wardrobe and also took care of the hats, gloves, furs, shoes and bags. He made no charge. Whatever came after, I was going to make a stunning first entrance, looking confident and RICH. No trouble or expense was spared. John's best cutter was on holiday and he looked at the white silk jersey dress that his *second*-best cutter had made and in a fury tore it off and flung it to the floor, lifting the phone and summoning the 'genius-with-the-scissors' back to London immediately. Naturally I had to do my bit as well and, weight dropping steadily, I stood for hours in the fitting room, one eye on my watch, with hours of work ahead, worrying desperately if I was up to any of this.

Stuart Hopps had the daunting task of teaching me to dance. Denis Lawson, who played Joey, was a very good dancer and an experienced singer. They were both endlessly patient, going over my routines in corridors and unoccupied corners of the shabby little rehearsal building – rat poison everywhere – over-run with confident, noisy youngsters who seemed to know exactly what *they* were doing. It was, for me, a time of total confusion. Every so often Robert would look at this revered script ('book by John O'Hara') and he'd say, 'Oh, I don't know about this' and set about turning it upside down, enthusiastically tearing out pages and rewriting. The only things that got rehearsed were production numbers, we scarcely looked at the scenes or my songs and I grew more and more despondent and more and more certain that I would never get to grips with the show. A week before we began previews I sang 'Bewitched' for Robert. Stuart Hopps who was waiting to 'set' the song said, 'Why are you singing it so high?' I told him that that was how it was written in the script. 'Put it in a key that suits *you*,' he insisted. 'Can I do that?' I asked John Fiske, the musical director. 'Yes,' he replied and began to rearrange the orchestrations. My teacher, Ian, optimistic and encouraging, was sure I could sing soprano. Maybe I could have managed it but it would have been a dreadful worry each time I opened my mouth. All my keys were changed down.

We moved in to the 'theater', the new premises of the Half-Moon in the Mile End Road, the conversion from Methodist Chapel barely accomplished. There was a block of seats 'raked' in the auditorium but they were wet with paint. The stage was just the flat bit at the end of the hall, the dressing room was a communal prefabricated building behind the chapel and there were portable toilets outside and duckboard walkways led to the Mile End Road. I realized that I would have to change for my first entrance at the front of the building under the stairs to what used to be the chapel gallery. They'd probably hang a cloth there later, I hoped. We were really short of funds. The production telephone was a red British Telecom kiosk on the pavement, and locals grew impatient as we received and made endless calls, and for a while our production company 'borrowed' electricity from the telegraph pole next to the telephone. Robert beamed, presiding over this mayhem like a prizefighter, hitching up his cotton slacks and executing a little shuffle from time to time, rubbing his hands with pleasure. I didn't doubt that he knew what he was doing but I had no idea what *I* was doing and he left me to get on with it.

It was hot July weather. Our first preview arrived. The paintwork in the auditorium was still wet. 'Send them away,' said Robert as a rather smart West End audience milled around in the Mile End Road. How *grand* he is, I thought. We still hadn't done a 'dress' run-through a few days later when we decided we *had* to open. (We simply couldn't keep sending people home.) As it was, we had to turn people away for lack of room. I'd tried to ignore the press interest in my involvement. I was playing a middle-aged socialite who'd taken up with a younger man. I was singing and dancing for the first time *and* I was past the great age of forty. The opportunities for column inches were limitless. By now, I *knew*, absolutely knew, that I was on a hiding to nothing. Only dour, dogged professionalism kept me chained to my post. I sat, wrapped in a shawl, eating sticks of celery and wishing I were dead. Outwardly, I smiled. My mother refused to attend the first performance. Sensing my mood (which no one else did) she said, 'I've no wish to be there to see her making a fool of herself.'

My mother . . . What I had feared had happened. My mother called and said she had to move out of Guyon House. She was shattered and could not speak of the circumstances. I told her to come and live with me right away. So, during the rehearsals of *Pal Joey* I had been making a flat for her on the garden floor of the house, buying furniture and making sure that the kitchen and the bathroom were in good working order. The big front bedroom was a half-basement, the large living room and kitchen at the back were light and airy, giving on to the garden. After work and at weekends, I obsessed over the floor, my worries about Pat and my mother and my part in the show projecting themselves on to this huge expanse of dingy tiles which were meant to be white. With a pail, soft wire wool and a sponge, I slowly scrubbed every inch of floor until it was blindingly clean.

My mother arrived at eight in the morning before we started previews at the theater. She hated the flat. I looked at it through her eyes and indeed it was a far cry from the luxury of Heath Street. This normally rational, practical woman refused to unpack and I had to leave her sitting, disconsolate, surrounded by luggage. She was almost eighty. It took her a couple of weeks to adapt to her new life; nothing to run and organize, no accounts, no cooking to speak of. She'd lost her role and she, like me, had lost her life in Connemara. Kate was twenty and had flown the nest and for the first time my mother was separated from Pat, her 'baby', who was now seventeen. She'd lived in Guyon House for seventeen years and, curiously, the change was harder for her than it had been for me. She began to smoke. Gradually, we made her comfortable but I wasn't sure that she would ever be entirely reconciled with her new life.

And that was the background to the opening of *Pal Joey* – a smash hit, which transferred in September to the Albery Theater in the West End and played there for over a year. There was enormous excitement, as is usual when one has a success, but I remember very little about the opening except the strange feeling of not being able to go on with the show and not knowing why (I had no idea what 'stopping the show' meant). Indelibly printed on my mind are the opening moments when, having dressed, hidden behind a blanket as the audience, inches away, filed into the theater, I emerged into the empty foyer in brilliant sunshine and stood just inside the double doors, open to the street. As I turned to make my first entrance, unseen down the side of the steeply raked bank of seats, I was joined by an extremely drunk local who wandered in through the unattended front door. Smiling broadly, he attached himself to me. We scuffled noiselessly, unseen by the spectators above and to the side of us, who were all looking straight ahead at the stage. My cue was approaching and I was desperate. Hitching up my skirt I jabbed him in the shin with my stiletto and hissed, 'Fuck off! I'm IN this.' He went reeling back into the lobby and, adjusting my furs, I sauntered on down the aisle and into the acting area with an assurance I was far from feeling.

I cannot recall one time of success that has not been counter-pointed by some kind of sadness or worry. Now, as I settled into a long run, I realized that with the arrival of my mother my time of kicking up my heels and living just as I pleased was once again at an end. Nevertheless, I felt pretty pleased with myself and with the way things were turning out.

Chapter Thirty-six

There is something about being in a long run that stabilizes one's life no end. My producer on *Pal Joey* was Ian Albery, son of Donald Albery who gave me my first West End job. We were playing at the Albery Theater which had been run by Ian's father and before that by his grandfather, Sir Bronson Albery, and his great grandparents, Charles Wyndham and Mary Moore who also ran the Criterion Theater, which dug deep into the bowels of Piccadilly Circus. Mary Moore was, to say the least, careful with money and a stingy employer. One day when workmen were seen digging up the pavement outside the Criterion and someone asked what they were doing, a disgruntled actor passing by replied bitterly, 'Disaster! Mary Moore's lost sixpence.'

When we were all young things in the fifties Ian, who was training in all branches of theater management, came out on the road for the first time as company manager when O'Toole and I were in *The Holiday*. He was anxious and zealous and O'Toole's antics exasperated him beyond endurance. The company report book was full of remarks along the lines of 'P. O'Toole *laughed* on stage and made S. Phillips laugh, as well. *Spoke* to them.' There was a lot of *speaking* to. All these years later, he's a very grown-up producer and I'm a very responsible leading lady and we get along just fine. The favorite performance of the week for me is Saturday matinée when a small boy occupies the stage-right box and sings along with the whole show. He knows every word. Stage-struck as ever, I find it very moving to be playing to a small Bronson Albery in the theater that until recently was named after his great great grandfather.

One always imagines that, once a show is up and running, there will be more leisure time in the week. The reality is that as the weeks go by, time shrinks as the need to stay fresh in order to keep the show fresh becomes paramount. Oddly enough, doing another job during the day can help to keep one fresh, but it goes without saying that there isn't a great deal of time left over for home life. However, domesticity – active, hands-on domesticity – was so novel to me that I shopped and cooked like a thing possessed. I was learning more and more about food and each Sunday I recklessly invited ten or twelve people to join us for brunch – lunch – dinner. Most of my recipes I learned from Bill Corlett, an expert in the kitchen. Every Sunday morning the telephone wires between Islington and the village of Great Bardfield rang with cries of '. . . but *how* do you get the bone out of the leg? Oh, okay – I've got it on the floor and – yes, it's out! – but it looks like a traffic accident.' 'How do I keep the stuffing from falling out? But my sewing's *terrible*. Oh Bill, it looks *awful*. Does it matter? Oh, yes what a good idea. I'll cover it with lots of parsley.' He more or less 'talked me down' from ambitious near-disasters for about two years.

It was one of the blessings of the early Eighties that Bill and I became fond of each other's partners. Grave, wickedly funny Bryn Ellis became as much my friend as Bill was and Robin was a treasured leavening and rising agent, egging us on to mild follies that we all loved even as we protested against them. We all went to Venice together and Robin very quickly cottoned on to the beneficial nature of an 'eye-opener' in the morning in cold weather. 'Spot of grappa to get us going, I think.' 'What? At nine in the morning? What are you thinking of? Oh, why not.' 'Another round of desserts?' 'Are you mad? But they *are* very nice. Oh, why not.' He was a mild lord of misrule and I loved being with him when we were with Bill and

Bryn. I loved it more, I realized, than I did when I was alone with him. We didn't have a great deal in common, now that the urgency of setting up home, getting divorced, and getting married had subsided. There was marvelous sex, of course, but I had never known anything less.

We did share some things; entertaining was a joint effort at this stage and it was enjoyable. Robin, having caught my passion for gardening, very quickly progressed from under-gardener to very capable, equal partner. Above all we shared a love of animals. He gave me my first Burmese cat, Spencer, a large, strong, blue tom cat with a loud, depressed voice. He was a present for me for the opening of *Pal Joey* but he bonded with Robin on their journey home from the breeder and he loved him evermore with ferocity. He was like the jealous cat in the story by Colette and I think that there were moments when he would have liked to murder me so he could have Robin all to himself. This didn't make me love him less and he, for his part, allowed me to feed him and love him and he grew to like me well enough, but passion he reserved for Robin. He came to think it was his right to sleep between us, so we decided to buy another Burmese so that he might spread his affections somewhat. And small, brown Barnaby came into our lives. Spencer 'mothered' him immediately. When Barnaby disappeared, we were frantic but our distress was nothing compared with Spencer's. He searched and searched for him, returning home dirty and dispirited, moaning loudly. Every day he led me around the house, pawing at closed doors, howling until I opened them so that he might check the interiors. He displayed all the symptoms of deep depression.

Barnaby had to be replaced in the hope of assuaging Spencer's grief. We found a breeder who could let us have a Burmese right away. So Rupert entered the house and took over, boxing Spencer's ears and appropriating the position of Top Cat in every sense. He sat high up on the tops of doors and bookshelves. He tormented us and Spencer. He was a force and he was wonderful, but he didn't replace Barnaby and Spencer became gloomier. For three weeks Robin and I spent all our spare time searching our neighbourhood and posting 'LOST' notes on trees and in shops and then I received a call from N19 (we lived in N1) from The Cat Protection League, saying that they had a very troublesome, noisy Burmese on their hands and it might be mine. A 'troublesome' cat, so far away, seemed an unlikely candidate for my small, quiet Barnaby, but off I shot with my cat box. There in the cat refuge, solitary in a cage, alone in a corridor, was a horrible-looking, screeching creature, his face all mouth, with a cut head and a misshapen leg. 'Oh no,' I began and then I saw a small defect on the right foot that told me that this unrecognizable creature had to be – 'Barnaby?' I said. The screeching stopped. The ferocity disappeared and the small cat quietly waited for me to open the cage, lift him out and take him home. He'd been screaming for help from home for three weeks and his screaming had worked or so he must think. As I thanked the staff of the N19 CPL and wrote the biggest check I could afford and carried him into the sunny street to look for a taxi, I thought how chancy were one's own hopes of a good result, of happiness, of getting what one wanted. It might seem as though we worked for things, won things, achieved things, but actually one's luck turned on being in when the phone rang.

Barnaby never spoke again. When I opened the front door, Spencer was waiting in the hall. I dropped to my knees, thinking I was going to witness a fantastic reunion. I opened the cat box and lifted Barnaby out. Spencer looked at the smelly, dirty, bloody animal, backed away and walked through the house into the garden. He never 'mothered' Barnaby again and became the slightly deranged outsider in the trio of cats dominated by Rupert. And they dominated us, as well. From this time on our lives revolved around that of the cats; we rarely went away at the same time. My mother, a dog woman, with her own dog in her flat, learned to become a cat person and took over Spencer's position in Barnaby's life. He demanded her undivided attention and gradually he won her over. At home, in Wales, cats were workers and lived outside. When Bill, on a visit to the farm, asked my small cousin, Mair, what the cat was called, she looked at him in astonishment and replied 'Cat'. My cousins were disgusted that the cats sat around in the kitchen, watching the cooking, stealing what they could (not Barnaby). Robin and I were slaves to these beautiful creatures – blue, brown and 'red' blonde – and we were completely at one in our care for them. Sometimes, animals keep a relationship flourishing more efficiently than children.

When *Pal Joey* ended I went to Ireland to film for television a play based on Jennifer Johnston's book *How Many Miles to Babylon?*. Ms Johnston, who came to visit us in Wicklow, was the epitome of my ideal Irish woman; independent, slightly racy, too stylish to be a victim of fashion or dietary whim. Meeting authors you admire is one of the big bonuses of being an actor *and* I was working in Wicklow *and* I was working for Moira Armstrong again (for the first time since *Shoulder to Shoulder*) *and* I acquired a new 'son'. Now that I'd begun playing mothers in earnest, my children were becoming a distinguished, beautiful bunch. Here was one of the most fascinating; Daniel Day-Lewis, whom I knew as Jill Balcon's son (Jill Balcon, so respectable and rather intimidating, who only a few months before, had along with me got the giggles so badly during recording of a Greek tragedy that we were both asked to leave the studio and not return until we could control ourselves). I hoped her son was as good, and as joky, as she was. He was playing his first decent part and within minutes it was evident that he was not only good, but very special (though *not* as joky.) Alec McNaughton was my husband (very joky). It didn't make me sad, being in Wicklow and Dublin. It was Connemara that had held me in thrall; I couldn't go west.

357

Afterwards, back in London, I went on working, slowly consolidating my financial position and continuing to improve the house. I bought myself a grand piano and made a second sitting room at the top of the house, next to the guest room; from there a staircase led to a roof garden that extended over the whole area of the house: white floor, white walls, it was like a Mediterranean garden. I was playing house. There was still something adolescent about my life during these years, in spite of the fact that I was taking care of my mother and seeing more of Pat and her friends than I had when we were living together in Hampstead. Kate I rarely saw these days. She was living with her current boyfriend in Islington, had decided against taking up a place at university and dropped out completely, but finally I tracked her down in Soho where she was working at Ronnie Scott's jazz club. I had made friends with Lynda La Plante while I was playing *Pal Joey* and I now persuaded her and her husband and Robin to come there with me on Kate's birthday so that I could deliver her a present. If there is such a thing as a star waitress, she was certainly it and I was sincere in my admiration as she whizzed around, placing well-heeled customers as far away from the bar as possible, thereby obliging them to tip her heavily as she made the long journey, carrying heavy trays to them. I was amazed and intrigued; she was good at her job and while I didn't think she should spend a lifetime being a waitress, it would never have occurred to me to try to divert her at this point. She was quick and smart and observant and sassy – all qualities I would dearly like to possess and never would. Now that I was no longer trying to influence her I found her totally enchanting; I didn't totally understand her but I really admired her. Nor did I have fears for her. Looking at her, only slightly put out by my presence, I realized that, bringing the whole of my personality to bear on her, I had made little impression on her. And that cheered me up enormously as I sat there in the dark, noisy club, wanting to leave for the relative quiet of the street. We made no plans to meet but I was sure that she would be in touch when the time was right. She got on well with Robin but I had a feeling that she found my relationship with him slightly comical, not embarrassing, not irritating, just faintly amusing.

Pat, on the other hand, may have been only too susceptible to the advice lavishly handed down by my mother and, to a lesser extent, myself. She was still the Good Girl that she had been all her life; schoolteachers, tutors, chaperons, nannies, all hated to see her go away from them. Her school reports were glowing, but she also decided against taking up her university place – and this hurt my mother, I know – and chose instead to go into the backstage side of the entertainment business. I wasn't displeased. She went on the road with her father as an ASM, and played a small part in *Pygmalion*. In very little time she was stage managing a West End show and I was amazed by her expertise in a field I knew nothing about. I was still uncertain in all things practical and one Sunday when I was making heavy weather of serving a three-course lunch for twelve people and standing in the kitchen, dithering, Pat, sensing trouble, rose from the table and joined me. Taking in the situation and speaking a theater language she felt I might understand, she said forcefully in stage management speak, 'Okay! Go Roast Lamb!' Lunch was on the table in a trice.

I had believed O'Toole when he told me that when our parting became public knowledge I would find work difficult to come by but that hadn't happened and, looking back, I couldn't believe that I had been so credulous and so nervous. Weekends, as often as possible, were spent in Bill and Bryn's country cottage in Great Bardfield. There were more friends in my life than ever before and there was fun now along with all the hard work. The dancer and choreographer, Anton Dolin, whom I'd known slightly for years, became a staunch friend and he tried to teach me a little grandeur, which would be good for me – and then gave up and allowed me to be his *un*glamorous chum. John Bates and his partner, John Siggins, became firm friends and saw to it that, though I couldn't always afford it, I was decently turned out – spectacularly turned out, when the occasion demanded.

Lynda La Plante made me laugh more than anyone I'd met since Maggie Smith. She said to me while we were rehearsing something or other, 'I'm giving up acting.' (She was a wonderful comedienne.) 'I'm going to be a writer.' 'Oh, yes,' I replied, hardly listening from this point on. 'Oh yes, I've got this idea and I've written the story *here* – do you have one of these? You must. It's a Chisholms – from the stationers in Kingsway. Can't live without it.' 'It' was a smallish, leather-bound address book, notebook, account book, diary – combined. 'You organize your life with this.' I made a mental note to go and buy a 'Chisholms'; it did look lovely. 'Here, you want to see? This is called *Widows* and I'm going to put it on television.' I glanced at the notebook; huge writing with lots of spelling mistakes sprawled over the pages. I looked at her pretty features fired with excitement and felt a pang of sympathy for her. What disappointments lay ahead. How many actors at this moment were saying, 'I've written a film script – a TV series – a novel.' Poor Lynda. Why not stick to what she was good at. Then she told me the story and I thought, 'Heavens, that's good.' Even so, I was astonished when, within a year, *Widows* appeared on TV and Lynda became a star.

She and her husband, Richard, and Robin and I spent much of our leisure time together now. The men began to focus their attention on the gymnasium; on weightlifting, or karate. Neither Lynda nor I could summon much enthusiasm for this preoccupation, or for the spectacular, muscled results. She and I worked like beavers while the men perfected their physiques. We never discussed it but I think we were both relieved that they had something with which to occupy themselves. Lynda worked hard because she loved writing and I worked so hard partly because I, too, loved my job and partly because I felt I had to prove myself – not least as a bread winner – and I thought I had to make up for lost time. Sara was a friend as well as my agent and she knew and understood my need to be constantly employed and colluded with me on this. Wiser heads maybe said, 'Don't panic. Wait for the better jobs.' I couldn't and I did miss a lot of prestigious work because of my infernal drive to work all the time. I was so busy I didn't always pay attention. Maureen Duffy and I met for lunch at old Bianchi's (with Elena presiding) and she and I discussed the possibility of doing a show about Karen Blixen. I had loved *Out of Africa* for some time and thought the show to be a good idea but I wasn't really listening properly and the script wasn't going to be ready for a while and I wanted to get *on*. Fool that I was. I should have listened to Maureen and played that part.

Instead, I found a play which would come 'in' quite quickly. The director was Frith Banbury, a great name from the heyday of the West End in its glory days of Binkie and John and Ralph and Peggy and Edith. It was a play about Bernard Shaw and Mrs Patrick Campbell and it was *Dear Liar* by Jerome Kilty. A 'letters' play. Not too much acting, I thought, and nice to play Mrs Pat again; I had played her in a TV series about Jenny Churchill in the early Seventies. Robert Hardy would play Shaw, Bob Ringwood would design the set and John Bates would make me three outfits (one of which ought to get a round of applause for itself). We rehearsed in Knightsbridge and I turned up just before ten to be greeted by an immaculate Frith ('beautifully shod', as Coral Browne, the personification of elegance, would have remarked) who checked his watch, sat straightbacked and said 'Begin' on the stroke of ten. It was like joining a boot camp. Elegant, charming, polite Frith, associated with elegant, charming, polite theater, was a bloody-minded slave-driver. No director that I ever met before or since expected so much hard work. The hours between

10 a.m. and 1 p.m. and 2 p.m. and 6 p.m. held nothing but work; no chats, no anecdotes, no breathers. He spotted my weaknesses very early on and was unremitting in his efforts to eradicate them. It was a wonderful experience, working for Frith. ('Frothy' Frith I had heard some acquaintance from the early Forties call him – Frothy? Hah!) He did a wonderful job on the play as did Bob Ringwood and John Bates (whose dress *did* get a round). Robert Hardy and I were pretty good too, by the time Frith had finished with us, but not all the elements for a success were in place. We came 'in' into the new Mermaid. Our producer became mortally ill, the theater did not have permission to advertise its existence outside the building, there was no way of crossing the road near the theater (Griff James, the famed company manager, used to go out into the busy highway to escort people across in safety). Frith had to go away on family business after the opening. We subsided quietly and Frith returned to a very sad scene. Good notices and a good show are not enough to ensure success in the West End. Without a well-managed advertising campaign and a good 'shop' one might as well not bother opening. But Ingrid Bergman came to see us one night with Ann Todd! And on the same night April Ashley blew in from – where? She was a vision. Sometimes the dressing room scenes should have been on stage. We came off.

Almost at once I was given a chance to work again with Peter Gill, now a great figure at the National, but I hadn't worked with him since we were at Nottingham Rep in the late Fifties. My room under the stage was next to Peter's stage manager's room, with the poisonous coke boiler (renowned in repertory circles) between us.

'Next week we will give '*Amlet*. I myself will play the moody Dane and me wife will play Ophalia.'

'Your wife's an old whore.'

'Nevertheless, she will play Ophalia.'

Each night we would chant these ancient theatrical jokes

through the cotton sheet that divided us in our gloomy, noxious, underground booths.

Now – how smart – I would play Lady Britomart for Peter in his production of *Major Barbara*. And Penelope Wilton would play Barbara and best of all, Brewster Mason (my Petruchio from the early Sixties) would play my husband again. It all seemed too good to be true. Penelope was one of O'Toole's favorite actresses. I had seen her, wonderful in his *Vanya* and alongside him when he played a brilliant Darcy Tuck in *Plunder* in his season at the Bristol Old Vic which Sara had helped put together. Penelope was now married to my old friend Dan Massey. I had longed to play at the National but none of the possibilities had ever worked out. I was delighted.

Rehearsals with Peter were so entertaining that I never wanted them to stop (they did go on for months). They didn't take place at the National because Peter didn't much like working there, so we rehearsed in Hammersmith at the Riverside Studio. I would have liked to have been at the National but Peter was a law unto himself and I was his willing slave. He must be one of the few 'teaching' directors of his generation. There was a time when almost all directors were able to teach actors how to play their parts. Then, as they relinquished lighting to lighting designers and sound to sound designers, many of them relinquished teaching as well, relying on casting directors to find actors who were 'right' for the parts. I watched Peter coax a great performance out of an actor that had neither the technique nor the natural aptitude for it. As for us girls, well, you can always spot a Peter Gill woman. He somehow reminds one of one's femininity and that confidence is retained long after the engagement is over.

We shifted over to the National a week before we opened and I found it very hard to 'learn' the building and never did become entirely confident that I could find my way to the right auditorium at the right time. I wished I had been able to rehearse there. (Subsequently, I fell in love with the confusing building and felt it to be the best place in the world in which to work.) Stage terror strikes at strange times. *Major Barbara* opens with a long duologue between Lady Brit and her son. David Yelland and I – both petrified – met each night before the show and ran the fiendish opening. We *never* felt confident enough to just come in and get on and do it.

Penelope Wilton was a wonderful colleague. Later, when the National went on tour, we both looked after Brewster who, by this time, was unwell and not good at looking after himself. She called herself Nurse Wilton. She and I went on a health kick and ran in the show each morning before breakfast. And it was in Aberdeen, returning from our run along the riverside, that I learned that my friend Marie-Liese Grès – John Hurt's partner – had died in a riding accident. We were friends and had been close neighbors in Hampstead. I had no idea how John was or where he was and I sat there, looking out at the bright, cold Scottish morning, snow on the ground, with no one to share my shock and I remember Liese and that view as if it were yesterday.

As we were about to open *Major Barbara* at the National, Sara had rung up, very excited, to say that a producer would like to see me about being in a major movie. As usual, at that time, I was stupidly underwhelmed by the prospect of the movies. Although I had been bitterly disappointed many years previously by the collapse of a plan to make *The Lonely Passion of Judith Hearne* and also very cast down when the director of *Ashes and Diamonds*, who had seen me in a play, failed to get finance for his film with me, I had never found it to be a problem turning down movies that didn't excite me. (Robert Atkins's command 'Don't go into the fillums' still sounded in my ears.) I asked the National for permission to go and see the producer. 'Not a chance,' was the reply. We were in the throes of technical rehearsals. 'Sorry,' I told Sara, 'can't go. We have to turn it down.' To my embarrassment, the producer and the director came over the river to see *me*. I slunk into the foyer with a white scarf over my wig and met – of all people – my friend Silvana Mangano's daughter, Raffaella de Laurentiis. She was the big film producer! (I hadn't seen her since she was a typical naughty teenager in her mother's house in the South of France) and with her was David Lynch, the director ('*Eraserhead*,' I realized). 'Oh God,' I thought. 'This is the most embarrassing thing that has ever happened to me. I've dragged them all the way down here to sit on a window ledge and have a drink of water.' I apologized and apologized – I couldn't bear to think they'd had to trek over Waterloo Bridge. We parted, I still apologizing. 'Have you got the part?' said Sara. 'Heavens, I've no idea,' I replied. '*I feel so bad* they had to come all this way.' 'Oh, be quiet,' she snapped and hung up.

We went on tech-ing. Days later, I remembered the incident in the foyer. 'Hey, have I got the part?' 'Yes, yes, yes,' said Sara, fed up with the whole thing.

'The part' in *Dune* took me to Mexico for almost a year off and on. Mexico. When Jack Hawkins was first diagnosed with throat cancer, after his surgery he and his wife, Doreen, and O'Toole and I had taken a cruise to Mexico and had fallen in love with the country. Later we had co-produced films at Churubusco Studio in Mexico City. O'Toole had made it his refuge when we were estranged. This was my chance to come to terms with another piece of my past. A thought: Was coming to terms with and overcoming my past taking up too much of my time? While I was playing *Major Barbara* I had time enough in which to review my personal situation and there was something not quite convincing about it. When one says 'Now I can be *me*,' what, exactly, is meant? In my case it meant being a person enjoying an absence of strain. Yes, that certainly. And freedom from the fear of disapproval. The subsequent increase in confidence, of course, but then ease and confidence tipping over maybe into complacency, self-indulgence, misplaced confidence – *over* confidence? Relaxation – verging on sloppiness, maybe? Simply getting rid of problems was not the answer to this great step forward that I had had in mind. And furthermore, who was this 'me' that I was now free to be? So many years spent trying to adapt to difficult circumstances not of my choosing had left me strangely diffident about realizing 'my' personality. I was having no trouble at all adjusting to the massive change in lifestyle. I travelled by public transport and loved it. Robin adored driving and I bought him cars that reflected my gradually improving financial position, culminating in a BMW which gave him inordinate pleasure that I did not share. With a sinking heart, I realized that in a much more easy-going, pleasure-driven way, I was again adapting; this time to Robin's congenial idea of what our life together should be. And it wasn't his fault, not in any way. I had divined the scenario and, as well as I was able and without being asked to, I was living it out. There is more, however, to being yourself than changing your circumstances. If one is not careful a change of circumstance can be like a change of scenery; nothing much. ('*A groeso fôr Ni newid onid air.*' Crossing the ocean only gives you a change of air.)

Even work was slightly unreal. I now had to find a few friends who would help me with performances. Wilfrid Lawson used to say that one of the secrets to being a good performer was to 'find a friend'. Alas, not easy. People are very reluctant to be brutally frank and however self-critical you are, you can't see all the things that you're doing wrong, and the director is often too close to his part of the job to be able to help. I had been accustomed to long, fascinating debriefings at home with O'Toole and it was a two-way road, one of the few areas where I was free to speak my mind. No matter how well a show had gone, O'Toole and I spent hours the following day gently pulling the performance to pieces in order to reassemble it better. It was a totally absorbing, interesting process – occasionally painful but over-ridingly enjoyable. I learned more about acting from O'Toole than I had done from any of my teachers. Once, when I was playing mad Queen Juana of Spain in a play by Montherlant and was struck down by flu, he actually 'fed' me the performance on my sick bed, phrase by phrase, inflection by inflection and I got up and went to perform the play, virtually with no rehearsal and it worked like a charm. I trusted him implicitly. Knowing I would never speak to him again (and neither he nor I would wish to attempt a meeting) I treasured the few words of advice I had had the sense to commit to paper; they proved to be the most useful pieces of acting advice I ever received.

The first time I saw Robin in a play I obligingly read the play carefully beforehand and made notes throughout. He was pleased that I'd liked the performance but looked aghast when I offered to go through the play the following day for improvements. I could see that the sight of my sheets of notes offended him, so I crumpled them up and hastily threw them away and we never discussed acting ever after. It was odd not to be able to share such a huge part of my life.

Now I was to spend the best part of a year in Mexico. Robin would not accompany me; he needed to find work in England. I knew I would be homesick for my house and my cats and our easy life and our friends, but I also wanted to get away. In the small hours of the morning I could not escape the fear that our relationship, Robin's and mine, was close to ending its course. Born in a series of random chances against a background of confusion and need, the attraction had been real enough but after seven years the differences between us were becoming more marked. I think it irritated Robin to find all the radios in the house retuned from Radio One to Radio Four as much as it irritated me to walk into a room to find, nine times out of ten, a quiz show playing on television. But these were small things, I told myself, and marriage was a big thing. I couldn't bear to be seen to fail again.

Chapter Thirty-seven

Robin and I have a Venetian holiday with Bill and Bryn before I leave for Mexico. Bill and I have tried to acquire the rights to the E. F. Benson books featuring Mapp and Lucia and George and mad Irene. No success. London Weekend Television has the rights and is just sitting on them. It's maddening. I don't necessarily want to *play* in the show but I would love to be a part of getting it done properly – properly, as I see it, that is. Ah well. Our other attempts at producing are also unsuccessful. We both love a book by Russell Hoban called *Turtle Diary* but we miss the rights by a day. Our other obsession is J. R. Ackerley and we buy the rights to *My Sister and Myself* but it's regarded as too 'depressing'. It is, in fact, hilariously despondent. We spend a fair bit of money on this before we give up and go on holiday. It's good to share my insider's view of Venice. All the Venetian friends and acquaintances come through magnificently and we have a wonderful time. Then Bill starts a novel and I go to Mexico.

For a month I sat in my bedroom on the twenty-first floor of the Century Hotel in Mexico City waiting vainly to be called to work. The budget was so enormous that they could afford to call actors and pay them to sit in the hotel doing nothing for weeks on end. It was a bizarre experience living at the Century; the lift was out of order, so it took a long time to reach the street by the staircase. The building, like most of the fashionable Zona Rosa, was constructed of artificial fabric; nylon, vinyl, plastic, concrete – all totally unsuited to the climate. I walked to the zócalo, the big square at the center of the city, and wandered enviously through the

Majestic Hotel, made, Spanish-style, of wood and stone and marble, the deep-set windows catching every breeze. For the whole of that month I stalked through the city, visiting every art gallery and museum, speaking to no one. No one from the production office telephoned me and one day I felt so isolated and unnerved that twice I fell over from a standing position. Robin, in the interest of economy, had ordained that we shouldn't speak on the phone except in the case of emergencies. (It was *very* expensive calling England.) What constituted an emergency, I wondered? The fear that one was losing the power of speech? Driven in on myself, I kept my eyes open and watched everything around me. On Grasshopper Hill, below Maximillian's Palace, I saw a family, out for a Sunday picnic, with a bald turkey on a leash. He seemed very content. One very small obscure exhibition pricked my imagination into seeing Mexico City in a new light. It was an exhibit of drawings and watercolors from the nineteenth century, all executed by the wives and daughters of diplomats from Europe. I had no idea that Mexico City had remained luxurious beyond Parisian standards well into the nineteenth century, when it was still a city built on water – as it had been to a greater extent when the Conquistadors crossed the causeway to be greeted as gods by the inhabitants of the beautiful island. When I was there, Mexico City contained seventeen million inhabitants and the pollution was unbearable. At night I leaned out of my window and watched the smart streets gently invaded by beautiful Indian families who slept in the doorways of the expensive shops. One became sick merely by breathing the foul air but the romance of the location had gripped me, thanks to those watercolors and drawings, and I never lost my 'inner' view of the city and grew to love living in it.

I was, however, lonely for a few months, we worked very long hours and returned to the city too tired to go out. I spent long hours at night learning new songs, listening to Peggy

Lee and Mabel Mercer hour after hour. Why? I wondered. Just for fun? Maybe. Work was slow and the script was difficult to follow but director David Lynch and the actors were wonderful to work with and I learned something about being a lone lady traveller; I learned not to travel light. I had observed Kate Hepburn arriving in Provence for the filming of *Lion in Winter* with her books and her food and her companion and her record player and her easel and her canvases and paints and special china. At the time I'd thought she was being a trifle eccentric. Now, I saw the good sense of carrying one's world on one's back, like a snail. I acquired books and drawing paper and tapes and a recording machine and vowed never to be caught short far from home again.

During the year I was able to return to London a few times and Robin flew out for a holiday once. We had different ideas about how to spend a holiday, so it was only partially successful; he wanted to lie on a beach and I wanted to explore. I found it hard to spend days on the beach and Robin didn't relish the long, hot journeys in rickety buses into the interior. We compromised. Towards the end of that year Robin got his first really good job in a TV series with Terence Stamp, whom he came to admire enormously. It gave his morale a huge boost and I hoped it would be a turning point in his fortunes.

By now both my daughters had gone into the theater. I, alone, was surprised by this which indicates that, far too much, I accepted things at face value; they displayed no interest in drama while they were growing up so I assumed they *weren't* interested. Now, belatedly, I realized that it must have been hard for them to declare themselves in that intensely theatrical household. Pat had got herself into a drama school in London (informing me of this after the event). When Kate came to the unhappy end of a love affair, her father took her to New York and she began a new life in America, first running somewhat wild in Manhattan and then, effecting a major change, entering Yale where she studied to be a dramaturge and was side-tracked into acting, leaving Yale to study in San Francisco and then in New York, where she began acting professionally at the Irish Arts Centre. She now came home to stay with me for the first time in years and I was mightily impressed by her appearance; drop-dead chic and, typically quirky, combining an elegant wardrobe with a startling punk haircut, and rolling her own cigarettes with flair and skill (one hand). I had watched Pat develop into the radiantly pretty girl she was and wasn't surprised by her control and her enviable insight and good sense, but now I *was* surprised to be getting along so well with this elegant creature whom I had spent so many years trying to alter. Thank goodness I'd had no success at all, I thought again, and counted myself lucky in my grown-up children. It did occur to me, not for the first time, that maybe I wasn't at my best trying to communicate with *small* children.

I was in a musical which was not a success but which was running in spite of its cool reception by the critics. It often happens that a poor show can lead to something wonderful. In this instance *Peg* led to two important friendships, one with musical director Kevin Amos, with whom I began an enduring musical collaboration and the other with an actor who became my very close friend and with whom I later shared my house – Edward Duke. At the moment when I met him he had been gathering praise and awards – and lots of money – for his portrayal of P. G. Wodehouse's Jeeves in a play he'd written himself, *Jeeves Takes Charge*.

A nice, eccentric man called Lou Bush Hager was obsessed with a show, which we always referred to as 'Peg-the-Musical'. (It was *Peg*, a musical version of the Laurette Taylor vehicle 'Peg o'My Heart'.) Lou was the scion of not one but two wealthy American families. Someone explained to me that innumerable people drink the Bush beer, Budweiser, and that every home has Hager's hinges on its doors and windows, so there was money raining down from all directions. His wife was sane and lovely but his mother gave one pause. She was called 'Poomey' (or 'Pumi' or 'Poomi'). We presented the show when it wasn't ready to be seen, because Poomey had flown over on her birthday with a Concorde-ful of friends. In the event, she passed on the opening but when she did decide to come she sat there, squat and bejewelled, occasionally, when pleased, letting out a loud whoop and exclaiming, 'That's mah boy!', compounding the confusion in the stalls of the Phoenix Theater.

David Heneker was the composer and musically the show was first rate. Edward became, like Bill and Bryn and Ricci, one of my adopted brothers. We met on a nasty February morning in Pimlico. We'd already been rehearsing for a week and Edward had been detained in America. I'd obligingly written down his moves and what little dialogue we possessed from a threadbare book, which was to be whisked away and rewritten. He was hugely tall, jet-lagged and barely coordinated, long legs and arms and narrow patrician feet and hands shooting off in all directions. During the morning we rehearsed a scene and I told him I'd 'filled in' a script for him. He looked at it as though he'd never seen a script before. (Well, it wasn't *much* of a script at this point and already he'd realized that this was going to be a *sauve qui peut* job.) 'Don't think I want that, love pot. How about a spot of lunch?' Scarcely pausing to shake his head reprovingly at the nourishing grains and fruit generously provided by Lou, he took me by the hand and ran me from the gastronomic wasteland in which we were rehearsing in the direction of the only good restaurant for miles. 'If I don't have a decent lunch I get – unhappy,' he remarked, as we tucked into a large meal at Pomegranate. From that moment on we were inseparable, eating and drinking *far* too much each day, spending most of our salary at the Caprice at night. Never in my entire life had I eaten 'proper' food so regularly. Never in my life had I laughed so much.

When we moved into town the company manager, whom we cordially disliked, had appropriated what should have been his dressing room on the ground floor, so we shared my number one suite and our blossoming friendship made the whole trying experience bearable. Lou gave me orchids instead of the rewritten script and amazingly didn't take offense when, exasperated, I threw them down the corridor. Sir Ronald Millar, who for some reason was engaged to write a new version of a perfectly good book by Robin Miller, delivered bits of text after we'd actually opened on tour. Infuriated by one – as I thought – useless contribution written on the back of an envelope, I was panicked into yelling, furious and exhausted, 'This just won't DO!' He rounded on me. 'How many authors do *you* know,' he demanded, 'who drive a *Rolls-Royce*?' As I struggled to shape a reply I could hear the strangled noise of a hysterical Edward Duke going back to a darkened dressing room for a lie down.

It was an unusual experience in all respects but it had another happy outcome. By the terms of my divorce, the girls were to be supported until they'd finished their higher education. Kate's allowance had stopped when she left Yale and she was now living on a shoestring and also needed to pay off her student loan. I was happy to be able to turn over to her my earnings from a show I hadn't been proud of. Of course, if I hadn't spent so much time and money in the best West End restaurants with Ed, I would have had money left over for me as well. As it was, after my grand gesture to Kate and her current boyfriend who was also short of funds, I had to go back to work – fast.

Sara found a play for me that might be suitable for Robin as well and for that reason I agreed to try it. I was to play an older, professional woman who dumps her long-term middle-aged lover (wonderful Moray Watson) for a delivery boy on roller skates (Robin). I noted gloomily that it was *French* and what kind of luck did I ever have with French plays? None. Charles

Savage was to direct – very bright and very handy with rewrites so we might stand a chance. Edward, before he left the country, read it and said bluntly, 'Absolutely *no*, sweetie.' But when did I ever listen to reason? Too late now, anyway.

The play goes its long, predictable way. We try. We really do. Charles is valiant. In the end, after months of struggling, we fail.

The only nice things that happened during the latter part of 1984 were, firstly, that I was to meet Irene Handl and she came to the house for lunch – big hat and all. It so thrilled me, to see her sitting there, eating *my* food at *my* table, that I was struck dumb. I love her acting and her two novels and her love for Elvis Presley. The other was that I was able to do the best thing imaginable for my mother. The University of Wales made me a Doctor of Literature and I took my mother to the ceremony in North Wales and was able to invite her sister, Meriel, as well. The two old women had the time of their lives, seeing people they hadn't met for fifty years. No one paid much attention to me and I stood back and watched Sally and Meriel queening their way demurely around Bangor.

I was moved by the ceremony but as we were waiting to march into the hall and organs were playing and trumpets were beginning to sound, Sheikh Yamani reached under his Doctor of Law gown and, producing what looked like a medicine bottle, said, 'This is very special perfume – only for my family – made for *me* only, in *my* factory.' I was standing there with five or six distinguished academic gentlemen and we nodded and stood frozen by surprise as he liberally splashed the scent all over our robes, so that, when the doors opened, we marched into the great hall on a tidal wave of what smelled suspiciously like Jungle Juice.

A few weeks later I had reason to feel that my debt of gratitude for that weekend in North Wales could never be repaid. My mother was diagnosed with lung cancer and her doctor told me that she would not live more than six months. Meriel, her sister, was magnificent and navigated her way from Carmarthenshire all over the outer margins of North-East London to be with her sister as they waited for the results of tests and queued endlessly to be seen by a succession of doctors. The first hospital my mother went to was Dickensian and I came upon her, stripped and wrapped in a blanket, sitting up, cold and scared and confused after one of those painful lung-draining injections. She was confirmed in her fear and dislike of hospitals and I noticed that whenever we drove past a hospice in North-East London – remarkable for its cheerful exterior – she pointedly turned her head away until we were well past it. I took the hint. Hospices were out. I began to plan her last six months. My sitting room was slightly raised above street level and caught whatever sun there was. Her bed could sit in the window. My National Health Service doctor put me in touch with the Islington Social Services and I had good reason to regret joining in the criticisms of the 'Looney Left' which abounded at the time. They asked me if I needed cleaning help – I didn't, or Meals on Wheels – no, or help with bathing and lifting – it might come to that later. Should someone help with shopping? No, but I outlined my plan to bring my mother's bed into the sitting room where she would feel part of our lives and have a good view of the street. The social worker's eyes lifted from her notepad. She looked surprised. 'Have you consulted your family about this?' 'No,' I answered, thinking what is there to consult about? She nodded and said that I was over-confident to think that I could keep my mother at home until her end but that she would monitor our progress and provide me with extra help, when it was needed.

After she'd gone, I thought again of her question about the reaction of 'the family' to my decision and realized that I was going to keep my mother at home for as long as possible, no matter what Robin's reaction might be. I could see that my decision would cause trouble in our relationship and I was prepared for that. My mother regarded him with a cool eye and he, for his part, seemed divided between fearing and patronizing her. He was also anxious that we should move upward in the property market and our choices were limited by my insistence that any house we bought should contain an apartment for my mother and space for at least one daughter. For the moment she was able to live independently in her flat.

Christmas came, uneasy this year and for me everything was colored by the awareness that it was Sally's last winter. I discussed my domestic plans with no one. There seemed no sense in precipitating a row with my mother who wouldn't wish to be dependent and with Robin who would not welcome the inconvenience.

February was a month of birthdays in the family. The women took turns in preparing the birthday dinners. It was my mother-in-law Eleanor's turn to prepare Robin's party at their family home in Bayswater. I privately commemorated my father's birthday and filmed some musical sequences for a *Life of Siân* that was being prepared by an independent TV company. But glittering and being gay did not come easily.

On February 10, the day of Robin's birthday party, I got ready to leave for Eleanor's house. It was so cold. Robin went to the car and I ran down the side path to the garden entrance and knocked at my mother's apartment door. When she opened it I saw that she was looking very chic in a Jean Muir outfit; hard to believe that she had ever been chronically overweight. She was shivering, 'I don't think I should come. I'm *so* cold.' 'Oh, come *on*,' I said, bossily. 'Let me get you a warm wrap. You're coming, so there.' We got into the car. She was in the front and she took a long look at the house as we drove off, turning her head to keep it in her vision. Sometimes my mother's sense of drama really annoyed me. I thought to myself, 'I'll bet she's counting the times she'll drive away down Oakley Road never to see it again. *Damn* the drama!'

The Sachs's house in Kildare Terrace was brightly lit on every floor. I noticed my mother straighten her back as we climbed the steps. Glitter and be gay. We were nine for dinner and Eleanor – a wonderful cook – was busy in the basement kitchen. I went to offer help but she didn't need it. She was looking as pretty and as unruffled as if she'd just popped in for a cocktail. As usual I marveled at her powers of organization and her sense of perfect presentation. In the first-floor drawing room, Leonard was dispensing champagne cocktails and my mother, glass in hand, was deep in conversation with her favorite of Robin's relations, his Aunt Toffee – not in show business; bad legs, a slave to her cats, indomitably coping with her long, lonely widowhood. My daughter, Pat, arrived. Because she was taking drama classes in Bayswater she had taken to popping in regularly to Eleanor and Leonard's house. I sat next to Toffee and Sally in the first-floor drawing room. 'D'you know,' said my mother to me in Welsh, 'I don't feel so wonderful.' 'Would you like to lie down?' 'Maybe, for a minute.' There was a day-bed in the closed off 'L' of the drawing room and she lay down while I fetched a glass of water. Pat – devoted to her grandmother – began to say, 'Let's get a doctor.' 'Oh, don't be silly, Pat,' I said. 'Just make her comfortable.'

Pat and I sat on either side of the narrow day-bed and I began to think that something unusual was occurring. Robin and then Eleanor looked around the door and went away. Pat and my mother and I were alone in the room. Sally began to breathe more urgently, deep, rasping breaths. Pat became agitated and I told her to be calm and hold her grandmother's hand. Again she said, 'We should call a doctor.' I was sure that we shouldn't. Then my mother spoke for the first time. Her voice was strong and magisterial. 'Take off these clothes,' she said. I had a moment of not knowing what to do. 'Undress me,' she said in the same strong voice, the voice that as a child, I had obeyed without question. I looked at Pat and we both

rose and began to take off the Jean Muir coat and blouse
and skirt. Then the petticoat. Then the spotless white corset
with its myriad hooks – how had she ever done them up I
wondered. I had never seen my mother's bare flesh and I
hesitated now before dealing with the straining hooks and
eyes. Pat took the initiative and loosened the suspenders and
rolled down the stockings. 'Go on,' said the voice – it seemed
there was nothing of my mother except her voice – and I
began to push and tug at the hooks and eyes. We discarded
the bits of metal and rubber and steel and nylon and elastic
and silk and wool. They lay on the floor and Pat and I stood
one each side of the smooth, smooth white body. 'We're here.
We're with you,' I repeated inadequately. I had a feeling that
it no longer mattered to my mother whether or not we were
here with her in this back room in Bayswater. Her breathing
changed. I had never heard a death rattle but I recognized it
now. I clutched my mother's hand and lowered my head. And
after a while, knowing she was gone, I looked up and saw Pat
staring, staring at her dead grandmother.

I looked at my watch. Barely fifteen minutes had passed.
My mother's dying seemed to have taken longer, a great deal
longer.

I did everything badly for the remainder of the night. It
was as though I'd lost any sense of how to behave properly.
Pat was now the person who needed attention and I didn't
give it to her. Eleanor gave me a loose robe and I dressed
my mother in it. I was all daughter, nothing of a mother.
Unbelievably, after calling the undertaker, I said we should
go ahead with dinner. Who knows what everyone wanted to
do? I, in my distraction, imposed a form of behavior on them
all. Conversation was impersonal and polite. The men arrived
to take my mother away. Sitting across from the dining room
door, I saw the bound body as they carried it down and out of
the front door. After dinner we went home. I find it hard to
believe that we took Pat home to her flat and left her there

instead of bringing her home with us. But we did. I find it painful to imagine how she got through the night. When I got home I began to weep for the first time. Robin patted me sympathetically. Later he reminded me that we were now free to move house. I felt a small canker of disdain for him which never went away.

In my mind I relived that February night in Bayswater and over and over again I picked and worried at that fifteen minutes. Something had happened that I hadn't noticed, something momentous had occurred when I wasn't paying attention and I'd missed it.

After the funeral in London, a tear-drenched, crowded affair, conducted partly in Welsh and attended not only by our small family, but by Kate's former boyfriend all the way from Clifden in Ireland (my favorite but never-to-be son-in-law) and undergraduates of Kate's and Pat's generation and staff from the North London Collegiate School, I was swamped with letters and, this being a Welsh occasion, poems written for the occasion. Meriel's bore a card saying in Welsh 'One small step behind'. Kate was back in America and unable to return but as Pat and I stood to say goodbye to the people who had attended the funeral I was surprised to find myself face to face with O'Toole. I hadn't spoken to him since we parted on the pavement outside the costumier Nathan and Bermans and now we shook hands and he left. We hadn't exchanged a word since we'd parted.

Pat and I went back to work the following morning. Robin had made all the arrangements, dealt with the technicalities of death in a city. There were times when I couldn't imagine how I would manage without him. Now he set me house-hunting. It was something to do when the acting stopped.

Chapter Thirty-eight

R icci got married! Consternation fought with rejoicing among his many friends, mostly women, to whom he was indispensable and to whom he was always available. Who could not wish him happiness? Nevertheless, it was going to be something of an exercise in timing and limiting one's phone calls and one's demands on his time and attention. House-hunting alone, I found a house on the day of his wedding and rushed on foot from Ripplevale Grove in Islington to the Registry Office in W1. Oh, I *was* unreservedly happy for him. His bride, Rachelle, was ravishing and as eccentric as he. Her small child was a dark beauty. After the brief service we lunched rather grandly and privately, and I was proud to be part of the small and select wedding party. Looking at the two of them, I had a feeling that they were going to achieve an unusual and successful union. Almost in passing, I noted that *my* third attempt at marriage seemed to be faltering. I put the thought out of my head and raised my glass to Ricci and Rachelle and J. J., their small boy.

And so in 1985 began the process of buying another house, a house which was at once a dream and a nightmare. Ripplevale Grove was one of those pretty roads, nestling in a conservation area, immaculately tended, always 'desirable' in the estate agents' lexicon. The houses were late Georgian, two stories high, double fronted, like doll's houses, with front paths leading to neat front doors, fanlights intact. In fact, the houses were surprisingly intact inside as well as out. There were modern extensions leading into the large gardens overhung with tall, mature trees. It wasn't until I talked to Jack

Pullman, the writer of *I, Claudius*, that I realized why the house retained its windows and shutters and was very little affected by ugly 'improvements'. When Jack and his wife, Barbara Young, arrived for dinner in the new house Jack said, 'I have to sit down with a stiff drink. I haven't been back here since I was a boy.' I gave him a drink and he said, 'I swore I'd never come back. I was so glad to get out. This was the roughest area in Islington. Boy Scouts needed police protection to get to the club house.' I couldn't credit what he was saying and, seeing my astonished face, he said, 'When we left our house in Hemingford Road to go out and play, the last thing my mother would shout was "DON'T GO UP RIP!"' (which was what they called Ripplevale Grove). No one had been able to *afford* to improve the houses until they were slowly bought up by sympathetic people from the class of chatterers – of which I was one. I could only just afford to buy the freehold of Number 15 and I suspect that I was able to buy it – heftily mortgaged – only because it needed a new roof, new plumbing, new wiring, new floors, new walls in some rooms and there was dry-rot and rising damp as well. It was a gem but it was to keep me poor for the next five years as I worked incessantly and poured all I earned into fixing the house and garden. The constant work and the strain of living in a building site was also to put an intolerable burden on my marriage.

The house bought and the builders engaged, I went to Northern California to make a film about Ewoks. The producer was George Lucas. On the plane I developed acute sciatica. Surrounded by beauty and hospitality, courtesy of Edward Duke's incomparable address book, I was in such pain that I slept standing up for a month and suffered appallingly as we worked the long hours six days a week. Kate joined me for a brief holiday and on the day she nearly missed her plane back to New York I found that although I couldn't lie down or sit or walk, I could *run*. Thereafter I cranked myself up each day and ran around the quiet neighborhood in Marin County where people didn't walk *or* run.

Painfully, I flew home and moved house. Having a 'bad back' didn't quite convey the pain of sciatica and I couldn't explain to Robin why suddenly I didn't want to carry heavy objects. My back had been giving out a few days before opening night for almost ten years and I had survived a couple of weeks of bearable pain and then snapped back to normal. Now, it took almost two months of truly severe pain before I recovered. I was worried. I had managed to get through a month's filming but I could never have opened a play in this acute distress. I saw doctor after doctor, got myself X-rayed, talked to chiropractors and surgeons and, having been told that I was stuck with this condition for life, '. . . look at the X-rays. Wear and tear I'm afraid, my dear' I couldn't accept it.

I baulked at surgery, bided my time. We moved, with an army of builders, to the new house and I began rehearsing *Gigi* in Chiswick. It was to move to the Lyric in Shaftesbury Avenue. I was not getting on with my director, John Dexter but, mercifully, I was on the best of terms with my 'sister', Beryl Reid, and Jean-Pierre Aumont and Geoffrey Burridge and Amanda Waring who was *Gigi* (and Dorothy Tutin's daughter). Although my sciatica had run its course I knew that, come opening night, I might fall ill again. I was desperate. Robin had been annoying me – playing at helping the builders when it suited him; slowing them up, entertaining them to breakfast. I stood drinking a coffee in what would, one day, be the kitchen while the men sat on the only chairs in the dining room and talked about 'manly' things before starting work. I could have done with a lift part of the way but our car sat in the street outside and there was murder in my heart as I left the house and ran past it on my way to the tube to Chiswick and to difficult John Dexter. Within a few weeks Robin and his brother were given a gift of money by their parents and decided to spend all of it going on a wonderful holiday. Robin left a list of things I was to make sure the builders finished before he returned and off he swept to Maui. His behavior so embarrassed me that I couldn't think of anything to say to him. He didn't notice that I was less than chatty.

After he left, rehearsals became more and more unpleasant. John Dexter antagonized each member of the company in turn – I wondered when it would be mine. Every night I cleaned up after the builders, left a list of things I'd like them to do on the morrow (I had actually built a house so I could see what they were or were not doing) and tried to keep myself reasonably clean and tidy despite the dust and dirt that enveloped me and my clothes. When Robin returned after two weeks, tanned and fit and deeply critical of the lack of progress, I looked at him and wished him buried under the rubble that was the house, with John Dexter for company, but I didn't know how to confront him and could only back further and further away, hiding behind a veneer of good behavior, implacably determined to keep my distance from him. Unfairly, I blamed him for not seeing that I was angry with him. Unreasonably, I blamed him for not being telepathic. Stupidly, I blamed him for qualities which had drawn me to him in the first place, a kind of sweet laziness.

By Christmas, the show was on in the West End. My turn to be worked over had come, so had Jean-Pierre Aumont's – I'll never forget the look on his face when he realized that he was being insulted. A polite, impenetrable shutter descended shutting out John Dexter forever. I think John had an idea that breaking people down was in some way good for them and he was also patronizing about the show, looking down his nose at its middle-of-the-road appeal. I met Alan J. Lerner in the wings as I was bracing myself to begin a dress rehearsal. 'You leaving?' 'Oh, yes, for good.' 'What do you mean?' 'Look.' He raised his hands; the nails had bitten into the palms of his hands and left a red, bleeding line. 'I have to clench my fists or I'll knock him out – and he's got diabetes, so I can't.' Dexter had just slung the great lyricist out of the theater where his own show was to play and he was going, deeply, deeply hurt.

I was assured that John Dexter had once been a wonderful director. Right now I could only rejoice at the story that the opera star Julia Migines had chased him out of the Met in New York when he was running the theater – she got rid of him for showing disrespect! I hoped I would meet the glorious creature one day. Jean-Pierre and Beryl both wanted to leave, but we all calmed down and I fell completely under Beryl's spell and had more fun on stage than I'd had for a long time. She improvised, flirted with the audience, doubled the playing time of our scenes if they were going well, cut out bits if they were going badly but never ever took her eyes off me to see if I was coping. I'd been a comic's 'feed' for six months when I was a young girl, so I was accustomed to a comic's lust for the audience's love and approval and laughter. I rather shared that feeling and felt privileged to be part of this great comedienne's nightly love affair with the house. Every weekend she bought presents of game and fish for me from Berwick Street and I bought fruit and veg for her and we couldn't have had a better time. And John Dexter never came near us after opening night.

Christmas arrived and the whole family came to visit me in the only-just completed house. I had Christmas day off and would have liked to have gone to bed for the holiday. The Burmese cats, Spencer, Barnaby and Rupert, sat high up on the tops of cupboards, fascinated by my seasonal efforts down below. As I was trying to stow away the dishes from the turkey part of the meal and tearfully retrieving my mother's Christmas pudding (injected with potheen, illicit, clear, raw Irish spirit) made the previous year, from its long, cloth-bound boil, Spencer decided to descend for a better view and somehow landed in the white rum sauce, at which I dropped the hot pudding. The three cats and I stared at the wreckage on the floor.

'Anything wrong?' cried someone from the dining room. 'No. No. No,' I responded, on my hands and knees, trying to rescue pudding and sauce and leave out the slivers of glass.

As I presented the dish to an unsuspecting table, I hoped I'd got all the glass out. I hoped. But I didn't really care, I was too tired and sadly I never exchanged a straightforward word with Robin after that year, 1985. The year of my mother, Sally's, death.

Chapter Thirty-nine

How do people end relationships 'amicably'? I wish there were a manual. After all these years and all these liaisons I'm at sea, rudderless. The awful thing is I suspect Robin feels as badly as I do, but when I try to broach the subject he backs off and won't discuss it.

There is a practical problem. No matter how grand or carefree one might try to be, money can be a terrible source of discontent. Robin has always said that he doesn't mind that I am the breadwinner – and at first I was grateful for that. Now, after some twelve years, I'm less grateful. Occasionally, he says that if things don't pick up he's going to have to 'get a job' (meaning a non-acting job); this is offered as the most awful move imaginable, but I think that getting an honest job, *any* sort of job might help us both feel better. And he does feel awful, I can tell. He and Richard La Plante build their bodies to perfection. He learns karate and does well, and then stops at the point of gaining his black belt. Why? I feel sorry for him as he comes home from the gym and retreats to the garden room to lie on the couch and watch game shows. There is nothing I can do for him – or for myself. He's begun to gamble regularly; he really enjoys it so I have little objection. I think I understand this desire to have a smart car and be seen in smart clothes at the gaming tables. I may be harassed and overworked but I am doing a job I love and spend my days with people that are the best possible company. The life of a chronically out-of-work actor is truly awful. The specter of unemployment terrifies me so much – a legacy of my childhood in Wales – and I can't discuss the problem but pick up the bills and cover the debts. Also, I did take the wedding promises seriously; this is worse rather than better and poorer rather than richer and there is sickness at the heart of our life, but this is what it is. The future seems hopeless.

A few things helped me along the way. Fenella Fielding, when I told her about my despair of ever curing my treacherous back, had suggested that I should consult a friend of hers from Israel, Lily Cohen, who had been a dancer and now taught T'ai Chi and the Feldenkreis exercise system and did a lot of voluntary work with old, disabled people. Feeling older than God's mother and twice as disabled and having exhausted all other avenues, I now embarked on a three-year course of treatment with Lily. We worked in her apartment in Bayswater three times a week and gradually my back grew stronger and I just knew that one day I was going to be completely 'normal' again. The regular exercise also improved my mood and, as an added protection against depression, I joined a drawing class so when I wasn't rehearsing or playing, I nipped into the Mary Ward Centre in Holborn and did a spot of bad but absorbing sketching – anything rather than sit at home. When I had a play to learn, I made that an excuse for going out of town; once I went to stay, alone, in a hotel near Lincoln Cathedral and another time Sara allowed me to use her country house in Norfolk where I learned lines and painted and became cheerful until my return home. I also got it into my head that the whole family should learn to meditate and that was an astounding success. Kate, who was back from America and now working in England, really loved the discipline but Pat was not so sure; Robin persevered and I added it to my cocktail of activities designed to keep me on an even keel. The garden thrived, the house improved gradually as I acquired well-paid television jobs. I was by no means out of the wood financially because our future seemed so precarious and the house continued to be a heavy drain, but when I got an unexpectedly large check, I was able to go back to St Laurent after a considerable absence and outfit myself out grandly for the first time in years.

I was working really hard on the TV series *The Snow Spider* in Wales when I was asked to go and see Milos Forman and was delighted to have the chance to meet a man I admired so much. Trailing a lot of luggage and destined for Paddington, I made a detour past Blake's Hotel where he was staying. Would I read, asked the Czech fascinator; 'Well sure,' I purred, having rolled over on my back, charmed. And having read, I pushed off to mid-Wales. Sara was furious. 'You didn't have to *read*. You've *never* had to read.'

A few weeks later I was asked back. Again, on my way to work in Wales, I dragged my suitcases down to Blake's and had another enchanting meeting with Mr Forman. Would I read a scene *with* someone? 'Oh, of course,' I crooned, rolling over again. Sara was fit to be tied. 'What are you *doing*?' 'Well, it was fun.' I forgot all about it.

A few weeks later Milos wondered if I could assemble a kind of costume and learn a *scene* and do it with a few people and he would film it. This time I didn't dare tell Sara what I was up to. It was another Monday meeting and again I toiled down with my luggage and a token costume. This time Milos *directed* a scene and it was massive fun. I pushed off to Builth Wells again. Ages later I was told that I was the first person Milos had cast for the movie, *Valmont*. Never can a part have been obtained more light heartedly or more pleasantly (or more secretly).

So, it was to be Paris for six months. I hadn't been in Paris since I was a rich person, living at the Meurice or in our apartment at the George V, dining out every night at the best restaurants, the newest night clubs. This was a very different life. I no longer knew anyone there and I lived quietly, but I was ravished anew as, this time, I walked and walked around the city and we worked in the most beautiful locations. And I met Annette Bening (playing Mme de Merteuil). She was not only beautiful and talented but good and wise and lots of fun, and I learned a great deal from watching her. She was patient and friendly to everyone in that enviably open American way. When bad things happened she dealt with them by going for a long run along the banks of the Seine. She possessed formidable discipline and a huge sense of the ridiculous. We both loved and admired Milos Forman who, when he was working, was the most tactless person imaginable. He was so intent on the work in hand that his thoughts sprang from his mouth uncensored and uttered in endearing Mittel European. One day as we were working on an endless tracking shot in the Musée Camondo (which was 'my' house in the film), we repeated our scene over and over and over and over again. The unit grew apprehensive as it looked as though we girls were going to cop it any minute. Sure enough, an anguished scream from Milos: '*Why* are you behaving like ziss? *Why* are you talking in such a peculiar way? *Why* do you *walk* like zat? *Why* can you not be like *peeple*? *Why* not be *natural*? *Tell* me *why* you do it?'

Disconsolate, we turned to go back to our first marks and begin again, and Annette under her breath said to me, 'We do it like *ziss*, Milos, because we want you to hate us. And we do it like *ziss* because we want never to work again.'

I stored her in my mind as an example of good behavior and there she stayed.

At Christmas, Annette's then husband, Steve Black, came to visit her from America and Robin joined me. It was an uneasy time. Robin was veering between low spirits and the sort of extra high spirits which none of us could match. The long separation was tearing apart the already threadbare fabric of our life together. When I returned to London, Kate came to stay and that helped somewhat. Robin was very well mannered and more good-humored when she was around. Even so the atmosphere became more and more strained. I had very little idea now what made up Robin's daily routine. Where did he go in his BMW? What did he do when he wasn't at the gym or the casino? Once, in a family crisis, I needed to find him and I called the place where he'd said he was spending the day – he'd not been there since early morning. When he returned at night I asked if his day had gone well. 'Oh yes,' he replied and I found I had neither the will nor the inclination to question him further. Perversely, I felt guilty about the episode, as though *I* was the one leading a secret life. As I went through the motions of being a 'good' wife I wished that something or someone would happen along radically to alter everything. Since I lacked the courage to force a discussion there was nothing for it but to hope feebly for a theatrical, *ex-machina* solution. Something along the lines of 'with one bound she was free'.

Robin was marooned in a comfortable world, but dependant on me, where the phones rang for me, a world in which, at almost forty years of age, he was still referred to by journalists as a 'toy-boy', where strangers called him 'Mr Phillips'. He no longer kept my accounts as he used to. It was as though by distancing himself from the practicalities of life he distanced himself from all responsibility for the mortgage payments, the taxes, the insurance and the day-to-day task of maintaining a life.

Gradually, the house grew glossier and the cats thrived; when they weren't fighting each other, they lay on the most comfortable chairs, a beautiful heap of shining brown, grey and red-blonde fur but I looked at them and myself and felt that they, the house and I had all lost our luster in Robin's eyes.

There was very little time for moping. I was always busy and the girls were both acting as well and when I went to see them I found, to my surprise, that watching them brought nothing but pleasure, with none of the fear and torment I used to feel when watching their father (or when I was a child, my father) on stage. Out of the blue I had been commissioned to write a book about needlepoint. Coral Browne had taught me the basic stitches in the Sixties and I had made some large pieces;

now I struggled to complete the book (sewing to a deadline was much worse than writing) and continued to film the TV *Life of Siân* that had begun so many months ago. It was meant to be a story told without narrative or interviewer's questions; just pictures and songs, shots of me opening a play, rehearsing, performing songs. This was a difficult concept, made doubly difficult by my unwillingness to reveal anything about my crumbling private life and it seemed to drag on interminably. Edward Duke came to stay and developed a new hobby – cooking. It was a measure of my fondness for him that I didn't turn a hair as my immaculate kitchen became an impenetrable no-go area, piled high with blackened pots and dirty dishes and spilled sugar, flour and gravy. (The food, though, was spectacular.)

I piled on more and more work – besides writing and sewing and filming musical segments for *The Life*, I began to rehearse a play by Loleh Belon, *Thursday's Ladies* ('Another French play,' I thought with misgiving). The other Ladies were to be played by Eileen Atkins and Dorothy Tutin, the one handsome young man by Jeremy Brudenell. I was delighted to be directed again by Frank Hauser. It was too much to resist. We played ourselves as toddlers, children, teenagers, young women, switching from one age to another with no warning or preparation. Frank didn't want to help the changes by making lighting adjustments so we did our level best to age or rejuvenate in an instant, switching from one age to another with startling suddenness, concentrating like mad. The three of us worked hard – and happily – but the play which was so much fun to do, wasn't, we gathered, nearly as much fun to watch. One of my faithful fans said to me at the stage-door, 'Oh, Miss Phillips, some of these foreign plays you're in – I do *dread* them.'

It was a short run but one night I met a great friend of Eileen's, an actor whom I hadn't met since the Fifties, Ken Parry, a rotund, Dickensian figure, with shiny, round eyes that missed nothing and rosy, pursed lips that conveyed disapproval or disbelief in hefty quantities. We realized that we were neighbors and began to visit each other and became friends. From Wigan, but born in Wales of Welsh extraction, Ken's English was eloquent, sonorous and magisterial and I began to collect his more ornate tirades against the sheer bloodiness of life. Some of his pronouncements were startling. 'Albert Finney was on a bicycle as I came down the street with me teeth in, and there were six nuns passing.' 'I first met Charlie Kay with a parrot in the Edgware Road.' 'Gloria Swanson told me all those lies. For instance: she told me Rudolph Valentino wasn't gay.'

I moved straight from the play to a musical at the Donmar. Bill Bryden and Sebastian Graham Jones were going to write the show, called simply *Brel*, as we rehearsed the sixteen or so Jacques Brel songs that would make up the evening and Bob Crowley would design the sets and costumes and the company was to consist of two 'mature' voices to sing the songs of experience and a young man and woman to sing the love songs. In the event they failed to cast an older man so I sang all the 'mature' songs, including one for which I was totally unsuited though I struggled (manfully) with it, and Alex Hansen and Kelly Hunter sang the songs of youth. Dressed by Bob in leather, I walked on to his ravishing set (three full grown trees set on an empty stage and the walls of the Donmar painted Gauloise blue right up to the roof) and opened the show singing 'Amsterdam', a tough song about tough, louche sailors. 'Go on. You can do it! Don't fuss!' they cried and in the end I didn't fuss, although I wasn't convinced I could do it (I think the meditating was taking effect). I loved doing the show and during the run something inside me changed. Then, just before Christmas, I experienced one of my rare, strong, Technicolor dreams.

Bob's set for the second half of the show was dominated by a vast dining table covered in a white tablecloth, with huge gilded dining chairs set around it. There was a picture of Brel propped on the chair at the head of the table, which was set with large crystal goblets. (One of the songs in Part Two was called '*Le dernier repas*'.) One Saturday night Robin picked me up after the second show and we set off to spend the weekend with Bill and Bryn, now living in Herefordshire. I strapped myself into the back and fell asleep instantly. Over an hour later I woke and saw that we were travelling very fast and that Robin was drinking from a hip flask. He was a responsible driver and this was very unlike him and for a moment I was speechless before finding far too loud a voice and demanding to know what the hell he thought he was doing. The 'Don't Drink and Drive' campaign was still in its infancy but, given my early experiences of being terrified in the car of a drunken driver, it was understandable that I should greet the campaign with enthusiasm. Absurdly, I demanded to be put out on the deserted roadside and Robin, refusing, insisted that he was perfectly capable of driving. The flask was, however, put away and we pitched up at the house silent and angry but unharmed at about two in the morning. Sizing up the situation, Bill and Bryn nervously suggested a quick bowl of soup and bed. I awoke from my dream at five in the morning. In it I had been singing and dancing Brel's 'Funeral Tango' which Alex Hansen and I used to do as a duet while Kelly Hunter looked on and at one point, dancing down the length of the dining table, as I looked down to check where I put my feet, I saw in the dream that all ten goblets were filled with salt instead of wine. The salt was as white as the tablecloth, and the chairs, upholstered in red brocade which was meant to echo the red of the wine, stood out shockingly as the only splash of color in the 'room'. I lay there thinking that the goblets held the bitter taste of a souring marriage. I had no glimpse of resolution but at least I had been brought sharply to a state of awareness. My temporary solution was pretty useless: work harder.

Simon Stokes asked me to play Amanda in Tennessee Williams's *Glass Menagerie* – another of those parts, along with Hermione in *Heartbreak House*, that I was always being told I was 'born' to play. I'd had my fingers burned with some of the 'born to play' parts but the combination of Simon and Tennessee convinced me to accept the job at the Arts Theater in Cambridge and after that on tour. Once again, I came to the conclusion that I appeared to do better in roles that seemed unsuitable for me. I never convinced myself as Amanda and also committed the ultimate sin of taking against my character. All my sympathy was with the boy, Tom, who escaped his family; Laura, the lame daughter, got on my nerves and I would have liked to shake Amanda until her teeth rattled. I just couldn't make a 'case' for her and that is a recipe for failure. I wasn't helped by the fact that I smashed my foot on a concrete block while I was running to have lunch with Colin Firth's mother in Winchester. By the evening my foot had swollen to double its size and we had to cut away half of my stage shoe (off-stage I wore a man's sock on my right foot). We were playing on a vertiginous raked stage – so fashionable in the Eighties – and I could scarcely hobble across it. What the audience made of the play in which the daughter's limp is one of the main features, when her mother's limp – never referred to – was much worse than hers, I can't imagine. The huge foot was extremely painful and showed no signs of subsiding.

The play ended in June and I had a few weeks only in which to pray that I got better soon because I'd agreed to do a play in London for Christopher Renshaw, with whom I'd been working on the score of a musical by Jerry Herman called *Dear World*, which we hoped to do together. Meanwhile, the play we were engaged on was a French comedy, set on the Avenue Foch, which meant clothes from Paris and *very* high heeled shoes. In the nick of time, the swelling went down and I managed to squeeze my foot into a smart shoe. Another French play, *Paris Match*. Will I never learn? Stephen Murray,

Leslie Ash and I bore the brunt of the action and we did everything to that play short of blowing it up and jumping up and down on the bits. The great Ray Galton came in to help and gave me some wonderful, sure-fire laughs which helped me, but nothing could help the play and a month after we'd opened in town I gratefully hung up my stilettos for the last time. But I couldn't take a break, unable to face the prospect of spending time at home.

Chris and I doggedly went on working on the musical (which never did happen) and at the same time I went into another play, *Vanilla*, this time an American play by Jane Stanton-Hitchcock which was to be directed by Harold Pinter. It was extremely incorrect politically and very funny and that, coupled with Harold's name and the prospect of working with a wonderful cast under the management of Michael Redington lured me on board against the advice of friends who now (rightly) sensed an element of panic in my choices. We came into the Lyric on Shaftesbury Avenue and as though doing the play was not enough, after the performances on Saturday night a car would pick me up and take me on the long journey to mid-Wales where I would work each Sunday and Monday morning on a television series, *Emlyn's Moon*, returning in time for the show at the Lyric on Monday night. During the weekdays I busied myself with broadcasts and recordings. The fact that I loved what I was doing couldn't disguise the fact that it was largely displacement activity. Taking on more and more responsibility at work was the only way I could hide from myself the truth that my life was out of control. The play did not succeed but I made enduring friendships with the author Jane Stanton-Hitchcock and one of my favorite Irish actors, Niall Buggy, with whom I shared a dressing room. We co-existed – I, pin neat and he, unbelievably untidy – without flying at each other's throats and continued to keep company harmoniously ever after.

After a long illness, Robin's father died and left him a

substantial sum of money. He genuinely forgot to tell me that he was proposing to go to Los Angeles for the period in the spring of the year, known in the television world as the 'pilot season'. For two or three months there is huge activity as innumerable new shows are cast and tried out. Most fall by the wayside but it is a time to see people and be seen and, of course, some people are lucky and get very lucrative work. Robin was comically mortified when he realized that he had discussed his plans with everyone except me. (I *was* out most of the time.) I considered this to be a good move on his part and helped him all I could, compiling a book of useful addresses and contacts. Ricci, when I told him the news, said, 'Well, that's the last we'll see of *him*.' I was so exasperated; such a glib, superficial, over-dramatic reaction, I thought. On January 6, 1991, I went to Heathrow and waved Robin off. After he'd passed through the barrier I stood unseen, watching his figure grow smaller as he descended a long ramp before disappearing from view. He looked vulnerable and very alone and I prayed that things would go well for him.

The atmosphere at home had been more friendly than it had been for a very long time and the parting had been easy because I was due to visit New York, Los Angeles and Washington within a matter of days, as a guest of Mobil Oil who presented much of our TV output in America. We were to celebrate the birthday of Masterpiece Theater on Channel 13. We were flown to New York and went on to L.A. where Robin and I were reunited. He came to stay with me at my smart hotel for a few days. Waking early near Venice Beach, I stood on the balcony and wondered why no one had mentioned that the city was framed by beautiful pale purple mountains. Robin was unexpectedly sweet and affectionate, shedding a tear as we parted after a few days, he to resume settling into his life of flat and job hunting and I to do a dinner in Washington. He was due home in three months.

Our caravan moved on to Washington, where we arrived

on the eve of the Gulf War to be entertained by Mobil Oil in the beautiful reception rooms at the top of the State Department Building. There must have been some local doubt about the wisdom of this event but it was decided to go ahead and some thirteen of us British actors went up in the modern lift through the modern building and stepped out into the eighteenth century – it was *such* a coup de théâtre and we were suitably stunned into open-mouthed, silent admiration. The veteran broadcaster Alistair Cooke gave us a tour of the rooms and we sat down to eat, two actors to each table of eight Americans. The tables were charmingly decorated with appropriate 'props' from plays in which we'd appeared. Jeremy Brett was at my table and he shamelessly switched place cards so that he could sit next to me and, as he explained, 'that halves the talking I have to do'. He ate nothing, I remember, and when I urged him to taste something he muttered, 'No, no, no, this is much too impressive and I want to concentrate on it.' We were given a tour of the city late that night and there was a light at every window in every government building. It was overwhelming, being in a place that would see no rest, where the lights would not be extinguished throughout the night. In the morning the United States went to war and we flew home, subdued.

Chapter Forty

I remained subdued until Edward Duke came to stay with me while we worked together at the BBC on a series of Noël Coward playlets, hardly distinguishing ourselves, alas, but having a lovely time at home cooking and watching incomprehensible Indian musical movies late at night, playing with the three cats, enjoying a spot of domesticity. We were juvenile, if not childish – and we were happy. Edward had become ill and I was aware that with the close of the pilot season my problems would reappear as urgent and as fresh as ever, so – so we ignored the future and took care to keep each other amused. When we finished the long job at the BBC we went our separate ways and for some time to come the laughter ended for both of us.

Before I embarked on another stage play I went to visit Robin in L.A. As I made my travel arrangements I found myself wondering why I was going on the visit; he was due home in a few weeks' time. He wasn't there to meet me when I arrived. I waited, feeling anew that this trip was a stupid mistake. My fellow passengers had all left when he appeared, eating. He explained that – waiting for me – he'd felt hungry and nipped out for some Mexican food. No apology. My uneasiness grew and stayed with me for the whole week. We were in an odd situation, partly estranged and partly over-familiar. I was genuinely pleased for him that he'd done an episode of a TV series and pleased also that he seemed so at home. He'd rented what I thought was a rather nice house which he shared with another English actor but he didn't like the neighborhood, not smart enough, I gathered, and hadn't done anything much to brighten up his part of the house. He seemed to be abstracted, waiting for something else to happen. We made a trip to San Diego but he was anxious to return to L.A. We saw friends for lunches and dinners but I felt he was eager to resume his 'normal' life – whatever that might be. I couldn't work out what he did all day. I was uneasy.

It was a long week. My spirits rose slightly as he drove me to the airport. 'See you in a month's time,' we chorused too brightly. The plane was delayed. I suspected that neither of us could endure to be locked together in the intimacy of waiting for a plane and I asked if he'd mind if I went through so I could do a little work on the play (an adaptation of *The Manchurian Candidate*.) Robin made a small show of reluctance and we parted. Miserable as I had been, now I fairly skipped through passport control and I imagined that he, too, must be happy to be driving alone through his beloved city. It really was dear to him. A few days previously, as we'd driven down a hideous road – gas stations, low, shoddily built shops, fast-food restaurants stretching for miles, disaffected youth lounging on the pavements – and I was wondering how this endless, messy sprawl had come about, Robin broke the silence saying, 'Isn't it *wonderful*?' I smiled, not speaking. It was charming and disarming, his genuine love of the place. As I pottered about in the airport, feeling better than I'd felt all week, I wondered again what form our future life could possibly take. Was he dreading a return to the poor weather and lack of excitement of London N1? Did London seem dull? Was the British actor's life of lower rewards, lower expectations, dreary in his eyes? When I tried to talk to him about the future he'd protested that London was 'his' town – his home. But I was sure that he'd fallen in love with Los Angeles. When he'd run out of money, would he want us – me – to maintain a home there? Should I embark on such a costly enterprise? How could I live in L.A. when I didn't drive? I had a score of questions and no answers so I settled down to work on the play until my flight was called.

The stewardess tapped me on my shoulder as I sat in my economy seat and asked me to come through to the first-class section of the plane. I was nonplussed until I saw Suzanne Bertish. I didn't know her but of course I recognized her. She was returning to London after doing a stage play in L.A. Forceful and authoritative, she'd just *told* someone to move me forward. I was impressed and grateful. I would never have thought of asking. As we talked, I mentioned that I didn't drive and instead of sympathizing as everyone else did with my horrible experiences culminating in car-phobia, she reared up and said that it was *ridiculous* not to be able to drive and that doubtless my fears had nothing to do with cars or traffic and that I ought to *address* the problem and why hadn't I already *done* so? Losing interest in that, she moved on to other areas where I might smarten up a bit – chiefly, as well she might be, astonished that I'd never read anything by Robertson Davies. We talked and talked all the way across the Atlantic and it was one of the most lively and agreeable of long flights. But driving? Despite Suzanne, I couldn't see myself behind the wheel of a car.

The play to which I returned was a version of the novel *The Manchurian Candidate* by Richard Condon (father of my friend Debbie). John Lahr had cleverly adapted and updated the book. I would play the hateful mother and Gerard Murphy, an actor I much admired, would play my son. We were to tour the play before bringing it to London for a season at the Lyric Hammersmith. Apart from anything else, I thought that this would give me a chance, once and for all, to perfect a good Southern American accent and I began to work with Joan Washington, my favorite accent and dialogue coach.

Neither the play nor the accent was easy and I had no time in which to worry about myself until, a month later, it was time for Robin's mother and me to collect him at Heathrow.

It was morning when we met him and Eleanor drove us back to Islington where I served a very quick lunch of pasta and salad. Robin exclaimed how wonderfully 'Californian' it was. It was evident that anything that might even remotely be considered Californian would be wonderful in his eyes. I felt a little defensive and was glad that it was a lovely spring day and that the garden, while not Californian, was looking very beautiful in its damp English way. Within days I left to open the play in the South of England, rushing home on the last train on Saturday night in order to spend the weekend there before travelling on to the next 'date' in Manchester. I was glad that Kate was staying at the house so that Robin – somewhat disoriented – wasn't all alone. I suspected that he hadn't wanted to leave California. He'd been gone five months, two months longer than he'd intended to be away. As I lunched at a friend's house while I was on tour in Manchester, Kate telephoned, very excited, to say that Robin had auditioned over the phone for a part in the mini-series of *Dynasty*. The actor playing one of the sons had dropped out for some reason and he'd got the part and was needed immediately in L.A. He'd gone while I played a matinée! It was like a fairy tale. Kate and I were beside ourselves with excitement. It was so *American*; the unexpectedness, the speed of it all. Although it wasn't long in duration, this job somehow justified all the time and money he'd spent in L.A. since January.

Later, I sat on my bed back at the little hotel where the company was staying and found myself writing a description of the room with its cheap bamboo furniture, cunning use of small space – the pretty bedside lamp just that bit too small and too low to make reading in bed comfortable, the little ornaments from Spain – noting the dull weather and the view from the window over the suburban backyards and knowing that this was the watershed of our life together. Nothing would henceforth be the same. I looked at the page and thought that maybe I was over-reacting. Robin's last message had been to wish me well and to say that he would be back for the opening of the play in London. I was unreservedly happy for him and if this job went well then it might follow that our lives might begin to make some kind of sense. It wasn't a job I would much want to do but it *was* a job and it might, with luck, help him on the way to a viable career.

As he dashed to the airport, returning to the balmy weather and the smart hotel, with his car waiting for him, I walked through the drizzle and caught a bus to the Opera House. My life was the usual combination of job satisfaction and anxiety and discomfort. It was not a life that Robin had ever truly embraced. And now he had a job in the beautiful climate that made him happy.

Chapter Forty-one

O ur set for *The Manchurian Candidate* – a huge piece of scaffolding – was difficult to work on and rather dangerous. Actors with vertigo had a particularly terrible time as they clung on to their moorings near the top of the proscenium arch. Clive Carter saved Gerard Murphy from plunging twenty feet to his death or horrible injury by grabbing at his waistband and praying that the wardrobe department had done a good job on the seams. We ran out of money in Cardiff. Our director had to leave to do another job. John Lahr was valiant (and generous with cash), and his friend Karel Reiz kindly stepped in to direct us. It was business as usual; part of the rough and tumble of putting on a play, but it was wearing and I was tired when we returned to London. The mini-series was soon over and Robin was expected back any day so I hastily organized a celebratory garden party for him. Then he called to say that although the show was over he was detained in L.A. I cancelled the party. His mother, however, was not pleased with him. After my opening night she and I went out for a small dinner with friends and I made excuses for him. In all fairness, I didn't totally disbelieve him. He might be evasive, protective of his privacy – I sympathized with that – but he had always laid great store by truthfulness and honesty.

Not only did he not return for the opening, he didn't return for the whole run of the play at the Lyric. There were 'people to see', hopes of 'another job' – it was all very understandable, I thought and moved on to another job, a television series called *The Chestnut Soldier*. One day I astonished myself as I lifted the telephone receiver and dialed a driving school that was offering a week's intensive, residential driving course, culminating in a test at the end of it. I arranged a place for myself the day after I finished the television series. I replaced the handset and wondered why it had taken so long for Suzanne's words to goad me into action.

Now as I nervously got ready for my driving course, I called Robin for reassurance and couldn't locate him. At last he called me and I was relieved to talk to him because he was a brilliant driver and I especially needed his encouragement and advice. I wasn't nervous – I was petrified; and what was propelling me forward? Was it Suzanne or a wish to make it possible for me to live in L.A.? I had no idea. Robin seemed bemused as well and wasn't quite as impressed and helpful as I'd hoped he would be. He seemed distracted. When I hung up, the phone rang and a woman from the driving school said that there had been a clerical error and my place was not available after all. I stood in the dining room in Ripplevale Grove, unable to move or think. If I couldn't begin this feared, dreaded venture and begin it at precisely the moment I'd planned, I didn't think that I would ever be able to begin it. It was established, like a challenging rock-face, in my mind and I couldn't imagine not climbing it.

Barely coherent, I called my daughter Pat and she, sensing that I'd lost my grip, told me to hang up and do nothing until she called me back. In less than half an hour she'd found me an alternative (non-residential) course, an instructor with whom I'd work all day and every day for a week and she had booked me into a small, quiet boarding house in Chester. She'd found the times of trains and I was to leave London in a few hours. I don't know that I thanked her properly but I did exactly what she'd told me to do. Before I left, I ran round to the shops at the Angel and my wallet was stolen. Back at the house, cancelling credit cards, I felt defeated before beginning; what if I sat in the car and burst into tears? What if I ran it into a wall? What if I killed someone? What if I simply couldn't move at all?

What if in twenty minutes I couldn't leave the house? I called Morag Hood and told her how bad I felt. She had a brain wave. 'Shall I consult the I-Ching?' she asked. This seemed to have a wonderfully calming effect on me and later she told me that she realized at that moment that I was fairly demented. When, before hanging up, I thanked her for her help and remarked that I had been quite sure she would be able to offer 'practical, down to earth' help, she had stood there with the I-Ching in her hand half laughing and half seriously concerned for the innocent people of Chester.

I don't recall what the I-Ching said but it should have told me that I was going to meet an angel in the guise of a driving instructor. He told me on the first day that there was no possibility that I could sit and pass the driving test at the end of a week; such boasts on the part of the driving schools were stupid. Occasionally a young man of around nineteen might pull it off but the rest of us didn't stand a chance. 'But you'll be driving in a couple of days,' he said matter of factly. It was a milestone week in my life. I was so anxious to live up to this lovely man's expectation that I became calm and methodical once I was behind the wheel. My feelings of unease were very near the surface the rest of the time. One day in the break between a daylight and a night driving lesson I went into a church and sat listening to an organist practicing for a concert later in the day and found myself overcome with sadness and apprehension. Something was terribly wrong and I felt that if I sat there for another moment I would see clearly what is was that was stalking me. Drying my tears, I hurried into the narrow, busy street. I wasn't ready to confront the beast. Not yet.

I returned to London, having driven with my instructor to Warrington and back – at night! I felt that I *had* climbed the North Face of the Eiger. Bill Corlett, as he did many times, urged me to enjoy my accomplishment for a day or two but, as usual, I could only think how much more I had to learn and went to the BSM to arrange a course of lessons in London starting at once. I would never again find an instructor like my savior in Chester but I no longer needed an angel – I was almost normal.

Robin was not in the flat I'd found for him (Gwen Humble's apartment – a smart address, more to his liking) and I had to wait to tell him the incredible news that I was actually up and driving. I had given him the address of an Anglophile with a lovely ranch in Santa Barbara, who had been married to a rich man and, parted from him, had fallen into a lucrative career doing voice-overs. Her ranch – the Red Rooster – was a haven for depressed foreigners, especially Englishmen. I had been urging Robin to call her and finally, after a lot of nagging, he did and was invited to spend a weekend there. He'd gone back to the Red Rooster for a last visit before coming home for good. He was still there when his niece was taken ill and I had to reach him a few days later. Morag Hood, who'd lived in Santa Barbara for many years, said that it was understandable he should linger there as it was one of the most beautiful, seductive places in the world. I urged him to make the drive up to San Francisco as well before returning.

It was October and Bill, Bryn and I made a trip to mid-Wales to visit a wonderful house where I'd spent some time filming in the summer. We always had a good time together but this visit was cold and dark and wet and we were in unusually low spirits. Robin was due back in two weeks' time and there were preparations to make for his return. Excepting a week at home in May he'd been gone for ten months during 1991.

I'd convinced myself that life in London would be dull for Robin, so I'd accepted some smart invitations I might otherwise have declined. On his return, as soon as he'd caught up on some sleep, we had a perfectly hideous night out at a smart charity ball, then we were taken to the Ivy by the producer of *Valmont*. I went on with my driving lessons and a dull week went by, during which I went to an award ceremony in Manchester. Understandably, Robin felt he needed some time at home to reactivate his London life so he didn't accompany me. I was nominated for an award for *The Manchurian Candidate* and Sara and I made the trip together. After a few hours of hilarity at the lunch, I realized how little light-heartedness there had been at home during the past week. Before I set off for London, I called Robin from the station in Manchester and he sounded surprised to hear my voice. I told him that I hadn't won and he seemed confused and confessed that he hadn't realized that I'd even gone to an awards ceremony. 'He must be very jet-lagged,' Sara said. It didn't occur to me that he might meet my train and he didn't. 'Are you all right?' I had asked him from time to time – too often to judge from his impatient reaction. I resolved to stop asking.

On the first day of the second week we arranged to meet a friend near Regent's Park and took a walk beforehand. He was abstracted and hating the weather. The day was just about as raw and as unpleasant as it ever gets in November in London. Everything compared unfavorably with California. I had run out of excuses but I felt protective towards the dozy waitress, the tepid coffee slopped into the saucer, the miserable geese in Regent's Park, the low, grey sky, the litter drifting about the pavement. I wanted to stand between him and them so he couldn't look down on and despise them. We met his friend Clive. 'Are you looking after this lovely woman?' Clive asked, as he often did in his kind-hearted, unthinking way. Robin didn't respond at all. Usually, he made a joke in reply. I began to collect myself and grew quieter. Quite suddenly, I felt very uneasy indeed. The beast was coming close.

At home I made a simple supper which we ate on trays in the garden room, while watching a video of *The Bonfire of the Vanities*. 'You look very sad,' said Robin rather accusingly, and there, in that moment, I felt the thing which had been lurking about the edges of my life detach itself from the shadows, visible only from the corner of my eye, and emerge into the bright light. I looked at it and heard a voice – my own. 'Is there someone else?' Even as I spoke the little cliché, I began to feel the beginning of a surge of energy. The reply hardly mattered but it would come, after a move into the dining room and a great deal of displacement activity and huffing and puffing and bluster. 'Yes,' he said in the end and his relief was palpable. How long, I wondered, would he have gone on saying everything was fine and he was glad to be home?

As he grew almost elated after his admission, I grew despondent and my resolve to clean up this mess as fast as possible wavered. I felt weak and unconfident and it was common sense alone that got me through the next hour. Life, I reminded myself, had been unsatisfactory and unhappy for years. Since we moved house five years ago, after my mother's death, and since Robin had caught a glimpse of the promised land in America, our life had disintegrated beyond repair. He'd found a new 'family' in Santa Barbara, complete with stepson, dogs, cats, garden pond. We had been wretchedly unhappy. There was nothing to salvage, no loss to regret, nothing worth keeping. Better to end quickly. '*Llosga fe mas. Paid llusgo fe mas*' – 'Burn it out, don't drag it out', was the Welsh saying that came to my mind.

He was so excited now that he showed me snapshots of the ranch – very nice; himself and a very nice-looking woman in fine-weather clothes doing fine-weather things – very nice. I felt that he would like me to enthuse more. 'Very nice,' I said and told him that he should go back there at once. He looked alarmed. As a matter of fact, I told him, I had to be out of the house early in the morning and it would be a good move on his part to move to his mother's apartment before I got home in the evening. He began to protest that we should consider what we were doing and not do anything hasty. I told him I had no intention of taking the scenic route towards the divorce which loomed ahead and that was as nasty as I got that night.

In the morning I had promised to be at a press conference for the launch of the TV series I had made for HTV so I had to take my hopeless, fine hair to the hairdresser very early. There scarcely seemed any point in going to bed but I had a bath and changed and we sat up in the bedroom talking and now that all the ties had been loosened and we weren't *supposed* to be getting along with each other, I felt quite well disposed towards him. He was no soul-mate, not even a real friend, but I didn't dislike him at all that night.

In the morning I called Bill and Bryn and Sara and she said that Bryn Newton, her partner, would meet me and take me to the press conference for *The Chestnut Soldier*. I pasted a smile on my face which stayed in place until I saw Bryn and we went for a chilly coffee in Covent Garden. He was so whole-heartedly on my side, so unashamedly supportive that it shook my composure. At the press conference there were many of the usual questions concerning the difficulty of maintaining a marriage and a career. Bryn's handsome face was grim but he knew that I wouldn't falter in public. He and Peter Murphy, the producer, and I drank a great deal of coffee and I went for a driving lesson, surprising my instructor as I charged between the buses at the Angel with unaccustomed brio and resolution.

The day was far from over and I went home to change before joining Ricci and Rachelle for a dinner party we'd arranged for Robin in the Caprice in Mayfair. Robin was in the house; he'd almost finished moving out and he said he'd drive me into the West End. As we left, I asked him for the house keys and he seemed startled, but gave them to me without comment. And what would happen to his BMW? It had been an expensive purchase and he said he'd sell it as best he could and return me the money. Arriving at Ricci's house, he came in and asked if he could still come to the Caprice for dinner. He was navigating without a map and his responses were bizarre. Ricci explained to him that it would be quite inappropriate for us all to spend

the evening together. He added that Robin would be much
better off in California and that we should never have married
in the first place and what a blessing it was all over. Robin
looked more and more glum and finally left us and drove off.
I was exhausted I realized but there was no doubt in my mind
that I was experiencing a lucky escape. And there *had* after all
been a *deus* – or *dea – ex machina*. I hadn't had to do anything
except indicate the exit.

I had arranged a series of dinners at home for Robin
and now I decided not to cancel them. I had better start
getting used to entertaining alone – officially alone, that
is. Robin came to finish his packing as I rushed around
preparing dinner. I hitched up my skirt and realized that my
waistband was hanging around my hips. I had unbounded
energy and I'd lost a huge amount of weight in twenty-four
hours. I was shocked when Robin made to embrace me and
I flinched away from him, offended. I couldn't even muster
a smile and realized that today I was disliking him rather.
Was nothing going to remain the same for more than a few
hours? He told me to 'go easy' on myself and not push the
driving or force myself to go to all the Christmas parties we
went to every year – and maybe cancel some dinner parties.
He probably meant well but I was seized with rage and
resolved to redouble my efforts to become a driver and that
the stove at home should scarcely be allowed to cool between
meals and that I'd get Ricci to find me a new wardrobe for
gadding about. I kept my fury well under wraps as I wished
him well and told him that he'd be free as soon as I could
arrange it and that he shouldn't worry unduly about me.
'Anything you want to ask me?' he asked. I couldn't think
of anything at all.

I never saw him after that. He went to America and six
weeks after his departure – exactly a year after he first went
to California – we were divorced. Ricci had been right, in
principle, when he'd said in that January of 1991 that that

was the last we'd see of him. Now he said, 'You'll never hear from him again.' I tried on my new wardrobe; I was almost two sizes slimmer than I'd been six weeks previously. Large mercies.

Chapter Forty-two

After a roller-coaster life of much happiness and many troubles, a woman of a certain age makes a break for freedom. She makes a critical error of judgment and against all expectations enjoys some years of uncomplicated happiness but thereafter finds it very difficult to pay for this pleasure when the bill arrives, as it surely does. She is released from her impossible life with the minimum of blame, the maximum of sympathy, some hurt pride and public humiliation and a greatly improved financial situation and she recovers her health, not to mention her figure, and knows in every part of her being that what happened is for the best. She proceeds with life. She is content.

For a moment or two it seemed that that was the story but almost immediately in that winter of 1992, something went terribly wrong. My shiny new clothes hung in my dressing room where I had expanded into all the capacious cupboards. Now that I had only myself to think of, my hair and nails were expensively groomed and tended. The house had the air of 'my house', the phone rang constantly, I was surrounded by new friends as well as the group of friends that I called my 'family'. My real family was solidly there for me. Everyone was relieved for me. Everyone took care of me. The welcome-home dinners for Robin went on, although he was probably back in California. Sara must have called the girls and they both turned up unexpectedly during a dinner party, Kate all the way from Ireland where she now lived, blowing in, dishevelled. I was dangerously overwhelmed with gratitude for my daughters and I looked around the table at them and my friends and thought myself fortunate.

One of my chief tasks in those early days was to console someone who had become a close friend during Robin's absence in America. Kevin Moore's dismay was almost comical. He was the person who had provided me with the Santa Barbara address which I had given to Robin, with much urging to use it. Now he blamed himself for what had happened at the Red Rooster. I tried to convince him that what had happened wasn't his fault at all and that in any case it really was for the best. He had been helping me learn to drive and now he continued to do so. Tart of tongue, maliciously funny, he was also a man of principle and distressed to find someone he had thought to be a friend had behaved shoddily, as he thought. Missing little, he probably sensed that I was not quite as serenely over the upheaval as I thought myself to be. Bill and Bryn monitored my days by telephone.

Sara called me every morning before she opened the office and Bryn (Newton) called later in the day with a carefully prepared, hilarious piece of gossip. Kate stayed with me and was wonderfully, unfairly partisan. Pat was close at hand – all strength and health and sanity. Ken Parry summoned me to his flat and lectured me on how to live my life with the minimum of pain; evidently, and rightly, he wasn't one of the friends who anticipated a problem-free time ahead. I listened to his warning of trials to come without really understanding it.

Ricci and his mother, Lilian, were pleased at the turn of events and Ricci expected me to snap back to normal at once. For the first time in our friendship he made a misjudgment and it caused our only estrangement. It was temporary but it came at a bad time for me. He so wanted to see me happily established and looked after that he began to cast around for a new partner ('not necessarily to *marry*') for me. We didn't see each other until he promised to stop introducing me to strange men whom he considered 'suitable'. His childlike hope would have been to see me reconciled to O'Toole and it was very difficult to explain to him that such a thing was unfeasible and undesirable. In any case, we were unlikely ever to be in touch again. The divorce wasn't through when suddenly I began to feel bad. Very bad. For the first time in my life I couldn't sleep more than a few hours a night and would wake at four o'clock in the morning – three cats on the counterpane – and lie there shaking with fright. What was I afraid of? I didn't know. Weeping silently, I would ask myself what I was crying for? I didn't know. Kate would say, 'Why didn't you wake me?' But what would I wake her for? I had no idea what – fear aside – I was feeling. It was clear to me that something bad was overtaking me and I had no idea how to deal with it. By day, I was all right for a great deal of the time, then suddenly I would be overcome with sadness and fright. The hours between four and seven a.m. were hideous. Edward Duke called from San Francisco. He'd just finished a performance and his dressing room seemed jammed with *I, Claudius* fans. A stranger to economy at the best of times, he put them all on the phone to me in this worst of times. He had his own problems but he spent hours on the phone every week and knowing, somehow, that I wasn't doing very well, he drew me a road map for getting through miserable days. On his advice I bought a small note book and when I felt I couldn't continue some ordinary activity, like walking across the concourse of Waterloo Station, I would stop, duck into an empty doorway and write down exactly how I felt; after a few pages I'd find I could, as he'd promised, resume everyday life again. The only truly 'safe' time for me was late at night, when I returned home after an evening out or after work. 'Home to an empty house', words of misery and foreboding for many, was, and always had been, for me, a happy phrase of promise. Now, the moment of knowing myself to be completely alone for a few hours was one of the truly happy times in what had become an unhappy life.

I didn't know what to do but I began to realize what I must *not* do. I dimly understood that the perception of me by many was that I was good wife material. Wrong though that was, I could see how my industry, good manners, sense of responsibility, cheerful temperament and general deceitfulness would have brought about such a belief. Once again, as had happened when O'Toole and I parted, I began to receive proposals of marriage – mostly from people I had known years previously (and many of those were, I felt, polite gestures) but some, comically, were from total strangers. (One man enclosed a statement of his assets with letters from his bank manager.) It became obvious to me that people thought I *ought* to be married and looked after, partly, I suppose, because for over thirty years I had *been* married. I myself knew that no one needed less looking after in that married way than I, and I saw clearly that the one thing I must not do now was to fudge whatever was happening to me with the distraction of a close relationship. For the first time in my life I was going to stand alone.

Things took an unexpected and hateful turn and I struggled between genuine misery and true annoyance. What happened seemed monstrously unfair and I didn't like it one bit. Every bad thing I had ever done came back to haunt me. Every mean thought and malicious deed reared up as though it had happened only yesterday. At first I sat up in bed in the ugly, small hours and wrote notes about my sins of omission, my careless cruelties. After a few months of that, I couldn't bear it any longer and just lay there, appalled at myself. But it seemed so unfair, to be visited in this way. *Why* was this happening to me, I wondered, resentfully? I confided this to no one. Someone would be sure to say that actually I was quite a nice person and I wanted to be the one to decide that, sometime, maybe never. Conversely, during the days, memories of great *happiness* intruded, no matter where I found myself. I had lived in London for a very long time and had been happy and sad in almost every part of it. Every miserable moment forgotten, I was assailed by recollections of intensely happy times with the children when they were small, with friends, lovers, husbands – even with Robin. I was cursed with the remembrance of the happy years when we first met and the contrast with my present state was torture.

Everything went wrong at home; the vacuum cleaner broke, the washing machine 'died', the downstairs loo jammed and one rainy day a plumber came and dug up the yard and £400 later was about to begin taking up the utility room tiles, when a kindly builder across the road took pity on me, came in and fished out a small deodorant container which had lodged in the 'S' bend. I shed tears of self-pity and gratitude. I felt so *clueless*, and kept cutting myself accidentally and then, worst of all, Spencer, the oldest of the three Burmese cats, became very ill. It rained and rained and Kate and I went to and fro on foot to the vet. Finally, I took him to live in my bedroom, coaxing him to eat from my hand. He was the cat that adored Robin and now I fancied he must sense that Robin was never coming back and for the first time I was filled with real anger. Spencer spent the last week of his life in the vet's surgery, on a drip. He died on the night of December 13. I asked for his body, not his ashes, and went to Upper Street to fetch him. It was raining when I carried the heavy burden back to be buried in the garden. The ground was hard and Kate and I had to use my mother's favorite gardening tool, a small pickaxe, to dig the grave. We were so cold and wet that we had to keep suspending work to come indoors for cups of hot tea. We cut ridiculous figures – dirty, laughing and crying and shivering and hacking out a grave. We buried Spencer wrapped in the cover of his favorite velvet cushion, broke his feeding bowl and put in the bits and added a few olives, to which he was very partial. He was twelve years old. Rupert and Barnaby slept, warm and dry, throughout the miserable afternoon.

I planted a rose on Spencer's grave. 'Isfahan' sounded good

and it was only after I installed it that I learned that its
alternative name was 'Pom Pom des Princes' – just about
as unsuitable a name as could be imagined for big, grave,
humorless Spencer. The thought of Robin with his new
family of cats, taking his ease in the sunshine while we buried
Spencer in the rain, so infuriated me that I broke a lot of
china that he'd been fond of and felt better immediately. I
realized that I was teetering on the brink of very foolish
behavior.

Before Christmas I began rehearsing *Painting Churches* by
Tina Howe, a play I had agreed to do before Robin's return.
It didn't go well in any sense and Tina, whom I admired and
liked enormously, didn't even stay in London for the opening,
leaving for Paris in order to avoid what she was sure would be
a disastrous production. We were underfunded and came very
close to being forbidden by Equity to perform, which would
have been a shaming experience. In spite of the difficulties at
work, riding home from the Playhouse on the Embankment to
Barnsbury and my 'empty house', I realized that I was content
to be working, doing what I was meant to do. That was no
small thing, I told myself.

Kevin and Kate and I went to the country to Bill and Bryn's
for Christmas. People say that however bad things are, they
seem worse at Christmas but I didn't feel that at all and we all
had a lovely time. But even I smiled as I unpacked and laid my
bedside reading on my night table and wondered how many
people would have included *Living with Grief* along with the
Christmas presents. Bill was one of the few people (Edward
was another) with whom I could be totally honest and he bore
the brunt as I talked and talked. He and Kenny and Kevin all
let me ramble on and on during those months when I needed
to be allowed to ramble and I could only hope that they had
a mechanism which filtered some of the nonsense I must have
been speaking. I had never before confided in anyone, had
always had a horror of boring people or embarrassing them or

being a nuisance and now that I'd begun to talk, the floodgates opened and washed over my closest friends. John Erman, the director, sent me books and advice from America. I clutched at everything indiscriminately and gratefully.

After months of this I wondered desperately whether I would ever again be free of fear. All the while I meditated night and morning and never missed doing the Feldenkreis back exercises I'd been taught by Lily Cohen, though I found I was at my most vulnerable and sad during the solitary twenty minutes of exercise. I longed to escape from the house but, ironically, work now kept me chained to London. Kate went home and before Edward returned, I schooled myself to live quietly with my unhappiness and to accept and come to terms with my own deficiencies, turning over and over in my mind the harm I'd inflicted on other people, the absence of kindness I'd shown only too often. My mother had never asked me for anything, but I knew what she would have liked to have and what mean-spirited arrogance it was that made me deny her a fur coat for her old age. I knew what she had in mind when she talked of fur; a musquash, no shape, grey, smooth and warm, as worn by the senior mistress at my grammar school. The coat of a woman who, though she could not afford a motor, went to Bruges for her holiday and once to Oberammergau for the passion play and who, if she chose, could go to see an Ivor Novello show in London. It was the coat of the woman my mother could have been. 'Fur? No, no liberal minded, caring person wears FUR nowadays!' My mother, transported from the Welsh countryside to the expensive shops of Hampstead, struggled politely with this glimpse of fashionable caring and nodded her thanks for the gift of a lovely and costly woollen cape. What mean impulse made me deny her the thing that would have made her harmlessly proud? It wasn't a small thing and it was one of a host of misdeeds that crowded into my mind, clamoring for attention. I was being brought very low.

My strongest resource, my reasonableness, was useful now, if only to preserve the framework of 'normal' life, enabling me to work and even to play a little. What I thought of as 'real' (hidden and secret) life was all tumult and confusion and I moved through the unfamiliar territories guided only by instinct; I neither questioned nor challenged the rhythms of this interior existence. As I sat alone with myself, I grew less appalled by myself and less interested in myself, but I knew that this miserable period was not over by a long shot. Less and less I wished that I knew where I was going or what I hoped to achieve and I stopped worrying about my lack of purpose. The natural world exerted the same power over me as it always had and I didn't worry at my inconsistency in finding myself in a sad mood, then suddenly engulfed for a moment or two in happiness; a change in the weather, a trick of the light in the garden was still enough to surprise me into delight. The cats made me laugh. I laughed a great deal the day a blackbird walked portentously into the kitchen and looked at me and two inscrutable Burmese faces hanging over cupboard tops, before turning tail and walking out again.

The days began to lengthen and I vigorously reclaimed the garden for myself, uprooting without a qualm all the plants that Robin had chosen and which I rather disliked. It was deeply satisfying to be rearranging and replanting and learning the workings of the lawnmower (previously considered too 'difficult' for me). As I wrestled with the pond and its pump (also too difficult), I realized as well that I would never achieve Robin's way with animals. The fish ignored me; they used to feed from his hand. But it was deeply satisfying to see the garden looking just as *I* wanted it. I turned my attention to the house, which for a while had become an object of hatred, and gradually I came to like it again as I rearranged it and altered it. On impulse, one day I heaved the matrimonial bed into the front garden and bought a lovely new one from Heal's. Recalling Bob Crowley's set for *Brel*, I had the front hall and the staircase and the landing painted the color of a Gauloise cigarette packet. Every morning I felt a surge of energy as I stepped into the wonderful blast of blue.

I still felt fear and pain but I had lost the wish to chatter and the need to validate everything I saw or did by sharing it. I was content to look and then stop looking and it didn't hurt me when what I did went unseen and unremarked upon, except in exceptional circumstances; when I passed my driving test I came home and telephoned everyone I knew, demanding astonishment and praise.

Chapter Forty-three

Sara thinks it a good idea for me to accept a job in America. I think she's probably right but I'm scared. I've only visited New York briefly in the Sixties and Seventies as a celebrity wife, living in the grandest hotels, travelling by limo, insulated from the frightening city outside. I remember the terrifying wave of traffic surging down Fifth Avenue. Will I get around safely? Will I learn to live with the noise? The film is *The Age of Innocence* which Martin Scorsese will direct. Daniel Day-Lewis and Michelle Pfeiffer will play the lovers and I suspect they need a fair number of actors who will look comfortable in period clothes and appear and sound like well-heeled, turn-of-the-century Americans, as they munch their way through lengthy and complicated meals which feature so heavily in books of that period.

Early spring in Troy in upstate New York. Location catering is wonderful and I've eaten rather more than my period stays will allow. The leaves on the trees will soon be in bud and Alec McCowen and I are making our way back to our trailers. I can't help myself and I blurt out, 'Oh, isn't this all *wonderful*?' Alec, mildly surprised and mildly pitying, shakes his head and says, 'Oh Siân, you're *very* easily pleased.' I suppose I am – thank God. I'm so pleased that nothing awful is happening, that I'm actively *not* suffering what Edward Duke has christened 'NDs' – nameless dreads.

There's a rail strike so I'm put in a taxi to travel to New York where most of the filming will take place. My driver is appalled that he has to go to New York which is full of 'bad people', he says. He's so frightened that I become quite brave and when he gets lost somewhere in the Bronx, I take over the map and begin navigating and have no trouble in getting us safely to the Wyndham Hotel. I'm impressed by myself. He's too scared to say thanks or stop for a coffee and heads off to Troy, never to return if he can help it, he assures me.

The Wyndham is a smallish hotel, home from home for English actors. I walk around my 'neighborhood' and very soon it begins to feel like home. Where is that intimidating city which used to scare me so much? Debbie Condon's friend from schooldays, Louise Emmett, calls me and takes me on a smart outing and teaches me a bit about the bus system. I feel as though I'm mastering demotic Aramaic as I board my first bus and then *change* buses.

The early rising and the long hours of work are familiar and soothing. When I'm not working I take huge walks and realize that I'm writing very little in my notebooks these days. It's also soothing to be with people who know nothing about me. This is most unexpected but New York is being just that – soothing. I begin to make friends. Meeting Louise was a piece of luck. She and Debbie attended a ladies' seminary here in the city. They wore white gloves and learned lovely manners, which have endured. I had not expected just yet that anyone would make me laugh uncontrollably, then I met Alexis Smith. We had to be separated because of bad behavior during the party scene in the film. The first assistant was cross and I avoided Daniel's eye; I don't suppose he'd believe me if I told him that the last person to be evicted with me from a studio for laughing was his mother, Jill.

I loved watching Martin Scorsese at work. He wore crisp, rather military-looking cotton shirts and belted slacks and bounced through the day on the balls of his feet. Never did we see him looking doubtful or uncertain or even dissatisfied. From the first moment of the day's work, for twelve or fourteen hours, he knew exactly what would happen next and all precautions were taken to make sure that everything was exactly as he wished it to be. His sets had a cloister-like quiet – even his carpenters seemed to be able to hammer noiselessly. Occasionally, if there was an unauthorized snatch of conversation in the distance, he would stop what he was doing and, smiling, say, 'Did I hear something? Sh! Listen! No. Nothing. My imagination.' Those smiling moments were blood chilling but I liked and admired him.

Jane Stanton-Hitchcock, the author of *Vanilla*, invited me to stay with her on the Upper East Side. We were both wary of the venture. Jane was a full-time novelist and filming hours make actors unsatisfactory guests. Also, I wasn't at all sure that I wanted to *be* a guest; hotel life was undemanding and I'd become used to living in the Fifties. When I arrived at Jane's duplex on the East River, I realized that she lived in breathtaking style. I had my own entrance to the prettiest guest suite imaginable. I adjusted my ideas. 'Jane, I had no idea. Are you wonderfully rich!' Simple, sweet thing, she merely smiled. I stayed with Jane for the rest of my time in New York. She didn't want a guest and I didn't want to be one so we got on famously. Occasionally, Jane would stop writing and we'd chat. I told her about heaving the king-size mattress into the street. When she stopped laughing she asked, 'Have you ever been in therapy?' I saw what she meant. It *was* rather extreme behavior. (I was blissfully Freudianly unaware of myself.) '*Don't* go into open-ended therapy,' she counselled. 'Do a sixteen hour course of *cognitive* therapy when you get home. It's called *CAT* and it will polish you up nicely!' I admired Jane for her chic, her industry, her expensive allure, her brains and her furniture. It would never have occurred to me not to promise to do as she told me.

Sara arranged for me to go and stay with June Havoc in Connecticut. Ageless at over eighty years, beautiful and gallant, she lived with her friend and assistant, Tana, in a wonderful farmhouse; the outhouses and fields full of the halt, the maimed and the blind of the animal world and in the barn stood her sister, Gypsy Rose Lee's, piano. It was all a bit too much for me and I lay on the grass and slept for a whole afternoon. June let me do some gardening for her and then took advantage of Tana's absence for a day, visiting her family nearby, to move a great deal of huge, heavy furniture from one room to another. Exhausted – I more than she – we had an early supper and went to bed. I woke very early, not knowing where I was for a moment and lay there looking at the New England sky, aware that something was different. I sat up abruptly and grinned broadly as I realized that for the first time in ages I wasn't scared, I was just awake. It wasn't a wonderful, exciting moment, it was lovely that something bad was absent. I went downstairs and sat with June and Tana and wished I could tell them what had happened but I couldn't because they didn't know my story and nothing *had* happened. Something had stopped, that was all. Tana took us to visit her enormous Italian/American family and for a moment I felt a pang of envy as I watched them cooking and playing and interfering in each other's lives but, standing alone on the veranda overlooking the sea, I reminded myself that my life was programed to be very different and that we cannot have everything or do everything. Having It All had been too exhausting and time-consuming and finally it had defeated me. It was a relief to stop trying.

Back in the city, I begin to think about going back to London. I shan't be there for more than a few days because I've arranged to do a job in Austria. I've started packing. Walking along Seventy-first Street towards the park, I find I'm suddenly running from high spirits, as I can't remember running since I was a girl at home, but I don't have anywhere to run to and although I have a house in London, I no longer know where 'home' is. Since Central Park is ahead of me I run there and go on running until, winded, I flop down on a bench. Bending over, catching my breath, I'm glad to have a moment where my face is hidden because I can't stop smiling and feel I look foolish. Finally, I sit up, exhausted. Two young men passing by smile at me sitting there, smiling. As they pass on I realize that at this moment I am not merely *not unhappy* I am perfectly *happy* and secure, surrounded by strangers, my suitcases half-packed at Jane's and a sheaf of travel arrangements in my bag. I haven't any idea what will happen to me. Will I ever get another, 'proper', exciting job? Will I go on working? How will I live? What country shall I live in? Shall I live alone? Why do I feel terrific?

Rising and, still moving fast, going east towards the river and up towards Gracie Square, I realize that I don't really care to look for answers to these questions; I no longer have an impulse to look into the future, but there is a swing in my step that I had not thought to feel again as I continue my way through the smart neighborhood; Seventy-fifth, Seventy-ninth, Eighty-first. Streets that are a world away from the places where I grew up but they feel as familiar and safe under my feet as the tracks across the low, Welsh mountains of my first home. The skies, the houses, the trees – green overnight in the swift astonishing New York spring – are improbably bright today with the Pre-Raphaelite clarity of a world seen with the eyes of youth – or of love.

When I was a girl, a moment ago, Saunders Lewis told me to 'Learn to live on the knife edge of insecurity'. It seemed to me an uncomfortable place to want to be but maybe that is where I have arrived and it begins to seem that maybe he was right; to live perilously is to live safely. Maybe. This is so undramatic, this afternoon in New York. So undramatic, so wonderful. No event has taken place. Nothing of significance has been said, but my life has changed. There is no solution, no resolution, no conclusion; but I am happy and I am at home and unafraid of what the future will bring.

Siân Phillips

1959 *Siwan* (Theater and TV), *Land of Song* (TV series), *The Garden of Loneliness* (TV), *Granite* (TV), *Treason* (TV and Radio), *The Tortoise and the Hare* (TV), *Game for Eskimos* (TV)

1960 *The Taming of the Shrew* (Theater), *The Duchess of Malfi* (Theater), *Strangers in the Room* (TV)

1961 *The Duchess of Malfi* (Theater cont.), *Ondine* (Theater), *The Lizard on the Rock* (Theater)

1962 *Don Juan in Hell* (TV), *The Maids* (Radio), *Afternoon of M Andesmas* (Radio)

1963 *Gentle Jack* (Theater), *This is not King's Cross* (TV), *Becket* (Film), *The Other Man* (TV Film), *Espionage* (Film)

1964 *Gentle Jack* (Theater cont.), *Maxibules* (Theater), *The Sex Game* (TV)

1965 *The Night of the Iguana* (Theater), *Ride a Cock Horse* (Theater)

1966 *Ride a Cock Horse* (Theater cont.), *Man and Superman* (Theater), *Man of Destiny* (Theater), *Eh Joe* (TV)

1967 *Man and Superman* (Theater cont.), *The Burglar* (Theater)

1968 *The Beast in the Jungle* (TV Film)

1969 *Goodbye Mr Chips* (Film), *The Cardinal of Spain* (Theater), *City 69* (TV), *Vessel of Wrath* (TV), *The Eccentricities of a Nightingale* (Theater)

1970 *Murphy's War* (Film)

1971 *Under Milk Wood* (Film), *Platonov* (TV)

1972 *Lady Windermere's Fan* (TV), *Epitaph for George Dillon* (Theater), *Alpha Beta* (Theater)

1973 *Gloriana* (Theater), *A Nightingale in Bloomsbury Square* (Theater), *Shoulder to Shoulder* (TV series)

1974 *Shoulder to Shoulder* (TV series cont.)

1975 *Pilgrim Fathers* (TV Film), *How Green Was My Valley* (TV series), *The Gay Lord Quex* (Theater)

1976 *How Green Was My Valley* (TV series cont.), *The Achurch Letters* (TV), *I, Claudius* (TV series)

1977 *Heartbreak House* (TV), *Off To Philadelphia in the Morning* (TV mini series), *Boudicca* (TV series)

1978 *Spine Chiller* (Theater), *Clash of the Titans* (Film), *Oresteia* (TV)

1979 *Crime and Punishment* (TV), *The Doctor and the Devils* (Film), *A Woman of No Importance* (Theater), *Tinker Tailor Soldier Spy* (TV), *The Inconstant Couple* (Theater)

1980   *You Never Can Tell* (Theater), *Sean* (TV series), *Pal Joey* (Theater),
       Barriers (TV series), *Churchill – The Wilderness Years* (TV series)
1981   *Pal Joey* (Theater cont.), *How Many Miles to Babylon* (Film), *Barriers*
       (TV series)
1982   *Dear Liar* (Theater), *Major Barbara* (Theater), *Smiley's People* (TV)
1983   *Dune* (Film)
1984   *Peg* (Theater), *Love Affair* (Theater)
1985   *Gigi* (Theater), *Return to Endor* (Film), *'Life of Siân'* (TV docu-
       mentary)
1986   *Gigi* (Theater cont.), *The Two Mrs Grenvilles* (TV), *A Painful Case*
       (TV Film), *Lost In Time* (TV), *The Snow Spider* (TV series)
1987   *Thursday's Ladies* (Theater), *Brel* (Theater), *Vanity Fair* (TV series),
       George Borrow (TV), *A Killing on the Exchange* (TV series)
1988   *Brel* (Theater cont.), *Mother Knows Best* (TV), *Shadow of the Noose*
       (TV), *Emlyn's Moon* (TV series)
1989   *Valmont* (Film), *The Glass Menagerie* (Theater), *Dark River* (Film),
       Paris Match (Theater)
1990   *Perfect Scoundrels* (TV), *Freddie and Max* (TV), *Red Empire* (TV),
       Vanilla (Theater), *Landscape and Legend* (TV)
1991   *The Manchurian Candidate* (Theater), *Emlyn's Moon* (TV series),
       Tonight At 8.30 (TV), *The Chestnut Soldier* (TV series)
1992   *Painting Churches* (Theater), *The Age of Innocence* (Film), *The Bor-
       rowers* (TV series), *Heidi* (Disney Film)
1993   Novello Concert, Ghosts (Theater), *Covington Cross* (TV)
1994   *The Lion in Winter* (Theater), *Marlene* (Theater), *The Borrowers* (TV),
       A Mind to Kill (TV series), *Nearest and Dearest* (TV)
1995   *An Inspector Calls* (Theater US), *A Little Night Music* (Theater)
1996   *A Little Night Music* (Theater US), *House of America* (Film), *Marlene*
       (Theater)
1997   *Marlene* (Theater US), *The Scold's Bridle* (TV), *Nikita* (TV)
1998   *Marlene* (Theater cont.), *Alice Through the Looking Glass* (Film),
       Aristocrats (TV series), *Falling in Love Again* – Cabaret (Theater
       Israel), *The Magician's House* (TV series)
1999   *Marlene* (Theater cont.), *Falling in Love Again* – Cabaret (Theater),
       The Magician's House (TV series)
2000   *Falling in Love Again* (Theater cont.), *Coming and Going* (Film),
       Ballykissangel (TV)
2001   *Lettice and Lovage* (Theater), *Falling in Love Again* (Theater cont.),
       The Leopard in Autumn (Radio series), *Almost Like Being in Love* –
       Cabaret (Theater), *Divas at the Donmar* – Cabaret (Theater)

Index

Index

Index

Meagher, Declan 165, 166
Meagher, Pam 317
Measure for Measure (Shakespeare) 134
Medmenham, Berkshire 109
Mercer, David 198–9, 201
   Ride a Cock Horse 198–203, 212
Mercer, Mabel 370
Merchant, Moelwyn 52
The Merchant of Venice (Shakespeare) 50,
   52, 66, 67, 70–73, 89, 92
Meriel (Siân's aunt) 54, 57, 374, 375, 379
Mermaid Theatre, London 362
Mestre, Italy 40, 215
Metropolitan Opera, New York 384
Meurice Hotel, Paris 388
Mexico 301, 305, 311, 316, 324, 325, 365,
   367, 368–70
Mexico City 365, 368–9
Michael (Kate's boyfriend) 319, 379
Mifune, Toshiro 226, 227, 228
Migines, Julia 384
Milan 46, 47, 215
Millar, Sir Ronald 373
Miller, John 244
Miller, Ronald 373
Milton, Ernest 132
Mirabelle restaurant, London 329, 330
Mirren, Helen 316, 319
Miss Venezuela 244
Miss World competition 244
Mitchell, Yvonne 198, 199
Mobil Oil 396, 397
Moeurs, Hélène Van 47–8, 60
Molière 47
Mon Oncle 182
Monroe, Marilyn 30
Montherlant, Henri de 367
A Moon for the Misbegotten (O'Neill) 89
Moore, Kevin 413, 417
Moore, Mary 353
Morocco 148
Morris, James 213
Morris, Ossie 204
Mortimer, Penelope 199
Mount Pleasant, Stratford-upon-Avon 56–7,
   59, 62–3, 67, 70, 78, 88, 89, 103, 104
Murphy, Gerard 400
Murphy, Peter 409
Murphy, Richard 282
Murphy's War (film) 242, 244, 246,
   248, 255
Murray, Stephen 394–5
Musée Camondo, Paris 389
Muzak, Mme Claude de 180

My Sister and Myself (Ackerley) 368

Naples Airport 1, 5
Nathan and Bermans 175, 334, 379
National Eisteddfod, North Wales 37
National Health Service (NHS) 243
National Theatre 171, 362, 363–4
Neal, Patricia 24
Neath station 53
Netherlands *see* Holland
New End Hospital, London 150, 274
New Mexico 299
New (later the Albery) Theatre, St Martin's
   Lane 22
New York 96, 155, 175, 176, 188, 370,
   371, 381, 396, 421–5
Newman, Paul 288
Newman, Sidney 23
News Chronicle 111
Newton, Bryn 409, 413
Night of the Generals (film) 236
The Night of the Iguana (Williams) 193–6,
   197–9, 203
Nina 171
Niven, David 167
No Man's Land (Pinter) 304
Noar, Doriah *see* Griffith, Doriah
Noh Theatre 228
Noiret, Philippe 246, 248
Non-Conformism 86–7
Norah (prompter) 171
Norfolk 387
North Acton, west London 317, 323
North London Collegiate School for Girls
   242, 255, 312, 314, 315, 379
Northumbria 346
Nottingham 199, 200
Nottingham Rep 362
Nureyev, Rudolf 11, 149–52
Nutting, Anthony 108–9, 135, 156

O'Casey, Sean 343
   Pictures in the Hallway 158
Off to Philadelphia in the Morning (TV
   serial) 334
O'Flaherty, Liam 35
Oh Mein Papa 158–9
O'Hara, John 349
Old Vic, London 171, 234, 272
Oliver, Anthony 129
Olivier, Sir Laurence (later Lord Olivier)
   171, 172, 205, 206, 304
O'Malley, Eileen 283
O'Malley, Matcher 283

436

Index

Index

Index

Praise for
THE KILL SWITCH

"Exceptional . . .
A spin-off from bestseller Rollins' Sigma Force
series introduces U.S. Army Ranger Tucker Wayne
and his four-footed partner, a small Belgian Shepherd
named Kane . . . The action careens across Russia and
into South Africa, where Tucker and Kane must go
underground to find a deadly life form. Rollins
and Blackwood succeed brilliantly."
Publishers Weekly (★Starred Review★)

"Rollins knows how to deliver a terrific page-turner.
The mix of Blackwood's military knowledge and
Rollins' background as a veterinarian makes the
narrative seem authentic. While Tucker Wayne is
a terrific character, the star of the novel is Kane,
a Belgian Malinois and one of the best dogs in thriller
literature. *The Kill Switch* is the start of a new series,
and the next book cannot come soon enough."
Huffington Post

"A fantastic adventure story with non-stop action
[that] shows the close bond between dog and partner,
and the readers will fall in love with this
canine and his handler."
Crimespree Magazine

P9-BXZ-901

Also by James Rollins

THE 6TH EXTINCTION
THE EYE OF GOD
BLOODLINE
THE DEVIL COLONY
ALTAR OF EDEN
THE DOOMSDAY KEY
THE LAST ORACLE
THE JUDAS STRAIN
BLACK ORDER
MAP OF BONES
SANDSTORM
ICE HUNT
AMAZONIA
DEEP FATHOM
EXCAVATION
SUBTERRANEAN

Also by Grant Blackwood

THE END OF ENEMIES
THE WALL OF NIGHT
AN ECHO OF WAR

JAMES ROLLINS

AND

GRANT BLACKWOOD

THE KILL SWITCH

A TUCKER WAYNE NOVEL

HARPER

An Imprint of HarperCollinsPublishers

HARPER

An Imprint of HarperCollins*Publishers*
195 Broadway
New York, New York 10007

Copyright © 2014 by James Czajkowski and Grant Blackwood
Map provided and drawn by Steve Prey. All rights reserved. Used by permission of Steve Prey.
Excerpt from *War Hawk* copyright © 2015 by James Czajkowski and Grant Blackwood
ISBN 978-0-06-213526-1

First Harper premium printing: January 2015
First William Morrow special paperback printing: May 2014
First William Morrow paperback international printing: May 2014
First William Morrow hardcover printing: May 2014

Visit Harper paperbacks on the World Wide Web at
www.harpercollins.com

10 9 8 7 6 5 4 3 2 1

To all the four-legged warriors out there . . .
And those who serve alongside them.

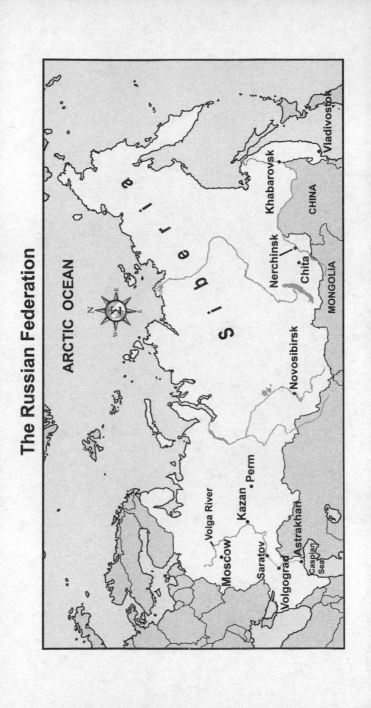

The Russian Federation

PROLOGUE

Doctor Paulos de Klerk packed the last of the medical supplies into the wooden trunk and locked the three brass clasps, mumbling under his breath with each snap. "*Amat . . . victoria . . . curam.*"

Victory favors the prepared.

Or so he prayed.

"So, my good doctor, how goes the effort?" General Manie Roosa's voice boomed from the fort's watchtower above.

De Klerk shielded his eyes from the blazing sun and stared up at the bearded figure leaning over the railing, grinning down. Though not physically imposing, Roosa had a commanding presence that made him look seven feet tall; it was in the man's eyes. The general always looked eager for a fight.

And he was about to get one if word from up north held true.

"Are we ready?" Roosa pressed.

De Klerk returned his attention to the other trunks, cases, and burlap sacks. Though the general's words had indeed ended with a question mark, he knew Roosa was not making an inquiry. At various times throughout the day their leader had posed the same "question" to almost every Boer soldier under his command, all of whom bustled around the plateau on which the fort sat, cleaning weapons, counting ammunition, and generally preparing for the upcoming march.

With an exaggerated sigh, De Klerk replied, "As always, I will be ready to leave five minutes before you are, my general."

Roosa let out a booming laugh and slapped the log railing. "You amuse me, Doctor. If you were not so good at your profession, I might be tempted to leave you behind, out of harm's way."

De Klerk stared around the bustling fort. He hated to leave its security, but he knew where he was best needed. As primitive as the fort was, with its palisade walls and crude buildings, this place had withstood countless British attacks, making it a bastion for Boer troops. Leaving the confines of its protective walls likely meant he and his medical aides would be seeing a brisk business in the coming days.

Not that he wasn't accustomed to the horrors of battle.

Though only thirty-two years old, this was De Klerk's fifth year of war in the past decade. The first *Vryheidsoorloë*, or *freedom war*, was fought back in 1880 and had mercifully lasted but a year, ending well for the *Boers*—the Dutch/Afrikaans word for *farmers*—as they won their sovereignty from British rule in the Transvaal. Eight years later, the second

Vryheidsoorloë started, involving not only the Transvaal but also the neighboring Orange Free State.

Same issues, more soldiers, he thought sourly.

The British wanted the Boers under their colonial thumb, and the Boers were not keen on the idea. De Klerk's ancestors had come to the savannahs and mountains of Africa to be free, and now the *Engelse* wanted to take that away. Unlike the first *Vryheidsoorloë*, this war was protracted, with the British implementing a scorched-earth policy. Though neither De Klerk nor any of his comrades verbalized it, they knew their own defeat was inevitable. The one person who seemed oblivious to this was General Roosa; the man was an irrepressible optimist when it came to matters of war.

Roosa pushed himself away from the railing and climbed down the rough-hewn ladder to the ground and walked over to where De Klerk was working. The general straightened his khaki uniform with a few well-experienced tugs. He was the same height as the doctor, but burlier of physique and bushier of beard. For the sake of hygiene, De Klerk kept himself clean-shaven and insisted his aides did the same.

"So I see many bandages are being packed," Roosa said. "Do you think so little of my leadership, Doctor? Or is it you think too highly of the *Engelse* soldiers?"

"Certainly not the latter, my general. I simply know that before long I will be treating throngs of enemy prisoners wounded by our bullets."

Roosa frowned and rubbed his beard. "Yes, about that, Doctor . . . about supplying succor to the enemy . . ."

It was a sore point between them, but De Klerk refused to relent. "We are Christian, are we not? It is our duty to provide such help. But I also understand that our men must come first. I will only provide enough aid so that a British soldier might survive long enough to be reached by his own doctors. If we do not do that, we are no better than them."

Roosa clapped him on the shoulder—not necessarily agreeing, but acknowledging the sentiment.

For reasons he had never fully understood, Roosa had come to think of him as a sounding board. The commander frequently shared information with De Klerk that had nothing to do with his medical duties—as if the general also saw him as his own conscience.

Still, he knew there was another reason Roosa took such an interest in his preparations. The men under the general's command had become his family, a surrogate to his own wife, three daughters, and two sons, all who'd been taken by smallpox two years earlier. The loss had nearly destroyed Roosa and left lasting scars. When it came to bullet and bayonet wounds, the general was phlegmatic and optimistic; when it came to disease, he was frighteningly anxious.

Changing the touchy subject, Roosa pointed to the leather-bound diary that was never beyond De Klerk's reach. "Cataloging more flowers, I see."

He touched the worn cover both affectionately and protectively. "Providence willing, yes. If we are going where I think we are going, there will be many species I have never encountered."

"We are indeed heading north, into the mountains of the Groot. My scouts tell me a brigade of *Engelse* soldiers are headed west from Kimberley, led by a new commander—a colonel fresh from London."

"And in a hurry to prove himself no doubt."

"Aren't they all? If we leave in the morning, their lead elements will spot us by early evening."

And then the chase will be on. Though not a military strategist by any means, De Klerk had been with Roosa long enough to recognize the general's favorite tactic: let the British scouts spot them, then draw the enemy north into the mountainous Groot, where the harsh terrain could be used to set up an ambush.

The British preferred to fight on the savannah, where their tidy formations and overwhelming firepower always won the day. The enemy commanders hated hills and mountains and ravines, hated that Roosa and his band of backward farmers refused to fight on their terms. And it was exactly such a strategy that Roosa had used many times to lure the British into murderous engagements. And still the enemy did not learn.

But how long would such arrogance last?

A chill iced through De Klerk as he gathered his research journal and pocketed it away.

The troops were up and on the move well before dawn, traveling northward without incident as the sun climbed higher. Then at noon, one of the Boer scouts overtook the formation from the south, pounding up to them on a sweating, heaving horse. He joined Roosa at the head of their formation.

De Klerk didn't need to hear the conversation to know its content.

The enemy had found them.

As the scout wheeled away on his horse, the general rode back to the medical wagon. "The British will soon be giving chase, Doctor. Your comfortable cart may see some jostling."

"I am less concerned with the wagon than I am my delicate internal organs. However, as always, I will survive."

"Fine mettle, Doctor."

Minutes slid into hours as the general led their unit north, steadily closing the gap between them and the Groot, whose foothills smudged the horizon, the details blurred by waves of heat rising from the savannah.

Two hours before dusk, another scout appeared. The expression on his face and the posture of his body as he rode past the medical wagon told De Klerk something had gone wrong. After a brief consultation, the scout rode off.

Roosa turned on his horse and shouted back to his leaders, "Prepare the wagons for fast travel! Five minutes!" He then rode back to De Klerk. "This new *Engelse* colonel is trying to be clever. He has disguised the size of his brigade and split them into two forces—one the hammer, the other the anvil."

"With us the pig iron in the middle."

"Or so they hope," Roosa replied with a broad smile. "But hope fades with the light, Doctor. Especially once we lure them into the Groot."

With a jaunty wave, Roosa wheeled his horse and rode off.

A few minutes later the general's booming voice echoed throughout the Boer formation. "Fast travel . . . go!"

De Klerk's wagon handler snapped the reins and barked a "Hah . . . hah!"

The horses bucked slightly, then broke into a gallop. De Klerk grasped the sideboard and held on, his eyes fixed on the distant Groot Karas Mountains.

Too far, he thought grimly. *Too far and not enough time.*

And an hour later, his fear proved true.

A trail of dust marked the return of a pair of riders sent north by Roosa to scout the way ahead, but as the dust settled, it became clear only *one* rider had come back. He leaned askew in his saddle and fell from his horse as he reached the unit, wounded twice in the back by rifle fire.

Roosa ordered a halt, then signaled for De Klerk to come forward. Armed with his medical bag, he rushed to the fallen man and knelt down. Both bullets had torn through vital organs before punching through the front of the young man's torso.

"Collapsed lung," he told Roosa, who cradled the man's head.

The scout, a boy of eighteen, was named Meer. He clutched at Roosa's sleeve, tried to speak, but coughed up frothy blood before he could find any words.

"My general," the boy croaked out, "an *Engelse*

battalion . . . north of us. Heavy cavalry . . . with cannons on fast caissons."

"How far away, son?"

"Eight miles."

Meer coughed harshly. A fresh gout of blood sprayed from his mouth. His body arched, fighting the inevitable, then went limp.

De Klerk checked him and shook his head.

Roosa closed the boy's eyes and gave his hair a few strokes before standing up. A pair of soldiers carried Meer's body away.

De Klerk joined the commander.

Roosa murmured, "All my talk of *Engelse* arrogance . . . it is I who was the arrogant one. This new British colonel is trying to stop us from reaching the Groot. If they can catch us out here in the open . . . well, then, my good doctor, you are going to have more work than you can handle in a lifetime."

He didn't respond, but Roosa must have noted his paling face.

The general gripped De Klerk's shoulder hard. "This *Engelse* colonel is clever, but the tongs of his pincer are still wide enough for us to escape through. And soon the night will swallow us."

An hour later, from the back of the bucking wagon, De Klerk watched the sun's upper edge dip below the horizon. Night was nearly upon them, but to the east, a plume of dust—red and gold in the setting sun—covered a quarter of the sky. He estimated the number of cavalry horses it would take to create such a cloud.

Two hundred riders at least.

And behind them, wagons upon wagons of troops and cannon-bearing caissons.

God help us . . .

But at least they had safely reached the foothills of the Groot, escaping through the enemy's pincers. With a final buck, the wagon rattled into a shadowy ravine, and the view of the British forces vanished.

He swung around and studied the broken landscape ahead, a veritable maze of hills, dry washes, and caves. Roosa had extolled many times about the "pocket fortresses" hidden in the mountains, Boer strongholds from which they could wait out any British siege.

Or so they all hoped.

Time ground slowly under the wheels of the wagon and the hooves of their horses. Finally, one of the scouting parties Roosa had dispatched to the south returned. After a brief consultation, the rider took off again, and Roosa ordered the formation to slow.

The general rode back to De Klerk's wagon.

"We have bought some time, Doctor. But this *Engelse* colonel is not only wily, but also stubborn. His troops still remain on our trail."

"What does that mean for us?"

Roosa sighed. He took a rag from his tunic pocket and wiped the dust from his face. "To quote Shakespeare's Falstaff, *discretion is in fact the better part of valor.* It is time we hole up. One of our pocket fortresses is nearby. Hidden, but easy to defend. We will tuck ourselves away, wait for the *Engelse* to tire of the Groot, then attack them from the rear when they leave. You are not, uh . . . what is the word? Afraid of tight places?"

"Claustrophobic? No, I am not."

"Good to hear, Doctor. I hope the others share the same fortitude."

For another half hour, Roosa led them deeper into the mountains, eventually turning into a narrow ravine before stopping at a large cave entrance. The men began transferring supplies into the cave.

He joined Roosa at the mouth of the tunnel and asked, "What of the horses and wagons?"

"All will go inside, Doctor. We shall have to partially disassemble the wagons, but there is room enough inside for a small paddock."

"And supplies?"

Again Roosa offered a confident smile. "I have been stocking this cave for some time, Doctor, and I have a few tricks up my sleeve as well. Unless this *Engelse* colonel is willing to loiter in these mountains for months, we have nothing to fear. Now, Doctor, if you will, take two men and begin transporting your supplies inside. I want to be safely settled within the hour."

As usual, Roosa got his way. As the last of the supplies were carried inside under the flickering glow of lanterns, the general oversaw the placement of black powder charges at the mouth of the cave. Having already set up a surgery of sorts in a side cave, De Klerk wandered back to the entrance to watch.

"Good, good!" Roosa called to one of the sappers. "Move that charge on the left a few feet higher.

Yes, there!" The general turned as he approached. "Ah, Doctor, are you settled in?"

"Yes, General. But may I ask . . . is that wise? Sealing us in here?"

"It would be distinctly *unwise*, Doctor, if this were the only entrance. But this cave system is vast, with many smaller, well-concealed exits. I have given this tactic much thought."

"I can see."

From outside the entrance came the pounding of hooves. One by one, the marksmen who had been dispatched earlier to harass the British forces entered the cavern, each man leading a lathered, panting steed. The last rider to enter stopped beside Roosa.

"We slowed them considerably, my general, but their scouts are less than an hour behind us. I estimate three hundred cavalry, two hundred foot soldiers, and forty 12-pound cannons."

Roosa took this in, then rubbed his chin. "An impressive force. It seems the British have put a large bounty on our heads. Well, even if they manage to find us, the fight will be on our terms. And then, comrades, we will see how good the *Engelse* are at digging graves."

After blowing and collapsing the cavern entrance, the night passed without event—as did the next day and the six days after that. Most of the Boer troops settled into their new stronghold and went about the business of making the cave system not only comfortable, but as defensible as possible, too.

Meanwhile, Roosa's scouts used secret exits to slip from the caverns under the cover of darkness and returned with the same report: the British battalions remained in the mountains and appeared to be searching intently, but so far, they had failed to find the hidden fortress.

After a week, a lone scout returned at dawn and found the general sitting in the officers' mess hall, a small cavern in which one of the disassembled wagons had been turned into a trestle table with benches. Roosa and De Klerk sat at one end, going over the day's sick report under the glow of a hanging lantern.

Exhausted and disheveled, the scout stopped beside Roosa. The general stood up, called for a water skin, then forced the scout to sit down and waited as the man quenched his thirst.

"Dogs," the scout said simply. "Bloodhounds. Coming this way."

"Are you sure?" Roosa asked, his eyes narrowing.

"Yes, my general. I could hear them baying, not two miles away. I believe they are coming toward this position."

"Could they be jackals instead?" De Klerk offered. "Or wild African dogs?"

"No, Doctor. My father had bloodhounds when I was a child. I know well their sound. I do not know how they would—"

"They captured three of our men," Roosa explained, as if expecting this news. "Their scent is our scent. And concentrated as we are in this damned cave . . ." The general's words trailed off. He looked down the length of the table at the faces of his concerned unit commanders. "Gentlemen, let us man the ramparts, such as they are. It appears the *Engelse* will be here for tea."

The first hidden entrance the British found was on the cave system's southern side, a hole disguised by a jumble of boulders.

And so it started.

De Klerk found Roosa kneeling before a sandbag barrier with one of his unit commanders, a man named Vos. Beyond the sandbags the cavern's ceiling descended to shoulder height; at the far end, some fifty feet away, was the horizontal shaft that led to the secret exit. A dozen soldiers were stationed across the cavern floor, each one kneeling with his rifle behind a stalagmite.

As they waited, De Klerk glanced up. Finger-width fissures split the cavern's ceiling, casting slivers of bright sunlight across the stone floor.

Roosa turned, placed an index finger to his lips, then pointed to his ear.

De Klerk nodded and said nothing. In the silence of the cavern, he strained his ears. In the distance, he could make out the faint baying of the British bloodhounds. After several minutes, the bawling fell silent.

Everyone held his breath. A soldier behind one of the forwardmost stalagmites signaled back to the barrier.

Roosa nodded. "He hears voices. Multiple men coming through the shaft. Vos, you know what to do."

"Yes, my general."

Vos scratched his bayonet along the rock floor, and the men stationed behind the stalagmites turned toward him. Using only hand signals, Vos gave them their orders. Though De Klerk knew what was coming, he dreaded it.

Led by the faint glow of a lantern, the first British soldier appeared in the shaft. He crawled out of the entrance, then turned left and stopped, making room for the man behind him. One by one, the British scouts crawled out of the tunnel until there were six crouched at the far end of the cavern. Silently, the enemy played their lanterns across walls and ceiling and the stalagmites across the floor.

De Klerk watched, continuing to hold his breath.

Seeming to find only an empty cavern, the trespassers clipped the lanterns to their belts, then started moving forward, their rifles at the ready.

Vos let them get within twenty feet—then, with a double tap of his bayonet on the rock floor, his men sprang the ambush and opened fire. The fusillade lasted but seconds, killing all but one of the British scouts instantly. Moaning, the surviving soldier began crawling back toward the shaft, trailing a slick of blood behind him.

De Klerk grabbed his medical bag and stood up. Roosa grasped his forearm and shook his head.

"But, General, he is—"

"I said *no*, Doctor. The more terrifying we make this for the *Engelse*, the sooner they will leave. Vos, see to it."

At Roosa's nod, Vos hopped over the sandbag wall, drew a knife, then walked across the cavern to the crawling soldier. He knelt down and slit the man's throat.

Roosa turned to him. "I am sorry, Doctor. I do not enjoy ordering such a thing, but if we are to survive this, we must be brutal."

Such butchery settled like a cold stone in De Klerk's chest. He turned away, despairing, knowing one certainty.

Nothing goes unpunished under the eyes of the Lord.

Days passed, and still the British came. Soon the enemy had found all but one of Roosa's secret entrances. Small but fierce battles raged at the *ramparts*, as Roosa had taken to calling them. It became clear the British colonel was not only willing to send his troops into Roosa's meat grinder, but he was also willing to make terrible sacrifices—five, six, seven of his troops for one Boer wounded or killed.

De Klerk did what he could to help the injured or dying, but as the days turned into weeks, the Boer death count continued to rise—at first from British bullets, then from illness. The first ailing soldier appeared in his surgery complaining of intense stomach cramps. The medical staff treated him with herbs, but within hours the man became feverish and writhed in agony. The next day, two more men appeared with the same symptoms; then four more the day after that.

His surgery became a madhouse of incoherent screams and squirming patients. Roosa walked into the surgery on the twenty-fourth day to check on the wounded, like he did every morning. De Klerk gave the general a grim status report.

Roosa frowned as he finished. "Show me."

Carrying a lantern, he led Roosa to a corner of the cavern where the sick men were quarantined. Together, they knelt beside the first patient who'd appeared with symptoms, a blond-haired boy named Linden. The boy flailed on the makeshift cot. His face was deathly pale. His arms had been secured to the sides of the cot with leather straps.

"Are those necessary?" Roosa asked.

"A new symptom," De Klerk explained and reached down to show the general.

He lifted the thin cotton tunic away from the man's torso. The patient's belly was covered in wart-like nodules, but instead of dotting the exterior skin of his stomach, the protrusions appeared to be coming from beneath the flesh.

"My God. What is that?"

He shook his head. "I don't know, General. Without these restraints, he would be clawing open his belly. Look here."

Together, they leaned over the boy's body. Using the tip of a scalpel, he pointed to one of the larger nodules, about the size of a pea. "Do you see the milky green color, just beneath the skin?"

"I see it. It's as if something is growing inside him."

"Not *as if*, General. Something *is* growing inside him. All of them. And whatever it is, it is doing its best to break *out*. They are all showing signs of it. Look here!"

Roosa brought a lantern closer. The pea-sized nodule seemed to be writhing, wormlike, beneath the skin. As they watched, a red blister grew at the edge of the nodule and quickly expanded to the size of a ripe plum.

"What in the world . . . ?" Roosa whispered.

"Stand back."

The doctor grabbed a nearby rag and draped it over the nodule. The scrap of cloth bulged for a few seconds—then came a hollow *pop*. A yellow-tinged crimson stain spread across the rag. The patient began to buck wildly, banging the cot's legs on the rock floor.

One of the medical aides ran over to help them hold Linden down. Still, the boy's back arched high under them, his head pressed against his pillow. Suddenly dozens of nodules appeared beneath the skin of Linden's throat and belly, the blisters growing before their eyes.

"Get back, get back!" De Klerk shouted, and the three of them backpedaled.

They watched, horrified, as the blisters began bursting, one after another. In the flickering lantern light, a yellowish mist hung in the air before slowly settling back over the boy's body.

With a final convulsion, Linden arched off the bed until only his heels and the crown of his head were touching the bedroll. The boy's eyes fluttered open, staring sightlessly, then his body collapsed and went still.

De Klerk did not need to check, and Roosa did not need to ask. Linden was dead. The medical aide draped a blanket over his ravaged corpse.

"How many are afflicted so far?" Roosa asked, his voice cracking.

"Seven."

"And the prognosis for them?"

"Unless I can discover the source and counteract it, I fear they will all die. Like this boy. But that's not the worst news."

Roosa finally tore his eyes away from the boy's draped body.

"This is only the beginning. More will surely get sick."

"You suspect a contagion."

"I must. You saw the airborne discharge from the blisters. We have to assume it is a mechanism of some sort—the disease's way of spreading itself at the end."

"How many do you think are already infected?" Roosa asked.

"You must understand. I have never seen or read of anything like this. And the incubation is short. The boy here was the picture of health three days ago. Now he is dead."

"How many?" Roosa pressed. "How many will become sick?"

De Klerk kept his gaze fixed to the commander, so he could see his certainty. "Everyone. Everyone in this cave." He reached and gripped Roosa's wrist. "Whatever is killing these men, it is virulent. And it is in here with us."

A SIMPLE PROPOSITION

1

His job was to protect the bad from the worst.

Not exactly the noblest of ventures, but it paid the bills.

Crouched at the edge of the Russian docks, Tucker Wayne let the weight of his duty fall over him. The icy wind and pelting sleet slowly faded from his attention, leaving him focused on a dark, quiet winterscape of cranes, haphazardly stacked shipping containers, and the hazy bulk of boats lining the pier. In the distance, a foghorn echoed once. Mooring lines creaked and groaned.

Tucker's training as a U.S. Army Ranger was always at the ready, but it was particularly necessary this morning. It allowed him to home in on two very important issues.

First: The port city of Vladivostok, which was a vast improvement over the deserts of war-torn Afghanistan—though he'd never add this frigid place to his list of retirement locations.

Second: The assessment of the threat risk—such as, who might try to assassinate his employer today, where would they be hiding, and how would they do it?

Prior to his taking this job three weeks earlier, two attempts had already been made against the Russian industrialist's life, and his gut told Tucker the third would happen very soon.

He had to be ready—they *both* did.

His hand reached down to offer a reassuring touch to his companion and partner. Through the snow-covered fur, he felt the tense muscles of the small Belgian shepherd. Kane was a military working dog, a Belgian Malinois, paired years ago with Tucker back in Afghanistan. After Tucker left the service, he took Kane with him. They were bound together tighter than any leash, each capable of reading the other, a communication that went beyond any spoken word or hand signal.

Kane sat comfortably beside him, his ears erect and his dark eyes watchful, seemingly oblivious to the snow blanketing the exposed portions of his black-and-tan fur. Covering the remainder of his compact body and camouflaged to match his coat, he wore a K9 Storm tactical vest, waterproofed and Kevlar reinforced. Hidden in the webbing of Kane's collar were a thumbnail-sized wireless transmitter and a night-vision camera, allowing the two to be in constant visual and audio contact with each other.

Tucker returned his full attention to his surroundings.

It was early in Vladivostok, not yet dawn, so the docks were quiet, with only the occasional laborer shuffling through the gloom. Still, he did his best to keep a low profile, trying to blend into the background: just another dockworker.

At least, I hope I look the part.

He was in his late twenties, taller than average, with slightly shaggy blond hair. He further masked his muscular physique under a thick woolen coat and hid the hardness of his eyes beneath the furred brim of a Russian *ushanka*, or trapper's hat.

He gave Kane a thumb stroke on the top of the head and got a single wag of his tail in response.

A far cry from home, eh, Kane?

Then again, if you took away the ocean, Vladivostok wasn't much different from where he'd spent the first seventeen years of his life: the small town of Rolla, North Dakota, near the border with Canada. If anyplace in the United States could give Siberia a run for its money, it was there.

As a kid, he had spent his summers canoeing Willow Lake and hiking the North Woods. In winter, it was cross-country skiing, snowshoeing, and ice fishing. But life wasn't as perfect as that postcard image made it seem. His parents—two schoolteachers—had been killed by a drunk driver when he was three, leaving him in the care of his paternal grandfather, who had a heart attack while shoveling snow one hard winter. Afterward, with no other immediate surviving relatives, he'd been dumped into foster care at thirteen, where he stayed until he petitioned for early emancipation and joined the armed services at seventeen.

He pushed those darker years away, down deep.

No wonder I like dogs better than people.

He brought his focus back to the business at hand.

In this case: assassination.

He studied the docks.

From where would the threat come? And in what form?

Against his advice, his principal—the Russian billionaire and industrialist Bogdan Fedoseev—had scheduled this early-morning visit to the port. For weeks there had been rumors of the dockworkers attempting to unionize, and Fedoseev had agreed to meet with the leaders, hoping to quash his employees into submission. If that tension wasn't enough of a threat, Tucker suspected a fair number of the workers were also Vladikavkaz Separatists, political terrorists whose main victims were the prominent capitalists in the Russian Far East, making Bogdan Fedoseev a high-value target.

Tucker cared little about politics, but he knew understanding the social landscape came with the job—as was knowing the *physical* landscape.

He checked his watch. Fedoseev was due to arrive in three hours. By then, Tucker needed to know every nook and cranny of this place.

He looked down at Kane. "What do you say, pal? Ready to work?"

In answer, Kane stood and did a full-body shake. Snow billowed off his fur, and the wind whipped it away.

Tucker started walking, with Kane trotting alongside him.

9:54 A.M.

By midmorning, Tucker had located six of the eight workers he suspected of being Vladikavkazists. The remaining two had called in sick that morning, something neither had done before.

Standing in a warehouse doorway, he studied the docks. The port was fully alive now, with forklifts moving here and there, cranes swinging containers onto outbound ships, all accompanied by a cacophony of hammering, grinding, and shouted orders.

Tucker pulled out his phone and scrolled through his list of PDF dossiers and found the two men who had called in sick. Both were former soldiers, petty officers in the Russian Naval Infantry. Worse still, they were both trained snipers.

Two and two equals a credible threat.

He set the men's faces in his memory.

His first instinct was to call Yuri, the head of Fedoseev's protective detail, but it would do no good. *I do not run*, Fedoseev had proclaimed loudly and frequently. But most damning of all, Tucker was an interloper, the American none of the other security detail wanted here.

Tucker's mind shifted again, visualizing Fedoseev's route through the docks. He judged the exposure windows, the angles of fire. He surveyed for any likely sniper perches. There were a half-dozen spots that would work.

He glanced at the sky. The sun was up now, a dull white disk above the horizon. The wind had also died, and the sleet had turned to big fat snowflakes.

Not good. Much easier to make a long-range shot now.

Tucker looked down at Kane, knowing they couldn't sit back and wait.

"Let's go find some bad guys."

10:07 A.M.

The six potential sniper nests were spread across the dockyard, some twenty acres of warehouses, catwalks, narrow alleys, and crane towers. Tucker and Kane covered the ground as quickly as possible without appearing hurried, using shortcuts wherever possible, never staring too long at any one spot.

As the pair passed a warehouse front, Kane let out a low growl. Tucker turned in a half crouch, going tense. Kane had stopped in his tracks and was staring down an alleyway between a pair of stacked containers.

Tucker caught the barest glimpse of a figure slipping out of view. Such a sighting would be easy to dismiss, but he knew his dog. Something in the stranger's body language or scent must have piqued Kane's interest: *tension*, *posture*, *furtive movements*. Kane's instincts were razor honed after several dangerous years in Afghanistan.

Tucker recalled his mental map of the dockyard, thought for a moment, then flipped Kane's collar cam into its upright position.

"Go scout," he ordered tersely.

Kane had a vocabulary of a thousand words and

understanding of a hundred hand gestures, making him an extension of Tucker's own body.

He pointed forward and motioned for Kane to circle around the bulk of containers to the far side.

Without hesitation, his partner trotted off.

Tucker watched him disappear into the gloom, then turned and jogged directly into the nest of giant container boxes where his target had vanished.

Reaching the first intersection, he stopped short and glanced around the corner of the container.

Another alley.

Empty.

He sprinted along it and arrived at the next intersection, this one branching left and right. It was a damned maze back here among the giant containers.

Easy to get lost, he thought, *and even easier to lose my target*.

He pictured Kane somewhere on the far side, hunkered down, watching this pile of containers. He needed his partner's eyes out there, while he hunted within this maze.

Tucker punched up Kane's video feed on his modified satellite phone. A flickering, digital image appeared on the tiny screen, live from Kane's camera.

A figure suddenly sprinted out of the line of containers, heading east.

Good enough.

Tucker ran in that direction. He caught a glimpse on the screen of Kane doing the same, tracking the man, still scouting as ordered.

Both were on the hunt now—which is what army rangers did. Aside from rare exceptions, rangers didn't patrol or provide humanitarian relief. They were single-minded in purpose: *find and destroy the enemy.*

Tucker had enjoyed the simplicity of that.

Brutal, true enough, but pure in a strange way.

He emerged from the container maze in time to draw even with Kane. He motioned the shepherd to him. Kane came trotting up and sat down beside him, awaiting his next command, his tongue lolling, his eyes bright.

They were now near the eastern edge of the dockyard. Directly ahead, across a gravel lot, lay a set of train tracks, lined with abandoned and rusted freight cars. Their quarry had vanished among them.

Beyond the train yard, a perimeter barbed-wire fence rose high—and beyond that, a dense pine forest.

Aside from the muffled dock sounds in the distance, all was quiet.

Suddenly Kane's head snapped to the left. A section of the barbed-wire fence shook violently for a few moments, then went still. In his mind's eye, Tucker envisioned a second target wriggling through a gap in the fencing to enter the dockyards from that direction, using the cover of the forest.

Why?

Searching farther to their left, he spotted a tall crane tower, once used to load the freight cars. The tower was one of the six potential sniper perches he had marked in his head.

Tucker checked his watch. Fedoseev would arrive in six minutes. Hurrying, he pulled out a pair of small binoculars from his jacket's pocket and focused on the top of the crane. At first he saw nothing but indistinct scaffolding in the swirling snow. Then a shadowy figure appeared, slowly scaling the ladder toward the high platform.

That's who came through the fence just now—but where's the guy I was following?

He considered calling Yuri with the abort code, but even if his message got past that gatekeeper, his boss's careless bravado would win out. Fedoseev would not back down from a threat. Bullets would have to be flying before the industrialist would consider a retreat.

It was the Russian way.

Tucker dropped to his belly and scanned beneath the freight cars. He spotted a pair of legs moving to the right, disappearing and reappearing as the figure passed the steel wheels. Whether this was in fact his guy, he didn't know, but it seemed likely.

He reached back and drew the Makarov PMM pistol from the paddle holster attached to his waistband. A decent weapon, but not his preference.

But when in Rome . . .

He looked over to Kane, who was crouched on his belly beside him. His partner's eyes had already locked on to the target jogging down the rail line, heading away from the man climbing the crane.

Tucker gave a one-word command, knowing it would be enough. He pointed to the target moving on the ground.

"TRACK."

Kane took off, silently sprinting after the man on foot.

Tucker angled toward the left, toward the crane tower.

Hunched over, he swept across the gravel lot, reached the train yard, and belly-crawled beneath a freight car and down the sloped ballast into a drainage ditch beyond. From the meager cover, he spotted the gap in the perimeter fencing; the cut was clean, recent.

To his left, a hundred yards away, rose the crane tower. Rolling to his side, he zoomed his binoculars and panned upward until he spotted his target. The assassin was perched on a ladder a few feet below the crane's glassed-in control cab. A gloved hand reached for the entry hatch.

Tucker quickly considered taking a shot at him but immediately decided against it. With a rifle, perhaps, but not with the Makarov. The distance and the scaffolding made a successful hit improbable. Plus the snow fell heavier now, slowly obscuring the view.

He checked his watch. *Three minutes before Fedoseev's limousine entered the main gate.* Fleetingly, he wondered about Kane, then brought his mind back to the task at hand.

One thing at a time, Ranger. Work the problem. Let Kane be Kane.

Kane runs low to the ground, his ears high, picking out the crunch of boot through ice-crusted snow. The command given to him is etched behind his eyes.

TRACK.

He sticks to the shadows of the rusted cars, following the dark shape through the whiteness, which grows thicker. But his world is not one of sight alone. That is the dullest of what he perceives, a shadow of a larger truth.

He stops long enough to bring his nose to a treaded print, scenting rubber, dirt, and leather. He rises higher to catch the wafting trail of wet wool, cigarette smoke, and sweat. He smells the fear in the salt off his prey's skin; distantly his ears pick out the rasp of a hurried breath.

He moves on, keeping pace with his quarry, his paws padding silently.

As he follows, he draws the rest of his surroundings inside him, reading the past and present in the flow of old and fresh trails. His ears note every distant shout, every grind of motor, every wash of wave from the neighboring sea. On the back of his tongue, he tastes frost and winter.

Through it all, one path shines brightest, leading to his prey.

He flows along it, a ghost on that trail.

10:18 A.M.

From his vantage in the drainage ditch, Tucker watched *his* target slip through the hatch at the top of the crane and close it with a muffled *snick*.

With the man out of direct sight, Tucker stood up and sprinted toward the tower, holstering the Makarov as he went. Discarding stealth, he jumped onto the ladder's third rung and started climbing. The rungs were slick with snow and ice. His boots slipped with every step, but he kept going. Two rungs beneath the hatch, he stopped. The hatch's padlock was missing.

Holding his breath, he drew the Makarov and

then gently, slowly, pressed the barrel against the hatch. It gave way ever so slightly.

Tucker didn't allow himself a chance to think, to judge the stupidity of his next action. Hesitation could get you killed as easily as bravado.

And if I have to die, let it be while I'm still moving.

In the past, he had pushed blindly through hundreds of doors in countless Afghan villages and bunkers. On the other side, something was always waiting to kill you.

This was no different.

He shoved the hatch open, his gun tracking left and right. The assassin knelt two feet away, crouched over an open clamshell rifle case. Behind him, one of the cab's sliding windows stood open, allowing snow to whip inside.

The assassin spun toward Tucker. The look of surprise on his face lasted only a microsecond— then he lunged.

Tucker fired a single shot. The Makarov's 9 mm hollow-point round entered an inch above the bridge of the man's nose, killing him instantly. The target toppled sideways and went still.

One down . . .

Tucker didn't regret what he'd just done, but the contradiction flashed through his mind. Though not a religious man, Tucker found himself attracted to the Buddhist philosophy of live and let live. In this case, however, letting this man *live* wasn't an option. Odd that he found the necessity of taking a human life defensible, while killing an animal was an entirely different story. The conundrum was intriguing, but pondering all that would have to wait.

He holstered the Makarov, climbed into the cab, and closed the hatch behind him. He quickly searched the assassin, looking for a cell phone or radio; he found neither. If he had a partner, they were operating autonomously—probably a fire-at-will arrangement.

Time check: *sixty seconds*.

Fedoseev would be prompt. He always was.

First order of business from here: keep the Russian out of the kill zone.

He turned his attention to the assassin's rifle, a Russian-made SV-98. He removed it from the case, examined it, and found it ready to fire.

Thanks, comrade, he thought as he stepped over the body and reached the open window.

He extended the rifle's bipod legs, propped them on the sill, and aimed the barrel over the sea of shipping containers and warehouse rooftops toward the main gate. With the cold stock against his cheek, he brought his eye to the scope's eyepiece and peered through the swirling snow.

"Where are you, Fedoseev?" Tucker muttered. "Come on—"

Then he spotted the black shadow sailing through the white snow. The limousine was thirty feet from the main gate and slowing for the cursory check-in with the guard. Tucker focused on the limousine's windshield, his finger tightening on the trigger. He felt a moment of reluctance, then recalled the SV-98's specifications. The weapon didn't have enough juice to penetrate the limousine's ballistic glass—or so he hoped.

He fired once, the blast deafening in the tight cab

of the crane. The 7.62 mm round struck the limo's windshield directly before the driver's seat. As an extra measure, Tucker adjusted his aim and fired again, this time shattering the side mirror. To his credit, the driver reacted immediately and correctly, slamming the limousine into reverse, then accelerating hard for fifty feet before slewing into a Y-turn.

Within seconds, the vehicle was a hundred yards away and disappearing into the snow.

Satisfied, Tucker lowered the rifle. Fedoseev was safe for the moment, but someone had tried to kill Tucker's principal. He'd be damned if he was going to let the second assassin escape and try again later.

Tucker ejected the rifle's box magazine and pocketed it before pulling out his satellite phone. He checked the video feed from Kane's camera. Between the wet lens and thickening snowfall, all he got for his effort was a blurry, indecipherable image.

Sighing, he opened another application on the phone. A map of the dockyard appeared on the screen. West of Tucker's location, approximately four hundred yards away, was a pulsing green blip. It was Kane's GPS signal, generated from a microchip embedded in the skin between his shoulder blades.

The dot was stationary, indicating Kane was doing as instructed. The shepherd had followed his quarry and was now lying in wait, watching.

Suddenly the blip moved, a slight jiggle that told him Kane had adjusted position, likely both to remain hidden and keep his quarry in sight. The blip moved again, this time heading steadily eastward and picking up speed.

It could only mean one thing.

The second assassin was sprinting in Tucker's direction.

Hurrying, he scaled down the ladder, sliding most of the way. Once his boots hit the ground, he trudged through the thickening snow, his Makarov held at ready, following the rail line. He hadn't covered thirty feet before he spotted a hazy figure ahead, crouched beside the cut in the fencing. His quarry leaped through the gap and sprinted into the trees.

Damn it.

Kane appeared two seconds later, ready to give chase. But once the shepherd spotted Tucker, he stopped in his tracks, ears high, waiting for further orders.

Tucker gave it.

"TAKE BRAVO!"

Playtime was over.

Kane lunged through the fence and took off in pursuit, with Tucker at his heels.

Though now in takedown mode, Kane didn't get too far ahead of him. The shepherd wove between trees and leaped over fallen trunks with ease, while simultaneously keeping his quarry and Tucker in view.

Engulfed by the forest, the sounds of the shipyard had completely faded. The snow hissed softly through the boughs around him. Somewhere ahead, a branch snapped. He stopped moving, crouched down. To his right, forty feet ahead, Kane was also frozen, crouched atop a fallen trunk, his eyes fixed.

Their quarry must have stopped.

Tucker pulled out his phone, checked the map screen.

Two hundred yards away, a narrow canal cut through the forest, a part of the dockyard's old layout when it had belonged to the Russian Navy. His quarry was former naval infantry, smart enough to have planned for an escape route like this, one by water.

But was that the plan?

According to the map, there was also a major road on the far side of the canal.

What if the man had a vehicle waiting?

Decide, Tucker.

Would his quarry flee by land or sea?

He let out a soft *tsst*, and Kane turned to look at him. Tucker held up a closed fist, then forked fingers: *Track.*

Kane took off straight south.

Tucker headed southeast, hedging his bet, ready to cut the man off if necessary.

As he ran, he kept half an eye on Kane's position using the GPS feed. His partner reached the canal and stopped. The blip held steady for a few seconds—then began moving again, paralleling the canal and rapidly picking up speed.

It could only mean one thing.

Their quarry had boarded a boat.

Tucker took off in a sprint, darting and ducking through the last of the trees. He burst out of the forest and into an open field. Ahead, a tall levy hid the canal's waterway. To his right came the grumble of a marine engine. He ran toward the noise as Kane came racing hard along the top of the levy.

Tucker knew he couldn't hope to match the dog's speed. According to the map, the canal was narrow, no more than fifteen feet.

Doable, Tucker thought.

He shouted, "TAKE DOWN . . . DISARM!"

The shepherd dropped his head lower, put on a burst of speed, then leaped from the levy and vanished beyond the berm.

Kane flies high, thrilled by the rush of air over his fur. Here is what he lived for, as ingrained in his nature as the beat of his heart.

To hunt and take down prey.

His front paws strike the wood of the deck, but he is already moving, shifting his hind end, to bring his back legs into perfect position. He bounds off the boards and toward the cabin of the boat.

His senses swell, filling in details.

The reek of burnt oil . . .

The resin of the polished wood . . .

The trail of salt and fear that lead to that open door of the cabin . . .

He follows that scent, dragged along by both command and nature.

He bolts through the door, sees the man swing toward him, his skin bursting with terror, his breath gasping out in surprise.

An arm lifts, not in reflexive defense, but bringing up a gun.

Kane knows guns.

The blast deafens as he lunges.

10:33 A.M.

The gunshot echoed over the water as Tucker reached the top of the levy. His heart clenched in concern. Fifty yards down the waterway, a center-cabin dredge boat tilted crookedly in the canal, nosing toward the bank.

Tucker ran, fear firing his limbs. As he reached the foundering boat, he coiled his legs and vaulted high, flying. He hit the boat's afterdeck hard and slammed into the gunwale. Pain burst behind his eyes. Rolling sideways, he got to his knees and brought the Makarov up.

Through the open cabin door, he saw a man sprawled on his back, his left arm flailing, his legs kicking. His right forearm was clamped between Kane's jaws. The shepherd's muscled bulk was rag-dolling the man from side to side.

The Russian screamed in his native tongue. Tucker's grasp of the language was rudimentary, but the man's tone said it all.

Get him off me! Please!

With his gun trained on the man's chest, Tucker stepped through the cabin door. Calmly he said, "Release."

Kane instantly let go of the man's arm and stepped back, his lips still curled in a half snarl.

The Russian clutched his shattered arm to his chest, his eyes wide and damp with pain. Judging by where Kane had clamped on to the man's forearm, the ulna was likely broken and possibly the radius as well.

Tucker felt no pity.

The asshole had almost shot his partner.

A few feet away lay a revolver, still smoking in the cold.

Tucker stepped forward and looked down at the man. "Do you speak English?"

"English . . . yes, I speak some English."

"You're under arrest."

"What? I don't—"

Tucker drew back his right foot and heel-kicked the man squarely in the forehead, knocking him unconscious.

"More or less," he added.

2

March 4, 12:44 P.M.
Vladivostok, Russia

"You owe me a new windshield," Bogdan Fedoseev boomed, handing Tucker a shot glass of ice-cold vodka.

He accepted it but placed the glass on the end table next to the couch. He was not fond of vodka, and, more important, he didn't trust his hands right now. The aftermath of the shoot-out at the shipyard had left Tucker pumping with adrenaline, neither an unfamiliar nor unpleasant rush for him. Even so, he wondered how much of that rush was exhilaration and how much was PTSD—a clinical acronym for what used to be called shell shock or battle fatigue, a condition all too common for many Iraq and Afghanistan veterans.

Compared to most, Tucker's case was mild, but it was a constant in his life. Though he managed it well, he could still feel it lurking there, like a monster probing for a chink in his mental armor. Tucker found the metaphor strangely reassuring. Vigilance was something he did well. Still, the Buddhist in him whispered in his ear to relax his guard.

Let go of it.
What you cling to only gets stronger.
What you think, you become.

Tucker couldn't quite nail down when and where he'd adopted this philosophy. It had snuck up on him. He'd had a few teachers—one in particular—but he suspected he'd picked up his worldview from his wanderings with Kane. Having encountered people of almost every stripe, Tucker had learned to take folks as they came, without the baggage of preconceptions. People were more alike than different. Everyone was just trying to find a way to be happy, to feel fulfilled. The manner in which they searched for that state differed wildly, but the prize remained the same.

Enough, Tucker commanded himself. Contemplation was fine, but he'd long ago decided it was a lot like tequila—best taken only in small doses.

At his feet, Kane sat at ease, but his eyes remained bright and watchful. The shepherd missed nothing: *posture, hand and eye movements, respiration rate, perspiration.* All of it painted a clear picture for his partner. Unsurprisingly, Kane had picked up on the anxiety in the air.

Tucker felt it, too.

One of the reasons he had been paired with Kane was his unusually high empathy scores. Military war dog handlers had a saying—*It runs down the lead*—describing how emotions of the pair became shared over time, binding them together. The same skill allowed Kane to read people, to pick up nuances of body language and expression that others might miss.

Like now, with the tension in the room.

"And the side mirror of the limo," Fedoseev added with a strained grin. "You destroyed both windshield and mirror. Very costly. And worst of all, you could have killed Pytor, my driver."

Tucker refused to back down, knowing it would be a sign of weakness. "At that distance and angle, the rifle I used didn't have enough foot-pounds to penetrate the limo's ballistic glass. Maybe if I was standing on the hood of the car, Pytor might have had something to worry about."

Stymied, Fedoseev frowned. "Still, very expensive things to fix on limousine, yes?"

"You can take it out of my bonus," Tucker replied.

"Bonus! What bonus?"

"The one you're going to give me for saving your life."

Standing behind Fedoseev, Yuri said, "We would have handled the—"

Fedoseev held up his hand, silencing his subordinate. Yuri's face flushed. Behind him, the pair of bodyguards at the door shifted their feet, glancing down.

Tucker knew what Yuri and his security team were thinking. *Would haves* were worthless when it comes to personal protection. The fact was, this outsider—this American and his dog—had saved their boss. Still, Yuri had intervened on Tucker's behalf with the police, smoothing over the complications that could have risen over killing the first shooter. Russian bodyguards taking down a would-be assassin was a simple matter; a former U.S. Army Ranger, not so much.

Ninety minutes after apprehending the second man, who was now in police custody, Tucker met Fedoseev and his entourage back at the Meridian Hotel, where the Russian had rented the top floor of VIP suites. The decor and furnishings were comfortable, but overly ornate. Shabby Soviet chic. Outside, snow still fell, obscuring what would have been a stunning view of Peter the Great Bay and mainland Russia.

"I do you better than bonus," Fedoseev offered. "You become part of my team. Permanent part. I am generous. Your dog will eat steak every night. He would like that, yes?"

"Ask him yourself."

Fedoseev's gaze flicked toward Kane, then he smiled and wagged his finger at Tucker. "Very funny." He tried a different angle. "You know, these two *suka* may have had a helper. If he is still around—"

Suka was one of Fedoseev's favorite slang terms. Roughly and politely, a *suka* meant *scumbag*.

Tucker interrupted. "If you're right, I'm sure Yuri will find anyone else involved in this attempted assassination."

Especially with one of the attackers already in custody.

Up here, torture was as common a tool as a knife and fork.

Fedoseev sighed. "Then your answer is?"

"I appreciate the offer," he said, "but my contract's up in two days. Past that, I've got somewhere to be."

It was a lie, but no one called him on it.

The truth was he had *nowhere* to be, and right now he liked it that way. Plus Yuri and his team were all ex-military and that background infused everything they did and said. He'd had his fill of them. Tucker had done his time in the military, and the parting had been less than amicable.

Of course, he'd loved his early days in the army and had been contemplating going career.

Until Anaconda.

He reached for the abandoned glass of vodka as the unwanted memory of the past swept over him. He hated how the cubes rattled against the crystal as he lifted the tumbler. PTSD. He considered it merely a piece of psychic shrapnel lodged near his heart.

He sipped at the liquor, letting the memory wash through him.

Not that he had any choice.

Tucker again felt the pop of his ears as the rescue helicopter lifted off, felt the rush of hot air.

He closed his eyes, remembering that day, drawn back to that firefight. He had been assisting soldiers from the Tenth Mountain Division secure a series of bunkers in Hell's Halfpipe. He had been flanked by *two* partners that day: Kane and Kane's littermate, Abel. If Kane had been Tucker's right arm, Abel was his left. He'd trained them both.

Then a distress call had reached his team in the mountains. A Chinook helo carrying a team of Navy SEALs had been downed by RPG fire on a peak called Takur Ghar. Tucker and his squad were dispatched east and had begun the arduous climb to Takur Ghar when they were ambushed in a ravine.

A pair of IEDs exploded, killing most of Tucker's squad and wounding the rest, including Abel, whose left front leg had been blown off at the elbow.

Within seconds, Taliban fighters emerged from concealed positions and swarmed the survivors. Tucker, along with a handful of soldiers, was able to reach a defensible position and hold out long enough for an evac helicopter to land. Once Kane and his teammates were loaded, he was about to jump off and return for Abel, but before he could do so, a crewman dragged him back aboard and held him down—where he could only watch.

As the helo lifted off and banked over the ravine, a pair of Taliban fighters chased down Abel who was limping toward the rising helo, his pained eyes fixed on Tucker, his severed leg trailing blood.

Tucker scrambled for the door, only to be pulled back yet again.

Then the Taliban fighters reached Abel. He squeezed those last memories away, but not the haunting voice forever in the back of his mind: *You could've tried harder; you could have reached him.*

If he had, he knew he would have been killed, too, but at least Abel wouldn't have been alone. Alone and wondering why Tucker had abandoned him . . .

Back in his own skin, he opened his eyes and downed the rest of the vodka in a single gulp, letting the burn erase the worst of that old pain.

"Mr. Wayne . . ." Bogdan Fedoseev leaned forward, his forehead creased with concern. "Are you ill? You've gone dead pale, my friend."

Tucker cleared his throat, shook his head. Without looking, he knew Kane was staring at him. He reached out and gave the shepherd's neck a reassuring squeeze.

"I'm fine. What were we talking—?"

Fedoseev leaned back. "You and your dog joining us."

Tucker focused his eyes on Fedoseev and on the present. "No, as I said, I'm sorry. I've got somewhere to be."

Though it was a lie, he was ready to move on, *needed* to move on.

But the question remained: What would he do?

Fedoseev sighed loudly. "Very well! But if you change your mind, you tell me. Tonight, you stay in one of the suites. I send up two steaks. One for you. One for your dog."

Tucker nodded, stood, and shook Fedoseev's hand.

For now, that was enough of a plan.

11:56 P.M.

The chirp of his satellite phone instantly woke Tucker in his room.

He scrambled for it, while checking the clock.

Almost midnight.

What now? With nothing on Fedoseev's schedule for that evening, Tucker and Kane had been given the night off. Had something happened? Yuri had already informed him earlier that the Vladikavkaz Separatist taken into custody had broken and talked, spilling everything.

So Tucker had expected a quiet night.

He checked the incoming number as he picked up the phone: a blocked number. That was seldom good.

Kane sat at the edge of the bed, watching Tucker.

He lifted the phone and pressed the talk button. "Hello?"

A series of squeaks and buzzes suggested the call was being filtered through a series of digital coders.

Finally, the caller spoke. "Captain Wayne, I'm glad I could reach you."

Tucker relaxed—but not completely. Suspicion rang through him as he recognized the voice. It was Painter Crowe, the director of Sigma Force, and the man who'd tried to recruit Tucker not so long ago after a prior mission. The full extent of Sigma's involvement in the U.S. intelligence and defense community was still a mystery to him, but one thing he did know: Sigma worked under the aegis of the ultrasecretive DARPA—the Defense Advanced Research Projects Agency.

Tucker cleared the rasp of sleep from his voice. "I assume you know what time it is here, Director?"

"I do. My apologies. It's important."

"Isn't it always? What's going on?"

"I believe your contract with Bogdan Fedoseev is almost up. In two more days, if I'm not mistaken."

Tucker should have been surprised that the caller had this information, but this was Painter Crowe, who had resources that bordered on the frightening.

"Director, I'm guessing this isn't a casual call, so why don't you get to your point?"

"I need a favor. And you've got forty-two days still left on your Russian visa."

"And something tells me you want those *days*."

"Only a few. We've got a friend I'd like you to meet."

"I've got enough friends. Why is this one so special?"

There was a pause, one that took too long. He understood. While the call was encrypted, Tucker's room could have been bugged—probably *was* bugged, knowing the Russians. Any further details would require additional precautions.

He couldn't say such subterfuge didn't intrigue him.

He also suspected this lapse in the conversation was a test.

Tucker proved his understanding of the need for privacy by asking another question. "Where?"

"Half a mile from your hotel—a pay phone on the northeast corner of the Grey Horse Apartments."

"I'll find it. Give me twenty minutes."

He was there in eighteen, stamping his feet against the cold. Using a prepaid calling card, Tucker dialed Sigma's cover trunk line, then waited through another series of encoder tones before Crowe's voice came on the line.

The director got straight to the point. "I need you to escort a man out of the country."

The simple sentence was fraught with layers of information. The fact that Crowe didn't think their *friend* was capable of accomplishing this feat on his own already told Tucker two things.

One: The man was of high value to Sigma.

Two: Normal travel options were problematic.

In other words, someone didn't want the man leaving the country.

Tucker knew better than to ask *why* this target needed to leave Russia. Crowe was a firm believer in the need-to-know policy. But Tucker had another question that he wanted answered.

"*Why* me?"

"You're already in-country, have an established cover, and your skill set matches the job."

"And you have no other assets available."

"That, too—but it's a secondary consideration."

"Just so we're clear, Director. This is a favor. Nothing more. If you're trying to court me to join—"

"Not at all. Get our friend out of the country, and you're done. You'll make twice your usual retainer. For this mission, I'm assigning you an operations handler. Her name is Ruth Harper."

"Not you?" This surprised him, and he didn't like surprises. "Director, you know I don't play well with others, especially those I've never met face-to-face."

"Harper is good, Tucker. Really knows her stuff. Give her a chance. So will you do it?"

Tucker sighed. While he had little trust in government agencies, Crowe had so far proven himself to be a stand-up guy.

"Give me the details."

3

The door to Tucker's private berth on the train slid back, and a head bearing a blue cap peeked through.

"Papers, please," the train porter ordered, tempering his KGB-like request with a friendly smile. The sliver-thin young man could be no more than twenty, his coal-black hair peeking from under his crisp hat. He kept the buttons of his uniform well polished, clearly very proud of his job.

Tucker handed over his passport.

The porter studied it, nodded, and handed it back. The man's eyes settled nervously on Kane. The shepherd sat upright in the seat opposite Tucker, panting, tongue hanging.

"And your animal?" the porter asked.

"Service animal."

Tucker handed over Kane's packet, courtesy of Painter Crowe. The papers certified his furry companion was a working dog, adept at sensing Tucker's frequent and debilitating epileptic seizures. It was a ruse, of course, but traveling with a seventy-pound military war dog tended to raise unwanted questions.

The porter reviewed the papers and nodded. "*Da*, I see. My second cousin suffers same sickness." His gaze returned to Kane, but with more affection and sympathy now. "May I pet him?"

Tucker shrugged. "Sure. He doesn't bite."

Not unless I tell him to.

Tentatively, the porter reached out and scratched Kane under the chin. "Good doggy."

Kane regarded him impassively, tolerating the familiarity.

Tucker resisted the urge to smile.

Satisfied, the porter grinned and returned the documents to Tucker.

"I like him very much," the young man said.

"I do, too."

"If there's anything you need, you ask, *da*?"

Tucker nodded as the porter exited and slid the door closed.

He settled back, staring at the Russian scenery passing by the window, which mostly consisted of snowy trees and Soviet-bloc-era buildings as the train headed out of Vladivostok. The port city marked one end of this route of the Trans-Siberian Railway; the other was Moscow.

Not that he and Kane were traveling that far.

For reasons Crowe hadn't explained, Tucker's target wouldn't be ready for extraction for a week. So after completing his final two days with Bogdan Fedoseev, Tucker had boarded the famous Trans-Siberian Railway and settled in for the five-day journey to the city of Perm. Once there, he was to meet a contact who would take him to his target, a man named Abram Bukolov.

Tucker still had no idea *why* the man needed to leave Russia in such a clandestine manner—especially such a high-profile figure. Tucker had recognized his name as soon as Crowe had mentioned it on the phone. Tucker's previous employer, Bogdan Fedoseev, had had business dealings with this man in the past.

Abram Bukolov was the owner of Horizon Industries and arguably the country's pharmacological tycoon. A frequent face on magazine covers and television shows, Bukolov was to prescription drugs what Steve Jobs had been to personal computing. In the years following the breakup of the Soviet Union, the pharmaceutical industry in Russia disintegrated into disarray and corruption, from the quality of the drugs themselves to the distribution networks. Thousands were thought to have died from tainted drugs or faulty doses. Through sheer force of will and inherited wealth, Abram Bukolov slowly and steadily bent the system to his benevolent will, becoming the keeper of Russia's pharmacy.

And now he wanted out, all but abandoning a multibillion-dollar empire he had spent his entire adult life building.

Why?

And what could possibly drive such a man to run so scared?

According to the encrypted dossier sent by Painter Crowe, the only clue lay in Bukolov's mysterious warning: *The Arzamas-16 generals are after me . . .*

The man refused to explain more until he was safely out of Russia.

Tucker had studied the rest of the files for this mission over and over again. Bukolov was a well-known eccentric, a personality trait that shone in every interview of him. He was clearly a driven visionary with a zealous passion to match, but had he finally snapped?

And what about these Arzamas-16 generals?

From the research notes included in the dossier, there was once a city named Arzamas-16. During the rule of Joseph Stalin, it was home to the Soviet Union's first nuclear weapons design center. The U.S. intelligence community simply referred to it as the *Russian Los Alamos*.

But it was only the first of the many *naukograds*, or "closed science cities," that popped up across the Soviet Union, secured by ironclad perimeters. In such places, top-secret projects under the aegis of the best Soviet scientists were conducted. Rumors abounded during the Cold War of biological weapons, mind control drugs, and stealth technology.

But Arzamas-16 no longer existed.

In its place, the region had become home to a couple of nuclear weapons test facilities—but what did anything like that have to do with Abram Bukolov?

And who could these nefarious *generals* be?

It made no sense.

He glanced over at Kane, who wagged his tail, ready for whatever was to come. Tucker settled back, deciding that was probably the best course of action from here.

Just be ready for anything.

4

The large man stepped around his desk and settled into his chair with a creak of leather. He had the call up on his speakerphone. He had no fear of anyone listening. No one dared, especially not here.

"Where is the target now?" he asked. Word had reached his offices that an operative—an American mercenary with a dog—had been assigned to help Dr. Bukolov leave Russian soil.

That must not happen.

"Heading west," the caller answered in Swedish-accented Russian. "Aboard the Trans-Siberian. We know he is booked through to Perm, but whether that's his final destination, we don't know yet."

"What makes you think it would be otherwise?"

"This one clearly has some training. My instincts tell me he wouldn't book a ticket straight to his ultimate destination. He's too clever for that."

"What name is he traveling under?"

"We're working on that, too," the Swede answered, growing testy.

"And where are *you* now?"

"Driving to Khabarovsk. We tried to board the train at Vladivostok but—"

"He gave you the shake, *da*?"

"Yes."

"Let me understand this. A man and a large dog lost you and your team. Did he see you?"

"No. Of that we're certain. He is simply careful and well trained. What else have you learned about him?"

"Nothing much. I'm making inquiries, trying to track his finances, but it appears he is using a credit card that has been backstopped—sanitized. It suggests he's either more than he seems to be or has powerful help. Or both. What came of the hotel search in Vladivostok?"

"Nothing. We couldn't get close. His employer—that bastard Bogdan Fedoseev—rented out the entire penthouse. Security was too tight. But if we can reach Khabarovsk before the train does, we'll board there. If not . . ."

The Swede's words trailed off.

Neither of them had to verbalize the problems such a failure would present.

The railway branched frequently from there, with routes heading in many different directions, including into China and Mongolia. Following their target into a foreign country—especially China—would exponentially multiply their surveillance challenges.

The speakerphone crackled again as the caller offered one hope. "If he is using sanitized credit cards, we should assume he has several passports and travel documents. If you have any colleagues in the FPS, it may be helpful to circulate his photo."

He nodded to himself, rubbing his chin. The caller was referring to Russia's Federal Border Guard Service.

"As you said," the caller continued, "a man and a large dog are hard to miss."

"I'll see what I can do. I would prefer to keep the scope of this operation limited. That's why I hired you. Sadly, I am beginning to question my judgment. Get results, or I'll be making a change. Do you understand my meaning?"

A long silence followed before a response came.

"Not to worry. I've never failed before. I'll get the information you need, and he'll be dead before he ever reaches Perm."

5

A voice over the intercom system called out first in Russian, then in English.

"Next stop, Khabarovsk."

A scrolling green LED sign on the wall of Tucker's berth repeated the multilingual message along with: DEPARTING AGAIN IN 18 MINUTES.

Tucker began gathering his things, tugging on his coat. Once done, he patted Kane. "What do you say we stretch our legs?"

They'd been cooped up in the car for most of the day, and he knew he could use a bit of fresh air. He pulled on his fur trapper's cap, attached Kane's lead, then opened the berth door.

He followed the slow trudge of fellow passengers down the corridor to the exit steps. A few eyebrows were raised at the sight of his unusual traveling companion. One matronly babushka gave him what he could best describe as the evil eye.

Taking heed of the unnecessary attention, he avoided the terminal building—a whitewashed, green-tiled Kremlin-esque structure—and guided

Kane across the train tracks to a patch of scrub brush. A chest-high fence, missing more pickets than it retained, bordered the area.

As Kane sniffed and marked his territory, Tucker stretched his back and legs. Aboard the train, he had caught up on his sleep, and he had the muscle kinks to prove it.

After a few minutes, the screech of tires drew his attention past the terminal. The frantic blare of a car horn followed. He spotted a line of cars stopped at the intersection as a departing eastbound train cleared the station. As the caboose clunked over the road and the barriers rose, a black sedan swerved to the head of the line and raced into the terminal parking lot.

He checked his watch. Four minutes to departure.

Whoever was in the sedan was cutting it close.

He let Kane wander for another full minute, then walked back over the tracks to their train car. Once returned to their berth, Kane jumped into his usual seat, panting, refreshed.

A commotion out on the terminal platform drew his attention, too. A trio of men in long black leather dusters strode purposefully along the length of the train, occasionally stopping porters and showing them what looked to be a photo before moving on again. None of the men offered any credentials.

Faint alarm bells sounded in Tucker's head. But there were hundreds of people on the train, he told himself, and so far all the porters had merely shrugged or shook their heads when shown the photo.

Clearly frustrated, one of the men pulled out a cell phone and spoke into it. Thirty seconds later, he was joined by his partners, and after a brief discussion, the trio hurried back into the terminal and disappeared from view.

He watched and waited, but none of them reappeared.

He sighed in relief when the train whistle blew and the *All Aboard* was called. The train lurched forward and slowly pulled away from the station.

Only then did he settle back in his own seat.

But he was hardly settled.

7:38 P.M.

An hour later, too full of nervous energy to remain inside the berth, Tucker found himself seated in the dining car. Around him, the tables were draped with linen; the windows framed by silk curtains; the place settings china and crystal.

But his attention focused on the car's best feature.

While he had never been the type to ogle the opposite sex, the woman sitting across the aisle and one booth down was challenging his discipline.

She was tall and lithe, her figure accentuated by a form-fitting skirt and a white cashmere turtleneck sweater. She wore her blond hair long and straight, framing high cheekbones and ice-blue eyes. Picking at a salad and occasionally sipping from a glass of wine, she spent most of the meal either reading a dog-eared copy of *Anna Karenina* or staring out the window as dusk settled over the Siberian landscape.

For one chance moment, she looked up, caught Tucker's eye, and smiled—genuine, pleasant, but clearly reserved.

Still, her body language was easy to read.

Thank you, but I'd prefer to be alone.

A few minutes later, the woman signaled for the check, signed her bill, then swished past Tucker's table and through the connecting door to the berth cars.

Tucker lingered over his coffee, oddly disappointed, more than he should be, then headed back to his own berth.

As he stepped into the corridor, he found the blond woman kneeling on the floor, the contents of her purse scattered at her feet, some of it rolling farther away with each jostle of the train's wheels.

Tucker walked over and dropped to a knee beside her. "Let me help."

She frowned, tucked a strand of blond hair behind her ear, and offered him a shy smile. "Thank you. Everything seems to be getting away from me lately."

Her accent was British, refined.

Tucker helped her gather the runaway items, then stood up. He nodded at her copy of *Anna Karenina*. "The butler did it, by the way."

She blinked at him, momentarily confused.

Tucker added, "In the library, with a lead pipe."

She smiled. "Well, goodness. Then there's not much point in my finishing it, is there?"

"Sorry if I ruined it for you."

"You've read it?"

"In high school," he said.

"And your verdict?"

"Certainly not beach reading. I liked it—but not enough to wade through it a second time."

"It's my *third* time. I'm a glutton for punishment, I suppose." She extended her hand. "Well, thank you again . . ."

He took her hand, finding her fingers soft, but firm. "Tucker," he said.

"I'm Felice. Thank you for your help. I hope you have a pleasant night."

It had certainly turned out *pleasant*.

She turned and started down the corridor. Ten feet away, she stopped and spoke without turning. "It doesn't seem quite fair, you know."

Tucker didn't reply, but waited until she turned to face him before asking, "What isn't?"

"You spoiling the end of a perfectly good Russian novel."

"I see your point. I take it that an apology isn't enough?"

"Not even close."

"Breakfast, then?"

Her lips pursed as Felice considered this a moment. "Is seven too early for you?"

He smiled. "See you in the morning."

With a slight wave, she turned and headed down the corridor. He watched until she vanished out of sight, enjoying every step she took.

Once alone, he opened the door to his berth and found Kane sitting on the floor staring up at him. The shepherd must have heard his voice out in the passageway. Kane tilted his head in his customary *What's going on?* fashion.

He smiled and scratched Kane between the ears. "Sorry, pal, she didn't have a friend."

6

The next morning, Tucker arrived five minutes early to find Felice already seated at a booth in the rear of the dining car. For the moment, they had the space to themselves. This time of the year, the sun was still not up, just a rosy promise to the east.

Tucker walked over and sat down. "You're a morning person, I see."

"Since I was a little girl, I'm afraid. It drove my parents quite mad. By the way, I ordered coffee for two, if you don't mind. I'm a much better morning person with caffeine in my system."

"That makes two of us."

The waiter arrived with a pair of steaming mugs and took their orders. Felice opted for the closest semblance to a standard big English breakfast. He nodded his approval, appreciating a woman with a good appetite. In turn, he chose an omelet with toasted black bread.

"You're the owner of that large hound, aren't you?" Felice asked. "The one that looks smarter than most people on this train."

"Owner isn't the word I would use, but yes." He offered up his service dog story, explaining about his epilepsy. "I don't know what I'd do without him."

At least that last part was true.

"Where are you two headed?" she asked.

"I'm booked to Perm, but I'm flexible. Plenty to explore out here. We might get off and sightsee if the mood strikes us. And you?"

She gave him a sly smile. "Is that an invitation?"

He gave her a shrug that was noncommittal with a hint of invitation, which only widened her smile.

She skirted over to tamer topics. "As to me, I'm headed to Moscow, off to meet some friends from my university days."

"You went to school there?"

"Goodness, no. Cambridge. Arts and humanities. *Hinc lucem et pocula sacra* and all that. *From here, light and sacred draughts.* Latin motto. Very highbrow, you see. Two of my girlfriends moved to Moscow last year. We're having a small reunion."

"You boarded in Khabarovsk?"

"Yes. And almost got run over in the parking lot for my trouble. A big black car."

"I remember hearing some honking, saw some commotion. Was that them?"

She nodded. "Three men, dressed like old-school KGB thugs. Quite gloomy looking. Very rude, marching around the platform like they owned the place, flashing their badges."

Tucker struggled to keep his brow from furrowing. "Sounds like the police. Perhaps they were looking for someone."

She took a dismissive sip of coffee. "I can only imagine."

"It's not you, is it? I'm not having breakfast with an international art thief?"

She laughed, tilting her head back and slightly to the side. "Oh, my cover has been blown. Stop the train at once."

He smiled. "According to my guide, Khabarovsk's Fedotov Gallery is a must-see for art connoisseurs. Especially for any sightseeing arts and humanities graduates from Cambridge. I almost wish I'd gotten off the train to go. Did you visit?"

She nodded, her eyes shining. "Absolutely stunning. Wish I'd had more time myself. You must go back sometime. And you, Mr. Wayne, what's your secret? What do you do when you're not traipsing around Siberia?"

"International art thief," he replied.

"Ah, I thought as much."

He patted his jacket pocket. "Excuse me," he said and pulled out his phone, glancing at the screen. "Text from my brother."

He opened the phone's camera application and surreptitiously snapped a shot of Felice's face. He studied the screen for a few more seconds, pretended to type a response, then returned the phone to his pocket.

"Sorry," he said. "My brother's getting married in a month, and he's put me in charge of his bachelor party. His wife is worried it's going to be too risqué."

Felice raised an eyebrow. "And is it?"

"Absolutely."

"Men," she said, laughing, and reached across the table and gave his forearm a squeeze.

8:35 A.M.

After finishing breakfast and lingering over coffee for another half hour, the two parted company with a promise to share another meal before Tucker disembarked at Perm.

Once free, he returned quickly to his berth, pulled out his satellite phone, and speed-dialed the new number Painter Crowe had given him. It was answered immediately.

"Tucker Wayne, I presume," a female voice answered.

"Ruth Harper."

"Correct." Harper's speech was clipped, precise, but somehow not quite curt. There was also a distinct southern accent there, too.

"What do you have for me?" Harper asked.

"No *nice to meet you* or *how are you*?"

"Nice to meet you. How are you? How's that? Warm and fuzzy enough for you?"

"Marginally," Tucker replied.

As he paced the small space, he tried to picture what she looked like. She sounded young, but with a bite at the edges that spoke of some toughness. *Maybe late thirties*. But he knew Sigma operatives had prior military experience, and Harper was likely no exception, so some of that *toughness* could be from hard lessons learned young, an early maturity gained under fire. From her seriousness, he imagined her dark-haired, wearing glasses, a battle-weary librarian.

He smiled inwardly at that image.

"So what's your take on the situation?" she asked.

"I think I've picked up a tail."

"Why do you think that, Captain Wayne?" Her tone grew grave with a trace of doubt.

"Just call me Tucker," he said and explained about the leather-jacketed men on the Khabarovsk train platform and Felice's insistence they were flashing badges.

"And they weren't?" Harper asked.

"No. They were just showing a photograph. I'm sure of it. She also claims she visited the Fedotov Gallery in Khabarovsk. It's been closed for renovations for the past month."

"And you know this detail how?"

"There's not much else to do on this train but sleep and read travel brochures."

"Anything else that makes you suspicious of her?"

"She's pretty, and she finds me fascinating."

"That certainly is odd. Are you sure she's in possession of her faculties?"

He smiled at her matter-of-fact tone. "Funny."

He decided he might—*might*—like Ruth Harper.

"Your accent," Tucker said. "Tennessee?"

She ignored his attempt to draw her out, but from the exasperated tone of her next words, he guessed he was wrong about Tennessee.

"Give me Felice's pedigree," she said, staying professional.

Tucker passed on the information he had gleaned: her name, her background at the University of

Cambridge, her friends in Moscow. "And I have a picture. I assume your wizards have access to facial-recognition programs."

"Indeed we do."

"I'm sending it now."

"Okay, sit tight and I'll get back to you."

It didn't take long. Harper called back within forty minutes.

"Your instinct was sound," she said without pre-amble. "But you've picked up *more* than a tail. She's a freelance mercenary."

"I knew it was too good to be true," he muttered. "Let's hear it."

"Her real name is Felice Nilsson, but she's trav-eling under Felice Johansson. Swedish citizenship. She's thirty-three, born in Stockholm to a wealthy family. She didn't graduate from Cambridge, but from University of Gothenburg, with a master's in fine arts and music. And here's where things get in-teresting. Six months after graduating, she joined the Swedish Armed Forces and eventually ended up in *Särskilda Inhämtningsgruppen*."

"SIG?"

As a member of the U.S. Special Forces, Tucker had to know the competition, both allied and enemy alike. SIG was the Swedish Special Reconnaissance Group. Its operatives were trained in intelligence gathering, reconnaissance, and covert surveillance, along with being superb, hardened soldiers.

"She was one of the group's first female mem-bers," Harper added.

"What was her specialty?"

"Sniper."

Great.

"I urge you to approach her with extreme caution."

"Caution? Never would have thought of that."

Harper let out what could be taken as a soft chuckle, but it disappeared so quickly that Tucker couldn't be sure.

"Point taken," she said. "But do not underestimate her. After six years in the SIG, Nilsson resigned her commission. Eight months later, she started popping up on intel radars, first working small-time stuff as a mercenary, mostly for established groups. Then, two years ago, she struck out on her own, forming her own team—all former Swedish Special Forces. Last estimate put her roster at six to eight, including herself."

"Bored rich girl goes rogue," Tucker said.

"Maybe that's how it started, but she's got a real taste for it now. And a solid reputation. For now, the question remains, *Who hired her and why?*"

"You're in a better position to answer that than I am. But this must have something to do with your operation. Otherwise, it would be about me personally, and that doesn't seem likely."

"Agreed."

"And if that's true, if they're already on my tail, I don't have to tell you what that means."

"We've got a leak," Harper replied. "Word of your involvement must have reached those who are hunting for Dr. Bukolov."

"But who leaked that information? For the moment, let's assume it didn't come from anyone inside Sigma command. So who in Russia had my itinerary? Who knew I'd be aboard this train."

"The only person with that information was the contact you're supposed to meet in Perm."

"Who's that?"

She didn't answer immediately, and Tucker knew why. If Felice Nilsson got her hands on Tucker, the less he knew, the less he could divulge.

"Forget I asked," he said. "So the leak is either my contact or someone he told."

"Most likely," she agreed. "Either way, it has to be Abram Bukolov they're after. But the fact that Ms. Nilsson is on that train rather than out in Perm, pursuing our contact, that tells us something."

"It tells us whoever is paying her wants this to play out for some reason. This isn't all about Bukolov himself. Maybe it's something he has . . . something he knows."

"Again, I agree. And trust me when I tell you this: I don't know what that could be. When he contacted us, he was tight-lipped. He told us only enough to make sure we'd get him out." A moment of contemplative silence stretched, then she asked, "What's your plan? How do you want to play this?"

"Don't know yet. Assuming those leather jackets I saw at Khabarovsk were hers, they were in a hurry, and I think I know why. The next stop on this route is at the city of Chita, a major hub, where trains spread out in every direction. They had to tag me in Khabarovsk or risk losing me."

"Do you think her men got aboard?"

"I don't think so, but I'll have a look around. I wonder if part of their job was a distraction—a spectacle to let Felice slip aboard without fuss."

"Either way, you can bet she's in contact with

them. You said there were no other stops before Chita?"

"Afraid not." Tucker checked his watch. "We'll arrive in two and a half days. I'm going to check the route map. If the train slows below thirty miles per hour, and the terrain is accommodating, we can roll off. It's the surest way to shake Felice off my trail."

"You're getting into the mountains out there, Tucker. Take care you don't tumble off a cliff."

"Glad to know you care, Harper."

"Just worried about the dog."

He smiled, warming up to this woman. His image of the battle-weary librarian was developing some softer edges, including a glint of dark amusement in her eyes.

"As to Felice Nilsson," she continued, "don't kill her unless you have to."

"No promises, Harper, but I'll keep you posted."

He disconnected and looked down at Kane, who was upright in his seat by the window. "How does a little backcountry romp sound to you, my friend?"

Kane tilted his head and wagged his tail.

So it's unanimous.

As the train continued chugging west toward Chita, Tucker spent the remainder of the day strolling the train, twice bumping into Felice. They chatted briefly. Both times she deftly probed him about his plans.

Would he be heading directly on to Perm?

What would he do when he got there?

Which hotel had he booked?

He deflected his way through her questioning with lies and vague responses. Then he spent the rest of the afternoon seeking an easy place to jump from the train.

Unlike Hollywood portrayals, one could not simply open a window or slip out between cars. While in motion, all the train's exits were locked, either directly or behind secure doors. Such security left Tucker with two choices. Either he remained aboard and attempted to shake loose of Felice at the Chita station, where she likely already had accomplices lying in wait—or he discovered a way to get through those locked exits and leap blindly from the train in the dead of night.

Not great choices.

Still, in the end, he had little trouble making the decision, leaning upon his military training and mind-set. It came down to a simple adage drilled into him as an army ranger.

Act, don't react.

7

With the night darkening the berth's windows, Tucker made his final preparations. He had spent the last few hours of daylight walking through his plan, both mentally and physically, rehearsing his movements, along with timing and tracing the routines of the staff.

After one final task—a bit of breaking and entering—he called Ruth Harper.

"Did you get the photos I took of Felice's papers?"

Earlier in the day, he had snuck into her berth while she was out. He rifled carefully through her bags and compartments, discovering four passports, her credit cards, and a Swedish driver's license. He took photos of them all with his cell phone, left the room as tidy as he had entered it, and sent them to Sigma command. He wanted to know all he could about his opponent.

"Yes, we got the pictures and are running them through our databases."

"Hopefully, by the time you finish that, whatever you find will be irrelevant." Because he didn't plan to still be on the train by then. "In forty minutes, the train will have to slow down for a hairpin turn along the river outside Byankino."

"Which is *where* exactly in the vast expanse that is Siberia?"

"About three hundred miles east of Chita. A lot of small villages lie nearby and even more forest. That means lots of territory to lose ourselves in."

"I assume you don't mean that literally. The downside of such isolation is that you're going to have trouble finding transportation to Perm—at least low-visibility transport."

"I think I've got an idea about that."

"You know the saying: *No plan survives first contact with the enemy.*"

Tucker pictured Felice's face. "We've already made contact with the enemy. So it's time to get proactive."

"Your call. You're on the scene. Good luck with—"

From the door to his berth came a light knocking.

"I've got company," he said. "I'll call when I can. In the meantime, nothing to our friend in Perm, agreed?"

He didn't want his new itinerary—improvised as it was—leaked out to the wrong ears.

"Understood," Harper acknowledged.

He disconnected, walked to the door, and slid it open.

Felice leaned against the frame. "I trust it's not past your bedtime?"

The expression on her face was one of coy invitation. Not too much, but just enough.

Well practiced, he guessed.

"I was just reading Kane a bedtime story."

"I had hoped you'd join me for a late-night snack."

Tucker checked his watch. "The dining car is closed."

Felice smiled. "I have a secret cache in my berth. We could debate the literary merits of *Anna Karenina*."

When Tucker didn't immediately reply, Felice let a little sparkle into her eye and turned up the corners of her mouth ever so slightly.

She was very good, doing her best to keep her quarry close.

"Okay," he said. "Give me ten minutes. Your berth is . . . ?"

"Next car up, second on the left."

He closed the door, then turned to Kane. "Plans have changed, pal. We're going *now*."

Kane jumped off his seat. From beneath it, Tucker pulled free the shepherd's tactical vest and secured it in place. Next he opened his wardrobe, hauled out his already-prepped rucksack, and shoved his cold-weather gear—jacket, gloves, cap—into the top compartment.

Once ready, Tucker slowly slid open his berth door and peeked out. To the right, the direction of Felice's berth, the corridor was clear. To the left, an elderly couple stood at the window, staring out at the night.

With Kane at his heels, Tucker stepped out, slid the door shut behind him, and strode past the couple with a polite nod. He pushed through the glass connector door, crossed the small alcove between the two carriages, and pushed into the next sleeper car. The corridor ahead was thankfully empty.

Halfway down, he stopped and cocked his head. Kane was looking back in the direction they'd come.

Somewhere a door had opened, then banged shut.

"Come on," Tucker said and kept walking.

He crossed through the next sleeper car and reached a glass door at the end. Beyond it, he spotted the small alcove that connected this carriage with the baggage coach.

As he touched the door handle, a voice rose behind him, from the far end of the corridor. "Tucker?"

He recognized her voice but didn't turn. He slid open the door.

"Tucker, where are you going? I thought we were—"

He stepped into the alcove with Kane and slid the glass door closed behind him. The shepherd immediately let out a low growl.

Danger.

Tucker swung around and locked eyes with a porter sharing the same cramped space, standing in the shadows off to the side. He immediately recognized the man's hard face, along with his deadly expression. It was one of Felice's team. The man had exchanged his black leather duster for a porter's outfit. Equally caught by surprise, the man lunged for his jacket pocket.

Tucker didn't hesitate, kicking out with his heel, striking the man in the solar plexus. He fell back into the bulkhead, hitting his skull with a crack and slumping to the floor, knocked out.

He reached into the man's pocket and pulled out a Walther P22 semiautomatic; the magazine was full, one round in the chamber, the safety off. He reengaged the safety and shoved the P22 into his own belt, then rummaged through the man's clothes until he found a key ring and an identification badge.

The picture it bore didn't match the slack face before him, but Tucker recognized the photo. It was the porter who had shyly petted Kane when they had first boarded. With a pang of regret, he knew the man was likely dead. Felice and company were playing hardball.

Tucker took the keys, spun, and locked the connector door just as Felice reached it.

"What are you doing?" she asked, feigning concern, a hand at her throat. "Did you hurt that poor man?"

"He'll be fine. But what about the *real* porter?"

Doubt flickered in Felice's eyes. "You're talking crazy. Just come out and we can—"

"Your English accent is slipping, Ms. Nilsson."

Felice's face changed like a passing shadow, going colder, more angular. "So what's your plan then, Mr. Wayne?" she asked. "Jump from the train and go where? Siberia is hell. You won't last a day."

"We love a challenge."

"You won't make it. We'll hunt you down. Work with me instead. The two of us together, we can—"

"Stop talking," he growled.

Felice shut her mouth, but her eyes were sharp with hatred.

Tucker stepped away from the door and unlocked the baggage car. He pointed inside and touched Kane's side. "SCENT. BLOOD. RETURN."

His partner trotted into the darkened space. After ten seconds, Kane let out an alert whine. He reappeared at Tucker's side and sat down, staring back into the baggage car.

Tucker now knew the true fate of the unfortunate porter.

"We're leaving," he said to Felice. "If you're lucky, no one will find the body before you reach Chita."

"Who's to say you didn't kill him?" Felice said. "He caught you burglarizing the baggage car, you killed him, then jumped from the train. I'm a witness."

"If you want to draw that kind of attention to yourself, be my guest."

Tucker turned, stepped over the limp body of her partner, and entered the baggage car, closing the door behind him.

Kane led him to the porter's body. The man had been shoved under a set of steel bulkhead shelves. Judging from the bruising, he had been strangled to death.

"I'm sorry," Tucker murmured.

He donned his jacket, gloves, and cap, then slung his rucksack over his shoulder. At the rear of the car, he used the porter's keys to unlock the metal door. It swung open, and a rush of wind shoved him sideways. The rattling of the train's wheels filled his ears.

Directly ahead was the caboose door.

With Kane following closely, Tucker stepped

onto the open platform, shut the door behind him, then unlocked the caboose and stepped into the last car. He hurried across to the rear, through the last door—and a moment later, they were at the tail end of the Trans-Siberian Express, standing on a railed catwalk.

Beneath them, tracks flashed past. The sky was clear and black and studded with stars. To their right, a slope led to a partially frozen river; to their left, scattered snowdrifts. The locomotive was chugging up a slight grade, moving well below its average speed, but still much faster than Tucker would have liked.

He tugged the collar of his jacket up around his neck against the frigid night.

At his knee, Kane wagged his tail, excited. No surprise there. The shepherd was ready to go, come what may. Tucker knelt and cupped Kane's head in both of his hands, bringing his face down close.

"Who's a good boy?"

Kane leaned forward, until their noses touched.

"That's right. You are."

It was a routine of theirs.

Standing but keeping a grip on Kane's vest collar, Tucker navigated the catwalk steps until they were only a few feet above the racing ground. He poked his head past the caboose's side, looking forward, waiting, watching, until he saw a particularly thick snowdrift approaching.

"Ready, boy?" he said. "We're gonna jump! Steady now . . . steady . . ."

The snowdrift flashed into view. Tucker tossed his rucksack out into the darkness.

"Go, Kane! Jump!"

Without hesitation, the shepherd leaped out into the night.

Tucker waited a beat, then followed.

8

Tucker immediately realized all snowdrifts were not alike, especially in Siberia. Having gone through weeks of thawing and freezing, the drift's face had become armored by several inches of ice.

He hit the frozen surface hip-first, hoping to transition into a roll.

It was not to be.

He crashed through the top of the berm before his momentum flipped his legs up and over his head, sending him into a somersault down the drift's rear slope. He slammed onto his back and began sliding on his butt down the long, steep surface, his heels stuttering over the ice-encrusted snow. He tried jamming his elbows into the drift, to slow himself, but got no traction. To his right, alarmingly close, rose a lizard-back of boulders.

Above him, he heard a growl. He tipped his head back in time to see Kane's sleek form come galloping down the slope. The shepherd was there in seconds and clamped his teeth into Tucker's jacket collar. Once latched on, Kane sat down on his haunches and lifted his head, his strong back-muscles straining to take Tucker's weight.

Ahead and a few feet to the right, a sapling jutted from the snow. On impulse, he swung his left leg out, curled it, and hooked the trunk with his ankle. The momentum whipped him around, dragging Kane along, too, before jerking them both to a sudden stop.

All was quiet.

Tucker lay perfectly still and mentally scanned his body. Nothing seemed broken. He could feel Kane's weight hanging from his collar.

"Kane? How're you doing, pal?"

The shepherd replied with a muffled growl that Tucker recognized as roughly, *Okay, but now it's time for you to do something about this.*

"Hang on, give me a second . . ."

Tucker lifted his hips, freeing his right leg from under his butt, then extended it and hooked it around the sapling trunk above the other ankle. He set his teeth, flexed his legs, and dragged himself and Kane up the slope until he could reach out and grab the sapling with his left hand. He then reached back with his other arm and snagged Kane's vest.

The shepherd unclamped his jaws, and with Tucker's help, Kane scrabbled up the slope, his nails scratching on the ice until he reached the sapling.

Finally, Tucker let his legs uncurl and swung his body around, his feet again facing downhill. He slammed his heels into the ice several times until he had formed adequate footholds, then sprawled back to catch his breath.

Kane gave his hand a lick: relief and reassurance.

Tucker sat up and got his bearings. While plunging headlong down the slope in almost complete darkness, the angle had seemed precipitous. Now he could see the grade was no more than twenty-five degrees.

Could be worse . . .

To their right, fifty feet away, a line of skeletal birches and heavy Siberian pines snaked down the slope. Far below, a dark smudge ran perpendicular to the incline.

A river. But which one? For every charted stream and lake in Siberia, a dozen more were unrecorded and unnamed. Still, rivers meant civilization. Follow one and you'll inevitably find the other.

But first he had to find his rucksack. All his supplies were inside it.

He looked around, scanning the snow, but saw nothing. It was too dark to make out any fine details. And unimpeded, his rucksack could have rolled all the way down to the river, taking with it everything he needed to survive in this harsh climate.

He had only one hope: to borrow someone's keener eyes.

Tucker turned to Kane. "Spot rucksack," he ordered.

Thankfully, *rucksack* was one of Kane's thousand-word vocabulary. When traveling, most of Tucker's worldly possessions—and survival tools—were contained in that pack.

After twenty seconds, Kane let out a low-key yelp.

Tucker twisted around and followed Kane's gaze uphill and sideways, toward the tree line. Even with Kane's guidance, it took Tucker another thirty seconds to spot it. The rucksack had become wedged into the fork of a white-barked birch tree.

He rolled onto his hands and knees, grasped Kane's vest collar with his left hand, then began sidling toward the tree line, kicking toeholds into the ice as he went. It was slow work, eating up too much time. Halfway there, Tucker realized Kane needed no support. The shepherd's nails worked as natural pitons.

Working together, they reached the forest of Siberian pines and birches. Under the shelter of the bower, the snow was powdery and soft. Leaving Kane propped against a trunk, he climbed upward and angled toward the tree into which the rucksack was wedged.

In the distance, a branch snapped.

The sound echoed across the night's stillness—then faded.

Tucker froze. Where had the sound come from? *Above*, he decided.

Slowly Tucker reached forward, grasped the nearest trunk, and laid himself flat. He scanned uphill, looking for movement. After ten seconds of silence, there came another distinctive sound: a muffled *crunch* of a footstep in the snow.

He strained as silence followed—then another *crunch*.

Somewhere above, a person was moving—not casually, but with purpose. Either a hunter or Felice. If so, she was even more dangerous than he'd anticipated. Almost fifteen minutes had passed since he and Kane had leaped from the train. Felice would have had to pinpoint their position, choose her own jumping-off point, then backtrack here at a running pace.

Possible, he realized, but such speed spoke to her skill as a hunter.

But was it her?

He turned his head. Twenty feet below, Kane lay on his belly, half buried in the softer snow. His eyes were fixed on Tucker, waiting for orders.

He signaled with his free hand: *move deeper into the trees and hunker down.*

On quiet feet, Kane moved off. Within seconds he was lost from sight.

Tucker returned his attention to their visitor. Using his elbows and knees, he burrowed himself into the powdery snowpack until only his eyes were exposed. Two minutes passed. Then five. The footsteps continued moving downhill at a stalking pace: step, pause . . . step, pause. Finally, a shadowy figure appeared from behind a tree, then stopped and crouched down.

The person's build was slim and athletic in a form-fitting dark jacket, a cut that was too modern, too tactical. Definitely not a local rural hunter. The head turned, and from beneath a dark wool cap, a wisp of blond shone in the stark starlight.

Along with something else.

A rifle barrel poked from behind a shoulder. How had Felice smuggled a sniper rifle onto the train? As he watched, she unslung her weapon and cradled it against her chest.

She was forty feet up the slope and to his right. If she kept to her line, she would pass within feet of his trapped rucksack. Not good. He was now playing cat and mouse with a SIG-trained sniper. The solution was simple if not so easily executed: kill Felice while he still had the element of surprise.

Moving with exaggerated slowness, he reached to his belt and withdrew the stolen P22. He brought it up along his body and extended it toward Felice. He aimed the front sight on her center mass, clicked off the safety, and took up the slack on the trigger.

What happened next Tucker would write off later as a soldier's intuition.

Still crouched, Felice pushed backward and disappeared behind a tree.

Crap.

He kept his gun steady, waiting for a clear shot, but from the stealthy noise of retreat, Felice was on the move, heading back up the slope, using the trunks to screen herself. After five minutes she was gone, but he could guess her plan. She intended to head deeper into the trees, then back down in a flanking maneuver. She must be gambling that he and Kane hadn't made it to the river yet, and that they didn't know she was tracking them. She would set up an ambush down below and wait.

She would be in for a *long* wait, Tucker decided.

He gave Felice another frigid five minutes' head start, then pocketed the P22, eased himself sideways out of his burrow, and began crawling toward his rucksack. He reached the tree, grabbed the bag's strap, and pulled it down to him.

He then went dead still to listen.

Silence.

He donned the rucksack, then aimed his hand

toward Kane's last known position and signaled, trusting the shepherd had followed his training and kept Tucker in view.

Return, he motioned.

He waited, but it did not take long. A hushed footfall sounded above him. He craned his neck and found Kane crouched in the snow a few feet away. Tucker reached up, grabbed a handful of neck fur, and gave his partner a reassuring massage.

"FOLLOW," he whispered in his partner's ear.

Together, they began the slow climb upward, back toward the rail line.

11:50 P.M.

It took longer than he'd hoped to reach the top of the slope—only to discover that a towering, wind-swept drift blocked the way to the tracks, a sheer wall, three times as tall as Tucker. He would have to sidestep his way across the slope and hope to find where he had originally crashed through it so they could cross back to the railway.

Tucker took only a single step away from the tree line and out onto that treacherous, icy expanse— when he felt something shift beneath his boot. In the back of his mind he thought, *log*, but he had no time to react. The thigh-sized chunk of tree trunk, buried under a few inches of snow and held fast by the thinnest film of ice, broke free and started rolling downhill, taking Tucker and a swath of snow with it.

Avalanche.

Tucker pushed Kane aside, knowing the shepherd would try to latch on to him again. "EVADE!" he hissed.

The order countermanded Kane's instinct to protect him. The shepherd hesitated only a moment before leaping sideways and back into the shelter of the tree line.

Tucker knew he was in trouble. The sliding mass of snow was bulldozing over him, propelling him faster and faster down the slope. With the rucksack preventing him from rolling over, Tucker paddled his arms and legs, trying to mount the snow wave, to ride its tumult, but it was no use. Doing his best to survive, he drove one elbow into the ground, leaning into it. He spun on his belly until he was aimed headfirst down the slope, still on his belly.

Fifty yards away, the river loomed. The surface was black and motionless. With any luck, it was frozen over. If not, he was doomed.

Tucker's mind raced.

Where was Kane? Where was Felice?

No doubt she'd heard the miniavalanche—but was he visible within the snowy surge? He got his answer. Ahead and to his right, an orange flare spat in the night, coming from a clump of scrub bushes near the waterline.

A muzzle flash.

If nothing else, his headlong plunge had made Felice miss her first shot. The second would be closer. The third would be dead-on. Tucker reached back, freed the P22 from his pocket with a struggle, and pointed it toward the site of that flash.

He felt a sting at his neck.

Grazed by a bullet.

Ignoring the pain, he squeezed the trigger twice, wild potshots, but maybe enough to discourage the sniper.

Then he hit the river's berm and launched into the air. His heart lurched into his throat. A heartbeat later, he belly-flopped onto the ice, bounced once, then found himself rolling, flat-spinning across the river's surface. He slammed into a clump of trees jutting from the ice and came to an abrupt, agonizing stop.

Gasping for air, he rolled onto his side and fought the urge to curl into a painful ball.

He swept his arms across the ice, searching for his pistol. It had been knocked from his cold fingers as he struck the river.

Where—?

Then he spotted it. The P22 lay a few feet away in a tangle of dead branches. He reached toward it.

A chunk of ice exploded at his fingertips, shards stinging his face. The gunshot sounded like the muffled snap of a branch. She was using a noise suppressor.

"Not another inch!" Felice Nilsson called from somewhere to his right.

He craned his neck and spotted her. She was forty feet away, kneeling at the river's edge, the rifle tucked to her shoulder. At this range, she could put a bullet in his ear.

Instead, she shifted her rifle ever so slightly, from a kill shot to something that would maim and hurt. The moon, reflecting off the ice, cast the scene in stark contrast.

"Tell me where you were scheduled to meet Bukolov," she demanded.

In answer, Tucker slowly lifted his hand from the ice.

"Careful!" she barked. "I'll take it off. Don't doubt it for a moment."

"I don't," Tucker replied, raising his palm, as if pleading for her to be calm, but instead he pointed one finger at her.

"What are you—?"

Tucker rotated his hand, fingers pointing toward the ice.

"Good-bye, Felice," he said through chattering teeth.

From out of the forest behind her, Kane burst forth.

A moment ago, Tucker had noted the shepherd's furtive approach, a mere shift of shadows lit by the reflected moonlight. Kane obeyed Tucker's signal, a simple one.

Attack.

Kane races across the gap, bunching his haunches at the last moment.

He has followed the trail of the woman, catching her scent in the woods, picking it out of the spoor of deer and rabbit. He recognizes it from the train, remembers the hatred in her voice. Next came the muffled shots of the rifle and the sharper cracks of a pistol.

His other was in danger, threatened.

The last command remained etched behind his eyes.
Evade.

So he kept hidden, following the whiff of gun smoke, the musk of the hot skin, ever down toward the flow of water and creaking ice.

There, beyond the woman, he sees his partner out on the ice. He holds back a whine of concern, wanting to call out.

Then movement.

A hand raised.

A command given.

He obeys that now.

The woman turns, fear bursting from her skin. As she swings, her gun barrel dips slightly.

He sees and explodes with his hind end, springing high.

As Tucker watched, Kane slammed into Felice like a linebacker, his jaws clamping on to her arm before the pair hit the ice. Felice screamed and thrashed, but she held tight to the rifle's stock.

A sniper to the end, Tucker thought. *Lose your rifle, lose your life.*

He shoved up, ready to help his partner—only to hear a sharp *crack* erupt beneath him. A rift snaked outward from his body and headed toward Kane and Felice. Dark, icy water gushed through the fault line.

"Felice, stop struggling!" Tucker called. "Lie still!"

Panicked, deaf to his warning, she continued to struggle, her left hand still clenched around the rifle stock.

He forced himself to his knees, then his feet. The ice shifted beneath him, dipping sideways. He leaped forward, balancing on the teetering slabs as the river broke under him. He hopscotched toward Kane and Felice.

The crack reached them, then spider-webbed outward, enveloping them. With a whoosh, the ice opened up. The pair dropped headlong into the water.

With his heart thundering in his ears, Tucker stumbled forward. Fifteen feet from the hole, he threw himself into a slide, on his belly, his arms extended, trying to distinguish between the two shapes thrashing in the icy water. He saw a pale white hand slapping at the ice, spotted Kane's head surge from the water, his snout pointed at the sky.

The shepherd gasped, coughing.

Sliding parallel to the hole, Tucker grabbed Kane's vest collar and jerked hard, plucking the wet dog from the water.

From the corner of his eye, Tucker saw Felice's rifle jut out of the water; the barrel swung toward them.

Even now, she hadn't given up the fight.

She slapped at the ice with a bloody arm, while trying to bring her rifle to bear with the other hand.

Tucker rolled onto his side and kicked off with his heel, spinning on his hip. He snapped out with his other leg and struck the rifle, sending it skittering across the ice and into the snow along the opposite bank.

With a final, spasmodic flailing, Felice's arm vanished underwater, her body pulled down by the current, and she disappeared from view.

Together, Tucker and Kane crawled to the bank,

but both kept watch on the shattered hole. He half expected Felice to reappear. Only after two minutes did he feel confident enough to state, "I think she's gone."

Still, he kept a vigil at the bank, probing his neck wound. The gouge was narrow but deep. Beside him, Kane did a full body shake, casting out a shower of icy water, his tail wagging off the last few drops.

Tucker checked over his partner for injuries. For his efforts, he earned a warm lick to his cold cheek, his dog's message easy to read: *Glad we're still alive.*

"I know, pal, me too," he muttered.

He shrugged off his rucksack, unzipped the side pocket, and dug out his first-aid kit. Working from feel alone, he squeezed a thick stripe of surgical glue into the wound and pinched the edges together, clenching his teeth against the sting.

Once finished, a shiver shook through him. Kane's haunches also quaked against the cold. In this weather, the effects of cold water were amplified. Hypothermia couldn't be far off.

"Let's go," he said, ready to set off, but not before completing one last duty.

Moving fifty yards downriver, he found a patch of thicker ice that easily bore his weight, allowing him to cross to the opposite bank. He walked back upstream and retrieved Felice's rifle. He examined his prize. It was the Swedish Army's standard sniper rifle: a PSG-90—variant D. After a quick inspection for damage and followed by a few quick twists and turns, he had the weapon broken down into its four component parts, none of which was longer than eighteen inches.

"Now to get warm."

He and Kane found a cluster of trees and made a temporary camp. An abandoned bird's nest and some scraps of birch bark served as perfect kindling. Within a few minutes, he had a fire blazing.

He stripped off Kane's vest and hung it over the fire to dry.

With no prompting, the shepherd stretched out beside the flames and gave a contented *hmmph*.

Settled and warm, Tucker did a quick check of his GPS unit, pinpointing their location. "Time to find out how big of a mess we're in," he mumbled.

According to the map, they were within easy walking distance of two villages: Borshchovka and Byankino. It was tempting to head for one of them, but he decided against it. Felice was clever. She surely had given her partners—or whoever hired her—a situation report after jumping from the train. If so, the two nearby villages would be the first places any search party would visit.

Of the hundreds of axioms that the army had drummed into his head, one matched this situation perfectly: *Avoid being where your enemy expects you to be.*

So he extended his search on the map. Ten miles to the northeast was the small town of Nerchinsk. There, he could regroup and decide how best to reach Perm and his contact.

He stared at the dog, at the crisp stars.

It would be easy to abandon this mission.

But blood had been spilled.

He pictured the dead porter's ashen face, remembering his smile, his joy while petting Kane. The memory, the responsibility, reminded him of another adage, burned into every ranger's mind: *Take the initiative, and get the mission done.*

He intended to do just that.

9

Their day hike to Nerchinsk quickly became a slog.

Around them, the landscape slowly changed from highland forest into a series of low, snow-blanketed hills, one stacked upon another, before dropping into a valley east of the town of Nerchinsk.

For the first five miles, he and Kane found themselves wading through thigh-high snow punctuated by snowdrifts twice as tall as Tucker. By early afternoon, they found themselves walking into a strong wind that found its bone-chilling way into every nook and cranny of Tucker's parka. For his part, Kane was in heaven, plowing through the powdery snow, occasionally popping to the surface, his eyes bright and tongue lolling.

Only twice did they see any signs of life. The first was a hunter, spotted in the distance, walking along a tree line. The second was a rusted fifties-era armored personnel carrier loaded down with dozens of laughing children. The rumble of the diesel engine reached them from a narrow road headed toward Nerchinsk.

Finally, eight hours after they set out and with only a few hours of daylight left, they crested a hill and the first signs of civilization came into view: a gold-domed, white-walled Russian orthodox church surrounded by a dilapidated split-rail fence that marked off a small graveyard. Many of the church's windows were boarded over, and the eaves drooped in several spots.

Tucker found a safe position behind a nearby boulder and pulled out his binoculars. A few hundred yards east of the church spread a collection of saltbox-style homes, painted in a variety of pastel blues, yellows, and reds. The town of Nerchinsk appeared quiet, with only a handful of pedestrians in view, along with a couple of boxy economy cars that puttered down the icy streets spewing clouds of exhaust.

He panned his binoculars beyond the town's outskirts, taking in the lay of the land. To the northwest, he spotted what looked to be a dilapidated airfield.

No, he realized on closer inspection.

Not air*field*, but air *base*.

Several of the base's buildings and hangars bore the red-star roundel of the Russian Air Force. Had it been abandoned? Focusing on the hangars, he was pleased to see the doors were clear of snowdrifts. *Someone* was maintaining the place, which in turn raised his hope that there might be operational aircraft.

He returned his attention to the small town, searching for either a motel or a general store. He glimpsed a soldier in an olive-drab greatcoat standing on a corner, smoking. This was no old veteran, but someone on active duty. His uniform was tidy and clean, his cap settled squarely on his head. The man finished his cigarette, tossed away the butt, then turned and headed down a side street.

"Where'd you come from?" Tucker muttered.

He kept scanning, following what he hoped was the man's path—then spotted a second anomaly. The main rotor hub of a helicopter jutted above one of the buildings at the edge of town. The chopper was big, tall enough to dwarf the building that shielded it. From the hub's mottled gray paint, it had to be military.

He didn't know what such a presence here implied, but either way, he and Kane needed to find shelter. They were both cold, tired, and with nightfall coming, the temperatures would soon plummet below zero.

He returned his attention to the ramshackle church. For the next thirty minutes, as darkness slowly enveloped them, he watched for any signs of life.

Nothing.

Still, he used the cover of snowdrifts and trees to make his way down to the churchyard. With Kane at his side, he crawled through the fence and walked around to the porch. He tried the knob. Unlocked. They slipped through and into the dim interior.

They were greeted by a wave of warmth and the tang of smoke and manure. Directly ahead, a wood-burning stove cast the interior in a flickering orange glow. A metal flue led upward from the stove toward a second floor.

Tucker kept near the door, waiting for his eyes to adjust, then called out in Russian. "*Dobriy večer?*"

No reply.

He tried again, a little louder this time, and again got no response.

Sighing, he followed the faded red carpet runner down to the domed nave. Beyond a small altar, a flaking, gold-painted wall bore religious icons and tapestries. There, he found a door, one likely leading to the church's administrative area.

He opened it with a protest of old hinges and discovered a spiral staircase. With Kane in tow, he scaled up it, ending in a small office area. Seeing the wood-slat cot in the corner, the freestanding wardrobe, and a closet-sized kitchenette, Tucker surmised it also served as a living space.

Judging by the cobwebs, no one had been up here for months. Above his head, the woodstove's pipe gushed warm air.

It would do.

He shrugged off his pack and cold-weather gear and tossed them on the cot where Kane had already settled. He spent a few minutes searching the kitchenette but found nothing save a few broken plates, a rusty tool chest under the sink, and a tarnished silver fork. In the wardrobe, he discovered an old patched greatcoat, its shoulders piled with dust.

"Looks like it's home sweet home, eh, Kane?"

The shepherd gave a tired wag of his tail.

Starving, Tucker fixed a quick meal of coffee and

dehydrated camping rations, preparing enough food for both him and Kane. An upper-story window, frosted with grime, allowed him to study the village as he ate. A stranger would stand out like a sore thumb here—and raise too much suspicion—especially one who could not speak Russian with flawless fluency.

He needed a remedy, a cover.

After a bit of thought, Tucker rummaged through the tool chest and found a spool of wire. He clipped four short pieces and, using duct tape from his rucksack, sculpted the pieces into a crude equivalent of a teenager's orthodontic mouth guard. He slipped the construction between his lower lip and gum, packing it in tightly. He checked himself in the room's grungy mirror, fingering his face.

To the casual eye, it would appear Nerchinsk's latest visitor had a badly broken jaw. It would give him an easy excuse not to talk.

"Time to see a man about a plane ride," Tucker said, testing out his contraption. The sound he emitted was barely intelligible.

Perfect.

Next, he donned the dusty greatcoat from the wardrobe and tugged his *ushanka* cap back on. He pulled its brim lower over his eyebrows.

"You stay here," he ordered Kane. "Out of sight."

The shepherd, fed and warm, didn't argue.

Tucker climbed back down and slipped out the church's front door. With his shoulders hunched, he shuffled toward Nerchinsk along a road of slush and mud. He adopted what he hoped was the posture of a man who'd spent his life in the gray, frozen expanse of Siberia. The weather made that easier. The temperature had plummeted another twenty degrees. His breath billowed thickly in the air, and the icy mud squelched under his boots.

By now, the streets were empty. The yellow glow of life shone through a few dirty windows, along with the occasional flicker of neon signs, but nothing else. He made his way to the corner where the soldier had been smoking earlier. He did his best to trace the man's steps until he was a block from the helicopter.

He studied its bulk surreptitiously.

It was certainly a military aircraft: an Mi-28 Havoc attack helicopter. He knew such a craft's specs by heart. It had racks and pods enough to carry forty rockets, along with a mounted 30 mm chain gun.

But this Havoc's exterior bore no Russian roundels or emblems. Instead, it had been painted in a jagged gray/black pattern. He didn't recognize the markings. It could be the FSB—formerly known as the KGB. But what would such a unit be doing out here, in the back end of nowhere?

Tucker knew the most likely answer.

Looking for me.

Two figures stepped out from behind the chopper's tail rotor. One was dressed in a uniform, the other in civilian clothes.

Tucker retreated out of sight—but not before noting the shoulder emblems on the uniform. A red starburst against a black shield.

He had been wrong.

These men weren't *FSB*, but rather *GRU. Glavnoye*

Razvedyvatel'noye Upravleniye served as the intelligence arm of the Russian Ministry of Defense. For covert operations, the GRU relied almost solely on Spetsnaz soldiers—the Thoroughbreds of the already-impressive Russian Special Forces stable.

If they're after me . . .

He hurried down the street, knowing his departure from this region was even more urgent—as was his overdue call to Ruth Harper.

7:55 P.M.

Tucker wandered the streets until he found a lively tavern. The neon sign above the door was in Cyrillic, but the raucous laughter and smell of beer was advertisement enough for the establishment.

This was as good a place as any to start.

He took a moment to make sure his mouth prosthetic was in place, then took a deep breath and pushed through the door.

A wall of heat, cigarette smoke, and body odor struck him like a fist to the face. A babble of country Russian—punctuated by loud guffaws and scattered curses—greeted him. Not that anyone paid attention to his arrival.

Tucker hunched his shoulders and wove his way through the mass of bodies toward what he assumed was the bar. With a bit of jostling and occasional grunting through his prosthetic, he found himself standing at a long, knotty pine counter.

Miraculously, the bartender noted his newest customer immediately and walked over. He barked something that Tucker assumed was a request for his order.

As answer, Tucker grunted vaguely.

"Eh?"

He cleared his throat and mumbled again.

The bartender leaned forward, cocking an ear.

Tucker opened his lips a little wider, exposing his mouth guard, then pantomimed a fist striking his jaw, ending it with a tired shrug.

The bartender nodded his understanding.

Tucker jerked his thumb toward a neighboring mug of beer. A moment later, a glass was pounded down in front of him, sloshing froth over the rim. He passed over a wad of rubles and pocketed the change.

Tucker felt a wave of relief. Providing no one else demanded a higher level of exchange, this might just work.

Clumsily sipping beer through his mouthpiece, he began scanning the bar for soldiers. There were a dozen or more, all army, but from the state of their clothes, none of these were active duty. In Russia, many veterans kept and wore their uniforms after leaving service, partly for necessity and partly for economic leverage. It was common practice for citizens to slip a former soldier a coin or pay for a drink or a meal. This was as much for charity as it was for insurance. Having impoverished or starving killers roaming the streets was best avoided.

Satisfied the bar was free of GRU operatives, he returned his attention to his primary interest: getting out of this place and reaching Perm. He searched for anyone who might be connected to the neighboring air base, but he spotted nothing overt. He might have to do this the hard way and—

"Your dog is beautiful," a gruff voice said at his shoulder. He spoke passable English, but heavily accented. "German shepherd?"

Tucker turned to find a short man in his sixties, with long white hair and a grizzled beard. His eyes shone a sharp ice-blue.

"Eh?" Tucker grunted.

"Oh, I see," the stranger said. "Let me guess, you are a traveling prizefighter."

Tucker's heart pounded as he glanced around. None of the other patrons seemed to be paying attention.

The man crooked his finger at Tucker and leaned closer.

"I know you are not Russian, my friend. I heard you talking to your dog at the church. You'd best follow me."

The older man turned and picked his way through the crowd, which seemed to part before him, the patrons nodding deferentially at him.

Nervous, but with no other choice, Tucker followed after him, ending up at a table in the bar's far corner, beside a stone-hearth fireplace.

With the table to themselves, the man stared at Tucker through narrow eyes. "A good disguise, actually. You have mastered the Siberian stoop—you know, the hunched shoulders, the lowered chin. The cold grinds it into you up here, bends you. So much so, if you live here long enough, it becomes one's posture."

Tucker said nothing.

"A cautious man. Good, very good. You have seen the soldiers, I assume? The Moscow boys, I mean, with the commandos and the fancy helicopter. It's the first time in years we've seen anyone like them here. And it's the *only* time an American with a giant dog has set up camp in my home. Not a coincidence, I am guessing."

Tucker said nothing.

"If I were going to turn you in, I would have already done so."

He considered this, recognized the truth of it, and decided it was time to take a chance. Covertly he removed his mouthpiece, then took a sip of beer.

"Belgian Malinois," Tucker said.

"Pardon me?"

"He's not a German. He's Belgian. And for your sake, he better be safe and sound where I left him."

"He is," the stranger said with a smile, holding out a hand. "I am Dimitry."

"I'm—"

"Do not tell me your name. The less I know, the better. I am Nerchinsk's bishop. Well, for this town and a few other villages nearby. Mine is a small flock, but I love them all the same."

The old man glanced affectionately across the crowded bar.

Tucker remembered how the others had deferred to the man, stepping out of his way. "Your English is very good."

"Satellite dish. I watch American television. And the Internet, of course. As for your Russian, well, it is—"

"Crap," Tucker finished with a smile. "But how did you know about me and my dog?"

"I was out hunting and spotted your tracks outside of town. I followed them back to my church."

"Sorry for the intrusion."

"Think nothing of it. Orthodox churches are intended as sanctuaries. The heat is always on, so to speak. And speaking of heat . . ." The man nodded to the bar's front door. "It seems you've drawn a fair share of your own heat."

Tucker shrugged. "I'm not sure if the soldiers are in town because of me, but I'm not a big fan of coincidences either."

"The last time we saw such a group in the area was before the wall came down. They were looking for a foreigner, an Englishman."

"What happened to him?"

"They found him two miles out of town. Shot him and buried him on the spot. I do not know any of the details, but he was on the run, like you and your dog."

Tucker must have paled.

Dimitry patted his arm. "Ah, but you have an advantage the Englishman lacked."

"Which is?"

"You have a friend in town."

Tucker still felt ill at ease and expressed his concern. "Do you know the phrase *look a gift horse in the mouth*?"

"As in being suspicious of good luck?"

"More or less."

"I understand your concern. So let me dispense with the formalities and settle things. Have you or do you intend to wreak havoc on Mother Russia?"

"No."

"Will you harm my flock?"

"Not unless they try to harm me."

"*Nyet*, of course not." Dimitry waved his hand dismissively. "So with that business dispensed of, I am going to assume you are simply a lost traveler, and those Moscow thugs were chasing you for stealing soap from your last hotel."

"Fair enough."

"I had my fill of the government back in the eighties, when I served as a paratrooper in Afghanistan. I killed a lot of jihadists, and the army gave me a lot of shiny ribbons. But now I am forgotten, like most of us from that war—at least the ones who truly got our knives dirty. I love my country, but not so much my government. Does that make sense to you?"

"More than you'd imagine."

"Good. Then that, my wayward friend, is why I am going to help you. I assume you and your keen-eyed partner spotted the air base?"

"We did."

"Do you know how to fly a plane?"

"No."

"Neither do I. But I have a friend who does. In fact—" Dimitry looked around the bar, half standing, before spotting what he was looking for. "There he is."

Dimitry pointed toward a pine table near the window where two men were sitting.

"Which one?"

"No, no, *underneath*."

Tucker peered closer until he could make out a figure under the table. His legs were splayed out, and his head sharply canted to accommodate for the tabletop pressing against his skull. A ribbon of dribble ran from the corner of his mouth to his coat sleeve.

"That is Fedor," Dimitry said as introduction. "Our postman. He flies in our mail."

"He's drunk."

"Massively," Dimitry agreed. "It is night, after all. In the morning, though, Fedor will be sober. Of course, that does not entirely solve your problem, does it? The Moscow thugs will be patrolling the skies during the day. Your departure must wait until tomorrow night, which means we must keep Fedor sober for, well, longer than he is accustomed." He paused with a frown. "Now I begin to see a flaw in our plan. No matter. This is a bridge we will cross later."

"Let's cross it now," Tucker said. "Fedor can't be your only pilot."

"*Nyet*, but he is the most experienced. And he is a first-rate smuggler. Nerchinsk does not live on bread alone, you see. For the right amount of money, he will get you out, right under the noses of these government men, and never tell a soul. And, as it happens, he loves dogs very much."

Tucker wasn't reassured one bit.

Dimitry downed his drink and stood up. "Come, let us collect him!"

10

Tucker woke just before dawn—a soldier's habit. With a groan from his back and a twinge of pain from his grazed neck, he pushed up from the church's attic cot and swung his bare feet to the floor.

The prior night, he and Dimitry had hauled the drunken postman across town to the church. On the way here, they had run into a trio of Spetsnaz soldiers, but none of them paid any heed, save for a few laughing gibes at the inebriated state of their companion. At the church, Dimitry offered Tucker and Kane his cot and rolled out a pair of hay-filled bedrolls for him and Fedor.

Tucker searched the attic space now, realizing he was alone.

Fedor and Dimitry were gone, along with Kane.

Quashing his panic, he went downstairs to find a naked Fedor sitting before the blazing wood-stove, seated in a puddle of his own sweat. Beside him stood a plastic milk jug half filled with a clear liquid. Sober now, the man looked younger, more midthirties than forties, with dark lanky hair and a wrestler's build, most of it covered in a mat of fur, a true Russian bear.

A few feet away, Kane sat on his haunches, watching curiously. He acknowledged Tucker's arrival with a wag of his tail.

Fedor lifted the jug, tipped it to his mouth, and took a long gulp.

Bleary eyed, Fedor sloshed the container in Tucker's direction and croaked, "*Vaduh. Natural-naya vaduh.*"

Tucker pieced together the words.

Natural water.

This must be part of Fedor's sobering ritual: extreme heat and copious amounts of water.

"Priest tells me fly," Fedor added in badly broken English. "Fly you tonight."

Tucker nodded. "*Spasiba.*"

"*Da.* Your Russian bad." He held his head between his palms. "Make my head hurt."

I don't think it's from my bad accent.

"Your dog beautiful. I love. May buy him, yes, please?"

"No, please."

Fedor shrugged and guzzled more water. "Trade fly for dog, *da?*"

"*Nyet.* Money."

Dimitry arrived, carrying in some firewood. "You see, he is already much better. Let us discuss arrangements. I will translate. It will go much faster." Dimitry spoke to his friend in rapid-fire Russian, then said to Tucker, "He will fly you tonight, but there will be surcharges."

"Go ahead."

"It does not translate well, but first you must pay him extra for missing his drinking tonight. Next, you must pay him extra because you are foreign. Finally, you must pay him extra because the Moscow men are looking for you."

"Did you tell him they were looking for me?"

"Of course not. Fedor is a drunk, not an idiot."

"Next?"

"He likes your dog—"

"Forget it. Next."

Dimitry said something to Fedor, listened, then replied to Tucker, "Where do you wish to go?"

He had already considered this. They'd likely never reach Perm in Fedor's plane. It was too far. Besides, he wasn't inclined to give away his final destination. The best hope was to reach a closer major city, one that offered plenty of options for his final leg to Perm.

"I need to reach Novosibirsk," he said.

"Very far," Dimitry translated. "It will take a lot of fuel."

Tucker waited while Fedor continued to mutter, making a big show of counting on his fingers and screwing up his face. Finally he said, in English, "Nine thousand ruble."

Tucker did the rough conversion in his head: 275 U.S. dollars. A bargain. Struggling to keep the smile off his face, he considered this for a bit, then shrugged. "Deal."

Fedor spit into his hand and held it out.

Reluctantly, Tucker shook it.

1:15 P.M.

After the fierce negotiation, Tucker and Kane spent the remainder of the morning in the church, while Dimitry and Fedor ran various errands, gathering supplies and readying the plane.

Early in the afternoon, Dimitry returned with provisions and news. "I learned there are *two* other GRU units in the region."

Tucker stood up from the woodstove. "What? Where?"

"They are positioned *west* of here, around the town of Chita. But like here, they are lazy, just smoking and lounging in hotels, *da*?"

Chita?

That was the next major stopover along the Trans-Siberian Railway. But what did that mean? He gave it some thought and came to only one conclusion. The fact that the search teams weren't actively patrolling for him, only lounging about, suggested Felice might not have had time to get out word that he had escaped the train. She must have hoped a sniper's bullet could correct her failure before her superiors learned the truth.

That was good—at least for the moment.

But as soon as the train reached Chita, and it was discovered he wasn't aboard, the search units would shift into high gear, including the unit here.

Tucker pulled out his train schedule and checked his watch. The train would reach Chita in three hours, about four hours before sunset. That meant he and Fedor couldn't wait for nightfall before departing.

"We need to take off early," he told Dimitry. "Now, if we can."

"Not possible, my friend. The fuel bowser is broken down. Fedor is working on it."

"How long?"

"I don't know, but I will go find out."

As Dimitry left, Kane walked over, sat down, and leaned against Tucker's leg, sensing the tension.

Tucker patted Kane's neck, reassuring his partner. "We've been in worse spots than this."

Not much worse, but worse.

He set his watch's countdown timer.

Three hours from now, when it was discovered he was no longer aboard the train, Nerchinsk would be swarming with Spetsnaz soldiers, all hunting for him.

2:36 P.M.

An hour later, Dimitry burst through the church's doors. The panic in his face drew both Tucker and Kane to their feet.

"They are coming!" Dimitry called out, quickly shutting the doors behind him. "The Spetsnaz."

Tucker checked his watch. It was too early. The train hadn't reached Chita yet. "Slow down. Tell me."

Dimitry crossed to them. "The soldiers are out patrolling the rest of the town. They do not seem to be in a hurry, but one is coming here nevertheless."

What did this sudden change mean? If the GRU unit had been activated, the Spetsnaz would be breaking down doors and moving Nerchinsk's inhabitants into the open. Maybe the local commander was only trying to break up the monotony.

Bored soldiers are ineffective soldiers, he thought.

Still, as Dimitry had said, it didn't matter. One of them was coming.

Tucker donned his pack and tightened the straps on Kane's vest.

"This way," Dimitry said.

He led them toward a side corner of the sanctuary and knelt before a tapestry-draped table. He scooted the table aside, lifted the rug beneath, then used the hunting knife in his belt to pry up a section of planking. It lifted free to reveal a vertical tunnel.

"What—?"

"Cossacks, Nazis, Napoleon . . . who can say? It was here long before I arrived. Get in!"

"Jump down, Kane," Tucker ordered.

Without hesitation, the shepherd dove into the opening. He landed in the dirt, then disappeared to the left.

Tucker followed, discovering the shaft was only a meter tall.

Dimitry hovered over the opening. "Follow the tunnel. It exits about two hundred meters north of here. Make your way to the east side of the air base and wait for me there. There is a shack near a crushed section of fence. Easy to find."

With that, Dimitry shut the hatch. A moment later, what little light filtered through the slats was blotted out as the rug and table were slid back into place.

A stiff pounding on the church's door echoed down to him.

Dimitry's footsteps clopped across the wooden floor, followed by the creak of hinges. "*Dobriy den!*" the bishop called out.

A sullen voice replied in kind, but Tucker didn't wait to hear what followed.

He headed off in a low crouch with Kane. After ten paces, he felt it safe enough to pull out his LED penlight and pan the cone of light down the tunnel. The dirt walls bristled with tree roots, while the roof was shored up with planks, some rotten, others new. Clearly someone had been maintaining the tunnel.

They continued on. For Kane, the going was easy as he trotted forward, scouting. Tucker had to move in a low waddle that had his thighs burning after only a few minutes. He ignored the pain and kept going. After another ten minutes, the tunnel ended at a short ladder entangled with tree roots.

A few inches above his head was a hatch. He craned his neck and pressed his ear against the wood and listened for a full minute. He heard nothing. He crouched back down beside Kane and checked his watch.

In a little over an hour, the train would reach Chita.

He had to be airborne by then.

Tucker recalled his mental map of the area. If Dimitry was correct, the hatch above his head should exit somewhere in the patch of forest that bordered the church grounds. From there, the air base lay more than a mile away, through scrub forest and open fields. Normally an easy hike, but he would have to contend with deep snowdrifts, while keeping out of sight of the newly patrolling soldiers.

He was not normally a pessimist, but he could not dismiss the pure logistics of the situation.

We'll never make it.

11

Tucker crouched beside Kane and carefully swung the hatch closed. The tunnel had exited beneath the shelter of a pine. Still, he swept fresh snow over the hatch to keep it hidden. Once satisfied, he wriggled his way out from beneath the boughs and into the open.

Kane followed, shaking snow from his fur.

"Ready for a little jog?" Tucker asked, acknowledging the press of time. He pointed east through the edges of a scrub forest. "Scout."

Kane took off, bounding through the snow, bulldozing a path.

Tucker trotted after him.

They made relatively quick progress, covering three-quarters of a mile in an hour. He could have gone faster, but he did his best to stay below snowy ridgelines, out of direct sight of the town proper. Now was not the time to be spotted by a stray soldier.

As they reached a stand of birches, within a few hundred yards of the airbase, Tucker's watch vibrated on his wrist.

He glanced down, seeing the countdown timer had gone off.

Grimacing, he pictured the train pulling into the Chita station.

How long until someone realizes I'm not on board?

With no choice, he urged Kane onward and followed, pushing through his exhaustion, focusing on his next step through the deep snow.

After another ten minutes, they reached the edge of the air base. The perimeter fence lay fifty meters ahead, topped by barbed wire.

Suddenly, Kane stopped in his tracks, cocking his head.

Then Tucker heard it, too.

A rhythmic clanging.

He waited, then heard it again, recognizing it.

A hammer striking steel.

The sound came from ahead and to the left, not too far away. He pushed to a break in the trees, where Kane had stopped.

Beyond the fence stretched a single long runway, lined by six hangars and twice as many outbuildings, most of which seemed to be bolstered by a patchwork of sheet metal. The eastern side of the base lay a little farther to the right, out of direct view. Somewhere over there was the shack where he was supposed to rendezvous with Dimitry.

But the loud clanging continued, closer at hand, coming from the base.

Curious, Tucker pulled out his binoculars, zoomed in on the buildings, and began panning. He searched for the source of the clanging and found it at the side door of a rusty hangar.

"You've got to be kidding me," he muttered.

Standing in the doorway was Fedor. Under one arm, he clutched an aircraft propeller; in his opposite hand, an eight-pound steel mallet, which he slammed down on the propeller's leading edge.

Gong.

The sound echoed across the base to where Tucker was lying.

Gong gong gong.

He lowered the binoculars and squeezed the bridge of his nose between his index finger and thumb. It was too late now. For better or worse, he'd hitched his wagon to this Russian bear.

He set out again, aiming right, searching ahead for the crumpled section of fence that marked the shack. At least, from here, the terrain offered decent cover. The air base had been abandoned long enough for the surrounding forest, once cut back for security purposes, to encroach upon the fence line. He kept to those trees, moving steadily, circling around to the eastern side of the base.

Tucker had just stopped to catch his breath when be heard the thumping sound of helicopter rotors. Swearing, he pushed into the shadowy bower of a Siberian pine. He whistled for Kane to join him.

As the shepherd rushed to his side, he craned his neck to the sky. The noise grew thunderous, making it difficult to discern the direction. Then the dark belly of the Havoc streaked overhead at treetop level.

The rotor wash stirred the powdery snow into a stinging whirlwind. Branches whipped overhead.

Had they been spotted?

What about their tracks through the snow?

There was something especially unnerving about being hunted from the air. His every primitive instinct was to run, but he knew that path was the quickest way to get cut in half by the Havoc's chain gun.

So he stayed hidden.

The chopper moved past, slowly circling the air base, seeming to follow the perimeter fence. He watched its slow passage, staying hidden, until he could no longer hear the rotors.

Tucker waited another ten minutes, just to be sure. He used the time to reassemble Felice's PSG-90. Once completed, he did a final check of the sniper rifle. Only then did he set out again, comforted by its weight.

In less than a hundred feet, he reached a corner of the air base. He stopped and used his binoculars to survey the eastern perimeter.

As Dimitry had promised, a section of fence had been flattened beneath a fallen tree. It lay about three hundred meters away—and there stood the shack.

The impulse was to hurry toward its relative safety, but he ignored it. Instead, he took a mental bearing and headed deeper into the trees, intending to circle wide and come at the shack from behind. He took his time, using the deepening shadows and snowdrifts as cover.

Finally, the shack came into view again. It was small, twelve feet to a side, with a mossy roof and timber walls. He saw no light and smelled no woodsmoke.

Satisfied, he bent down and pulled up Kane's camera stalk. He also made sure the radio receiver remained secure in the shepherd's left ear canal. Once done, he did a fast sound-and-video check with his phone.

With the GRU unit on the hunt, he wasn't taking any chances.

And he certainly wasn't going to enter that cabin blind.

Tucker pointed at the shack, made a circling motion with his arm, and whispered, "QUIET SCOUT."

Kane slinks from his partner's side. He does not head directly for the cabin, but out into the woods, stalking wide. His paws find softer snow or open ground, moving silently. He stays to shadow, low, moving under bowers that burn with the reek of pine pitch. Through the smell, he still picks out the bitter droppings of birds. He scents the decaying carcass of a mouse under the snow, ripe and calling out.

His ears tick in every direction, filling the world with the smallest sounds.

Snow shushes from overburdened branches, falling to the ground . . .

Fir needles rattle like bones with every gust . . .

Small creatures scrape through snow or whisper past on wings . . .

As he moves, he sights the cabin, glances back to his partner, always tracking. He glides to the far side of the shack, where the shadows are darkest, knowing this is best for a first approach, where fewer eyes will see him.

A command strikes his left ear, brash but welcoming.

"HOLD."

He steps to the nearest cover: a fallen log musky with rot and mold. He drops to his belly, legs under him, muscles tense and hard, ready to ignite when needed. He lowers his chin until it brushes snow.

His gaze remains fixed to the structure. He breathes in deeply, picking out each scent and testing it for danger: old smoke, urine of man and beast, the resin of cut logs, the taint of thick moss on shingles.

He awaits the next command, knowing his partner watches as intently as he does. It finally comes.

"MOVE IN. CLOSE SCOUT."

He rises to his legs and paces to the cabin, scenting along the ground. His ears remain high, bristling for any warning. He comes to a window and rises up, balancing on his hind legs. He stares through the murky glass, deeply and long, swiveling his head to catch every corner.

He spots no movement in the dark interior—so drops back to his paws.

He turns to stare at where his partner is hidden among the trees and keeps motionless, signaling the lack of danger.

It is understood.

"MOVE OUT. QUIET SCOUT AGAIN."

He swings away, angling around the corner. He checks each side, spies through another window, and sniffs intently at the closed door. He ends where he started.

"GOOD BOY. RETURN."

He disobeys, instead dropping again to his belly by the rotten log.

A low growl rumbles in his chest, barely heard with his own ears.

A warning.

. . . .

Tucker watched the video feed jostle as Kane lowered to his belly, his nose at the snow line. He heard the growl through the radio and noted the pointed stare of the shepherd toward the deeper forest to the right of the shack.

He studied the video feed on his phone. Even with the camera, his eyesight was no match for Kane's. He squinted at the screen, trying to pick out what had seized Kane's attention. After ten long seconds, he spotted movement, fifty yards away.

A lone figure, hunched over, moved through the trees, heading toward the shack.

Tucker swore silently and dropped quietly to his chest. He shifted the sniper rifle to his shoulder, flicking off the safety.

The trespasser was also carrying a gun—an assault weapon from its shape and angles. The figure moved through thick shadows, hard to make out, camouflaged from head to toe in a woodland winter suit. He moved deftly, someone well familiar with hunting in a forest, every cautious step cementing Tucker's certainty that this was one of the Spetsnaz soldiers, not a local hunter.

Thank God for Kane's keen perception.

But why only *one*?

If there had been others, Kane would have alerted him.

It made no sense. If the Spetsnaz knew he and Kane were here, they would have come in force. This had to be a lone scout. He remembered the Havoc helo circling the perimeter of the air base.

Apparently the unit commander must have sent a man or two to do the same on foot.

He raised the sniper rifle to his shoulder and peered through its scope, getting a sight picture. Once fixed, he subvocalized into the radio mike taped to his throat, passing on yet another command to his partner.

"TARGET. QUIET CLOSE."

It was an order Kane knew all too well from their time together in Afghanistan: *get as close to the enemy as possible and be ready.*

Kane began creeping toward the man.

With his partner on the move, Tucker laid his cheek against the rifle's stock and peered through the scope. The target was forty yards off, moving with practiced economy. He never paused in the open, only when behind a tree. His current line of approach would take him straight to Kane's position.

Thirty yards.

Given the angle of the man's body, Tucker knew a head shot would be tricky, so he adjusted the rifle's crosshairs and focused on a point a few inches below the man's left nipple.

The soldier stepped behind a tree and paused, ever cautious. Two seconds passed. The man emerged again from cover, ready to close in on the cabin.

It was Tucker's best chance. He squeezed the trigger ever so slightly, took a breath, let it out—and fired.

In the last millisecond, the soldier's arm shifted forward. The bullet tore through the man's elbow, shattering bone and cartilage, but veering wide from a kill shot.

The man spun counterclockwise and disappeared behind the trunk of a spruce.

"TAKEDOWN!" he called out to Kane.

He didn't wait to track his partner. Instead, he dropped the sniper rifle and charged forward, drawing his P22 pistol on the run.

Ahead and to his left, Kane leaped through the air and disappeared behind the spruce. A scream burst out, followed by a spatter of automatic fire that shred needles from the tree.

Tucker reached the spruce, grabbed a passing branch, and whipped himself around with his pistol raised. The soldier struggled on the ground, on his back. Kane straddled him, his jaws clamped on his right wrist. The assault rifle lay nearby, but the soldier had a Makarov pistol gripped in his free hand.

Time seemed to slow for Tucker. The man's gun hand turned, straining to bring the weapon to bear on Kane. Then the Makarov bucked. Kane was strobe-lit by orange muzzle flash but unharmed. In his panic and pain, the man had shot too soon.

Tucker refused to give him another chance.

Stepping sideways, he took aim and fired once. The bullet drilled a neat hole in the soldier's right temple. His body went slack.

"RELEASE," Tucker rasped out.

Kane obeyed and backed away a few steps.

Tucker placed his boot on the Makarov, which lay half buried in the snow. There was no sense in checking the man's pulse; he was dead. His mind switched to their next worry. The gunfire would have carried through the trees.

But how far? Who might have heard?

Tucker took a moment to double-check Kane for injuries. Finding none, he gave the shepherd a quick neck ruffle, then pointed in the direction the man had come.

"QUIET SCOUT."

He had to know if reinforcements were on their way.

As Kane moved off, he pocketed the Makarov, stripped off the man's camouflage suit, and stuffed it into his own pack. Though pressed for time, he spent a minute hand-shoveling snow over the corpse. The grave wouldn't stand close scrutiny, but it might buy him precious seconds.

Finally, Tucker retrieved his rifle and moved deeper into the trees, where he found a tangle of fallen logs. If necessary, it would serve as a good sniper's roost.

He checked Kane's camera, but all seemed quiet out there. Satisfied for the moment, he radioed to his partner.

"RETURN."

Thirty seconds later, Kane crouched next to him, panting.

"Good work, pal."

Kane licked Tucker's cheek.

Using the momentary lull, Tucker pulled on the camouflage suit.

"Now we wait."

4:39 P.M.

After several long minutes, the snap of branches alerted Tucker. Someone was approaching from his eight o'clock position. As he listened, the plod of footsteps grew louder, distinctly different from the soldier's cautious approach.

Not Spetsnaz.

A moment later, Dimitry appeared, lumbering through the forest.

Still, Tucker stayed hidden, waiting, suspicion ringing through him.

When Dimitry was ten feet away, seemingly alone, Tucker called out to him.

"Stop!"

Dimitry jumped, genuinely startled. He lifted both arms, showing empty hands. "Is that you, my friend?"

Tucker kept hidden. "You're making a lot of noise."

"Intentionally," Dimitry replied with a half smile. "I didn't feel like getting shot, *da*? I heard the gunfire."

"We had a visitor," Tucker admitted, relaxing somewhat. "Spetsnaz."

"Is he—?"

"Dead. Dimitry, did you turn us in?"

"*Nyet.* But you are smart to ask. I swear I have told no one about you."

"And Fedor?"

The old man shook his head. "He has his flaws, but he has never betrayed me or a customer. Besides, you must trust someone or you'll never get out of here."

Tucker both believed him and knew he was right. Even Kane wagged his tail, wanting to greet Dimitry. He finally stood up out of his blind.

Dimitry joined him, eyeing his winter suit. "New clothes, I see."

"Someone no longer needed them." Tucker pointed toward the air base. "Is Fedor ready to fly? Matters are getting a little tense out here."

"I think so. When I called him, he had just finished making some adjustments to the plane's propeller. Fine-tuning, he called it."

Tucker smiled, remembering the crude hammering. "I saw."

Together, they headed past the cabin and across the air base. Dimitry took him along a circuitous path that mostly kept them hidden, working their way toward the hangar.

"I am glad you are safe," Dimitry said. "At the church, when I left you in that tunnel—"

"What exactly is that tunnel?" Tucker interrupted, remembering the fresh boards shoring it up.

"I found it by accident one morning. I felt a strange draft coming up from the floor and started prying up boards."

"And you've been maintaining it?" he asked.

The suspicion must have been plain in his voice.

Dimitry smiled. "Myself and Fedor. I told you he was a smuggler."

Tucker raised an eyebrow toward the town's old bishop, suddenly remembering how deferential everyone in the bar had been toward Dimitry, more than could be explained by religious affection.

"Okay, perhaps Fedor has a partner," Dimitry

admitted. "It is hard to maintain my flock on faith alone. But, mind you, we don't smuggle anything dangerous. Mostly medicine and food, especially during winter. Many children get sick, you understand."

Tucker could not find any fault in such an enterprise. "It's a good thing you're doing."

Dimitry spread his hands. "Out here, you do what you can for your neighbor. It is how we survive, how we make a community." He pointed ahead. "There is Fedor's hangar. I will check first. Make sure it is clear, *da*?"

With Kane at his knee, Tucker waited while Dimitry went ahead. He returned two minutes later and gestured for them to follow.

"All is good."

Dimitry led them through the main hangar doors. Lit by a lone klieg light, a single-engine prop plane filled the small space. Tucker couldn't make out the model, but like everything else at the air base, the craft seemed a hodgepodge of bits and pieces. But at least the propeller was in place.

He found Fedor kneeling beside a red toolbox on the floor.

Before they could reach him, Kane let out a low growl. The shepherd still stood by the door, staring out.

Tucker hurried to the shepherd's side, careful not to show himself. He drew Kane back by his collar. Across the base, a pair of headlights passed through the main gate, turned, and headed in their direction. It was clearly a military vehicle.

He drew his pistol and crossed to Fedor. He

raised the gun and aimed it at the man's forehead. "We've got visitors. No matter what else happens, you'll be the first one to go."

Fedor's eyes got huge, and he sputtered first in Russian, then English. "I tell no one! No one!" He stood up—slowly, his palms toward Tucker. "Come, come! Follow. I show where to hide."

Tucker weighed his options as the grumble of a diesel engine grew louder. He remembered Dimitry's earlier words: *you must trust someone or you'll never get out of here.*

With no choice but to heed that wisdom, Tucker pocketed his weapon. "Show me."

Fedor hurried toward the rear of the hangar, towing everyone with him.

The big man led them to a giant orange storage tank, streaked with rust, that sat on a set of deflated rubber tires. A hose lay curled next to it. Tucker recognized an old fuel bowser used to fill the tanks of planes.

Fedor pointed to a ladder on one side. "Up! Through hatch on top."

Having already cast his dice, Tucker stepped to the ladder and crouched down. He turned to Kane and tapped his shoulder. "Up."

Backing a step, then leaping, Kane mounted Tucker's shoulder in a half-fireman carry. Together, they scaled the ladder and crawled across the bowser's roof to the hatch.

Fedor headed toward the hangar door, leaving behind a warning. "Quiet. I come back."

Hurrying, Tucker spun the hatch, tugged it open, and poked his head inside. The interior seemed dry.

At least, I won't be standing hip-deep in gasoline.

He pointed down and Kane dove through the hatch, landing quietly. Tucker followed, not as deftly, having to struggle to pull the hatch closed, too. His boots hit the bottom of the empty tank with a clang. He cringed, going still, but the rumbling arrival of the military vehicle covered the noise.

In complete darkness, Tucker drew his gun, his nose and eyes already stinging from fuel residue. But he also smelled bananas, which made no sense. He shifted to a better vantage, but his foot hit something that sounded wooden.

What the hell . . . ?

He freed his tiny penlight and flicked it on. Panning the narrow beam, he discovered the back half of the bowser's tank was stacked with crates and boxes, some marked in Cyrillic, others in various languages. He spotted one box bearing a large red cross. Medical supplies. On top of it rested a thick bunch of bananas.

Here was more of Dimitry and Fedor's smuggling operation.

It seemed he was now part of the cargo.

From outside, he heard muffled Russian voices moving around the hangar—then they approached closer. He clicked off his penlight and gripped the pistol with both hands. It sounded like an argument was under way. He recognized Fedor's tone, which sounded heated, as if in the thick of a furious negotiation. Then the conversation moved away again and became indiscernible.

After another ten minutes, an engine started,

rumbling loudly, wheels squelched on wet tarmac, and the sounds quickly receded. Seconds later, feet clomped up the ladder, and the hatch opened.

Tucker pointed his pistol up.

Fedor scolded, "No shoot, please. Safe now."

Tucker called out, "Dimitry?"

"They are all gone, my friend!"

Fedor groaned. "*Da, da*. As I say, safe."

Tucker climbed up, poked his head out, and looked around. Once confident the hangar was clear, he dropped back down, collected Kane, and climbed out.

"Price higher now," Fedor announced.

Dimitry explained, "They were looking for you, but mostly they learned about our operations here. Not unusual. Every village in Siberia has such a black-market system. So people talk. The soldiers came mostly to collect what could be most kindly described as a tax."

He understood. The roving soldiers weren't above a little extortion.

"Cost me best case of vodka," Fedor said, placing a fist over his heart, deeply wounded.

"We told them that we were about to leave on a postal run," Dimitry explained. "After collecting the tax, there should be no problem getting through. Even soldiers know the mail must flow. Or their vodka here might dry up."

Tucker understood. "'Neither snow, nor rain, nor dark of night . . .'"

Fedor looked quizzically at him. "Is that poem? You write it?"

"Never mind. How much more do I owe you?"

Fedor gave it much thought. "Two thousand rubles. You pay, *da*?"

"I'll pay."

Fedor clapped his hands together. "Happy! Time to go. Put dog in plane. Then *you* push plane out, I steer. Hurry, hurry!"

Tucker rushed to comply.

Not exactly first-class service, but he wasn't complaining.

PART II

HUNTER/KILLER

12

"And how confident are you of Dimitry and Fedor?" Ruth Harper asked.

Tucker stood at a pay phone next to an open-air fish market. The pungent smell of sturgeon, perch, and smelt hung heavily in the cold air. He had spent the previous ten minutes bringing Harper up to speed. He was surprised how happy he was to hear that southern lilt to her voice.

If not Tennessee, then maybe—

"Do you trust those Russians?" she pressed.

"I wouldn't be making this call if either of them had ratted me out. Plus, I've been strolling the snowy streets of Novosibirsk for the past two hours. I'm clean. And it's still another twelve hundred miles to Perm. If I pick up a tail, I'll have plenty of time to shake it loose."

"Still, you're cutting the rendezvous close."

"Bukolov will keep. If they—whoever they are—had any idea where he was, they wouldn't be after me. Which reminds me, any further word about the source of that leak?"

"No luck, yet. But from the story you just told me—one involving GRU and Spetsnaz—we know the enemy has powerful connections in either the Russian government or military. I'm looking hard at the Ministry of Defense, or maybe someone at a cabinet level of the government."

"Maybe you'd better be looking at *both*."

"A scary proposition. Do you want help out there?"

Tucker considered it for a long moment. "For now, no. We've got enough players in the field. Makes it confusing enough."

Plus he liked working alone—well, not quite alone.

He gave Kane, seated at his knee, a reassuring pat.

"If I change my mind, Harper, I'll let you know."

"Do that. As it happens, I've got nobody to give you right now."

"Busy on the home front?"

"Always. World's a dangerous place. At least Sigma can offer you some logistical support. Do you have a wish list for me?"

Tucker did. After reciting the provisions he needed, he signed off. He would find all he asked for once he reached the city of Perm, secured and cached in a safe house.

But first he had to get there.

Harper had arranged clean papers and seemed confident that Russian immigration and customs did not have him on any watch list, making it safe for him to fly. Furthermore, Sigma's intelligence team had arranged another level of countermeasures, booking false tickets, hotel rooms, and car rentals. He was everywhere and nowhere.

Still, whether it was his inherent wariness of all things governmental or simply a tactical change of mind, Tucker called a local car rental agency after hanging up with Harper and booked an SUV for a one-way trip to Omskaya, some four hundred miles to the west. He had no reason to distrust Sigma, but there was no mistaking the reality of his current situation. He and Kane were out here alone, without any hope of reinforcements.

Harper had tasked him with getting Abram Bukolov safely out of Russia and to the United States. How exactly he accomplished that was his decision.

And he preferred it that way.

With Kane on a leash, he walked the mile to the rental car office and picked up the vehicle, a Range Rover of questionable age, but the engine purred and the heater worked.

Tucker took it and left Novosibirsk at midday, heading west down the highway to Omskaya. Three hours later, he pulled off the highway and drove six miles north to his *true* destination, Kuybyshev.

It never hurt to employ his own countermeasures. Following the pictograph signs, he pulled into the local airport. Using a map and a smattering of Russian, he booked a flight to Perm.

Sixteen hours after he left Novosibirsk, his flight touched down at Perm's Bolshoye Savino Airport. He waited in cargo claim for Kane to emerge from the belly of the plane, then another hour for immigration to clear them both.

Minutes later, he and Kane were in another rental vehicle—this one a Volvo—and headed into the city proper.

From the car, he called Sigma for an update.

"Still no blips on immigration or customs," Harper informed him. "If they're still actively hunting you, they're not doing it that way."

Or they're giving me enough time to get to Bukolov before snapping shut the trap.

"Is this safe house I'm heading to manned?" he asked, intending to collect the provisions he had requested without delay.

"It won't be. It's an apartment. Call the number I gave you, let it ring three times, then again twice, then wait ten minutes. The door will be unlocked. Five minutes inside, no more."

"Are you kidding me?"

"Simplicity works, Tucker, and this is a lot simpler than meeting someone on a park bench with a flower in your lapel and your shoelace untied."

Tucker realized this made sense. In fact, one of the acronyms soldiers lived by was KISS—*Keep It Simple, Stupid.*

"Fair enough," Tucker said, but he gave voice to another troubling matter. "It's South Carolina, isn't it?"

"Pardon?"

"Your accent."

She sighed heavily, giving him his answer.

Wrong.

"Tucker, the details for your meeting tonight will also be in the safe house."

"And my contact?"

"His name and description are included in the dossier you'll find there. He's hard to miss."

"I'll call you after it's done."

"Keep out of trouble," she said.

"Are you talking about both of us, or just Kane?"

"Kane would be much harder to replace."

Tucker glanced to his partner. "Can't argue with that," he said and signed off.

Now came the hard part—grabbing Abram Bukolov without getting caught.

13

His visit to the safe house was thankfully anticli-
mactic. He left with four new passports—two for
him and two for Bukolov—along with a roll of cash,
a pair of credit cards, a second satellite phone, and
the location of his meeting with Sigma's contact, the
one who was supposed to lead Tucker to Bukolov.

This mysterious contact was also high on his list
of suspects as the source of the intelligence leak that
almost got him killed. The man's dossier rested on
the seat next to him. He planned on studying it in
great detail.

Next, Tucker took advantage of a list of local sup-
pliers left at the safe house. He traveled to a bakery
whose basement doubled as an armory. The baker
asked no questions but simply waited for Tucker to
make his weapon selections from a floor-to-ceiling
pegboard. He then wrote down the price on a piece
of paper, which he handed to Tucker with a gravelly,
"No negotiate."

The next supplier, the owner of a car lot, was
equally taciturn and effective. Through Harper,

Tucker had preordered a black Marussia F2 SUV. Of Russian manufacture, it had a front end that only a mother could love, but it was a brute of a vehicle, often modified for use by first responders or as a mobile command center.

After paying, Tucker told the owner where to leave the vehicle—and when.

With six hours still to spare before he was supposed to meet with his contact, Tucker proceeded to the neighborhood in question: the Leninsky District on the northern side of the Kama River. Once there, he parked the Volvo and began walking. In between scouting locations and routes, he was able to relax and take in the sights.

Straddling the banks of the Kama and within the shadow of the snow-topped Ural Mountains, Perm was home to a million people. While the city had its share of Soviet-gray architecture, the older Leninsky District continued to maintain its original European charm. It was a cozy neighborhood of tree-lined streets and secluded garden courtyards, spattered with small cafés, butchers, and bakeries. To top it off, the sun shone in a cloudless blue sky, a rare sight of late.

As he strolled, no one seemed to pay much attention to him: just a man walking his dog. He wasn't alone in that regard. Much of Perm was taking advantage of the handsome day. Kane took particular interest in a pair of leashed dachshunds that passed by on the sidewalk, all three dogs doing the customary greeting of sniffing and tail wagging. Tucker didn't mind, as attached to the other end of the leash was a buxom, young beauty in a tight sweater.

The day certainly had brightened.

Eventually, as they crossed the half-mile-long bridge spanning the Kama, he abruptly found himself in a different world. On this side of the river, it was distinctly seedier and less populated. The area was mostly forest, with roads that were either dirt or deeply potholed. The few inhabitants he encountered stared at the pair as though they were alien invaders.

Luckily, where he was supposed to meet his mysterious contact was only a quarter mile from the river. He studied it from a distance, getting the lay of the land. It was a bus stop shelter across from a sullen cluster of businesses: a grocery store, a strip club, and a body shop.

Tucker finished his reconnoiter, then gladly crossed back over the bridge.

He and Kane returned to the Volvo, found a nondescript hotel in the area, checked in, and took a fast nap. Tucker knew that once he had Bukolov in hand, he might not get a chance to sleep again until he delivered the man across the border.

That is, if he ever reached the border.

In the end, he didn't sleep well at all.

8:12 P.M.

By nightfall, Tucker found himself parked in an elementary-school lot on the wrong side of the tracks—or in this case, the wrong side of the *river*. The school had boarded-up windows with a playground full of rusty, broken equipment that looked perfect for spreading tetanus.

He had picked this spot because it lay within a hundred yards of the bus stop where he was supposed to meet his contact. He shut off the engine and doused the lights and sat in the darkness for five minutes. He saw no other cars, and no one moving about. Again no one seemed to be following him. This made him feel more uneasy, not less.

It was what you *couldn't* see that usually got you killed.

He turned to Kane, motioning with a flat palm. "STAY."

He had debated the wisdom of leaving Kane behind, but if the meeting went awry, he wanted to make sure he had an escape vehicle. And considering the neighborhood, Kane's presence in the Volvo was better than any car alarm.

He often wrestled with this exact quandary. With the memory of Abel's death never far, he had to fight the temptation to keep Kane out of harm's way. But the shepherd loved Tucker, loved to work, and he hated to be separated for long.

They were a pack of two.

Even now, Kane displayed his displeasure at Tucker's order, cocking his head quizzically and furrowing his brow.

"I know," he replied. "Just mind the fort."

He took a moment to check his equipment: a Smith & Wesson .44-caliber snubnose in his belt, a hammerless Magnum revolver in his coat pocket, and a similar .38-caliber model in a calf holster. Additionally, he kept a pair of quick-loaders for each in his pockets.

This was as close to *armed to the teeth* as he could manage.

Satisfied, he got out, locked the car, and started walking.

He hopped a chest-high fence and crossed the school's playground to the north side. He followed a line of thick Russian larch trees, bare and skeletal, around a vacant lot that was dominated by mounds of garbage.

On the other side, fifty yards away, stood the bus stop. The curbside shelter was little more than a lean-to over a graffiti-scarred bench.

Across the street, under the strip club's neon sign—a silhouette of a naked lady—four thugs lounged, laughing, smoking, and chugging bottles of beer. Their heads were shaved, and they all wore jeans tucked into black, steel-toed boots.

Staying out of their sight line, Tucker checked his watch. He still had twenty minutes.

Now came the waiting.

Back at the hotel, he had read the dossier on his contact, a man named Stanimir Utkin. He was Bukolov's former student and now chief lab assistant. Tucker had memorized his face, not that it took much effort. The man stood six and a half feet tall but weighed only one hundred fifty pounds. Topped by a shock of fiery-red hair, such a scarecrow would be hard to miss in a crowd.

Right on time, a cab pulled to a stop before the bus shelter.

The door opened and out climbed Stanimir Utkin.

"Come on," Tucker mumbled. "Don't do this to me."

Not only had Utkin arrived by cab to the exact spot of their meeting—displaying a reckless lack of caution—he had come wearing what appeared to be an expensive business suit. His red hair glowed in the pool cast by the streetlamp like a beacon.

The cab pulled away and sped off.

The driver was no fool.

Like sharks smelling chum, the four thugs across the street took immediate notice of Utkin. They pointed fingers and laughed, but Tucker knew this phase wouldn't last long. Utkin was too tempting of a target, either for a mugging or a beating—or more likely, *both*.

Tucker jammed his hands into his pockets and tightened one fist around the Magnum. Taking a deep breath, he started walking fast across the open lot, keeping out of sight as he headed toward the back of the bench. He covered the distance to the bus shelter in thirty seconds, by which time Utkin had begun glancing left and right like a rat who had spotted a snake.

One of the thugs threw a bottle across the street. It shattered on the curb near Utkin's toes.

The skinny man stumbled backward, falling to his seat on the bus bench.

Oh, dear God . . .

Ten feet behind the shelter, Tucker stopped in the shadows and called out, keeping his voice low enough so only Utkin could hear him. According to the dossier, the man spoke fluent English.

"Utkin, don't turn around. I'm here to meet you."

Another beer bottle sailed across the street and shattered in the street. Harsh laughter followed.

"My name is Tucker. Listen carefully. Don't think, just turn around and walk toward me, then keep going. Do it now."

Utkin stood, stepped out from under the shelter, and headed into the abandoned lot.

One of the thugs called out, and the group started across the street, likely drawn as much out of boredom as larceny.

Utkin drew even with Tucker, who hid behind a stack of tires and trash.

He waved him on. "Keep going. I'll catch up."

Utkin obeyed, glancing frequently over his shoulder.

By now, the thugs had reached the bus stop and entered the lot.

Tucker stood up, drawing out his Magnum. He took three paces into the light, showing himself. He raised the pistol and drew a bead on the lead thug's chest.

The group came to a fast stop.

Tucker summoned one of the Russian phrases he'd been practicing. "Go away, or I will kill you."

He raised the Magnum, a mean-looking weapon. His Russian language skills might be lacking, but some communication was universal.

Still, the leader looked ready to test him, until they locked gazes. Whatever he saw in Tucker's eyes made him change his mind.

The leader waved the others off, and they wisely retreated.

Tucker turned and hurried after Utkin, who had stopped at the fence that bordered the schoolyard. He was bent double, his hands on his knees, hyperventilating.

Tucker didn't slow. He couldn't trust the thugs wouldn't rally up more guys, additional firepower, and come after them. He grabbed Utkin's arm, pulled him upright, and shoved him toward a neighboring gate.

"Walk."

Coaxed and guided by Tucker, they reached the car quickly. He opened the front passenger door and herded Utkin inside. The man balked when he spotted Kane in the back. The shepherd leaned over the seat to sniff at the stranger.

Tucker placed a palm atop Utkin's head and pushed him inside. Still panicked, the man balled up in the passenger seat, twisted to the side, his eyes never leaving Kane.

Not the most auspicious introduction, but the man had left him little choice.

Tucker started the engine and drove off.

Only once back over the bridge and in more genial surroundings did Tucker relax. He found a well-lit parking lot beside a skating rink and pulled in.

"The dog won't hurt you," Tucker told Utkin.

"Does *he* know that?"

Tucker sighed and turned to face Utkin fully. "What were you thinking?"

"What?"

"The taxi, the business suit, the bad part of town . . ."

"What should I have done differently?"

"All of it," Tucker replied.

In truth, Tucker was partly to blame. From the dossier, he had known Utkin was a lab geek. He knew the meeting site was dicey. He should have changed it.

Utkin struggled to compose himself and did a surprisingly admirable job, considering the circumstances. "I believe I owe you my life. Thank you. I was very frightened."

Tucker shrugged. "Nothing wrong with being frightened. That just means you're smart, not stupid. So before we get into any more trouble, let's go get Bukolov. Where is your boss?"

Utkin checked his watch. "He should still be at the opera."

"The opera?"

Utkin glanced up, seemingly not bothered that someone seeking to escape the country, someone being hunted by Russian elite forces, should choose such a public outing.

Tucker shook his head. "You remember when I said don't be *stupid* . . ."

Over the next few minutes, he got the story out of Utkin. It seemed—faced with the possibility of never seeing the Motherland again—Abram Bukolov had decided to indulge his greatest passion: *opera*.

"They were doing one of Abram's favorites," Utkin explained. "*Faust*. It's quite—"

"I'm sure it is. Does he have a cell phone?"

"Yes, but he will have it turned off."

Tucker sighed. "Where is the opera house and when does it end?"

"In about an hour. It's being held at the Tchaikovsky's House. It's less than a mile from here."

Great . . . just great . . .

He put the Volvo in gear. "Show me."

10:04 P.M.

Ten minutes before the opera ended, Tucker found a parking spot a few blocks from the Tchaikovsky's House. As angry as he was at Bukolov for choosing to preface his defection by dressing up in a tuxedo and attending a public extravaganza, the deed was done. Still, this stunt told him something: Bukolov was either unstable, stupid, or arrogant—any of which did not bode well for the remainder of their journey.

Tucker left Kane in the car and accompanied Utkin down the street. He stopped across from the opera's brightly lit main entrance and pointed toward its massive white stone façade.

"I'll wait here," he said. "You go fetch the good doctor and walk to the car. Don't hurry and don't look at me. I'll meet you at the Volvo. Got it?"

"I understand."

"Go."

Utkin crossed the street and headed toward the main entrance.

As he waited, Tucker studied the crimson banner draped down the front of the theater. The fiery sign depicted a demonic figure in flames, appropriate for *Faust*, an opera about a scholar who makes a pact with the devil.

I hope that's not the case here.

A few minutes later, Utkin emerged with Abram Bukolov in tow. The billionaire leader of Russia's burgeoning pharmaceutical industry stood a foot shorter and forty pounds heavier than his lab assistant. He was bald, except for a monk's fringe of salt-and-pepper hair.

Following Tucker's instructions, Utkin escorted the man back to the car. Tucker gave them a slight lead, then followed. Once he was sure no one was tailing them, he joined them at the car.

"Hello!" Bukolov called, offering his hand.

Irritated, Tucker skipped the formal introductions. Instead, he used the remote to unlock the doors. "Utkin in front, Bukolov in—"

"*Doctor* Bukolov," the man corrected him.

"Whatever. *Doctor*, you're in the back."

Tucker opened the driver's door and started to climb in.

Behind him, Bukolov stopped and stared inside. "There's a dog back here."

"Really?" Tucker said, his voice steeped in sarcasm. "How did he get back there?"

"I'm not sitting next to—"

"Get in, or he'll drag you inside by your tuxedo lapels, Doctor."

Bukolov clamped his mouth shut, his face going red. It was doubtful many people had ever spoken to him like that. Still, he got in.

Two blocks later, the pharmaceutical magnate found his voice. "The opera was tremendous, Stanimir—though I doubt you would have appreciated the subtleties. Say, you, driver, what's your name? Is this your dog? He keeps staring at me."

Tucker gave Utkin a narrow-eyed glance, who got the message.

"Doctor Bukolov, why don't we talk about the opera later? We can—"

The man cut him off by tapping on Tucker's shoulder. "Driver, how long until we reach Kazan?"

Resisting the urge to break his fingers, Tucker pulled to the nearest curb and put the Volvo in park. He turned in his seat and faced Bukolov. "Kazan? What are you talking about?"

"Kazan. It's in the *oblast* of—"

"I know where it is, Doctor." The city of Kazan lay about four hundred miles to the west. "Why do you think we're going there?"

"Good God, man, didn't anyone tell you? This is unacceptable! I am not leaving the country without Anya. We must go to Kazan and collect her."

Of course we do.

"Who's Anya?" he asked.

"My daughter. I will not leave Russia without her."

11:22 P.M.

Sticking to his original plan, Tucker headed out of town, stopping only long enough to trade the Volvo for the new Marussia F2 SUV. They found the brute of a vehicle parked where he had instructed it to be left on the south end of town. It was fully gassed and carried a false license plate.

Reaching the P242, he continued west for an hour, doing his best to tune out Bukolov's rambling monologue, which ranged from the mysterious Anya, to the industrial history of the region, to Kane's *disturbingly intelligent mien.*

On the outskirts of the small town of Kungur, Tucker pulled into the hotel parking lot and decided he'd put enough distance from Perm to regroup.

He got out and called Harper and brought her up to speed.

"This is the first I've heard of this Anya," Harper said.

"You described the doctor as eccentric. You were being generous."

"He may be a bit"—she paused to consider her words—"out of touch, but there's no mistaking his brilliance. Or his desire to leave Russia. And to answer your unspoken question, we're convinced he's on the up-and-up."

"If you say so."

"Where is he now?"

"In the backseat of my SUV, having a staring contest with Kane. I had to get some air. Listen, Harper, if Anya is the brideprice to get Bukolov out of the country, that's fine, but let's make sure she's real before I head to Kazan. That's a good seven-hour drive from here."

"Agreed. Give me her full name."

"Hang on." Tucker opened his door. "Doctor, what is Anya's last name?"

"*Bukolov*, of course! She's my daughter. What kind of question—?"

Tucker straightened and spoke to Harper. "You heard?"

"I did."

The professor added, "She works at the Kazan

Institute of Biochemistry and Biophysics. She's quite brilliant, you know—"

Tucker slammed the door, muffling Bukolov's ramblings.

On the phone, Harper said, "I'm on it."

Bukolov rolled down the window a few inches. "Apologies. How forgetful of me. Anya took her mother's surname—*Malinov*. Anya Malinov."

Harper heard that, too. "Got it. Name's Malinov. What's your plan, Tucker?"

"In the short term, to check into a motel. It's almost midnight here."

Tucker waited until Bukolov had rerolled up his window. He took a few additional steps away before broaching a touchier matter.

"Harper, what about Utkin?"

The lab tech continued to remain on the short list of potential leaks—but were such breaches accidental or done on purpose? Tucker trusted his gut, along with his ability to read people. He found nothing that struck a wrong nerve with the young man, beyond simple naïveté.

It seemed Harper had come to the same conclusion. "Our intelligence can find nothing untoward about Utkin. He seems as honest as they come."

"Then maybe it was a slip of the tongue. Something said to the wrong person. By Utkin . . . or maybe even by Bukolov. That guy seems a few fries short of a Happy Meal."

"I'll keep looking into it. In the meantime, I'll dig into this Anya business overnight and get back to you by morning."

With the call done, he led everyone to the hotel

for the night, booking a single room with two beds. Tucker parked Kane at the door, knowing the shepherd would keep guard for the night.

He half dozed in a chair, while Bukolov puttered around the room, muttering and complaining before eventually unwinding. Around one in the morning, he sat down on the edge of the bed. Utkin was already asleep in the other.

"I'm sorry," Bukolov said. "I've forgotten your name."

"Tucker." He nodded to his partner. "That's Kane."

"I must say your dog seems well mannered enough. Thank you for coming to get me."

"You're welcome."

"Did they tell you about my discovery?" Before he could answer, Bukolov shook his head dismissively. "No, of course not. Even I didn't tell them, so how could they know?"

"Tell me about it."

Bukolov wagged a finger. "In good time. But I will say this. It is *monumental*. It will change the world of medicine—among other things. That's why they're after me."

"The Arzamas generals."

"Yes."

"Who are they?"

"Specifically? I don't know. They're too crafty for that."

Tucker stared across, sizing the other up. Was this guy suffering from a paranoid delusion? A persecution complex? Tucker fingered the healing bullet graze in his neck. That certainly was real enough.

"Then tell me about Anya," he said.

"Ah . . ." Bukolov's face softened, holding back a ghost of a smile. "She's wonderful. She's means everything to me. We've been working in tandem, the two of us—at a distance of course, and in secret."

"I thought Stanimir was your chief assistant."

"Him? Hah! He's adequate, I suppose, but he doesn't have the mind for it. Not for what I'm doing. Few people do really. That's why I must do this myself."

With that, Bukolov kicked off his shoes, sprawled back on the bed, and closed his eyes.

Tucker shook his head and settled into the chair for the night.

Bukolov whispered, his eyes still shut. "I'm not crazy, you know."

"If you say so."

"Just so you know."

Tucker crossed his arms, beginning to realize how little he actually *knew* about any of this.

March 13, 6:15 A.M.
Kungur, Russia

Despite the discomfort of the chair, Tucker slept for a solid five hours. He woke to find both of his charges still sleeping.

Taking advantage of the quiet moment, he took Kane out for a walk, let the dog stretch his legs and relieve himself. While they were still outside, Harper called.

"Anya's real," she said as introduction.

"I don't know if that's good news or bad."

If Anya were a figment of the good doctor's imagination, they could get out of Dodge immediately.

Harper continued. "We were able to confirm there's an Anya Malinov working at the Kazan Institute of Biochemistry and Biophysics, but not much else. A good portion of her file is redacted. Kazan's not as bad as the old Soviet-era *naukograds*, their closed science cities, but large swaths of the place do fall under the jurisdiction of the Ministry of Defense."

"So not only do we need to go to Kazan, but I have to extract this woman out from under the military's nose."

"Is that a problem?"

"I'll have to make it work. Not like I have a whole lot of choice. You asked me to get him out of Russia, and that's what I intend to do—him and now his daughter apparently. Which presents a problem. I've only got new passports for Bukolov. Not for Anya. And what about Utkin, for that matter? He wouldn't survive a day after we're gone. I won't leave him behind."

He flashed to Abel, panting, tongue lolling, tail wagging.

He wasn't about to abandon another teammate behind enemy lines.

Harper was silent for a few seconds. Even from halfway around the world, Tucker imagined he could hear the gears in the woman's head turning, recalibrating to accommodate the change in the situation.

"Okay. Like you, I'll make it happen. When do you plan to go for Anya?"

"Within twenty-four hours. More than that and we're pushing our luck."

"That won't work. I can't get new passports for Anya and Utkin over to you that fast. But if you gave me your route from there—"

"I don't know it yet. Considering all that's happened, it's hard to plan more than a step in advance. All I know for sure is the next step: free Anya."

"Then hold on for a minute." The line went silent, then she was back. "After you fetch Anya, can you get to Volgograd? As the crow flies, it's six hundred miles *south* of Kazan."

Tucker pulled a laminated map from his back pocket and studied it for a few seconds. "The distance is manageable."

"Good. If you can get to Volgograd, I can get you all out. No problem."

Out sounded good. So did *no problem*.

But after all that had happened, he had no faith about the outcome of either proposition.

14

By that midafternoon, Tucker stood on a sidewalk in central Kazan, staring up at a bronze monolith topped by the bust of a dour-faced man. Predictably, the plaque was written in Cyrillic.

But at least I came with my own tour guide.

"Behold the birthplace of modern organic chemistry," Abram Bukolov announced, his arms spread. "Kazan is home to the greats. Butlerov, Markovnikov, Arbuzov. The list is endless. And this fine gentleman depicted here, you surely know who he is, yes?"

"Why don't you remind us, Doctor," said Tucker.

"He is Nikolai Lobachevsky. The Russian pioneer in hyperbolic geometry. Ring any bells?"

Maybe warning bells.

Tucker was beginning to suspect Bukolov suffered from bipolar disorder. Since leaving the hotel at dawn Bukolov had cycled from barely contained excitement to sullenness. But upon reaching Kazan's outskirts a short time ago, the doctor had perked up enough to demand that they go on a walking tour of the Kazan Institute of Biochemistry and Biophysics.

Tucker had agreed for several reasons.

One: To shut Bukolov up.

Two: To scout the campus.

Three: To see if he could detect a general alert for any of them. If they were being pursued, their hunters had chosen a more discreet approach.

But most of all, he needed to find out *where* on this research campus Anya Malinov resided or worked. He hoped to sneak her out under the cover of night.

Utkin followed behind with Kane. He had a phone at his ear, trying to reach Anya. He spoke in low tones. Matters would have been easier if her father, Bukolov, knew where she lived or where her office was located.

I've never been here was his answer, almost tearful, clearly fraught with worry for his daughter.

Not trusting Bukolov to be civil, Tucker had thought it best for Utkin to make an inquiry with the institution.

Utkin finally lowered the phone and drew them all together. "We have a problem."

Of course we do.

Bukolov clutched Utkin's sleeve. "Has something happened to Anya?"

"No, she's fine, but she's not *here*."

"What do you mean?" Tucker asked. "Where is she?"

"She's at the Kremlin."

Tucker took a calming breath before speaking. "She's in *Moscow*?"

Utkin waved his hands. "No, no. Kazan has a Kremlin also. It lies a kilometer from here, overlooking the Volga."

He pointed in the general direction of the river that bordered Kazan.

"Why is she there?" Tucker asked, sighing out his relief.

Bukolov stirred. "Of course, because of the archives!"

His voice was sharp, loud enough to draw the eye of a passing campus guard. Not wanting any undue attention, Tucker drew the group along, getting them moving back toward their hotel in town.

Bukolov continued. "She mentioned finding something." He shook his head as if trying to knock a loose gear back into place. "I forgot about it until now. Something she was going to retrieve for me. Something very important."

"What?" Tucker asked.

The doctor looked up with a twinkle in his eye. "The journal of the late, great Paulos de Klerk."

"Who is that?"

"All in good time. But De Klerk may have the last piece of the puzzle I need."

Tucker decided not to press the issue and returned his attention to Utkin. "How long until she returns to the institute?"

"Three or four days."

"We can't wait that long!" Bukolov demanded.

For once, Tucker agreed.

Utkin also nodded. "According to what I learned, security is actually tighter here on the campus than at the local Kremlin. Over where Anya lives and works at the institute, there are guards at every entrance, magnetic key card access, and closed-circuit television cameras."

Tucker blew out a discouraged breath.

Then it looks like we're breaking Anya out of the Kremlin.

3:23 P.M.

An hour later, Tucker followed a tour group onto the grounds of the Kazan Kremlin. He and a handful of others had been separated out and handed over to an English-speaking guide, a five-foot-tall blond woman who smiled a lot but tended to bark.

"Now stay close!" she called, waving them all forward. "We are passing through the south entrance of the Kremlin. As you can guess from the massive wall we are crossing under, the structure was designed to be a fortress. Some of these structures you'll see are over six hundred years old."

Tucker searched around him. He had already done an intensive study of the Kazan Kremlin: scouring various websites, cross-referencing with Google Earth, and scanning travel blogs. A plan had begun to take shape, but he wanted to see the place firsthand.

"Here we are on Sheynkman Street," the guide expounded, "the Kremlin's main thoroughfare. Above you stands the Spasskaya Tower, known as the Savior's Tower. It is one of thirteen towers. Going clockwise, their names are . . ."

This was the third-to-last tour of the day. Tucker had Utkin working on a project back at the hotel, assisted by Bukolov. He left Kane to watch over them both.

As the group continued across the grounds, he tuned out the guide's ongoing monologue, concentrating instead on fixing a mental picture of the grounds in his head. He'd seen the *Moscow* Kremlin twice, and while that had been impressive, the Kazan version seemed somehow more majestic.

Enclosed by tall snow-white walls and turrets, the interior of the Kazan Kremlin was a mix of architectural and period styles: from the brute practicality of medieval barracks to the showy majesty of an Eastern Orthodox cathedral. Even more impressive was a massive blue-domed mosque with skyscraping tiled towers.

Gawking all around, Tucker followed their guide for the next forty-five minutes, discovering a maze of tidy cobblestone streets, hidden courtyards, and tree-lined boulevards. He did his best to appreciate the ancient beauty, while also viewing it with the eye of a soldier. He noted guard locations, blind spots, and escape routes.

As the tour wrapped up, the group was allowed to roam relatively free in the public areas, even to take pictures for the next half hour. He sat in various places, counting the number of times he was passed by guards and visitors.

It might just work, he thought.

His phone finally rang. It was Utkin. His message was terse.

"We're ready here."

He stood and headed back to the hotel, hoping everything was in order. They had to move swiftly. One mistake and it could all come crashing down.

4:14 P.M.

Tucker studied Kane approvingly.

The shepherd stood atop the hotel bed, wearing his K9 Storm jacket, but over it, covering it completely and snugly, was a new canvas vest, midnight blue, bearing Cyrillic lettering. It spelled out KAZAN KREMLIN K9.

"Good job, Utkin," Tucker said. "You could have a new career as a seamstress."

"Actually I bought the vest at a local pet store and the letters are ironed on."

Looking closer, Tucker spotted one of the Cyrillic letters peeling off.

"I will fix that," Utkin said, stripping off the false vest.

It wasn't a great disguise, but considering Utkin had been working with Internet photos of the security personnel at the Kazan Kremlin, he had done a pretty damned good job. Besides, the disguise would only have to pass muster for a short time—and then mostly in the dark.

As Utkin finished his final touch-ups—both on the vest and on the winter parka Tucker had stripped off the dead Spetsnaz soldier—Tucker turned to Bukolov.

"Were you able to reach Anya?" he asked.

"Finally. But yes, and she will be ready as you directed."

"Good."

He noted how pale Bukolov looked and the glassy glaze to his eyes. He was plainly fearful for his daughter. It seemed hearing her voice had only stoked his anxiety.

Tucker sat down next to him on the bed, figuring the doctor could use a distraction. "Tell me more about those papers Anya was searching for. Did she find them?"

He brightened, ever the proud father. "She did!"

"And this De Klerk person, why are his journals so important?"

"If you're trying to wheedle something out of me—"

"Not at all. Just curious."

This seemed to satisfy him. "What do you know about the Boer Wars?"

"In South Africa?" Tucker frowned, taken aback by the turn of the conversation. "Just the basics."

"Then here's a primer so you'll understand the context. Essentially the British Empire wanted to keep its thumb on South Africa, and the Boer farmers disagreed, so they went to war. It was bloody and ugly and replete with atrocities on both sides, including mass executions and concentration camps. But Paulos de Klerk was not only a soldier, but a *doctor* as well. Quite a complex man. But that's not why I found him so fascinating—and certainly not why his diary is so critical to my work."

Bukolov paused and glanced around as though looking for eavesdroppers. He leaned forward and gestured for Tucker to come closer.

"Paulos de Klerk was also a *botanist*." Bukolov winked. "Do you see?"

Tucker didn't reply.

"In his spare time, in between plying his dual

trades, he studied South Africa's flora. He took copious notes and made hundreds of detailed drawings. You can find his work in research libraries, universities, and even natural history museums around the world."

"And here, too, in the archives at the Kremlin?" Tucker said.

"Yes, even before the institute in Kazan was founded, this region was considered a place of great learning. Russian czars, going back to Ivan the Terrible, who built the Kremlin here, gathered volumes of knowledge and stored them in its vaults. Vast libraries and archives, much of it poorly cataloged. It took many years to track down the various references to De Klerk, bits and pieces scattered across Russia and Europe. And the most valuable clue was found here, right under our enemies' noses. So you understand now why it's so important?"

"No, not entirely."

More like *not at all*, but he kept silent.

Bukolov leaned back, snorted, and waved him off.

That was all he would get out of the man for now.

Utkin called over to him, fitting the vest back onto Kane. "That should do it."

Tucker checked his watch.

Just enough time to catch the last tour of the day.

He quickly donned the military winter suit and tugged on a pair of black boots and a midnight-blue brigade cap. The latter items had been purchased by Utkin at a local army surplus store. He had Utkin compare the look to the photos he had taken of the guards at the Kremlin.

"It should pass," the lab tech confirmed, but he didn't sound entirely convinced.

No matter. They were out of time.

Tucker turned to his partner, who wagged his tail. "Looks like it's showtime, Comrade Kane."

15

"And this concludes the day's tour," the guide told the group clustered in the cold. "Feel free to wander the grounds on your own for another fifteen minutes, then the gates will be closing promptly at six P.M."

Tucker stood with the others in a red baseball cap and knockoff Ray-Ban sunglasses, just another tourist. The disguise was in place in case he had the same blond tour guide as before. In the end, it turned out to be a man, so maybe such a level of caution was unnecessary.

At his side, Kane had initially attracted some curious glances, but as he had hoped, the service animal documents passed muster at the ticket office. It also helped that Kane could be a charmer when allowed, wriggling happily and wagging his tail. He also wore a doggie backpack with I LOVE KAZAN printed in Cyrillic on it. The bored teenagers at the gate only gave Kane's pack a cursory exam, as they did with his own small bag.

Now free to roam, Tucker wasted little time.

As casually as possible, he strode with Kane down Sheynkman Street until he reached the green-roofed barracks of the old Cadets' Quarters. He walked under its archway and into a courtyard. He ambled around and took a few pictures of a fountain and a nineteenth-century cannon display. Once done, he sat down on a nearby stone bench to wait. Beyond the arch, tourists headed back down Sheynkman toward the main exit.

No one glanced his way. No guards came into view.

Taking advantage of the moment, he led Kane across the courtyard and through a door in the southwest corner. The corridor beyond was dimly lit, lined by barrack doors. He crossed along it, noting the polished walnut floors and the boot heel impressions in the wood outside each barrack. According to the guidebook, cadets of yore stood at attention for four hours each day as their barracks underwent inspection. Tucker had thought the claim a yarn, but apparently it was true.

He came to a flight of stairs at the end of the hall and stepped over a "no access" rope. He quickly climbed to the second floor, found it empty, and searched until he located a good hiding place: an unused and derelict storage room off one of the cadets' classrooms.

He stepped inside with Kane and shut the door behind him.

Standing there, he took a breath and let it out.

Phase One . . . done.

In the darkness, he settled with Kane against one wall.

"Nap time, if you feel like it, buddy," he whispered.

Kane dropped down and rested his head on Tucker's lap.

He used the next two hours to review his plan backward, forward, and sideways. The biggest unknown was Anya. He knew little about the woman or how she would behave in a pressure situation. Nor did he know much about the escorts who guarded her here on the Kremlin premises, except for what Bukolov had learned from her.

According to him, two men—both plainclothes GRU operatives—guarded her day and night. He had a plan to deal with them, but there remained some sketchy parts to it, especially in regard to the Kremlin's K9 patrol detachment.

Over the course of the day's two tours, Tucker had counted eight dog-and-handler pairs, mostly consisting of German shepherds—which Kane could pass for. But he'd also spotted a few Russian Ovcharkas, a type of mop-coated sheepdog used by Russian military and police units.

He feared confronting any of them. He didn't kill animals, and he desperately wanted to keep it that way. Dogs did what they did out of instinct or training. Never malice. Tucker's reluctance to harm was a chink in his armor, and he knew it. Ultimately, he truly didn't know what he would do if his back were against such a wall.

In the darkness, his watch vibrated on his wrist, letting him know it was time for Phase Two.

8:30 P.M.

Tucker and Kane changed into their uniforms, a process complicated by the enclosed space and the need for quiet. Tucker already wore the police boots, their height hidden under the legs of his jeans. The rest of the clothing was split up between their two packs. He slipped into his winter military suit and tugged on the brigade cap and stuffed his old clothes into the backpack, which he stashed in the closet's rafters.

With care, he emerged back into the classroom and strode over to the windows overlooking the darkened boulevard below. At this late hour, with the temperature dropping, a light icy mist had begun to fill the streets, glistening the cobblestones under the gas lamps.

Tucker stood still for another fifteen minutes, partially because he wanted to observe the routes of the night guards—but also because his arrangement with Anya required precise timing.

At nine o' clock, she would be escorted from the private research archives to the Governor's House, one of the nonpublic buildings under intense Kremlin security. Once she crossed inside there, Tucker would have no chance of reaching her.

As the time neared, Tucker attached Kane's leash and left the classroom. He went downstairs and out onto the misty boulevard. With Kane tightly heeled beside him, Tucker put a little march into his step.

At an intersection, he spotted a guard and his dog coming in his direction. Tucker called out an order in Russian to Kane, one taught to him by Utkin, though he had to practice the local accent. Kane didn't speak Russian, so Tucker reinforced the order with a hidden hand signal.

Sit.

Kane dropped to his haunches.

As the guard approached the intersection, Tucker's heart pounded.

Keep walking.

Unlike Kane, the guard refused to obey. Both man and dog suddenly stopped, staring suspiciously at the pair.

Taking a risk, Tucker raised his hand and gave the man a curt wave. The man didn't respond. *Press it*, he thought. He took two strides forward and called out brusquely in one of the phrases Utkin had taught him, which translated roughly as, "Is everything okay?"

"*Da, da*," the guard replied and finally returned the wave. "*A u vas?*"

And you?

Tucker shrugged. "*Da.*"

The pair continued walking again, passing by Tucker and Kane.

The two quickly headed in the opposite direction, south toward the Spasskaya Tower. He had to concentrate on his steps until the acute tension worked out of his legs.

After a hundred meters, he drew even with his destination. It was called the Riding House, once a former stable, now one of the Kremlin's exhibition halls.

Thirty meters away, the guard at the Spasskaya

Tower gate waved to him. He was barely discernible through the thickening mist.

Tucker lifted his arm high, acknowledging the other.

Sticking to his disguise, Tucker put on a show, shining his flashlight into the Riding House's windows and over its walls. He spotted another K9 unit crossing the square surrounding the neighboring mosque.

Tucker waved and got one in return.

"One big happy family," he muttered and kept walking.

As Anya had promised, he found the pedestrian door at the northeast corner of the building unlocked. He swung it open and scooted inside, closing the door behind him.

The interior was what he'd imagined a *riding house* would be: horse stalls lined both sides of a central hall. Only now the spaces were dominated by glass cases displaying artifacts of the cadet corps's past: saddles, riding crops, lances, cavalry swords. The room's main halogens were off for the night, but emergency lighting allowed him to see well enough.

Anya was working in the archives located in the building's cellar, the genesis of what was soon to become the Kremlin's Museum of Ancient Books and Manuscripts. How the diary of a Boer botanist had come to rest here Tucker didn't know. It was a long way from South Africa to Kazan.

He leaned down and unclasped Kane's leash.

Time to get to work.

He pointed ahead. "SCOUT AND RETURN."

He didn't want any surprises.

On quiet paws, Kane trotted off and disappeared around one of the display cases. It took him ninety seconds to clear all the former stalls. He returned, sat beside Tucker's legs, and looked up at him.

Good boy.

Together, they crossed the central room to the south wall. A door there opened to a staircase leading down. At the bottom, milky light glowed, accompanied by the distinctive hum of fluorescent lighting.

He and Kane started down.

A couple yards from the last step, an order barked out in Russian. "Who's there?"

Tucker had been expecting this and whispered to Kane, "PLAY FRIENDS."

The shepherd loved this command. He perked up his ears, sprung his tail jauntily, and trotted down the remaining steps into the corridor beyond.

Tucker followed. Ten feet down the corridor, a thick-necked man in an ill-fitting business suit frowned at the wriggling dog.

It was one of Anya's escorts.

"*Dobriy večer,*" Tucker greeted him, wishing him a good evening.

Taking advantage of the guard's divided attention, Tucker kept walking forward.

The man held up a stiff arm and rumbled something in Russian, but Tucker made out only one word—*identify*—and the tone was demanding.

Tucker gestured at Kane, playing the chagrined guard and a misbehaving dog. "Sasha . . . Sasha . . ."

When Tucker was two strides away, the man had had enough and reached into his jacket.

Tucker dropped the act and called to Kane. "PANTS."

Kane clamped his jaws on the man's pant leg and jerked backward, using every ounce of his muscled frame. The guard tipped backward, one arm windmilling, the other still reaching for his gun.

Tucker was already moving. He closed the gap and grabbed the hand going for the concealed weapon. He lashed out with his opposite fist, punching the man squarely in the center of the throat.

The guard croaked as he fell to his back, still conscious, his eyes bulging, his mouth opening and closing spasmodically as he tried to draw breath.

Tucker slipped the man's gun out of its shoulder holster—a GSh-18 pistol—and cracked its steel butt across his temple.

His eyes finally fluttered shut.

Tucker dropped to one knee and aimed the pistol down the corridor. Although the takedown had gone relatively quietly, there was no way of knowing the second escort's proximity.

When no one immediately came running, Tucker pointed ahead. "SCOUT CORNER."

Kane trotted down the corridor and stopped at the next intersection. He peeked left, then right, then glanced back with the steady stare that meant *all clear*.

Tucker joined him and searched ahead.

Unlike the floor above, the storage cellar had undergone little renovation. The walls consisted of crumbling brick, and the floor was rough-chiseled granite. The only illumination came from fluorescent shop lights bolted to the exposed ceiling joists.

On the left, stacks of boxes blocked the corridor. To the right, it was open. At the far end, a rectangle of light was cast on the opposite wall.

A door.

Tucker led the way down the hall. He flattened himself against the wall and peeked around the corner of the door.

Inside was a massive storeroom with an arched roof. It occupied the length and breadth of the main floor above. Bookcases covered all the walls. In the center, row upon row of trestle tables lined the hall, stacked with books, manuscripts, and sheaves of paper.

A raven-haired beauty in a red blouse stood at the nearest table, partially turned from the door. With her arms braced on the table, she studied an open manuscript. To her left, the second guard sat at another table, smoking and playing solitaire.

Tucker drew back, motioned for Kane to stay. Keeping to the hallway, he stepped past the open door to the opposite side. He shoved the stolen pistol into his side pocket. He signaled Kane—*distract and return*—then pointed through the open door.

Kane trotted a few yards into the massive storeroom and began barking.

A gruff voice shouted in Russian, accompanied by the sound of a chair scraping on the stone floor.

Kane trotted back through the door, and Tucker waved for him to continue down the corridor, back the way they'd come.

A moment later the guard emerged, hurrying to catch up. Tucker let him get two steps ahead, then rushed forward and swung a roundhouse punch into his kidney. Gasping, the man dropped to his knees. Tucker wrapped his right arm around the guard's throat and used his left palm to press the man's head forward. Five seconds of pressure, squeezing the carotid artery, was all it took. The man went limp in his arms. To be sure, Tucker held on for another thirty seconds before lowering him to the floor.

Kane returned to his side, wagging his tail.

Tucker patted the shepherd's side, then turned and stepped into the storeroom.

The woman was facing him now, a worried hand at her throat. Her striking blue eyes stared at him, glassy with fear, making her look even younger than her midtwenties. She took a couple of wary steps away from him, plainly skittish. But he couldn't blame her, considering the circumstances.

"You . . . you are Tucker, yes?" she asked in lightly accented English.

He held both palms toward her, trying to calm her. "I am. And you're Anya."

She nodded, sagging with relief, while also quickly composing herself. "You were almost late."

"Almost doesn't count . . . I hope."

Kane trotted forward, his tail high.

She stared down with a small, shy smile. "I must say he startled me with that sudden barking. But, my, he is a lovely animal."

"His name is Kane."

She glanced up at Tucker with those bright eyes. "As in Cain and Abel?"

His voice caught. "Just Kane now." He turned back to the door. "We should get moving."

He quickly led her back upstairs, pausing to frisk

both men on the way out, taking their identification cards.

Anya followed, clutching to her chest a leather shoulder bag studded with rhinestones. It was large enough that she could've carried Kane in it. Not exactly inconspicuous. She caught him staring as they climbed up from the cellar.

"A Prada knockoff. I'm leaving my entire life behind, my career. Is one bag too much to ask?" As they stepped back into the main hall of the Riding House, she turned to him. "So what's your plan, great rescuer?"

He heard the forced humor in her voice, masking nervousness, but perhaps deeper down even a glint of steel. Now rallying, she seemed tougher than she first appeared.

"We're walking out the front gate," replied Tucker.

"Just like that?"

"As long as you can act worth a damn."

9:09 P.M.

Tucker spent a few minutes rehearsing with Anya in the main hall of the Riding House, running through what was to come. Once ready—or ready enough—he led her toward the exit door.

Before stepping back into the misty night, he reattached Kane's leash, straightened his military coat and brigade cap, then took her by the arm.

"All set?" he asked.

"This would be easier if I was *really* drunk." But she smiled and waved him on. "Let's do this."

Together, they slipped out of the Riding House and onto the boulevard. He headed immediately for the Spasskaya Tower and the main gate. He held Kane's leash in one hand, and with his other arm, he attempted to balance a struggling and stumbling Anya.

When he was thirty feet from the gated exit, the guard stepped out of his shack and called something that probably meant, *"What's going on?"*

"She was sleeping in the cadet quarters!" Tucker called out in Russian, repeating a preset phrase taught to him by Utkin for this very situation.

Anya began her performance, jabbering in Russian and generally making a fuss. Though Tucker understood none of it, he hoped the gist of her obscenity-laced tirade was what he had instructed her to say: *this guard was a thug . . . his dog stunk . . . there were no laws against sleeping in the Kremlin, let alone drinking . . . the visiting hours were much too short . . . and that her father was the vengeful editor of the* Kazan Herald.

Tucker manhandled her roughly toward the gates and yelled to the guard in another of his memorized stock phrases. "Hurry up! The police are on their way! Let's be rid of her!"

Behind them, farther down the boulevard, a voice called out to them. A glance over his shoulder revealed another K9 unit hurrying toward the commotion.

Biting back his own litany of curses, he turned and gave the approaching guard a quick wave that was meant to convey, *I've got it under control.*

Under his breath, he whispered to Kane, "NOISE."

The shepherd began barking loudly, adding to the frantic confusion.

All the while, Anya never slowed her tirade.

Still, the other K9 unit closed toward them.

Improvising, Anya went red-faced and bent over double, hanging on to Tucker's arm and covering her mouth with her other hand. Her body clenched in the universal posture of someone about to toss their cookies all over the ancient cobblestones.

"Hurry up!" Tucker yelled, repeating the little Russian he knew.

Finally, turning away from the young woman about to vomit, the guard fumbled with the keys on his belt and crossed to the gate. He unlocked it and swung it open—then he waved his arm, swearing brusquely, and yelled for him to get her out of there.

Tucker hurried to obey, dragging Anya behind him.

The gate clanged closed behind them. The Kremlin K9 unit reached the exit and joined the other guard, staring after them.

Tucker waved back to the pair in a dismissive and sarcastic manner, as if to say *Thanks for leaving me to clean this mess up*.

From the ribald laughter and what sounded like Russian catcalls, his message must have translated okay.

Twenty feet from the gate, Anya started to cease her performance.

Tucker whispered to her, "Keep it up until we're out of sight."

She nodded and began shouting and tried to pull

free of Tucker's grasp. He recognized the words *nyet* and *politsiya*.

No and *police*.

More laughter erupted behind him at her weak attempt at resisting arrest.

"Good job," he mumbled under his breath.

He dragged her along, angling right, until they were out of the guards' view.

Once clear, Anya stood straight and smoothed her clothes. "Should we run?"

"No. Keep walking. We don't want to draw any attention."

Still, they moved in tandem briskly and reached the forested lawn on the north side of the Church of Ascension. He pointed to the black Marussia SUV parked under a nearby tree.

They piled into the front, with Kane in the back.

Tucker started the engine, did a U-turn, and headed south. He dialed Utkin's cell phone.

"We're out. Be ready in five."

As planned, Utkin and Bukolov were waiting in the alley behind their hotel. Tucker pulled up to them, they jumped into the back with Kane, and he immediately took off.

Bukolov leaned forward to hug Anya, to kiss her cheek, tears in his eyes.

Tucker let them have their brief family reunion— then ordered everyone to keep low, out of sight. Without a glance back, he fled Kazan and headed south.

Now to get the hell out of Russia.

16

"I can't believe you did it," Bukolov said thirty minutes later. "You really did it."

Tucker concentrated on the dark, icy road, steering the SUV south on the P240 with the heater on full blast.

"Do you think we're safe now?" Utkin asked, leaning up from the backseat, looking shell-shocked. "Everything happened so fast."

"Fast is good," said Tucker. "Smooth is better."

Truth be told, he was surprised his scheme had gone largely to plan. Still, he resisted the urge to let down his guard and relax.

The sign for a rest area flashed past his high beams.

That will do.

Two miles south of here, they would reach a major highway junction. Before that, he wanted to do a little housekeeping. He took the ramp to the rest area, which consisted of a small bathroom and a couple of snow-mounded park benches nestled among ice-encrusted birches.

"Stretch your legs," Tucker said as he swung into a parking spot. He turned to face the others. "But first I need your cell phones, laptops, anything electronic that you're carrying."

"Why?" asked Bukolov.

Anya told him. "He thinks one of us will call someone."

"Who?" Bukolov demanded. "Who would we call?"

"It's not just that," Tucker explained. "Electronics can be tracked, even if they're not active. Hand them over."

Slowly they all complied, passing over their cell phones.

"What if one of us needs to make a call?" Anya asked.

"Then I'll arrange it," Tucker replied.

Once we're safely out of the country, and I've handed you over to Sigma.

Tucker took Kane out for a stroll and a bathroom break and let the others work some blood into their limbs after the rushed flight out of Kazan. While no one was looking, he threw all the electronic gear, including the laptops, into a creek that abutted the rest area. He kept only his own satellite phone buried in his pocket.

Ten minutes later, they were back on the road.

"What happens now?" Anya asked. "Where do we go? Are we looking for some airport?"

"We'll see," he replied cryptically, refusing to show his hand.

Tucker drove south for six hours, using the P240's relatively good condition, and put as much distance between them and Kazan as possible. Throughout the night, he headed deeper into rural farmlands, eventually crossing from one Russian *oblast* to another. At least the borders between the Russian provinces didn't have checkpoints. It would have made things much harder.

A couple of hours before dawn, Tucker reached the small town of Dimitrovgrad, a place that had never strayed far from its Soviet-era roots. He circled the major thoroughfares, looking for a hotel with the right mix of anonymity and accommodations. Discovering a suitable location, he booked adjoining rooms on the second floor, one for Anya and her father, the second for Utkin and himself. He posted Kane at the pass-door between the two rooms.

Tucker didn't want to stay in one place too long. So four hours later, he was already up and about again. He allowed the others a little more sleep and took a short stroll. He also wanted to be alone. As he drove into town last night, he had spotted an Internet café and headed over there. The place smelled of sausages and hot plastic, but at least it was empty at this hour. Five card tables bore nineties-era IBM computers, so old that the modems consisted of rubber cradles into which telephone handsets had been stuffed.

Thankfully, the proprietor, an older man who looked welded to his stool, wasn't the talkative type. Tucker deciphered the rates from a handwritten sheet on the counter and handed the fellow a hundred rubles. The man waved his arm as if to say *take your pick*.

The connection was predictably slow. He surfed several Russian newspaper websites. Using the translate feature, he found what he had been looking for—or, more accurately, what he had hoped *not* to find.

He returned to the hotel to discover both Anya and Utkin had left. Kane was sitting on the bed, watching him expectantly. A moment of frustration fired through him, but it passed quickly. He should have given Kane instructions to keep everyone in their rooms.

He shook Bukolov awake. "Where's Anya? And Utkin?"

"What?" Bukolov bolted upright in bed. "They're gone? Have they come for me?"

"Relax."

Tucker had begun to turn toward the door when it opened. Utkin and Anya stepped through. They were both carrying a cardboard tray filled with steaming Styrofoam cups.

"Where'd you go?" he snapped at them.

"To get tea," Anya replied, lifting the tray. "For everyone."

He pushed down his irritation. "Don't do it again, not without telling me."

Utkin mumbled an apology.

Anya looked embarrassed and set her tray down.

Bukolov defended his daughter, putting a protective arm around her. "Now see here, Tucker, I won't have you—"

He pointed a finger at the doctor's nose and swung it to include the others. "Once you're out of the country, you can all do as you please. Until then, you'll do as I say. Innocent blood has already been shed to get you this far, Doctor Bukolov. I won't have it wasted by stupidity. Not on anyone's part."

He stormed into the next room to cool off. Kane followed, tail low, sensing his anger.

Tucker ruffled the shepherd's fur. "It's not you. You're a good boy."

Utkin joined him, closing the door between the rooms. "I'm sorry, Tucker. I wasn't thinking."

He accepted the young man's apology, but he had another nagging question. "Were you two together the whole time?"

"Anya and I? No, not the entire time. I was up earlier than her. Went for a walk around the block. Sorry, I just needed to get out. All of this is . . . it's nerve-racking. I couldn't just sit in this quiet room while the others were sleeping."

"When did you and Anya meet up?"

He scrunched his nose in thought. "I met her in the parking lot. She had just come from the coffeehouse down the block, carrying the two trays of tea."

"Which direction was that?"

He pointed. "West."

"Did you see anyone with her? Talking to her?"

"No. You seem upset. Has something happened— something other than this, I mean?"

He sized the young man up, trying to decide if he was fabricating his side of the story or not. A liar always gave away tells, if you knew where to look. In the end, he decided his opinion of Utkin hadn't changed. He couldn't read a shred of artifice in the man's character.

Tucker explained, "I checked the Kazan news. They're reporting that Anya Malinov was kidnapped."

"Well, she was in a way."

"The reports state that she was taken from an alley outside a nightclub, by a man who killed her male companion."

Utkin sank to the bed. "Why the cover-up?"

"So they can shape events. But what strikes me as odd is that the fabricated story hit the newswires less than two hours after we left Kazan."

"That seems very fast. But does it mean something?"

"Maybe, maybe not."

"Do the reports have your description?"

"No, but by now someone is surely connecting the dots: Anya and her father and me."

"What about me?"

"They'll connect that dot, too, eventually."

Utkin paled. "That means they'll come after me once you're all gone."

"No, they won't."

"Why?"

He put a hand on the man's shoulder. "Because you're coming with us."

"What? Really?" The relief on his face gave him a puppy-dog look.

Was I ever that simple and innocent?

Tucker knew the guy needed to toughen up. "But I'm going to need you to pull your weight. Have you ever fired a gun?"

"Of course not."

"Then it's time to learn."

March 14, 9:12 A.M.

Tucker stood out on the balcony of their second-story room to get some air. He heard the pad of feet behind him and glanced over to find Anya leaning against the wall, arms crossed.

"May I speak with you?"

He shrugged.

"I'm sorry for what I did, for what my father said before . . . he was just being defensive. Protective."

"Your father is . . ." He did his best to sound diplomatic. "He's not an easy man to get along with."

"Try being his daughter."

Tucker matched her smile.

"He might not show it, but my father likes you. That's rare."

"How can you tell?"

"He doesn't ignore you. Earlier, I was just feeling boxed in. I had to get out for a while. Claustrophobic, is that the word?"

"Maybe stir-crazy?" Tucker offered.

She smiled. "This is certainly *crazy*. But let me ask you, why are you helping us?"

"I was asked to."

"By whom?" She immediately waved her hands. "Never mind. I should not have asked. Can you at least tell me where we are going?"

"South. With any luck, we'll make Syzran by morning. My people will meet us there."

Anya looked reassured.

"I'll drop you off at a rendezvous point in town—the Chayka Hotel. Have you thought about what you'll do once you're in the States?"

"I don't know really. I suppose that depends on what happens with my father. I have not had time to think much about it. Wherever he goes, I will go. He needs my help with his work. Where do you live?"

The question caught Tucker off guard. He had a P.O. box in Charlotte, North Carolina, but he hadn't had a permanent place to lay his head for a long time. His way of life was tough to describe to most people. He'd tried it a few times but gave up. What could he say? *I don't much like people. I travel alone with my dog and do the occasional odd job. And I like it that way.*

To shorthand the conversation now, Tucker simply lied. "Portland, Maine."

"Is it nice there? Would I like it?"

"Do you like the ocean?"

"Yes, very much."

"Then you'd like it."

She stared wistfully across the parking lot. "I'm sure I would."

Then you can send me a postcard and tell me about it.

He'd certainly never been there himself.

They chatted for a few more minutes, then Anya walked back inside.

Taking advantage of the privacy, Tucker dialed Harper. When the line clicked open, he spoke quickly.

"Tomorrow morning. Chayka Hotel in Syzran."

7:05 P.M.

With the sun fully down, the group set out again, driving south in the darkness. Tucker took a highway that skirted alongside the Volga River, the longest river in Europe. Navigating from memory, he headed for Volgograd, a city named after the river. As a precaution, he followed a mixture of main and secondary roads.

At four in the morning, he pulled into a truck stop at the edge of the city of Balakovo. "Need a caffeine fix," he said drowsily, rubbing his eyes. "Anyone else?"

The others were half asleep. He got dismissive tired waves and irritated grunts. He headed out and returned to the SUV with a boiling cup of black coffee.

As he climbed back inside, he noted his satellite phone remained in the cup holder, where he'd left it on purpose. It appeared untouched.

Satisfied, he kept driving, covering the last hundred miles in two hours. By the time he crossed into the town of Saratov, the sun was fully up.

From the backseat, Anya roused, stretched, and looked around. "This isn't Syzran."

"No."

"I thought you said we were going to Syzran? The Chayka Hotel."

"A last-minute change of plans," he replied.

He pulled off the highway and headed to a hotel near the off-ramp.

"Won't your friends be worried?" she asked.

"Not a problem. I called them."

He turned into the parking lot and shut off the engine. Utkin stirred. Anya had to shake Bukolov awake.

Tucker climbed out. "I'll be right back with our room keys."

On his way to the lobby, his satellite phone chirped. He pulled it from his pocket and checked the screen:

No activity at the Chayka Hotel.
No activity on this phone for the past eight hours.

Satisfied, Tucker crossed through the lobby and headed toward the restroom. He relieved himself, washed his hands, finger-combed his hair, and took a breath mint from a jar near the sink. Only after five minutes did he exit the hotel and cross back to the SUV.

"No vacancies, I'm afraid," he said. "Might as well push on to Volgograd."

Utkin yawned and motioned to the new day. "I thought you told us it wasn't safe to drive during the day."

"No matter. We're pushing through."

Utkin was right. It was a risk, but with only a couple of hundred miles to go before Volgograd, it was a worthwhile gamble. And from his little test, it seemed none of his fellow travelers had taken his Chayka Hotel bait. Nor had they tried to use his phone.

So far, so good.

It seemed a safe bet to move on.

Besides, if the enemy had managed to track them, why hadn't they closed the net?

Sensing the light at the end of the tunnel, he headed out, trying to enjoy the passing scenery of this sunny morning. They were almost home free and his suspicions about Anya and the others had proven unwarranted.

Out the driver's-side window, the morning sun reflected brilliantly off the Volga River. On the other side spread rolling hills and farm tracts lying fallow under pristine blankets of snow. He rolled down the window to smell the river and fresh snow.

Everyone seemed in better spirits, talking among themselves, laughing.

"Time for a Russian history quiz," Bukolov declared merrily. "Is everyone game?"

Tucker smiled. "It's not my best subject."

"Duly noted," replied Utkin.

Anya chimed in. "Tucker, we could give you a point lead. To make it fair."

Tucker opened his mouth to reply, but the words never came out. Crossing through an intersection, he caught a glimpse of chrome, a flash of sun off a windshield, accompanied by the roar of an engine— followed by the sickening crunch of metal on metal.

Then the world rolled.

17

With his head ringing, Tucker forced open his eyelids and searched around. It took him several seconds to register that he was hanging upside down, suspended by his seat belt, a deflated airbag waving in front of his face.

The SUV had rolled and settled onto its roof. Water poured through the vents. Improbably, the wipers were sliding across the windshield.

Groaning, he looked right and found Utkin balled up below him on the overturned ceiling, not moving. He lay face-up in about six inches of rising water.

Tucker's next worry.

Kane.

He was about to call out, to check on the others, then stopped, remembering the collision.

Someone had hit them—purposefully.

He squeezed his eyes shut and tried to think.

They'd ended up in the roadside ditch. He remembered seeing the wide drainage canal paralleling the road. The cut had looked deep—thirty feet or so—and steep sided. Though at this time of year, the bottom flowed with only a shallow creek of icy water.

He fought through gauzy thoughts to focus on two things.

First: Whoever hit them was coming.

Second: Survive.

He patted his jacket pocket. The Magnum was still there.

A splashing sounded behind him. He craned his neck and spotted a pair of furry front legs shifting through the water. He also saw Bukolov and Anya tangled and unconscious on the overturned roof. One of the woman's legs was still caught in the seat belt above.

"Kane," Tucker whispered. "Come here."

The shepherd climbed over the inert forms of Bukolov and Anya.

Fumbling, Tucker released the latch on his belt and fell as quietly as possible into the cold water. Kane joined him, bumping his nose against Tucker's cheek, giving a worried small lick.

That's my boy.

Thankfully, except for an inch-long gash above his eye, Kane seemed uninjured.

"Out," he ordered and shoved Kane toward the open driver's window. "Hide and cover."

Kane squeezed through and disappeared into the high grass covering the shadowy bank of the ditch. Tucker dove out after him. Staying low and using his elbows to propel him, Tucker dragged himself through the mud and weeds. He followed Kane's trail for ten feet up the embankment before running into the shepherd's backside.

Kane had stopped, crouched on his belly. He must have a good reason to stop. Taking a cue from the dog, he went still and listened.

Russian voices.

Two or three, farther down the canal to his left.

"STAY," Tucker whispered breathlessly to Kane.

He rolled to the right—once, twice, then a third time. He then sidled backward to the canal, putting the SUV between him and the voices. Once behind the bumper, he crouched and peeked along the vehicle's side.

Beyond the SUV, farther down the ditch, a trio of men in civilian clothes descended a shallow section of the embankment, aiming for the overturned vehicle. Each one carried a compact submachine gun—a PP-19 Bizon.

He hid away again, thinking quickly.

Something didn't make sense, jangling him with warning.

Three men, he thought. *They would be operating in pairs, which meant there had to be . . .*

Tucker risked another glance—back up toward the road.

A fourth man suddenly stepped to the highway's edge, training his Bizon down at the vehicle below.

Tucker slid back into hiding before being spotted. If the man had come a few seconds earlier, he would have caught the two exiting the SUV.

Damned lucky—but he couldn't count on such good fortune to last.

It would take skill.

He lowered to the waterline at the corner of the SUV and stuck his hands back into view, hoping the shadows there hid his signal to Kane. He placed a palm over a fist, then stuck out one finger and swung it to the right.

Stay hidden . . . move right.

He hoped Kane was watching, knowing the shepherd's sharp eyes would have no trouble discerning the movement in the darkness. It was the best he could do to communicate, especially since his partner wasn't wearing the tactical vest.

Done, Tucker shifted to the opposite corner of the bumper, farthest from the man on the road. He lowered flat to the canal, sinking to the bottom. The depth was only a foot and a half. He did his best to drape himself fully underwater. His fingers clung to weeds to help hold his belly flat. He set off with the meager current away from the SUV, heading downstream. With the morning sun still low in the sky, the steep-sided ditch lay in deep shadows, hopefully hiding his efforts. He prayed the shooter kept his focus on the SUV. Still, Tucker expected to feel rounds slam into his back at any moment.

When nothing came, he angled across the canal, to the same side as Kane and the gunman. He glided up to the bank and rolled to his back in the water. He lifted his head and blinked away the muddy residue.

Due to a slight bend in the waterway and the precipitous slope of the canal's side, the shooter on the road was out of direct view now. Closer at hand, he spotted a shifting through the grasses, coming his way, easy to miss unless looking for it.

His trick hadn't fooled Kane.

Keeping to the tallest weeds and shadows, his partner had tracked and followed him.

Like a beaching seal, Tucker slid out of the water and into the icy mud and weeds. Kane joined him. Together, they worked straight up the side of the ditch, moving as silently as possible, sticking to the thickest grasses. He heard the other three gunmen reach the SUV and start talking loudly.

He was running out of time.

He finally reached the top, peered down the road, and spotted the shooter to the left, his attention still focused on the SUV.

Tucker sank back and whispered in Kane's ear, "WAYPOINT, COVER, QUIET CLOSE, TAKE ALPHA."

He repeated the complex chain of commands.

While Kane's vocabulary was impressive, he also had an amazing ability to string together actions. In this case, Kane would need to cross the road, find cover, close the distance between himself and their target—then attack.

"Got it, buddy?" Tucker asked.

Kane bumped his nose against Tucker's. His dark eyes twinkled with his answer: *Of course I do, you stupid ass.*

"Off you go then."

Kane sweeps on silent paws across the cold pavement. On the far side, he squeezes into the deep brush, frosted brittle by the winter. He is cautious not to rattle the grasses and branches of scrub bushes. He finds the ground is a mix of ice and mud and keeps moving, slowly at first, testing the placement of each paw.

Growing confident, he moves faster.

A wind blows across the road, carrying to him the scent

of his partner—as familiar as his own. It is warmth and heart and satisfaction.

He also catches a whiff of his prey ahead: the sour ripeness of unwashed flesh, the tang of gunmetal and oil, the rot of bad teeth. He fixes every slight movement with minute movements of his ears: the scuff of boot on pavement, the creak of a strap of leather, the wheeze of breath.

He moves along the edge of the road, staying hidden, weaving the darkest path.

At last, he draws even with his target. He drops low and shimmies to the road's edge, watching. The other's back is to him, but he turns every few fetid breaths to look around, even back toward where Kane hides.

Dangerous.

But the command burns behind his eyes.

He must attack.

He shifts his back legs to best advantage, firing his muscles for the charge to come. Waiting for his moment—

—then movement to the left.

His partner steps out of hiding, onto the road's shoulder. He moves wrong, tilting, stumbling. Kane knows this is false, a feigned flailing. He picks out the glint of steel held at his partner's hip, out of sight of the other.

Across the road, his target turns toward his partner and focuses fully upon him. Kane feels a surge of bone-deep approval and affection. The two are a pack, one tied to the other, working together.

With his target distracted, Kane bursts out of hiding.

Tucker stared down the barrel of the submachine gun, trying his best not to flick his gaze toward Kane, as his partner charged across the pavement.

This had been the dicey part. Much of it depended on the enemy not killing Tucker on sight. Once Kane had reached his vantage point across the road, Tucker had limped out of hiding, stumbling forward, weaving and dazed, looking like a disoriented crash victim. He held his Magnum against his thigh and kept that side turned away from the shooter.

As expected, the man had spun toward him, swinging his Bizon up.

Time slowed at that moment.

Tucker lunged forward, leading now with his Magnum.

He had to put his full faith in Kane. The pair had worked for so long together, the shepherd could read Tucker's tone and body language to infer much more than could be communicated by word or hand signal. Additionally, Kane also took in environmental cues to make astute judgments on how best to execute any orders.

All that training came to a perfect fusion now.

Kane never slowed and closed the last ten feet with a leap. Seventy pounds of war dog slammed into the man's side, and together they crashed into the dirt. Even as they landed, Kane's jaws had found their mark, closing down on his target's exposed throat with hundreds of pounds of force.

Still on the run, Tucker knee-skidded to a stop beside the man, pivoted, and fired an insurance round into the shooter's hip.

He switched the Magnum to his left hand, snatched up the Bizon with his right, and leaped over Kane. He landed on his butt in the grass and began sliding down the ditch's steep embankment.

He took in the situation below with a glance, fixing the position of the three remaining enemy combatants.

One to the left, twenty feet away . . .

One kneeling at the SUV window . . .

One standing at the bumper . . .

The grass whipped Tucker's face, and rocks slammed into his buttocks and thighs. As he plummeted, he aimed the Magnum at the man beside the bumper and opened fire, squeezing the trigger over and over again. His first shot went wide, the second caught the man in the leg, and the third in the sternum.

One down.

Tucker turned his attention next to the kneeling man, who lay directly below him. He tried to bring the Bizon to bear, but he was sliding too quickly and hit the bottom of the embankment first.

At the last moment, he kicked out with his legs and flew, body-slamming the second man against the side of the SUV. Pain burst behind his eyes—but he had the other pinned, now underwater. A blind hand rose and slapped at him, fingers clawing. Then a mud-covered face pushed out, gasping, coughing. As the man tried to gulp air, Tucker shouldered his face back underwater.

He held him down, while he swung his Bizon and pointed it toward the far side of the SUV. The third enemy appeared, still about ten feet beyond the SUV, out in the open. Tucker fired a burst of rounds. His aim was wild, but it forced the other back out of sight.

By now, the man under him had stopped struggling, drowned.

Tucker crouched up, certain the last man would come charging at him.

Nothing came for a full five count.

He heard rustling in the grass and looked up to see Kane picking his way down the embankment.

With his partner coming, Tucker sidled along the edge of the SUV and took a fast look past its bumper.

The last man was stumbling away, his back to Tucker. The Bizon hung loosely from his right hand. His feet splashed heavily in the water. Out in the open, he knew he was defeated.

"Damn it," Tucker muttered.

He couldn't let the man go, but he refused to shoot a victim in the back.

"*Stoj!*" he hollered and fired a burst into the air. *Stop!*

The man obeyed, but he didn't turn around. Instead, he dropped to his knees and threw his weapon to the side. He placed his hands on top of his head.

Kane reached him, but Tucker held him back.

"Stay, pal."

Tucker walked down the ditch to where the man was kneeling. He realized the *man* was a *boy* of about nineteen or twenty.

"Turn around," he ordered.

"I will tell no one," the boy begged in heavily accented English.

Yes, you will. Even if you don't want to, they'll make you.

Tucker was suddenly tired, spent to his core. "Turn around."

"*Nyet.*"

"Turn around."

"NYET!"

Tucker swallowed hard and raised the Bizon. "I'm sorry."

18

As ugly as the Marussia SUV had been, Tucker had no complaints about the vehicle. In the end, it had saved their lives.

That, and the soft mud at the bottom of the ditch.

Tucker turned his back on the overturned vehicle. The others wobbled along the shoulder of the road. After extracting them from the SUV and doing a quick triage, he managed to rouse Utkin, who helped him with Anya and Bukolov.

In all, the group had sustained bruises and a smattering of cuts and abrasions. Bukolov suffered the worst, with a dislocated shoulder and a slight concussion. Tucker had managed to pop the old man's shoulder back into place while the doctor was still asleep. The concussion would take time and rest.

But now was *not* the time to stop moving.

Tucker led them to their new car, their attackers' dark blue Peugeot 408. Aside from a dent in the front bumper, the sedan remained unscathed. Whoever had rammed them off the road knew what they were doing. Tucker searched the car for transmitters or GPS units but found none.

As Anya helped Bukolov into the car, Utkin pulled him aside.

"What is it?" Tucker asked, wanting to get moving.

Utkin acted rather furtive. "You'd better see this."

He slipped a cell phone into Tucker's hand. It was the only phone they had found amid the attackers' possessions.

"Look at the photo I found in the digital memory."

Tucker squinted at a grainy image of himself on the screen. He was seated at a computer workstation, his hands frozen in midair over the keyboard. With a sinking feeling in his gut, he recognized the location. It was that dingy Internet café in Dimitrovgrad.

Someone had taken a picture of me.

Not knowing what to make of it, Tucker e-mailed the photo to his own phone, then deleted the original. He scrolled to the phone's address book and found it empty; same with the recent calls. It had been sanitized. Frustrated, Tucker removed the phone's battery case and SIM card and crushed them both with his heel. He crossed the road and threw the remains down into the ditch.

He took a moment to consider the meaning of the photo. Clearly someone had been covertly following them. But how? And who? He glanced to the overturned SUV. Could there have been a hidden tracer planted on the Marussia?

He didn't know . . . couldn't know.

In fact, there were far too many unknowns.

He faced Utkin. "Have you shown the others this photo?"

"No."

"Good. Let's keep this between us for now."

A few minutes later, they were again racing south along the Volga River.

Aside from a desire to get off the main road and put some distance between themselves and the ambush site, Tucker had no immediate plan. After ten miles, he turned off the highway and onto a dirt road that led to a park overlooking the Volga. He pulled in and everyone climbed out.

Utkin and Anya helped Bukolov to a nearby picnic table.

Tucker walked to the rocky bluff above the thick-flowing river. He sat down, needing to think, to regroup. He let his legs dangle over the edge and listened to the wind whistle through the skeletal trees. Kane trotted over and plopped down beside him. Tucker rested his hand on the shepherd's side.

"How're you feeling, buddy?"

Kane thumped his tail.

"Yeah, I'm okay, too."

Mostly.

He had cleaned the gash on Kane's head, but he wondered about any psychic damage. There was no way of knowing how the shepherd felt about killing that man on the road. His partner had killed in combat before, and it seemed to have no lasting impact on him. While for Tucker, that particular onion was more layered. After Abel's death, after leaving the service, Tucker had come to appreciate certain parts of the Buddhist philosophy, but he knew he'd never match Kane's Zen mind-set, which, if put into words, would probably be something like *Whatever has happened, has happened.*

As he sat, he was torn between the instinct to run hard for Volgograd, and his desire to take it slow and cautious. Still, many things troubled him. It was why he had stopped here.

Four men, he thought. *Why only four?*

Back at the ambush site, he had checked them for identification and found nothing but driver's licenses and credit cards. But the tattoos they bore confirmed them as Spetsnaz. So why hadn't the enemy landed on them with overwhelming force? Where were the platoon of men and helicopters like back at Nerchinsk?

Somehow this current action reeked of *rogue* ops. Perhaps someone in the Russian Ministry of Defense was trying to snatch Bukolov without the knowledge of their bosses. But for now, that wasn't the most pressing question concerning Tucker.

He knew the ambush couldn't have been a chance accident.

So how did the enemy know where to find them?

He pictured the photo found on the phone.

What did that mean?

Utkin joined him, taking a seat at the bluff's edge. "Good view, yes?"

"I'd prefer to be staring at the Statue of Liberty."

That got a chuckle out of Utkin. "I would like to see that, too. I've never been to America."

"Let's hope I can get you there."

"So have you figured out a plan? Where to go from here?"

"I know we have to reach Volgograd."

"But you're worried about another ambush."

It didn't require an answer.

Changing the subject, Utkin waved an arm to encompass the river and region. "Did you know I grew up around here?"

Actually Tucker did. He'd read it from the man's dossier, but he remained silent, sensing Utkin wanted to talk, reminisce.

"It was a tiny village, along the river, about fifty miles south. My grandfather and I used to fish the Volga when I was a boy."

"It sounds like a nice childhood."

"It was, thank you. But I meant to make a point. You wish to reach Volgograd, yes?"

Tucker glanced over to him, crinkling his forehead.

"And you wish to stay off the highway," Utkin said.

"That would be good."

"Well, there is another way." Utkin pointed his arm toward the river below. "It worked for thousands of years. It can work for us now."

11:01 A.M.

Tucker had one last piece of business to address before moving on. He asked Anya to stay with Bukolov at the park. He instructed Kane to guard them. For this last chore, he needed Utkin's help.

Climbing back into the Peugeot, Tucker headed out into the tangle of the remote river roads. He followed Utkin's directions. It took less than an hour to find the abandoned farmhouse tucked away in a forest.

"This was once part of an old collective," Utkin explained. "It's at least a hundred and fifty years."

Tucker used the remote to pop the trunk.

They both stared down at the bound figure inside, his mouth secured with duct tape. He was the last of those who had ambushed them, the boy of nineteen or twenty.

"Why did you let him live?" Utkin whispered.

Tucker wasn't exactly sure. He simply couldn't execute someone in cold blood. Instead, he had clubbed the kid with the butt of his gun, bound him up, and tossed him in the trunk.

The boy stared at Tucker and Utkin with wide eyes. They pulled him out and marched him toward the farmhouse. Utkin opened the front door, which shrieked on its hinges.

The interior was what Tucker had imagined: knotty plank walls and floors, boarded-up windows, low ceilings, and layers of dust on every surface.

Tucker pushed the boy inside and sat him down on the floor. He peeled the tape from the boy's mouth.

"Can you translate?" he asked Utkin.

"Are you going to interrogate him?"

Tucker nodded.

Utkin backed up a step. "I don't want to be a part of any—"

"Not that kind of interrogation. Ask him his name."

Utkin cooperated and got an answer.

"It's Istvan."

Tucker took the boy through a series of benign personal questions designed to massage his defenses. After five minutes, the kid's posture relaxed, his rat-in-a-cage expression fading.

Tucker waved to Utkin. "Tell him I have no plans to kill him. If he cooperates, I'll call the local police and tell them where to find him."

"He's relieved, but he says you must beat him. For effect. Otherwise, his superiors will—"

"I understand. Ask him his unit."

"It's Spetsnaz, like you thought. But he and his team had been assigned to the Russian military intelligence."

"The GRU?"

"That's right."

The same as the Spetsnaz at Nerchinsk.

"Who did his unit report to at the GRU?"

"A general named Kharzin. Artur Kharzin."

"And what was their job?"

"To track down Bukolov. His group was told to intercept our car here."

"By Kharzin."

"Yes, the order came from Kharzin."

This guy must be one of Bukolov's mysterious Arzamas generals.

"And once they got hold of the doctor?" Tucker asked. "What were they to do?"

"Return him to Moscow."

"Why does General Kharzin want him?"

"He doesn't know."

Tucker pulled out his cell phone and showed the grainy image from the Internet café to their captive. "How and when did you get this?"

"By e-mail," Utkin translated. "Yesterday afternoon."

"How did they know where to intercept us?"

Utkin shook his head. "He was just given the order."

"Do you believe him?"

"Yes, I think so."

"Let's find out."

Abruptly, Tucker pulled the Magnum from his jacket pocket and pressed it against the boy's right kneecap. "Tell him I don't believe him. He needs to tell me *why* Kharzin wants Bukolov."

Utkin translated Tucker's demand.

Istvan started jabbering, white-faced and trembling.

"He says he doesn't know," Utkin blurted, almost as scared as the kid. "Something about a plant or flower. A discovery of some kind. A weapon. He swears on the life of his son."

Tucker kept the Magnum pressed against the guy's kneecap.

Utkin whispered, "Tucker, he has a son."

Tucker did his best to keep his face stony. "A lot of people have sons. He's going to have to give me a better reason than that. Tell him to think hard. Has he forgotten anything?"

"Like what!"

"Is there anyone else after us? Anyone besides the GRU?"

Utkin questioned the boy, pressing him hard. Finally, he turned and stammered, "He says there's a woman. She is helping Kharzin."

"A woman?"

"Someone with blond hair. He only saw her once. He doesn't know her name, but he believes that she was hired by Kharzin as some sort of mercenary or assassin."

Tucker pictured Felice Nilsson. She was old news. "Go on. Tell him I already know about—"

"He says after they pulled her from the river, she was taken to a hospital."

Tucker felt as though he'd been punched in the stomach.

"Has he seen her since?"

"No."

Could she truly have survived?

He remembered the strong current, the icy water. He pictured Felice swimming or being pulled along by the flow, maybe finding a break in the ice, maybe radioing for rescue. If the Spetsnaz had found Felice quickly enough, there was a slight chance she could have made it.

Tucker took the Magnum away from Istvan's knee and shoved it into his jacket pocket. The boy leaned back, gasping with relief.

Tucker was done here. As he turned away, he imagined that cunning huntress coming after him again, but he felt no fear, only certainty.

I killed you once, Felice. If I have to, I'll do it again.

19

Back in the Peugeot, Tucker continued working his way south, staying off the main road. Utkin's knowledge of the area came in very handy as he pointed to rutted tracks and cow paths that weren't on any map.

Anya broke the exhausted silence and expressed a fear she had clearly been harboring. "What did you do with the young man from the trunk?"

"Are you asking me if I killed him?" Tucker said.

"I suppose I am."

"He'll be fine."

Conditionally, he added silently. They had left Istvan duct-taped to a post at the old farmhouse. His parting words to the kid had been clear: *This is your one free pass. Appear on the field of battle again and I'll kill you.*

"Please tell me you didn't hurt him."

"I didn't hurt him."

Tucker glanced at her in the rearview mirror. Her blue eyes stared back at him in the reflection.

She finally turned away. "I believe you."

Following Utkin's directions, Tucker drove south for another thirty miles, reaching a farming community near the Volga's banks.

"The village of Shcherbatovka," Utkin announced.

If you say so . . .

Half the buildings were either boarded up or looked abandoned. At the far end, a narrow dirt road led in a series of sharp switchbacks from the top of a bluff to a dock that hugged the river.

They all unloaded at the foot of the pier, a ramshackle structure of oil-soaked pylons and gap-toothed wooden planks.

Utkin waved to a man seated in a lawn chair at the end. Floating listlessly beside him was what looked to be a rust-streaked houseboat. Or maybe *tent* boat was the better description. A blue tarpaulin stretched over the flat main deck.

Utkin talked with the man for a few minutes then returned to the car.

"He can take us to Volgograd. It will cost five thousand rubles, not including the fuel."

The price wasn't Tucker's concern. "Can we trust him?"

"My friend, these people do not have telephones, televisions, or radios. Unless our pursuers plan to visit every fisherman personally between Saratov and Volgograd, I think we are safe. Besides, the people here do not like the government. Any government."

"Fair enough."

"In addition, I know this man well. He is a friend of my uncle. His name is Vadim. If you are in agreement, he says we can leave at nightfall."

'Tucker nodded. "Let's do it."

After storing their gear in the storage shed of Vadim's boat, Tucker drove the Peugeot back toward Shcherbatovka. A mile past the village, following Utkin's crude map, he reached a deep tributary to the Volga. He drove to the edge, put the car in neutral before turning it off, and climbed out.

Kane followed him, stretching, while searching the woods to either side.

Tucker quickly tossed the keys into the creek, got behind the car, and shouldered it into the water. He waited until the Peugeot sank sullenly out of view.

He then turned to Kane.

"Feel like a walk?"

8:30 P.M.

Captain Vadim stood on the dock, a glowing stub of a cigar clenched between his back molars. The stocky, hard man, with a week of beard scruff and hardly more stubble across his scalp, stood a head shorter than any of them. Though it was already growing colder following sunset, he wore only a shirt and a pair of stained jeans.

He waved Tucker and the others toward a plank that led from the pier to his boat. He grumbled something that Tucker took as *Welcome aboard*.

Anya helped Bukolov tiptoe warily across the gangplank. Kane trotted across next, followed by Tucker and Utkin.

Vadim yanked the mooring lines, hopped aboard, and pulled the gangplank back to the boat's deck.

He pointed to an outhouse-like structure that led below to the cabins and spoke rapidly.

Utkin grinned. "He says the first-class accommodations are below. Vadim has a sense of humor."

If you could call it that, Tucker thought.

"I should take my father to his cabin," Anya said. "He still needs some rest."

Bukolov did look exhausted, still compromised by his concussion. He slapped at Anya's hands as she tried to help him.

"Father, behave."

"Quit calling me that! Makes me sound like an invalid. I can manage."

Despite his grousing, he allowed himself to be helped below.

Tucker turned to find Kane standing at the blunted bowsprit, his nose high, taking in the scents.

That's a happy dog.

To the west, the sun had set behind the bluffs. The afternoon's brisk wind had died to a whisper, leaving the surface of the Volga calm. Still, underneath the surface, sluggish brown water swirled and eddied.

The Volga's currents were notoriously dangerous.

Utkin noted his attention. "Don't fall in. Vadim has no life rings. Also Vadim does not swim."

"Good to know."

With everyone aboard, Vadim hopped onto the afterdeck and took his place behind the wheel. With a rumble, the diesel engine started. Black smoke gushed from the exhaust manifolds. The captain steered the bow into the current, and they were off.

"How long to Volgograd?" Tucker asked.

Utkin glanced back to Vadim. "He says the current is faster than normal, so about ten hours or so."

Tucker joined Kane, and after twenty minutes, Anya returned topside.

She stepped over to him. Chilled, she tugged her wool jacket tighter around her body, unconsciously accentuating her curves.

"How's your father doing?" he asked.

"Finally sleeping."

Together, they stared at the dark shoreline slipping past. Stars glinted crisply in the clear skies. Something brushed Tucker's hand. He looked down to find Anya's index finger resting atop his hand.

She noticed it and pulled her hand away, curling it in her lap. "Sorry, I did not mean to—"

"No problem," he replied.

Tucker heard footsteps on the deck behind them. He turned as Utkin joined them at the rail.

"That's where I grew up," the man said, pointing downstream toward a set of lights along the west bank. "The village of Kolyshkino."

Anya turned to him, surprised. "Your family were farmers? Truly?"

"Fishermen actually."

"Hmm," she said noncommittally.

Still, Tucker heard—and he was sure Utkin did, too—the slight note of disdain in her question and response. It was an echo of Bukolov's similar blind condescension of the rich for the poor. Such sentiment had clearly come to bias Bukolov's view of Utkin as a fellow colleague. Whether Anya truly felt this way, Tucker didn't know, but parents often passed on their prejudices to their children.

Tucker considered his own upbringing. While his folks had died too young, some of his antisocial tendencies likely came from his grandfather, a man who lived alone on a ranch and was as stoic and cold as a North Dakota winter. Still, his grandfather treated his cattle with a surprisingly warm touch, managing the animals with an unusual compassion. It was a lesson that struck Tucker deeply and led to many stern conversations with his grandfather about animal husbandry and responsibility.

In the end, perhaps it was only natural to walk the path trod by those who came before us. Still . . .

After a time, Anya drifted away and headed below to join her father.

"I'm sorry about that," Tucker mumbled.

"It is not your fault," Utkin said softly.

"I'm still sorry."

9:22 P.M.

Belowdecks, Tucker lounged in what passed for the mess hall of the boat. It was simple and clean, with lacquered pine paneling, several green leatherette couches, and a small kitchenette, all brightly lit by bulkhead sconces.

Except for the captain, everyone had eventually wandered here, seeking the comfort of community. Even Bukolov joined them, looking brighter after his nap, more his old irascible self.

Tucker passed out snacks and drinks, including some jerky he'd found for Kane. The shepherd sat near the ladder, happily gnawing on a chunk.

Eventually, Tucker sat across from Bukolov and placed his palms on the dining table. "Doctor, it's high time we had another chat."

"About what? You're not going to threaten us again, are you? I won't stand for that."

"What do you know about Artur Kharzin, a general tied to Russian military intelligence?"

"I don't know anything about him. Should I?"

"He's the one hunting us. Kharzin seems to think your work involves biological weapons. So convinced, in fact, he's ordered all of us killed—except you, of course." He turned to Anya. "What do you make of all of this?"

"You'll have to ask my father." She crossed her arms. "This is his discovery."

"Then let's start with a simpler question. Who are you?"

"You know who I am."

"I know who you *claim* to be, but I also know you've been pumping me for information since we met. You're very good at it, actually, but not good enough."

Actually he wasn't as confident on this last point as he pretended to be. While Anya had asked a lot of questions, such inquiries could just as easily be born of innocent curiosity and concern for her father.

"Why are you doing this?" Anya shot back. "I thought such suspicions were settled back in Dimitrovgrad."

"And then we were ambushed. So tell me what I want to know—or I can take this discussion with your father in private. He won't like that."

She stared with raw-eyed concern and love toward

Bukolov. Then with a shake of her head, she touched her father's forearm, moving her hand down to his hand. She gripped it tightly, possessively.

Bukolov finally placed his hand over hers. "It's okay. Tell him."

Anya looked up at him, her eyes glassy with tears. "I'm not his daughter."

Tucker had to force the shock not to show on his face. That wasn't the answer he had been expecting.

"My name is Anya Malinov, but I'm not Doctor Bukolov's daughter."

"But why lie about it?" Tucker asked.

Anya glanced away, looking ashamed. "I suggested this ruse to Abram. I thought, if he told you that I was his daughter, you would be more inclined to take me with you."

"You must understand," Bukolov stressed. "Anya is critical to my work. I could not risk your refusing to bring her along."

No wonder this part of the plan was kept from Harper.

"But I meant what I said before," Bukolov pressed. "Anya is critical to my work."

"And what is that *work*? I'm done with these lies. I want answers."

Bukolov finally caved. "I suppose you have earned an explanation. But this is very complicated. You may not understand."

"Try me."

"Very well. What do you know about earth's primordial history? Specifically about plant life that would have existed, say, seven hundred million years ago?"

"Absolutely nothing."

"Understandable. For many decades, a hypothesis has been circulating in scientific communities about something called LUCA—Last Universal Common Ancestor. Essentially we're talking about the earth's first multicellular plant. In other words, the *seed* or genesis for each and every plant that has ever existed on the earth. If LUCA is real—and I believe it is—it is the progenitor of every plant form on this planet, from tomatoes and orchids, to dandelions and Venus flytraps."

"You used the word hypothesis, not theory," said Tucker. "No one has ever encountered LUCA before?"

"Yes and no. I'll get to that shortly. But first consider stem cells. They are cells that hold the potential to become any other cell in the human body if coaxed just right. A blank genetic slate, so to speak. By manipulating stem cells, scientists have been able to grow an ear on a mouse's back. They've grown an entire liver in a laboratory, as if from thin air. I think you can appreciate the significance of such a line of research. Stem cell research is already a multibillion-dollar industry. And will only escalate. It is the future of medicine."

"Go on."

"To simplify it to the basics, I believe LUCA is to plant life what stem cells are to animal life. But why is that important? I'll give you an example. Say someone discovers a new form of flower in Brazil that treats prostate cancer. But the rain forests are almost gone. Or the flower is almost extinct. Or maybe the drug is prohibitively expensive to synthesize. With LUCA, those problems vanish. With LUCA, you simply carbon-copy the plant in question."

Bukolov grew more animated and grandiose. "Or, better yet, you use LUCA to replenish the rain forest itself. Or use LUCA in combination with, say, soybeans, to turn barren wastelands into arable land. Do you see the potential now?"

Tucker leaned back. "Let me make sure I understand. If you're right, LUCA can replicate *any* plant life because in the beginning, it *was* all plant life. It's as much of a genetic blank slate as stem cells."

"Yes, yes. I also believe it can *accelerate* growth. LUCA is not just a replicator species, but a *booster* as well."

Anya nodded, chiming in. "We can make flora hardier. Imagine potatoes or rice that could thrive where only cacti could before."

"All this sounds great, but didn't you say this was all an unproven hypothesis?"

"It is," Bukolov said, his eyes glinting. "But not for much longer. I'm about to change the world."

20

Tucker turned the conversation from world-changing scientific discoveries to more practical questions. Like why someone was trying to kill them?

"Back to this General Kharzin," Tucker said.

"Since we are done with the lies," Bukolov said, "I *do* know him. Not personally, just by reputation. I'm sorry. I do not trust people easily. It took me many months before I even told Anya about LUCA."

"What do you know about him? What's his reputation?"

"In a word. He's a monster. Back in the eighties, Kharzin was in charge of Arzamas-16, outside of Kazan. After that military weapons research facility was shut down, its archives were transferred to the Institute of Biochemistry and Biophysics in Kazan."

"And then, years later they were moved into storage vaults at the Kazan Kremlin," Anya added.

"All along, Kharzin was a true believer in LUCA—though his scientists called it something different back then. But he only saw its destructive potential."

"Which is?"

"What you must understand, the primordial world was once a much harsher place. In its original habitat, such a life-form would have been highly aggressive. It would have to be to survive. If let loose today, with no defenses against it, I believe—as did Kharzin—that it would be *unstoppable*."

Tucker was beginning to see the danger.

Bukolov continued. "LUCA's primary purpose is to hijack nearby plant cells and modify them to match its own, so it can reproduce—rapidly, much like a virus. It has the potential to be the world's most deadly and relentless invasive species."

Tucker understood how this could easily become a weapon. If released upon an enemy, it could wipe out the country's entire agricultural industry, devastating the land without a single shot being fired.

"So how far along are you with this research?" he asked. "You and Kharzin?"

"In the past, we've been running parallel lines of research, trying to reverse-engineer plant life to create LUCA or a LUCA-like organism in the lab. My goal was to better the world. His was to turn LUCA into a weapon. But we both ran into *two* problems."

"Which were what?"

"First, neither of us could create a viable specimen that was stable. Second, neither of us could figure out how to control such a life-form if we succeeded."

Tucker nodded. "For Kharzin, his biological bomb needed an *off* switch."

"Without it, he wouldn't be able to control it. He couldn't safely use it as a weapon. If it is released without safeguards in place, LUCA runs the risk of spreading globally, wiping out ecosystem after ecosystem. In the end, it could pose as much risk to Russia as Kharzin's enemies."

"So what suddenly changed?" Tucker asked. "What set this manhunt in motion? Why do you need to leave Russia so suddenly?"

Clearly the old impasse between the two of them had broken.

"Because I believe I know where to *find* a sample of LUCA . . . or at least its closest descendant."

Tucker nodded. "And Kharzin learned of your discovery. He came after you."

"I could not let him get to it first. You understand that, yes?"

He did. "But where is this sample? How did you learn about it?"

"From Paulos de Klerk. The answer has been under our noses for over a century."

Tucker remembered Bukolov's story about the Boer botanist, about his journals being prized throughout the academic world.

"You see, over the years, I've managed to collect portions of his diaries and journals. Most of it in secret. Not an easy process as the man created great volumes of papers and accounts, much of it scattered and lost or buried in unprocessed archives. But slowly I was able to start collating the most pertinent sections. Like those last papers Anya smuggled out of the Kremlin."

Tucker pictured the giant Prada bag clutched to her chest.

"He kept a diary for decades, from the time he

was a teenager until he died. Most of it is filled with the mundane details of life, but there was one journal—during the Second Boer War—that described a most fascinating and frightening observation. From the few drawings I could find, from his detailed research notes, I was sure he had discovered either a cluster of living LUCA or something that acted just like the hypothetical life-form."

"Why do you think that?"

"It wasn't just me. In one page I found at a museum in Amsterdam, he described his discovery as *die oorsprong van die lewe*. In Afrikaans, that means *the origin of life*."

"So what became of this sample? Where did he find it?"

"Some cave in the Transvaal. Someplace he and his Boer unit retreated to. They were pinned down there by British forces. It was during this siege that De Klerk found the cluster of LUCA. As a botanist and medical doctor, he was understandably intrigued. I don't have the complete story about what happened in that cave. It's like reading a novel with half the pages missing. But he hints at some great misery that befell their forces."

"What happened to him?"

"Sadly, he would die in that cave, killed as the siege broke. The British troops eventually returned his belongings, including his journals and diary, to his widow. But past that we know nothing. I'm still studying the documents Anya found. Perhaps some of the blanks will be filled in."

"Is there any indication that De Klerk understood what he found?"

"No, not fully," Anya replied. "But in the papers I was collecting when you came for me in the Kremlin, he finally named his discovery: *Die Apokalips Saad*."

"The Apocalypse Seed," Bukolov translated. "Whatever he found scared him, but he was also intrigued. Which explains his map."

"What map?"

"To the location of the cave. It's encrypted in his diary. I suspect De Klerk hoped he'd survive the siege and have a chance to return later to continue his research. Sadly that wasn't to be."

"And you have this map?"

"I do."

"Where?"

Bukolov tapped his skull. "In here. I burned the original."

Tucker gaped at the doctor.

No wonder everyone is after you.

10:18 P.M.

After the discussion, Tucker needed some fresh air to clear his head.

He and Kane stepped up on deck and waved to Vadim, who continued to man the boat's wheel. In return, he got a salute with the glowing tip of his cigar.

Settled into the bow, Tucker listened to the waves slap the hull and stared longingly at the pinpricks of lights marking homes and farmsteads, life continuing simply. He considered calling Ruth Harper. But after all that had happened, he was wary. His satellite phone was supposed to be secure, but was any communication truly safe? He decided to err on the side of caution until he got to Volgograd.

Footsteps sounded behind him. Kane stirred, then settled again.

"May I join you?" Anya asked.

Tucker gestured to the deck beside him. She sat down, then scooted away a few inches. "I'm sorry we lied to you," she said.

"Water under the boat."

"Don't you mean under the bridge?"

"Context," Tucker said, getting a nervous laugh out of the woman. "It's nice to see that."

"Me laughing? I'll have you know, I laugh all the time. You just haven't seen me at my best as of late." She hesitated. "And I'm afraid I'm about to make that worse."

He glanced over to her. "What is it?"

"Do you promise not to shoot me or throw me off the boat?"

"I can't promise that. But out with it, Anya. I've had enough surprises for one day."

"I'm SVR," she said.

Tucker blew his breath out slowly, trying to wrap his head around this.

"It stands for—"

"I know what it stands for."

Sluzhba Vneshney Razvedki. It was Russia's Foreign Intelligence Service, their equivalent of the CIA.

"Agent or officer?" he asked.

"Agent. For the last six years. But I do have a degree in biochemistry. That's real enough. It's why they sent me."

"Sent you to get close to Bukolov."

"Yes."

"And you're pretty," Tucker added. "Perfect bait for the older, widowed professor."

"It was never like that," Anya snapped. "They told me to seduce him if necessary, but I . . . I couldn't do it. Besides, it proved unnecessary. The doctor is consumed with his work. My interest and aid was enough to gain his trust."

Tucker decided he believed her. "What was the SVR after? LUCA?"

"No, not exactly. We knew Abram was working on something important. That he was close to a breakthrough. And given who he is, they wanted to know more about what he was working on."

"And now they do," Tucker replied. "When are they coming? Where's the ambush point?"

"That's just it. They're *not* coming. I've strung them along. Believe this or not, but I believe in what he is doing. When I found out what he was trying to accomplish, I changed my mind. I'm still a scientist at heart. He genuinely wants to use LUCA for *good*. Months ago, I decided I wasn't about to hand over something that important. Since then I've been feeding my superiors false information."

"Does Bukolov know?"

"No. It is a distraction he does not need. Completing his work must come first."

"What do you know about Kharzin?"

"This is the first I've heard of his involvement here, but I do know his reputation. He's ruthless, very old school, surrounds himself with like-minded ideologues. All Soviet hard-liners."

"What about your superiors? Have you been in contact with them since I got you out of the Kremlin?"

"No. You took our phones."

"What about in Dimitrovgrad . . . when you disappeared?"

"Tea," Anya replied. "I really was just getting tea. I didn't break communication silence, I swear."

"Why should I believe you? About any of this?"

"I can't offer any concrete proof. But ask yourself this: If I were still in contact with the SVR and my loyalties had not changed, why aren't they *here*?"

Tucker conceded her argument was solid.

"My real name is Anya Averin. You can have your superiors confirm what I'm saying. When we reach Volgograd, turn me over to your people. Let them debrief me. I've told you the truth!" Anya's voice took on a pleading but determined tone. "Only Abram knows where De Klerk's cave is. He never told me. Ask him. Once you get Abram out of the country and under U.S. protection, LUCA is safe from everyone—the SVR, General Kharzin—all of them."

Tucker stared across the waters at the small slumbering homesteads along the banks, free of such skullduggery. How did spies live in this world and keep their sanity?

"What are you going to do?" Anya asked.

"I'll keep your secret from Bukolov for now, but only until we reach the border."

She gave him a nod of thanks. For a second, he considered throwing her overboard anyway, but quashed the impulse.

After she left, Tucker grabbed a sleeping bag and

a blanket and found a nook on the boat's forecastle. Kane curled up on the blanket and closed his eyes. Tucker tried to do the same but failed.

He stared at the passing view, watched the moon-rise above the banks. Kane had a dream, making soft noises and twitching his back legs.

Tucker tried to picture their destination.

Volgograd.

He knew the city's infamous history, when it used to be called Stalingrad. During World War II, a major battle occurred there between the German Wehrmacht and the Soviet Red Army. It lasted five months, leaving Stalingrad in rubble and two million dead or wounded.

And that's where I hope to find salvation.

No wonder he couldn't sleep.

21

With sunrise still two hours away, the river remained dark, mottled with patches of fog, but a distant glow rising ahead, at the horizon line, marked their approach toward Volgograd. As they motored along the current, the lights of the city slowly appeared, spreading across the banks of the river to either side, then spilling out into the surrounding steppes.

Tucker checked his watch, then retrieved his satellite phone and dialed Sigma. Once Harper was on the line, Tucker brought her up to speed about everything, including Anya's confession from last night.

"I'll look into her," Harper promised.

"We should be in the city proper in another hour or so. What do you have waiting for us?"

Harper hesitated a moment. "Try to keep an open mind about this."

"Whenever a sentence starts that way, I get nervous."

"What do you know about ecotourism?"

"Next to nothing."

"Well, that area of Russia has become something of a mecca for it—especially the Volga. Apparently the huge river is home to plant and animal life that's found in few other places. Consequently, a cottage business has sprung up in Volgograd—submarine ecotours."

"You're kidding. The Russians don't strike me as the ecofriendly type."

"Still, at last count, there are eleven companies that offer such tours. They make up a fleet of about forty electric minisubs. Each holds six passengers and one pilot. With a depth rating of thirty feet. Aside from conducting monthly safety checks, the government is hands-off. The subs come and go as they please."

"I like the sound of that."

Tucker could guess the rest. Sigma must have found a tour company that was strapped for cash and was willing to take a private party on an *extended* tour of the Volga.

After she passed on the details, Tucker hung up and went aft to speak with Vadim.

"Do you speak English?" Tucker asked.

"Yes. Some. If speak slow."

Tucker explained as best he could, much of it involving pantomiming. He should have woken Utkin to help with the translation.

But finally Vadim grinned and nodded. "Ah! The Volga-Don canal. Yes, I know it. I find the boat you meet. Three hours, *da*?"

"*Da*."

"We make it. No worry. You and dog go now."

It seemed Tucker had been dismissed. He went

below to find everyone awake and eating a simple breakfast of tea, black bread, and hard cheese.

Bukolov asked, "So, Tucker, what is your plan? How are you going to get me out of the country?"

"It's all been arranged." He held off mentioning the unusual means of transportation—not because of fear that the information might leak to the wrong ears, but simply to avoid a mutiny. Instead, he bucked up as much confidence as he could muster and said, "We're almost home free."

8:13 A.M.

Ninety minutes later, Vadim called down the ladder, "We are here."

Tucker led the group topside, where they found the world had been whitewashed away, swallowed by a thick, dense fog. To the east the sun was a dull disk in the overcast sky. All around, out of the mists, buoys clanged and horns blew. Flowing dark shadows marked passing boats, gliding up and down the Volga.

Vadim had them anchored near the shore, the engine in neutral.

"It is eerie, all this fog," Anya said.

"But good for us, yes?" Bukolov asked.

Tucker nodded.

Vadim resumed his post at the wheel and said something to Utkin.

"He says your friends are late."

Tucker checked his watch. "Not by much. They'll be here."

They stood in the fog, not talking, waiting.

Then an engine with an angry pitch grew louder, coming toward them. A moment later, the sharp nose of a speedboat glided out of the fog off the port bow. The speedboat drew abeam and a gaff hook appeared and latched on to their gunwale.

With a hand on his pocketed Magnum, Tucker crossed to the port side and cautiously peeked over the rail.

A bald, round-faced man with two gold front teeth smiled and handed a slip of paper up to Tucker. Nine alphanumeric characters had been scrawled on it. Tucker checked them carefully, then handed across his own slip of paper with a similar string of symbols, which the stranger studied before nodding.

It was a coded means of verifying each other, arranged by Harper.

"You are Tucker?" the man asked.

"I am. That must mean you are Misha?"

He got another gold-tinged smile, and Misha stepped back and waved his hand to the speedboat. "Thank you for choosing Wild Volga Tours."

Tucker collected the others, paid Vadim, then herded everyone onto the other boat.

Misha eyed Kane skeptically as Tucker hauled him down.

"Is he wolf?"

"He thinks so sometimes. But he's well trained."

And all the more dangerous for it, Tucker added silently.

His reassurance seemed to satisfy the boatman. "Come. Follow me."

They set off into the fog, seeming to go much

faster than was wise considering the visibility. They wove in and around the river traffic. Even Tucker found himself clinging tightly to one of the boat's handgrips.

Finally, the engine changed pitch, and the boat slowed. Misha angled toward shore, and a dock appeared out of the mist. He eased them alongside the tire bumpers. Men appeared out of the fog and secured the mooring lines.

"We go now," Misha said and hopped to the pier.

Tucker led the others and followed their guide through the fog down a wide boardwalk that spanned a swampy area. At the end rose a Quonset hut with pale yellow walls and a riveted roof streaked with so much rust it looked like an abstract painting.

The group stepped inside. To their left, a pair of red-and-blue miniature submarines sat atop maintenance scaffolding. The subs were thirty feet long and seven wide with portholes lining the hull, including along the bottom. Amidships, a waist-high conning tower rose, topped by a hand-wheel-operated entry hatch. Below this, jutting from the subs' sides, were a pair of adjustable control-planes. At the bow was a clear, bulbous cone, which Tucker assumed was the pilot's seat.

Tucker turned to the others, who were staring openmouthed at the subs, and said, "Your chariots."

No one spoke.

"Impressive, *da*?" Misha said cheerily.

"You're joking, right?" Utkin asked. "Is this how we're leaving Volgograd?"

And this, from the most pliable of the group.

Bukolov and Anya remained speechless.

"They're so very small," Utkin continued.

"But comfortable, and well stocked," Misha countered. "And reliable. It may take a while to reach your destination, but we will get you there. To date, we have had only three accidents."

Anya finally found her voice. "Accidents? What kind of accidents?"

"No injuries or fatalities. Power outages." Misha shrugged. "We got craned out of the river before the Volga mud swallowed us."

Anya turned a pleading look toward Tucker. "This is your plan? I am not—"

Surprisingly, Bukolov became the voice of reason, stepping to Anya and curling an arm around her shoulders. "Anya, I am sure it is perfectly safe."

She did not look convinced.

Leaving the others in the maintenance bay to ogle the submarines, Misha led Tucker into a side office. There, Misha's friendly grin disappeared. "What your people have asked is very difficult. Do you know how far away the Caspian Sea is?"

"Two hundred eighty-two miles," Tucker replied. "Taking into account the cruising speed of your submarines, the average recharge time for the sub's batteries, and the seasonal current of the Volga, we should reach the Caspian in eighteen to twenty-four hours."

"I see," he grumbled. "You are well informed."

"And you're being *well* paid."

Before Misha could reply, Tucker added, "I understand the risk you're taking, and I'm grateful. So, I'm prepared to offer you a bonus: ten thousand rubles if you get us there safely. On one condition."

"I am listening."

"You're our pilot. *You* personally. Take it or leave it."

He wanted more than a financial gamble by the owner of Wild Volga Tours. He wanted his skin involved in the game, too.

Misha stared hard at Tucker, then stuck out his hand. "Done. We leave in one hour."

22

Misha led the group back the way they'd come, through the swamp to the speedboat. Once aboard, the crew shoved off and headed downriver toward the tour company's embarkation point. The fog remained thick as the weak morning sun had yet to burn it away.

"What's that stink?" Utkin asked after a few minutes.

Tucker smelled it, too, a heavy sulfurous stench to the air.

"Lukoil refinery over there," Misha replied and pointed to starboard. "Much oil businesses along the river."

"This close to the Volga?" Bukolov said. "Seems like a disaster waiting to happen."

Misha shrugged. "Many jobs. No one complains."

The speedboat slowly angled back toward shore, weaving through a maze of sandbars into the mouth of an estuary. Its bow nosed into a narrow, tree-lined inlet and pushed up to a wooden pier, where the boat was tied off. At the other end of the dock, one of Misha's minisubs bobbed with the waves from their wake, rubbing against the tire bumpers.

"The *Olga*," Misha announced. "Named after my grandmother. Lovely woman, but very fat. She too bobbed in the water. But never sank."

Misha led them to the end of the dock to the *Olga*. An employee in blue coveralls climbed out of the conning tower hatch and descended the side ladder. He shook Misha's hand and exchanged a few words.

After clapping the employee on the shoulder, Misha turned to the group. "Checked, stocked, and prepared for takeoff. Who goes first?"

"Me." Anya set her jaw and stepped forward.

Tucker felt a wave of sympathy and respect for her. Frightened though she was, she'd decided to face it head-on.

Without a word, she scaled the ladder. At the top, she dropped one leg into the hatch, then the other, and disappeared into the conning tower. Utkin went next, followed by Bukolov, who muttered under his breath, "Fascinating . . . what fun."

When it came to Kane's turn, Tucker double tapped the ladder's rung. Awkwardly but quickly, the shepherd scaled the ladder, then shimmied through the hatch.

"Impressive," Misha said. "He does tricks!"

You have no idea.

Tucker followed, then Misha, who pulled the hatch closed, tugged it tight over the rubber seals, then spun the wheel until an LED beside the coaming glowed green. With the sub secure, Misha dropped down and shimmied to the cockpit.

The sub's interior was not as cramped as Tucker

had expected. The bulkheads, deck, and overhead were painted a soothing cream, as were the cables and tubes that snaked along the interior. A spacious bench padded in light blue Naugahyde ran down the center of the space, long enough for each of them to lie down, if necessary.

Tucker leaned and stared out one of the portholes, noting that the sun was beginning to peek through, showing shreds of blue sky. Occasionally green water sloshed across the view as the sub rolled and bobbed. He straightened and took a deep breath, tasting the slight metallic scent to the air.

"If anyone's hungry," Misha called out from the cockpit, "there's food and drink at the back."

Tucker turned and saw that the aft bulkhead held a double-door storage cabinet.

"You'll also find aspirin, seasickness pills, and such. We'll stop every four hours for bathroom breaks. Are there any questions?"

"How deep will we be diving?" Bukolov pressed his face to one of the portholes, looking like a young boy about to go on an adventure.

"On average, eighteen feet. The Volga's main channel is at least twice that. Plenty of room for us to maneuver as needed. Plus I have a hydrophone in the cockpit. I'll hear any ships coming our way. If you'll take your seats, we will be under way."

Tucker sat on the forwardmost section of bench, and Kane settled in beneath it. The others spread out along its length, staring out portholes. With a soft whirring, the electric engines engaged, and the sub slid sideways away from the dock, wallowed a few times, then settled lower. The waters of the

Volga rose to cover the portholes and flooded the sub's interior in soft green light.

As Misha deftly worked the controls, the *Olga* glided out of the estuary and into the main river channel. They were still only half submerged.

"All hands prepare to dive." Misha chuckled. "Or just sit back and enjoy."

With a muffled *whoosh* of bubbles, the sub slid beneath the surface. The light streaming through the portholes slowly dimmed from a mint green to a darker emerald. Soft halogen lights set into the underside of the benches glowed to life, casting dramatic shadows up the curved bulkheads.

After a few moments, Misha announced in his best tour-guide voice, "At cruising depth. We are under way. Prepare for a smooth ride."

Tucker found his description to be apt. They glided effortlessly, with very little sense of movement. He spotted schools of fish darting past their portholes.

Over the next hour, having slept fitfully over the past days, exhaustion settled over everyone. The others drifted away one by one, draped across the bench, each with a wool blanket and inflatable pillow.

Tucker held off the longest, but after a quiet conversation with Misha who assured him all was well, he curled up and went to sleep, too. He hung one arm over the side of the bench, resting his palm on Kane's side. The shepherd softly panted, maintaining his post beside the floor's porthole, studying every bubble and particle that swept past the glass.

1:00 P.M.

Tucker startled awake as Misha's voice came over the loudspeaker.

"Apologies for the intrusion, but we are about to make our first stop."

The others groaned and stirred.

Tucker sat up to find Kane curled on the bench with him. The shepherd stood, arched his back in a stretch, then hopped down, and trotted to the entrance of the cockpit.

"Tell your friend he cannot drive," Misha called good-naturedly.

"He just likes the view," Tucker replied.

Bukolov waddled forward and sat down beside Tucker. "I must say, you impress me."

"How so?"

"I had my doubts that you could truly help me—us—escape Russia. I see now that I was wrong to doubt you."

"We're not out yet."

"I have faith," Bukolov said with a smile. He gave Tucker's arm a grandfatherly pat, then returned to his section of bench.

Miracles never cease.

He felt his ears pop as the *Olga* angled toward the surface. The portholes reversed their earlier transformation, going from a dark green to a blinding glare as the sub broached the surface. Sunlight streamed through the glass. A moment later, forward progress slowed with a slight grinding complaint as the hull slid to a stop on sand.

Misha crawled out of the cockpit, climbed the ladder, and opened the hatch. "All ashore!"

They all abandoned ship.

Misha's expert piloting had brought the *Olga* to rest beside an old wooden dock. Their tiny cove was surrounded by tall marsh grass. Farther out, up a short slope, Tucker could see treetops.

"Where are we?" Utkin asked, blinking against the sun and looking around.

"A few miles north of Akhtubinsk. We're actually ahead of schedule. Feel free to walk around. You have thirty minutes. I'm going to partially recharge the batteries with my solar umbrella."

Tucker crossed with Kane to the shore and surveyed the immediate area around the dock. He had Kane do a fast scout to make sure they were alone. Once satisfied, he waved the others off the dock so they could stretch their legs.

"Stay close," he ordered. "If you see anyone, even in the distance, get back here."

Once they agreed, Tucker headed back to the sub. Misha had the solar umbrella already propped over the sub, recharging the batteries.

As Misha worked, he asked, "Tell me, my friend, are you all criminals? I do not judge. You pay, I don't care."

"No," replied Tucker.

"Then people are following you? Looking for you?"

"Not anymore."

I hope.

Misha nodded, then broke into a smile; his gold

teeth flashed in the sun. "Very well. You are in safe hands."

Tucker actually believed him.

Anya returned early by herself and prepared to return below.

"Where are the others?" he asked.

"I . . . I did what I had to do," she said, blushing a bit. "I left the boys so they could have some privacy to do the same."

Tucker glanced down to Kane. It wasn't a bad idea. It would be another four hours before they stopped again. "How about it, Kane? Wanna go see a man about a horse?"

2:38 P.M.

As the *Olga* continued to glide down the Volga, the group dozed, stared out the portholes, or read. Occasionally Misha would quietly announce landmarks no one could see: a good spot for sturgeon fishing, or a mecca for crawfish hunting, or a village that had played a major or minor part in Russian history.

Utkin and Anya traded scientific journals and pored over them. Bukolov studied his notes, occasionally stopping to scribble some new thought or idea.

With nothing else to do himself, Tucker drifted in a half drowse—until Bukolov abruptly slid next to him and nudged him alert.

"What do you make of this?" the doctor said.

"Pardon?"

Bukolov pushed a thin journal into his hand. It was clearly old, with a scarred leather cover and sewn-in yellowed, brittle pages. "This is one of De Klerk's later journals."

"Okay, so?"

Bukolov took it back, scowled at him, and flipped the pages back and forth. He then bent the book open, spread it wide, and pointed to the inner seam. "There are pages missing from this last diary of De Klerk's. See here . . . note the cut marks near the spine."

"You're just noticing this now?" Tucker asked.

"Because the entries seemed to follow along smoothly. No missed dates, and the narrative is contiguous. Here, just before the first missing pages, he talks about one of the men in his unit complaining of mysterious stomach pains. After the missing pages, he begins talking about his Apocalypse Seed—where he found it, its properties, and so on."

Not able to read or speak Afrikaans, Tucker had to take the doctor's word for it, but the man was right. The cut marks were there.

"Why would he do this?" Tucker asked.

"I can only think of one reason," Bukolov replied. "Paulos de Klerk was trying to hide something. But what and from whom?"

7:55 P.M.

Misha announced another pit stop and guided the *Olga* toward shore. It was the third landfall of the day, near sunset. He wanted one more chance to stock up his solar batteries for the night. He pulled them up to another abandoned fishing dock. Clearly he had planned their route carefully, choosing backwater locations for their ports of call.

As the hatch was unsealed, Tucker was immediately struck by the cloying rotten-egg stench of the place, undercut by a heady mix of petroleum and burned oil.

"Ugh," Anya said, pinching her nose. "I'm staying inside. I don't have to use the bathroom that badly."

Tucker did, as did Kane. So they headed out with Utkin and Bukolov.

The cove here was surrounded by swamp, choked with densely packed grasses and reeds, interspersed with dead dwarf pines. A maze of wooden boardwalks zigzagged through the marshy area, paralleling aboveground pipes. At several intersections, car-sized steel cones protruded out of the oil-tinged water.

"Apologies for the ugly scenery," Misha called. "This is a Lukoil station—propane, I believe. Those metal funnels are burp valves. Sad. Before Lukoil bought the land, there was a fishing village here named Saray. Known for very good sturgeon. No more."

The group wandered around the dock area, which forked in several directions, all of which seemed to head inland toward the ghost town of Saray.

"Tucker, come look at this!" Utkin called somewhere to his right.

With Kane at his heels, Tucker followed the boardwalk to where the other two men were standing beside a section of submerged gas pipe. He noted the water roiling there. He plunged his hand into the marsh and slid his palm over the pipe's slimy surface until he found what he was looking for—an open control valve. He continued probing until his fingers touched a short length of chain. Dangling at the end was a padlock. Its hasp had been cut in half.

Sabotage.

"Go!" he yelled to the others. "Back to the sub!"

"What is it?" Utkin asked. "What—?"

He stiff-armed Utkin away. "Get Bukolov to the sub!"

Still kneeling, Tucker hollered to the sub, "Misha!"

"What is it?"

"A gas leak! Get under way!"

Tucker fought back the questions filling his head—like *who*, *how*, and *when*—and drew his gun. He searched the water and spotted a thumb-thick section of a pine branch floating nearby. He snatched it with his free hand and crammed it into the mouth of the leaking valve, like a cork in a bottle. The bubbling gas slowed to a sputter.

An ominous thumping echoed over the swamp, seeming to come from every direction at once.

Helicopter rotors.

Tucker burst to his feet and ran. Kane kept to his side.

Backlit by the setting sun, Misha was slipping through the sub's conning tower hatch. The others had already made it aboard. Misha paused when he spotted Tucker's flight.

Tucker waved his arm. "Go, go!"

Misha hollered back. "A cannery! Four miles downstream! I will wait!"

He vanished below, yanking the hatch.

Behind the *Olga*, a helicopter appeared across the river, streaking over the surface. It swooped over the sub, banked hard, then slowed to a hover above the marsh. It was a civilian chopper, not a Havoc assault bird. It seemed General Kharzin's influence and reach had limits this far from his home territory.

The helo's side door opened, and a slim figure appeared, carrying a fiery red stick in one hand. Leaning out, a long tail of blond hair whipped in the rotor wash.

Tucker's heart clenched into a tight fist.

Felice Nilsson.

Back from the dead.

From fifty yards away, he raised his pistol and fired. The bullet struck the fuselage beside Felice's head. She jerked back out of sight, but it was too late. As if moving in slow motion, the flaming flare dropped from her hand and spun downward.

Tucker swung away and took off at a sprint, Kane at his heels.

Somewhere behind he heard a *whoosh*, followed a split second later by a muffled explosion. Without looking, Tucker knew what was happening. The closely packed marsh grass had trapped the heavier-than-air propane as it leaked from the sabotaged pipe, creating a ground-hugging blanket of gas.

The flare had ignited it.

Orange-blue flames swirled through the swamp grass, chasing him. Heat seared his back. They reached an intersection and dodged left toward the river where the sub should have been. But it was already gone, sunk away.

The flames caught up with him, outpacing them, surging beneath the boardwalk. Fire spurted between the planks.

The end of the dock loomed ahead.

Tucker put his head down, covered the last few steps to the end of the boardwalk, then jumped. Kane brushed against him as they sailed through the air together—then a wall of fire erupted in front of them.

23

At the last moment, Tucker reached out and curled his arm around Kane's neck. Together, they plunged through the fire and into the river. While Kane had trained for sudden immersion, his core instinct would be to surface immediately. Cruel though it sounded, Tucker needed to prevent this.

As their plunging momentum slowed, Tucker stuck out his arm, his fingers grasping until he found a clump of roots. He clenched tight and pulled them both toward the mud. Under his other arm, Kane's body was rock hard with tension, but he did not struggle.

Tucker craned his neck backward and watched the worst of the fire blow out on the surface. The blanket of propane had quickly exhausted itself, but the swamp grass continued to burn. In his blurred vision, the flaming stalks along the marsh edges appeared like so many orange torches against the darkening sky.

One problem down, one big one to go.

Felice and the helicopter were still out there. He knew the Swede was too stubborn to assume the flames had done her work.

Tucker worked his way deeper into the swamp-lands bordering the river, pulling himself from one clump of roots to another. When his lungs could take no more, he let go and bobbed to the surface.

He immediately heard the thump of rotors back at the dock.

Felice continued to hunt for them, a hawk in the sky.

As he and Kane gulped air, the swamp grass crackled and smoked. Cinders hissed on the water's surface. Tucker looked at Kane. The shepherd's eyes were huge, darting left and right. Kane's animal instincts were screaming *Fire! Get away!* But his trust in Tucker and his training were holding him in place.

Tucker hugged his partner and whispered in his ear, "We're okay, we're okay . . . easy . . . hold on . . ."

The words themselves didn't matter. It was Tucker's tone and closeness that made the difference. They were together. The tension eased slightly from the shepherd's body.

Around them, the fire began dwindling as it devoured the dry tops of the marsh grass, filling the cove with smoke.

Tucker released Kane, and they half paddled, half crawled through the water, heading still deeper into the swamp, aiming for shore. Though it burned his lungs and stung his eyes, he did his best to hide their passage under the thick pall of smoke.

As they drifted into the shallows, the water was

only a foot or so deep. The grasses here were greener, still smoldering. Warning bells went off in his head. Though the smoking grass provided cover, it could also serve as a beacon. Their passage risked nudging aside stalks, causing the smoky columns to shift.

From the hovering helicopter, Felice would certainly spot the irregularity.

Slowly, Tucker lowered himself to his belly and wriggled deeper into the mud. He kept Kane close.

Now, wait.

It didn't take long. With the sun setting, the helicopter crisscrossed the marshes, stirring up the smoke. It finally settled into a gliding hover over the marshy cove. He spotted the shape of the chopper through the pall.

If he could see the helicopter . . .

Not a twitch, Tucker told himself. *You're part of the swamp . . . you're mud.*

After what felt like hours, the chopper finally moved on as dusk settled. Slowly, the thump of the rotors faded away. Still Tucker didn't move. With the sun down, the temperature dropped rapidly. The cold of the water seeped into his bones. He set his jaw against it.

Wait . . .

As he'd expected, the helicopter returned a few minutes later. Ever the hunter, Felice had hoped her quarry would have taken the invitation to bolt, but Tucker knew better.

There came a sharp crack of a rifle shot. Tucker flinched. His first fear was that Felice had spotted them, but he knew immediately this wasn't the case.

Felice wouldn't have missed.

She was trying to flush them out.

Crack!

Another shot, this one closer and somewhere to their left.

Tucker eased his hand over a few inches and laid his palm on Kane's paw. The shepherd tensed, then relaxed. If Tucker remained calm, so would Kane.

Crack! Crack!

The shots were even closer still. The feeling of utter helplessness was maddening. The shots were coming at irregular intervals now, moving ever closer to their position. Tucker closed his eyes and concentrated on his breathing. His survival was now down to dumb luck: the random squeeze of a trigger, a pilot's hand on the chopper's cyclic control, the vagaries of the wind.

Crack!

This shot was to the right.

Felice had finally passed them.

Afraid to jinx their luck, Tucker held his breath until the next shot came—again to their right, even farther out.

After another agonizing five minutes, the helicopter banked away, and the thump of its rotors slowly faded.

Fearing another return, Tucker remained in the cold water for ten more minutes. By now his limbs were trembling from the cold, his teeth chattering. Night had fully fallen. Above, the sky was clear and sprinkled with stars.

Tucker sat up and rolled onto his hands and knees. He patted Kane on the rump and together they began crawling toward shore.

Once on dry land, they set off south, hugging the shoreline where there were trees for cover and veering inland when there were none, ever wary of the helicopter's return.

As he hiked, Tucker considered the implications of the ambush. How had Felice found them? The most likely suspect was Misha. He had had time to sell them out during their brief stay at the headquarters of Wild Volga Tours, as well as during the sub's voyage via radio. But for that matter, any of the others—Utkin, Anya, even Bukolov—had access during one or another of their recharging stops. Any of them could have used the sub's radio. He hated to believe it, but he also couldn't afford to ignore the possibility that one of his companions was a traitor.

Once again he was letting himself slip into a wilderness of mirrors, where everyone and no one was suspect. But he did have one last ace up his sleeve. Only he and Ruth Harper knew the endgame of their evacuation scheme. All anyone else knew was that the sub's destination was the Caspian Sea.

If Felice wanted to ambush them again, she'd have to work hard for it.

10:37 P.M.

From the edge of a copse of trees across a broad starlit meadow, Tucker spied a plank-sided building the size of an aircraft hangar along the bank of the Volga. He recalled Misha's last words.

A cannery! Four miles downstream! I will wait!

"What do you think?" Tucker whispered to Kane. "Look like a cannery to you?"

His partner simply stared up at him.

Tucker nodded. "Yeah, me too."

They took a cautious approach, circling west through the trees to bring them within a few hundred yards. He discovered a narrow canal that cut from the river toward the structure. There was little water this time of the year, and its concrete sides were crumbling. Tucker dropped down into it and used the chunks of fallen rock and other debris as stepping-stones as he followed the canal and closed the remaining distance to the cannery building.

As he drew abreast of the exterior wall, he noted a lone, rusted crane looming over the canal, its hooked cable drooping like the line from a giant's fishing pole. The air smelled faintly of rotting fish.

He found stone steps leading out of the canal and took them. Crouched near the top, he scanned the area. Aside from the croaking of frogs and the buzz of cicadas, all was quiet. From Kane's relaxed posture, the shepherd's keen senses weren't discerning anything more.

He grabbed a few pebbles off the top step and tossed one against the cannery's wall. It plinked against the wood. Still, nothing moved.

Had Misha and the others made it here? Or had they come and gone?

Tucker tossed another pebble, then a third.

From somewhere inside the building came a scuffing sound—a footstep on concrete. Kane heard it, too, his body instantly going alert. Tucker prepared to send the shepherd scouting in the dark—but then a door creaked open and a lone figure leaned out.

"Tucker?" came Misha's voice.

Tucker didn't respond.

"Tucker, is that you?" Misha repeated.

Taking a chance, he stood up and walked over. Kane followed, stalking stiffly, sensing Tucker's anxiety.

Misha sagged with relief. "Good to see you, my friend."

Despite the cordiality of the greeting, Tucker could hear the tightness in the other's voice. It was not surprising, considering the man had narrowly escaped being roasted alive in his own sub. Still, Tucker kept a wary stance, not sure how much he could trust Misha.

"You made it," the man said, eyeing him up and down.

"A little crisp along the edges but I'm okay." Tucker glanced inside and saw that the dark cannery appeared empty. "Are the others waiting at the sub?"

"*Da.*"

"How's the *Olga*?"

"All is good. We dove before the explosion."

"They didn't shoot at you?"

"No."

"Your radio is operational?"

"Of course. Wait." He shook a finger at Tucker. "I see what you are really asking, my friend. You wonder how did they find us, *da*? You think I might have betrayed you."

Tucker shrugged. "Would you be any less suspicious?"

"Probably not." Misha's eyes stared hard into Tucker's own. "But I did not do such a thing. If I had known someone was going to firebomb my sub, I would have declined your generous offer to pilot the *Olga*. I have many other employees I don't particularly like, such as my lazy brother-in-law. But I took your money and came. And I take contracts seriously. We shook hands."

Tucker believed him. Mostly. But only time would tell.

"How can I prove this to you?" Misha asked.

"By *proving* how good of an actor you can be."

24

Misha had docked the *Olga* at the still-flooded mouth of the canal. Only the conning tower jutted above the surface, camouflaged in a nest of branches he'd cut from neighboring trees.

With Kane at his side, Tucker followed Misha into the shallows and up into the sub.

"You're alive!" Anya cried as he climbed down.

Utkin and Bukolov shook his hand vigorously, pumping his arm up and down, both smiling with an enthusiasm that seemed genuine.

"If everyone's done celebrating," Misha growled, "it's time we *talk*."

Tucker turned to him. "About what?"

"You lied to me. You told me there would be *no* danger—that *no* one was chasing you. I've had enough! I am turning around. I will return you safely to Volgograd and tell no one about this, but this voyage is over!"

Tucker took a step forward. "We had a deal."

"Not anymore."

He pulled the Magnum from his pocket and leveled it at Misha's chest.

Anya cried, "Tucker, don't."

"You're taking us the rest of the way."

"Shoot me," Misha said with a shrug. "And you'll be stranded here. Middle of nowhere. You think you can drive the *Olga*? Think you know the Volga? You will die in her mud!"

The two combatants glared at each other for a long ten seconds before Tucker lowered his gun and pocketed it. "The bastard is right."

Anya cried, "We cannot go back to Volgograd. Tucker, tell him!"

Bukolov chimed in. "This is lunacy."

"It's a setback," Tucker said, keeping his voice strained. "I'll call and arrange another means out of Volgograd." His next words were for Misha, full of menace. "If anyone is waiting for us in Volgograd, I'll put the first bullet in your head. Do we understand each other?"

"We do," replied Misha and headed for his cockpit. "Now everyone sit down so I can get under way."

As Misha eased the sub back toward the main channel, Tucker gathered the others at the rear. He kept his voice low. "Like I said, this is a setback, nothing more."

Bukolov groaned. "I will never leave this country alive. My discovery will die with me."

"Don't worry. I'll contact my friends at our next stop. Everyone try to get some sleep." He glanced back toward Misha. "I'm going to keep working on him, try to get him to change his mind."

Once the others settled to the bench, despondent and defeated, Tucker stoop-walked forward and ducked tightly next to Misha. The cockpit was cast in darkness, save the orange glow of Misha's instrument panels. Beyond the windscreen, the dark waters of the Volga swept and churned.

Tucker posted Kane two yards behind him, blocking anyone from coming forward.

"How did I do?" Misha whispered.

"An award-winning performance," replied Tucker. "Are you sure they won't notice that we're *not* heading north toward Volgograd?"

Misha pointed at the sub's windscreen, beyond which the Volga churned darkly. "How could they tell?"

True. Even Tucker was lost.

Tucker leaned forward, peering out. "How do you navigate through this sludge, especially at night?"

Misha reached above his head, pulled a sheaf of laminated paper from a cubbyhole, and handed it to Tucker. "Nautical chart of the Volga. You see the red squares along the shore? Those have been our stops so far. But usually I navigate by dead reckoning. Most of the Volga is in here." He tapped his skull. "Like a woman's body in the dark, I know her every curve and imperfection. Still, when I am a mile or so from a stop, I always broach the surface just enough for the sub's antenna to get a GPS fix."

"And how long do you think it will take us to reach Astrakhan?" Their destination lay within the Volga delta, where the river emptied into the Caspian Sea.

"We should reach the city by tomorrow afternoon, but I suspect you'd like me to stay submerged until nightfall."

"I would."

"Then that's your answer."

"And let's limit any more pit stops along the way to no longer than five minutes."

"I agree. But sometime in the morning, I'll need to dock for one more thirty-minute solar charge of the batteries in order to reach Astrakhan."

"Understood."

Tucker remained quiet for a moment, then said, "I hate to ask this, but, Misha, I need one more favor from you. Until we reach Astrakhan, no more radio communication."

Misha shrugged, clearly understanding the necessity. He reached up, unscrewed the head of the gooseneck microphone, and handed it to Tucker with a smile.

"I will now be free of my wife's nagging for a peaceful twenty-four hours."

March 17, 6:04 A.M.

The next morning, it was showtime again.

They had sailed southward for seven hours, for as long as they could manage before needing a pit stop. Misha found another quiet dark cove and put in.

Tucker ordered everyone to disembark, including Misha, who put on another display of feigned outrage.

"You disabled the radio. What do you expect me to do here by myself?"

"You could leave us. So get moving."

"Fine, fine . . ."

Everyone climbed out. While there was no dock, Misha had partially grounded the sub on a shallow sandbar. Having to wade through several inches of water in the predawn chill drew grumbled complaints as the group sought private spots amid the shrubs lining the bank.

Misha hung back with Tucker as he kept watch and whispered. "Are any of them good at astronomy?" He jerked a thumb toward the star-studded sky.

Tucker hadn't considered this. He didn't know if any of the group was adept at celestial navigation, but it probably didn't matter.

"Keep an eye on things," Tucker said to Misha and led Kane off to their own private spot. Once done, he stayed crouched in hiding and dialed Sigma's headquarters.

When Harper answered, Tucker passed on a fast request, risking only a few words. "I need a discreet airstrip near Astrakhan. I'll call back."

He hung up and stood. He made a dramatic pantomime of searching for a signal with his phone. He emphasized it by swearing softly under his breath.

Suddenly, Kane let out a low growl.

Tucker turned to find Utkin standing in the bushes ten feet away.

"Phone problem?" the man asked, zipping up his pants.

"Satellite interference."

Utkin stepped out of the shadows and walked closer. "I thought I heard you talking to someone."

"Kane. Old habit. How're you holding up?"

"Tired. Very tired. I don't think I'm suited for adventure." Utkin offered a smile, but it came out jaded. It was an expression Tucker had yet to see on the lab assistant's face.

Utkin shoved his hands in his jacket pockets and took another step toward Tucker.

Kane stood up, shifting between them.

Tucker found his fingers tightening on the butt of the Magnum.

Utkin noted the tension. "After the attack, you suspect all of us, don't you?"

"Part of the job description."

"Hmm . . ."

"If you were me, who would you suspect?"

"Any one of us," Utkin confirmed.

"Including you?"

"Including me."

"What about Bukolov and Anya? They're your friends, aren't they?"

Utkin looked at the ground and kicked a rock. "Maybe I thought so at one time. Not anymore. I was naive or maybe just wishful. How could I expect them to consider a poor fisherman's son their equal?"

Utkin turned and walked off.

Tucker stared after him.

What the hell just happened?

10:46 A.M.

The midmorning sun blazed down upon a secluded estuary where the sub had parked in the shallows, perfect for recharging the batteries.

While the solar umbrella was spread wide to catch every photon of energy, Tucker stood on the shore with his fellow passengers. "We have thirty minutes," he said. "Make the best use of it. We'll be in Volgograd soon and should be ready for anything."

The others set off amid the stands of bare willows, crowded with crows, who loudly complained at their trespass.

Tucker knelt down beside Kane and whispered, "SCOUT, HERD, ALERT."

For as long as this break lasted, the shepherd would discreetly circle the area, making sure that none of his *sheep* wandered off or drifted too close. Kane would bark a warning if there was a problem.

Satisfied, and out of direct sight, he climbed back aboard the *Olga* and started a thorough search of the group's belongings. Before reaching Astrakhan, he had to be sure that someone in the group wasn't leaking their position.

He dug through bags, shook out clothes, flipped through notebooks, everything. With experienced fingers, he probed the seams of pants, shirts, even the soles of shoes. He went so far as to pick through personal items, like thumbing through a bodice-ripper paperback of Anya's or the boxes of Utkin's playing cards—one empty, the other full of well-worn cards. He even dug through Bukolov's pouch of tobacco. As he did so, he felt a twinge of guilt, as if trespassing through the others' secret vices.

Still, for all his trespassing, he found nothing.

Next, he squeezed into the cockpit and scrutinized the instrument panel. He ran his palms over the console. Nothing anomalous jumped out at him.

He was stumped.

Only one possibility remained. Someone *had* to have used the sub's radio to transmit their position and set up that last ambush. How else could word have gotten out? He was glad he had asked Misha to disable the radio before they set off for Astrakhan. With the radio out of commission, their path from here should be unknown to their pursuers.

Tucker checked his watch, knowing he was running out of time. Ending his search, he climbed out of the conning tower and returned to the shore. Tucker whistled, raising more complaints from the nesting crows. He waved everyone back. They climbed aboard as Misha began breaking down and storing the solar array.

Tucker got Kane inside, then dropped back down next to Misha.

"Give me a minute," he said and walked a couple meters away from the sub.

Pulling out his phone, he dialed Sigma.

Harper came on the line immediately. "That was one hell of a cryptic message you left me," she said. "Had me worried."

"I'm in the wilderness, if you get my drift."

"Been there myself. I take it you don't want to go *straight* to the rendezvous as planned?"

Tucker recounted the helicopter attack. "I can't swear to this, but I suspect Felice let the sub go. Her attack was focused solely on me and Kane."

"With you gone, the rest would be easy pickings. Plus Bukolov is the prize. They don't dare risk killing him."

"Since I took out the sub's radio, it's been quiet,

but I don't want to take any more chances. Better to disembark as soon as we're within sight of Astrakhan."

"Agreed. I've found an aircraft that suits our needs." She passed on the coordinates. "They're part of a charter fishing company. They fly clients south into the Volga delta on a regular basis. With a little incentive, the pilot will take you to the new rendezvous."

"Which is where?"

"An island. Just outside Russian territorial waters—or what passes for marine borders in the Caspian Sea."

"Who's meeting us?"

"They're trustworthy. I've worked with them personally in the field. You reach them, and your worries are over."

"So says the woman who described this mission as a *simple escort job*."

25

As promised, Misha reached the outskirts of Astrakhan by the afternoon. With the sub still submerged, he announced this quietly to Tucker, who squeezed into the cockpit. They studied the nautical chart together.

Checking coordinates, Tucker tapped a spot where the Volga's main channel branched into Astrakhan.

"Stop there?" Misha asked.

"*Turn* there," Tucker corrected. "Follow it for three miles, then call me again."

It took forty minutes to reach the branch.

Tucker returned to the cockpit and pointed to another spot a mile farther west.

"You are being very cagey," Misha said. "I see a small cove. Is that our destination?"

"No. Call me when you reach the next waypoint."

After another twenty minutes, Misha summoned him again.

With a smile, Tucker placed his finger on the small cove that Misha had mentioned before. "That's our destination."

"But you said—oh, I see. You are very untrusting."

"It's a recent development. Don't take it personally. How long until nightfall?"

"To be safe, two hours. I will pull us into the undergrowth along this bank. It should shield us further as we wait."

It turned out to be the longest two hours of his life. The others attempted to question him about what he was doing, but he only gave cryptic reassurances, allowing them still to believe the sub was parked underwater at some destination near Volgograd.

Finally, he ordered everyone to collect their belongings and disembark. With Tucker directing, they gathered in a clump of bushes on the shore of the cove.

Overhead, the dark sky hung with low clouds, turning the waning moon into a pale disk. Aside from the trilling of insects and the occasional croak of a frog, all was quiet.

Across the cove, a few hundred yards off, a trio of squat cabins hugged the water. A lone light burned beside the door of one. Moored to its dock floated a pair of small seaplanes.

That was their ticket out of here.

"This is not Volgograd," Utkin whispered, scrunching his face. "The air smells too clean."

Tucker ignored him and joined Misha alongside the sub. The two shook hands.

"This is where we say good-bye," Misha said. He let go of Tucker's hand but continued to hold out his open palm.

With a smile, Tucker understood. He pulled a

wad of rubles from his pocket and counted out what he owed the sub's pilot—then he added an extra ten thousand on top of that. "Hazardous duty pay."

"I knew I liked you for a reason, my friend."

"You'll be able to get back to Volgograd safely?"

"Yes, I think so. And I hope you do the same—wherever you are going."

"I hope so, too."

"Because of the extra pay, I will wait here until you take off. Just in case you need me again."

"Thank you, Misha. If I don't see you again, safe sailing."

With Tucker in the lead and Kane bringing up the rear, the group headed around the curve of the cove, sticking to the trees and taller bushes.

Once near the cluster of cabins, he called a halt, knelt by Kane, and pointed forward. "SCOUT AND RETURN."

Kane skulked off and disappeared into the darkness.

Several minutes passed, then from back the way they'd come, a whispered call reached him.

"Tucker!"

It was Misha.

His heart thudding with worry, Tucker told the others to stay out of sight. He made his way back down the trail to where Misha was crouching.

"What is it?"

"This."

He passed over a black plastic object roughly the size and shape of a narrow bar of soap. A pair of insulated wires dangled from either side, ending in alligator clips.

Misha explained, "I was cleaning up after you all left, straightening and doing a systems check while I waited as promised. I found this tucked beneath my seat in the cockpit. Those clips had been spliced into the sub's antenna feed."

"It's a signal generator," Tucker muttered, his belly turning to ice. "It sends out frequency-specific pulses at regular intervals."

"Like a homing beacon."

"Yes." Tucker felt icy fingers of despair close around his heart. "That's how the enemy was tracking us."

He remembered Misha describing how he would surface the sub at regular intervals to get a GPS fix on their location, especially as they neared one of their ports of call. Each time he did it, the generator gave away their location, allowing the enemy ample time to set up an ambush once they figured out Misha's routine.

"Who put it there?" Misha asked.

Tucker glanced toward the trio hidden by the cabins.

Who indeed?

He ran everything he knew through his head—then his whole body clenched with a realization.

It couldn't be . . .

Misha read his reaction. "You know who the traitor is?"

"I think so." Tucker stuffed the signal generator into his pocket. "I suggest you shove off right now and put as much distance between you and us as possible."

"Understood. Good luck, my friend."

Tucker returned to where the group sat crouched in the darkness. By now, Kane was waiting for him. The shepherd's posture, the tilt of his ears, and the softness of his eyes told Tucker *all was clear*.

Like hell it was.

He crouched and draped an arm around Kane's neck, struggling to keep his composure.

Now what?

How much information had already been funneled to General Kharzin?

Since surfacing here, he had to assume the enemy knew where they had stopped. Surely Felice was on her way.

He didn't have the time to properly interrogate and break the traitor. That would come later. For now, by hiding his knowledge, he still had a slight upper hand.

He stared toward the seaplanes. The enemy didn't want to kill Bukolov, and with their agent sitting next to him on the plane, they'd be even less likely to try to shoot the craft down once it was airborne. In that way, both men could serve as unwitting human shields, increasing the group's chances of reaching the rendezvous point safely. But first he had to get them all into the air.

He also intended to keep a close eye on the traitor, an eye sharper than his own. He shifted next to Kane. Shielding his hand signals, he pointed and touched the corner of his own eye.

Keep a watch on the target.

Until Tucker lifted the order, the shepherd would be on close guard—watching his target for any aggressive movements or hostile actions, judging the tone of voice, listening for the cock of a hammer or the slip of a blade from a sheath. It was a broad tool, but Tucker trusted the shepherd's instinct. If his target made the wrong move, Kane would immediately attack.

"What was that all about with Misha?" Anya whispered, drawing back his attention.

"He wanted more money. To stay silent."

"And you paid him?" Bukolov asked, aghast.

"It was easier than killing him. And besides, we're leaving now anyway."

Tucker stood up and gestured for the others to remain hidden. He crossed to the lighted cabin and knocked on the door.

It opened a few moments later. Yellow light spilled forth, framing a young woman in denim overalls. She was barely five feet tall, with black hair trimmed in a pixie haircut.

Tucker tightened his grip on the Magnum concealed in his pocket, bracing himself for any attack.

"You are Bartok?" she asked in a surprisingly bold voice for such a small body.

Bartok?

He was momentarily confused until he remembered Harper's mention of a code name.

"Yes, I'm Bartok."

"I am Elena. How many come with you on plane? Costs three thousand rubles per passenger."

She certainly didn't waste any time getting down to business.

"Four and a dog."

"Dog cost more."

"Why?"

"He crap . . . I must clean up, no?"

Tucker wasn't about to argue—not with this little firebrand. She sort of scared him. "Fine."

"Get others," she ordered him. "The plane is prepared. We are ready to leave."

With that, she stalked toward the dock area.

Tucker waved the others out of hiding and hurried to keep up with Elena. She had stopped beside one of the planes. With one leg leaning on a float, she unlatched the side door and lowered it like a ramp onto the dock's walkway.

The twin-engine seaplane, painted azure, stretched about seventy feet long, with gull wings and oval stabilizers at the tail. The fuselage was deep chested, with a bulbous cockpit.

"I don't recognize this model," he said as he joined her.

She explained proudly, her hands on her hips. "This is a Beriev Be-6. Your NATO called it *Madge*. Built the same year Stalin died."

"That's sixty years ago," Anya noted, worried.

"Fifty-nine," Elena shot back, offended. "She is old, but a very tough bird. Well maintained. Board now."

No one dared disobey.

Once everyone was aboard, Elena unhooked the lines from their cleats, hopped inside, and pulled the door closed behind her with a resounding slam. She hurried forward to the cockpit.

"Sit down!" she yelled back. "Seat belts!"

And that was the extent of their preflight safety briefing.

Bukolov and Anya were buckled into the bench

along the right side of the fuselage, Utkin and Tucker on the left. Kane curled up between Tucker's feet, never letting his guard down.

The plane began drifting sideways from the dock.

Bukolov called over, "Tucker, you seem to have a proclivity for unorthodox methods of travel."

"One of my many idiosyncrasies."

"Then I assume we will be traveling to the United States aboard a zeppelin."

"Let's leave it as a surprise," he replied.

From the cockpit came a series of beeps and buzzes, accompanied by a short curse from Elena—then the sound of a fist striking something solid. Suddenly, the engines roared to life, rumbling the fuselage.

"Here we go!" Elena called.

The plane accelerated out of the cove and into the inlet. Moments later they were airborne.

7:44 P.M.

"*Bartok!*" Elena yelled once they'd reached cruising altitude. "You come up here!"

Tucker unbuckled his seat belt, scooted around Kane, and ducked into the cockpit. He knelt beside her seat. The copilot seat was empty. Through the windscreen, he saw only blackness.

"Now tell me the destination. The person on phone said *southeast*. Said you would have the destination once in air."

Tucker gave her the coordinates, which she jotted on her kneeboard.

After a few fast calculations, she said, "Fifty minutes. You know what we are looking for? A signal of some kind, *da*? The Caspian is big, especially at night."

"Once we are there, I'll let you know."

Tucker returned to the cabin. The roar of the engines had faded to a low drone. Aside from the occasional lurch as Elena hit a pocket of turbulence, the ride was smooth.

Now is as good a time as any.

Tucker stood between the two benches. "It is time we have a family meeting."

"A what?" Bukolov asked.

Tucker dove in. "Every step of the way, General Kharzin has been waiting for us. Until now I had no idea how he was doing it."

Tucker paused to look at each of them in turn.

Anya shifted under his scrutiny. "And? What are you saying, Tucker?"

He drew the signal generator from his pocket and held it up for everyone to see.

"What is that?" Bukolov asked, motioning for a closer look.

Tucker turned to Utkin. "Would you like to explain?"

The young man shrugged, shook his head.

"It's a signal generator—a homing beacon. It was attached to the *Olga*'s antenna feed. Since we left Volgograd it's been regularly sending out a signal until I disarmed it a few minutes ago. A signal that Kharzin has been listening for."

"You think one of us put it there?" Utkin asked.

"Yes."

"It could have been Misha," Anya offered. "He would know how to attach the device. It was his submarine."

"No, Misha brought this to me."

Anya's eyes grew rounder. "Tucker, you're scaring me. What do you know?"

Tucker turned to Utkin. "Is that your bag under your seat?"

"Yes."

"Pull it out."

"Okay . . . why?"

"Pull it out."

Utkin did so.

"Show me your playing cards."

"My what? I don't see why—"

"Show me."

Having noted the hardness of Tucker's tone, Kane stood up and fixed his gaze on Utkin.

"Tucker, my friend, what is going on? I do not understand, but fine, I will show you."

He unzipped his duffel and began rummaging around. After a few seconds, he froze, glanced up at Tucker, and pulled out his two boxes of playing cards. One empty, one full. Utkin held up the empty one.

Tucker read the understanding in the young man's eyes.

"But it . . . it is not mine," Utkin stammered.

Tucker grabbed the box, slid the signal generator into it, and resealed the flap. It was a perfect fit. Earlier this morning, during his search of the group's belongings, he'd found the empty box of playing cards in the young man's duffel.

Utkin continued shaking his head. "No, no, that is not mine."

Anya covered her mouth.

"Is it true?" asked Bukolov. "Tucker, is this true?"

"Ask him."

Bukolov had paled with shock. "Utkin—after all our time together, you would do this? Why? Is this tied to that past gambling problem of yours? I thought you had stopped."

Shame blushed Utkin's face to a dark crimson. "No! This is all a mistake!" He turned to Tucker, his eyes hopeless with despair. "What will you do to me?"

Before he could respond, Anya blurted out, "Tucker, do not kill him, please. He made a mistake. Perhaps someone forced him to do it. Remember, I know these people. Perhaps they blackmailed him. Isn't that right, Utkin? You had no choice. Tucker, he had no choice."

Tucker looked to Bukolov. "Doctor, how do you vote?"

Bukolov shook his head. Without looking at his lab assistant, he waved a dismissive hand. "I do not care. He is dead to me either way."

At this, Utkin broke down. He curled himself into a ball, his head touching his knees, and started sobbing.

Tucker felt sorry for Utkin, but he kept his face impassive. The lab assistant had almost cost them their lives—and he might still. Felice could already be on her way here.

That fear drew him back to the cockpit, leaving Utkin guarded by Kane.

"Can we circle?" he asked Elena. "To check our tail?"

She frowned at him. "You think we are being followed."

"Can you do it?"

Elena sighed. "Two hundred rubles extra for fuel."

"Deal."

"Okay, okay. Hold on."

She turned the wheel and the Beriev eased into a gentle bank.

After a lazy ten-minute circle above the Volga delta, Elena said, "I see no one. Easy to spot in the dark. But I will keep watching."

"Me, too." Tucker took the empty copilot's seat.

In the green glow of the instruments, he glimpsed a dark shape against the lower console between the seats. It was a machine gun, attached to the console with Velcro straps. It had a wooden stock and a stubby barrel. Just ahead of the trigger guard was a large, cylindrical magazine.

"Is that an old tommy gun?" he asked.

Elena corrected him. "That is a Shpagin machine gun. From Great Patriotic War. It was my father's. American gangsters stole the design."

"You're an interesting woman, Elena."

"*Da*, I know," she replied with a confident smile. "But don't get any ideas. I have a boyfriend. Okay, *three* boyfriends. But they don't know about each other, so it's okay."

As they neared their destination coordinates, everything still remained dark and quiet in the skies around them.

"What now, Bartok?" Elena asked.

"An island lies dead ahead at the coordinates I gave you. We're supposed to rendezvous on the eastern side, where there is a narrow beach. Once you land on the water, taxi in as close as you can, and we'll wade ashore. After that, you're done."

"Whatever you say. Best to strap in now. Touch-down in two minutes."

Tucker relayed the message to the others, then buckled in next to Elena.

"Beginning descent," she said.

The nose of the plane dipped, aiming for the dark waters below.

As they plummeted, Elena prepared for landing: flipping switches, adjusting elevator controls, tweaking the throttle. Finally, the plane straightened, racing over the water, until the pontoons kissed the surface. The Beriev shook slightly, bounced once, then settled. The seaplane's speed rapidly bled off, and the ride smoothed out.

Tucker checked his watch. They had made good time and were twenty minutes early.

"Very shallow here," Elena announced as she swung the plane's nose and headed toward the island's shore.

"Again, just get as close as you can." Tucker unbuckled and stood up. "Thanks for the ride. I—"

Over Elena's shoulder, out the side window, a dark shape appeared out of nowhere. Disoriented, Tucker's first thought was *rock*. They were passing some storm-beaten shoal sticking out of the water.

Then a strobe of navigation lights bloomed, hovering there, revealing its true nature.

Helicopter.

Tucker shouted, "Elena . . . get down!"

"What—?"

As she turned toward him, her forehead disappeared in a cloud of red mist.

26

Tucker dropped to his knees, then his belly. He felt wet warmth dripping down his face and swiped his hand across it.

Blood.

He turned his head and yelled through the cockpit door. "Everyone flat on the deck!"

Kane came slinking toward him, but Tucker held up his hand, and the shepherd stopped.

"What's happening?" Anya called out, sounding terrified.

"The pilot's dead. We've got company."

He rolled and rose to his knees behind the pilot's seat. He craned his neck over Elena's slumped body and peeked out the side window.

The helicopter was gone.

Smart, Felice . . . kill the pilot and the plane's grounded.

Now she and her team could take their sweet time at capturing or killing them.

Tucker peered through the windscreen. A hundred yards ahead, the black silhouette of the island blotted out the stars. At its base, a gentle crescent of white sand beckoned.

Only then did he note that the Beriev was still moving toward their goal. He scanned the control panel, looking for—*there*. The pictogram of a spinning propeller glowed, bracketed by a plus and minus sign.

Easy enough to interpret.

Reaching around the seat, he shoved the twin throttles forward. The engines roared, and the nose lifted slightly, then settled as the Beriev's speed climbed. The plane raced for the island, skimming the water, rapidly closing the distance. He knew they would never be able to escape the more agile chopper by air.

That wasn't his plan.

He goosed the wheel, keeping them angled toward the beach.

"Brace for impact!" he shouted. "KANE, COME!"

The shepherd sprinted forward. Tucker curled his left arm around Kane's chest and turned them both so they were tucked against the bulkhead. He propped his legs against the pilot's chair and squeezed his eyes shut.

Beneath his rear end, the Beriev's fuselage shuddered as it passed the shallows. Next came a shriek, followed by a grinding of metal on sand.

The plane violently lurched left, catching a pontoon on something—a rock, a sandbar—then flipped up on its nose and cartwheeled across the beach.

Glass shattered.

From the cabin, screams and shouts.

The copilot's seat tore free and seemed to float in midair before crashing into the side window above Tucker's head.

Then the plane hit the trees, shearing off one wing. They slammed to a teetering stop, the plane stuck up on its side, the remaining wing pointed to the sky.

Tucker looked around. A pair of emergency lights in the overhead bathed the cockpit in a dull glow. Tree branches jutted through the side window. Above him, over his left shoulder, he saw a sliver of dark sky through the windscreen.

He took personal inventory of his condition and ran his hands over Kane's flanks and limbs, getting a reassuring lick in return.

Think, he commanded himself.

Felice was still out there, but her helicopter lacked pontoons, so it could not land in the water. He pictured the tree-lined beach. He didn't believe it was wide enough to accommodate the chopper's rotor span.

We have time—but not much.

They just had to survive until the plane Harper sent got here.

He called, "Everyone okay back there?"

Silence.

"Answer me!"

Bukolov called weakly, "I am . . . we are hanging in the air. Anya and myself. She hurt her hand."

"Utkin!"

"I am here, pinned under my seat."

"No one move. Let me come to you."

Tucker ordered Kane to stay put and pulled himself to the cockpit door. He swung his legs until he was sitting on the door coaming. With the plane on its side, the left bulkhead was now the floor. He found an emergency flashlight strapped to the wall. He snagged it free, turned it on, and took a moment to orient himself.

Utkin was still buckled into his seat, but it had broken loose and rolled atop him. Above him, Bukolov and Anya were strapped in place and suspended in midair.

No one seemed to be direly injured, except Anya clutched her hand to her chest, her eyes raw with pain. For now, there was nothing he could do to help her.

"Utkin, unbuckle yourself and crawl to me."

As he did so, Tucker hopped down next to him and stoop-walked aft until he was beneath Bukolov and Anya. He shined his flashlight up.

"Anya, you first. Press the buckle release with your good hand, and I'll catch you. It's not as high as it seems."

After a moment's hesitation, she hit the release and fell. Tucker caught her and lowered her to her feet.

He repeated the procedure with Bukolov.

Once down, the doctor leveled a finger at Utkin's face. "You! You almost got us killed. Again."

"Abram, I did not—"

"Quiet!" Tucker barked. "We have only a few minutes before Felice finds a way to reach us. We need to get out of here without being seen."

"How?" Anya asked, wincing. It appeared she had either sprained or broken her wrist.

"A window in the cockpit is smashed. That's our way out."

He turned and clambered back through the door that led to the cockpit. He swung his legs until he was straddling the coaming.

"Grab our packs!" he ordered. "Then Anya up first."

Moving quickly, Tucker shuttled everyone out of the cabin, past the cockpit, and through the broken window. It was a tight squeeze amid the broken branches, but it allowed them to exit directly into dense forest, keeping off the open beach.

Utkin was the last of the three to leave. He looked at Tucker. "You're wrong about me. I wish you would believe that."

"I wish I could."

As the man shimmied out, Tucker turned to Kane. "Ready to go, pal?"

Kane wagged his tail and belly-crawled after the others.

Tucker followed, but not before grabbing Elena's Shpagin machine gun. He slung it across his back, while staring down at the young woman's lifeless body.

"I'm sorry . . ."

The words sounded idiotic to him.

I'm sorry you're dead. I'm sorry I dragged you into this.

Anger stabbed into him, fiery and fierce. He used it to steady the edge of panic, to clear his head to a crystal focus.

Felice, you're dead.

He made a silent oath to make that happen.

For Elena.

Turning away, he crawled out and joined the others huddled together in the darkness of the forest. The neighboring beach looked like polished silver under the moonlight that pierced the clouds.

"What now?" Bukolov asked. "I don't see the helicopter. Perhaps they think we are dead."

"It's possible, but you're their prize, Doctor. They won't leave without knowing your true fate."

"What about your people?" Anya asked.

He checked his watch. It was still a few minutes until they were supposed to arrive.

Tucker dug through his duffel until his fingers touched the satellite phone. Even without looking, he knew the phone was shattered. The casing had split open, and the innards lay in pieces at the bottom of his pack.

"Stay here," he ordered and crawled to the edge of the sand. He scanned the sky, while straining to listen. He thought he heard the distant thump of rotors, but when he turned his head, the sound faded.

Options, Tucker thought. *What do we do?*

Felice had them pinned down.

Again, Tucker heard thumping.

The helicopter was definitely out there, moving with no lights, like before, lying in wait.

And not just for us, he suddenly realized.

No wonder she didn't immediately come after them.

He pushed back to the others. "Kharzin *knows* this is the rendezvous point, that others must be coming. Felice is out there waiting for them, intending to take them out, to catch them off guard like she did us, leaving her free to deal with us after that."

"What are we going to do?" Anya said.

"I don't know—"

Utkin suddenly bolted past Tucker, his heels kicking up sand as he broke from cover and stumbled out onto the open beach.

Tucker's first instinct was to raise the Shpagin, but he stopped himself. He still couldn't shoot an unarmed man in the back.

"Stop!" he called out to Utkin. "There's nowhere to run!"

A strobe of navigation lights burst above the treetops at the northern tip of the island. A floodlight bloomed, stabbing down to the beach. The helicopter's nose followed the beam down, picking up speed.

Utkin got caught in the light, sliding to a stop. He lifted his arm against its blinding glare and waved his other arm.

"What is that idiot doing?" Bukolov said. "Does he think they'll pick him up?"

"He'll get away," Anya cried.

Skimming the trees, the chopper reached the beach in seconds and banked over the crashed Beriev. All the while, the floodlight kept Utkin pinned down.

Suddenly fire winked from the chopper's open cabin door.

Bursts of sand kicked up, and a bullet struck Utkin's leg. He toppled forward, lay for a stunned moment, then started crawling in agony toward the trees, pushing with his good leg.

The gun flashed again from the helicopter's doorway.

A second bullet struck Utkin's other leg. He pitched flat to the sand. His arms paddled as he tried to push himself back up.

From the precision of the shooting, it had to be Felice.

He knew what she was doing, torturing Utkin to draw him out. She didn't know that the traitor had been exposed—or maybe she didn't care.

A part of Tucker knew Utkin had brought this upon himself.

But another part railed against such brutality.

He felt his ears pop, a rush of hot air, the screams of his fellow rangers filled his head. He saw a mirage of a limping dog, bloodied and in pain—

No, not again . . . never again . . .

He broke from cover, sprinted past the wreckage of the Beriev, and across the sands. He charged forward, eating up the distance until he was twenty yards away. He dropped to one knee, jerked the Shpagin to his shoulder, and took aim.

He fired a short three-round burst. The Shpagin bucked in his grip. The bullets went wide. He tucked the weapon tighter to his shoulder and fired again, squeezing and holding fast. Bullets shredded into the chopper's tail.

Smoke gushed.

The helicopter pivoted, exposing its open doorway. A lone figure stood there. Though her lower face was hidden behind a scarf, he knew it was Felice.

He opened fire again, stitching the fuselage from tail to nose.

She stumbled out of view.

Abruptly the chopper banked hard left and dove for the ocean's surface and picked up speed, heading away, trailing oily smoke.

Furious, blind with rage, he kept firing after it until it had vanished into the darkness. Critically damaged, the helicopter wouldn't be returning any time soon.

He swung over to Utkin, dropping to his knees beside him.

During the firefight, the young man had managed to roll onto his back. His left thigh was black with blood. His right poured a crimson stain into the sand, spurting from his leg, with a brightness that could only be arterial.

Tucker pressed his palm against the wound and leaned on it.

Utkin groaned heavily. One hand rose to touch the hot barrel of the machine gun. "Knew you could do it . . ."

"Quiet. Lay still."

"Someone . . . someone had to flush out that evil *suka* before she ambushed your friends . . ."

Hot blood welled through his fingers.

A sob rose in Tucker's chest, escaping in shaking gasps. "Hold on . . . just hold on . . ."

Utkin's eyes found his face. "Tucker . . . I'm sorry . . . my friend . . ."

Then he was gone.

9:02 P.M.

Tucker sat on the sand, hugging his knees. Kane lay tight against his side, sensing his grief. A small fire burned on the beach, created by igniting driftwood with some of the leaking fuel from the wreckage, a signal to those who were coming.

It seemed to have worked.

The drone of an engine echoed over the water. A moment later, a seaplane swept above the beach. Anya waved with her good arm. From the plane's side window, a flashlight blinked back at her, signaling the identity of their rescuers.

As the plane circled for a water landing, Bukolov wandered over to him. "I still don't understand why he did that."

Off to the side, Utkin's body was covered by a tarp.

"Redemption," Tucker said. "I think he purposefully drew the chopper out of hiding, so I'd have a chance to take it out before the others arrived."

"But why? Did he do it out of guilt?"

Tucker remembered his last words.

. . . *my friend* . . .

Tucker laid a hand on Kane's side. "He did it out of friendship."

PART III

ROUGH COUNTRY

27

Tucker followed the embassy aide into the conference room. The space looked ordinary enough: white walls, burgundy carpet, maple table. Someone had set out glasses and pitchers of ice. He also smelled coffee, one of life's necessities at this early hour after such a long night.

Bukolov and Anya joined him as he settled into one of the leather chairs. They all squeaked heavily into place for this private meeting.

Anya's left arm was in a cast from midforearm to her knuckles. She had broken two bones in her wrist as a result of the plane crash. Her eyes were still glassy from pain relievers.

For this meeting, it would just be the three of them, seated around a speakerphone.

"Your call is being routed," said the aide, a young man in a crisp suit. He promptly left, sealing the door behind him.

Despite the unassuming decor, Tucker knew this room in the U.S. consulate was soundproofed and electronically secure. No one else would be listening in.

Tucker stared across the table at the other two.

Anya looked haunted.

Bukolov defeated.

They'd flown straight from the Caspian Sea to Turkey, arriving well after midnight. They'd been given rooms here, but it looked like none of them had slept well. Tucker had left Kane behind to give the shepherd some extra downtime.

The conference phone on the table trilled, and a voice came over the speaker. "Your party is on the line. Go ahead."

After a series of beeps, followed by a burst of static, Ruth Harper's voice came on the line.

"Tucker, are you there?"

"Yes." Again he felt the comfort of her familiar soft twang. "I have Doctor Bukolov and Anya here also."

"Very good."

In Harper's usual brusque manner, she got right down to business. "Let's start with the most pressing concern of the moment. Stanimir Utkin. How much information do you believe this mole shared with his superiors? With this General Artur Kharzin?"

Tucker had already given Harper a condensed version of the last twenty-four hours, including the betrayal and ultimate redemption by Utkin.

Bukolov answered angrily. "How much information? How about *all* of it? He had access to all my research material. I never suspected him in the slightest." He glanced over to Anya, his voice dropping further into defeat. "I never suspected anyone."

Tucker stared between them.

Anya looked down at the table. "I told Abram last night. About my involvement with Russian SVR. About my assignment. I thought he should hear it from me first."

"Anya *Averin*," Bukolov muttered. "I didn't even know your real name."

Harper spoke into the awkward silence that followed. "I made some discreet inquiries. As far as I can tell, Anya's story checks out. She *was* falsifying intelligence to her superiors."

Anya glanced to the doctor. "In order to protect you, Abram, to protect your research, so it wouldn't be abused." She reached her right hand to him. "I'm sorry. I should have told you sooner."

Bukolov turned slightly away from her. "Does she need to be here? She's of no use to me now. I have all of De Klerk's diary. I can handle the rest on my own."

"Not your decision to make, Doctor," Tucker replied.

"Not my decision? How can you say that? She betrayed me!"

Anya said, "Abram, please. I gave them nothing of your work. I protected—"

"I am done with you! Mr. Wayne, I refuse to allow her to accompany us."

Harper cleared her throat. "Let's put a pin in this, Doctor, and get back to Stanimir Utkin. For now, we must assume he gave Kharzin everything. Including the information from Paulos de Klerk's diary. Is that correct, Doctor Bukolov?"

"Unfortunately, yes."

"Then let's move on to the threat posed by that information, about the danger of LUCA falling into the hands of Kharzin?"

Bukolov took on a defensive tone. "You must understand, that if handled properly, LUCA could be an unprecedented boon to humanity. We could turn deserts into—"

"Yes, I understand that," Harper said, cutting him off. "But it's the phrase *handled properly* that worries me. Correct me if I'm wrong, but even if we're able to find a viable specimen of LUCA, we still have no way of controlling it—not you, not Kharzin's people. Is that right?"

Bukolov hesitated, frowned. "Yes," he said slowly. "No one has developed a kill switch. But I am convinced the mechanism for controlling LUCA *does* exist. So is Kharzin convinced. The general would only have to introduce a few ounces of LUCA in a handful of strategic locations, and without a kill switch in our possession, the organism would spread like wildfire, destroying all native plant life. There would be no stopping it. But the larger threat is *weaponization*."

"Explain, Doctor," said Harper.

"Take smallpox, for example. It's one of the most feared biological weapons known to man, but that threat alone is not enough. To be sure of infecting the maximum number of victims, smallpox must be weaponized—it must be deliverable over a wide area in a short period of time, so it overwhelms the population and the medical infrastructure. Kharzin will see LUCA in the same light. He's a military man. It is how they think. Weaponized LUCA, delivered strategically, could reach critical mass in hours. Yes, yes, LUCA in its raw form is dangerous, but not necessarily catastrophic. There would be a chance we might be able to stop it. If he weaponizes it . . . it's an endgame move."

"End?" Harper asked. "As in end of the world?"

"Without a kill switch, a way of controlling what's unleashed, yes. We're talking about the fundamental destruction of the earth's ecosystem."

Harper paused, digesting the information. Tucker pictured her removing her thick set of librarian glasses and rubbing her eyes. Finally she spoke again. "How confident are you about this kill switch, Doctor?"

"I'm sure I can develop it. Even De Klerk hinted at the possibility in his diary. I just need a sample."

"From some lost cave in South Africa?" Harper added.

"Yes."

"And you think you can find this cave?"

"I believe so. Before I burned the page that explained its location, I set it to memory. But De Klerk plainly feared this organism, even bestowing it with the ominous title *Die Apokalips Saad*. He was so frightened that he encrypted his words, couching the route to the cave in obscure terms."

"Can you recite it now? Give us an example?"

"Here is how it starts." Bukolov formed a steeple of his fingers as he concentrated. "*'From Grietje's Well at Melkboschkuil . . . bear twenty-five degrees for a distance of 289,182 krags . . . there you find what is hidden beneath the Boar's Head Waterval.'*"

Harper didn't speak immediately. Tucker could

almost feel the frustration coming through the speakerphone. "Does that mean anything to you?"

"Not a damned thing," Bukolov said. "I tried for a solid week after finding this page. None of the locations are on any map. Not Grietje's Well. Not Melkboschkuil. Not that Boar's Head Waterfall. And as far as I could ascertain, there is no unit of measurement called a *krag*."

Bukolov tossed his arms in the air. "It's one of the reasons I called out to you all. Surely you've got cryptographers and map experts who could decipher it. Get us on the right path to that cave."

"I will see what I can do," Harper said. "Give me a couple of hours—let me do some research—and we'll reconvene here."

The line went dead.

As they all headed out, Anya reached an arm toward Bukolov, clearly wanting to talk, to smooth matters between them. When he ignored her, Tucker read the pain in her face, the crush of her posture. She stood in the hall for a long breath, watching the man stalk off.

When she turned away, he caught a glimpse of a single tear roll across a perfect cheekbone.

It seemed betrayal wore many faces.

10:22 A.M.

Tucker used the break to walk Kane amid the courtyards of the embassy. He had been ordered not to venture beyond its gates. The multilevel compound—with its industrial white walls and rows of cell-like windows—looked more like a maximum-security prison than a consulate.

Still, the small gardens inside were handsome, blooming with purplish-pink crocuses and tangled with roses. But best of all, the warm Turkish sun helped melt the residual Russian ice from his bones and thoughts.

Even Kane had more of a dance to his step as he sniffed every corner and bush.

But soon Tucker was back inside, back at the conference table.

"I may have a couple pieces of the puzzle worked out," Harper announced as she came back on the line. "But I fear until we have boots on the ground in South Africa, the location of the cave will remain a mystery. From these obscure references, I believe De Klerk was trying to hide some meaning or significance that would only make sense to another Boer of his time."

Bukolov leaned closer. "Understandable. The Boer were notorious xenophobes, suspicious of other people and races, and especially paranoid about the British. But you said you had a couple of the clues solved. What did you learn?"

"It took consulting with a handful of Smithsonian historians, but we may have figured out De Klerk's reference to *krag* as a unit of measurement."

"What is it?" Anya asked.

"During the fighting back then, a common weapon used widely by Boer troops was a Norwegian rifle called an M1894 Krag-Jørgensen. Over time, it became simply known as a *krag*. The rifle was thirty-nine inches long. If we assume that was

De Klerk's unit of measurement, the distance he described is around 178 miles."

Bukolov sat straighter, some of his normal spunk returning. "So we now know the distance from Grietje's Well to the Boar's Head Waterfall!"

"And not much else," Harper added, quickly popping that balloon. "I suspect the Boar's Head Waterfall—where this cave is hidden—is not so much a *name* as what the place *looks* like, some local landmark that you have to see to recognize."

"So obviously something that looks like the head of a boar," Tucker said.

"And that's why we'll need boots on the ground. We need someone scouring that location, likely on foot or horseback."

"To view the place from the same vantage as De Klerk did in the past," Anya said.

"Exactly." Harper shifted the topic. "But to even get there, we need to know where to *start*, where to set out from. Without that information, we're nowhere."

Bukolov nodded. "We must figure out what De Klerk meant by *Grietje's Well at Melkboschkuil*."

"Which brings me to the *second* piece of the puzzle we've solved. The historians determined that there once was a farm called *Melkboschkuil*, owned by the Cloete family, located in the Northern Cape province of South Africa. It's historically significant because the farmstead eventually prospered and grew into the present-day city of Springbok."

"Then that's where we must go!" Bukolov slapped a palm on the table. "To Springbok . . . to find this Grietje's Well. Then it's a simple matter to measure out 178 miles at a compass bearing of twenty-five degrees, like De Klerk wrote, and look for this Boar's Head near a waterfall. That's where we'll find the cave!"

Is that all we have to do? Tucker thought sourly.

Harper also lacked the good doctor's confidence. "The only problem is I could find no reference to a place called Grietje's Well. It's likely a place known only to the locals of De Klerk's time. All we've been able to determine is that *Grietje* is Dutch for 'Wilma.'"

"So then we're looking for Wilma's Well," Tucker said.

"That's about it," Harper conceded. "Like I said. We need boots on the ground."

"And I intend to be a pair of those boots," Bukolov said. "My knowledge of De Klerk may prove the difference between success and failure out there."

Anya stirred, too, clearly wanting to go. Like the doctor, she was also well versed in De Klerk's work—and if anything, more stable.

"Understood," Harper said. "But all this presents one other problem."

Tucker didn't like the note of warning in her tone; even her southern lilt grew heavier.

"If you draw a line from Springbok along De Klerk's bearing, it puts you squarely into the Groot Karas Mountains—in the country of Namibia."

Tucker took a deep breath and let it out audibly.

"What?" Anya asked. "What's wrong?"

"Namibia is in the middle of a bloody war," Tucker explained. "Between government forces and guerrillas."

"And those guerrillas," Harper added, "hold those mountains. They're particularly fond of kidnapping foreigners and holding them for ransom."

Bukolov puffed loudly, clearly frustrated. "There has to be a way. We cannot abandon the search now."

"We're not, but if you go, I wanted you to understand what you could be facing out there. I'll arrange some local assets to assist you in Africa, but it'll be far from safe."

Bukolov shook his head. "I must go! We must try! Before Kharzin finds some other means to discover that cave. Utkin only saw that map page briefly before I burned it, but I don't know how much he retained or shared. And maybe I inadvertently mentioned something to him. I simply don't know."

Anya spoke with more certainty. "What I do know is that General Kharzin *won't* stop. Most everyone at the SVR detests him. He's a Cold War–era warrior, a real dinosaur. He believes Russia's brightest days died with Stalin. If Utkin has been feeding him intelligence all along, then he understands LUCA's potential as a weapon. Properly introduced into an ecosystem—like a rice paddy in Japan—a single speck of LUCA would systematically destroy that ecosystem. And not just that rice paddy, but *all* of them."

"That must not happen," Bukolov pressed.

"I agree," Harper said. "I'll begin making arrangements."

11:10 A.M.

After settling some minor issues, Harper asked to speak to Tucker alone.

"Have we made a devil's deal here, Tucker? Part of me thinks we should just firebomb this cave if we find it."

"It may come down to that. But you've also made one hell of an assumption."

"Which is what?"

"That Kane and I are going to Africa."

"What? After everything we just discussed, you'd consider bailing out?"

Tucker chuckled. "No, but a girl likes to be *asked* to the dance."

Harper laughed in return. "Consider yourself asked. So what's your assessment of Anya and Bukolov. He plainly doesn't want her along."

"I say that's his problem. Anya's earned her place on this mission."

"I agree. She seems to know almost as much about LUCA as he does. And considering the stakes, it wouldn't hurt to have a different perspective on things. But the good doctor will not like it."

Tucker sighed. "The sooner Bukolov learns that his tantrums will get him nowhere, the better it will be for everyone once he reaches the United States."

"How soon can you get me a list of supplies you'll need?"

"A couple hours. I want to be under way tonight. In Springbok by noon."

"Understood."

"And I need to ask a couple of favors."

"Name them."

"First, find the family of the Beriev pilot." *Elena.* "Make sure they know where to find her body and reimburse them for the Beriev."

"And second?"

"Make sure Utkin's body is returned to his family. They're in a village called Kolyshkino on the Volga River."

"Why? The man betrayed you—almost got you all killed."

"But in the end, he saved us. And I respect that last act."

Naive or not, Tucker wanted to believe that maybe Anya was right. That Utkin had been forced against his will to betray them. But he would never know for sure. And maybe it was better that way.

"Sounds as though you liked him." Harper's voice went unusually soft, as if sensing the depth of his regret.

"I suppose I did. It's hard to explain."

Thankfully she let it go at that.

"Okay, I'll handle everything. But what about sending additional muscle your way, something beyond a few local assets?"

"I think small is better."

Besides, Tucker had all the help he needed and trusted in the form of his four-legged partner.

"You may be right," Harper agreed. "South Africa's security agencies run a tight ship. You show up big and loud, and they'll be all over you."

"I can't argue with that."

"Now, I have to ask something difficult of you," she said.

"Go ahead."

"If you get to that cave and things go sour, you make damned sure LUCA doesn't see the light of day. No matter the cost. Or casualties. Is that understood?"

Tucker inhaled deeply. "I'll get it done."

3:34 P.M.

A soft knock on his door woke him out of a slight drowse. Kane lifted his head from Tucker's chest as the two lay sprawled on the bed, napping in the day's heat.

Tucker, still in his clothes, rolled to his feet and placed his face in his hands.

Who the hell . . .

Kane hopped down, sidled to the door, and sniffed along the bottom. His tail began to wag. Someone he knew.

"Tucker, are you awake?" a voice called through the door.

Anya.

He groaned, stepped over, and unlocked the door. He wiped his eyes blearily. "What's wrong?"

Something better be *wrong*.

Anya stood in the doorway, wearing a peach-colored sundress. She smoothed it over her hips self-consciously with her good hand. "One of the consulate wives gave it to me. I'm sorry, you were sleeping, weren't you?"

She began to step away.

"No. It's all right. Come in."

"I should probably be sleeping, too. But every time I lie down . . ." She walked over to the side chair across from the bed and sat down. "I'm frightened, Tucker."

"Of going to South Africa?"

"Of course, that. But mostly about what happens *after* all this. Once we're in America."

"Anya, the government will give you a new identity, a new place to live. And with your background, you'll have no trouble finding work. You'll be fine."

"I'll be *alone*. Everything I know will be gone. Even Bukolov. You heard him. He'll barely talk to me now."

"Maybe he'll calm down and eventually understand."

She picked slightly at her cast, her voice growing pained. "He won't. I know him."

Tucker knew she was right. Bukolov was single-minded and emotionally inflexible. Now that he had De Klerk's diary in hand, Anya was no longer indispensable to his work. And in addition she had proven herself untrustworthy. For Bukolov, both of these sins were unpardonable.

Anya was right. Once in America, she would be alone. Rudderless. She would need friends.

With a sigh, he reached across and squeezed her hand.

"You'll know at least *one* person in the States," he reassured her.

Kane thumped his tail.

"Make that *two*," he added.

28

As Tucker set foot off the plane's stairway and onto the hot tarmac of Cape Town's International Airport, a shout rose ahead. They had landed at a private terminal, shuttled here by corporate jet—a Gulfstream V—arranged by Harper.

"Mr. Wayne, sir! Over here!"

He turned to see a tall, thin black man in his midtwenties trotting toward him. He wore charcoal slacks and a starched white shirt. He gave Tucker a broad smile and stuck out his hand.

"Mr. Tucker Wayne, I presume."

He took the man's hand. "And you are?"

"Christopher Nkomo."

Kane came trotting down behind him, sliding next to Tucker, sniffing at the stranger, sizing him up.

"My goodness," the man said, "who is this fine animal?"

"That would be Kane."

"He's magnificent!"

No argument there.

Bukolov and Anya came next, shielding their eyes, as they joined him. Introductions were made all around.

"What tribe are you?" Anya asked, then blurted out, "Oh, is that impolite to ask? I'm sorry."

"Not at all, missus. I am of the Ndebele tribe."

"And your language?"

"We speak Xhosa." He waved and guided them across the tarmac toward a nest of parked Cessnas and other smaller aircraft. "But I went to university here, studying business administration and English."

"It shows," said Tucker.

"Very kind of you." He finally stopped before a single-engine plane, a Cessna Grand Caravan. It was already being serviced for flight. "With your patience, we will get all your baggage loaded quickly."

Christopher was a man of his word. It was accomplished in a matter of minutes.

"Your pilot will be with you shortly," he said, clambering up the short ladder and through the Cessna's side door. A moment later, he hopped back out, his head now adorned with a blue pilot's cap. "Welcome aboard. My name is Christopher Nkomo, and I will be your pilot today."

Tucker matched his grin. "You'll be flying us?"

"Myself and my older brother, Matthew."

A thin arm stuck out from the side window next to the copilot's seat.

"No worries," Christopher said. "I am a very good pilot and I know this land and its history like the palm of my hand. I hear you all are Boer historians, and that I am to assist you however I can."

From the tone of the man's voice, he knew they weren't historians. Harper clearly must have debriefed Christopher about the goal of their mission here.

"I am especially familiar with Springbok. My cousin has a home there. So if we are all ready, let us get aboard."

Bukolov and Anya needed no coaxing to climb out of the sun and into the dark, air-conditioned interior. Bukolov took the seat farthest from Anya. The doctor was not happy to have her along, but back in Istanbul, Tucker had left him no choice.

Tucker hung back with Christopher. "The supplies I asked for?"

"Come see."

Christopher lifted a hatch to reveal a storage space neatly packed with supplies. He pulled out a clipboard and handed it to Tucker. It listed the contents: potable water, dehydrated meals, first-aid kits, maps and compasses, knives, hatchets, a small but well-stocked toolbox.

"As for weapons and ammunition," the man said, "I was not able to provide all the exact models you requested. I took the liberty of using my own judgment."

He pulled that list out of a back pocket and passed it over.

Tucker scanned it and nodded. "Nicely done. Hopefully we won't need any of it."

"God willing," Christopher replied.

1:38 P.M.

Tucker stared at the passing landscape as the Cessna droned toward their destination. Buckled opposite Tucker, Kane matched his pose, his nose pressed to the window.

The scenery north of Cape Town was hypnotically beautiful: a dry moonscape of reddish-brown earth and savannah, broken up by saw-toothed hills. Tiny settlements dotted the countryside, surrounded by brighter patches of green scrub.

At last, Christopher swung the Cessna into a gentle bank that took them over Springbok. The town of nine thousand lay nestled in a valley surrounded by rolling granite peaks, called the *Klein Koperberge*, or Small Copper Mountains.

The plane leveled out of its banking turn and descended toward Springbok's airstrip. As they landed, the tires kissed the dirt tarmac without the slightest bounce. They rolled to the end of the runway and turned right toward the terminal, administrative offices, and maintenance hangars.

Christopher drew the Cessna to a smooth stop alongside a powder-blue Toyota SUV. A man bearing a striking resemblance to Christopher and his brother waved from the driver's seat.

Tucker called toward the cockpit, "Another brother, Christopher?"

"Yes, indeed, Mr. Wayne. That is Paul, my youngest brother. He flew up here last night to arrange things and make inquiries."

When the engines had come to a complete stop,

Christopher walked back, opened the side door, and helped them out.

A palpable blast of heat struck Tucker in the face. Anya gasped at it.

Bukolov grumbled his displeasure. "What is this fresh hell you have brought us to, Tucker?"

Christopher laughed. "Do not worry. You will get used to the heat." He stepped away, embraced his brother Paul, and motioned them into the SUV. "My brother has arranged accommodations at a guesthouse not far from here."

"Why?" Bukolov said. "How long will we be staying here?"

"At least the night. Matthew will remain here and guard your supplies. If you'll climb aboard, please."

Soon they were heading north on a highway marked R355. Barren foothills flanked both sides, their eroded reddish-orange flanks revealing black granite domes.

"This place looks like Mars," Bukolov said. "I've seen no water at all in this godforsaken land. How are we supposed to find a *well* out here?"

"Patience, Doc," Tucker said.

They finally reached the outskirts of Springbok. It could have passed for a small town in Arizona, with narrow, winding streets bordered by modest ranch homes.

Paul turned into a crescent-shaped driveway lined by thick green hedges. A hand-painted placard atop a post read KLEINPLASIE GUESTHOUSE. The SUV stopped beneath a timbered awning. A set of stone steps led up to French doors bracketed by a pair of potted palms.

After speaking to a bellman in white shorts and a crisp polo shirt, Christopher led his charges, including Kane, into the lobby.

"Oh, this is glorious," Anya said, referring more to the air-conditioning than the accommodations—though they were handsome, too.

The lobby consisted of leather armchairs, animal-hide rugs, sisal runners, and framed drawings of famous African explorers. Above them, huge rattan-bladed ceiling fans hung from exposed beams and churned the already-cool air.

Christopher checked them in, then led them to a private meeting space down the hall. They gathered around a mahogany table. Sunlight streamed through the tilt of plantation shutters. Sparkling pitchers of water, floating with sliced lemons, awaited them.

Paul eventually stepped inside and crossed to the head of the table. "Mr. Wayne," he said. "Christopher informed me of your interest in a local feature. Grietje's Well. I've been making discreet inquiries, but no such place seems to exist, I'm afraid."

"It must," Bukolov snapped, still out of sorts from the travel and heat.

"Mmm," Paul said, too gracious to argue. "However, the relationship between Springbok and water is a long and bloody one. Water was quite treasured here and fought over, as you can well imagine with the heat. So natural sources were often hidden. In fact, the town's original Afrikaans name is *Springbokfontein*."

"What does that mean?" Anya asked.

"*Springbok* is a local antelope. If you keep a sharp eye, you will see them hopping about. And *fontein* means fountain. But a fountain here simply refers to a natural spring or a watering hole."

"Or perhaps a well," Tucker added.

"Exactly so. But *man-made* wells are relatively modern features here in Springbok. Before the middle of the twentieth century, locals relied upon *fonteins*. Natural springs. That is why my brother and I believe what you are actually seeking is not a *well* but a *spring*."

"But how does this fact help us?" Tucker asked.

"Perhaps much, or perhaps not at all," Christopher replied. "But there is a man who might know that answer. Reverend Manfred Cloete."

The name struck Tucker as familiar—then he remembered a detail from the briefing back in Istanbul.

"*Cloete*," Tucker said. "That's the name of the family that once owned *Melkboschkuil* farm. The one Springbok was founded upon."

Christopher nodded. "That's correct. Manfred is indeed a descendant from that distinguished lineage, making the man not only Springbok's reverend, but the keeper of its unwritten history as well."

Paul checked his watch. "And he's waiting for us now."

2:15 P.M.

Crossing through the historic center of Springbok, Christopher turned into a paved parking lot surrounded by a low stucco wall and shaded by lush green acacia trees. Nestled within those same walls stood a sturdy stone church, with a single square steeple and a large rosette window in front. It resembled a miniature Norman castle.

"Springbok's *Klipkerk*," Christopher declared. "The Dutch Reformed Church. Now a museum."

He waved his three passengers out.

Tucker and Kane clambered from the backseat. Anya slid out the front passenger door. They had left Bukolov back at the guesthouse. The travel and the sudden heat had proved too much for the Russian's reserves. As a precaution, Paul had been left behind to watch over the doctor.

Anya waited for Tucker to join her before following Christopher toward the church. She smiled at him, slightly cradling her casted arm. She must still be in some pain, but she hadn't made a single complaint. Perhaps she feared her injury might be used as an excuse to leave her behind. Either that, or she was a real trouper.

Christopher led them along a path that took them to the rear of the church and across a broad, well-manicured lawn.

To one side, a barrel-chested man with wild white hair and a bushy beard knelt beside a bed of blooming desert flowers. He wore Bermuda shorts and nothing else. His torso was deeply tanned and covered in curly white hair.

"Manfred!" Christopher called.

The fellow looked over his shoulder, saw Christopher, and smiled. He stood up and wiped his soiled palms on a towel dangling from the waistband of his shorts. As he joined them, Christopher made the introductions.

"Ah, a pair of fellow historians," Manfred Cloete said, shaking their hands. His light blue eyes twinkled. "Welcome to *Springbokfontein*."

His accent was pure South African, a blend that sounded both British and Australian with a bit of something mysterious thrown in.

"I appreciate you seeing us, Reverend," Tucker replied.

"Manfred, please. My goodness, is that your hound?"

Kane came bounding past, doing a fast circuit of the yard.

"He is indeed. Name's Kane."

"Might tell him to be careful. Got some snakes about. Can't seem to get rid of them."

Tucker whistled, and Kane sprinted over and sat down.

"Follow me, all of you," Manfred said. "I've got some lemonade over in the shade."

He led them to a nearby picnic table, and everyone sat down.

As Manfred tinkled ice and lemonade into Anya's glass, he asked, "So, Ms. Averin—"

"Anya, please."

"Of course, always happy to accommodate a lady's request. Especially one with a wounded wing." He nodded to her cast. "What is this interest in the Boer Wars?"

She glanced to Tucker, letting him take the lead.

He cleared his throat. "It's my interest actually. A personal one. I recently discovered one of my ancestors fought during the Second Boer War. He was a doctor. I know very little else about him except that he served most of his time during the fighting at a fort somewhere around here."

"If he was a *doctor*, that would most likely put him at the Klipkoppie fort. That's where the local medical unit was stationed. It was under the command of General Manie Roosa. Tough old bird and a bit crazy, if you ask me. The British hated fighting him. You'll find the ruins of the fort just outside of town."

Tucker frowned. On the flight down here, he had already studied the locations of various old forts, hoping for a clue. "Outside of town?" he asked. "But according to my research, the ruins of Klipkoppie are in the *center* of town."

"Pah! That dung heap beside the shopping center? That was only a forward outpost, nothing more. The ruins of the *real* Klipkoppie are two miles to the northwest. Christopher knows where."

"Then why—?"

"Easier to suck tourists into the gift shops and restaurants if it's in the center of town. Besides, the real Klipkoppie isn't much to look at, and it's hard to get to. Can't have tourists getting themselves killed." He clapped his palms against his thighs. "Right. So tell me the name of this ancestor of yours."

"De Klerk. Paulos de Klerk."

Manfred leaned back, clearly recognizing the name, staring at Tucker with new eyes. "The famous botanist?"

"You know him."

"I do. Though I can't say more than that. I actually forgot until you reminded me just now that he was a field medic. He's much better known for those flower drawings of his."

"It's actually one of his journals that drew us down here. In one of his diaries, he mentioned Grietje's Well several times. It seemed important to him."

"Water was back then. It was the difference between life and death. Especially during the wars. When the Brits laid siege to a Boer fort, one of the first things they did was try to cut off access to water. A man can go weeks without food, but only a few days without water. For that reason, the Boer started building forts atop natural springs. Because of the importance of such water sources, the troops came to name them after loved ones, usually women: wives, daughters, nieces."

Anya stirred. "And *Grietje* is Afrikaans for 'Wilma.'"

Manfred nodded. "Wilma must have been dearly loved by whoever named that spring. But like I said, the springs of most forts bore women's names. The key is to find out *which* fort it might be. Because your ancestor was a doctor, I'd still start with the ruins of Klipkoppie."

Anya stared out toward the horizon, at the dry hills. "Do you know of any wells or springs up there?"

"No, but if this spring hasn't dried up, there'll be evidence of erosion on the surface from where the waters seasonally rise and fall. Christopher will know what to look for."

Christopher appeared less convinced. "It will be hard to find. And we're still not certain Klipkoppie is the right fort. With all the old Boer strongholds around here, it could be like finding a needle in a haystack."

"Still, it gives us somewhere to start," Tucker said.

"And in the meantime," Manfred said, "I will look more deeply into the local history of your ancestor. Paulos de Klerk. Come by tomorrow afternoon and we'll talk again."

2:55 P.M.

"Should we head to the Klipkoppie fort now?" Christopher asked as they pulled out of the parking lot.

"How hard is it to reach?"

"It's not far to the base of the fort's hill, but there are no roads to the top. We must hike. Very steep, but I know the way."

Tucker checked his watch. "When does the sun set here?"

"Remember you are south of the equator. It is our late summer, the end of our rainy season. So the sun won't go down until a bit past seven o'clock."

"That gives us roughly four hours." He turned to Anya. "We can drop you back at the guesthouse on the way out of town. Let you rest. I'm not sure your orthopedist would approve of you going hiking."

"And miss this chance?" She lifted her bad arm. "It's fine. Besides, I've got my boots on. Might as well use them."

Tucker heard happy thumping on the seat next to him.

"Sounds like it's unanimous."

Christopher turned the SUV and headed away from the guesthouse. He wound through the streets to the edge of Springbok, then out into the sun-blasted countryside.

They had traveled a couple of kilometers when Christopher's phone rang.

Tucker felt a clutch of fear, wondering if they should have checked on Bukolov before setting out. But there was no way the old man could make the hike in this heat.

Christopher spoke in hushed tones on the phone, then passed the handset over his shoulder. "It's for you. It's Manfred."

Both surprised and curious, he took the phone. "Hello?"

"Ah, my good fellow, glad I was able to reach you." His words were frosted with excitement and pride. "I did some digging as soon as you left. It seems General Manie Roosa, your old ancestor's commander, had a daughter. Named Wilhelmina."

"Another version of Wilma."

"Quite right. And listen to this. In one of Roosa's field reports, he states and I quote, 'Without Wilhelmina, that British bastard MacDonald would have been successful in his siege of our fort.' I suspect he's referring to Sir Ian MacDonald, a British regimental commander back then. But I doubt Roosa's young daughter had any hand in breaking that British siege."

"He must be referring to the fort's water supply! Named after his daughter."

"And surely your ancestor would have known of this secret nickname for the well."

Tucker thanked Manfred and hung up. He relayed the information to the others.

Christopher smiled. "It seems our haystack has gotten considerably smaller."

29

Eleven miles outside of Springbok, Christopher turned onto a narrow dirt driveway that ended at a tin-roofed building. The billboard atop it read HEL-MAN'S GARAGE. Christopher parked in the shadow of the building, then got out and disappeared through an open bay door.

When he returned, he opened the passenger side for Anya and waved Tucker and Kane out. "Helman says we can park our vehicle here. If we are not back in three weeks, he says he will alert the police."

"Three weeks?" Anya asked, then noted Christopher's smile. "Very funny."

Christopher pulled a trio of daypacks from the SUV's trunk and passed them out. He also unzipped a rifle case and handed Tucker a heavy, double-barreled gun, along with a cartridge belt holding a dozen bullets, each one larger than his thumb.

"Nitro Express cartridges," Christopher said. "Four-seventy caliber. Are you familiar with weapons, Mr. Wayne?"

Tucker broke the rifle's breech, checked the

action, and gave it a quick inspection. He pulled a pair of Nitros from the belt, popped them into the breech, and snapped the weapon closed.

"I'll manage," he said.

"Very good." Christopher's expression grew serious. "It is unlikely we will encounter anything, but there are lions in this area. I recommend that Kane stays close to us."

"He will."

"If we encounter lions, we shall try to back out of the area slowly. Lions are typically inactive during the day and mostly sleep. But if there is a charge, stay *behind* me. I will take the first shot. If I miss the shots with both barrels, or the lion fails to yield, I will drop to the ground to give you a clear field of fire. The lion will likely stop to maul me. When he does, take your shot. Do not hesitate. This is very important. Aim a few inches below the lion's chin, between the shoulders, if possible. Or if from the side, just past the armpit."

"Understood," Tucker replied.

"And finally, if you miss your shots, do not under any circumstances run."

"Why not?" asked Anya.

"Because then you will die exhausted, and that is no way to present yourself to God."

With that, Christopher prepped his own rifle and donned his pack. He also pulled out a tall walking stick with a tassel of steel bells at the top.

"Ready?" he asked.

"Hold on," Anya said. "Where is my gun?"

"I am sorry, missus. I did not think . . . I have very

few female clients, you see. Plus your wrist. Please forgive me."

"It's okay, Christopher. Once one of you two drops from exhaustion, I'll have my rifle." Anya smiled sweetly. "Which way are we headed?"

"South to the trailhead, missus, then northeast into the hills."

Anya turned on her heel and headed off. "Try to keep up, boys."

She led them across a patch of scrubland to where the thin trail headed northeast. From that point, she wisely let Christopher take the lead. Almost immediately, the grade steepened, winding its way higher into the hills.

Tucker kept up the rear.

He tapped Kane's side. "CLOSE ROAM."

As was his habit, Kane trotted to either side, sometimes drifting ahead, sometimes dropping back, but he never strayed more than fifty feet in either direction. The shepherd's ears looked especially erect, his eyes exceptionally bright. Here were smells he'd never before experienced. Tucker imagined it was something of a sensory kaleidoscope for Kane.

After a kilometer or so, they passed into a narrow ravine and found themselves in shadows. A riotous profusion of desert flowers in dusty shades of pink and purple bloomed from the rock faces around them, casting out a sweet perfume, not unlike honeysuckle. The deep thrum of insects greeted them as they moved through, amplified by the tight space.

Kane stood before the wall of blooms, watching petals and leaves vibrate, his head cocked with curiosity.

"Cape honeybees," Christopher announced. "Fear not. If we do not bother them, they will not bother us."

"There must be thousands," Anya murmured.

"Many, many thousands, missus."

A quarter of a mile later, they exited the ravine and found themselves on a plain of red soil and scattered scrub brush. To their left, rolling granite hills towered hundreds of feet into the air.

Abruptly, Christopher let out a barking yelp, then another one thirty seconds later, then one more. In between yelps, he shook his walking stick, tinkling the bells attached to the handle.

"What's he doing?" Anya whispered back to Tucker.

"Letting everyone know we're here. Most wildlife doesn't want anything to do with us."

Cocking his head, Christopher stopped. He held up a closed fist and pointed to his ear: *Listen*.

After a few moments of silence came a deep huffing grunt. It echoed over the hills and faded.

Without a sound, Kane padded to the head of the column, halting several feet in front of Christopher. The shepherd angled his body to the right and sat down, his eyes fixed in the distance.

The huffing came again, then stopped.

"Male lions," Christopher said and pointed off to the left. "A few miles away. They should stay there until nightfall."

Kane continued to stare—but in the opposite direction from where Christopher had been pointing. Tucker dropped to a knee next to his partner.

"Maybe those male lions will," Tucker murmured. "But look beyond that line of scrub trees over there."

"What? I do not see . . ." Christopher's words trailed, ending with a whispered, "Oh, my."

A hundred yards away, a trio of lionesses, each well over three hundred pounds, slipped from the brush and began slowly stalking toward their group. As if by some unseen cue, the trio parted to change their angle of attack. The largest of the group took the center position.

"This is unusual," Christopher muttered. "They usually do not behave this way."

"Tell them that. They're trying to flank us."

Anya said, "What should I do?"

"Stay still," Christopher said. "Tucker, if they get around us—"

"I know."

Even as Tucker said the words, Kane stood up. The shepherd arched his back, his fur hackling up in a ridge along his spine, bushing out his tail. He dropped his head low to the ground and bared his fangs. A deep, prolonged snarl rolled from his chest. He began padding toward the lead lioness.

Christopher said, "Tucker, stop him."

"He knows what he's doing," he said, putting his faith in Kane. "Follow me. Gun ready. Anya, stay behind us."

"This is ill-advised," Christopher whispered.

Tucker rose to his feet and followed Kane, pacing carefully but steadily.

The center lioness suddenly stopped, a three-hundred-pound mountain of muscle, claw, and teeth. She crouched low, her tail slashing back and forth behind her. The other two also stopped, settling to Tucker's two and ten o'clock positions.

"What's happening?" Anya whispered.

"Kane's letting them know we're not an easy meal."

"This is remarkable," Christopher rasped. "Did you teach him this?"

"This isn't teachable," Tucker replied. "This is instinct."

The lead lionesses began huffing.

Kane let out a snapping growl and took three fast paces forward. Saliva frothed from his jaws.

Tucker murmured, "HOLD."

"Let's give our visitors a little nudge," Christopher said. "A single shot each, above their heads."

Tucker nodded. "You call it."

"Understand, if they do not bolt, they will charge."

"I'm ready."

Anya said, "I think I'm going to be sick."

"Swallow it," he warned.

Christopher turned to face the lioness to the left flank; Tucker did the same to the right. Kane stayed put, his gaze fixed to the beast in the center.

"Fire!"

Tucker lifted his rifle, propped the butt against his shoulder, and blasted over the lioness's head. She jumped, then dropped low and slunk away, back through the line of scrub bushes. Christopher's did the same as he fired.

The big lioness never budged, holding her ground

as the others retreated. She stared at Kane for a few more seconds, let out another huffing grunt, then turned and walked after the other two. With a final backward glance, she disappeared from view.

Christopher wasted no time in leading them off. After putting a few hundred yards between them and the lionesses, they stopped for a water break under a rock ledge. Kane sat comfortably in the shade as though nothing unusual had happened.

No one spoke for a few minutes, then Anya said, "I've never been so terrified in my life. The look in those eyes . . . we were simply meat to them."

"Essentially, yes," Christopher said.

"I am not even sure I understand what happened."

"Lions are to be feared, but they are not stupid. Given a choice between ambushing easy prey or engaging in a fight, they will always choose the former. It is a simple matter of practicality. An injured lion is a weak lion. Tucker's dog was simply reminding them of that point. Plus it is just past the main rutting period, so plenty of young animals are around. They have abundant food. If prey had been scarce, our encounter back there would have ended badly."

4:45 P.M.

Rehydrated and with nerves calmed, the group headed out again.

After another twenty minutes, Christopher stopped and pointed into the hills. "The ruins of Klipkoppie fort are over that ridge. Now we climb a bit."

"How far?" asked Anya.

"Half a kilometer. As we go, stomp your feet occasionally so we do not surprise any snakes."

Christopher led them up a shallow gully awash with boulders, scrub brush, and the occasional tree. The trees had wide trunks that narrowed to a cluster of leafless branches that ended in single star-shaped buds.

"Looks like broccoli," Anya said.

"*Kokerboom*," Christopher called over his shoulder. "Also called Quiver trees. The San people use the hollow branches as arrows."

As the gully grew narrower, it eventually required hopping from boulder to boulder to continue the steep ascent. A few spots required Tucker to haul Kane up or assist Anya. Finally, clawing their way up the last few yards, they reached a half-crescent-shaped plateau overlooking Springbok.

They were all breathing heavily, gulping water, sweating.

"What a view," said Anya, leaning over the edge.

A sheer cliff dropped away at her toes. Behind them climbed a steep-walled granite dome. Across the plateau, the stubbed ends of timbered pillars stuck up out of the ground. More sprouted across the curve of the dome.

Squinting his eyes, Tucker could almost make out the bases of old fortifications and the foundations of long-lost buildings.

"This is the Klipkoppie," Christopher announced.

"Not much left of it," he said.

"No. Time and erosion have done their job. A hundred twenty years ago, this was a massive fort.

The watchtower sat atop the dome. From here, Boer soldiers could see the entire valley below. The only access was up that narrow ravine we climbed."

"A natural choke point."

"Exactly so."

Tucker began to wander into the ruins, but a shout from Christopher halted him.

"Step carefully! This plateau is riddled with tunnels and old cellars."

"Here?" Anya asked. "This looks like solid rock."

Tucker knelt and probed the earth with his fingers. "Sandstone. Definitely workable. But it would've taken hard labor and patience to excavate here."

Christopher nodded. "Two qualities the Boers were known for. The entrances are covered by old planks—probably very fragile by now. Below us are sleeping quarters and storage areas."

Tucker called to Kane, who had wandered off to explore. "COME."

The shepherd galloped over and skidded to a stop.

Kneeling, Tucker opened his canteen and filled his cupped hand. He rubbed the water over Kane's snout and under his chin. He held his damp palm to his nose. "SEEK. EASY STEP."

Nose to the ground, Kane padded off, following the edge of the plateau.

"What's he doing?" asked Anya.

"Setting up a search parameter."

Kane began working inward, crisscrossing the dirt with his nose to the ground. Occasionally he would stop suddenly and circle left or right before resuming course.

"Tunnel openings," Tucker explained to Anya and Christopher.

"Remarkable," Christopher murmured.

Kane suddenly stopped a quarter of the way across the plateau. He circled one spot, sniffing hard, stirring up dust eddies with his breath. Finally, he lay down and shifted around to face Tucker.

"He smells moisture there."

The trio worked cautiously toward him. Christopher led the way, thumping his walking stick against the ground, testing each step.

Once they reached Kane, Tucker gave his partner a two-handed neck massage. "Attaboy."

Christopher lifted his walking stick and drove the butt of it hard into the dirt, at the spot where Kane had been so vigorously sniffing.

There came a dull *thunk*.

"Impressive beast of yours!" Christopher said.

Unfolding the small spades in their packs, the trio dug and swept away the packed dirt until a square of planking was exposed. It looked like a trapdoor into the earth. Luckily, the rough-hewn wood was rotted, desiccated by a century of heat. Jamming their spades into crannies and splits, they slowly pried the planks free and set them aside, exposing a dark shaft, about a yard across.

Lying on his belly, Tucker pointed his flashlight down the throat of the tunnel. Kane crouched next to him, panting, sniffing at the hole.

"Looks to drop about eight feet," he said, rising to his knees. "Then it branches off to the left."

"Who goes first?" Anya asked.

As if understanding her, Kane gained his feet and

danced around the hole, his tail whipping fast. He looked up at Tucker, then down at the shaft.

"Take a guess," Tucker said.

"You're sending him down there?" Anya crossed her arms. "That seems cruel."

"Cruel? I think Kane was a dachshund in a former life, a breed built to flush badgers out of burrows. If there's a hole, Kane wants to crawl in and explore."

Tucker pulled the shepherd's tactical vest out of his backpack. Anticipating what was to come, Kane shook and trembled with excitement. Tucker quickly suited up his partner, synching the feed into the new sat phone Harper had supplied. He ran through a quick diagnostics check and found everything working as designed.

"Ready, Kane?"

The shepherd walked to the shaft and placed his front paws on the lip. Tucker played the beam of his flashlight across the sides and down to the floor of the tunnel. He pointed.

"Go."

Without hesitation, Kane leaped into the darkness, followed by a soft *thump* as he landed at the bottom.

"SOUND OFF."

Kane barked once in reply, indicating he was okay.

Tucker punched buttons on his phone, and Kane's video feed came online. Shading the screen with his hand to reduce the sun's glare, he was able to make out the horizontal tunnel that angled away from the shaft. The camera had a night-vision feature, but Tucker tapped a button, and a small LED lamp flared atop the camera stalk, lighting Kane's way.

The sharper illumination revealed coarse walls, shored up by heavy timber. Out of the sun and wind, the wood looked solid enough, but *looks* could be deceptive. Back in Afghanistan, he'd witnessed several tunnel collapses while hunting for Taliban soldiers in their warren of caves.

Fearing the same now, he licked his lips, worried for Kane, but they both had a duty here.

Speaking into his radio mike, he said, "FORWARD. SEEK."

Hearing the command, Kane stalks forward. He leaves the glaring brightness of the day and heads into darkness, led by a pool of light cast over his shoulders. His senses fill with dirt and mold, old wood and stone—but through it all, he fixes on a trail of dampness in the air.

It stands out against the dryness.

He needs no lights to follow it.

But he goes slowly, stepping carefully.

His ears pick out the scrunch of sand underfoot, the scrabble of chitinous legs on rock, the creak of timber.

He pushes through faint webs of dust.

He reaches another tunnel, one that crosses his path.

Which way?

A command whispers in his ear. His partner sees what he sees.

SEEK.

He steps to each direction, stretching his nose, breathing deeply, pulling the trail deep inside him, through his flared nostrils, past his tongue, to where instinct judges all.

He paces into one tunnel, then another, testing each.

Down one path, to the left, the air is heavier with moisture.

His ears hear the faintest tink of water falling to stone.

He heads toward it, his heart hammering inside him, on the hunt, knowing his target is near. The tunnel drops deeper, then levels. Several cautious paces farther and the passage opens into a cavern, tall enough to jump and leap with joy within.

He wants to do that.

But instead he hears, HOLD.

And he does.

He stares across the sloping floor of the cave, to a pool of glassy blackness. The sweep of his light bathes across the surface, igniting it to a clear azure blue.

Water.

"Eureka," Christopher murmured.

Tucker turned to the others and passed Anya his phone. "I'm going down there. When I reach Kane, I'll check in, using his camera."

He turned, fished through his pack, and pulled out his handheld GPS unit. He stuffed it into a cargo pocket of his pants.

"I don't understand," Anya said. "Why do you have to go down there? It doesn't look safe for someone as big as you."

Tucker scooted to the hole and swung his legs over the edge. "We need accurate coordinates."

"But why?" Concern shone on her face. "We know the well is below this plateau. Isn't that close enough?"

"No. We need a compass bearing from that *exact*

spot. Any miscalculation of the well's location will be compounded exponentially two hundred miles away." He pointed toward the horizon. "Make a hundred-yard mistake here, we could be off by a mile from De Klerk's coordinates. And out in the broken and inhospitable terrain of the Groot Karas Mountains, we could spend months up there and never find it."

Anya looked stunned. "I didn't think about that."

Tucker smiled. "All part of the service, ma'am." He prepared to lower himself down, then stopped. "Wait, I just realized I can't get any GPS lock underground. I'm going to have to go old school. Christopher, lend me your walking stick."

Their guide understood. "To act as a yardstick. Very clever."

"Give me thirty minutes. Unless there's a cave-in."

"If that happens," Christopher said, clapping him on the shoulder, "I'll alert the proper authorities to recover your body."

"And Kane's, too. I want him buried with me."

"Of course."

Anya frowned at them. "That's not funny."

They both turned to her. Neither of them was trying to be humorous.

That realization made her go pale.

Twisting around, Tucker lowered himself over the edge and dropped below. As his boots hit the ground, he crouched, turned on his flashlight, then ducked into the side tunnel. As he crawled on his hands and knees, he slid the walking stick end to end and counted as he went, mapping his route on a pocket notebook.

Occasionally, his back scraped the ceiling, causing miniavalanches of sand. In the confined quiet of the tunnel, the cascade echoed like hail peppering a sidewalk. He reached the intersection of tunnels and followed Kane's path to the left. Working diligently, it still took him an additional five minutes to map his way down to the cavern.

Kane heard him coming, trotted over, and licked his face.

"Good boy, good job!"

Tucker shined his flashlight around the room. Clearly the Boer troops must have spent a lot of time down here. The surrounding sandstone walls had been carved into benches and rudimentary tables, along with dozens of pigeonhole shelves. Ghosts of men materialized in his mind's eye: laughing, lounging, eating, all during one of the bloodiest and most obscure wars in history.

After jotting down the final measurements, Tucker lifted the page of his notebook toward Kane's camera and passed on a thumbs-up to the others above. He wanted a visual record of his calculations, of the coordinates of Grietje's Well, in case anything happened to him.

Satisfied, with his knowledge secure, he knelt and dipped his fingers into the water. It was cold and smelled fresh.

How long had people been using this spring?

He pictured ancient tribesmen coming here, seeking a respite from heat and thirst.

He decided to do the same. It felt like an oasis—not just from the blazing African sun, but from the pressures of his mission. The events of the past days came rushing back to him, a tumult of escapes, fire-fights, and death. At the moment, it all seemed surreal.

And now I am here, huddled in the bowels of a century-old Boer fort?

All because of a plant species almost as old as the earth itself.

He looked at Kane. "Can't say our lives are boring, can we?"

Confirming this, a sharp *crack* exploded, echoing down to the cave.

Tucker's first thought was *rifle fire*.

Another lion attack.

Then a deeper grumble came, a complaint of rock and sand.

He knew the truth.

Not a gunshot.

A crack of breaking timber.

A cave-in was starting.

30

Tucker shoved Kane into the tunnel as the rumbling in the earth grew louder, sounding like the approach of a locomotive.

"ESCAPE! OUTSIDE!"

Kane obeyed the frantic, breathless command and dove out of the cave. The shepherd could move faster, so had a better chance of surviving.

No sense both of them dying.

Tucker did his best to follow. He abandoned his flashlight, freeing one hand. But he dared not discard Christopher's walking stick. He had failed to measure it before jumping down here. To do his final calculations of the spring's coordinates, he needed the stick's exact length.

Ahead, the LED lamp from Kane's camera bobbled deeper down the tunnel, outdistancing him as he scrambled on his hands and knees. Skin ripped from his knuckles as he clenched the walking stick. His knees pounded across rough rocks and hard stone.

He'd never make it.

He was right.

A grinding roar erupted ahead, accompanied a moment later by a thick rolling wash of dust and fine sand through the air.

The tunnel had collapsed.

Through the silt cloud, Kane's lamp continued to glow, jostling, but not seeming to move forward any longer. Coughing on the dust, Tucker hurried to his partner's side.

Past Kane, a wall of sand, rock, and pieces of broken timber blocked the tunnel. There was no way past. The shepherd clawed and dug at the obstruction.

Tucker pushed next to him. With his free hand against the wall, he felt the vibration of the earth. Like a chain of dominoes, more collapses were imminent. With his palm on the wall, his fingertips discovered a *corner* at the edge of the obstruction.

"HOLD," he ordered Kane.

As the shepherd settled back, Tucker twisted the dog's vest camera to shine the light on his hand, still pressed against the wall. He glanced over his shoulder, then back to his fingers, regaining his bearings.

He realized they had reached the *intersection* of the two tunnels.

The collapse had occurred in the passageway to the right, the one leading from the entry shaft to here. What blocked them was the flood of sand and rock that had *washed* into this intersection by the cave-in. That meant there was no way to get back out the way they'd come in. But with some luck, they might be able to dig through this loose debris to reach the tunnel on the far side. Of course, there was no guarantee that such a path would lead to freedom, but they had no other choice.

"Dig," he ordered Kane.

Shoulder to shoulder, they set to work. Kane kicked rocks and paw-fulls of sand between his hind legs. Tucker grabbed splintery shards of wood and tossed them back. They slowly but relentlessly burrowed and cleared out the debris.

With raw fingers, Tucker rolled away a large chunk of sandstone down the slope of debris. He reached into the new gap and found—nothing. He whooped and scrambled faster. He soon had enough of a path for the two of them to belly-crawl through the wash of debris and into the far tunnel.

Kane shook sand from his coat.

Crouched on his hands and knees, Tucker did the same—though his shaking was a combination of relief and residual terror.

"Scout ahead," he whispered.

Together, they set out into the unknown maze of subterranean tunnels of the old Boer fort—and it was a labyrinth. Passageways and blind chambers met them at every turn. Tucker paused frequently to run his fingertips along the roofs or to shine Kane's lamp up.

Distant booms and rumbles marked additional cave-ins.

At last, he found himself standing in a square space about the size of a one-car garage. From the carved shelves and the decayed remains of smashed wooden crates, it appeared to be an old cellar. More tunnels led out from this central larder.

He bent down and turned Kane's lamp up.

He sighed in relief.

The low ceiling was held up with wooden planks.

As he straightened, Kane growled, a sharp note of fury—then bolted for the nest of crates. He shoved his nose there, then came backpedaling, shaking his head violently. After a few seconds, he trotted back to Tucker's side, something draped from his jaws.

Kane dropped it at his feet.

It was a three-foot black snake with a triangular head that hinted at its venomous nature.

Only now, past the hammering of his heart, did he hear a low and continuous hissing. As his eyes adjusted, he saw shreds of shadow slithering over the floor, wary of the light. From the other tunnels, more snakes spilled into the chamber. The trembling of the earth was stirring them out of their nests, pushing them upward.

Tucker used the butt of the walking stick to push one away from his toes, earning a savage hiss and the baring of long fangs.

Time to get out of here.

"PROTECT," he ordered Kane.

He gripped the pole two-handed and slammed the stick upward, striking into the planks with a jangle of the rod's bells. Wood pieces showered down. He kept at it, pounding again and again through the decay and rot above his head, while Kane kept watch on the snakes.

He continued to work on the ceiling, trying to force his own cave-in, knowing he had to be near the surface. He pictured Kane's earlier cautious search of the plateau and Christopher tapping the ground as they crossed, watching for pitfalls underfoot. By now, debris had begun to fall faster: wood, sand, rock. The rain of rubble only served to further piss off the roiling snakes.

With his shoulders aching, he smashed the stick into the ceiling again, cracking a thick plank, splitting it in two.

That was the straw that broke the camel's back.

A good chunk of the roof collapsed, crashing down around Tucker's ears. A piece of wood caught him in the face, ripping a gash. Sand and dirt followed. He did his best to shelter Kane with his body.

Then a blinding brilliance.

He risked a look up to see blue sky and sunlight, as the dome of his dark world broke open. He heard surprised shouts rise outside, from Anya and Christopher.

"I'm okay!" he hollered back.

Blowing out his relief, he sank to a knee next to Kane.

"We're okay," he whispered.

Kane wagged his tail, peacocking a bit, plainly proud of the scatter of dead snakes around him. The sudden sunlight had driven the rest into hiding.

"You're enjoying all this a little too much," Tucker scolded with a smile.

6:13 P.M.

In short order, using the nylon ropes in Christopher's pack, Tucker helped evacuate Kane by hooking the rope through the dog's vest, then he followed, climbing out, hand over hand.

Once topside, Anya cleaned the gash on his cheek, slathered it with antibacterial ointment, and pasted a bandage over it.

Any further ministrations could wait until they reached the hotel.

With the sun close to setting, they hurried out of the hills. As the way was mostly downhill, they made quick progress, goaded on by the distant huffing of lions.

"Did you get what you needed?" Anya asked, marching beside him.

"Down to the inch."

This time, he had measured Christopher's walking stick.

"Good," she replied. "I'm starving, and I've had enough of a nature walk for one day."

He couldn't agree more.

Once they reached the SUV parked at Helman's Garage, Christopher headed back toward Springbok. It was a quiet, exhausted ride. Christopher called his brother Paul, confirmed all was calm at the guesthouse. Or at least mostly calm. Bukolov had rested enough to become his normal irascible self, demanding to know everything about the day's discoveries, irritated at being left out.

Tucker did not look forward to that. He wanted nothing more than a long, hot soak, followed by a dip in the guesthouse pool.

As they pulled into the parking lot, Christopher's phone rang. He balanced it to his ear as he rolled up to the hotel's steps.

Once stopped, he turned to Tucker. "It's Manfred. He asked if he could speak to you at the church.

Tonight. Says he has some news that might interest you." He covered the mouthpiece. "I could put him off until tomorrow."

"I should go," Tucker said, postponing his bath and dip.

Anya rebuckled her seat belt, determined to come, too, but he leaned forward and touched her shoulder.

"I can handle this," he said. "If you handle Bukolov. Someone needs to bring him up to speed, or he'll be on the warpath."

A look of uncertainty crossed Anya's face.

Tucker said, "He'll behave. Just keep it short."

Anya nodded. "After your day, I'll take the bullet with Bukolov."

"Thanks."

As Anya disappeared through the French doors, Tucker drove back with Christopher to the church. They found the good reverend lounging where they'd last left him: at the picnic table in the yard. Only now, he was fully clothed, all in colonial white, except he remained barefoot. He smoked a pipe, waving it at them as they joined him.

"How went the expedition?" Manfred asked.

"Very well," Tucker responded.

"I believe that bandage on your face says otherwise."

"Knowledge always comes with a price."

"And apparently this one was blood."

You have no idea.

Tucker shifted forward. "Reverend, Christopher mentioned you had news."

"Ah, yes. Quite mysterious. It seems Springbok has suddenly become very popular."

"What do you mean?"

"About an hour ago, I received a call from a gene-alogist. She was asking about your ancestor, Paulos de Klerk."

"She?" Tucker replied, warning bells jangling inside him. "A woman?"

"Yes. With an accent . . . Scandinavian, it sounded like."

Felice.

Manfred narrowed his eyes. "Tucker, I can see from your expression, this is not welcome news. At first, I assumed the woman was part of your research team."

He shook his head. "No."

"Competition then? Someone trying to steal your thunder?"

"Something like that," he said, hating to lie to a man of the cloth. "But can you tell me if this was a local call?"

He shook his head. "The connection was made through an international operator."

So likely not local.

A small blessing there.

"What did you tell her about De Klerk?" Tucker asked.

"I told her I knew very little. He was a doctor, a botanist, and likely was stationed at Klipkoppie."

He bit back a groan, sharing a glance with Christopher.

"What about me?" Tucker asked. "Did she inquire about us?"

"Not a word. And I wouldn't have told her anything anyway. By midway into the conversation, I sensed something awry. I wanted to speak to you before I offered her any further cooperation. That's why I called you."

"Did she ask about Grietje's Well?"

"Yes, and I did mention Klipkoppie fort."

This was disastrous.

Sensing his distress, Manfred patted his hand. "But I didn't tell her *where* Klipkoppie fort was."

"Surely she'll learn—"

"She'll learn what *you* learned. That Klipkoppie fort is located in the center of Springbok. It's in all the tour books."

Tucker remembered Manfred's earlier disdain for the tourist trap. He felt a surge of satisfaction. Such a false trail could buy them even more time.

He calmed down. Mostly. Knowing Felice was on her way, he wanted to immediately return to the hotel, haul out his maps, and calculate De Klerk's coordinates to his cave based on the location of the spring.

But he also had a font of local knowledge sitting across from him, and he did not want to waste it.

"Reverend, you mentioned De Klerk was under the command of General Roosa. In your research did you encounter any mention of a siege in the Groot Karas Mountains. It was where, I believe, my ancestor died."

"No, but that doesn't mean it didn't happen. It wasn't like today's wars, with embedded journalists and cameras and such. But I can look into it."

"I'd appreciate it."

Manfred stared hard, releasing a long puff of pipe smoke. "From that hunger in your voice, I worry that you're thinking of going up into the Groot mountains."

"And if we are?"

"Well, if you discount the guerrillas, the Namibian military, the poachers, and the highway bandits, there's always the terrain, the heat, and the scarcity of water. Not to mention the indigenous wildlife that would like to eat you."

Tucker grinned. "You need to be hired by the Namibian tourist board."

"If you go," Manfred warned, eyeing him seriously, "don't look like a poacher. The Namibian military will shoot first and ask questions later. If rebels or bandits ambush you, fight for your life because if they get their hands on you, you're done. Finally, take a reliable vehicle. If you break down, you'll never reach civilization on foot."

He nodded, respecting the man's wisdom. "Thanks."

Tucker stood up and shook Manfred's hand.

As he and Christopher headed across the yard, Manfred called after them, "If your *competition* comes calling, what should I do?"

"Smile and point her to that tourist trap in the center of town."

It wasn't exactly the *trap* he wished for Felice.

That was more of a razor-sharp bear trap.

But it would do for now.

31

"Welcome to wine country," Christopher announced as the Cessna's tires touched down at the airport of Upington, a picturesque town two hundred miles northeast of Springbok. "Here is where you'll find the production fields of South Africa's finest vintages. Some quarter-million pounds of grapes are harvested each year."

Tucker had noted the rolling swaths of vineyards hugging the lush banks of the Orange River. This little oasis would also serve as their group's staging ground for the border crossing into Namibia. Not that he wouldn't mind a day of wine tasting first, but they had a tight schedule.

Last night, he had completed his calculations and had a fairly good idea of the coordinates of De Klerk's cave. Knowing Felice would not be too far behind, he had everyone up at dawn for this short hop to Upington. He intended to stay ahead of her.

Once they deplaned, Paul Nkomo chauffeured them in a black Range Rover. He drove them up out of the green river valley and off into a sweeping savannah of dense grasses, patches of dark green forest, and rocky outcroppings. After twenty minutes of driving, the Rover stopped before a steel gate. A sign beside the gate read SPITSKOP GAME PARK.

Leaning out the open window, Paul pressed the buzzer, gave his name, and the gate levered open. Paul followed the road into an acre-sized clearing and parked before a sprawling, multiwinged ranch house. A trio of barns outlined the clearing's eastern edge.

They all got out, stretching kinks.

"Not nearly as hot here," Bukolov commented cheerily, on an uptick of his mood swings.

"It is still morning," Paul warned. "It will get hot, very hot."

"Are there any lions around here?" Anya asked, staring toward the savannah.

"Yes, ma'am. Must be careful."

She looked around, found Kane, and knelt down next to the shepherd, scratching his ear appreciatively, clearly remembering his heroics yesterday and intending to stick close to him.

Christopher drew Tucker aside as the others went inside. He led Tucker to one of the barns. Inside was another Range Rover, this one painted in a camouflage of ochre, brown, and tan. Stacks of gear were strapped to the roof rack or piled in the rear cargo area.

"Your ride, Mr. Wayne."

"Impressive," Tucker said. He walked around the Rover, noting it was an older model. "How're the maintenance records?"

He recalled Manfred's warning about the dangers of getting stranded in Namibia.

"You will have no problems. Now, as for when we should depart, I—"

Tucker held up a hand. "What do you mean by *we*?"

"You, your companions, and *myself*, of course."

"Who says you're going with us, Christopher?"

The young man looked puzzled. "I thought it was understood that I was to be your guide throughout your stay in Africa."

"This is the first I've heard of it."

And he wasn't happy about it. While he would certainly welcome Christopher's expertise, the body count of late had already climbed too high. He and the others had to go, but—

"You didn't sign up for this, Christopher."

He refused to back down. "I was instructed to provide whatever assistance you required to travel into Namibia. It is my judgment that *I* am the assistance you will require most." He ticked off the reasons why on his fingers. "Do you speak any of the dialects of tribal Namibia? Do you know how to avoid the Black Mamba? How many Range Rovers have you fixed in the middle of nowhere?"

"I get your point. So let me make mine."

Tucker walked to the Rover's roof rack, pulled down a gun case, and lifted free an assault rifle. He placed it atop a blanket on the hood.

"This is an AR-15 semiautomatic rifle with a 4x20 standard slash night-vision scope. It fires eight hundred rounds per minute. Effective range four hundred to six hundred meters. Questions?"

Christopher shook his head.

"Watch carefully." Tucker efficiently field-stripped the AR, laid the pieces on the cleaning blanket, then reassembled it. "Now you do it."

Christopher took a deep breath, stepped up to the Rover, and repeated the procedure. He was slower and less certain, but he got everything right.

Next Tucker showed him how to load, charge, and manage the AR's firing selector switch. "Now you."

Christopher duplicated the process.

One last lesson.

Tucker took back the weapon, cleared it, and returned it to Christopher. "Now point it at my chest."

"What?"

"Do it."

Tentatively, Christopher did as Tucker ordered. "Why am I doing this?"

Tucker noted the slight tremble in the man's grip. "You've never done this before, have you?"

"No."

"Never shot at anyone?"

"No."

"Been shot at?"

"No."

"Never killed anyone?"

"Of course not."

"If you come along, *all* of those things will probably happen."

Christopher sighed and lowered the AR to his side. "I am beginning to see your point."

"Good. So you'll wait here for us."

"You assume too much." He handed the AR back to Tucker. "If anyone tries to shoot at us, I will shoot back. What happens to them is God's will."

"You're a stubborn bastard," Tucker said.

"So my mother tells me. Without the *bastard* reference, of course."

11:45 A.M.

"How confident are you about your coordinates?" Harper asked.

Tucker stood in the barn next to the Range Rover. He had just finished an inventory check. Everyone else had retired out of the noonday heat for lunch, leaving him alone. He used the private moment to check in with Sigma.

"Ninety percent. It's as good as it's going to get, and it puts us ahead of the competition."

"Speaking of them, a woman matching Felice Nilsson's description and bearing a Swedish passport arrived in Cape Town this morning. Four men, also with Swedish passports, cleared customs at roughly the same time."

"Not surprising. But we've got a big head start on her. Without Utkin feeding them info, they're in the dark. And they still have to figure out the Klipkoppie mystery."

"Hope you're right. Now one last thing. You know that photo you forwarded us—the one of you in the Internet café in Dimitrovgrad?"

"Yes."

"There's something off about it."

"Define *off.*"

"Our tech people are concerned about artifacts in the image's pixel structure. It may be nothing, but we're dissecting everything you sent—including all of Bukolov's data."

"Any verdict in that department?"

"We've got a team of biologists, epidemiologists, and botanists looking at everything. There's not a whole lot of consensus, but they all agree on *one* thing."

"That it's all a hoax. We can turn around and go home."

"Afraid not," she replied. "They all agree that LUCA, if it's the real deal, could have an r-naught that's off the scale."

"And that would mean *what* in English?"

"R-naught is shorthand for *basic reproductive ratio*. The higher the number, the more infectious and harder an organism is to control. Measles has a known r-naught value between 12 and 18. If Bukolov's estimates and early experiments are valid, LUCA could clock in at 90 to 100. In practical terms, if a strain of LUCA is introduced into an acre of food crops, that entire plot of land could be contaminated in less than a day, with exponential growth after that."

Tucker took in a sobering breath.

"Find this thing," she warned, "and make sure Kharzin never gets his hands on it."

Tucker pictured the plastic-wrapped blocks of C-4 packed aboard the Rover.

"That I promise."

After they signed off, Tucker circled around to the front of the Rover and leaned over a topographical map spread across the hood. It depicted the southern Kalahari Desert and eastern Namibia.

He ran a finger along the Groot Karas Mountains. He tapped a spot on the map where De Klerk's cave should be located. Once there, they had to find a feature that looked like a boar's head. But first the group had to *get* there.

"I've brought you lunch," Christopher said behind him. "You must eat."

He came with a platter piled with a spinach-and-beetroot salad and a club sandwich stuffed with steak, chicken, bacon, and a fried egg—the four essential food groups.

Kane—who had been lounging to one side of the Rover—climbed to his legs, sniffing, his nose high in the air. Tucker pinched off a chunk of chicken and fed it to him.

"What is troubling you?" Christopher asked.

Tucker stared at the map. "I'm trying to decide the best place to cross the border into Namibia. With our truckload of weapons and explosives, it's best we try to sneak across at night."

"Most correct. It is very illegal to bring such things into Namibia. Long prison sentences. And because of the smuggling operations of guerrillas and bandits, the border is patrolled heavily."

"So you understand my problem; how about a solution?"

"Hmm." Christopher elbowed him slightly to the side and pointed to the plate. "You eat. I'll show you."

He touched a town not far from the border. "Noenieput is a small agricultural collective. The South African police are lax there. Should be no problem to get through. Might have to pay . . . a tourist surcharge."

Tucker heard the trip over the last. "In other words, a bribe."

"Yes. But on the other side of the border, the Namibia police are not lax at all. Bribe or no bribe. All the paved roads are blockaded. We will have to go overland at night, like you said."

Christopher ran his finger north and tapped a spot. "This is the best place to make a run for the border."

"Why is that?"

"It's where the guerrillas most often cross. Very dangerous men."

"And that's a good thing?"

Christopher looked at him. "Of course." He pointed to the plate. "Now eat."

For some reason, he no longer had an appetite.

32

As Christopher drove, the landscape slowly changed from savannah to a mixture of rust-red sands, stark white salt flats, and scattered, isolated tall hillocks called *kopjes*. With the sun sitting on the horizon, those stony escarpments cast long shadows across the blasted plains.

Far in the distance, the crinkled dark outline of the Groot Karas Mountains cut across the sky. How were they going to reach those distant peaks? As flat as the terrain was here, a border crossing at night seemed impossible. Confirming this, small black dots buzzed slowly across the skies. They were spotter planes of the Namibian Air Force. By standing orders, they shot smugglers first and asked questions later.

Tucker tried to coax Christopher's plan out of the man, but he remained reticent. Perhaps out of a secret fear that Tucker might leave him behind once he knew the plan.

"Noenieput," Christopher announced, pointing ahead to a scatter of whitewashed homes and faded storefronts. "It has the only police station for a hundred miles. If they search our cargo, things will go bad for us."

Anya slunk lower in the front seat, clutching the door grip.

Bukolov gave off a nervous groan. The doctor shared the backseat with Tucker and Kane.

"Down," Tucker ordered the shepherd.

Kane dropped to the floorboards, and Tucker draped him with a blanket.

Ahead, a white police vehicle partially blocked the road, its nose pointed toward them. As they neared, the rack on top began flashing, plainly a signal.

But of what?

Christopher slowed and drew alongside it. He rolled down his window and stuck out his arm in a half wave, half salute. An arm emerged from the driver's side of the police vehicle, returning the gesture.

As Christopher passed, he reached out and slapped palms with the officer. Tucker caught the flash of a folded bill pass hands.

The tourist surcharge.

The Rover rolled onward.

"We made it," Anya said.

"Wait," Christopher warned, his eyes studying the side mirror. "I have to make sure I paid him enough. *Too much*, he could get suspicious and come after us. *Too little*, he might be offended and hassle us."

Thirty seconds passed.

"He's not moving. I think we're okay."

Everyone relaxed. Kane hopped back into the seat, his tail wagging as if all this was great fun.

"Three more miles," Christopher announced.

"Three miles to what?" Bukolov grumbled. "I wish you two would tell us what the hell is going on."

"Three miles, then we'll have to get off the highway and wait for nightfall," Tucker explained. Though he was no happier than the doctor at being kept in the dark about what would happen from there.

As that marker was reached, Christopher turned, bumped the Rover over the shoulder, and dipped down a steep slope of sand and rock. As it leveled out, he coasted to a stop in the lee of a boulder that shielded them from the road. They sat quietly, listening to the Rover's engine *tick tick tick* as it cooled.

Within minutes, the sun faded first into twilight, then into darkness.

"That didn't take long," Anya whispered.

"Such is the desert, miss. In an hour, it will be twenty degrees cooler. By morning, just above freezing. By midday, boiling hot again."

Tucker and Christopher grabbed binoculars, walked west a hundred yards, and scaled the side of a *kopje*. They lay flat on their bellies atop the hill and scanned the four miles of open ground between them and the border.

A deadly no-man's-land.

It seemed too far to sneak across, especially because of—

"There!" Christopher pointed to the strobe of airplane lights in the dark sky. "Namibian Air Force spotter. Each night the guerrillas do what we are doing, only in reverse. They use the cover of darkness to sneak into South Africa, where they have supporters here that provide supplies and ammunition."

Tucker watched the plane drone along the border until it finally faded into the darkness. "How many are there? How often do they pass?"

"Many. About every ten minutes."

It didn't seem possible to cross that open ground in such a short time.

"And what happens when they catch you crossing?" Tucker asked.

"The spotter planes are equipped with door-mounted Chinese miniguns. Capable of firing six thousand rounds per minute. The Namibian Air Force averages three kills a night along the long border. When we go across, you will see the wreckage of many trucks whose drivers timed their run poorly."

"Here's hoping our timing is better," Tucker said.

"Tonight, *timing* does not matter. We just need to find a rabbit." Upon that cryptic note, Christopher rolled to his feet. "We must be ready and in position."

But ready for what?

Back behind the wheel, Christopher set out with the Rover's headlights doused. Milky moonlight bathed the dunes and *kopjes*. Farther out, the Groot Karas Mountains appeared as a black smudge against the night sky.

Christopher kept the Rover to a pace no faster than a brisk walk, lest the tires create a dust wake. Christopher steered the Rover into a narrow trough between a pair of dunes, keeping mostly hidden. After a mile, they emerged beside a line of scrub-covered *kopjes*.

Crawling forward, Christopher drove alongside the row of hillocks until they ended. He then parked in the shelter of the last *kopje*, camouflaged against its rocky flank.

Only open flat ground lay ahead.

"Now we wait," Christopher said.

"For what?" Tucker asked.

"For a rabbit to run."

8:22 P.M.

Tucker held the binoculars fixed to his face. He had switched places with Anya, taking the passenger seat, so that he had a sweeping view of the open land ahead. Through the scope, he picked out the blasted wreckage of unlucky smugglers and guerrillas. Most were half buried in the roll of the windswept dunes.

Then off to the northwest, he caught a wink in the distance.

He stiffened. "Movement," he whispered.

Christopher leaned next to him, also using binoculars. "What do you see?"

"Just a glint of something—moonlight on glass, maybe."

They waited tensely. Christopher had finally revealed his plan a few minutes ago. Tucker no longer believed the young man had held off telling him as some sort of insurance plan against being abandoned. He had kept silent because his plan was pure insanity.

But they were committed now.

No turning back.

"I see it," Christopher said. "It is definitely a vehicle—a pickup truck. And he's gaining speed. Here, Tucker, this is our rabbit."

Run, little rabbit, run . . .

Through his binoculars, Tucker watched the pickup careen at breakneck speeds, heading toward South Africa. No wonder Christopher had picked an area regularly frequented by guerrillas. For his plan to work, they needed traffic.

Illegal traffic, in this case.

"If the spotters are in the area," Christopher warned, "it won't be long now."

The rebel truck continued to sprint, trying to reach the highway on the South African side. Tucker no longer needed his binoculars to track its zigzagging race through the dunes.

It had covered a mile when Christopher whispered, "There, to the south!"

Lights blinked in the sky. A Namibian spotter plane streaked like a hunting hawk across the foothills on the far side, going after the fleeing rabbit. It dove, picking up speed, drawn by the truck's dust plume. Soon the plane was flying seventy yards off the desert floor. On its current course, it would sweep past their *kopje*, where they hid.

"Time to get ready," Christopher whispered. "Buckle up and hold on."

"This is madness!" Bukolov barked.

"Be quiet, Abram!" Anya ordered.

"Any moment now . . ." Tucker mumbled.

Suddenly the plane streaked past their position and was gone.

Christopher shifted into gear and slammed the

accelerator. The Rover lurched forward and began bumping over the terrain.

"Tucker, keep a close eye on that plane. If they finish off that other truck too quickly, we might still draw the spotter's attention."

"Got it." He twisted around in his seat, climbed out the open passenger window, and rested his butt on the sill. With one hand clutching the roof rack, Tucker watched the pickup truck's progress.

"Doesn't look like he's going to make it!" he called out.

"They rarely do! Hold on tight!"

The Rover picked up speed, slewing around obstacles, bouncing over rock outcroppings, and dipping into dune troughs. The cooling desert wind whipped through Tucker's hair. His heart pounded with the exhilaration.

"How far to the border now?" he shouted.

"One mile. Ninety seconds."

Tucker watched the plane suddenly bank right, running parallel now to the racing truck.

"Almost there!" Christopher called.

Fire arched from the plane's doorway and streamed toward the truck. The aircraft's minigun poured a hundred rounds per second into its target, tearing the vehicle apart in an incendiary display that lit the black desert.

The engagement quickly ended.

Smoke and flames swirled from the wreckage.

Above, the plane banked in a circle over the ruins. As it turned, their dust trail would surely be spotted.

"He's coming about," Tucker called.

He turned forward to see a waist-high stone cairn flash by the right bumper of the Rover. Any closer and it would have knocked Tucker from his perch.

"Border marker!" Christopher called. "We're across! Welcome to Namibia!"

Tucker ducked back inside and buckled up.

From the backseat, Kane crowded forward and licked his face.

"Are we safe?" Anya asked.

"We're in Namibia," Christopher replied. "So *no*."

Bukolov leaned forward, red-faced and apoplectic. "For God's sake! Are you two trying to get me killed? Actually *trying*?"

Tucker glanced back. "No, Doctor, but the day's not over yet."

33

"Should be just over that next dune," Tucker said.
He had a map on his lap and his GPS unit in hand.

"What are we looking for?" Anya asked, leaning forward between the two front seats, careful of her cast.

After their flight across the border, Christopher kept the Rover at a cautious pace, proceeding overland, using the terrain to cover as much of their movement as possible.

"There should be a paved road," Tucker replied. "One heading west into the mountains."

"Is that wise?" she asked. "Won't there be traffic?"

"Perhaps, but a vehicle with South African plates in Namibia isn't unusual. As long as we don't attract attention to ourselves, the odds are in our favor."

Christopher glanced over to her. "And on the road, we're less likely to encounter guerrillas or bandits."

"That is, until we reach the mountain trails," Tucker added. "Once we're off the paved roads and climbing into the badlands, then all bets are off."

With his headlamps still dowsed, Christopher picked his way over the last of the dunes. A blacktop road appeared ahead, cutting straight across the sands. They waited a minute, making sure no traffic was in sight, then bumped over the shoulder and out onto the smooth pavement.

Christopher flipped on his lights and headed west.

Despite its remote location, the road was well maintained and well marked but completely devoid of traffic. For the next twenty-five miles, as the road wound higher into the mountain's foothills, they saw not a single vehicle, person, or sign of civilization.

The road finally ended at a T-junction. Christopher brought the Rover to a stop. In the backseat, Bukolov was snoring loudly. Anya had also fallen asleep, curled in the fetal position against the door.

"She is lovely," Christopher said. "Is she your woman?"

"No."

"I see. But you fancy each other, yes?"

Tucker rolled his eyes. "It's complicated. Mind your business."

Still, he considered Christopher's words. Anya certainly was attractive, but he hadn't given much thought to any sort of relationship with her. She would need a friend once she reached America, and he would be that for her, but beyond that . . . only time would tell. He felt pity for her, felt protective of her, but those feelings might not be the healthiest way to start a romance. And, more important, this was the wrong place and time to think about any of it.

Especially in guerrilla-infested Namibia.

Tucker checked their GPS coordinates against the map. "We're on track," he said. "We should turn right here, go a quarter mile, then turn northwest onto a dirt trail."

"And then how far to our destination?"

"Eighteen miles."

At least he hoped so. If his bearing and range measurements were off by even a fraction of a degree, the cave could be miles from where he thought it was. Plus even if his calculations were accurate, the landmark they needed to find—the Boar's Head—could have been obliterated by time and erosion. He felt a flicker of panicky despair. Tucker tried to shove it down.

Deal with what's in front of you, Ranger, he reminded himself again.

"That's a long distance to cover," Christopher said. "And the terrain will only get rougher."

"I know." Tucker checked his watch. "It's almost midnight, and I don't want to tackle the mountains until daylight. Once we're a little higher in the foothills, we'll start looking for a place to camp and get some rest. At dawn, Kane and I will do some reconnoitering."

In the backseat, Bukolov snorted, groaned, then muttered, "My ears hurt."

"We're at three thousand feet of elevation, Professor," Christopher said. "Your ears will adjust soon. Go back to sleep."

A short time later, they were off the blacktop and bouncing slowly along a rutted dirt road. They followed the ever-narrowing tract higher into the foothills.

After an hour of this, Tucker pointed to a craggy hill with a clump of scrub forest at the top. "See if you can find a way up there."

"I'll do my best."

Christopher turned right off the trail and down an embankment. He followed a dry riverbed that wound to the hill's southern face and discovered a natural ramp that headed up. After another hundred yards, they reached a clearing surrounded by a crescent of boulders, shaded by stubby trees.

"This'll do," Tucker said, drawing Christopher to a stop.

Tucker climbed out with Kane and pointed. "SCOUT AND RETURN."

The shepherd trotted off into the darkness, exploring the edges of the clearing and what looked like several game trails. Tucker did the same, circling completely around the Rover. In the distance, he heard the huffing grunt of lions, accompanied by several roars. Other creatures screeched and howled.

He waved Anya and Bukolov out and turned to Christopher.

"Let's get the tents set up. But what do you think about a fire?"

"The flames are good at keeping curious animals at bay, but also good at attracting rebels and bandits. I vote no."

Tucker agreed. They quickly set up camp; even Bukolov pitched in before finally retiring, almost collapsing into the tent. Anya soon followed him.

"I'll take first watch," Tucker said to Christopher. "You've been driving all day. Get some sleep."

"I don't need much sleep. I'll relieve you in a couple of hours."

Tucker didn't argue.

He drifted to the Rover and leaned a hip against the bumper. Overhead, a brilliant display of crisp stars flushed the sky, accompanied with the glowing swath of the Milky Way. He listened to the cacophony of the African night: the trill of insects, the distant hoots and hollers, the rustle of wind.

It was hard to believe such beauty hid such danger.

March 21, 1:24 A.M.

As Tucker kept a drowsy guard, Kane stirred from where he'd curled beside the Rover's tire.

Tucker heard the *zip* from the tent.

He turned to see Anya push out, wrapped in a blanket. Her breath misted in the cold desert air. She slowly, shyly joined him.

"Couldn't sleep?" he whispered. "Is your wrist bothering you?"

"No. It's not that—" She ended in a shrug.

He patted the hood next to him.

She sat down, shifted closer, and tugged the blanket around Tucker's shoulders. "You looked cold."

He didn't object. He had to admit the warmth was welcome . . . as was the company.

Kane glanced at them and made a deep *harrumphing* sound, then lay back down.

"I think someone is jealous," Anya said, hiding a grin.

"He can get grumpy when he's tired."

"You know each other's moods very well."

"We've been together a long time. Since Kane was a pup. And after the years of training, we've learned each other's tics and idiosyncrasies."

He suddenly felt foolish talking about this with a beautiful woman at his hip.

But she didn't seem to mind. "It must be nice to have someone so close to you in life, someone who knows you so well."

At that moment, he realized how little he knew about the real Anya Averin—and how much he wanted to know more.

"Speaking of getting to know someone," he whispered, "I don't know anything about your past. Where did you grow up?"

There was a long pause—clearly it was hard for her to let her guard down, especially after so many years of wearing a false face.

"Many places," she finally mumbled. "My father was in the Russian Army. He was a . . . a hard man. We moved around a lot."

He heard pain there as she looked down. After a long awkward silence, she shifted away. He had clearly touched a sore point.

"I suppose I should try to sleep," she mumbled, hopping down and drawing the blanket with her. With a small wave of a hand, she headed back to the tent and ducked inside.

The night was suddenly much colder.

34

Christopher shook Tucker awake while it was still dark. He instantly went alert, muscles going hard, shaking off the cobwebs of fitful dreams.

"It's okay, Mr. Wayne," the man reassured him. "You asked me to wake you before the sun was up."

"Right, right . . ."

He slithered out of his sleeping bag and grabbed the AR-15 rifle resting next to it.

As he followed Christopher out of the tent, Bukolov snorted and woke from the commotion. "What's going on? What's happening?"

"Nothing, Doctor," Tucker said. "Go back to sleep."

"I could if you two would stop bumbling around like a pair of elephants." He rolled over, putting his back to them.

Across the dark tent, Anya's eyes shone toward him, then she turned away, too.

With Kane in tow, Tucker pushed out into the predawn chill. He stomped circulation back into his feet, while Kane darted over to a bush and lifted his leg.

Once the shepherd had returned, Christopher asked, "Which way will you two go and how far?"

He pointed east. "We'll scout a few miles ahead. We can move quieter than the Rover. We'll make sure nothing stands between us and the coordinates. If it looks safe, we can continue with the Rover. I should be back before noon. If I run into any trouble or you do, we've got our radios."

"Understood."

"Have the Rover packed and ready. Run if you need to. Don't fight unless you have no other choice."

"I would much prefer to come with—"

"I know you would, but someone has to guard Anya and Bukolov. That's why we're here. They're more important than me."

"I don't agree, sir. Every life is precious in the eyes of God."

Tucker knew it was foolish to argue with the young man. He just prayed that when it came to a firefight that Christopher placed *his* precious life above that of his enemy's.

With matters settled, Tucker suited up Kane, then thoroughly checked his rifle and strapped a Smith & Wesson .44-caliber snubnose to his belt. As an additional precaution, knowing he might encounter guerrilla forces, he wanted something extra in his back pocket, something with a little more bang. He fished out a block of C-4 plastic explosive from their reserves and shoved it into the cargo pocket of his pants.

That'll have to do.

Ready now, he and Kane took to a game trail that led them down the steep north face of the hill and into a short valley. He took a compass bearing, marked his map, then they set out east. The terrain of the Groot Karas Mountains was as unique and strange as the desert that bordered it. From satellite images, it appeared as though a giant hand had poured molten metal across the mountain's slopes: rock formations looped and whorled around one another forming a flowing maze, all of it broken up by plateaus, boulder-strewn ravines, and tiny crescent canyons tucked tightly against steep cliffs.

It was no wonder rebels and bandits had marked off this harsh terrain as their base of operations. Hidden here, they would be difficult to find, and harder still to root out and destroy. It seemed in both real estate and guerrilla warfare, one maxim ruled them all: location, location, location.

Tucker continued picking his way eastward, studying the detailed topographical map, judging the best course to keep parallel to the dirt road without being seen, searching for any evidence of a trap set by bandits or a bivouac of guerrilla forces. He wanted no surprises when he brought the others through here in the Range Rover.

He also relied heavily on Kane, outfitted with his tactical Storm vest.

The shepherd became an extension of his eyes and ears.

ROAM. SCOUT. RETURN.

Those were Kane's standing orders as they moved through the maze of cliffs, scrub brush, and sand. Padding silently, the shepherd explored every nook and cranny. He scaled slopes, peeked over crests, ducked into blind canyons, and sniffed at cave entrances, returning every now and again to pass on an *all clear*.

After three miles, the first glimmer of the new day appeared. He pictured the sun rising above the distant Kalahari Desert, firing the sands and stretching its light into the mountains. Tucker paused for a water break, sharing his canteen with Kane. He performed another compass check and updated his map.

Kane suddenly jerked his head up from the collapsible water bowl. Tucker froze, his eyes on the shepherd. Kane tilted his head left, then right, then took a few paces forward.

Though Tucker heard nothing, he implicitly trusted Kane's ears. Quietly, he tucked away their items and donned his pack.

"CLOSE LEAD. QUIET SCOUT."

While the shepherd's gait was naturally quiet, this order put Kane into a covert stalk mode. The shepherd took off at a fast walk, with Tucker following five paces behind. Kane slowly worked his way up a sandy ridge, moving from stone to stone so as not to trigger an avalanche of sand that could give away their position.

Tucker followed his example.

At the crest of the ridge, Kane lowered flat and stopped moving. From the intensity of the dog's gaze and the angle of his ears, Tucker knew his partner had homed in on the source of the noise.

Tucker joined him, dropping to his belly and

crawling the last few feet. He peeked over the ridge-line.

Before them spread a fan-shaped valley a quarter mile long. The far side vanished into a scatter of ravines that broke through a tall, flat-topped plateau. The site had great potential to serve as a guerrilla base or a bandit hideout. It was hidden and defensible, with several escape routes nearby.

As if on cue, a pair of dark compact pickup trucks rolled into the valley from the neighboring dirt road. The two picked their way overland across the floor below. Jutting from the bed of each truck was a tripod-mounted machine gun. The hair on Tucker's neck tingled. Whether these were bandits or guerrillas, he didn't know, not that it really mattered. They were a force of armed men.

That was enough.

That, and they're right where I don't want them.

He watched the trucks continue past his position, then vanish down one of the ravines. Tucker waited a few more minutes to ensure they weren't turning back. Once satisfied, he and Kane scaled down into the valley and made their way to where the trucks had first appeared. Down a short slope, he found the remains of a still-warm campfire not far from the dirt road. Refuse littered the area, including what looked like fly-encrusted entrails, the discards of a field-dressed deer or antelope.

Tucker approached the campfire. It was small and the coals only a few inches deep. That told him the site had not been used many times. It wasn't a regular base.

Just passing through then. Maybe hunting food before returning to their main base deeper in the badlands.

"Hopefully," he muttered.

He checked his watch, recognizing it was time to head back to the others.

At his side, Kane growled, hackles rising.

Tucker dropped low next to him.

Then he heard another growl—but not from Kane.

From across the neighboring road, a fleet of dappled shadows sped over the dirt tract, a pack of dogs—from their rounded ears and spotted flanks, they were African wild dogs, *Lycaon pictus*, the second-largest canid predators in the world, topping off at eighty pounds each. As a necessity, Tucker had read up on the natural threats he might face out here. These beasts had the highest bite strength relative to body size of any carnivore. Their most common means of attack: disembowelment.

He stared at the pile of entrails, at the trickle of smoke still rising from the embers. The scent had clearly drawn them. Until now, intimidated by the larger group of men from the trucks, the pack had kept hidden, biding their time. But now, with the larger force gone, the pack was not going to tolerate a single man and a shepherd stealing from their larder.

As the pack reached the far side of the road, Tucker quickly retreated, drawing Kane with him. He shouldered the AR-15, sweeping the rifle's barrel across the pack as they burst through the scrub and into the clearing.

He didn't want to shoot—not because they were dogs, but because the gunfire would surely be heard by the departing guerrillas, likely drawing them back to the road.

He continued to retreat, hoping such a non-threatening act would appease the dogs. Most of the pack went straight for the food, scattering a cloud of heavy flies to reach the entrails. Growls and yips rose from the feasting, amid much shouldering and complaints.

Two dogs ignored the easy pickings, clearly wanting fresh meat. They sped at Tucker and Kane. The first reached Tucker and lunged, leaping toward his groin. Expecting such an attack, he reversed his rifle and slammed the stock into the skull, catching the beast a glancing blow. The dog fell, tried to get up, stumbling and dazed. It was a male.

The female hesitated, shying from the sudden attack, juking to the side, watching them, stalking back and forth. Her lips rippled into a snarl, her hackles high. Kane paced her move for move, growling from deep inside.

Tucker knew that packs of African wild dogs were different from many other canids. An alpha female always led the pack, not a male.

Here was that leader.

Confirming this, she let out a short chirping burst from her throat, calling for support. Several of the pack lifted bloody muzzles from the feast.

Tucker knew running wasn't an option. The pack would be on them in seconds. They had to make a stand here—and make it before she got her pack fully rallied, which meant taking her out.

Still, he dared not shoot her, knowing the blast would echo far, likely to the wrong ears.

But he had another weapon.

He pointed toward the female.

"ATTACK."

Kane moves before the command leaves his partner's lips. He anticipates the instruction—and charges. Aggression already rages through him, stoked to a fiery blaze by the other. He has smelled her fury, read the territoriality in her posture, heard the threat.

She does not back down, lunging at him at the same time he leaps.

They strike hard, chest to chest, teeth gnashing at each other, catching air and fur. They roll, entangled, first him on top, then her.

She moves, fast, powerful, going for his exposed belly. She bites hard—but finds no flesh, only tough vest. He slides free from under her confusion and dismay. He lunges, snapping, shredding her ear.

She leaps back.

Now wary.

He smells her fear.

He growls deeper, from his bones. His ears lie back, his hackles trembling. He sets his front legs wider, challenging her. Saliva ropes from his curled lips, redolent with her blood.

It is enough.

She backs from his posture, from the toughness of his false hide.

One step, then another.

A new command reaches him, cutting through the crimson of his rage.

COME. FOLLOW.

He obeys, retreating but never backing down, locking eyes, still challenging the other until she falls out of view.

Tucker hurried away from the campsite, putting several hundred yards between them and the pack before slowing. He paused only long enough to run his fingers over Kane. Except for a few missing puffs of hair, he appeared unscathed.

As he'd hoped, Kane's tactical vest, reinforced with Kevlar, had not only protected the shepherd, but also clearly spooked the female with its strangeness. She was happy to let them retreat.

Backtracking along their old trail, the return journey went much faster. They arrived at the camp shortly before noon and were greeted happily by Christopher and Anya.

Bukolov offered a gruff but surprisingly genuine "Glad you are not dead."

While Anya and Bukolov prepared a cold lunch, Tucker recounted for Christopher his encounter with the guerrillas and wild dogs.

"You were lucky to survive that hungry pack, Mr. Tucker. And let us hope you are right about the soldiers, that they were simply passing through. Show me how far you mapped and we can plan the best course to avoid trouble."

Half an hour later, they were all gathered over

a set of maps and charts. Christopher and Tucker had settled on the safest route to reach De Klerk's coordinates. But that was only *one* problem solved.

"Once there," Tucker said, "we need to find that landmark De Klerk mentioned, something shaped like a boar's head near a waterfall."

He turned to Bukolov and Anya. They knew De Klerk's history better than anyone. "In his diary of that siege, did De Klerk give any further clues about that waterfall. Like maybe some hint of its height?"

"No," Bukolov said.

"How about whether it was spring fed or storm runoff?"

Anya shook her head. "De Klerk described the troop's route into these mountains in only the vaguest terms."

"Then we're just going to have to get there and check every creek, stream, and trickle, looking for that waterfall."

Christopher considered this. "We are at the end of our rainy season. That highland region will likely be flowing with many small creeks and waterfalls. Which is good and bad. *Bad* because there will be many spots to explore."

Making for a long search . . .

Tucker pictured Felice closing in on them.

How much time did they have?

"How is it *good*?" Anya asked.

"The terrain here is hard and unforgiving. As a consequence, the creeks and river basins rarely change course. Year after year, they are the same. If the waterfall was flowing when your man was here, it is probably still flowing now."

"So we won't be on a wild-goose chase," Tucker said. "The waterfall is somewhere up there."

It was little consolation, but in this desolate environment, that was the best he could hope for.

Tucker rolled up the maps.

"Let's go."

35

Following Tucker's map they made slow and steady progress—the operative word being *slow*.

Christopher steered the Rover eastward along the dirt road, slipping past the guerrillas' campsite where Tucker and Kane had encountered the African wild dogs. A couple of miles after that, the trail vanished under them, so gradually that they had traveled several hundred yards before realizing they were simply in the trackless wilderness now.

Their new pattern became one of faltering stops and starts.

Every half mile or so, Tucker and Kane would have to climb out, hike to the highest vantage point, and scout the terrain ahead for signs of hidden bandits or guerrillas. They also charted the best path for the Rover, using both their eyes and the topographical maps.

As Christopher bounced up a rocky ravine, testing the extremes of the Range Rover's off-road capabilities, Tucker's GPS unit gave off a chime. He checked the screen.

"Getting close to De Klerk's coordinates. Another quarter mile or so." He glanced from the screen to the path of the ravine, calculating in his head. "It should be at the top of this next pass."

The Rover climbed the last of the approach as the ravine's walls narrowed to either side. It was a tight squeeze, but they finally reached the top of the pass and rode out onto a flat open plateau.

"Stop here," Tucker said.

They all clambered from the Rover, exhausted but excited.

"We made it," Anya said, sounding much too surprised.

Beyond that plateau, the landscape looked like a giant's shattered staircase. Flat-topped mesas and fractured crooked-top plateaus spread outward, climbing higher and higher. Brighter glints reflected the sunlight, marking countless waterfalls cascading from the heights, draped like so much silver tinsel across the landscape.

Closer at hand, confronting them, rose a thirty-foot cliff. Two wide ravines cut into its face on either side, both large enough to drive the Rover into. Between them, they framed an unusual section of cliff, shaped like a triangular nose with a blunted tip. It stuck out toward them, but its slopes were still too steep to climb.

But it was the ravines that drew Tucker's attention. The canyons were twins of each other, angling away from each other, like a giant shadowy V, only the legs of the V were slightly curved, like the up-raised tusks of a—

"Boar's head," Bukolov muttered, sounding dis-appointed.

Tucker now appreciated the protruding cliff itself somewhat resembled a pig's flattened snout—with the twin canyons forming its tusks.

Still, Tucker understood the doctor's disenchant-ment. Somewhere buried in the back of his own head, he'd been picturing a magnificent granite boar's skull spewing a glittering stream of water between its tusks, spilling its bounty into a roiling pool surrounded by blooming desert flowers.

The reality was much more mundane.

Yet still just as dangerous.

Tucker urged them to grab their packs and get moving again. He pointed to the two canyons in the rock face. "While we still have daylight, we should check *both* sides. Doctor Bukolov with me. Anya with Christopher. Everyone stay on the radio. Questions?"

There were none.

With Kane at his heels, Tucker and Bukolov headed for the ravine on the right. The other pair aimed for the cleft on the left.

Tucker hiked into the gorge first, trailed by Bu-kolov. It was about eight or nine feet wide, filled with sand and loose rock.

"How are we going to find water in here?" Buko-lov asked.

"Kane."

The shepherd pushed to his side. Dropping to a knee, Tucker tipped his canteen over his cupped palm and brought the water to Kane's nose.

"SEEK."

Kane turned away, his nose sniffing high.

You did it before, my friend. Do it again.

As if reading his mind, Kane looked up at Tucker and sprinted away, deeper down the ravine.

"He's onto something. C'mon."

The two men followed the shepherd, going slower, having to pick themselves over rubble and around boulders. They discovered Kane squatted before a section of rock wall on the left. When Tucker appeared, Kane let out a single bark. The dog jumped up, planting his front paws against the wall.

"Does that mean he's found something?" Bukolov asked.

"Let's find out."

Tucker shrugged off his pack—then pulled out and unfolded a small shovel. Crossing to the wall, he jammed in the spade's tip and gouged out a chunk of sandstone. He kept digging until he'd chipped a hole about six inches deep. It took some time and effort—but he was rewarded when he noted the change in color of the stone. Reaching in, he fingered some of the darker reddish-brown sand. The granules clung together a bit.

"It's damp back here."

"What does that mean?" Bukolov asked.

He placed his hand on the wall. "There must be a source of water somewhere behind here."

"Like a cave."

"Maybe."

Bukolov frowned. "But this wall is clearly not De Klerk's *waterfall*."

"No. But there is a water source close by here."
He patted his dog's side. "Good boy, Kane."

The shepherd resisted his praise. He sniffed at
Tucker's sandy fingertips, barked three times rapidly, then jumped back on the wall.

"Shh!" Tucker said.

Kane obeyed, going silent, but he stayed with
his forepaws braced on the rock face, his nose
pointed up.

What are you trying to tell me?

Tucker backed away from the cliff face, shaded
his eyes with a hand, and looked up.

From behind them, Christopher called, "What's
happening?"

Anya was with him. "Our canyon came to a dead
end. Then we heard the barking."

As they closed the distance, Christopher clearly
hobbled on his left leg. "Twisted my ankle on some
loose shale," he explained. "Hurts but I'm fine."

Anya stared over at Kane. "What's he found?"

"I don't—"

Then he understood.

Craning his neck, he continued down the ravine.
He soon discovered what he was looking for: a
jumble of boulders piled against the left side of the
gorge.

"I should be able to climb that."

"Why? What the devil is going on?" Bukolov
asked, dragging everyone with him.

Tucker faced them. "I'm climbing up. Something
on top of the plateau has Kane all hot and bothered."

"Then I'm coming, too," Anya said.

He eyed her cast.

"I can manage. If I could climb to the top of Klipkoppie fort, I can scale this."

Christopher hung back, plainly compromised by his leg.

"Stay with Doctor Bukolov," Tucker instructed him. "We'll scout it out first."

Not knowing what was up there, Tucker wanted an extra set of eyes and ears. Bending down, he hauled Kane over his shoulders in a fireman's carry and started up the steps. It was a precarious climb in spots, but they reached the top.

Boulders littered the summit, a veritable broken maze. They had succeeded in mounting the section of cliff between the two tusk-shaped canyons. To their right, the plateau ended at the pig's snout. To the left, a pair of higher plateaus abutted against this one, like the raised shoulders of a monstrous beast.

"We're standing atop the Boar's Head," he realized aloud.

It had to be significant.

Tucker returned Kane to his feet with the instruction "SEEK."

Without hesitation, the shepherd sprinted in the direction of the taller mesas, dodging around boulders. Tucker and Anya followed, and after a few twists and turns, they found Kane sitting beside a pool of water. On the far side, a sparkling cascade poured into it, flowing along a series of cataracts from the neighboring, higher lands.

His tail wagged happily, as if to say: *This is what I was talking about*.

"What on earth . . ." Anya whispered and stared

at the dancing flow of water over rock. "Is that De
Klerk's waterfall? If so, where's the cave?"

"I don't know."

Tucker took a moment to orient himself. Something was wrong with this picture. The pool next to
Kane was kidney shaped, about twenty feet across.
He stared at the stream flowing into it—as it likely
had all season long. The pool seemed too tiny to
capture all that flow.

So why hasn't this pool overflowed by now?

Then he knew the answer.

36

Tucker knelt at the pool's edge with Kane. With his head cocked to the side, he stared across the surface, watching the gentle ruffle of ripples spread outward from the cascade on the far side.

"What are you looking for?" Anya asked.

"There!" He pointed near the center of the pond, where the flow of ripples slightly churned in on themselves. "See that swirl."

"Yes, I see it, but what does it mean?"

"It means the pool is draining into something *beneath* it. That's why it's not overflowing its banks as the waterfall continues to pour into it. It drains below as quickly as it fills above."

A lilt of excitement entered Anya's voice. "You're thinking it might be draining into a cave."

"Maybe *the* cave. We're exactly at De Klerk's co-ordinates here."

Tucker crossed back to the edge of the cliff and called down to Christopher. "I need the climbing rope from my pack. Can you toss it up?"

"Just a minute!"

"What did you find?" Bukolov yelled to them.

"That's what I'm about to find out!" he hollered down.

Christopher pulled out the nylon climbing rope, tied a monkey's fist in one end, and hurled the end up to Tucker. He caught it on the first try and reeled the rest of the length up. Before returning to the pond, he knotted the rope around one of the pool-side boulders.

Pulling on gloves, he stepped back to the water-line and flung the other end of the rope—the one with the monkey's fist still tied in it—out toward the center of the pool.

The knotted end sank—then after a few tense breaths, the remaining line between his fingers began uncoiling, snaking into the water. Slowly at first, then faster and faster. With a *twang*, the last of the line sprang taut in his fingertips, forming a straight line from the boulder to the whirlpool.

Tucker waded out a few feet, sliding his palm along the rope. When he was thigh deep, he felt a slight tidal pull of the drainage vortex. His fingers tightened on the line. He moved step by step. The tug on his legs became stronger. By the time he was waist-deep, his boots began to slide on the slippery rocks underfoot.

For safety's sake, he straddled the rope, grasped it with both hands, and began backing toward the center.

Step by cautious step.

Then his left foot plunged into nothingness. Gasping in surprise, he dropped to his right knee. Water foamed and roiled around his upper chest.

"Tucker! Careful." Anya stood on the bank, a worried hand at her throat.

Kane barked at him.

"I'm okay," he told them both.

He pulled on the rope and yanked his left foot back from the hole. He gained a firmer stance against the tide. With his right hand clutching the rope, he bent down and reached back with his left. He probed the pool's bottom until his fingers touched the rim of the hole.

"Seems wide enough," he called to Anya.

"Wide enough for what?"

"Me."

"Tucker, no. You don't know what's down there. Don't—"

He took a deep breath, sat down on his butt, slid both feet into the hole, and lowered himself downward.

The current of the vortex grabbed him hard and sucked him through the drain. His gloved fingers slid along the rope in fits and starts. Then he popped out of the flooded chute and found himself swinging in open air.

He dangled and twisted in the faucet of water pouring down from the ceiling of stone overhead. Watery light flowed down with it, but not enough to illuminate the cavernous space below him.

Spinning on the line, he lowered himself hand over hand.

Finally his boots touched solid ground. He found his footing, backed up a few steps out of the torrential stream, and let go of the rope. Bent double, gasping, he spit water, coughed, and wiped clear his eyes.

He finally straightened, expecting to see nothing but what little daylight filtered through the chute above, but as his eyes adjusted, he noted fiery slivers of sunlight shining around him—some four or five of them, coming through fissures in the roof or sloping walls.

Still, they offered scant illumination.

He plucked his flashlight out of a buttoned pocket and panned it around the roughly oval-shaped cavern. The waterfall, which marked the space's center point, flooded across the bottom of the cave, pooling in some places but mostly draining through fissures in the floor.

Turning slowly, he oriented himself with the outside landscape. *Above* his head was the boulder-strewn plateau. To his *left* would be the pig's snout, the cliff that was framed by the shadowy boar tusks. To his *right*, he spotted a pair of tunnel entrances that looked like the twin barrels of a shotgun. He imagined they led deeper into the higher plateaus that extended behind the boar's head.

Shining his light across the floor, he also saw evidence of prior habitation, washed up along the walls' edges. He spotted broken furniture that could have once been tables or beds. His beam picked out a couple of bayonets oxidized to black.

As in the cave at Klipkoppie, Tucker pictured the ghosts of soldiers coming and going here, sitting around tables lit with oil lamps, polishing those bayonets, joking and exchanging war stories.

Eyeing the shotgun tunnels, he wanted to explore further, to see where they might lead, but now was not the time to go wandering by himself.

He stared at the rope whipping within the cascade of water and sighed.

He needed the others.

Going *up* proved a hundredfold harder than the descent. Hand over hand, he hauled himself through the pounding cascade, out the hole, and back to the surface of the pool. Exhausted, he waded back to the rim and threw himself flat on the bank. He rolled to his back and let the sun warm him.

"Tucker?" Anya dropped to her knees next to him. "Are you okay?"

Kane came up on his other side, nosing him fiercely, half greeting, half scolding.

"What's down there?" Anya asked.

He only grinned at her and said, "You'll see."

5:23 P.M.

"Bless you, my boy!" Bukolov said by the bank of the pond. "And your dog!"

It took some effort to get the good doctor atop the plateau, but he proved fitter than he appeared. Even Christopher, after resting while Tucker took the plunge into the unknown, was walking more solidly on his left leg. He made it up the boulder staircase without any assistance.

Bukolov continued. "We stand at the entrance to De Klerk's cave! At the threshold of discovering the greatest boon known to mankind!"

Tucker allowed the doctor to wax purple and lay on the hyperbole.

For in fact, they *had* done it.

Christopher and Anya chuckled, standing next to the doctor.

Tucker stood off by the cliff's edge, inventorying the supplies they had shuttled up here by rope. There were still a few last items he wanted, but he could haul those by hand.

Straightening, he called to the others. "I'm going for another run to the Rover while we have daylight!"

He was acknowledged, but before he could step away, a buzzing rose from his pack. He fished out his satellite phone and answered.

"Tucker, I'm glad I could reach you." The tension in Harper's voice was obvious.

"What's wrong?"

"Where were you?"

"Down a hole. At De Klerk's coordinates. We found it. We found the—"

"*Who's* with you?"

"Everyone."

"How close?" she pressed.

"Fifty feet." Tucker withdrew farther from the others, sensing the need for privacy. He put a boulder between him and the others. "Now sixty feet. What's the matter?"

"We deconstructed that photo you sent—the one of you sitting at the computer in the Internet café in Dimitrovgrad. It was *shopped*. It's a fake. Don't ask me to explain the technicalities, but there were pixel defects in the image—something called integration artifacts."

"Go on."

"Integration artifacts are created when you extract part of one image and overlay it onto another. You follow?"

"Like replacing a horse's ass with your boss's face. I get it. Out with it."

"The photo of you at the Internet café was created by merging *two* different images. An interior shot of the café. And a photo of you taken elsewhere. Someone shopped them together. Faked it."

"What the hell?"

"Our techs were able to separate out the original photo of you, and through extrapolation and pixel capture, they were able to rebuild some of the old details that were erased, mostly details around your hands. In the faked photo, your hands are hovering over a computer keyboard. But when the techs were done, they showed your hands were really originally holding a *steering wheel*."

"So the picture of me that was Photoshopped was actually taken while I was driving."

"Exactly. It appears to have been taken by a cell-phone camera. It was a side profile of you, as if someone in the passenger seat shot it."

It took several pained seconds for Tucker's brain to register what Harper was telling him. He squeezed his eyes shut, her last words echoing in his mind.

. . . *a side profile of you, as if someone in the passenger seat shot it* . . .

"What was I wearing in the photo? I can't remember."

"Uh . . . a military winter suit."

That was the jacket he wore when he pulled Anya out of the Kazan Kremlin. After that, they fled the city. He pictured that ride.

Bukolov and Utkin had been sitting in the back.

Anya had been up front with him—in the passenger seat.

Tucker whispered, "It's Anya."

He closed his eyes, despairing. She must have covertly taken the photo with her cell phone as he drove them out of Kazan, then e-mailed it away before he ditched everyone's electronics.

He had to recalibrate his entire worldview of events—and brace a hand against the boulder to keep his legs steady.

She had lied about *just getting tea* in Dimitrovgrad. While loose, she must have made contact with Kharzin's people, told them where to arrange the Spetsnaz ambush. She must have also covertly followed Tucker, noted he had used that Internet café. Kharzin's people took advantage of that information to create the doctored photo. It was insurance, a red herring. It had been *planted* on the Spetsnaz people in case their ambush failed. In that worst-case scenario, Tucker was meant to find the photo, so he would believe the attackers had been tailing them or tracking them all along, so as to throw off suspicion from Anya.

But that was not the worst of it.

Utkin.

He suddenly found it hard to breathe. He felt sucker punched in the gut. He pictured the man bleeding to death on the beach, sacrificing himself to save them, the same people who had falsely accused and condemned him.

Still, you saved us.

And it had never been Utkin. Anya had set him

up. The signal generator was *hers*. The empty pack of cards in Utkin's bag was *hers*. She knew Utkin would have a set of cards. It was easy enough to plant that evidence in his duffel.

Harper's voice blared in his ear, drawing him back to his own skin. "Tucker!"

"I'm here." He took a deep breath. "It's Anya. She's the one working with Kharzin. I should have seen it."

"There's no way you could have."

"Either way, we have to assume she's been in contact with Kharzin's people since we touched down in Africa. She was with me when I found Grietje's Well. She knew the GPS coordinates to this spot. Which means Kharzin has them, too."

"Then that means you're likely to have company soon," Harper said. "What're you going to do?"

"We've found the cave, but not the specimens of LUCA."

"That doesn't leave you many options."

"Just one. Get Bukolov into the cave and let him go to work. While he's doing that, I'll get ready for a siege and rig the cave with C-4. If we can't hold off Felice and her team, I'll blow it all to hell."

There was a long silence on her end. "Let's hope it doesn't come to that," she finally said. "What about Anya? What are you going to do with her?"

"In the short term, I haven't decided yet."

"And the long term?"

He pictured Utkin's face. "I don't see her having a *long* term."

5:38 P.M.

Tucker knelt by his pack out of sight of the others, slicing two six-foot sections of rope.

He considered how smoothly Anya had duped him. Then again, she had done the same with her superiors at the SVR. All along she'd been a GRU mole planted there or groomed there by Kharzin. It was for *that* reason she'd been falsifying reports to the SVR—not to protect Bukolov, but to help Kharzin. Even her admission to Tucker that she was an SVR agent was clever: confess to a damning lie, throw yourself on your sword, and claim remorse. Then be a team player, struggling and suffering with everyone else. And then finally, when Utkin's treachery is revealed, come to his defense with sympathy and rationalization.

My God, Tucker thought.

He stood, stuffed the rope sections into his back pockets, and picked up his AR-15 rifle. He stalked back over to the group, all still gathered at the pond's edge.

Christopher greeted him with a wave. "I thought you were going back to the Rover to get more supplies."

Kane trotted over, his tail high, but he must have immediately sensed the black pall around his partner. The flagging tail drooped down. His entire body stiffened up, readying for action.

Anya was too skilled not to get worried. "Tucker, what's wrong?"

He lifted the rifle and pointed it at her. "Raise

your arms above your head. If you so much as twitch a finger, I'll shoot you."

"What are you doing?" she replied, feigning confusion, but he noted the microexpression of fury that momentarily flashed.

"Five seconds, Anya."

"Tucker, you're scaring me."

The shock that had initially struck Christopher and Bukolov wore off. They began to voice a similar chorus of confused complaints. He ignored them.

"Three seconds."

He raised the AR to his shoulder.

Anya pushed her arms high. She looked to Bukolov and Christopher for support, fixing an expression of suffering innocence. "Tell me what is happening."

"My people deconstructed the photo of the Internet café in Dimitrovgrad. It was *you*, Anya, from the very beginning. You were the traitor. Not Utkin. He was a just a boy, and you set him up to take the fall."

The complaints from Christopher and Bukolov died away.

"Tucker, please, I don't know what—"

"Deny it one more time, Anya. One more time and I'll put a round in your foot."

She stared up and must have read his seriousness. She kept her gaze fixed on him, showing no shame, but also no satisfaction. "It was not personal. I took no joy in the bloodshed. I liked Utkin. I truly did, but it was necessary. I was given a duty, and I performed it to the best of my abilities."

Her words lacked any coldness or disdain, only a calm self-assurance.

"How long until your people get here?" he asked.

"I will not tell you."

"How are they tracking you?"

She just stared.

"Drop to your knees, then to your belly, hands flat on the rock."

She complied, moving with surprising grace.

"GUARD," he ordered Kane.

As the shepherd stalked to her side, Tucker passed his weapon to Christopher. "Keep her covered."

With her under tight watch, Tucker quickly bound her hands and ankles. He frisked her, removing anything he found, including taking her boots and socks. He examined each item, but he found no electronics or trackers.

He was fairly certain she didn't have a phone, which meant Kharzin's people had to have been tracking her. But how? He would have to search through her entire pack, strip the Rover down, too.

Tucker noted Bukolov had wandered a few paces away, his back to them.

Concerned, Tucker crossed to him. He didn't need the guy falling apart. Bukolov wasn't the most stable of personalities even on his good days.

"Doc?"

Bukolov glanced to him and away, but not before Tucker noted the tears. "He died thinking I hated him."

Utkin.

"I was such a fool," Bukolov said. "How can I forgive myself?"

"Because Utkin would want you to." He placed a hand on the doctor's shoulder. "He knew our distrust of him was based on deceit. He saved us because he wouldn't let that lie define him. We have to honor that."

Bukolov nodded, wiping his eyes. "I will try to do that."

"Forget Anya. Forget all of it. I'm going to get you inside that cave, and you're going to find that sample of LUCA. That's all that matters now."

"What about Kharzin's team?"

"Let me worry about them. Concentrate on what you came here to do. The sooner you find LUCA, the sooner we can leave—with any luck, before the enemy arrives. Are you with me, Doc?"

Bukolov straightened, took a deep breath, and nodded firmly. "I am with you."

Tucker glanced back to Anya, still on her belly, her arms tied behind her back, guarded over by Christopher and Kane.

It was time to turn her betrayal to his advantage.

37

Standing at the edge of the pond, Tucker passed a gun to Bukolov. It was a Smith & Wesson .38-caliber revolver. Though it only held five rounds, it was a personal favorite: for its size, accuracy, and reliability. All too often, surviving a firefight relied more on the *quality* of the gun than the *quantity* of the rounds. He'd rather have five good shots than ten poor ones any day.

"Do you know how to use a gun?" Tucker asked.

Bukolov turned the revolver over in his hands. "Finger squeezes here. Bullets come out there. I think I can manage." He glanced down to Anya, still on her belly and bound up. "Can I shoot her?"

"Not unless she gets free and charges you. Otherwise, we're leaving you here to *guard* her until we get back."

Christopher stood off to the side. The pair of them were going to return to the Range Rover, where Anya's pack was still stored. He intended to search both it and the SUV thoroughly. They needed to find her tracking device, and the hunt would go faster with two people.

He stared toward the sky.

They had less than an hour of daylight left.

He crossed and checked Anya's bindings and knots one final time before leaving.

"You cannot win, Captain Wayne," Anya said matter-of-factly, as if discussing the weather, in this case a coming storm. "General Kharzin will have many men with him. Elite Spetsnaz."

"I believe you."

"You may hold them off for a time, but eventually you will lose. If you surrender, it will go better for you."

"Somehow I don't see that ending with anything less than a bullet in my skull." He gave the ropes around her ankle a snug pull. "Just answer one question."

Arching her back, she glanced over her shoulder toward him.

"Knowing what you do about LUCA, *why* would you want Kharzin to have it?"

"It is not my place to question. I know my duty, and I serve."

Tucker stared at her preternatural calmness, at her steady and simple gaze. It was beginning to unnerve him a little. Here was the true Anya.

"How does Kharzin plan to use it?" he asked.

"I do not know."

Oddly enough, *this* he believed.

6:33 P.M.

"Look here," Christopher said as he knelt on the ground next to Anya's open pack. He had already dumped the contents out and had been slowly going over them, item by item.

Tucker was performing a similar search upon the Rover, knowing a wireless transmitter could have been planted in a thousand places. As he worked, he felt the growing press of time as the sun sank toward the horizon.

"What did you find?" he asked, shifting over to Christopher.

Kane came sniffing, too.

Christopher passed over what looked like a thick-barreled ballpoint pen. "Twist it open."

He did, unscrewing it and pulling the two halves apart. Inside, he discovered a cluster of fine wires, a microcircuit board, and a strip of lithium-ion batteries the size of his pinkie nail.

He smiled. *Gotcha.*

"What about the Range Rover?" Christopher asked. "Do you want me to help you look for any additional transmitters?"

"In the end, they won't matter. I just need this one in hand."

"What next then?"

"You head back to the pond. We need to hide any evidence that we're still here. That means getting you, Bukolov, and Anya down into that cave."

Tucker quickly instructed Christopher on how to get everyone lowered through the vortex.

"I should be back around dusk to join you,"

Tucker finished. "Call me by radio if there is any trouble."

With Christopher headed back, Tucker climbed into the driver's seat of the Range Rover. Kane clambered into the passenger seat.

He engaged the engine and slowly reversed his way back down the ravine. Once at the bottom, he headed west for ten minutes, continuing their group's original trajectory, pushing the Rover as hard as he dared, hoping Kharzin was actively monitoring his progress.

He eventually found the perfect terrain.

Three-quarters of a mile from where he'd started, Tucker stopped the vehicle at the mouth of a narrow slot-canyon, much like the one back at the coordinates. He hopped out and entered the narrow ravine. Using his flashlight, he studied the rubble-strewn floor until he discovered a deep fissure in the ground. Peering down, he saw no bottom.

Good enough.

Reaching to his pocket, he pulled out Anya's pen and dropped it down the crack.

Dig for that, General.

He hurried back to the parked Rover. If there were any more transmitters aboard, he didn't care. He wanted to draw Kharzin here. He left the keys in the ignition and set to work on the second part of his plan: a surprise welcome for the general's team.

From the cargo pocket of his pants, he pulled out the waxy block of C-4 explosives that he'd been carrying all day.

Working quickly but cautiously, he sidled under the vehicle on his back and stuffed a half block of the explosive between the muffler and the floorboard. Next, he strung a length of detonation cord to the leaf springs behind the front tire and affixed a chemical detonator.

He crawled back out and surveyed his handiwork.

If anyone tried to move or even sit inside the vehicle, the stress on the tire springs would set off the charge. With any luck, the bomb would take out one or two of Kharzin's Spetsnaz.

And while the ruse wouldn't stop Kharzin forever, it should buy Tucker and the others some valuable extra time.

He turned to Kane. "Ready for a little run?"

The tail wag was answer enough.

7:18 P.M.

Setting a hard pace, it took only ten minutes to return to the canyon and up to the pond. He found Christopher waiting for him at the pool's edge. The sun had already disappeared, but the twilight's gloaming still allowed decent light.

"Are the other two down safely in the cave?" Tucker asked, huffing heavily. "And the supplies?"

"The doctor went first with his pistol. Then Anya, all trussed up and lowered like a Christmas goose. Doctor Bukolov radioed that he has her well in hand."

"Then we should get below, too."

"Before we do that," Christopher said, "I had a thought. If I call my brothers and—"

"No. I'm not going to involve them here."

"I do not mean to bring them *here*. I love my

brothers too much for that. I simply mean to ask them to wait for us at last night's campsite. I can pass on the coordinates. If we make it out of this alive, we'll still need a way *back* to civilization, especially if our Rover gets blown up."

It made sense.

Christopher talked with his brother for two minutes on the satellite phone, then disconnected. "They will be there tomorrow night."

With the matter settled, they set about getting themselves down into the cave. Christopher disappeared first through the vortex. Next, Tucker lowered Kane, cinching the line through a set of loops in his tactical vest. Tucker went last after reconfiguring the rope ties, so he could pull the rope down after him once inside.

A few moments later, soaked to the skin, Tucker stood in the cave with the others. Hauling with his shoulders, he reeled the rope down from above.

"What are you doing?" Christopher asked, watching the last of the line tumble down to the floor.

Bukolov stood up from where he sat atop their supplies next to Anya, his pistol still pointed at her head. She was flat on her belly as before.

Tucker had told no one about this last detail of his plan, or they might have balked at coming down here.

"I don't want to leave any evidence that we were ever *up* there. And I certainly don't want to leave behind any clue about how to get *down* here."

"But how are we supposed to get out of here?" Bukolov asked.

"According to De Klerk, this was an old Boer

bunker." He pictured the warren of tunnels and cellars back at the Klipkoppic fort. "So I wager there's more than one way out of this cavern system."

"You're *wagering* with our lives," Bukolov warned, but he ended it with an unconcerned shrug. "But you are right, the Boer were a crafty bunch."

"And even if I'm wrong, I have a contingency plan as backup."

"Which is what?" Christopher asked.

"Let's worry about that *after* we search this place."

Tucker realized one of their team had remained unusually quiet. He stepped over to Anya and dropped to a knee.

Bukolov shuffled his legs a bit. "She had a lot to say while you were all gone. Very sly, this one. Gets in your head. She kept wheedling, pressing, promising, until finally I had to put a sock in it."

Tucker smiled. In this case, the doctor was speaking literally. He had stuffed a rolled-up sock in Anya's mouth, gagging her.

Tucker straightened back up. "That's why you're a billionaire, Doctor Bukolov. Always using your head."

Or in this particular case, his foot.

Tucker pointed to her and renewed an order with Kane. "Guard."

The shepherd walked over to Anya and lowered his head until his snout was mere inches away, panting. Anya leaned back, her eyes flashing hatefully, finally showing cracks in that calm professional demeanor.

Bukolov chuckled. "I have grown quite fond of that dog."

7:55 P.M.

Preparing to explore, Tucker and Christopher donned headlamps. The cavern's only other illumination came from an LED lantern next to Bukolov. The doctor still sat among the supplies, guarding Anya. He had a pistol in one hand and De Klerk's diary in another, doing his best to get his bearings, to discern some clue about the whereabouts of the specimens of LUCA.

"There are many references in his damned diary," Bukolov had said a few moments ago. "To bunkrooms, officers' messes, medical wards, including a place grimly noted as the *Die Bloedige Katedraal*, or 'The Bloody Cathedral.' It seemed the Boer even brought their horses in here and wagons."

Tucker looked up at the falling chute of water.

Not through there they didn't.

"But I keep coming to one entry over and over again. It's simply noted as *Die Horro*, or 'The Horror.' It seemed important to De Klerk. But it would be easier to trace his steps through this subterranean world if I had some *map* of the place."

And that's what Tucker and Christopher intended to do, with Kane's help. Tucker figured this recon mission was a better use of the shepherd's skills than merely guarding Anya. She was already trussed up and under the baleful eye of Bukolov. Besides, where could she go?

So Christopher and Tucker headed over to the two passageways that looked like the muzzle of a double-barreled shotgun.

Tucker took the one on the right with Kane.

Christopher vanished into the other. After only sixty steps, Tucker's tunnel dumped into another cavern, this one massive, with a vaulted ceiling festooned with stalactites. The floor was likewise covered in a maze of towering stalagmites. Some of the two met to form columns like in a—

"Cathedral," Tucker mumbled.

Was this the place Bukolov had mentioned?

Die Bloedige Katedraal.

As he stepped farther out, he saw the walls to either side had been carved into tiers. They definitely looked man-made, likely the handiwork of the Boers.

A scuffle of boots sounded behind him. Christopher stumbled into view thirty feet away, his light shining blindingly into Tucker's face. His tunnel had also deposited him into the Cathedral.

"Whoa, whoa!" Christopher said, sweeping his headlamp across the cavern. "How big do you think this place is?"

"Side to side, fifty yards. Maybe twice again as deep." Tucker pointed to the tiered ledges on his side. "I want to check those out. Those aren't natural. See the chisel marks and ax strikes in the sandstone?"

Tucker crossed over and hopped up onto the first ledge, then the second, finally the third, like climbing tall steps. Kane followed him up. They were now ten feet off the ground. He found more Boer handiwork on top. The highest ledge had been excavated along its length to form a crude foxhole, enough room for a soldier to duck down out of sight from the floor below.

Shining his lamp into the foxhole, he saw the bottom littered with spent shell casings. Kane jumped down to explore, sniffing at the casings, shuffling through them.

Christopher had mirrored his climb on the far side of the cavern and discovered the same. They both walked along the top tier on their respective sides, heading down along the cavern, paralleling each other.

"I'm starting to see how the Boers did it," Tucker called out. "From these foxholes, they could strafe anyone passing through the cavern below. A perfect killing floor."

"Horrible to imagine," Christopher said.

Tucker now understood the *bloody* part of the room's nickname.

"Let's keep going."

They clambered back to the floor, met in the middle, and headed farther down the belly of the monstrous cavern.

Tucker noted the telltale pockmarks gouging a nearby stalagmite, evidence of gunfire. This killing floor had seen some use.

But if so, where were the bodies from that slaughter? Had the British buried them after clearing this place out—even the Boers' remains? Was there a mass grave somewhere in these hills?

As they continued through the Cathedral, the walls began narrowing and the roof descending, until the space was only thirty feet across. Near the end of the cave, they hit a waist-high wall of burlap sandbags that stretched from wall to wall. They high-stepped over it, while Kane hurdled it. In another ten feet, with the walls ever narrowing, they ran into another line of sandbags, then after that another. Beyond the last one, the Cathedral's walls and ceiling narrowed to a four-foot-wide funnel that became a tunnel.

"Defense in depth," Tucker whispered.

"Pardon me?"

He pointed to the dark tunnel. "Your enemy comes through there. The defenders hide behind the closest row of sandbags. If the enemy breaches that wall, the defenders fall back to the next barrier."

"And the next after that . . ."

"All the way across. If the enemy makes it through that gauntlet, they still have to face the killing floor behind us. No wonder the Boer lasted so long here, where only a few could withstand many."

Tucker stepped over the last sandbag and wondered if his team would soon face similar bad odds.

"Stay here with Kane," Tucker said. "I'll be right back."

Dropping to his hands and his knees, he crawled along the shaft ahead, which almost immediately began cutting sharply left and right. As he crawled, Tucker imagined a Boer sniper lying prone at each corner, picking off an advancing British soldier before retreating to the next corner, then repeating the process again.

After eight or ten bends Tucker reached a straight passageway. At the end of it, slivers of pale light glowed. Dowsing his headlamp, he crawled the last of the way and reached a pile of rock that blocked the path forward. He fingered the silvery light that pierced through the rubble and pulled a fist-sized rock from its edge. A few more fell with it, forming a watermelon-sized hole.

Cool night air flowed back to him.

He poked his head out and searched around outside, gaining his bearings.

He realized he had reached the other canyon— the other tusk of the boar—the one Christopher and Anya had explored earlier.

Interesting.

If nothing else, he'd found another exit.

After pulling his head back inside, he carefully returned the fallen rocks back into place, sealing the hole, making sure it remained camouflaged from the outside.

He didn't want any uninvited houseguests coming in the back door.

8:13 P.M.

Tucker returned to the sandbag barrier, where he found Christopher waiting, but he noted a missing member of their team. "Where's Kane?"

Christopher did a dance of searching around. "He was here a moment ago. That one, he is like a ghost."

True . . . and with a dog's curiosity.

He had forgotten to tell Kane to stay.

Tucker pursed his lips and let out a soft double whistle.

Kane responded with a double bark.

They followed the sound back into the Cathedral, only to discover Kane standing at the top ledge along the left wall. He stared square at Tucker—then jumped down into the foxhole and vanished out of sight. The shepherd's message was plain.

Come see what I found!

What now?

Tucker led Christopher up to the ledge. He shone his lamp's beam into the foxhole to find Kane seated before a barrel-shaped wooden door in the cavern wall.

"Seems there is more to this maze," Christopher said.

Tucker jumped down. He tested the four-foot-wide plank door. The wood was once stout, the iron joinery solid. No longer. He leaned against the other side of the foxhole and kicked out with his legs. The ancient door shattered under his heels. A passageway extended from it.

"Let's see where it leads."

He took Kane with him this time, but he had noted Christopher beginning to limp badly on the ankle he'd twisted before, so he left him to rest.

The crawl this time was mercifully short. The passageway ended at a crudely circular room, crowded with stacked boxes, but at least he could stand.

He noted *four* tunnels led out from here.

Tucker sighed.

The Boers apparently were ants in another life.

Tucker called back to Christopher. "If I'm not back in fifteen minutes, come after me."

He took a brief moment to examine the crates. Burned into their sides was the coat of arms for the

Boer Orange Free State. Same as De Klerk's unit. He pulled the lid off the top crate and looked inside. He found rifle shells, canned goods, tins of kerosene, candles, hammers, nails. He examined three more crates and found similar contents.

Though he had found nothing significant, a question nagged at him: *Why hadn't the British seized this bounty when they cleared this place out?*

Without an answer, he began his search of the four tunnels, starting from the left and working his way right.

The first passage led to a mess hall: a long, narrow gallery containing trestle tables constructed from what appeared to be the remains of wagons, all of them topped with abandoned plates and pewter cups.

The second tunnel ended at a bunkroom: a gallery-style cavern, with moldy lines of bedrolls flanking the walls and dark lanterns hanging above.

Again, there was no indication that the British had been here. Nothing was ransacked; nothing looked disturbed. Tucker felt as though he were touring an abandoned theater.

Down the third passageway, he found the unit's hospital: a ward lined by thirty or so makeshift cots and stacked with crates of medical supplies.

He was about to leave, when something struck him as off.

"No blankets, no mattresses, no pillows," he murmured.

The cots had been stripped.

And why so many of them?

According to Bukolov, the Boers had arrived here

with only a hundred men. This medical ward held cots for nearly a third of that number. Had that many soldiers been wounded?

With more mysteries raised than solved, Tucker moved to the fourth and final passageway. This one ended at a huge cavern, but it was barren: no crates, no equipment. Nothing. But something struck him as odd about its far wall.

Following his beam of light, Tucker crossed there and discovered a large wall of rubble. He noted blackened scorch marks to either side. Roosa must have blasted this entrance, collapsing and sealing it behind him. At least this discovery answered a question that had been nagging him: *How had Roosa gotten the horses into this cave system?* Of course, that raised in turn yet another question: *What became of the horses?*

Kane barked twice behind him.

The shepherd drew him to a tunnel opening off to the right. This one was blocked by a careful stack of boulders. Each stone wedged tightly together. Even the gaps had been stuffed with clumps of burlap.

"What the hell?" he murmured.

Using his hands and his knife, he pried at the wall of boulders until one slipped free. It crashed to the floor, almost hitting his toes. He began to lower his face to the opening, to shine his light through the gap, but yanked his head back, slapped in the face by a fierce stench.

He took a few involuntary steps backward, covering his nose and mouth with a hand. He recognized the stink immediately, flashing back to too many battlefields, to too much death.

Flesh and fire.

He took a full minute to steel himself, then he returned to the sealed door. He now detected a whiff of kerosene through the stench, the incendiary source for whatever horrors lay beyond this blockade.

He remembered the entry read by Bukolov from De Klerk's diary.

Die Horro . . .

Holding his breath, he shoved his head through the gap and swiveled the beam of his lamp. He pointed it down first, expecting to see floor. Instead, darkness swallowed his light. He was staring into the mouth of a shaft, a black pit.

Tucker pulled back out and sat down beside Kane.

He knew what he had to do, but he railed against it.

He had no doubt *what* lay at the bottom of the pit.

But he had no answer as to *why* and *who*?

Those answers lay below—along with perhaps the secret behind De Klerk's diary. He closed his eyes, struggling to rally. He'd come too far with too much blood shed. He could not balk now.

But I want to . . . dear God, do I want to.

8:41 P.M.

"Tucker, what did you find?" Christopher asked, looking worried, perhaps noting his sickened demeanor as he returned.

"I'm not sure. But I need you to go back to the supplies, grab a coil of climbing rope, and come back here."

Christopher returned two minutes later.

"Follow me," Tucker said and led Christopher

and Kane back to the large cavern and over to the doorway that closed off the pit.

"That stink . . ." Christopher said after peering through the hole. He had helped Tucker widen it by pulling out a few more rocks. "You're not going down there, are you?"

"I'm happy for you to take my place."

For once, Christopher didn't argue.

Working together, they anchored the rope around a nearby stalagmite and tossed the free end through the hole.

After ordering Kane to stay put, Tucker boosted himself through the opening and twisted around. With his gloved hands on the rope, he leaned back and braced his feet against the wall of the shaft. He took a calming breath. He tried to quiet the voice in his head that was shouting at him to go no farther.

In the end, he simply chose to ignore it.

Hand over hand, Tucker walked himself down into the pit. His headlamp danced off the rock. After ten feet he stopped, steadied himself, and looked below. The bottom of the pit was still beyond the reach of his headlamp's beam. He kept going. He stopped again at the twenty-foot mark and spotted the end of his rope coiled on a bottom of sorts, a rock ramp that tilted at a sharp angle.

Tucker lowered himself until his boots came to rest atop that ramp. He noted most of the shaft around him was scorched with an oily black soot. He kept one hand on the line—not trusting the rock's slippery surface or its steep grade. Crouching carefully, he peered over the lip of the ramp and discovered another drop-off.

Don't think, he commanded himself.

Swallowing hard, he leaned over the drop-off and shone his light down.

His beam revealed an outstretched arm, reaching up toward him, blackened to bone, fingers curled by old flames.

He shuddered, his heart pounding in his throat.

He panned the light down the forearm and biceps, where it disappeared into—

It took Tucker a few seconds for his mind to accept what he was seeing: a morass of skeletal remains and charred flesh. At the edges, he picked out scorched clothing and blankets, chunks of half-charred wood, and blackened tins of kerosene. Despite trying to avoid it, he discerned bits of individual remains.

—a torso jutting from the mire as though the man had been trying to claw his way out of quick-sand.

—the disembodied hoof of a horse, its steel shoe glinting dully.

—a pair of gentleman's spectacles caught on a higher spur of rock, looking unscathed by the con-flagration below, reflecting back his lamp's light.

"Good God," he murmured.

Sick to his stomach, his head full of the acrid stench of immolated flesh, he tore his eyes away and pulled himself back until he stood on trembling legs on the scorched ramp. Questions swirled.

What had happened here?

How deep was the pit?

How many were down there?

Tucker stared up, ready to escape this choked gateway to hell.

Two feet above his head, he found himself staring at the haft of a dagger. It was jutting from the rock face, so soot covered he hadn't noticed it when he first came down. He reached up, grabbed the haft, and gave it a wiggle. Dried soot flaked off and swirled in the beam of his headlamp. There was something beneath the soot, pinned by the blade into the rock.

Using his fingertips, he brushed away the soot to reveal a thick square of oilcloth. Carefully, he pried the packet off the wall and slipped it into his thigh pocket.

"Tucker!" Christopher's shout startled him. "What did you find?"

He glared up toward his friend's headlamp. "I'm coming up! Get that damned light out of my eyes."

"Oh, sorry."

He quickly and gladly hauled himself up the rock face and out of the shaft. Without saying a word, he strode several yards away from the charnel pit and finally sat down. Christopher joined him and offered a canteen.

He took a long gulp of water.

Kane slinked over, his tail low, the very tip wagging questioningly.

"I'm okay . . . I'm okay . . ."

The reassurance was as much for him as Kane.

"What was down there?" Christopher asked.

Tucker explained—though words failed to convey the true horror.

Christopher murmured, "Good Lord, why would they do that?"

"I don't know." Tucker withdrew the wrapped packet of oilcloth. "But this may hold some clue."

He turned the prize over in his hands. He found a seam in the cloth. Using the tip of his knife, he slit along it and unfolded the cloth. It was several layers thick. At the heart of the package rested a thick sheaf of papers, folded in half and perfectly preserved, showing no signs of soot or decay.

Written on the outside in what he immediately recognized as De Klerk's handwriting were two lines: one Afrikaans, the other in English, likely the same message.

> Aan wie dit vind...
>
> To whoever finds this...

He shared a glance with Christopher and unfolded the papers. What he found there was written in both languages. Tucker read aloud from the English section.

"*'However unlikely this eventuality, if this message is ever found, I feel compelled by my conscience to recount what has led to the awful events that took place here. Whether our actions will ever be recognized or understood by our loved ones is for God to decide, but I leave this life confident that He, in His infinite wisdom, will forgive us . . .'*"

The remainder of De Klerk's testament went on for several more pages. Tucker read through it all, then folded the paper and put it back in his pocket.

"So?" Christopher asked.

He stood up. "Bukolov must hear this."

38

With Kane leading the way, Tucker and Christopher made it back to the Cathedral. They had barely spoken after reading De Klerk's letter. As they turned toward the double-barrel tunnels leading out from the cavern, Kane stopped ahead of them and turned. He gazed down the length of the Cathedral, toward the distant walls of sandbags. His ears were up, his posture rigid.

What had he picked out?

"QUIET SCOUT," Tucker ordered.

Hunched low and padding softly, Kane took off across the former killing floor of the Cathedral. Tucker and Christopher followed, dodging through the forest of stalagmites. Near the end of the cavern, Kane leaped the sandbag barriers and stopped at the shaft leading out to the crooked corridor.

"HOLD," Tucker ordered softly.

Kane stopped and waited for him.

Tucker took the lead, crawling through the twisting shaft of the corridor. He reached the end, where it straightened out. The slivers of pale moonlight blazed much brighter ahead. Then he heard it—what had likely caught Kane's attention.

The faint rumble of a diesel engine.

Tucker picked his way along the last of the corridor. He dropped to his belly at the tumble of rocks. He peeked out one of the shining slivers and saw the canyon outside was lit up brightly from the headlamps of a truck parked in the canyon.

From that direction, a voice shouted in Russian.

Then a bark of laughter closer at hand.

A pair of boots stomped up to his hiding spot. A man, dressed in fatigues, dropped to a knee. Tucker froze, waiting for a shout of alarm, for gunfire.

But the soldier only tied up a loose bootlace, then regained his feet.

Tucker heard other men out there, too, moving about or talking quietly.

How many?

Then a deep baritone shouted harshly, gathering everyone back to the truck. A moment later, the timbre of the engine rose, rocks ground under turning tires, and darkness fell back over the canyon.

He listened, hearing the rumble fade slowly into the distance.

They were leaving.

These were clearly Kharzin's men. Had they come to check out where the Range Rover had stopped for a few hours? Finding nothing here, were they continuing on to where Tucker had parked the boobytrapped vehicle, drawn by the transmitter?

Tucker placed his forehead against the cool rock and let out the breath he'd been holding. Relieved, he made his way back to Christopher and Kane.

The three of them hurried back to the waterfall cavern.

Nothing had changed here.

Bukolov was where they had left him. Anya had rolled to her butt and leaned against a stalagmite, her arms still bound behind her. With her chin resting on her chest, she appeared to be asleep.

"How went the search?" Bukolov asked, standing and stretching.

"We need to talk," Tucker said.

After ordering Kane to guard Anya, Tucker drew Bukolov to the mouth of one of the shotgun tunnels. He recounted their investigation, ending with his discovery of the charnel pit.

"What?" Bukolov said. "I don't understand—"

"In that pit—staked to the wall of the shaft like a warning—I believe I found De Klerk's missing pages."

"What?" Shock rocked through the doctor.

Tucker passed the papers over. "He wrote this message in both Afrikaans and English. He must have been covering his bases, not knowing who might stumble upon that pit later: his fellow Boers or the British."

"You read it?"

Tucker nodded. "De Klerk was terse but descriptive. About three weeks after they entered these caves, several men began getting sick. Terrible stomach pains, fever, body aches. De Klerk did his best to treat them, but one by one they began dying. In the final phase of the disease, the victims developed nodules beneath the skin of their lower abdomen and throat. These eventually crupted through the skin, bursting. While the British troops laid siege to the cave, De Klerk found himself overwhelmed by patients. As hard as he tried, he couldn't find the source of the illness."

"What then?"

"On day thirty, General Roosa ordered the remainder of the cave entrances sealed shut. He had become convinced everyone was infected—or soon would be—by some kind of plague. He was afraid that if the British breached their defenses they would also become infected, and the plague would spread to the outside world."

"Not an unusual reaction," Bukolov said. "Paranoia of pandemics ran rampant during the turn of the century. Scarlet fever, influenza, typhoid. It made normally rational men do crazy things."

"I think it was more personal than that. According to De Klerk, General Roosa had lost his entire family to smallpox. Including his daughter Wilhelmina. He'd never quite gotten over it. According to De Klerk, the symptoms they saw among the men struck Roosa very close to home. It was too much like the pox that killed his family. In essence, the guy lost it."

"So everyone died here. Despite what the records show, the British never did overrun this cave?"

"That record was likely falsified by the British colonel waging this siege," Tucker said. "He came to kill Roosa and his men. And after what happened here, the end result was the same. Everyone dead. So the British colonel took credit and chalked it up as a victory."

"Craven opportunist," Bukolov muttered sourly,

clearly bothered that history was so unreliable and anecdotal.

Tucker continued the story. "Shortly after Roosa and his Boers entombed themselves, the British left. The dead were dropped into the pit and burned along with their clothing, bedding, and personal belongings. Many committed suicide and were burned as well—including Roosa himself. De Klerk was the last man to go down, but before he lowered himself into the pit and put a gun to his head, he gave his diary to a passing Boer scout who discovered their hiding place. De Klerk took care not to contaminate the outsider. This was the man who returned the journals and diary to De Klerk's widow."

"And what about what he pinned to the wall of the pit?" Bukolov lifted the sheaf of papers.

"A warning for anyone who came here. On the last page of his testament, De Klerk lays out his theory of this disease. He thinks it was something the men ingested—small white bulbs that the soldiers thought were some kind of local mushroom. He even includes some beautifully detailed drawings. He wrote the name under them. *Die Apokalips Saad.*"

Bukolov's eyes shone in the dark. "LUCA."

Tucker nodded. "So it sounds like your organism infects more than just *plants*."

"Not necessarily. You mentioned the worst of the victims' symptoms were concentrated to the throat and abdomen. The human gut is full of plant material and plantlike flora. LUCA could thrive in that environment very well, wreaking digestive havoc on the host."

"Does that mean LUCA poses a danger as a biological weapon, too?"

"Possibly. But only on a *small* scale. For humans to become infected, they would have to *eat* it or—like here—be confined in a closed space where airborne spores are concentrated."

"How sure are you about that, Doc?"

"The science is complicated, but believe me when I say this: as a biological weapon, LUCA is virtually useless on the large scale—especially when a thimbleful of anthrax could wipe out a city. But as an *ecological* threat, a weaponized version of LUCA is a thermonuclear bomb."

"Then let's make sure that never happens."

"In regards to that, I've made some progress."

10:48 P.M.

When Tucker and Bukolov rejoined the others, Anya was awake. Christopher guarded her with his AR-15 rifle, while Kane kept close watch.

Tucker ignored her and followed Bukolov to his makeshift office set up amid their stack of supplies. From the haphazard scatter of paper, notes, and journal pages, he had been busy.

"It's here," Bukolov said and grabbed De Klerk's old diary from atop one of the boxes.

With the skill of a magician cutting a deck of cards, the doctor opened to the spot where it looked like pages had been cut out. He compared it to the pages Tucker had discovered.

"Looks like a perfect match," Bukolov said.

Anya stirred, trying to see, to stand. But a deep-throated growl from Kane dropped her back to her butt.

"See. Here's a crude, early rendition of LUCA in the old diary, a hazy sketch. A first-draft effort. What we had to work from before." Bukolov fitted a sheet from Tucker's collection into place. "This page was the diary's next page. Before it was cut out. The finished masterpiece."

The page in question depicted a deftly drawn sketch of a mushroomlike stalk with ruffled edges sprouting from a bulb. Colors of each structure were called out in tiny, precise print. Other drawings showed the same plant in various stages of growth.

Bukolov pointed to the earliest of the drawings. "This is LUCA in a dormant stage. A bulblike structure. De Klerk describes it here as a butter-yellow color. His measurements indicate it's about the size of a golf ball. But don't let its simplicity fool you. This structure is pure potential. Each cell in the bulb is a blank slate, a vicious chimera, waiting to unleash its fury on the modern world. It reproduces by infection and replication, as invasive as they come, an apex predator of the flora world. But if we could tame it, unlock the keys to its unique primordial genetics, anything could be possible."

"But first we need to find it," Tucker said.

Bukolov turned to him, a confused expression on his face. "I already explained where to find it."

"When?"

"Just a moment ago, when I said, *It's here.*"

Tucker had thought the doctor was referring to De Klerk's diary. "What do you mean, it's here?"

"Or it should be." Bukolov stared around the cavern with frustration. "It is supposed to be *here*. In this cavern. At least according to De Klerk."

"Why do you think that?"

Bukolov flipped the diary to the page before with the crude drawing of LUCA. "Here he talks about finding the dormant bulbs, but he never says *where* to find them. He's a sly one. But see here in the margin of that section."

Tucker leaned over. He couldn't read the passage written in Afrikaans, but next to it was a crudely scribbled spiral.

"I always thought it was just an idle doodle," Bukolov said. "I do it all the time. Especially when I'm concentrating. My mind wanders, then so does my pen."

"But you think it's significant now."

"The drawing looks like water spilling down a bathtub drain." Bukolov pointed to the torrent of water across the room. "It wasn't a mindless squiggle. De Klerk was symbolically marking this passage about the discovery of the bulb with its location. As I said, *it's here*. Under the bathtub drain."

Bukolov closed the journal and tossed it aside. "I

just have to find it. And now that I don't have to play babysitter . . ."

With a glare toward Anya, Bukolov picked up an LED lantern and set off across the cavern.

For the moment, Tucker left the doctor to his search. Knowing now that Kharzin's team was in the neighborhood, he had to prepare for the contingency that Bukolov might fail. His ruse with the booby-trapped Rover would not stop the enemy for long . . . nor did he know how many of the enemy his trick might take out.

He pictured his last glimpse of Felice Nilsson, leaning out the helicopter door, her lower face hidden by a scarf, her blond hair whipping in the wind.

It was too much to hope that she would be caught in that blast.

He had to be ready.

He crossed to the pile of boxes and packs, knelt down, and pulled over the stiff cardboard box holding the blocks of C-4.

"Christopher, can you start measuring out six-foot lengths of detonation cord? I'll need about fifteen of them."

Anya stared at them, her face unreadable.

Ignoring her, he calculated the best spots to set his charges to cause the most destruction. If Bukolov couldn't find the bulbs of LUCA, he intended to make sure no one ever did, especially General Kharzin.

He unfolded the flaps of the box of C-4 and stared inside.

With a sinking drop of his stomach, he glanced

again over to Anya. Her expression had changed only very slightly, the tiniest ghost of a smile.

"How?" he asked.

The box before him was packed full of dirt, about the same weight as C-4.

Anya shrugged. "Back at the campsite this morning, after you left. All your C-4 is buried out there."

Of course, she had known of his contingency plan to blow the cave as a fail-safe and had taken steps to ensure it wouldn't happen.

But she was wrong about one fact: *all your C-4.*

He had taken a block of the explosive with him as he hunted for guerrillas and ran into the pack of dogs. Later, he used half of it to rig the Rover. He still had the other half, but it was far too little to do any real damage here.

And now they were running out of time.

If they couldn't blow the place up, that left only one path open to them: *find the source of LUCA before Kharzin's team returned.*

So there was still hope—not great, but something.

Bukolov dashed it a moment later as he returned with more bad news. "I found nothing."

11:12 P.M.

Fueled by anger and frustration, Tucker tossed the leg of an old broken chair across the cavern floor. It bounced and skittered away, splashing through a standing pool of water. Christopher and Bukolov worked elsewhere in the cavern, spread out, slowly circling the torrent of water falling through the room's center.

Tucker wasn't satisfied with Bukolov's cursory search.

He had them sifting through some of the old Boer detritus and flotsam tossed against the walls by prior flooding.

But it was eating up time and getting them nowhere.

If they had a sample of LUCA, Kane could have quickly sniffed out the dark garden hidden here, but they didn't. So he left the shepherd guarding Anya.

Christopher and Bukolov finally reached him. They'd made a complete loop of the cavern. He read the lack of success in their defeated expressions.

"Maybe I was wrong about the bathtub drain." Bukolov stared up at the water cascading through the vortex. "Maybe it was just a doodle."

Tucker suddenly stiffened next to him. "We've been so stupid . . ."

Christopher turned. "What?"

Tucker grabbed Bukolov by the shoulder. "De Klerk *was* marking the location. It *is* a drain."

The doctor looked up again toward the ceiling.

"No." Tucker pointed to the floor, to where the flood of water flowing down from above either pooled—or drained through fissures in the floor. "*That's* the drain depicted by De Klerk. The water must be going somewhere."

Bukolov's eyes went wide. "There's more cavern below us!"

Christopher stared across the cavern. "One problem. If you're right, how do we get down there?"

Tucker stared across the expanse of the room. "De Klerk has been cagey all along. He wouldn't have left the entrance open. He would have sealed or covered it somehow." Tucker circled his arm in the air. "One more time around. We need to find that opening."

It was accomplished quickly—now that they knew what to look for.

Christopher called him over. "See here!"

Tucker and Bukolov joined him beside a thigh-high boulder not far from the torrent. Excess water sluiced through a four-inch crack under it and vanished away.

"I believe the stone is covering a larger hole," Christopher said.

"I think you're right."

With both Christopher and Tucker putting their shoulders to it, they were able to dislodge and roll the boulder aside.

The hole was small, only two feet wide. All three of them leaned over the opening, shining their lights down into the depths. A cavern opened below, its floor about seven feet below them.

Tucker squinted, noting the protrusions sticking up from the floor.

For a few moments, he thought he was staring at a cluster of stalagmites, but they were too uniform, and the beam of his headlamp glinted off a hint of brass beneath a greenish patina.

"What the hell are those?" Bukolov said.

"Those are artillery shells."

39

Tucker lowered himself to his belly and hung his head through the opening. He panned his lamp around the space. The spread of upright shells looked like some giant's bed of nails. Turning, he faced the others.

"There're at least two dozen shells down there."

"What type of artillery are they?" Christopher asked.

"Can't be sure. Judging by the size, I'd guess twelve-pounders. British Royal Horse Artillery units used them in their cannons during the wars."

"Are they live?" said Bukolov.

"More than likely."

"Why are they here?" Christopher pressed.

Tucker considered it a moment. "I'm guessing because of the black powder inside them. The Boers were probably using the powder in the shells to reload bullets."

"The Boers had to be resourceful to survive," Bukolov commented.

So do we.

Tucker shifted around, swinging his legs toward the hole. Somewhere down below must be De Klerk's dark garden. "Doc, tell me again what to look for. Anything I should be watching for."

Bukolov shook his head. "I don't have the time to give you a crash course in botany. Nor have you read all of De Klerk's notes. I should go with you. Besides, why should you have all the fun?"

Christopher looked unconvinced. "Doctor Bukolov, perhaps you didn't hear Mr. Tucker correctly. Those shells are *live* and likely very unstable by now."

"I heard him, but how difficult can it be? I must simply avoid bumping into one of those things, correct?"

"That about covers it," Tucker said. "But it's tight down there. You'll have to crawl. It's going to be hard work."

"And I'm saving my stamina for what?" Bukolov asked. "I can do this. I have not come all this way to find LUCA only to blow myself up. God will guide my hand."

"I didn't know you believed in God."

"It's a recent development. Considering everything you've put me through."

"All right, Doc, let's do this."

"I'll need to gather a few things first. Tools, sample dishes, collection bags."

"Go get them."

As Bukolov hurried away, Tucker returned his attention to the array of shells down below. He told Christopher, "There's at least a couple of hundred pounds of black powder down there. It might just solve our explosives problem."

"Will it be enough to collapse this cavern system?"

"No, but it'll definitely take out this immediate set of caves."

Bukolov returned quickly, with everything collected into a brown leather kit with his initials on it. He eyed the hole.

"Gentlemen, I believe I could use some assistance getting down. It's not a far drop but now is not the time for a misstep."

Tucker agreed. He went first, using his arms to slowly lower himself, keeping well away from the first row of shells. Once down, he turned and helped ease Bukolov through the opening. Christopher held his arms, while Tucker guided his legs, planting the doctor's boots on firm footing.

"That should do, gentlemen." Bukolov ducked low, equipped now with his own headlamp. "Shall we proceed?"

Tucker crouched next to him. From here, there was only about four feet of clearance between the floor and the roof. The chamber extended in a gentle downward slope. The water, streaming down from above, trickled in small rivulets across the floor, carving the soft sandstone into tiny channels, like the scribblings of a mad god. The rows of shells were standing upright in the flatter and drier sections.

"We should follow the water," Bukolov said, pointing down the slope. "It's what we've been doing since we got here."

"I'll go first."

Dropping low, Tucker set the best course through the field of shells. He followed the trickles, wondering if he'd ever be dry again. The last pass through the deadly gauntlet required him to lie on his right hip and scoot through sideways. An inopportune thrust of an elbow set one tall brass round to rocking on its base. He was afraid even to touch it to stabilize it.

Both men held their breath.

But the shell steadied and went still.

Tucker helped Bukolov past this squeeze.

"I can do it," the doctor complained. "I may have gray hair, but I'm not an invalid."

Free of the artillery, they were able to slide next to each other and crawl onward. Slowly a soft light glowed out of the darkness ahead.

"Do you see that?" Bukolov asked. "Or are my eyes tired?"

Tucker shaded his headlamp with his hand. Bukolov followed his example. As the darkness ahead grew blacker, the glow brightened before their eyes.

Definitely something over there.

As Tucker set out again, the roof slowly dropped down on top of them, forcing them to their bellies. They slid alongside each other across the wet, sandy floor. Finally, the slope dumped them into a pool of water about a foot deep. It lay inside a domed chamber about the size of a compact car's cabin, with enough room to kneel up, but little more.

"Amazing," Bukolov said, craning his neck to stare around.

The arched roof glowed with a soft silvery azure, like moonlight, but there were no cracks in the roof. The light suffused from a frilly carpet of glowing moss.

"It's lichen," Bukolov said.

Okay, lichen . . .

"Some phosphorescent species. And look across the chamber!"

The pond they knelt in was shaped like a crescent moon, its horns hugging a small peninsula of sandstone jutting out into the water from the far wall. Atop the surface, a dense field of buttery-white growths sprouted about six inches tall. From bulbous bases, stalks formed thick flat-topped umbrellas, with fine filaments draping from them. They gave off a slightly sulfurous smell that hung in the still air.

"LUCA," Bukolov murmured, awed.

As they shifted closer, Tucker felt the cracks in the floor under his knees, sucking at the cloth of his pants, marking drainage angles for this pool. The smell also grew worse.

"It is okay to be breathing this?" Tucker said.

"I believe so."

Tucker wanted to believe so, too.

"They're exactly like the sketches from the diary," Bukolov said.

He had to admit the renderings by De Klerk showed a masterful hand.

The doctor splashed farther to the left. "Come see this! Look at where the field of bulbs and growths meet the wall."

Tucker leaned to look where he pointed. The bulbs and the edges of the mushrooms that touched the wall were a brownish black, as if burned by the glow of the lichen covering the wall.

"I think the lichen is producing something toxic

to the LUCA." Bukolov swung toward Tucker. "Here might be the secret of the kill switch."

Tucker felt a surge that was equal parts relief and worry.

Bukolov continued. "It's what I had hoped to find here. Something had to be holding this organism in check down here. It couldn't just be the isolation of the environment."

"Then collect samples of everything and—"

Bukolov knelt back and brushed his fingertips across the roof, causing the glow to darken where he touched. "You don't understand. We are looking at a microcosm of the ancient world, a pocket of the primordial history. I have so many questions."

"And we'll try to answer them later." Tucker grabbed Bukolov by the elbow and pointed from the collection kit over the man's shoulder to the field of growth. "Get your samples while you still can."

A sharp bark echoed to them—followed by a second.

Kane.

"Get to work, Doc," he ordered. "I'm going to find out what's going on."

Hurrying, he slid and crawled his way through the field of artillery shells and back to the water-fall chamber. He hauled himself out of the hole, and Christopher helped him to his feet.

"He just started barking," Christopher said.

In the pool of light cast by the single LED lamp, it appeared Anya hadn't moved. She was still tied securely. Kane stood next to her, but he was staring toward the twin shotgun tunnels.

"What is it?" Christopher asked.

"I don't know. Kane must have heard something."

Tucker remembered his earlier sighting of the Russian soldiers.

Anya called over to them. "It seems we owe you some thanks, Captain Wayne. We wouldn't have thought of this method without you. Upon your example in Russia, we decided to add another weapon to our arsenal."

She was staring at Kane.

Tucker suddenly understood her veiled implication.

Damn it, Anya, you are good.

The thought had never occurred to him. Barring technology, what was the best way to track someone?

Kane glanced back at him, clearly waiting for the order to pursue whatever he had sensed.

Tucker turned to Christopher. "Stay here and be ready to help Bukolov."

"Is there trouble?"

Isn't there always?

He pointed to Anya. "She moves . . . you shoot her."

"Understood."

Working quickly, Tucker crossed to their gear and prepared for the storm to come. He grabbed two spare magazines for his rifle, along with a red flare, stuffing them all into his thigh pockets. He then slung the AR-15 over his shoulder and picked up the Rover's plastic gas can.

Once ready, he headed for the tunnels with Kane on his heels.

It was time to test these old Boer defenses.

11:55 P.M.

Reaching the Cathedral, Tucker hurried across the stalagmite maze to the series of sandbag walls at the far end. He hurdled over the first two with Kane flying at his side—then he skidded to a stop at the third wall and dropped to his knees.

Echoing up from the crooked tunnel ahead, he heard a faint barking.

No, not barking—*baying*.

The enemy had come with hounds.

Kharzin must have sent his main body of troops, along with the dogs, straight to where he had hid the booby-trapped Range Rover. The other Russians—the ones he had spied upon earlier—were likely a smaller expeditionary force sent here to canvass the side trail as a precaution. No wonder they had seemed so lax and casual. But now that Tucker's trap had been sprung and his ruse discovered, Kharzin had returned here, bringing all his forces to bear.

But what was Tucker facing?

Only one way to find out.

He pointed to the tunnel. "QUIET SCOUT."

Kane jumped over the sandbags and dove into the shaft. Using his phone, Tucker monitored his partner's progress. Once Kane reached the straight corridor, Tucker touched his throat mike.

"HOLD. BELLY."

Kane stopped and lowered himself flat, well hidden by rubble.

Right now the corridor appeared empty with no evidence of trespass. The pile of rocks blocking the way outside looked untouched. So far, the hounds hadn't found this back door to the cavern system—at least not for the moment. But they would.

Through Kane's radio, the baying already grew louder.

Hurrying, Tucker began removing sandbags from the middle of the barricade. After creating a sufficient-sized hole, he wedged the gas can into the gap. He then replaced the sandbags, taking care to hide any trace of the can.

All the while, Tucker monitored the phone's screen, using Kane to extend his vision. Movement drew his full attention back to the screen. In the gray-green glow of Kane's night-vision camera, the slivers of light at the far end of the corridor began to break wider. More light blazed through as rocks were pulled away.

Shadows shifted out there.

They'd been discovered.

Tucker whispered to Kane, "QUIET RETURN."

The camera jiggled as the shepherd belly-crawled backward. After retreating for a spell, Kane finally turned and came running back. Moments later, he emerged and hurdled the sandbags.

Good boy.

After rechecking the placement of the gas can, Tucker pulled out a flare and jammed it between a pair of sandbags near the bottom. For now, he kept it unlit.

He turned to his partner. "STAY."

With a final rub along Kane's neck, he stepped over the sandbags, planted his rifle to his shoulder, and ducked into the shaft. He crawled until he was at the last corner of the crooked corridor. He kept hidden out of sight, peeking around the bend with his rifle extended. He quickly dowsed his headlamp and flipped the scope to night-vision mode. With his eye to the scope, he waited.

The first Spetsnaz appeared, peeking out from the straight passageway, bathed in the moonlight flowing from the open door behind him.

Tucker laid the crosshairs between the man's eyes and squeezed the trigger. The blast stung his ears. He didn't need to see the man crumple to know he was successful.

Tucker ducked away and retreated as the bullets peppered down the shaft, likely fired blindly by the second soldier in line. He knew the enemy dared not lob or fire a grenade into such a confined space, or it risked collapsing the very tunnel they had come to find and ruin any chances of reaching the prize. As far as they knew, this was the only way inside.

Still, he never trusted the enemy to think logically.

Especially with one of their comrades dead.

So he fled on his hands and knees.

If nothing else, the ambush would give the others pause, force them to move slowly, but it wouldn't last long.

He reached the end of the tunnel, regained his feet, and hopped over the first sandbag wall. Crouching down, he ruffled Kane's neck and did a quick inspection of the gas can and flare. Satisfied, he headed back over the series of sandbag fences.

As he hopped over the last one, a booming cry echoed from the far side of the Cathedral.

It was Christopher, calling from the mouth of the shotgun tunnels across the way.

"Tucker . . . watch out!"

40

Kane let out a deep snarl, leaped to his feet, and took off across the Cathedral floor, heading in Christopher's direction. For the shepherd to break his last command to *stay* could only mean one thing.

An immediate and real danger.

Tucker stared down the length of the dark Cathedral.

At the other end, a star glowed, marking Christopher's headlamp.

Between here and there lay a gulf of darkness. Kane vanished into it. Tucker lifted his rifle's scope and used its night-vision capabilities to pierce the blackness. Out there, he watched a figure dashing between the stalagmites. Kane rushed at full sprint toward the shape. The jittering flight of the other was difficult to track through the forest of tall rock.

Then the shape cleared a stalagmite, her face perfectly caught by the scope for the briefest instant—then gone as she dodged away, doing her best to stay in cover, knowing he was armed.

Anya.

Free.

How?

He caught another brief glimpse, watched her lift an arm, the flash of gunmetal in her hand, a revolver, the Smith & Wesson he had given to Bukolov.

Then gone again.

New movement to the left.

Kane.

Then he vanished, too.

Next came the gunfire.

Three shots in the dark, each muzzle flash an incendiary burst through his scope—followed by a strangled yelp that tore his heart out.

He watched a small shape skid across the floor, back into the glow of his headlamp, and come to a stop.

Kane.

Anya lunged out of the darkness, vaulted over the body, and came running straight at him, firing. Her first shot went wide. He shot back. Rock blasted behind her, his aim thrown off by the sight of Kane on the ground.

Undeterred, she fired again.

He felt a hammer blow on his hip that sent him spinning, pitching backward over the sandbags. He lost the rifle. He rolled, tried to rise to his knees, and reached for the weapon.

"Stop!" Anya shouted.

She was standing at the sandbag wall. The revolver was pointed at Tucker's head, only three feet away. He ignored her and lunged for his rifle. She pulled the trigger. He heard the click. Nothing else.

He had counted out her *five* shots, the limit of that Smith & Wesson model he had given Bukolov.

Not the usual six-shooter, Anya.

He grabbed the rifle, swinging it up—but too slowly, thinking he had the upper hand. He turned in time to see the revolver flying at his face, catching him across the bridge of the nose, momentarily blinding him with a flash of pain.

She threw herself over the sandbags and bowled into him.

They went down, her on top.

Tucker saw a glint of a black blade—one of the old Boer bayonets he had spotted when he first descended into the cave. She drove it in a sideswipe for his throat. Both as defense and offense, he head-butted her, his forehead striking her nose. The plunging bayonet struck the stone *behind* his head instead of his throat.

He rolled her, straddling her. He clamped her wrist and twisted until she screamed.

The bayonet dropped.

He snatched it and held the point to her throat.

She stared up, showing no fear.

Not of death, certainly not of him.

From their long journey together, she knew he couldn't kill in cold blood—no matter how much he wanted to.

A flick of her gaze was the only warning.

A shadow hurdled the sandbags behind him. The heavy weight struck his back, catching him by surprise and slamming him down atop Anya.

The shape tumbled off his shoulders and gained his four legs, wobbly, panting, dazed. Kane's lips curled in fury, his eyes fixed to his target. Even barely moving, his partner had come to his rescue, never giving up.

Tucker stared down at Anya.

Blood bubbled up around the bayonet plunged through her throat. When Kane had struck, with the sharp point poised under her chin, their combined weight had driven the blade home.

Her mouth opened and closed, her eyes stared in disbelief and pain.

"Tucker!" Christopher shouted again, sounding like he was running toward him.

"I'm okay! Go back with Bukolov!"

Tucker climbed off Anya, watching the pool of blood spread.

She no longer breathed; her eyes stared glassily upward.

Dead.

12:36 A.M.

He knelt and called Kane over to his side. The shepherd limped over with a soft whine and pressed himself against Tucker's chest. He ran his hands along Kane's belly but felt no blood. As he worked his fingers over the vest, the dog let out a wincing yelp.

"You're okay, buddy."

As gently as he could, he pried the flattened .38-caliber round from the Kevlar and tossed it away. He followed it with a hug.

Tucker then took inventory of his own damage.

Anya had clipped him with her last shot, tearing the flesh of his upper thigh. Blood soaked his pant leg, and the pain was coming on, but it was manageable for now. A few inches to the center and the high-powered .44 round would have shattered his hip, crippling him.

Such was the changeable nature of war, where life, death, disfigurement were measured by inches and seconds. He considered his own past. How many friends had he lost to the capriciousness of fate? Take a half step to your left and you get cut in half by an AK-47. A tossed grenade bounces to the right, and you live another day, but if it bounces to the left, your legs are blown off.

He felt an icy shudder run up his spine. His eyesight swirled. In some detached part of his mind, he thought: *classic symptoms of PTSD.*

He clung to that notion.

You know this enemy.

Tucker took a half-dozen calming breaths.

You're alive. Kane's alive. Get it together and do what you came here for.

Abruptly, Kane's ears perked up, accompanied by a low growl meant only for his ears.

Rustling rose from the tunnel.

He motioned for Kane to stay.

Clicking off his headlamp, he grabbed his rifle, rose to his knees, and found a break in the sandbags to peer through. Using his night-vision scope, he spied a Spetsnaz soldier edging toward the mouth of the tunnel, cautious, likely hearing the gunplay from a moment ago.

Tucker waited until he reached the tunnel's end

and shot him in the head. He followed it with a continuous barrage of fire into the tunnel to keep the others at bay. While doing this, he crossed forward, high-stepping the sandbags, knowing what he needed from the dead soldier.

He reached the corpse, clicking on his headlamp, and pulled the dead man's torso to the side.

Enemy fire blasted out of the tunnel, but he kept away from the direct line of sight. He quickly stripped off the man's portable radio. That's all he intended to grab, but he got greedy and yanked a couple of grenades off the man's tactical harness. He shoved the pilfered pair into his pocket—then he grabbed a third, pulled the pin, and threw it down the tunnel.

And ran.

He vaulted over the first wall of sandbags, stopping only long enough to yank the hidden flare's ignition loop, setting it sputtering to life. As he rolled over the second barrier, he dropped flat.

The grenade exploded, the flash bright in the darkness, the noise deafening.

Tucker gained his knees, stared back as smoke poured out, along with a sift of fine sand. The tunnel hadn't collapsed, but it would certainly discourage any more soldiers from coming through for a time.

Gathering Kane to his side, he fled across the Cathedral, his wounded leg on fire. By the time he reached the twin tunnels, his sock on that side was damp with blood. Exhausted, he reached the twin tunnels and sank to his rear with Kane.

Calling over his shoulder down the tunnel, he shouted. "Christopher!"

The young man appeared a moment later and knelt beside Tucker. "You are hurt."

"And Anya is dead. I'll take that deal. By the way, how did she get loose?"

"When Bukolov returned, I had to help him out of the hole. She came at us then. Caught us by surprise. She knocked me down and attacked Bukolov with an old bayonet she must have picked up. She tried to cut away the doctor's specimen collection kit and steal it. But he fought and the bag ripped open, scattering bulbs and sample dishes across the floor. She did succeed in grabbing Bukolov's gun. By the time I got to my rifle and fired at her, she was already running and gone."

"But how did she get loose to begin with?"

"Among her ropes, I found the ripped remains of her cast."

Tucker nodded slowly. During his fight with her, he hadn't noticed her cast was missing. While tying her up, he had bound her good wrist to her cast. He should've known better, but he never imagined her to be that tough and stoic. It had to be extremely painful to get the cast off, yet she showed not the slightest wince or bead of sweat.

With her back against the stalagmite and her hands hidden behind her, she must have slowly—using the fingers of her other hand and the rock's hard surface—broken through the plaster and worked the cast free. Afterward, she was able to tug her hands through the loose rope. From there, it was just a matter of waiting for the right moment to act.

"I'm sorry," Christopher said.

"Nothing to be sorry about. She was scary good. But I need a few things: two of the five-second chemical detonators and the first-aid kit."

As Christopher disappeared into the tunnel, Tucker put on the stolen headset and keyed the radio. "General Kharzin, come in. Are you there?"

There were a few seconds of silence, then a harsh voice answered. "This is Kharzin. I assume I am talking to Tucker Wayne?"

"That's right. I want to negotiate. We can all leave here with what we want."

"Which is what?"

"Against my advice, Bukolov wants to make a deal. A trade. Some of the LUCA samples for our lives."

"He has it then?" Kharzin asked. "He's found the source?"

"Almost," he lied. "He's in the tunnel digging as we speak. He sounds confident of success."

"Give me a few minutes to consider your offer."

That was a lie, too.

Tucker needed to teach the Russian a lesson before they could really talk.

Christopher reappeared, carrying the items Tucker had requested. "Thanks. Follow me."

He regained his feet and hobbled up the tiered steps to the right and dropped into the old Boer foxhole. He moved fifty yards along it. Christopher followed, carrying the supplies.

Once settled, Tucker pointed across the Cathedral to the small red glow, "Do you see the burning flare over there?"

"Barely, but yes."

"Put your rifle scope on the shaft entrance beyond it and tell me if you see anything."

With Christopher guarding, Tucker slit open his pant leg around the wound, then ripped open a QuikClot package from the first-aid kit and pressed it to the bullet gouge. He clenched his teeth against the burn and wrapped a pressure bandage around his thigh and knotted it in place.

He then took out the remaining half block of C-4 from his pocket. He divided what was left into two equal pieces. He returned one to his pocket, then shaped the other into a deadly pancake and carefully inserted a chemical detonator in its center. He passed the bomb over to Christopher.

"This half we'll use to blow the artillery shells."

"Hold on . . ." Christopher whispered. "I see movement. Two men, I think."

"Good. I'll take over. Take the C-4 back to the cavern and wait for me."

As he left, Tucker lifted his rifle and peered through the scope. A pair of Spetsnaz soldiers crouched at the entrance of the blasted shaft. They were in full body armor, weapons ready. Beyond them, another soldier crept out . . . and another. The last one carried an RPG launcher. An arm waved, preparing for a sweep of the cavern.

As if on cue, Kharzin's voice came over Tucker's headset. "Mr. Wayne, I have given your proposal some thought."

"And?"

"What assurances do I have that you will keep your word?"

"Hmm . . . good question." Tucker adjusted his

aim on the flaming flare, then lifted the crosshairs to where he had hidden the Rover's gas can. "This is my answer."

He squeezed the trigger. As the round struck the can, gasoline jetted from the bullet's holes, ran down to the flaming flare—and ignited. With a whoosh, flames engulfed the back of the Cathedral. The soldiers began screaming. Orange backlit shadows danced on the walls. After a few seconds, the screaming stopped.

Tucker spoke into his headset. "You heard?"

"Yes, I heard."

Kharzin had to learn this lesson. It was the Russian way. From his prior employment with Bogdan Fedoseev, Tucker knew how the general would respond to the inherent weakness expressed by Tucker's offer. As expected, he would try to gain the upper hand by force, to test how weak his opponent actually was.

Now he knew.

"General, I've had twelve hours to turn this place into a death trap for you and your men. If you want to keep sending your boys in, I'll be happy to keep killing them. But I don't think you came with a limitless supply."

"You set me up."

Tucker heard a note of respect buried in the outrage.

"Do we have a deal?"

Kharzin hesitated, then sighed. "We have a deal. What are your terms?"

"Let me check Doctor Bukolov's progress. I'll get back to you in ten minutes. Cross me again, General, and things will really start to get ugly. Do you understand?"

"I do."

"One last thing. Is Felice Nilsson with you?"

"And if she is?"

"She's part of the bargain. I want her."

"Why?"

"Take a guess."

"Well, as it happens, she's not with us. She had another assignment. And speaking of personnel, I want Anya returned untouched."

Tucker heard more than mere professional concern for a colleague in the Russian's voice. This was a personal matter for the general.

He knew better than to tell the truth.

"That can be arranged," he said.

"Then we have a deal."

"Stay by your radio, General."

Tucker signed off and hopped back down, one painful step at a time.

Though the back of the Cathedral still burned, he dared not leave his rear unguarded. He pressed his forehead to Kane's. "Sorry, buddy, but I need to ask even more from you."

Kane wagged his tail.

He pointed to the flames. "HOLD. WATCH."

The shepherd dropped to his belly and stared across the cavern, ready to watch for any further intrusions.

Ever his guardian.

12:55 A.M.

As Tucker limped back into the cave, Bukolov and Christopher joined him, both clearly wanting to know what the plan was from here.

"Have you secured your samples, Doc?"

"Yes, they're packed away. What now?"

"I told Kharzin we're willing to make a deal. We'd trade half of the LUCA samples for our lives." Bukolov opened his mouth to protest, but Tucker held up a hand. "I'm stalling for time. There are only two ways out of here. One we can't climb out since I pulled that rope. And the other is crawling with Spetsnaz. So we're going to have to make a third."

"How?" Christopher asked.

"Do you remember the first spot we dug—on the ravine wall outside?"

Both men nodded.

Tucker pointed across the cavern. "It's right on the other side of that wall. I estimate it's only three or four feet thick . . . mostly soft sandstone."

Bukolov looked there in dismay. "It would take us hours to dig—"

Tucker pulled the square of C-4 from his pocket. "But only seconds to blast through."

"Would that work?" Christopher said. "Truly?"

"It's our only shot."

So they all set to work. Tucker unfolded and handed Christopher one of the shovels and instructed him to dig a hole four feet off the ground, as deep as he could make it.

As he labored, Tucker prepared the new charge

and handed the C-4 patty to Bukolov. "Gently, Doctor. It's live. Just go stand by Christopher."

He then collected the first bomb he'd prepared earlier and planted it down the hole among the artillery shells.

With everything in motion, Tucker limped back over to the Cathedral and joined Kane. He put on his headset and keyed the radio. "General, are you there?"

After a few long seconds, he responded. "I am here."

"Bukolov has the samples."

"Good news."

"How many vehicles do you have?"

"Two."

"We're going to want one of them."

"I understand, considering the fate of your original vehicle." He heard the residual anger in the man's voice.

So at least his ruse with the Rover had worked.

Tucker asked, "Are both vehicles at the entrance to the cave?"

He pictured the SUV from earlier, parked in the canyon by the back door. As far as the Russian knew, that was the *only* entrance.

"Yes."

"Okay. We have wounded in here. Give me a few more minutes to get ourselves together, then I'll signal you to come in. You may bring two of your men as guards. So we're all on equal footing. I don't want any surprises. We'll make the trade in here, then you and *all* your men will get in one vehicle and drive off. Agreed?"

"Agreed. And you'll have Anya ready to travel."

"Yes. Stand by."

Tucker left Kane on guard and returned to the cavern. Bukolov was leaning against the wall, cradling the C-4 patty in his hands. "I am not enjoying this, Tucker."

"Hang in there. Christopher, how's it coming?"

Christopher stopped digging. "See for yourself. To be honest, I don't think we need that explosive. The sandstone is crumbling almost faster than I can chop at it."

Tucker examined the hole. It was already more than two feet deep.

"You're right. Over time, the moisture from this chamber must have weakened the stone, softening it. Keep going—but gently. I don't want to punch through quite yet. Doc, are you packed and ready to go?"

"I'm ready, but what am I going to do with this?" He raised the C-4 in his palms.

"It's okay to lay the C-4 patty down at your feet, just don't step on."

"I will step gingerly from here."

"Tucker, I am almost through!" Christopher called.

Tucker returned to his side and used a chisel to punch a hole through the wall. He pressed his ear to the opening and listened for half a minute. Satisfied no one was in this canyon, he widened the hole and peered out. Kharzin had all his men in the other gorge, guarding what he believed was the only entrance.

"Okay, everyone keep your voices low from here.

We don't want to turn any heads in this direction." He turned to Christopher. "Go ahead and widen the hole as quietly as you can, just large enough for both of you to climb through. Then I want you to take the packs and Kane and hightail it away from here; stay hidden and keep moving east. Kane can help you. I'll catch up and find you once I'm finished here."

"What are you going to do?" Bukolov said.

"I'm going to keep Kharzin looking at me, while you all make your escape. After that, I'm going to drop your C-4 patty down with the one I already planted among those artillery shells and run like hell. When those babies blow, this whole cavern will collapse in on itself."

Christopher whispered, "I'm finished."

"Then it's time for you all to vacate the premises."

Tucker helped gather their packs and drop them through the opening and out into the chilly night. He also gathered up Bukolov's abandoned bomb and repositioned it close to the hole in the floor.

With everything ready, he used the video feed on his phone to check on Kane, staring at the screen. All looked quiet out in the Cathedral, so he touched his mike and summoned his partner back to his side.

He gave Kane a warm greeting, then passed his phone to Christopher. "No matter what happens to me, keep hiking to last night's campsite and wait for your brothers. Once you're safely back over the border, hit number one on the speed-dial and ask for Harper. Tell her what's happened and she'll take it from there."

"I will."

"And take care of Kane."

"Tucker—"

"Promise me."

"I promise. He'll be like another brother to me."

"I couldn't ask for anything better."

Christopher extended his hand, shook Tucker's, then clambered through the hole and dropped low outside.

"Now you, Doctor," Tucker said.

Without warning, Bukolov wrapped Tucker in a bear hug. "I will see you out there, yes?"

"As soon as possible."

As Bukolov climbed out, Tucker knelt beside Kane. "You've done enough here, buddy," he said, his voice cracking. "I'm going to do this last part by myself."

Kane cocked his head and stared into Tucker's eyes. A soft whine flowed to him; he plainly sensed what was to come.

Tucker stood again and whispered, "Christopher, are you there?"

"I'm here."

He lifted Kane in his arms, gave him a final long squeeze, then guided him through the hole and into Christopher's waiting hands.

"I have him, Tucker. Good luck."

"You, too."

He waited for three minutes, making sure no shouts of alarm were raised as the others fled. He took an extra moment to cover the hole with a scrap of khaki tent canvas, securing the upper corners with duct tape. He didn't want the moonlight shining through the new window, giving away the ruse when he entertained guests in a few minutes.

He then crossed back to the Cathedral and tugged back on the radio headset. He kept his headlamp off, standing in the pitch darkness.

"General Kharzin."

"Yes, I'm here."

"You can come in."

"We are on our way."

1:58 A.M.

Keeping watch, Tucker raised his rifle and peered through the night-vision scope. After two minutes, the greenish haze of lights bloomed on the far side. Moments later, three men appeared. From their body posture, he could register the horror of finding the charred remains of their comrades. The trio stepped over the sandbags, only to discover Anya's body. They knelt there even longer, clearly calling for someone to collect her. Then they started across the Cathedral floor.

When they reached the halfway point, Tucker shouted, "Stop there."

The men halted.

Into his headset, Tucker said, "General, you're—"

The pain in the other's voice cut him off. "You told me Anya was still alive!"

"Let's call it even."

"It'll never be *even*. Never. She was my daughter."

Shocked by this revelation, Tucker felt a sickening twist in his gut. He remembered Anya talking about her father. He could still hear the buried pain in her words: *My father was in the Russian Army. He was a . . . a hard man.*

Tucker now wondered how much of that pain was feigned. He could only imagine what it was like to grow up with a father like Kharzin, to be used and groomed to be little more than a finely honed tool. He remembered that it had been Anya who had first suggested to Bukolov that she pretend to be the doctor's daughter. Perhaps that ruse had its roots here. To keep things easy, Anya simply shifted the lie about one father to another.

"I'm going to kill you," Kharzin said.

"I'm sorry for your loss, General. I truly am. And you certainly can come after me, but for now, do you want revenge or your LUCA samples?"

Kharzin didn't respond for a full ten seconds. His voice was tight with grief and fury. "We will settle this personal matter later then. But I promise you it will be settled. There will be an accounting."

"I look forward to it," Tucker said. "For now, come forward. Let's be done with this."

Kharzin and his two companions started walking, proceeding slowly, suspiciously. When they were thirty feet away, Tucker saw movement across the Cathedral.

"Halt," he yelled. "What is going on back there?"

One of the men glanced over to the commotion. "They are only collecting the bodies of my men . . . and my daughter. I will not leave them behind."

"Then keep coming," he said and added a lie.

"But be warned, I have other guns fixed on them if they try anything."

He took off his headset and began backing down the tunnel.

"Keep coming, General," he called out.

Tucker continued his retreat back to the waterfall cavern and didn't stop until he was a few steps from the hole.

Kharzin and his men entered the cave cautiously, searching thoroughly. The tallest man waved the other two to stand guard and continued forward alone.

This had to be General Kharzin. He was a bull of a man, stony-faced, much like his photos, but in person, he appeared younger than Tucker had expected.

Tucker raised the rifle level to the man's chest. "Nice to finally meet you, General."

Kharzin would not look at him, keeping his face averted, hard and angry. He simply thrust out his palm, even refusing to speak to the man who had killed his daughter. Perhaps not trusting himself to.

"Again, I am sorry for your loss," Tucker said.

The arm remained up, demanding. "Show me the LUCA."

Immediately, alarm bells went off in Tucker's head as the man spoke. The voice was *wrong*. He stared harder at the man's shadowy features. Though there was a resemblance to the photos he'd seen of Kharzin back in Istanbul, the man standing before him wasn't the general.

"Get on your knees!" Tucker shouted, shouldering his rifle. "Now!"

All three men knelt down.

Tucker put his headset back on. "General, this was a bad gamble."

"Did you really think I would risk handing myself over to you? And now none of this matters. Even in death, my beautiful girl did her job. She brought me what I wanted. I knew she would never fail me."

"What are you talking about?"

"You should have *searched* Anya after you killed her."

Tucker's belly turned to ice.

Kharzin said, "I'm kneeling beside my beautiful daughter right now. It appears Doctor Bukolov is missing one of his samples. Major Lipov, are you there?"

"I am here, General," the man said, speaking into his headset.

"Kill him!"

Lipov's arm shot behind his back.

Tucker shifted his rifle and fired, striking the man in the heart.

The two men on the slope yanked their guns up, but he was already moving as soon as he squeezed the trigger. The others opened fire, but he leaped sideways and slammed his heel down on the C-4 patty planted there—igniting its chemical fuse.

Five seconds . . .

With rounds ricocheting off the rock at his heels, he kicked the primed explosive down the neighboring hole and kept going.

Four . . .

Firing from the hip, he sprinted across the cavern for the canvas-covered hole.

Three . . .

He didn't slow and dove headfirst at the covering.

Two . . .

Ripping through the canvas, he sailed out the hole, landed hard on his palms, and rolled.

One . . .

He pushed himself to his knees, then his feet—and started running down the canyon.

Behind him he heard a *whomp*, followed by a second, sharper *boom*.

He kept sprinting as a string of firecrackers—the cache of artillery shells—began detonating.

Head down, legs pumping, he kept going.

Don't look back! Run!

The pressure wave hit him and sent him flying.

2:39 A.M.

Tucker landed in a heap, blinked hard, and spat out a mouthful of dirt, swearing under his breath. He had survived, gotten the others out safely—but still failed.

Kharzin had a sample of LUCA.

The rumble of engines echoed from the other canyon. The Russians were preparing to leave.

Tucker looked around. Behind him, the cliff face that he just jumped through showed little sign of damage, save for the gout of smoke and dust gushing through his exit hole. But he knew inside, that tiny microcosm of the primordial world was gone, incinerated.

But it was too little, too late.

He pictured Kharzin in one of those SUVs, clutching a buttery-white bulb.

Was there still time to catch him—and, more important, catch him by surprise?

Tucker would never make it out and around to the other canyon, and even if he did, he'd likely just be run over. Instead, he turned and headed back the way he had come, checking his pockets as he ran. He'd lost his rifle, so he would have to improvise. He sprinted, passing through the surge of smoke, and skidded to a stop beside the boulder steps that led up to the plateau. He scrambled like a monkey with his tail on fire. When he reached the top, he paused for a breath, picturing what lay below. He was now standing *atop* the cavern inside. If the blast there had weakened the structure, he might drop straight through.

Might, maybe, if . . . the hell with it.

He charged across the plateau toward the opposite canyon. As he neared the edge of the cliff, the rumble of the trucks ratcheted to twin roars. Tucker slid to a stop and looked down to see both of Kharzin's SUVs racing along the canyon floor, their headlights bouncing over the rock walls.

Tucker started running parallel to them, balanced on the cliff's edge: one eye on his footing, one eye on the SUVs. Somewhere directly ahead of him was the end of the cliff, the section shaped like a pig's snout. He ignored the voice in his head yelling for him to stop.

Instead, he ran faster and yanked out the two grenades he had stolen from the soldier he had shot. As he reached the cliff's edge, he dropped to his butt and began sliding down the steep slope of the snout. To his right, out of the corner of his eye, the first SUV raced past him. Skidding along, he pulled the pin with his teeth, but he kept the spoon pressed tightly.

Then he reached the blunted end of the snout and went airborne. The drop was only ten feet, but he was flying. He hit the ground hard and shoulder-rolled, hugging his limbs tightly, clutching the grenades to his belly. As his momentum bled away, he skidded to a stop and rose to his knees. He let the grenade's spoon pop and hurled it after the lead SUV as it swept past him.

Behind him, an engine roared. Headlights flashed over him. He spun to find the second SUV barreling straight at him. He dove right and rolled out of its way, barely making it. Flipping to his back, he pulled the pin on the second grenade and lifted his arm to throw—

Whomp.

The first grenade exploded, fouling his aim as he let loose with the second. The black chunk of armament bounced harmlessly past the second SUV's back bumper and rolled into the scrub. Escaping damage, the truck sped away, dropping down the ravine that led up here—and was gone.

Whomp.

Bushes blasted away, amid a choke of rock dust.

All that wasted fury . . .

Cursing, Tucker turned to the first SUV. Its right side was on fire, flames licking inside. From the cabin came screaming.

He ran toward the SUV, not knowing if Kharzin

was in this vehicle or the one that got away. There was only one way to know for sure. He ran to the far side of the burning SUV, where the flames were less intense, and yanked open the passenger door. Heat washed over him, accompanied by a few licks of fire that he dodged.

The driver lay slumped at the wheel, his back burning, his skin blackening and oozing. But his uniform marked him as a major, not a general. Same was true of the passenger. The second man had caught shrapnel in the chest and the side of his face. The man groaned and grabbed Tucker's wrist. His head turned, revealing a flayed cheek and an eye scorched black. His mouth opened, but only guttural sounds came out.

Tucker twisted his wrist, trying to free it from the man's viselike grip.

"*Nyet*," the man rasped finally. "*Nyet.*"

His other hand rose—clutching a grenade. He threw it over his shoulder into the backseat and held fast to Tucker, trapping him with a strength born of vengeance and pain.

Not hesitating, Tucker swung his fist and smashed it into the guy's face. As the man's head snapped back, he finally broke free and ran. He'd only taken a handful of steps when a sledgehammer struck him across the back.

Everything immediately went dark.

41

The world returned in fits and starts, fluttering pieces that lacked substance: a shadowy glimpse of a face, whispers near his ear, something cold poured through his lips.

Then something real: the lap of a warm tongue along his cheek.

I know that . . .

He forced his eyes to open, to focus, blinking several times, and found himself staring at a brown-black nose, whiskers, and the darkest amber eyes. The wet nose nudged him a few times.

He groaned.

"Sleeping Beauty awakes." That had to be Bukolov.

Tucker sensed he was somehow moving, bumping along, but his legs were immobile.

"Lie still, Mister Tucker," Christopher said as he hauled Tucker along in a makeshift travois, the sled made of branches and climbing rope.

Coming slowly alert, Tucker took in his surroundings. The sun was up, low in the sky, likely early morning from the residual chill. They were moving through forests that were too tall and thick for the upper highlands of the Groot Karas.

Nearing the foothills . . .

He finally pushed up on an elbow, causing the world to spin for a moment, then steady again. He spent another minute just breathing to clear the cobwebs from his head.

Kane sidled over, his tail wagging, a prance to his gait.

"Yeah, I'm happy to be alive, too." Tucker called to Christopher, "I think you've played oxen long enough, my friend. I can walk."

Christopher lowered the sled. "Are you sure?"

"I'll let you know when I'm back up on my legs." He reached out an arm. "Help me up."

They lifted him to his feet and held him steady as he regained his balance.

He looked around. "Where are we?"

"About a five-hour walk from the cavern," said Christopher.

Bukolov explained, "When we heard the grenades, we came as fast as we could and found you near the destroyed vehicle."

"I told you both to keep going," Tucker said. "Not to turn back, no matter what."

"I don't remember him saying that, do you, Christopher?"

"I'm sure I would have remembered that, Doctor Bukolov."

"Fine." He turned to Bukolov, his chest tightening as he relived the events of last night fully in his head. "Doc, where are your LUCA samples?"

"Right here in my satchel with the lichen—"

"Count them."

Frowning, Bukolov knelt down, opened his kit, and began sorting through it. "This isn't right. One is missing."

"What about the lichen samples?"

He counted again, nodding with relief. "All here. But what about the missing bulb?"

"Anya must have snatched it during the tumult of her escape. Kharzin has it now."

Her father . . .

"That is not good," Bukolov moaned. "With the resources at his disposal, he could wreak havoc."

"But he doesn't have the lichen. Which means he doesn't have the kill switch for controlling it."

Tucker pictured the burned bulbs and stalks that came in contact with the phosphorescent growth.

"And we do . . . or might." Bukolov looked determined. "I'll have to reach a lab where I can analyze the lichen, run challenge studies with the LUCA organism. Find out which component or chemical is toxic to our ancient invasive predator."

"Then that's what we'll do. We need that kill switch."

And soon.

10:02 A.M.

Two hours after they ditched the travois and slowly worked their way east toward their old campsite in the foothills, Kane came sprinting back from a scouting roam. He sat down in front of Tucker, stared up at him, then swung his nose toward the east.

"Something ahead," Tucker said.

Bukolov dropped back a step. "Bandits? Guerrillas?"

"Maybe. Christopher, you take the doctor into cover. Kane and I will go have a look."

Tucker followed the shepherd east down the next ravine to a string of low hills. He climbed one to gain a good vantage point and dropped to his belly.

Below and two hundred yards away, a lone SUV trundled across a salt flat, heading in their direction. He lifted his binoculars, but with the sun in his face, it took him a few moments to adjust. Finally, he was able focus through the vehicle's windshield.

He smiled when he recognized the driver.

It was the group's regular chauffeur.

Paul Nkomo.

"Fetch everyone," he instructed Kane.

As the shepherd raced back to the others, Tucker stood up and waved his arms over his head. The SUV stopped, and Paul leaned out the window. A glint of sunlight on glass told him Paul was peering back at him with binoculars.

Then a thin arm returned the wave.

Christopher joined Tucker a few moments later. He frowned down at the slow approach of his younger brother. "Little Paul. He was supposed to meet us at the campsite, but as usual, he didn't listen and kept heading this way. Always the impetuous one. Always getting himself into trouble."

Tucker glanced over at his bruised, sprained, and lacerated friend. "Yeah, right," he said sarcastically, "*he's* the troublemaker of the family."

8:42 P.M.

With the assistance of their regular chauffeur, Tucker and the others reached the Spitskop Game Park shortly after nightfall, where staff awaited them with food, drink, and first aid, including veterinary care.

A man in a clean smock who told wild stories of life as an African vet cleaned Kane's wounds, listened to his heart and lungs, and palpated the area of his ribs that had taken Anya's bullet. *Nothing broken just a deep bruise* was his verdict. Only after that did Tucker allow a nurse to stitch the four-inch-long gouge in his thigh.

Hours later, Tucker found himself visiting Bukolov in a private room. The doctor had his own unique needs that went beyond food and medicine. He had borrowed a dissecting microscope and some lab equipment from a group of scientists doing research locally. Though he and the others were due to depart for the United States at midnight, Bukolov had wanted to get a jump on his investigation into a potential kill switch for LUCA.

Tucker didn't blame him. After his brief encounter with General Kharzin, he knew they dared not waste a moment. He knew Kharzin would be working just as quickly to weaponize his prize.

"How are things going?" he asked Bukolov.

The man sat hunched over the dissecting microscope. A specimen of LUCA, sliced in half, lay on the tray under the lenses. "Come see this."

Bukolov scooted back to make room for Tucker to use the eyepiece.

He found himself staring at the edge of the specimen. The outer surfaces were peeling away like the layers of an onion, the tissue pinpricked with tiny holes.

"That is a sample of dying LUCA taken from the cave," Bukolov said.

Tucker pictured that glowing primordial garden.

"I'm fairly certain what you're looking at here is a chemical burn, something given off by the lichen. *What* that chemical is I do not know, but I have a hypothesis, which I'll get to in a moment. But first let me tell you about this mysterious glowing lichen." Bukolov looked at him. "Are you familiar with lichens?"

"Considering I thought it was moss . . ."

"Oh, my dear boy, no. Lichens are much more ancient and strange. They're actually made up of *two* organisms living in a symbiotic relationship. One is a fungus. The other is something that photosynthesizes."

"Like plants."

"Yes, but in the case of lichens, it's either an algae or cyanobacteria that pairs up with the fungus." He slid over a petri dish of the glowing organism. "In this particular case, it's a *cyanobacteria*. Cyanobacteria are three to four billion years old, same as LUCA. Both inhabitants of the strange and hostile Archean eon. And likely competitors for the meager resources of that time."

"Competitors?"

Bukolov slid the lichen sample and slices of bulbs resting in another petri dish next to each other. "You see, during that Archean eon, true land plants were yet to come. These two were the earliest precursors."

He tapped the lichen. "Cyanobacteria gave rise to modern chloroplasts—the engines of photosynthesis—found in today's plants."

He shifted the sample of LUCA. "And here we have the earlier common ancestor, the stem cells of the flora world, if you will."

Tucker pictured the microcosm of that ancient world found in the cave. "And the two were in competition?"

"Most definitely. In that harsh primordial time, it was a winner-takes-all world. And I believe it was that *war* that was the evolutionary drive for the rise of today's modern plants."

"And what we saw in the cave?"

"A snapshot of that ancient battle. But as in all wars, often common ground is found, cooperation necessary for short periods of time. What we witnessed below was an uneasy détente, two enemies helping each other survive in such strict isolation. Both needed the other to live."

"Why do you think that?"

"During my studies here, I found *healthy* LUCA bulbs with dead lichen melting deep inside, being consumed. I believe *living* lichen can kill LUCA and use it as some fertilizer source. While at the same time, as the lichen die and flake from the roof and walls, it feeds the LUCA below, raining down, landing on those broad mushroomlike growths."

"You're saying they were feeding off each other."

"That. And I'm sure the constant flow of water through the chamber brought a thin and steady flow of nutrients and biomatter to them as well. I also think their relationship was more nuanced, that they helped each other out in other ways. Perhaps the lichen's bioluminescence served some beneficial advantage to the LUCA, while the sulfur-rich gas—that stink we smelled down there—given off by the germinating bulbs helped the lichen in some manner. I don't know if we'll ever understand it fully. That unique relationship was formed as much by geology as it was biology."

"And how does that help us find the kill switch?"

Bukolov held up a finger. "First, we know that the *living* lichen can kill LUCA, but not *dead* lichen. So that knowledge alone will help me narrow my search for the chemical kill switch."

He raised a second finger. "Two, we know who won that ancient battle. LUCA was vanquished, all but this small isolated garden, leaving behind only its genetic legacy in the form of modern plants. But cyanobacteria survive today, going by their more common name: blue-green algae. Because of their versatility, you can find cyanobacteria in every aquatic and terrestrial location on the planet, from the coldest tundra to the hottest volcanic vent, from freshwater ponds to sun-blasted desert rock. They are masters of disguise, merging with other organisms, like with the lichen here, but also with other plants, sponges, and bacteria. They can even be found growing in the fur of sloths."

"It almost sounds like your description of LUCA from before. An organism with limitless potential."

"Exactly!" Bukolov stared over at Tucker. "That's because cyanobacteria are the closest living organisms to LUCA today. But from my studies—on a purely genetic scale—LUCA is a thousandfold more efficient, aggressive, and tough. Released today, unchecked and untamed, LUCA would wreak untold ecological havoc across every terrain on Earth, both land and sea."

"But, Doc, it *was* defeated in the past. Like you said, it didn't survive."

"And that's the second clue to discovering the kill switch: *Why didn't LUCA survive, while cyanobacteria did?*"

Tucker had to say he was impressed with how much Doctor Bukolov had learned in such a short time. He could only imagine what he could accomplish with Sigma's laboratory resources in the States.

"I have much to ponder," Bukolov said.

Tucker's satellite phone buzzed in his pocket. "Then I'll leave you to it."

He headed out of the room and answered the call.

"How are you all doing out there?" Harper asked as the line connected. He had already debriefed her about the past day's successes and failures. "Will you be ready to go at midnight?"

"More than ready."

"I talked to the military biologists over at Fort Detrick, and they wanted to know if Doctor Bukolov had any estimate on how long it would take Kharzin to weaponize his sample of LUCA."

"That's just it. According to Bukolov, it would take very little engineering. It's a ready-made weapon. All that he really needs to figure out is the method of delivery and dispersal."

"And how long would it take General Kharzin to do that? It seems Bukolov knows this man and his resources fairly well."

"No more than a week."

"Not much time," she said dourly. "And is Bukolov any further along with the kill switch?"

"Some progress, but any real answers will have to be worked out back in the States."

"Then I have one last question. From Bukolov's assessment of the general's personality, would Kharzin unleash this bioweapon without that kill switch."

"In other words, how much of a madman is he?"

"That's about it."

"I don't have to ask Bukolov." Tucker reviewed his dealings with Kharzin from Vladivostok to now. "He'll test it. And he'll do it soon."

PART IV

ENDGAME

42

With a puff of pressurized air, Tucker crossed out of an airlock into the BSL-3 laboratory. He wore a containment suit and mask, much like the men and women bustling within the long, narrow space. He imagined there were more Ph.D.s in this lab than there were test tubes—of which there were a *lot*. Across the vaulted space, tables were crowded with bubbling vessels, spiral tubing, glowing Bunsen burners, and slowly filling beakers. Elsewhere, stacks of equipment monitored and churned out data, scrolling across computer screens.

Orchestrating this chaos like a mad conductor was Abram Bukolov. The Russian doctor moved from workstation to workstation like a nervous bird, gesticulating here, touching a shoulder there, whispering in an ear, or loudly berating.

These poor souls are going to need a vacation after this.

The biolab lay in the basement of a research building on the grounds of Fort Detrick, a twelve-hundred-acre campus that once was home to the U.S. biological weapons program before it was halted in 1969. But that legacy lived on, as Fort Detrick continued to be the military's biodefense headquarters, home to multiple interdisciplinary agencies, including USAMRIID, the U.S. Army Medical Research Institute of Infectious Diseases. They were currently in the building that housed the Foreign Disease Weed Science Unit, part of the Department of Agriculture.

It seemed the U.S. military was already well aware of the national security threat posed by invasive species. Today that caution paid off, as they mobilized scientists from across the entire campus of Fort Detrick to tackle the threat posed by a weaponized form of LUCA.

Bukolov finally noted Tucker's arrival and lifted an arm, waving him to his side, which proved a difficult task as the doctor headed away from him, deeper into the lab. Tucker excused his way through the chaotic landscape, finally reaching Bukolov beside a table holding a five-liter glass beaker with a distillate slowly dripping into it from some condensation array. The liquid looked like burned coffee.

"This is it!" Bukolov expounded, his voice slightly muffled by his mask.

"Which is what?"

Tucker had been summoned here this morning by an urgent call from the good doctor, pulled from his temporary accommodations on base. He had been kept in the dark about what was going on at the labs here since they landed three days go in D.C. He and Bukolov had been whisked straight here under military escort.

"I was able to crack the lichen's code." He waved

a half-dismissive hand toward the team around him, giving them minimal credit. "It was just a matter of determining what it was in *living* lichen that became inert or dissipated after it died. I won't bore you with the technical details, but we were able to finally distill the chemicals that created that burn, that killed LUCA cells on contact. In the end, it wasn't just *one* chemical but a mix. A precise solution of sulfuric, perchloric, and nitric—all *acids*."

Bukolov's eyes danced, as if this last part was significant. When Tucker didn't question him, the doctor gave him an exasperated look and continued. "Not only is this the kill switch, but it explains *why* the genetically superior LUCA did not survive the Archean eon, but cyanobacteria did."

"What's the answer?"

"One of the turning points of that primordial era to the next was a shifting of atmospheric conditions, an acidifying of the environment. Remember, back then, oxygen-producing plants did not exist. It was a toxic hothouse. Acid rain swept in great swaths over the earth, tides and storms burned with it."

"And that's important why?"

"Cyanobacteria were perfectly equipped to deal with this acidification of the environment. They were already masters of organic chemistry, as evidenced by their control of photosynthesis, a process of turning sunlight into chemical energy. They rode that acid tide and adapted. Unfortunately, LUCA's mastery was in the field of *genetics*. It placed all its evolutionary eggs in that one basket—and chose wrong. It could not withstand that tidal change and stumbled from its high perch in the food chain. And like sharks sensing blood in the water, cyanobacteria took advantage, incorporating that acid into their makeup and burning LUCA out of the last of its environmental niches, driving it into evolutionary history."

Bukolov pointed to the steaming dark brown mire in the beaker. "That's the acid." A single drop splashed from the distillation pipe into the soup. "That's what passed for rain long before we were even single-celled organisms floating around in mud. What we're brewing here is a form of precipitation that hasn't been seen for 3.5 billion years."

"And that will kill LUCA."

"Most definitely." Bukolov stared at him. "But even still, we must catch any such environmental fires started by LUCA *early*, preferably as soon as they're set. Once it establishes a foothold and reaches critical mass, it will explode across an environment, a raging firestorm that even this ancient rain might not put out."

"So if we're too late stopping Kharzin, even this might not be enough."

Bukolov slowly nodded, watching the slow drip of acid. "The only good news is that we ran some preliminary estimates of the threat posed by the single bulb Kharzin possesses. In the long term, he could, of course, try to grow more bulbs, but that would take much patience."

"A virtue Kharzin is sorely lacking."

"In the short term, we estimate he could macerate and extract at best a liter or two of weaponized LUCA. But it's still enough to light a fire somewhere, a fire that would quickly become a storm."

So the only question remains: Where does he strike that match?

To answer that, Tucker had only one hope.

In the shape of a deadly assassin.

And so far, she was not being cooperative.

9:12 A.M.

"Felice Nilsson could have scrubbed her credit cards," Harper told him over the phone.

Tucker spoke to her as he crossed in long strides from Bukolov's lab and headed across Fort Detrick's campus for his dormitory. "Like I said from the start, Harper. It was a long shot."

Three days ago, he had informed Sigma about his radioed conversation with Kharzin and the conspicuous absence of a certain someone to that deadly party in the mountains of Africa. Kharzin had claimed Felice was on *another* assignment, which even back then struck him as odd. She had been Kharzin's point man in the field from the start, hounding Tucker since he'd first set foot aboard the Trans-Siberian Railway. Then as Kharzin's team closed in for the kill, she was suddenly pulled off and reassigned.

Why? And to where?

Tucker had proposed that perhaps Kharzin had pointed that particular blond spear in a new direction, sending her in advance to prepare for the next stage of his plan—and likely to execute it, too.

"It was a good idea," Harper said. "To search for her whereabouts by placing a financial tracer on her.

But so far we've failed to get any hits from the documents you photographed aboard the train. Not the four passports, not the five credit cards, not even the bank routing numbers you managed to find. She likely received a new set of papers."

Sighing, Tucker ran through his steps that day as he broke into her berth. He had carefully sifted through her belongings, photographed what he found, and returned everything to where he'd found them.

"Maybe I wasn't careful enough," he said. "She must have gotten wise to my trespass."

"Or she could have just gone to ground and is keeping her head low. We'll keep monitoring."

1:22 P.M.

Tucker briefly visited Bukolov after lunch and discovered the doctor was working with an engineer, devising an aerosol dispersal system for his acid solution, which to him looked like a backpack garden sprayer. But he heard phrases like *flow rate composition* and *contaminant filter thresholds*, so what did he know?

Bukolov had little time to chat, so Tucker left and decided to do something more important.

Standing on a windswept wide lawn, he hauled back his arm and whipped the red Kong ball across the field. Kane took off like a furry arrow, juking and twisting as the ball bounced. He caught up to it, snatched it in his jaws, and did a little victory prance back to Tucker's side, dropping the ball at his toes.

Kane backed up, crouching his front down, his hind end high, tail wagging, ready for more.

It was good to see such simple joy—though *obsession* might be the better word, considering Kane's current deep and abiding love for that rubber Kong ball. Still, the play helped temper the black cloud stirring inside Tucker.

If only I'd been more careful . . .

Tucker exercised Kane for another few minutes, then headed back to their dorm. As he crossed the lawn, his phone rang. It was Harper again.

"Looks like you have a future career as a cat burglar after all, Captain Wayne. We got a hit on Ms. Nilsson."

"Where?"

"Montreal, Canada. Hopefully you and Kane are up for a little more cold weather."

He pictured Felice's face, remembering Utkin in the sand, bloody and crawling.

"I'll grab our long johns."

43

Right back where I started . . .

Tucker stood on the hotel balcony, staring out at the frozen edges of Lake Huron. Snow sifted from a low morning sky. The rest of the view could best be described as *brittle*. It was below freezing with the forecasted promise of the day climbing a whole two degrees.

He'd started this adventure in Vladivostok, a frozen city by the sea.

And here he was again: cold and facing another assassin.

Bukolov called from inside the room. "Some of us don't have the hardy constitution of a young man. Perhaps if you close the balcony door, I won't catch pneumonia before your tardy guest arrives in the area."

He stepped back inside and pulled the slider and latched it. Kane lifted his head from where he curled on the bed.

"But for the hundredth time, Doc: you didn't have to come."

"And for the hundredth time: you may need my expertise. We have no idea how Kharzin plans to utilize his weaponized LUCA. And my solution has had no real-world field test. We may have to improvise on the fly. Now is not the time for inexperienced guesswork."

It had been two days since Sigma's cyber net had detected the credit card hit in Montreal. Unfortunately, Felice still remained a ghost, leaving only the occasional financial bread crumb behind: at a gas station outside of Ottawa, at a diner in the small town of Bracebridge. Her movements seemed headed straight for the U.S. border. Immigrations and Customs were alerted, but the northern border of the United States was an open sieve, especially in the dense woods nestled among the Great Lakes. She could easily cross undetected.

This was confirmed yesterday when they got a hit here in St. Ignace, the northernmost city in Michigan. Ominously, she had made a single purchase from the local Ace Hardware & Sporting Goods.

A plastic backpack sprayer.

Tucker stared toward their hotel room's closet. Inside rested the battery-powered chemical dispersant rig engineered by Bukolov and filled with his acid slurry.

Since then they had had no further hits indicating her whereabouts.

Was she still in town? Had she moved on?

Waiting in the wings, ready to mobilize in an instant, were *fourteen* two-person helicopter teams, each armed with their own canisters of the kill-switch solution. Six of these teams were located in Michigan; the other eight in the surrounding states.

Whether this was enough manpower or resources for the situation, Tucker didn't know, but he left it to Harper's best judgment. Harper feared that alerting the authorities at large would invariably turn into a brute-force manhunt that Felice would easily spot. If that happened, she would bolt, scrubbing those cards. They would never get a second chance at her. They had to do this right the first time and as surgically as possible.

So for now, the job of stopping Felice and her team—*of stopping LUCA*—fell to Tucker and the other quick-alert teams.

He hoped Harper's caution was not their downfall.

7:02 P.M.

As the sun sank toward the horizon, Tucker's phone finally trilled.

"We've got something," Harper said as soon as Tucker answered. "Picked up a report on a Harbor Springs police scanner. Fifteen minutes ago, a woman matching Felice's description, accompanied by three other men, were spotted stealing a speedboat from the marina. It was heading into Lake Michigan."

Tucker leaned over a map spread out on the coffee table. "Harbor Springs . . . that's thirty miles south of us."

"You're the closest team. Get to your extraction point. A helicopter is en route to pick you up."

Tucker disconnected. "Doc, we're moving!"

Bukolov was already heading for the closet. He grabbed the backpack holding their gear, including the dispersant rig. Tucker unzipped his duffel. He slid out a noise-suppressed Heckler & Koch MP-5 SD submachine gun, donned the gun's concealed chest rig, and harnessed the weapon in place. He then pulled his jacket on over it and shoved a Browning Hi-Power 9 mm into a paddle holster in the waistband at the back of his pants.

But his real firepower leaped off the bed and followed him to the door.

With Kane at their heels, Tucker and the doctor left the room and jogged across the icy parking lot. Off in the distance, helicopter rotors chopped the sky, coming in fast. The white-and-blue Bell 429 swooped over their heads, slowed to a hover, and then touched down.

As soon as the three of them had boots and paws inside, the Bell roared and sped upward. They banked hard over Lake Huron, passing above the Mackinaw City Bridge, and headed out across Lake Michigan.

Tucker tugged on a radio headset, and the pilot's voice came over it. "Fifteen minutes to Harbor Springs, gentlemen. I have incoming for you on channel five."

Tucker punched the proper frequency. "Up on channel five," he called over the rush of the engine.

Harper came on the line. "We have the make, model, and registration number of the boat. I gave it to the pilot. The last sighting put her on a heading of two-three-nine degrees. They should be passing the city of Charlevoix right about now. It's a fast boat, Tucker. Running at about forty knots."

"What's in front of it?"

"Mostly cargo traffic from the St. Lawrence seaway. The bulk of the ships are heading for either Milwaukee or Chicago."

"Carrying what?"

"I'm working on it."

Bukolov had his headset on. "I have an idea of what's happening here, Ms. Harper. I think Felice is targeting one of those cargo ships, one that's likely carrying something organic—fertilizer, seeds, even herbicide."

"What makes you say that?"

"Because it's what I would do if I were in Kharzin's shoes. He could not have produced more than a couple of liters of weaponized agent by now. Far too little to disperse via air. Such small amounts require him to *directly* contaminate a primary source in order to ensure suitable germination and propagation—but how do you get the most bang for your buck in such a scenario? Let's say Ms. Nilsson can contaminate a cargo of agricultural products and that ship docks in Chicago or Milwaukee or another major distribution hub—"

Tucker understood. "Planting season is starting throughout the Midwest. That infected cargo could incubate in the hold and then be spread throughout the nation's heartland." He imagined the havoc that would be wreaked. "Harper, what about the Coast Guard? Can we get them mobilized, to set up some sort of blockade? We can't let that ship reach shore."

"I'll sound the alarm, but I doubt we have enough

time. Doctor Bukolov, answer me this. What happens if the LUCA is introduced into a body of water?"

Tucker stared at the snow-swept lake racing under the helicopter, appreciating her concern.

"Simply speculating, much of the organism would survive. Lakes have plenty of vegetative matter to host or feed LUCA. This organism survived and thrived for millions of years during this planet's most inhospitable period. It's aggressive and highly adaptable. Nature always finds a way to go on, and LUCA is *Nature* at its most resilient."

"I was afraid you'd say that."

"What's got you worried, Harper?" Tucker asked.

"If Felice boards one of those ships and contaminates the cargo, we've got more ways to lose than win. If the ship is sunk or destroyed, LUCA still escapes."

Bukolov nodded. "Additionally, if the contamination does reach open water, it would be much harder to clean up with the kill switch."

"Then we need to stop Felice before she reaches one of those ships," Tucker said.

After signing off, he switched channels to the pilot, a young National Guard aviator named Nick Pasternak. "Give me all the speed you can, Nick."

"You got it. Hold tight."

The timbre of the engines climbed, and the Bell accelerated to its maximum speed. At 150 knots, the ice-crusted coastline rushed beneath them.

"Coming to Harbor Springs now," Nick called five minutes later. "The marina where your boat was stolen is on our nose, thirty seconds out."

"Once there, head out on the same bearing the boat took. Two-three-nine degrees. Then keep your eyes peeled. If they're still on this bearing, they've got a twenty-five-mile head start on us."

"I can close that in six minutes."

The helicopter passed over the frozen docks of the marina, turned its nose southwest, and headed out over the lake. As it raced away from the coast, Tucker watched the waters slowly change from green to blue. He strained for any sign of the stolen boat through the thickening snowfall.

Nick had better eyes. "Speedboat dead ahead! Make and model seem to be a match."

Tucker had to be certain. "Give us a close flyby."

"Will do."

The Bell swept down until it was a hundred feet off the water, speeding low over the water.

"Boat coming up in five seconds," Nick reported. "Four . . . three . . ."

Tucker pressed his face against the window. The speedboat appeared out of the storm mist. As the helicopter buzzed over it, he saw the deck was empty, no one behind the wheel.

What the hell . . .

7:33 P.M.

Bukolov stared out his window. "Nobody's aboard."

Ignoring him, Tucker radioed the pilot. "Keep on this bearing!"

The doctor turned to him. "Does that mean they already boarded one of the cargo ships?"

"Most likely."

Nick called out, "Cargo ship dead ahead!"

"I need her name," Tucker replied. "Can you get us close to—?"

"Yep, hold on. Descending."

"But don't crowd her!" Tucker warned.

If Felice was aboard that ship, he didn't want her spooked—at least not yet.

"I understand. I'll keep us a half mile out."

Tucker picked up a set of binoculars and focused on the boat.

Off in the distance, the gray bulk cut slowly through the storm, led by a tall well-lit wheelhouse, flanked by flying bridges. He imagined the pilot and crew inside there navigating the ship through the growing weather. At the stern rose a three-level superstructure, less bright. Between the two castles spread a flat deck interrupted by cranes and a line of five giant square cargo hatches. He adjusted his view down and read the name painted on the cargo ship's hull.

He radioed it to Harper. "I think we've got her. *Motor Vessel Macoma.* I need whatever you can get on her. Especially her cargo."

"Stand by." She was back in two minutes: "*Motor Vessel Macoma.* Capacity is 420 deadweight tons. It's bound for Chicago carrying fertilizer-enhanced topsoil and compost for agricultural use."

Tucker turned. "Doctor, would that fit the bill?"

"Yes . . ." Bukolov confirmed. "Such material would make the perfect incubation bed for LUCA."

Harper remained more cautious. "Tucker, are you sure this is the ship?"

"We spotted an abandoned speedboat, adrift a few miles astern of the *Macoma*. Listen, Harper, we're not going to find a neon sign guiding us. We have to roll the dice."

"I hear you. You're on scene. It's your call."

"How soon can we expect any help?" Tucker asked.

"The closest team to you is still forty minutes out. I'm working on the Coast Guard."

"Then I guess we're going in. If Felice is smart, and I know she is, she'll be rigging that ship with explosives. So the sooner we can intercede, the better."

"Then good luck to the both of you."

Tucker switched channels. "Nick, we need to get aboard that ship. Can you do it?"

"Watch me," he said, with the confidence of the very young and very foolish.

Nick descended again, a stomach-lurching drop to thirty feet. He banked until the chopper was dead astern to the *Macoma*. The dark ship filled the world ahead of them. He moved slower, closing the gap, buffeted by the storm's crosswind. The Bell's nose now lingered mere feet from the ship's rear railing.

Nick radioed his plan from here. "I'm gonna pop us higher, bring us to hover over the roof of that aft superstructure. You'll have to jump from there."

Tucker studied the towering castle rising from the ship's stern. The superstructure climbed three levels, its lights glowing through the snow.

"Go for it," he said.

"Hang on."

Nick worked the cyclic and throttle, and the Bell

shot straight up. Fighting the winds, the helicopter glided forward, bobbling, struggling.

Oh, God . . .

Bukolov agreed. "Oh, God . . ."

The landing skids bumped over a top railing—then came the sound of steel grinding on steel as the skids scraped across the roof. Crosswinds skittered the craft.

Crack . . . crack . . .

From the shattering blasts, Tucker thought something had broken on the helicopter.

Nick corrected him. "Pulling out! Somebody out there with a gun, taking potshots at us."

The helicopter lifted, rising fast.

Tucker unbuckled and leaned forward, searching through the cockpit's Plexiglas bubble. A man, cloaked in storm gear, stood on the roof deck below. He slung his rifle, picked up another weapon, and rested it atop his shoulder, something larger and longer.

A grenade launcher.

Tucker yelled, "Hard left, nose down!"

Nick worked the controls, pitching the nose and leaning into a bank.

Too late.

Below, a flash of fire, a trailing blast of smoke—

—and the rocket-propelled grenade slammed into the Bell's tail rotor, sending the bird into a hellish spin.

Tucker got pitched left and landed in a heap in the cockpit's passenger seat.

Nick screamed next to him, fighting for control, "Tail strike, tail strike . . . Ah, Jesus!"

Tucker shouted and pointed to the cargo ship's main deck. "Cut the engines! Crash us! We're going down anyway. Do it!"

"Okay . . . !"

"Doctor, grab Kane!"

"I have him."

Nick worked the cyclic, bringing the nose level, then took his hand off the throttle and flipped switches. "Engines off! Hold on!"

As the roaring died around them, the Bell dropped, falling crookedly out of the sky. Suddenly a tall davit crane loomed before the windscreen. Nick jerked the cyclic sideways, and the Bell pivoted. The tail section swung and slammed against the davit tower, whipping the helicopter around as it plummeted to the deck.

With a bone-numbing thud, the helicopter hit, bounced once on its skids, then slammed its side into the aft superstructure. The still-spinning rotor blades chopped against the steel, shearing off and zipping across the deck like shrapnel, severing cables and slicing off rails.

Then all went silent, save the spooling down of the Bell's engine.

44

"Who's hurt?" Tucker called out as he regained his senses after the wild plummet and crash.

"Bleeding," Nick mumbled, dazed. "My head. Not bad."

"Doc?"

"We're okay, Kane and I . . . I think."

Tucker untangled himself from his spot on the floor and crawled back to the passenger compartment. He checked on Kane, who jumped up and greeted him.

Bukolov gasped, aghast. "Dear God, man, the blood . . . your ear . . ."

Tucker carefully probed the injury. The upper part of his left ear hung down like a flap.

"Grab that first-aid kit behind—"

Nick shouted from the cockpit, "Another guy with a gun!"

"Where?"

"Left side! On the port side! Coming up the deck by the railing!"

Means I have to be on the starboard side . . .

Tucker crawled across Bukolov's legs and shoved at the side door. It was jammed. Tucker slammed into it with his shoulder a few times until the door popped open. He hurled himself out and landed hard on the roof of the cargo hold. Staying flat, he rolled away from the man climbing to the deck. As he reached the starboard edge of the raised cargo hold, he fell the yard down to the main deck.

He landed on his back, unzipped his jacket, and drew out his MP-5 submachine gun.

Bullets ricocheted across the cargo hold as the man on the far side took potshots at him from across its roof.

Tucker shouted to Kane, "CHARGE SHOOTER!"

He heard the shepherd land on the roof and begin sprinting toward the gunman. Tucker waited two beats—then popped up out of hiding. As planned, the shooter had turned toward the charging dog. Tucker fired twice, striking the guy in the chest and face.

One down . . .

"COME!" he called to Kane.

The shepherd skidded on the snow-slick surface, turned, and ran to him, jumping down beside Tucker.

Now to deal with the man who had shot their bird out of the air. The assailant with the RPG launcher had been atop the aft superstructure. But where was—?

Boots pounded to the deck from the ladder behind Tucker. He swung around. The assailant had his weapon up—but pointed at the helicopter. During the man's frantic climb down, he must have failed to witness the brief firefight, and now he missed Tucker lying in the shelter of the raised cargo only yards away in the dark.

Small miracle, but he'd take it.

He fired a three-round burst into the man's chest, sprawling him flat.

Two down . . .

That left Felice and how many others? The police report mentioned three men accompanying her on the boat, but were there more? Did she have other accomplices already on board, mixed with the crew, to expedite this takeover? Regardless, his most pressing question at the moment remained: *Where was she?*

He poked his head up and took five seconds to get the lay of the land. Their helicopter had crash-landed against the aft superstructure and on top of the rearmost cargo hold. He turned and stared down the length of open deck between him and the main bridge, studying the ship's wheelhouse and its two flying bridges.

The first order of business was to reach there, try to take control of the ship.

There was only *one* problem.

Between him and the bridge stretched two hundred yards of open deck. Aside from the other four raised cargo holds and a handful of davit cranes down the ship's midline, there was no cover.

Which meant they had *two* problems.

Somewhere aboard this ship was an expert sniper.

Tucker called toward the helicopter, "Nick . . . Doc!"

"Here!" the men called in near unison from inside the craft.

"Think you can make it over to me?"

"Do we have a choice?" Bukolov yelled back.

It seemed to be a rhetorical question. Both men immediately vacated the broken bird at the same time. Nick helped Bukolov, as the doctor was weighted down by the backpack over his shoulders. They ran low and fast together. Nick pushed Bukolov over the roof's edge to the deck, then jumped down after him.

They both collapsed next to him.

Nick had brought the first-aid kit with him and passed it over. "Looks like you could use this."

Tucker quickly fished out a winged pressure bandage. Using the pad, he pressed his ear back in place, then wound the strips around his forehead and knotted it off.

"What's this I overheard about the ship may be blowing up?" Nick asked as he worked.

"Just a possibility. The good news is that it hasn't happened yet. The bad news is that there's a highly trained sniper on board, and unless I miss my guess, she's probably looking for a decent perch to—"

A bullet zinged off the cargo hold beside Tucker's head.

They all dropped lower.

And there she is . . .

He rolled to face the others, while keeping his head down. "Nick, you stay put with the doctor."

"Wait! Do you feel that?" Bukolov asked.

Tucker suddenly did: a deep shuddering in the deck. He knew what that meant.

"The engines are picking up speed," he said. "And we're turning."

Tucker had spent the last two days studying a map of Michigan's Upper Peninsula. In his mind's eye, he overlapped the *Macoma*'s approximate position, picturing the ship slowly swinging to port. He suddenly knew *why* the ship was turning.

He yanked out his satellite phone and dialed Harper, who picked up immediately. "She's here!" he said. "On the *Macoma*. And she knows she's been exposed and knows the ship will never make Chicago now that the alarm has been raised. So she's gone to Plan B and is heading straight for land, to try to run this ship into the ground."

It also explained why her forces hadn't overwhelmed Tucker and the others by now. She and her remaining teammates must have turned their attention to the bridge and likely entrenched themselves there to keep anyone from thwarting them.

"If Felice is truly attempting to crash the ship," Harper said, "that might be good news."

"Good? How?"

"It means she hasn't had time to set up any explosives . . . or maybe she doesn't have any. Either way, I'm vectoring all teams to you now. The State Police and Coast Guard won't be far behind us. Still no one will reach you for another twenty minutes."

"We don't have that much time, Harper."

"Do what you can to delay her. Cavalry's coming."

Tucker disconnected.

"How long until we hit the coastline?" Bukolov asked after eavesdropping on the conversation. He crouched, hugging his body against the cold and snow.

"Twenty, maybe twenty-five minutes at most."

Tucker needed to get the others somewhere safer. A bit farther up the deck was a thick enclosed hinge for the cargo hold. It was only two feet high, but it offered additional shelter both from the wind and from direct view of the main bridge's wheelhouse, where Felice was surely perched.

"Follow me, but stay low," he said and got everyone into that scant bit of cover.

Nick clutched Tucker's elbow. "I was born and raised in Michigan. If this ship is heading to shore around here, that'll put them in Grand Traverse Bay, headed straight for Old Mission Point. The rocks there'll rip the hull to shreds."

"Must be why she chose that course," Bukolov said.

Tucker nodded grimly. "Doc, stay here with Kane, prep your dispersal rig, and do your best not to get shot. Felice is holed up there in the forward wheelhouse, with who knows how many others. She intends to make sure this ship stays on course for those rocks. I have to try to get to her before that happens."

Tucker also had to assume one or more of the holds was already contaminated by Felice and her team. Back at Fort Detrick, he had trained Kane to lock on to the unusual sulfurous smell of LUCA. But before that search could commence, Tucker first had to clear the way.

He poked his head an inch above the cargo hold's lid, aimed the MP-5's scope at the wheelhouse, then dropped down again. The wheelhouse had three aft-facing windows. They all appeared untouched, which meant Felice had probably fired upon them from one of its two open flying bridges—one stuck out from the port side of the wheelhouse, the other from the starboard, the pair protruding like the eyes of a hammerhead shark.

Perhaps he could use this to his advantage.

"What's your plan?" Bukolov asked.

"Run fast and hope she misses."

"That's not a plan. Why not go belowdecks and stay out of sight?"

He shook his head. "Too easy to get lost or boxed in, and I don't know how many men she's got."

His only advantage was that Felice would be surprised by his frontal assault. How much time that surprise would buy him was the big question.

Tucker took a deep breath and spoke to the others. "Everyone stay here. When the coast is clear, I'll signal you." He ruffled Kane's neck. "That means you, too, buddy."

Kane cocked his head, seemingly ready to argue.

Tucker reinforced it with an order, pointing to Nick and Bukolov. "HOLD AND PROTECT."

He stared across the open deck.

But who's going to protect me?

8:04 P.M.

Tucker took a few deep breaths—both to steady his nerves and to remind himself that he was alive and should stay that way.

Ready as he was ever going to be, he coiled his legs beneath him, then took off like a sprinter, a difficult process with the snow and wind. But the darkness and weather offered him some cover, and he was happy to take it. All the while, he kept a constant watch on the wheelhouse for movement.

Clearing the rearmost cargo hold, he shifted a few steps to the left and ran across the deck toward the cover of the next hold. He was twenty feet from it when he spotted movement along the flying bridge on the starboard side. He threw himself in a headfirst slide and slammed against that next hold's raised side.

A bullet thudded into the lid above his head.

Not good.

He crawled to the right and reached the corner of the cargo hold and peeked around—just as another round slammed into the steel deck beside his head. He jerked back.

Can't stay here . . .

Once a sniper had a target pinned down, the game was all but won.

He crawled left, trying to get as far out of view of the starboard bridge wing as possible. When he reached the opposite corner, he stood up and started sprinting again, his head low.

Movement . . . the *port* bridge wing, this time.

Felice had anticipated his maneuver, running from the starboard wing, through the wheelhouse, to the port side, but she hadn't had time to set up yet.

Tucker lifted his MP-5 submachine gun and snapped off a three-round burst while he ran. The bullets sparked off a ladder near a figure sprawled atop the wing. Dressed in gray coveralls, the sniper rolled back from Tucker's brief barrage. He caught a flash of blond hair, the wave of a scarf hiding her face.

Definitely Felice.

Tucker kept going, firing at the wing every few steps.

Movement.

Back on the *starboard* bridge wing.

Felice had crossed through the wheelhouse again.

Tucker veered to the right, dove, and slammed into the third hold's edge, gaining its cover for the moment.

Three holds down, two to go.

He stuck his MP-5 over the edge and fired a burst toward the starboard wing—then something slapped at his palm. The weapon skittered across the deck. He looked at his hand. Felice's bullet had gouged a dime-sized chunk from the flesh beneath his pinkie finger. He stared at it for a moment, dumbfounded, and then the blood started gushing. Waves of white-hot pain burst behind his eyes and made him nauseated.

Sonofabitch!

He gasped for breath, swallowing the pain and squeezing the wound against his chest until the throbbing subsided a bit. He looked around. The MP-5 lay a few feet away, resting close to the railing.

As if reading his thoughts, Felice put a bullet into the MP-5's stock. His weapon spun and clattered—then went over the ship's edge, tumbling into the water.

Felice shouted, muffled by her scarf. "And that, Tucker, is the end!"

45

Tucker tried to pin down the direction of her voice, but it echoed across the deck, seeming to come from all directions at once. He didn't know where she was. Unfortunately, the same couldn't be said for Felice. She had her sights fixed on him. Even a quick pop-up would be fatal.

He still had his Browning in its paddle holster tucked into his waistband, but the small-caliber pistol at this distance and in this weather was as useless as a peashooter.

With his heart pounding, he tried to guess Felice's approximate position. She was likely still on the starboard wing of the bridge, from where she'd shot both his hand and the MP-5. Considering him weaponless and pinned down, Felice had no reason to move. She wouldn't give up that advantage.

On the other hand, she seemed talkative and overconfident. First rule in the sniper's handbook: *You can't shout and shoot at the same time.*

Tucker yelled over to her, "Felice, the Coast Guard knows your course! They're en route as we speak!"

"Makes no difference! The ship will crash before—"

Tucker jumped up and mounted the top of the cargo hold lid. He sprinted directly toward Felice, toward the starboard wing. As he'd hoped, in replying to his taunt, she'd lifted her scarf-shrouded head from the weapon's stock—breaking that all-important *cheek weld* snipers rely upon. She tucked back down.

He dodged right—as a bullet sparked off the metal by his heels—and in two bounding steps, he vaulted himself off the lid, rolled into a ball across the main deck, and crashed into the next cargo hatch, finding cover again.

"Clever!" Felice shouted. "Go ahead . . . try it again!"

No thanks.

He had one hatch to go before he could duck under the wheelhouse bulkhead as cover. To reach there, he had no good choices and only one bad—an almost unthinkable option.

Not unthinkable—just heartbreaking.

But he couldn't let the LUCA organism escape.

Using his left hand, Tucker drew the Browning from its paddle holster. He squeezed his eyes shut, then shouted above the wind.

"KANE! CHARGE TARGET! FAST DODGE!"

The loud command strikes Kane in the heart. Up until then, he has heard the blasts, knows his partner is in danger. He has strained against the last order; it still blazes behind his eyes: HOLD. Another's hand has even grasped the edge of his vest, reeking of fear, sensing his desire.

But the shout finally comes. He leaps the short obstruction, ripping out of those fingers. Wind, icy and full of salt, strikes his body hard. He ducks his head against it, pushing low, getting under the wind. He sprints, finding traction with his rear pads to propel him forward.

He obeys the order, the last words.

. . . FAST DODGE.

As he flies across the deck, he jinks and jukes. He makes sudden shifts, feinting one way and going another. But he never slows.

He races toward where his ears had picked out the blasts. Nothing will stop him.

Tucker heard Kane pounding across the deck. His heart strained toward his friend, now a living decoy, sent out by his own command to draw deadly fire. He regretted the order as soon as it left his lips—but he didn't recall it.

It was too late now. Kane was already in the line of fire. The shepherd knew his target, knew he needed to evade, but would it be enough? Were Kane's reflexes faster than Felice's?

Miss . . . miss . . . dear God, miss . . .

From the starboard bridge wing, a single shot rang out. Kane had drawn her fire, her attention . . .

Good boy.

Tucker popped up, took aim on the starboard wing, and started running that way. Felice crouched up there, rifle up to her shoulder.

He shouted to Kane. "TAKE COVER!"

. . . .

Kane instantly reacts to the new order and pivots off his left front paw. He slides on the wet, icy deck, up on his nails, spinning slightly to slam into the next raised metal square.

He stays low.

He ignores the searing pain.

But the blaze of it grows.

Felice had heard Tucker's shouted order. She pivoted toward him, bringing her rifle barrel to bear, her scope's lens glinting for a flash through the storm.

Tucker fired, three quick shots in that direction with no real hope of hitting her. The rounds pounded into the steps and railing around Felice. Not flinching, she pressed her eye to the scope.

"CHARGE TARGET!" he screamed.

Kane pushes the pain deep into his bones and lunges back out of hiding. He runs straight, gaining speed with each thrust of his back legs, with each pound of his front.

He stays low against the sleet and snow, his entire focus on the steel perforated steps leading up. His target lurks above, in hiding, and dangerous.

Still he runs forward.

Then a new order is shouted, but he does not know this word. It flows through him and away, leaving no trace.

As meaningless as the wind.

So he keeps running.

• • • •

"KILL!" Tucker hollered, using all his breath.

To his right, Kane passed his position and raced toward the starboard stairs, taking no evasive action as ordered. The shepherd sprinted along the deck, his head down, his focus fixed on the objective. He was pure muscle in motion, an instinctive hunter, nature's savagery given form.

"KILL!" Tucker shouted again.

It was a hollow, toothless order—the word had never been taught to Kane—but the command was not meant for the shepherd, but for Felice. It was intended to strike a chord of terror in Felice, igniting that primal fear in all of us, harkening to a time when men cowered around fires in the night, listening to the howling of wolves.

Tucker continued his sprint across the cargo hatch, firing controlled bursts in her direction. Felice shifted back, lifted her face from the stock, and glanced to her left, toward Kane.

The shepherd had closed to within twenty feet of the steps and was still picking up speed.

Felice swung her rifle around and began tracking the shepherd.

Firing upward, Tucker covered the last few feet of the cargo hatch, leaped off, and headed for the shelter of the wheelhouse bulkhead.

"KANE! BREAK TO COVER!"

Crack! Felice shot as Tucker's body crashed into the bulkhead. He bounced off it and stumbled along its length until he was in the shadows beneath the starboard bridge wing. He pointed his gun up, searching through the ventilated steel, looking for movement above.

Nothing.

He peeked behind him.

No sign of Kane.

Had his last order come in time?

No matter the dog's fate, Kane had done as asked, allowing Tucker to close the gap and get inside Felice's bubble. Her primary advantage as a sniper was gone. Now she was just another soldier with a rifle.

Which was still a dangerous proposition.

She was up there, and he was down here—and she knew it. All she had to do was wait for Tucker to come to her.

With his gun still trained on the wing above him, Tucker slid over to a neighboring hatch, one that led into the main bridge's tower. He tried the handle: *locked*. He slid farther around the bulkhead, searching for another.

As he stepped cautiously around an obstruction, leading with his Browning, a dark shape lunged toward him. He fell back a step, until he recognized his partner.

Kane ran over to Tucker, panting, heaving.

Relief poured through him—until he saw the bloody paw print in the snow blown up against the bulkhead.

Buddy . . .

He knelt down and checked Kane. He discovered the bullet graze along his shoulder. It bled thickly, matting the fur, dribbling down his leg. He would live, but he would need medical attention soon.

A growl thundered out of Kane.

Not of pain—but of *warning*.

Behind Tucker, the hatch handle squeaked, and the door banged open against the bulkhead. He spun, bringing the Browning up, but Kane was already on the move, leaping past Tucker and onto the man in three bounds. The shepherd clamped on to the hand holding the gun and shook, taking the assailant down with a loud crack of the guy's forearm.

The pistol—a Russian Makarov—clattered to the deck.

Tucker stepped to the fallen man and slammed the butt of his Browning into his temple. He went limp—only then did Kane release his arm.

"Good boy," he whispered. "Now HOLD."

Tucker moved to the hatchway and peeked past the threshold. Inside was a corridor leading deeper into the bridge's superstructure, but to his immediate right, a bolted ladder climbed up toward the wheelhouse above.

Then came a clanking sound.

A grenade bounced down the ladder, banked off the wall, and landed a foot from the hatch.

Crap . . .

He backpedaled and stumbled over the splayed arm of the downed assailant. As he hit the deck hard, he rolled to the right, to the far side of the hatch.

The grenade exploded, the blast deafening.

A plume of smoke gushed from the doorway, along with a savage burst of shrapnel. The deadly barrage peppered into the steps leading up to the bridge wing, some pieces ricocheting back and striking the wall above his body.

Both he and Kane remained amazingly un-scathed.

Tucker strained to hear, perhaps expecting some final taunt from Felice—but there was only silence. She had the upper hand, and she knew it.

If that's how you want to play this . . .

8:18 P.M.

Working quickly, Tucker holstered his Browning and returned to the unconscious man. He slipped out of his own hooded parka and wrestled the man into a seated position. He then forced his coat over the man's torso, tugging the hood over his head.

The man groaned blearily but didn't regain his senses.

Straightening, Tucker hauled his limp body over a shoulder and carried the man to just inside the hatch, leaning him against the bulkhead. He took a step past him—then leaned forward, grabbed the ladder railing, and gave it a tug.

The aluminum gave a satisfying squeak.

Immediately, he got a response.

Clang . . . clang . . . clang . . .

The grenade dropped, bounced off the last step, and rolled toward him.

Twisting around, he vaulted over the seated man and dodged to the left of the hatch. The grenade exploded. More smoke blasted, and shrapnel flew, finding a target in the man at the door.

As the smoke rolled out, Tucker peeked around the hatch and kicked the macerated body deeper inside. It landed face-first on the deck, coming to a bloody rest at the foot of the ladder.

He backed out again.

Five seconds passed . . . ten seconds . . .

Felice was a hunter. He knew she would want to inspect her handiwork.

At the first scuff of boot on metal rung, he signaled to Kane and they both climbed the outside stairs to reach the open starboard wing of the bridge. Reaching the last step, he leaned forward and peered through the open hatch of the wheel-house. It appeared empty.

He pictured Felice on the ladder, abandoning the bridge to gloat over his body.

Good.

With the Browning up and ready, Tucker quietly stepped across the threshold into the wheelhouse. He slipped to the head of the ladder, took a breath, and pointed the Browning down the rungs.

No Felice.

No one.

Just the corpse on the floor in a widening pool of blood.

Kane growled at his side.

On instinct alone, Tucker spun on his heel, jerked the Browning up, and fired—as Felice stepped through the wheelhouse's port hatch.

His sudden shot went slightly wide, catching the woman in the side, just above her hip bone. She staggered backward and landed hard on the deck.

Rushing forward, he reached the hatch in time to see her rifle rising.

"Don't," Tucker said, cradling the Browning in both hands, centered on her face. "You're done."

She lifted her head, her scarf fallen away, revealing the ruin of her handsome face. Part of her nose was gone, sewn with black suture, along with a corner of her upper lip, giving her a perpetual scowl. A thick bandage covered her left cheek.

He recalled his last sight of her, as she vanished into the icy waters. She had been found later, saved, but it seemed not before frostbite ravaged her.

She snapped her rifle up, trying to take advantage of his momentary shock—but he also remembered feisty Elena and poor Utkin. It tempered any shock and revulsion. All he saw in the ruin of her face was justice.

Holding steady, he squeezed the trigger and sent a single round through her forehead.

46

From behind Tucker, boots clanked on the outside stairs. He turned and spotted a shotgun-wielding figure charging up the ladder toward the starboard wing. Here were the boots he had heard descending the ladder earlier—not Felice.

As the man reached the top stair, his shotgun up, Kane bounded into the hatchway before him, hackles raised, growling.

The sudden materialization of the large dog knocked the man back, his shotgun barrel dropping toward Kane.

Tucker shot once, placing a bullet through his sternum. The gunman tumbled backward down the ladder. Tucker followed him out, covering with his Browning, but the man lay on his back, snowflakes melting on his open eyes.

Tucker took a fast accounting. He'd shot three men, along with Felice, the same number as reported stealing the speedboat.

But was that all of them?

He waited a full minute more—but no other threat appeared.

Satisfied, he moved farther out onto the bridge wing and cupped his hands around his mouth. "Doc! Nick! Come forward quickly!"

As the two men joined him, running forward against the sleet and snow, Tucker peeled off the pressure bandage from his ear and called Kane to him as he knelt. He secured the bandage to the shepherd's wound and wrapped it snugly, patching his friend up as best he could for now.

Bukolov joined him in the wheelhouse as he finished. The doctor's gaze shifted across the dead bodies. "Is that all of them?"

"I think so. Time for you all to get to work. Take Kane and use his nose to sniff out which cargo holds might have been contaminated by Felice's team."

From an inner pocket of his jacket, Tucker removed a gauze sponge prescented with the sulfurous discharge from Bukolov's specimen of LUCA. He held it to the shepherd's nose.

"TRACK AND FIND."

He next turned to Nick. "Go with them," he ordered. "Keep them safe."

"Will do."

The three took off, heading belowdecks.

Remaining in the wheelhouse, Tucker crossed quickly to the computerized helm console. He hoped to find some way to turn the *Macoma*, to stop its collision course with the rocky coastline.

Off in the distance, a light glowed through the

snowfall. It had to be Old Mission Point, dead on the bow.

Maybe two miles, probably a little less.

He glanced at their speed on a gauge and calculated swiftly.

Eight minutes to impact.

Tucker studied the helm. Dozen of additional gauges, switches, knobs, and readouts spread across its console—but no wheel.

Instead, he spotted a joystick with a handgrip—beside it, an LED readout marking the ship's course. He grasped the stick and eased it slightly to the right, while keeping his eyes on the course readout.

"Come on, come on . . ."

The LED digits refused to change. Frustrated, he shoved the stick all the way to the right, but to no effect. The *Macoma* continued its relentless charge for the coast.

The glow in the distance grew brighter.

What am I doing wrong—?

Backing a step to consider his options, his boot crunched on something on the floor. He glanced down to find the deck beneath the console strewn with circuit boards, each one broken in half.

Felice had sabotaged the helm.

Even in death, she continued to thwart him.

Kane suddenly appeared at the port bridge hatch, followed a half minute later by a panting Bukolov and Nick.

"We found it!" Bukolov declared. "Or rather Kane did. Remarkable nose on that fellow. They contaminated hold number five, just behind us. But

it's sealed like a bank vault. Looks like someone sabotaged the locking mechanism."

Felice.

Nick stared out the window, looking ill. "That's
Old Mission Point," he confirmed. "Dead ahead."

"That's awful close," Bukolov said. "If we crash
before we can decontaminate that hold . . ."

LUCA would be let loose into the world.

8:27 P.M.

After explaining his inability to turn or slow the
ship, Tucker wasted a full precious minute as he
scanned the helm, clenching his fist all the while.
There had to be *something*: an override, an emergency shutdown . . .

Where's a damned plug when you need to pull one?

His eyes skipped over a gauge—then returned to
it, reading it more carefully.

HOLD FIRE SUPPRESSION

Tucker suddenly stiffened and swung to Nick and
Bukolov.

"Follow me!"

He slid down the ladder, followed by the two men
who scrambled after him. Kane used the outside
stairs to join them below. At the bottom, Tucker
grabbed the shotgun from the last man he had killed.

Nick looked around. "What are we—?"

"We need to find the crew," he said.

"Why?"

"I'll explain later. Kane can help us."

Tucker searched the next few rooms on this level and found a crewman's cabin. He grabbed some dirty clothes from a hamper and placed it in front of Kane's muzzle, ruffling it to raise the scent and gain Kane's full attention.

"TRACK AND FIND," he ordered again.

The shepherd buried his nose in the garments, snuffling deeply. He finally backed a step, lifted his nose high in the air—then bounded through the door.

The three men ran after him. Kane led them on a chase deeper into the ship's bowels, but in short order, the shepherd skidded to a double set of doors, sniffing furiously along the bottom.

The door was labeled CREW DINING.

Tucker pounded on it. "Anybody there?"

Multiple voices shouted back, both frantic and relieved, overlapping one another.

He tried the knob and found it locked. "Move as far to your right as you can! And turn away from the door!"

After getting a confirmation, he waved Bukolov and Nick farther down the hall, along with Kane. He then pointed the shotgun at the door's hinges from about six inches away and turned his head.

The blast stung his ears.

He moved immediately to the second hinge and did the same. With his ears ringing, he kicked the door the rest of the way open.

Seven or eight crewmembers stood huddled together in the far corner. Felice must have rounded them up when Tucker arrived by helicopter, knowing her hopes of contaminating the cargo without anyone's knowledge were ruined.

A tall, auburn-haired woman stepped from the group. "Who are you? What's going on?"

"No time," Tucker said. "We're working with national security. Who's the engineer?"

A wiry man in a thick wool sweater and suspenders raised his hand. "I am. John Harris."

"You're familiar with the ship's fire suppression system for the cargo holds?"

Tucker pictured the label on the helm's gauge: HOLD FIRE SUPPRESSION.

Of course, a cargo ship must be equipped with a sophisticated means of controlling fires, especially those that broke out in their cavernous holds. Fire was a ship's worst enemy.

"Yes, certainly," the ship's engineer confirmed. "It's a high-pressure water mist system."

"Where is it?"

"One deck down, right below us."

"Can you isolate hold number five?"

"Yes."

"Great. This is Doctor Bukolov. Take him to the fire suppression controls—then purge the water out of the tank and refill it with what the good doctor gives you. Can you do that?"

"Yes, but—"

He turned to Bukolov. "Doc, do you have enough?"

"Yes, more than adequate, I believe."

"John, you've got your orders. Get moving."

As they set out, Tucker turned back to the other crewmembers. "Who's the captain?"

The tall woman stepped forward again and introduced herself. "Captain Maynard."

"Captain, the *Macoma* is going to run aground in about three minutes, and the helm console is locked. Where's the safest place on the ship?"

"At the stern. Chart Library. One deck below the navigation bridge."

"Go there now!" he ordered.

As the crew filed past him, the last in line, a bald man wearing a cook's apron, suddenly wobbled into him. He was holding a bloody towel up to his mouth, and there was a deep gash in his forehead. Dried blood caked his eyebrows, nose, and mouth.

Tucker asked, "What happened to you?"

The man moaned and removed the towel to reveal a split lip and a flattened nose.

More of Felice's handiwork.

"I'll get you medical help as soon as we can." He turned to Nick. "Help get this guy to safety."

Nick nodded and hooked the man around the shoulders, helping him move faster. The pair hurried after the others.

Tucker turned and slid down the ladder to the next deck, following Bukolov and Harris, the ship's engineer. He found the pair standing before a wall console, with a panel open next to it. Bukolov's dispersal tank rested nearby, a hose running from it through the open panel.

"The fire-suppression tanks are here," Bukolov said as Tucker joined them. "He just finished siphoning the kill switch into the right one."

Tucker checked his watch.

Two minutes.

He asked Bukolov, "Will this really work?"

"In an enclosed space like that hold? Without a doubt—that is assuming their fire suppression system works as described to me."

"It'll work," Harris said and started pressing a series of buttons, then turned a lever clockwise. A button marked with the number 5 began flashing red on the board. "It's ready."

"Punch it."

Harris stabbed it with his thumb. From the tank closet, a *whoosh* sounded, followed by a gurgling.

"It's flowing," the engineer confirmed.

"How long until it's empty?"

"It's high pressure, high volume. Forty-five seconds and the compost in that hold will be soaked thoroughly."

Tucker clapped him on the shoulder. "Good job. Now we need to reach the Chart Library and join the others."

They scrambled up the ladder, where Tucker found Kane waiting. They took off as a group down the passageway with Harris leading the way.

The deck began shivering beneath their feet.

The engineer called over his shoulder, "The keel's scraping the sandbar!"

"Keep running!"

At a sprint, Harris led them toward the stern, passing intersection after intersection. As they passed one, movement drew Tucker's attention to the right. For a fleeting second, he spotted a white-smocked figure sprint past, heading the opposite direction along a parallel corridor.

The man was wearing a backpack.

Tucker skidded to a stop, as did Kane.

A backpack . . . ?

Bukolov looked over his shoulder. "Tucker . . . ?"

"Keep going! Go, go!"

The running figure in white had been the ship's cook. He was sure of it. But why—?

Tucker went momentarily dizzy as he fixed the man's broken visage before his mind's eye: *give him thick salt-and-pepper hair, a mustache, and clean the blood off his face . . .*

General Kharzin.

No, no, no!

Tucker remembered the subterfuge back in Africa, when Kharzin had sent in a body double to take his place. This time around, he had flipped that scam on its ear: disguising himself to look like an injured member of the crew. From the fact that the crew seemed to accept Kharzin as their cook meant that the general must have assumed the role of ship's cook at some prior port, coming aboard under false pretenses in order to expedite Felice's team: to get them aboard unseen, to help them contaminate the hold, and likely to help get them back off the ship unseen.

Clever.

But once Tucker arrived and the gig was up, Felice must have beaten the man to further disguise his features. Kharzin was the mission's final layer of security. If the ship was saved, he could still slip away with a final canister of LUCA and wreak what damage he could.

Tucker couldn't let that happen.

He backtracked, turned left at the intersection,

and took off after the fleeing man with Kane. When he reached the parallel corridor, he stopped short and peeked around. There was no sign of Kharzin, but somewhere forward a hatch banged against steel.

He broke from cover and kept going. The deck gave a violent shake. He lost his balance and slammed against the bulkhead.

As he righted himself, he heard faint footsteps pounding on aluminum steps.

He pointed ahead. "SEEK SOUND."

Kane sprinted down the corridor, turned right at the next intersection, and down another corridor. It ended at a set of stairs, heading toward the main deck.

Ten feet from the stairs, a hatch door banged open far above.

As he closed the distance, Tucker dropped to his knees and skidded forward with his shotgun raised. As his knees hit the bottom step, he blasted upward—just as Kharzin's rear foot disappeared from the opening.

The hatch banged shut.

Tucker bounded up the steps, watching the locking wheel begin to spin. He hit the hatch before it fully engaged. He shouldered into it, bunching his legs and straining. Finally it popped up, sending him sprawling outside onto his chest.

Kane clambered next to him.

Tucker pushed himself to his feet and looked around. To his left, General Kharzin was running forward along the deck.

Tucker shouted, "Kharzin!"

The man never looked back.

He took off after the general—then suddenly his feet flipped out from under him. He landed hard on his back. The deck bucked again, accompanied by the sound of steel scraping against sharp rocks.

Tucker and Kane went flying.

47

*The Macoma's nine hundred thousand pounds of iron
and steel plow into the cold sands of Old Mission Point,
its bow bulldozing trees, rocks, and bushes ahead of it.
Debris crashes over the bow railing and smashes into the
forecastle. A hundred feet inland, the bow strikes a boulder off center, heaving the ship onto its starboard side,
dragging the forward third of its hull across a row of
jagged rocks along the shoreline before finally lurching to
a heavy stop.*

Tucker knew none of this.

As the world became a herculean roar of rent steel
and churning rock, he recalled snatching hold of
Kane's collar, of tucking the shepherd to his chest,
and the pair of them tumbling over the *Macoma*'s
deck. They had bounced across the cargo hatches,
pinballed off the davits, and slammed into the
wheelhouse's bulkhead. They finally slid across the
last of the canted deck and came to rest entangled
on the starboard railing.

Christ Almighty . . .

With his head hammering, he forced open his eyes and found himself staring down into a well of blackness. He blinked several times, bringing the world into focus.

A world of mud.

He stared dazedly down through the starboard rails that had caught them as the ship rolled to its side. Below him rose a giant pile of black mud, its summit less than seven feet under his nose.

He smelled the ripeness of manure and the earthiness of rot.

Compost.

Kane licked Tucker's chin. The shepherd still sprawled half on top of him. The only thing keeping them from a plunge below were the struts of the rail.

"I got you, buddy," Tucker said. "Hang on."

Under him, the hull outside hold number five—where Felice's team had introduced LUCA—looked as though a giant had taken a pair of massive tin shears to the steel. Spilling from the gash was a massive wave of slurry compost, forming a mountain under him and spreading like dark lava across the landscape of Old Mission Point.

Fifty yards away a wood sign jutted from the sludge:

LIGHTHOUSE PARK—OLD MISSION POINT

A few yards past that marched a familiar figure, mucking calf-deep through the edge of the debris, a backpack hanging off one shoulder.

Kharzin.

Tucker disentangled his left arm from the railing, reached across his body to Kane, and drew the shepherd more tightly to him.

They had to find a way *down*—not that there was a way *up*.

He saw only one possibility, a *messy* possibility.

He stared below at the steep-sloping mountain of wet compost.

"Hold on, buddy, it's going to be a bit of a drop."

Tucker shifted them to the edge of the railing and rolled off. As they fell, he clutched Kane tightly against his body. They hit hard, especially for landing in mud—then they were tumbling down the slick surface of the mire. The smell filled his every sense. Muck soon covered them in a heavy coat.

In a matter of a few moments, they rolled free of the compost mountain and out across a mix of snow and sand. Tucker stood up, weaving and unsteady. His left shoulder throbbed. Kane limped a few steps, his left rear leg tucked up against his body, but as his partner worked the kinks out of his muddy body, he brought the limb down and tentatively took a few hops.

Sprained perhaps, but not broken.

Now where was General Kharzin? He was nowhere in sight.

Kane limped forward, ready to go, but Tucker forced the shepherd down with a firm, "STAY."

You've done plenty, buddy.

Tucker drew the Browning from its holster and edged forward, sticking to the deeper shadows of the *Macoma*'s canted hull. Now out of the wind and snow, he could hear the pop and metallic groan of the dying ship. It loomed above him, like a building frozen in the process of collapsing.

He noted a rope dangling from a railing ahead, marking Kharzin's exit from the ship. The end hung a good ten feet off the ground. He pictured Kharzin dropping from it.

Continuing onward, he climbed the bulldozed wave of sand and rock at the ship's bow. The tip of the ship hung like a massive shadowy hatchet in the storm overhead, waiting to fall.

Tucker reached the crest of the stony tide and peered cautiously over its lip.

Fifty yards away, a figure moved through the storm, his back to Tucker and favoring one leg. Apparently Kharzin's descent hadn't gone any easier. The man slowly limped toward a snowy tree line, marked by park benches and gravel pathways.

Tucker cautiously picked his way down the backside of the rocks and started stalking toward his target, not wanting to spook him. Whether Kharzin heard his approach or not, the man suddenly shrugged off his backpack, knelt down near a copse of leafless maples, and unzipped the bag.

A stainless steel tank shone brightly within the muddy pack. Kharzin unscrewed the nozzle hose of the sprayer and tossed it away.

Uh-oh . . .

Tucker moved swiftly forward, incautiously snapping a twig.

Kharzin turned his head.

The two of them locked eyes.

Tucker raised his pistol and charged Kharzin. The

other swung around, shaking free the tank from the pack and hugging it to his chest like a shield.

Kharzin confronted him, dared him. "Go ahead! Shoot! Hit the tank or hit me . . . it doesn't matter! Either way, the corruption inside will spill free upon your precious soil. And I'll have my revenge for my daughter, for my country!"

Tucker lowered the Browning and slowed his run to a walk.

Off in the distance came the wail of sirens.

The pair stood staring at each other, neither speaking.

Tucker considered his options. First of all, he had no idea whether Bukolov had succeeded in decontaminating the ship's hold. He smelled the ripe sludge covering his body. The monster could already be out of the bag, set loose upon the shores of Lake Michigan.

If so, the tank in Kharzin's arms was irrelevant.

Still, Tucker waited, wanting extra insurance for his next move.

Then he heard it: *thump, thump, thump*—multiple helicopters echoed over the water behind him.

Good enough.

He shot Kharzin in the right kneecap, breaking the stalemate. The man's leg buckled, and he pitched forward. As he hit the ground, the canister knocked from his arms and rolled free. Yellow liquid spilled out its open spigot, blazing a toxic trail, mapping its trajectory. As the tank came to a rest, it continued to leak weaponized LUCA.

Tucker moved forward, taking care not to step on any of the yellow lines.

Kharzin rolled onto his back, his face twisted with rage and pain.

Behind him, a helicopter swept over the bulk of the *Macoma*, then hovered for a landing at a neighboring open stretch of beach. Others buzzed higher, circling wider, stirring through the storm.

"The cavalry has arrived," he said to Kharzin.

As the skids of the first helicopter touched the rocky beach, the side door popped open, and a pair of men jumped out, both wearing anorak parkas and shouldering backpack sprayers. They should be able to quickly clean up and decontaminate the brief spill. Behind them followed another trio of men armed with assault rifles.

The group began jogging toward Tucker's position.

He returned his attention to Kharzin. "Do you see the men with the rifles?"

The general remained silent, his gaze burning with hatred.

"They're going to take you into custody, whisk you off somewhere for a long talk. But I'm not officially *with* them, you see. So before they take you away, I want you to know something."

Kharzin's eyes narrowed, showing a glint of curiosity past the pain.

"You're going to need new shoes."

He shot Kharzin in the left foot, then right—then turned away from the screaming and the blood. He'd had enough of both.

Time to go home.

He headed back to where he had left Kane.

That was home enough for him.

48

Footsteps entered the barn.

Now what?

Lying on his back, Tucker scooted his roller board out from beneath the Range Rover. He wiped the oil from his hands onto his coverall, but there was nothing to do about the splatters on his face. No doubt about it, the Rover needed a new oil pan and gasket.

As he rolled free of the bumper, he found himself staring up at the worried face of Christopher Nkomo.

"My friend," he said, "I am not comfortable accepting such a large gift."

Tucker sat up and climbed to his feet.

Kane stirred from where he had been curled on a pile of straw, patiently waiting for his partner to realize he was not an auto mechanic.

Tucker scratched at the bandage over his ear. The sutures had returned his ear to its proper place on his head and were due to come out now.

It had been ten days since the crash of the *Macoma*. It seemed Bukolov's kill switch had proved successful, the site declared LUCA free, although monitoring continued around the clock. The entire event was reported to the media as a mishap due to a fault in the ship's navigation systems during a severe winter storm. Additionally, the cordoning of the site was blamed on a hazardous spill. Under such a cover, it was easy for teams to move in with electric-powered dispersion sprayers and swamp the entire area with the kill switch as an extra precaution. It also explained the continued environmental monitoring.

The rest of the crew, along with Bukolov, were discovered safe, except for a few broken bones and lacerations. Even Nick Pasternak, the pilot, was found with only an egg-sized knot behind his ear, where Kharzin had clubbed him and made his attempted escape.

In the end, with no one reported killed, the media interest in the crash quickly faded away into lottery numbers and celebrity weddings.

Life moved on.

And so did Tucker.

Two days after the events, he and Kane landed in Cape Town. Bruised, battered, and stitched up, they both needed some rest—and Tucker knew just where he would find it.

He waved Christopher toward the shaded veranda of a colonial-era mansion. The three-story, sprawling home was located in a remote corner of the Spitskop Game Preserve, far from the tourist area of the park where he and the others had originally stayed with its bell captains and its servers dressed all in house whites. This mansion had been abandoned a decade ago, boarded up and forgotten, except by the snakes and other vermin, who had to be evicted once the restoration process began.

A crew worked busily nearly around the clock. Ladders and scaffolding hid most of the slowly returning glory of the main house. New boards stood out against old. Wide swaths of lawn—composed of indigenous buffalo grass—had already been rolled out and hemmed around the home, stretching a good half acre and heavily irrigated. Cans of paint were stacked on the porch, waiting to brighten the faded beauty of the old mansion.

Farther out, the twenty-acre parcel was dotted with barns and outbuildings, marking future renovation projects.

But one pristine sign was already up at the gravel road leading here, its letters carved into the native ironwood and painted in brilliant shades of orange, white, and black. They spelled out the hopes and dreams for the Nkomo brothers:

LUXURY SAFARI TOURS

Tucker crossed the damp lawn and climbed the newly whitewashed porch steps. Overhead, wired outlet boxes marked the future site of porch fans. Kane trotted up alongside him, seeking shade and his water bowl.

"Truly, Mr. Tucker, sir," Christopher pressed, mounting the steps as if he were climbing the gallows. "This is too large a gift."

"I had the funds and quit calling it a *gift*. It's an investment, nothing more."

Upon completing the affair with Sigma, Tucker

had noticed a sudden large uptick in his savings account held at a Cayman Island bank. The sudden largesse was not from Sigma—though that pay had been fair enough—but from Bogdan Fedoseev, the Russian industrialist whose life Tucker had saved back in Vladivostok. It seemed Fedoseev placed great stake in his own personal well-being and reflected that in the *bonus* he wired.

Tucker took that same message to heart and extended a similar generosity to the Nkomo brothers, who, like Tucker with Fedoseev, had helped keep him alive. From talking to Christopher during the long stretches of the journey to the Groot Karas Mountains, he knew of the brothers' desire to purchase the mansion and the tract of land, to turn it into their own home and business.

But they were short on funds—so he corrected that problem.

"We will pay you back when we can," Christopher promised. Tucker knew it was an oath the young man would never break. "But we must talk interest perhaps."

"You are right. We should negotiate. I say *zero* percent."

Christopher sighed, recognizing the futility of all this. "Then we will always leave the presidential suite open for you and Kane."

Tucker craned his neck up toward the cracked joists, the apple-peel curls of old paint, the broken dormer windows. He cast Christopher a jaundiced eye.

The young man smiled in the face of his doubt. "A man must hope, must he not? One day, yes?"

"When the presidential suite is ready, you call me."

"I will certainly do that. But, my friend, when will you be leaving us? We will miss you."

"Considering the state of the Rover, you may not be missing me anytime soon. Otherwise, I don't know."

And he liked it that way.

He stared again at this old beauty rising out of the neglect. It gave him hope. He also liked the idea of having a place to lay his head among friends when needed. If not a home, then at least a *way station*.

Kane finished drinking, water rolling from his jowls. His gaze turned, looking toward the horizon, a wistful look in his dark eyes.

You and me both, buddy.

That was their true home.

Together.

Tucker's phone vibrated in his pocket. He pulled it out and answered, guessing who was calling. "Harper, I hope this is a social call."

"You left in a hurry. Just wanted to check on you and Kane."

"We're doing fine."

"Glad to hear it. That means you might be up for some company."

Before Tucker could respond, a black Lincoln town car pulled into the dirt driveway, coasted forward, and came to a stop in front of the house. The engine shut off.

"I assume it's too late to object," Tucker said.

As answer, the driver's door popped open, and a woman in a dark blue skirt and white blouse exited. She was tall, with long legs, made longer as she stretched a bit on her toes, revealing the firm curve of her calves. She pushed a fall of blond hair from her eyes, sweeping it back to reveal a tanned face with high cheekbones.

Though he had never met the woman face-to-face, he knew her.

Ruth Harper.

He stood straighter, trying to balance the figure before him with the image formed in his mind from their many phone conversations.

This certainly was no *librarian*.

The only feature he got right was the pair of thick-rimmed rectangular eyeglasses perched on her nose. They gave her a studious, even sexier look.

Definitely no librarian he had ever met.

Tucker called down to her from the top. "In some lines of work, Harper, this would be considered an ambush."

She shrugged, looking not the least bit chagrined as she climbed the steps, carrying a small box in her palms. "I called first. In the South, a lady does not show up on a gentleman's doorstep unannounced. It just isn't done."

"Why are you here?" he asked—though he could guess why, sensing the manipulation of her boss, Painter Crowe.

"First," she said, "to tell you that Bukolov sends his regards—along with his thanks."

"He said the *last* part? Doctor Bukolov?"

She laughed, a rare sound from her. "He's a new man now that he has his own lab at Fort Detrick. I even saw him smile the other day."

"A minor miracle. How's he getting along?"

"His studies are still in the rudimentary stages right now. Like with human stem cell research, it might take years if not decades to learn how to properly manipulate that unique genetic code to the benefit of mankind."

"What about to the *damage* to mankind? What's the word out of Russia?"

"Through back channels, Kharzin's superiors at the GRU have insisted they knew nothing about his actions. Whether it's true or not, we don't know. But word is that the Russian Defense Ministry is turning the GRU upside down, purging anyone associated with Kharzin."

"How about Kharzin? Is he cooperating?"

She turned and balanced the small box she had been carrying onto the porch rail. "I don't know if you heard before you left, but he lost one of his feet. He must have rolled after you shot him, contaminated the wound with some of the spilled LUCA organism. By the time anyone realized it, the only option was amputation."

"Sorry to hear that," he lied.

"As to cooperation, he knows the fate that would befall him if he ever did return to Russia, so he's grudgingly beginning to bend, revealing small details to fill in some of the blanks. Like revealing the name of a port authority agent who was paid to look the other way when and if the *Macoma* reached port in Chicago. The man's in custody now."

Good riddance.

"And it seems Kharzin's paranoia has finally proven of benefit. Prior to leaving for the States, he set up a fail-safe at his lab outside of Kazan. Without an abort code from him personally every twenty-four hours, his lab's remaining samples of LUCA would be automatically incinerated. He didn't want anyone else gaining access to them."

"So they're all gone then?"

"That's the consensus. His lab did indeed burn down. And if we're wrong, we're still the only ones who have the kill switch."

"So it's over."

"Until next time," she warned, arching an eyebrow. "And speaking of next time—"

"No."

"But you don't know—"

"No," he said more firmly, as if scolding a dog.

She sighed. "It's true, then. You and the Nkomo brothers are going into some investment together? Luxury safari adventures?"

"As always, Harper, you're disturbingly well informed."

"Then I guess the only other reason I made this long trip was to deliver *this*." She pointed to the box on the porch rail. "A small token of my appreciation."

Curiosity drew him forward. He fingered the top open, reached inside, and pulled out a coffee mug. He frowned at the strange gift—until he turned the cup and spotted the gnarled face of a bulldog on the front. The dog was wearing a red-and-white-striped cap with a prominent G on it.

He grinned as he recognized the mascot for the University of Georgia, remembering all of his past attempts at placing Harper's accent.

"Never would've taken you for a fan of the Georgia Bulldogs," he said.

She reached down and scratched Kane behind an ear. "I've always had a special place in my heart for dogs."

From the arch of her eyebrow, he suspected she wasn't only referring to the four-legged kind.

"As to the other matter," she pressed, straightening up, "you're sure?"

"Very sure."

"As in forever?"

Tucker considered this.

Kane picked up his rubber Kong ball and dropped it at Tucker's feet. The shepherd lowered his front end, hindquarters high, and glanced with great urgency toward the endless stretch of cool grass.

Tucker smiled, picked up the ball, and answered Harper's question.

"For now, I have better things to do."

AUTHOR'S NOTE TO READERS: TRUTH OR FICTION

As with my Sigma books, I thought I'd attempt here at the end of this story to draw that fine line between fact and fiction. I like to do this, if for no other reason than to offer a few bread crumbs to those who might be interested in learning more about the science, history, or various locations tread by Tucker and Kane.

But first let's start with that illustrious duo.

Military War Dogs and Their Handlers

The first recorded use of war dogs goes back to 4000 BC, to the Egyptians who used them in battle. But the modern use of dogs in the U.S. military really started in World War I. Since then dogs have become an integral part of the U.S. military, including the dog Cairo who was involved with the take-down of Osama bin Laden.

During a USO tour of authors to Iraq and Kuwait, I got a chance to observe a few of these fighting teams in action. While in Baghdad, I also met a fellow veterinary classmate who was with the U.S. Veterinary Corp. He was able to give me great insight into the technology, the psychology, and even the aftermath of such a unique fighting team.

All the MWD (military working dog) technology found in this book is real: from the Kevlar-reinforced K9 Storm tactical vest worn by Kane to his amazing communication gear. I also tried to capture that unique and intimate psychological connection between dog and handler, described as "it runs down the lead," where over time the two learn to read each other's emotions and understand each other beyond gesture and spoken command. I also learned about how PTSD afflicts not only the soldier but also the dog, and how efforts are being undertaken to combat and treat both sufferers.

As to Kane's amazing talent, that's also based on real stories. Even Kane's vocabulary, while stellar, has been demonstrated by a dog named Chaser, a border collie who has been shown to understand over a thousand words, including grammatical structure.

Last, after three decades of working with dogs as a veterinarian, I knew I wanted to portray these stalwart war heroes as they really are—not just as soldiers with four legs, but as *real* dogs. In this book, there are scenes written from Kane's perspective. Here, I wanted readers to experience what it's like to be a war dog—to be in their *paws*—to paint an accurate portrayal of how a dog *perceives* the world, how he *functions* in combat with his unique talents and senses. I hope I did them justice.

. . . .

On to the central scientific concept and threat of the novel . . .

LUCA and Cyanobacteria

LUCA (Last Universal Common Ancestor) is a scientific concept concerning the origin of life, the proverbial seed from which all life sprang. There are many different theories about how that ancient lifeform might have presented itself, whether its origin is rooted in DNA or RNA, whether it needs extreme heat to survive or moderate temperatures. It remains a great unknown. In regard to the concepts of cyanobacteria as a progenitor for modern plants, all the science and details regarding this ubiquitous form of life are true, including that you can find cyanobacteria in every environmental niche on the planet, including the fur of sloths.

The Threat of Invasive Species

This is a real and ongoing threat across the globe, where foreign species invade an established ecosystem and wreak great harm: from the introduction of pythons in the Everglades, where those snakes are creating untold damage, to Asian carp in the Mississippi, which are wiping out native fish populations and sweeping toward the Great Lakes. Such threats have not escaped the notice of federal counterterrorism officials. Alarm bells are being raised that terrorists could very well use invasive species as biological weapons, where the introduction of a single virulent organism into an environment could cause great economic and physical harm, possibly irreversibly so.

Let's move on to the main history topics.

The Boer Wars

All the details of this bloody conflict are true, including the military tactics related in the prologue and the weapons used (like the "krag"). The character General Manie Roosa was very loosely based on the real-life Boer leader Manie Maritz. And you can still find such "pocket camps" of the Boers hidden throughout South Africa, and the archaeological ruins of their forts still dot the countryside.

Arzamas-16

The Russians did indeed have closed science cities, called *naukograds*, including one named Arzamas-16, which was home to the Soviet Union's first nuclear weapons design. The U.S. intelligence community did indeed refer to it as the *Russian Los Alamos*.

Last . . .

Location, Location, Location

One of the great thrills of writing is being able to shine a light on various regions of the world.

And *The Kill Switch* was no exception. Grant and I strove to make sure every detail of each location was as accurate and illuminating as possible: from life in Siberian villages to the historical magnitude of the Kazan Kremlin. Even such details like the submarine ecotours of the Volga River are factual. I also wanted to paint an accurate picture of South Africa, its wildlife, and the regional strife of Namibia, while capturing the raw beauty of the Groot Karas Mountains. Over the course of writing this book, I grew to love these places, and I hope you enjoyed the journey, too.

Finally, let me leave you with one last *fact:* Tucker and Kane will be back—because their *true* adventure is just beginning!

**Don't miss Tucker and Kane's
next exciting adventure!**

Tucker Wayne's past and present collide when a former army colleague comes to him for help. She's on the run from brutal assassins hunting her and her son. To keep them safe, Tucker must discover who killed a brilliant young idealist—a crime that leads back to the most powerful figures in the U.S. government and to a mystery from World War II that is suddenly redefining what it means to be human. With no one to trust, Tucker will be forced to break the law, expose national secrets, and risk everything to stop a madman determined to control the future of modern warfare. But can Tucker and Kane withstand a force so indomitable that it threatens our very future?

**Keep reading for a sneak peek of
the heart-pounding sequel,**

WAR HAWK

**Coming April 2015 in hardcover
from William Morrow**

PROLOGUE

Spring 1940
Buckinghamshire, England

Failure was not an option.

The spy went by the codename Geist, the German word for ghost. Few in the *Abwehr's* military intelligence knew his true name, nor even his intent here on British soil.

Geist lay on his stomach in a muddy ditch, with ice-encrusted cattails stabbing at his face. He ignored the midnight cold, the frigid gusts of breezes, the ache of his frozen joints. Instead, he concentrated on the view through the binoculars fixed to his face.

He and his assigned team lay alongside the banks of a small lake. A hundred yards off, on the opposite shore, a row of stately rural mansions sat dark, brightened here and there by the rare sliver of yellow light peeking through blackout curtains. Still, he spotted the glint of moonlight off the rolls of barbed wire mounted atop the garden walls of one particular estate.

Bletchley Park.

The place also went by a codename: Station X.

That seemingly nondescript country house masked an operation run by British intelligence, a joint effort by MI6 and the Government Code and Cypher School. In a series of wooden huts set up on those idyllic acres, the Allied forces had gathered the greatest mathematicians and cryptographers from around the globe, including one man, Alan Turing, who was decades ahead of his peers. Station X's goal was to break the German military's Enigma code, using tools built by the geniuses here. The group had already succeeded in building an electrome-chanical decrypting device called The Bombe, and rumors abounded about a new project already underway to build Colossus, the world's first programmable electric computer.

But none of that was his goal this night.

Hidden upon those grounds was a prize beyond anything his

superiors could imagine: a breakthrough that held the potential to change the very fate of the world.

And I will possess it—or die trying.

Geist felt his heart quicken.

To his left, his second-in-command, Lieutenant Hoffman, pulled the collar of his jacket tighter around his neck as an icy rain began to fall. He shifted, cursing his complaint. *"Gott verlassenen Land."*

Geist kept his binoculars in place and scolded the head of the commandos. "Silence. If anyone hears you speaking German, we'll be stuck here for the rest of the war."

Geist knew a firm hand was needed with the eight-man team under his charge. The members had been handpicked by the *Abwehr* not only for their superb martial skills, but also for their grasp of English. Whatever the British might lack in military presence out here in the rural regions, they made up for by a vigilant citizenry.

"Truck!" Hoffmann rasped.

Geist glanced over his shoulder to the road passing through the woods behind him. A lorry trundled along, its headlights muted by blackout slits.

"Hold your breaths," Geist hissed.

He wasn't about to let their presence catch the attention of the passing driver. He and the others kept their faces pressed low until the sound of the truck's puttering engine faded away.

"Clear," Hoffman said.

Geist checked his watch and searched again with his binoculars. *What is taking them so long?*

Everything from here depended on clockwork timing. He and his team had been offloaded by U-boat five days ago. Splitting up into groups of two or three, they worked their way across the countryside, ready with papers identifying them as daylaborers and farmhands. They'd regrouped at a nearby hunting shack, where a cache of weapons awaited them, left by sleeper agents who had prepped the way in advance for Geist's team.

Only one last detail remained.

A wink of light caught his attention from the grounds neighboring the Bletchley Park estate. It shuttered off once, then back on again— then finally darkness returned.

It was the signal he had been waiting for.

Geist rolled up to an elbow. "Time to move out."

Hoffman's team gathered their weapons: assault rifles and noise-suppressed pistols. The largest commando—a true bull of a man named Kraus—hauled up an MG42 heavy machine gun, capable of firing twelve hundred rounds a minute.

Geist studied the black-streaked faces around him. They had trained for three months within a life-sized mock-up of Bletchley Park. By now, they could all walk those grounds blindfolded.

The only unknown variable was the level of onsite defense. The research campus was secured not only by soldiers, but also by guards in civilian clothes.

Geist gave his team final instructions. "Once inside the estate, torch the assigned buildings with your incendiaries. Cause as much panic and confusion as possible. In that chaos, Hoffman and I will attempt to secure the package. If shooting starts, take down anything that moves. Is that understood?"

Each man nodded his head.

With everyone prepared—ready to die if need be—the group set off and followed the contour of the lake, sticking to the mist-shrouded forest. Geist led them past the neighboring estates. Most of these old homes were shuttered, awaiting the summer months. Soon servants and staff would be arriving to prepare the country estates for the leisure season, but that was still a couple of weeks away.

It was one of the many reasons this narrow window of opportunity had been chosen by Admiral Wilhelm Canaris, head of German military intelligence. Including one other time-critical element.

"Access to the bunker should be just up ahead," Geist whispered back to Hoffman. "Ready the men."

The British government—aware that Adolf Hitler would soon launch an air war against this island nation—had begun constructing underground bunkers for its critical installations, including Bletchley Park. The bunker at Station X was only half completed, offering a brief break in the secure perimeter around the estate.

Geist intended to take advantage of that weakness this night.

He led his team toward a country house that neighbored Bletchley Park. It was a red-brick Tudor with yellow shutters. He approached the stacked-stone fence that surrounded the grounds and waved his team to flatten against it.

"Where are we going?" Hoffman whispered. "I thought we were going through some bunker."

"We are." Only Geist had been given this last piece of intelligence.

He crouched low and hurried toward the gate, which he found unlocked. The winking signal earlier had confirmed that all was in readiness here.

Geist pushed open the gate, slipped through, and led his team across the lawn to the home's glass-enclosed conservatory. He found another unlocked door there, hurried inside with his men, and crossed to the kitchen. The all-white cabinetry glowed in the moonlight streaming through the windows.

Wasting no time, he stepped to a door beside the pantry. He opened it and turned on his flashlight, revealing a set of stairs. At the bottom, he found a stone-floored cellar; the walls were white-painted brick, the exposed ceiling a maze of water pipes running through the floor joists. The cellar spanned the width of the house.

He led his team past stacks of boxes and furniture draped in dusty sheets to the cellar's eastern wall. As directed, he pulled away a rug to reveal a hole that had been recently dug through the floor. Another bit of handiwork from Canaris's sleeper agents.

Geist shone his flashlight down the hole, revealing water flowing below.

"What is it?" Hoffman asked.

"Old sewer pipe. It connects all the estates, circling the lake."

"Including Bletchley Park," Hoffman realized with a nod.

"And its partially completed bunker," Geist added. "It'll be a tight squeeze, but we'll only need to cross a hundred meters to reach the construction site of that underground bomb shelter and climb back up."

According to the latest intelligence, those new foundations of the bunker were mostly unguarded and should offer them immediate access into the very heart of the estate's grounds.

"The Brits won't know what hit them," Hoffman said with a mean grin.

Geist again led the way, slipping feetfirst through the hole and dropping with a splash into the dank water. He kept one hand on the moldy wall and headed along the old stone pipe. It was only a meter-and-a-half wide, so he had to keep his back bowed, holding his breath against the stink.

After a handful of steps, he clicked off his flashlight and aimed for the distant glow of moonlight. He moved more slowly along the curving pipe, keeping his sloshing to a minimum, not wanting to alert any possible guards who might be canvassing the bunker's construction site. Hoffman's teammates followed his stealthy example.

At last, he reached that moonlit hole in the pipe's roof. A temporary grate covered the newly excavated access point to the old sewer. He fingered the chain and padlock that secured the grate in place.

Unexpected but not a problem.

Hoffman noted his attention and passed him a set of bolt cutters. With great care, Geist snapped through the lock's hasp and freed the chain. He shared a glance with the lieutenant, confirming everyone was ready—then pushed the grate open and pulled himself through.

He found himself crouched atop the raw concrete foundations of the future bunker. The skeletal structure of walls, conduits, and plumbing surrounded him. Scaffolding and ladders led up toward the open grounds of the estate above. He hurried to one side, ducking under a scaffold, out of direct view. One by one the remaining eight commandoes joined him.

Geist took a moment to orient himself. He should be within forty meters of their target: Hut 8. It was one of several green-planked structures built on these grounds. Each had its own purpose, but his team's goal was the research section overseen by the mathematician and cryptanalyst, Alan Turing.

He gestured for the men to huddle together.

"Remember, no shooting unless you're intercepted. Toss those incendiaries into Huts 4 and 6. Let the fire do the work for us. With any luck, the distraction will create enough confusion to cover our escape."

Hoffman pointed to two of his men. "Schwab, you take your team to Hut 4. Faber, you and your men have Hut 6. Kraus, you trail us. Be ready to use that machine gun of yours if there is any trouble."

After getting nods of agreement, the lieutenant's men scaled the ladders and disappeared out of the open pit of the bunker. Geist followed on their heels with Hoffman and Kraus trailing him.

Staying low, he headed north until he reached Hut 8 and flattened against the wooden siding. The door should be around the next corner. He waited a breath, making sure no alarm had been raised.

He counted down in his head until finally shouts arose to the east and west. *"Fire, fire, fire!"*

Upon that signal, he slid around the corner and climbed a set of plank steps to reach the door into Hut 8. He turned the knob as the night grew brighter, flickering with fresh flames.

As more shouting rose, he pushed through the doorway and into a small room. The center was dominated by two trestle tables covered in stacks of punch cards. The whitewashed walls were plastered with propaganda posters warning about ever-present Nazis' eyes and ears.

With his pistol raised, he and Hoffman rushed across and burst through the far doorway into the next room. Seated at a long table, two women sorted through more piles of punch cards. The woman to the right was already looking up. She spun in her chair, reaching for a red panic button on the wall.

Hoffmann shot her twice in the side. The suppressed gunfire was no louder than a couple of firm coughs.

Geist took out the second woman with a single round through her throat. She toppled backward, her face still frozen in an expression of surprise.

They must be Wrens—members of the Women's Royal Naval Service—who were assisting in the work being conducted here.

Geist hurried to the first woman, searched her pockets, and came up with a thumb-sized brass key. On the second woman, he found a second key, this one iron.

With his prizes in hand, he hurried back to the main room.

From outside, there arose the *wonk-wonk-wonk* of an alarm klaxon.

So far their subterfuge seemed to be—

The rattling blasts of a submachine gun cut off this last thought. More gunfire followed. Hoffman cursed.

"We've been discovered," the lieutenant warned.

Geist refused to give up. He crossed to a waist-high safe along one wall. As expected, it was secured by two keyed locks, top and bottom, and a combination dial in the center.

"Need to hurry, sir," Hoffmann rasped next to him. "Sounds like we got a lot of foot traffic outside."

Geist pointed to the door. "Have Kraus clear a path for us back to the bunker."

The large soldier obeyed, vanishing quickly out the door with his heavy weapon. As Geist inserted his two keys, Kraus's MG42 opened up outside, roaring into the night.

He focused on the task at hand, turning one key, then the other, getting a satisfying *thunk-thunk* in return. He moved his hand to the combination lock. This was truly the test of the *Abwehr's* reach.

He spun the dial: 9 … 29 … 4.

He took a breath, let it out, and depressed the lever.

The safe door swung open.

Thank God.

A quick search inside revealed only one item: a brown accordion folder wrapped in red rubber bands. He read the name stenciled on the outside.

THE A.R.E.S. PROJECT

He knew *Ares* was the Greek god of war, which was appropriate, considering the contents. But that connotation only hinted at the true nature of the work found inside. The acronym—A.R.E.S.—stood for something far more earth-shattering, something powerful enough to rewrite history. He grabbed the folder with trembling hands, knowing the terrifying wonders it held, and stuffed the prize into his jacket.

Hoffman had already moved to the door, cracking it open and yelling. "Kraus!"

"*Komm!*" the man shouted back in German, forsaking any need for further subterfuge. "Hurry! Before they regroup!"

Geist joined Hoffman at the door, pulled the pin on an incendiary grenade, and tossed it back into the center of the room. Both men lunged outside as it exploded behind them, blowing out the windows with gouts of flames.

To their left, a pair of British soldiers sprinted around the corner of the hut. Kraus cut them down with his machine gun, but more soldiers followed, taking cover and returning fire, forcing Geist's team away from the excavated bunker—away from their only escape route.

As they retreated deeper into the grounds, smoke billowed more thickly, accompanied by the acrid stench of burning wood.

Another set of figures burst through the pall. Kraus came close to carving them in half with his weapon, but at that last moment, he halted, recognizing his fellow commandos. It was Schwab's team.

"What about Faber and the others?" Hoffman asked.

Schwab shook his head. "Saw them killed."

That left only the six of them.

Geist quickly improvised. "We'll make for the motor pool."

He led the way at a dead run. The team tossed incendiaries as they went, adding to the confusion, strafing down alleyways, dropping anything that moved.

Finally they reached a row of small sheds. Fifty meters beyond, the main gate came into view. It looked like a dozen soldiers crouched behind concrete barriers, guns up, looking for any targets. Spotlights panned the area.

Before being seen, Geist directed his group into a neighboring Quonset hut, where three canvas-sided lorries were parked.

"We need that gate cleared," Geist said, looking at Hoffman and his men, knowing what he was asking of them. For any chance of escape, many of them would likely die in the attempt.

The lieutenant stared him down. "We'll get it done."

Geist clapped Hoffman on the shoulder, thanking him.

The lieutenant set out with his remaining four men.

Geist crossed and climbed into one of the lorries, where he found the keys in the ignition. He started the engine, warming it up, then hopped back out again. He crossed to the remaining two trucks and popped their hoods.

In the distance, Kraus's machine gun began a lethal chattering, accompanied by the rattle of assault rifles and the overlapping *crump* of exploding grenades.

Finally, a faint call reached him.

"Klar, klar, klar!" Hoffman shouted.

Geist hurried back to the idling lorry, climbed inside, and put the truck into gear—but not before tossing two grenades into each of the open engine compartments of the remaining lorries. As he rolled out and hit the accelerator, the grenades exploded behind him.

He raced to the main gate and braked hard. British soldiers lay dead; the spotlights shot out. Hoffman rolled the gate open, limping on a bloody leg. Supported by a teammate, Kraus hobbled his way into the back of the lorry. Hoffman joined him up front, climbing into the passenger seat and slamming the door angrily.

"Lost Schwab and Braatz." Hoffman waved ahead. "Go, go."

With no time to mourn, Geist gunned the engine and blasted down the country road. He kept one eye on the side mirror, watching for any sign of pursuit. He took a maze of turns, trying to further confound their escape route. Finally, he steered the lorry down a narrow dirt tract lined by overgrown English oaks. At the end was a large barn, its roof half collapsed. To the left was a burned-out farmhouse.

Geist parked beneath some overhanging boughs and shut off the engine. "We should see to everyone's injuries," he said. "We've lost enough good men."

"Everybody out," Hoffman ordered, rapping a knuckle on the back of the compartment.

After they all climbed free, Geist surveyed the damage. "You'll all get the Knight's Cross for your bravery tonight. We should—"

A harsh shout cut him off, barked in German. *"Halt! Hände hoch!"*

A dozen men, bristling with weapons, emerged from the foliage and from behind the barn.

"Nobody move!" the voice called again, revealing a tall American with a Tommy gun in hand.

Geist recognized the impossibility of their team's situation and lifted his arms. Hoffman and his last two men followed his example, dropping their weapons and raising their hands.

It was over.

As the Americans frisked Hoffman and the others, a lone figure stepped from the darkened barn door and approached Geist. He pointed a .45-caliber pistol at Geist's chest.

"Tie him up," he ordered one of his men.

As his wrists were efficiently bound in rope, his captor spoke in a rich southern twang. "Colonel Ernie Duncan, 101st Airborne. You speak English?"

"Yes."

"Whom do I have the pleasure of addressing?"

"Schweinhund," Geist answered with a sneer.

"Son, I'm pretty sure that isn't your name. I'll assume that slur is intended for me. So then let's just call you Fritz. You and I are going to have a talk. Whether it's pleasant or ugly is up to you."

Over his shoulder the American colonel called to one of his men. "Lieutenant Ross, put those other three men into the back of their truck and get them ready for transport. Say goodbye to your team, Fritz."

Geist turned to face his men and shouted in German, *"Für das Vaterland!"*

"Das Vaterland!" Hoffman and the others shouted back in unison.

The American soldiers herded the commandos into the back of the lorry, while Colonel Duncan marched Geist over to the barn. Once inside, he closed the doors and waved to encompass the piles of hay and manure.

"Sorry for our meager accommodations, Fritz."

Geist turned to face him and broke into a smile. "Damned good to see you, too, Duncan."

"And you, my friend. How'd it go? Find what you were looking for?"

"It's in my jacket. For whatever it's worth, those Germans fight like the devil. Bletchley's burning. But they should be up and running again in a week."

"Good to know." Duncan used a razor blade to free his bound wrists. "How do you want to play this from here?"

"I've got a small Mauser hidden in a crotch holster." He stood up and rubbed his wrists, then unwound his scarf and folded it into a thick square. He reached into the front of his pants and withdrew the Mauser.

Geist glanced behind him. "Where's the back door?"

Duncan pointed. "By those old horse stalls. Nobody'll be back behind the barn to see you *escape*. But you'll have to make it look convincing, you know. Really smack me good. Remember, we Americans are tough."

"Duncan, I'm not keen on this idea."

"Necessities of war, buddy. You can buy me a case of scotch when we get back to the States."

Geist shook the colonel's hand.

Duncan dropped his .45 to the ground and smiled. "Oh, look, you've disarmed me."

"We Germans are crafty that way."

Next Duncan ripped open the front of his fatigue blouse, popping buttons off onto the straw-covered floor. "And there's been a struggle."

"Okay, Duncan, enough. Turn your head. I'll rap you behind the ear. When you wake up, you'll have a knot the size of a golf ball and a raging headache, but you asked for it."

"Right." He clasped Geist by the forearm. "Watch yourself out there. It's a long way back to D.C."

As Duncan turned his head away, a twinge of guilt swept through him. Still, he knew what needed to be done.

He pressed the wadded scarf to the Mauser's barrel and jammed it against Duncan's ear.

The colonel shifted slightly. "Hey, what are you—"

He pulled the trigger. With the sound of a sharp slap, the bullet tore through Duncan's skull, snapping his friend's head back as the body toppled forward to the ground.

Geist stared down. "So sorry, my friend. As you said before, *necessities of war*. If it makes you feel any better, you've just changed the world."

He pocketed the pistol, walked to the barn's back door, and disappeared into the misty night, becoming at last … a true ghost.

GHOST HUNT

1

October 10, 6:39 P.M. MDT
Bitterroot Mountains, Montana

All this trouble from a single damned nail…

Tucker Wayne tossed the flat tire into the back of his rental. The Jeep Grand Cherokee sat parked on the shoulder of a lonely stretch of road through the forested mountains of southwest Montana. These millions of acres of pines, glacier-cut canyons, and rugged peaks formed the largest expanse of pristine wilderness in the lower 48 states.

He stretched a kink out of his back and searched down the winding stretch of blacktop, bracketed on both sides by sloping hills and dense stands of lodgepole pines.

Just my luck. Here in the middle of nowhere, I pick up a nail.

It seemed impossible that this great beast of an SUV could be brought low by a simple sliver of iron shorter than his pinkie. It was a reminder how modern technological progress could still be ground to a halt by a single bit of antiquated hardware like a roofing nail.

He slammed the rear cargo hatch and whistled sharply. His companion on this cross-country journey pulled his long furry nose out of a huckleberry bush at the edge of the forest and glanced back at him. Eyes the color of dark caramel stared back at him, plainly disappointed that this roadside pit stop had come to an end.

"Sorry, buddy. But we've got a long way to go if we hope to reach Yellowstone."

Kane shook his heavy coat of brown-and-tan fur, his thick tail flagging as he turned, readily accepting this reality. The two of them had been partners going back to his years with the Army Rangers, surviving multiple deployments across Afghanistan together. Upon leaving the service, Tucker took Kane with him—not exactly with the Army's permission, but that matter had been settled in the recent past.

The two were now an inseparable team, on their own, seeking new roads, new paths. Together.

Tucker opened the front passenger door and Kane hopped cleanly inside, his lean muscular seventy pounds fitting snugly into the seat. He was a Belgian Malinois, a breed of compact shepherd used more and more by the military and law enforcement. The breed was known for their fierce loyalty and sharp intelligence. They were also well-respected for both their nimbleness and raw power in a battlefield environment.

But there was no one like Kane.

Tucker closed the door but lingered long enough to scratch his partner through the open window. His fingers discovered old scars under the fur, reminding Tucker of his own wounds: some easy to see, others just as well hidden.

"Let's keep going," he whispered before the ghosts of his past caught up with him.

He climbed behind the wheel and soon had them flying through the hills of the Bitterroot National Forest. Kane kept his head stuck out the passenger side, his tongue lolling, his nose taking in every scent. Tucker grinned, finding the tension melting from his shoulders as it always did when he was moving.

For the moment, he was between jobs—and he intended to keep it that way for as long as possible. He only took the occasional security position when his finances required it. After his last job—when he had been hired by Sigma Force, a covert branch of the military's research-and-development department—his bank accounts continued to remain flush.

Taking advantage of their down time, he and Kane had spent the last couple of days hiking the Lost Trail Pass, following in the footsteps of the Lewis & Clark expedition, and now they were moving onto Yellowstone National Park. He timed this trip to that popular park for the late fall, to avoid the crush of the high season, preferring the company of Kane to anyone on two legs.

Around a bend in the dark road, a pool of fluorescent lights revealed a roadside gas station. The sign at the entrance read FORT EDWIN GAS AND GROCERY. He checked his fuel gauge.

Almost empty.

He flipped on his turn signal and swung into the small station. His motel was three miles farther up the road. His plan had been to take a fast shower, collect his bags, and continue straight toward Yellowstone, taking advantage of the empty roads at night.

Now he had a snag in those plans. He needed to replace the flat tire as soon as possible. Hopefully someone at the gas station knew the closest place to get that done in these remote hills.

He pulled next to one of the pumps and climbed out. Kane hopped through the window on the other side. Together they headed for the station.

Tucker pulled open the glass door, setting a brass bell to tinkling. The shop was laid out in the usual fashion: rows of snacks and food staples, backed up by a tall stand of coolers along the far wall. The air smelled of floor wax and microwaved sandwiches.

"Good evening, good evening," a male voice greeted him, his voice rising and falling in a familiar singsong manner.

Tucker immediately recognized the accent as Dari Persian. From his former years in the deserts of Afghanistan, he knew the various dialects of that desert country. Despite the friendliness of the tone, Tucker's belly tightened in a knot of old dread. Men with that very same accent had tried to kill him more times than he could count. Worse still, they had succeeded in butchering Kane's littermate.

He flashed to the bounding joy of his lost partner, the flagging tail, the tongue lolling with happiness. It took all of his effort to force that memory back into that knot of old pain, grief, and guilt.

"Good evening," the man behind the counter repeated, smiling, oblivious to the tension along Tucker's spine. The proprietor's face was nut-brown, his teeth perfectly white. He was mostly bald, save for a monk's fringe of gray hair. His eyes twinkled as though Tucker was a friend he hadn't seen in years.

Having met hundreds of Afghan villagers in his time, Tucker knew the man's demeanor was genuine. Still, he found it hard to step inside.

The man's brow formed one concerned crinkle at his obvious hesitation. "Welcome," he offered again, waving an arm to encourage him.

"Thanks," Tucker finally managed to reply. He kept one hand on Kane's flank. "Okay if I bring my dog in?"

"Yes, of course. All are welcome."

Tucker took a deep breath and crossed past the front shelves selling packets of beef jerky, Slim Jims, and corn chips. He stepped to the counter, noting he was the only one in the place.

"You have a beautiful dog," the man said. "Is he a shepherd?"

"Actually he's a Belgian Malinois … a type of shepherd. Name's Kane."

"And I am Aasif Qazi, owner of this fine establishment."

The proprietor stretched a hand across the counter. Tucker took it, finding the man's grip firm, the palm slightly calloused from hard labor.

"You're from Kabul," Tucker said.

The man's eyebrows rose high. "How did you know?"

"Your accent. I spent some time in Afghanistan."

"Recently, I am guessing."

Not so recently, Tucker thought, but some days it felt like yesterday. "And you?" he asked.

"I came to the States as a boy back in the late seventies. My parents wisely chose to emigrate when the Russians invaded. I met my wife in New York." He raised his voice. "Freba, come say hello."

From an office in the back, a petite, gray-haired Afghani woman peeked out and smiled. "Hello. Nice to meet you."

"So how did you both end up here?"

"You mean in the middle of nowhere?" Aasif's grin widened. "Freba and I got tired of the city. We wanted something that was exact opposite."

"Looks like you succeeded." Tucker glanced around the empty shop and the dark forest beyond the windows.

"We love it here. And it's not normally this deserted. We're between seasons at the moment. The summer crowds have left, and the skiers have yet to arrive. But we still have our regulars."

Proving this, a diesel engine roared outside, and a white, rust-stained pickup truck pulled between the pumps, fishtailing slightly as it came to a stop.

Tucker turned back at Aasif. "Seems like business is picking—"

The man's eyes had narrowed; his jaw muscles, clenched. The army had handpicked Tucker as a dog handler because of his unusually high empathy scores. Such sensitivity allowed him to bond more readily and deeply with his partner, and to read people. Still, it took no skill at all to tell Aasif was scared.

Aasif waved to his wife. "Freba, go back into the office."

She obeyed, but not before casting a frightened glance toward her husband.

Tucker moved closer to the windows, trailed by Kane. He quickly assessed the situation, noting one odd detail: the truck's license plate was covered in duct tape.

Definitely trouble.

No one with good intentions blacked out his license plate.

Tucker took a deep breath. The air suddenly felt heavier, crackling with electricity. He knew it was only a figment of his own spiking adrenaline. Still, he knew a storm was brewing. Kane reacted to his mood, the hackles rising along the shepherd's back, accompanied by a low growl.

Two men in flannel shirts and baseball caps hopped out of the cab; a third jumped down from the truck's bed. The driver of the truck sported a dirty red goatee and wore a green baseball cap emblazoned with I'D RATHER BE DOIN' YOUR WIFE.

Great … not only are these yokels trouble, they also have a terrible sense of humor.

Without turning, he asked, "Aasif, do you have security cameras?"

"They're broken. We haven't been able to fix them."

He sighed loudly. *Not good.*

The trio strutted toward the station entrance. Each man carried a wooden baseball bat.

"Call the sheriff. If you can trust him."

"He's a decent man."

"Then call him."

"Perhaps it is best if you do not —"

"Make the call, Aasif."

Tucker headed to the door with Kane and pushed outside before the others could enter. Given the odds, he would need room to maneuver.

Tucker stopped the trio at the curb. "Evening, fellas."

"Hey," replied Mr. Goatee, making a move to slip past him.

Tucker stepped to block him. "Store's closed."

"Bull," said one of the others and pointed his bat. "Look, Shane, I can see that rag head from here."

"Then you can also see he's on the phone," Tucker said. "He's calling the sheriff."

"That idiot?" Shane said. "We'll be long gone before he pulls his head outta his ass and gets here."

Tucker let his grin turn dark. "I wouldn't be so sure of that."

He silently signaled Kane, pointing an index finger down—then tightening a fist. The command clear: THREATEN.

Kane lowered his head, bared his teeth, and let out a menacing growl. Still, the shepherd remained at his side. Kane wouldn't move unless given another command or if this confrontation became physical.

Shane took a step back. "That mutt comes at me and I'll bash his brains in."

If this mutt comes at you, you'll never know what hit you.

Tucker raised his hands. "Listen, guys, I get it. It's Friday night, time to blow off some steam. All I'm asking is you find some other way of doing it. The people inside are just trying to make a living. Just like you and me."

Shane snorted. "Like us? Them towel-heads ain't nothing like us. We're Americans."

"So are they."

"I lost buddies in Iraq—"

"We all have."

"What the hell do you know about it?" asked the third man.

"Enough to know the difference between these storeowners, and the kind of people you're talking about."

Tucker remembered his own reaction upon first entering the shop and felt a twinge of guilt.

Shane lifted his bat and aimed the end at Tucker's face. "Get outta our way or you'll regret siding with the enemy."

Tucker knew the talking part of this encounter was over.

Proving this, Shane jabbed Tucker in the chest with the bat.

So be it.

Tucker's left hand snapped out and grabbed the bat. He gave it a jerk, pulling Shane off balance toward him.

He whispered a command to his partner, "GRAB AND DROP."

Kane leaped and clamped his bone-breaking jaws onto Shane's forearm. Upon landing on his paws, Kane twisted and threw the off-balance combatant to the ground. The bat clattered across the concrete.

Shane screamed, froth flecking his words. "Get him off, get him off!"

The second man charged forward, his bat swinging down toward Kane. Anticipating this, Tucker dove low, taking the hit with his own body, expertly blunting the blow by turning his back at an angle. As the wood struck, he reached up and wrapped his forearm around the bat, pinning it in place—then side kicked.

His heel slammed into the man's kneecap, triggering a muffled pop. The man hollered, released the bat, and staggered backward.

Tucker swung his captured weapon toward the third attacker. "It's over. Drop it."

The last man glared, but he let the bat fall—

—then reached into his jacket and lashed out with his arm again.

Tucker's mind barely had time to register the glint of a knife blade. He backpedaled, dodging the first slash. His heel struck the curb behind him, and he went down, crashing into a row of empty propane tanks and losing his bat.

Grinning cruelly, the man loomed over Tucker and brandished his knife. "Time to teach you a lesson about—"

Tucker reached over his shoulder and grabbed a loose propane tank as it rolled along the sidewalk behind him. He swung it low, cutting the man's legs out from under him. With a pained cry of surprise, the attacker crashed to the ground.

Tucker rolled to him, snatched the man's wrist, and bent it backward until the bone snapped. The knife fell free. Tucker retrieved the blade as the man curled into a ball, groaning and clutching his hand. His left ankle was also cocked sideways, plainly broken.

Lesson over.

He stood up and walked over to Shane, whose lips were compressed in fear and agony. Kane still held him pinned down, clamped onto the man's bloody arm, his teeth sunk to bone.

"RELEASE," Tucker ordered.

The shepherd obeyed but stayed close, baring his bloody fangs at Shane. Tucker backed his partner up with the knife.

Distantly sirens echoed through the forest, growing steadily louder.

Tucker felt his belly tighten. Though he'd acted in self-defense, he was in the middle of nowhere awaiting a sheriff who could arrest them if the whim struck him. Flashing lights appeared through the trees, and a cruiser swung fast into the parking lot and pulled to a stop twenty feet away.

Tucker raised his hands and tossed the knife aside.

He didn't want anyone making a mistake here.

"SIT," he told Kane. "BE HAPPY."

The dog dropped to his haunches, wagging his tail, his head cocked to the side quizzically.

Aasif joined him outside and must have noticed his tension. "Sheriff Walton is a fair man."

"If you say so."

In the end, Aasif proved a good judge of character. It helped that the sheriff knew the trio on the ground and held them in no high opinion. *Been raising hell for a year now. So far, nobody's had the sand to press charges against them.*

That changed this night, much to the delight of Sheriff Walton, who took down their statements and noted the truck's blacked-out license plate with a sad shake of his head.

"I believe that would be your third strike, Shane. And from what I hear redheads are very popular at the state pen this year."

The man lowered his head and groaned.

After another two cruisers arrived and the men were hauled away, Tucker faced the sheriff. "Do I need to stick around?"

"Do you want to?"

"Not especially."

"Didn't think so. I've got your details. I doubt you'll need to testify, but if you do—"

"I'll come back."

"Good." Walton passed him a card. Tucker expected it to have local sheriff's department's contact information on it, but instead it was emblazoned with the image of a car with a smashed fender. "My brother owns a body-repair shop in neighboring Wisdom. I'll make sure he gets that flat tire of yours fixed at cost."

Tucker took the card happily. "Thanks."

With matters settled, Tucker was soon back on the road with Kane. He held out the card toward the shepherd as he sped toward his motel. "See, Kane. Who says no good deed goes unpunished?"

Unfortunately, he spoke too soon. As he turned into his motel and parked before the door to his room, his headlight shone upon an impossible sight.

Sitting on the bench before his cabin was a woman—a ghost out of his past. Only this figment wasn't dressed in desert khaki or the dress blues of the Navy. Instead, she wore jeans, a light-blue blouse, with an open wool cardigan.

Tucker's heart missed several beats. He sat behind the wheel, engine idling, struggling to understand how she could be here, how she had found him.

Her name was Jane Sabatello. It had been over five years since he'd last set eyes on her, but even now he found his gaze sweeping over her every feature, each triggering distinct memories, blurring past and present: the softness of her full lips, the shine of moonlight that turned her blond hair silver, the joy in her eyes each morning.

Tucker had never married, but Jane was as close as he'd come.

And now here she was, waiting for him—and she wasn't alone.

A child sat at her side, a young boy tucked close to her hip.

For the briefest of moments, he wondered if the boy—

No, she would have told me.

He finally cut off the engine and stepped out of the vehicle. She stood up as she recognized him in turn.

"Jane?" he murmured.

She rushed to him and wrapped him in a hug, clinging to him for a long thirty seconds before pulling back. She searched his face, her eyes moist. Under the glare of the Cherokee's headlamps, he noted a dark bruise under one cheekbone, poorly obscured by a smear of cosmetic concealer.

Even less hidden was the panic and raw fear in her face.

She kept one hand firmly on his arm, her fingers tight with desperation. "Tucker, I need your help."

Before he could speak, she glanced to the boy.

"Someone's trying to kill us."